Dear Grieve

MacDiarmid by William Johnstone.
By permission of Alan Riach.

Dear Grieve

Letters to Hugh MacDiarmid
(C. M. Grieve)

Selected and Edited
by John Manson

With an introduction
by Alan Riach

Editorial Assistants

Kirsten Matthews
David Kelly

Kennedy & Boyd

Kennedy & Boyd
an imprint of
Zeticula Ltd
The Roan
Kilkerran
KA19 8LS
Scotland

http://www.kennedyandboyd.co.uk
admin@kennedyandboyd.co.uk

First Edition published in 2011
Reprinted 2012

Letters © as listed on pages ix to xii
Introduction © Alan Riach 2011
Apparatus Copyright © John Manson 2011
Front Cover Photograph © Cyril Maitland 2011
Back cover Photograph © Ayrshire Writers and Artists Society 2011

ISBN 978-1-84921-078-2

For the Life and Times of Hugh MacDiarmid

Contents

Acknowledgements

The editor and publisher gratefully acknowledge permission to print copyright letters as follows:

Christine Davis for two letters from W.R. Aitken; William Anderson for two letters from John G. Anderson; Jean MacWhirter for two letters from Roy Armstrong; R.A. Atkinson for one letter from Tom Atkinson;

Alasdair Barke for one letter from Nan Barke; Logie Barrow for one letter; David M. Black for one letter; Rona Taylor for three letters from Robert ('Robin') MacKelvie Black; David Higham Associates Limited for four letters from George Blake; Scirard R. Lancelyn Green for one letter from Gordon Bottomley; Jessica Sutcliffe for one letter from Ern Brooks (with Barbara Niven); David Bruce for two letters from George Bruce; John Halliday for four letters from Basil Bunting;

Clara Young for two letters from Stewart Carmichael; Deborah Kaplinsky and Harriet Wilson for six letters from Catherine Carswell; The Estate of Sean O'Casey for three letters; Joy Chiari for one letter from Jo Chiari; Pollinger Limited and The Estate of Richard Church for one letter from Richard Church; Duncan Clark for three letters from Aonghas Cleireach/Angus Clark; David Craig for one letter; Timothy Cribb for one letter; Patrick Crotty for one letter; Flora Hunter for three letters and one poem from Helen Cruickshank; Anthony R.A. Hobson for one letter from Nancy Cunard;

David Higham Associates Limited for one letter from David Daiches; Deirdre Grieve for one letter from Elizabeth Dawson, formerly Grieve, neé Graham; the late George Elder Davie for four letters; Douglas Dunn for one letter;

The Estate of T.S. Eliot for six letters;

The Estate of Ian Hamilton Finlay for one letter;

Janet MacDonald for four letters from Edward Gaitens; The Trustees of the National Library of Scotland for one letter from Sir Patrick Geddes; the late Duncan Glen for two letters; Michael and Margaret Snow for one letter from W.S. Graham; Morag Enticknap for one letter from Andrew Graham Grieve; Christine MacIntosh for five letters from Margaret ('Peggy') Grieve; Deirdre Grieve for four letters from Michael Grieve and six letters from Valda Grieve; Walter Grieve for one letter; The Neil Gunn Literary Estate for eight letters;

The Heirs of George Campbell Hay and the Lorimer Trust for five letters; Seamus Heaney for one letter; R.R. Calder for one letter from J.F. Hendry; The Estate of Christopher Hill for one letter; The Estate of Ted Hughes for one letter;

Sandra Ross for one letter from N.C. Jack; A.D. Currie for three letters from William Johnstone; Meic Stephens for three letters from Glyn Jones; Heledd Hayes and Nia Harper for two letters from Gwyn Jones;

Sheila Triggs for one letter from Peter Kerrigan; Julie Whelan for one letter from B.C.J.G. Knight; Vincent Kosman for one letter from Jessie Kocmanová;

David Higham Associates Limited for one letter from Jack Lindsay; Joyce Lindsay for one letter from Maurice Lindsay; Peter Rankin for four letters from Joan Littlewood (one with Jimmie Miller/ 'Ewan MacColl');

Ewen McCaig for five letters from Norman MacCaig; Margaret McCance for five letters from William McCance; Neil MacCormick for one letter from John M. MacCormick; Jean McCrindle for one letter from Alex McCrindle; Margery Palmer McCulloch for one letter; Francesca Hardcastle for two letters from Mary MacDonald and three letters from T. Douglas MacDonald ('Fionn MacColla'); Christine MacIntosh, née Grieve, for two letters; six letters from Sir Compton MacKenzie by permission of The Society of Authors, on behalf of the estate of Compton MacKenzie; John Mackie for one letter from Albert D. Mackie; Renée MacLean for eight letters from Sorley MacLean; John MacLellan for one letter from Robert MacLellan; Janet MacDonald for six letters from William MacLellan; Gordon McLennan for one letter; Nigel Leask for one letter from Joseph MacLeod; H M Book Trust- Copyright and Archives Fund for one letter from Harold MacMillan;

Mrs Mearns for one letter from Tommy Mearns; Ellice Milton for two letters from Nan Mercer, later Milton, neé MacLean; Peggy Seeger for two letters from Jimmy Miller ('Ewan MacColl'), one with Joan Littlewood; Rhea Martin for six letters from James Leslie Mitchell ('Lewis Grassic Gibbon') and one letter from Rebecca ('Rhea') Mitchell; David Higham Associates Limited for one letter from Naomi Mitchison; Alexander Moffat for one letter; John Montague for one letter; Edwin Morgan for one letter; Jim Hastie, Margaret Morris Movement, for one letter from Margaret Morris; Kenneth T. Ross for five letters from Edwin Muir and one letter from Willa Muir; Roderick Watson for one letter, from David Murison;

Zoe Readhead for two letters from A.S. Neill; Gwyneira James for one letter from T.E. Nicholas; Caroline Neuburg for one letter from Victor Neuburg; Jessica Sutcliffe for eight letters from Barbara Niven (one with Ern Brooks);

A. M. Orr for one letter from Robin Orr (with J. B. Caird);

Cécile Triat-Saurat for one letter from Marguérite and Félix Paknadel; Pollinger Limited and New Directions Publishing Corporation for four letters from Kenneth Patchen; Mark Pitter for one letter from Ruth Pitter; Judith Hein for one letter from Sadie Pritchard;

David Higham Associates Limited for one letter from Sir Herbert Read; George N. Reid for one letter; Eva Rhys for one letter from Keidrych Rhys; Alan Riach for one letter; P. Jane Grubb for two letters from Edgell Rickword; Carl Spadoni for Bertrand Russell Permissions Committee for one letter from Bertrand Russell;

Donald G. Saunders for one letter from R. Crombie Saunders; Cécile Triat-Saurat for five letters from Denis Saurat and one letter from Ella Saurat; The Trustees of the late Benno Schotz for one letter; Crombie Scott for three letters from Alexander Scott; Lillias Scott Forbes for twenty letters from Francis George Scott; Heather Scott for five letters from Tom Scott; Douglas Sealy for one letter; David Higham Associates Limited for one letter from Sir Sacheverell Sitwell; Donalda Henderson for two letters from Iain Crichton Smith; Katharine M. Pal for three letters from Sydney Goodsir Smith; The Sorabji Archive for three letters from Kaikhosru Shapurji Sorabji; The Trustees of the National Library of Scotland for five letters from William Soutar; Ronald Stevenson for one letter; Ian Sutherland for three letters from Robert Garioch Sutherland;

Nathaniel Tarn for two letters; Alan N. Taylor for two letters from Grant Taylor; Rona Taylor for one letter from Ronald K.R. Taylor; Kunjana Thomas for two letters from R.S. Thomas; Johnson & Alcock for one letter from Henry Treece; The Alexander Trocchi Archive for three letters from Alexander Trocchi;

Taylor & Francis for two letters from Fredric J. Warburg; Roderick Watson for one letter; Kenneth White for two letters; Tappan Wilder for one letter from Thornton Wilder; Cora Cuthbert for two letters from Wendy Wood;

Clara Young for four letters from Douglas Young.

The editor and publisher also gratefully acknowledge permission from the MacDiarmid Estate to include in notes four extracts from letters of Hugh MacDiarmid which were parts of his M.I.5 file (TNA KV2/2010); and also his oration at the interment of the ashes of James Barke.

Every effort has been made to trace copyright holders. In instances where these efforts have been unsuccessful, the editor and publisher would be grateful if the omissions were pointed out, and undertake to make acknowledgement at the earliest appropriate opportunity.

The letters of James Bridie are reproduced by permission of The Agency (London) Ltd 1943, 1945, 1946 and 1949 © James Bridie. All rights reserved and info@ theagency.co.uk. Enquiries to The Agency (London) Ltd, 24 Pottery Lane, London W11 4LZ.

The letter of J. D. Fergusson © The Fergusson Gallery, Perth & Kinross Council.

The letters of John Gawsworth © Javier Marías, the estate of John Gawsworth.

The letter by Eric Linklater (© Eric Linklater) is reproduced by permission of PFD (www.pfd.co.uk) on behalf of The estate of Eric Linklater.

The letters of Ezra Pound © 2011 by Omar S. Pound and Mary de Rachewiltz. Used by permission of New Directions Publishing Corporation.

Letter of March 4th 1934 to Hugh MacDiarmid from *Collected Letters* (online resource) (1986) by Yeats, WB edited by Kelly, J (ed.) By permission of Oxford University Press.

The editor and publisher have appreciated the full support of Deirdre Grieve and Dorian Grieve of the MacDiarmid Estate who have encouraged this project at all stages; of Professor Alan Riach who has given it his positive backing from the outset; and of Kirsten Matthews and David Kelly for their skill and patience in scanning the text.

They are grateful to Edinburgh University Library (Special Collections Department) and to The Trustees of the National Library of Scotland for kind permission to publish letters from their collections. They acknowledge the courtesy and helpfulness of the staff on all occasions. They also thank the Poetry Collection of the University Libraries of the State University of New York at Buffalo for two letters.

Thanks are also due to the British Film Institute; Ewart Library, Dumfries; Glasgow Caledonian University (William Gallacher Memorial Library); Glasgow University Library (Special Collections Department); Mitchell Library, Glasgow; The National Library of Ireland ; The National Library of Wales; Scottish Poetry Library; Scottish Screen Archive; Stirling University Library, and their staffs.

The editor thanks the undernoted for their indispensable help in various ways:

Chris Allen; Gavin Bowd; Michel Byrne; Duncan Clark; Josie Comas i Riu; David M. Craig; Béatrice Duchateau; Lillias Scott Forbes; Graham Gibson; the late Duncan Glen; Joan Ham; Stefanie Kinz; Nigel Leask; Margaret McCance; Margery Palmer McCulloch; Hugh K. Mackay; the late Jean MacPherson; John MacLellan; Angus MacMillan; George Philp; Sophie Mamattah; Carla Sassi; Bob Purdie; John Purser; Tatiana Romanova; Heather Scott; Douglas Sealy; Margaret and Michael Snow; Meic Stephens; Andrew Steven; Ronald Stevenson; and Gordon Wright.

The editor acknowledges the award of a Scottish Arts Council grant which enabled him to spend ten four-day weeks in Edinburgh in 2004 in order to research in Edinbugh University Library (Special Collections Department) and in The National Library of Scotland.

Hugh MacDiarmid: Put it to the Touch

An Introduction to *Dear Grieve*

Alan Riach

In a letter of 5 November 1968, Iain Crichton Smith writes to Christopher Grieve, Hugh MacDiarmid, that he sees the essential problem in his work: 'To select is to be untrue to life. Not to select is to face the possibility of extinction.'

The affinity Crichton Smith is describing between his own poetry and MacDiarmid's indicates the profundity and commonality of poetic commitment in all major work: 'The poet must remain open to all possible experiences but in doing this his psyche is bombarded by forces of such intensity as might / would destroy him.' Crichton Smith himself faced up to this and went through a dark depression in the 1980s, and he saw clearly in MacDiarmid a major poet who had experienced this before: he knew what it was like.

MacDiarmid's poem 'I Wha Aince in Heaven's Height' ('I Who Once in Heaven's Height'), from *To Circumjack Cencrastus* (1930), expresses the position with piercing clarity. It is a poem about the fall of Lucifer, who once 'in Heaven's height' gathered into himself all the light of the cosmos, but now he cannot respond to fire, the burning illumination of the world, as he is buried in the depths and filth, beneath dead leaves and mould. Yet he is a cousin of – related to, possessed of visceral closeness with – 'dewdrop, rainbow, ocean' – even as he knows their 'hues and motion' are not for him: he cannot take the forms or shapes or movements of these watery identities, because the 'foul clay' – the earth itself, the clay that grew tall in humankind – has infiltrated him so deeply that it's impossible to say that he isn't also connected to water even now. In other words, all the elements: earth, water, fire, the air the light inhabits and through which the angel is cast down, are all constituents of his singular identity. There is hope in this, just as Milton's Satan, in line 106 of Book 1 of *Paradise Lost*, resolutely comments, 'All is not lost'. The setting of MacDiarmid's poem by the composer F.G. Scott, who figures crucially in the letters collected in this book, is one of the most beautiful, strong and subtle of modern songs, and can be heard on the CD *Songs of F.G. Scott: Moonstruck* (signum: SIGCD096).

MacDiarmid remains one of the greatest of all modern poets, important as a cultural and political warrior, a catalyst, an energising force, and of lasting value as an exemplary life: setting examples both good and bad, not always to be followed, and never followed blindly. The pioneering biography by Alan Bold (1988, revised edition 1990), the *Illustrated Biography* by Gordon Wright (1977), biographical essays and interviews by Duncan Glen, Nancy Gish, critical studies by Kenneth Buthlay, Roderick Watson, and others, letter-collections (*The Letters*, edited by Alan Bold and *New Selected Letters*, edited by Dorian Grieve, Owen Dudley Edwards and Alan Riach), books of his correspondence with George Ogilvie, Sorley MacLean, his second wife Valda, all these together with his own autobiographical books, *Lucky Poet* (1943) and *The Company I've Kept* (1966) and various essays, amount to a multi-faceted compendium, a vade mecum of stories and characters, a life whose trajectory crossed through so many constellations, encountered so many fascinating people, was engaged by innumerable movements, battles, signs and wonders, no single selection is adequate. But not to select risks extinction. Dinosaurs were too big to survive, and even the hippopotamus is a sizeable beast in a modern world enthralled by sound-bite-sized commodities. (MacDiarmid entitled the 'Author's Note' to his autobiography, 'On Being a Hippopotamus': 'The hippopotamus is a big beast, and that explains why I should have difficulty in getting it all on to a certain size of canvas, and even then cannot present it "in the round", but only from one angle at a time, and far from life-size.')

John Manson's collection of letters to MacDiarmid, or to Christopher Grieve, or to Hugh or Chris or Christie or Hughie, is a major work. It is the fruit of a lifetime of dedicated scholarly research, meticulous, self-effacing study in libraries, most deeply in the National Library of Scotland and Edinburgh University Library, and follows his initial co-editorship with David Craig of the first Penguin paperback edition of MacDiarmid's *Selected Poems* (1970), and his later co-editorship of *The Revolutionary Art of the Future: Rediscovered Poems*, with Dorian Grieve and Alan Riach (2003). He is a fine poet and translator himself, and his small-press publications are to be sought out and read closely. However, this is a monumental achievement: a collection so rich in diversity, covering historical epochs, strata of human character, social engagement, political motivation and accomplishment, that it will take some time before its impact and value really sinks in and embeds itself in modern literary and political culture – especially in Scotland!

To introduce the book, it may be helpful to give some idea of the world MacDiarmid came from, the nature of his engagement and achievement, the crises in politics, the domestic scene of family and friends, some notion of the complex nets of interconnection MacDiarmid falls through like Lucifer, and these letters emerge from. The critic and theorist Homi Bhabha once said that out of every emergency there comes an emergence: MacDiarmid is proof of that, and these letters chart a series of emergences that cover an epoch in time and continue to supply us here in the twenty-first century with vital information, things that are needed most.

He was born in 1892 in Langholm, a small town in Dumfriesshire, twelve miles north of the Scottish border with England. His father was the local postman, his mother's people lived in neighbouring towns and villages. As a boy he roamed the hills and forests surrounding the town, and read all the books in the extensive library housed in the same building they lived in. In essays he recollected the loveliness of the country around him and claimed to be able to identify his location by the sound alone of the three rivers that ran into a confluence in Langholm: the Wauchope, the Esk and the Ewes. His reading was omnivorous. His appetite was large. He became intimately knowledgeable with the details of geography and the natural world around him, and also with what book-learning could bring him, undirected by educational dictatorship. At school, in fact, he was of a company of pupils all too lively. The composer F.G. Scott was his English teacher, administering corporal punishment (strapping him with a leather belt), at least once. MacDiarmid, or Grieve, later said he couldn't remember what it had been for, but he was sure that he deserved it: 'We were all delinquents.' (He recounts some gloriously hairy tales of their school activities in *Lucky Poet*.)

He was going to be a teacher but decided on journalism instead, went to South Wales and reported on the riots and resistances of the coal miners, writing for the socialist newspaper run by Keir Hardie, the Scottish leader and foundation-figure in the newly-formed Labour Party. 'It's like living on the top of a volcano down here,' he wrote home. When the First World War began, he signed up like thousands of other young men, eager to fight, imagining the end of the world and wanting to march right into the centre of Armageddon. But his political consciousness was developing fast. These early years of the twentieth century were full of war and revolution. MacDiarmid – from here on we shall refer to him thus, though Chris Grieve was what he was called personally by most who knew him – was thinking about what was happening through the Easter Rising in Ireland in 1916: a Celtic nation violently asserting independence from the British Imperial centre. And he was thinking about the Russian Revolution in 1917: a socialist ideal, a Communist revolution, an act of defiance towards the class system, social hierarchy, economic discrimination. He said in a late interview that if it had been possible for him to have left the British army and joined the Irish fighting British imperialism he would have done so. He was to join the Communist Party, believing in the ideal of international socialism, and he was to be a founder-member of the National Party of Scotland in 1928, believing in the cultural difference and value of Scotland, other than and oppressed by the Anglocentric or British imperial ethos, and latterly what he called 'American trash-culture' and my grandfather referred to as 'Yankee-doodle'.

For MacDiarmid, as a young man, the core ideas were Empire and Nation. Empire had led directly to the slaughter of the First World War. Not competing nations, but competing uber-nations, empires: imperial authorities, sending their mustered troops from various nations collectively to kill each other in the service of the uber-nation, the expansionist empire, to serve the wealthy and maintain a social hierarchy of privilege. Nation, however, meant something else: a cultural identity made up of different component parts, not motivated by competition but rather by collaborative curiosity. All the arts are ways of exploring the world, of representing reality, of criticising what is taken for granted. His own national cultural identity, which he found, when he began to explore it seriously, included different languages: Gaelic, Scots and English, different geographical terrains: borderlands, industrial cities, fertile heartlands, stretching Highland moors and mountains, island archipelagoes, landscapes, seascapes, cityscapes: this could not be accommodated within a single British state. On cultural terms alone, Scotland warrants statehood. But nationalism would be nothing without socialism. Separatism that reinforced economic discrimination and a hierarchy of privilege would be useless. He spells his position out in *Lucky Poet*:

The Social Revolution is possible sooner in Scotland than in England. The working-class policy ought to be to break up the Empire to avert war and enable the workers to triumph in every country and colony. Scottish separation is part of the process of England's Imperial disintegration and is a help towards the ultimate triumph of the workers of the world. (p.144)

So he had a vision. What was required now, after he was demobilized and returned to Scotland, was a strategy.

He went to the north-east seaside town of Montrose, became a journalist on the local newspaper, a socialist Justice of the Peace, gave public lectures on Lenin, and wrote his first poems in the language we call Scots. He had written in English, eerie poems and deliberately crafted short stories, many set in Salonika and France, where he had been a Sergeant in the Royal Army Medical Corps and contracted cerebral malaria. Now he began writing in Scots, using words and phrases he knew from boyhood and acquired from reading in dictionaries and works of Scottish literature from earlier eras. The poems were shocking, startling, adult, wry, rebarbative, difficult, piercingly sweet, unsentimental and brutal. They established a new dispensation for Scottish literature, and modernist lusts: for the body and the sexually explicit cognate with Joyce and Lawrence, for the local and demotic, cognate with William Carlos Williams, for the difficult, cognate with Eliot, for the vatic and austere, cognate with Yeats and Pound, for the intellectually demanding, cognate with Stevens and Valéry, but uniquely, also, for the national, Scots, reclaiming a literary history that had fallen into neglect and obfuscation. Forget about Burns, he advised, that annual gluttony of guilt, go back to Dunbar and Henryson, recover and reclaim a national tradition that goes back through millennia. Use the precedents that are of use to you: he picked up from past, pre-war masters: his English teachers, F.G. Scott and George Ogilvie, had drilled into him an understanding of respect for literary quality, the value of great art, but he went further back to the 1890s, to Patrick Geddes (1854-1932), the social architect and town-planner, scientist and biologist, founder of the understanding of ecology, who first used the term 'Scottish Renascence' in his magazine *The Evergreen* in 1895. MacDiarmid championed him, and finally met him in the 1920s. His vision was deepening. What of the strategy?

His newspaper job was a breadwinner but also taught him tactics. He wrote the poems, but he also wrote articles, polemical and analytical essays, cultural, literary and political journalism, publishing in general newspapers and specialised periodicals throughout Scotland, in London (especially in the highbrow *New Age*, alongside Pound and other luminaries of modernity) and occasionally in America. He edited anthologies of poetry, *Northern Numbers*, three collections representing the old guard (yearning for golden days in the Hebrides) alongside the younger generation (noting the price of 'that woman's body' in the post-war industrial city), with the third book publishing poems by ten men and ten women: positive discrimination indeed. He edited his own periodicals and magazines: *The Scottish Chapbook*, *The Scottish Nation*, others, and contributed to many more. The strategy was to get the ideas out into circulation as widely as possible, to stir things up, not to let the dead hand – the mortmain – of the establishment reassert its authority.

In this context, we read the letters gathered here from Scottish correspondents who were his friends and allies: the novelists Lewis Grassic Gibbon, Neil Gunn, Catherine Carswell, poet Edwin Muir, sculptor Pittendrigh MacGillivray who refers to his fellow-sculptor William Lamb, the artists J.D. Fergusson and William McCance; and internationally, the composer Kaikhosru Shapurji Sorabji (1892-1988), poets Ezra Pound, T.S. Eliot, W.B. Yeats; and in politics, Nan Mercer regarding her father, the Communist John Maclean (1879-1923), appointed Bolshevik representative in Scotland by Lenin. The range of interests is wide, and impressive also for their depth and the activities they sparked and fuelled.

Two essays demonstrate the interconnectedness of these interests: 'A Theory of Scots Letters' (1923) which MacDiarmid published himself in three successive issues of his journal *The Scottish Chapbook* and 'English Ascendancy in British Literature' (1931) which T.S. Eliot published in *The Criterion*. In the first, MacDiarmid proposed that the language we call Scots possessed a validity in speech and a value in literature unique and misunderstood, that it was a vast quarry of possibility for modern writing, in two ways: in its capacity to draw on the experience of its users in Scotland across generations and geographies, and in its potential in literary modernism. First, it might spring from a physical intimacy in observation – its sound-qualities, its velar fricatives, the ichs, ochs and achs, all utilise bodily parts standard English finds rebarbative, and its history is predominantly rural, where the hard practicalities of farm life, raw humour and irony, sexual and bodily functioning in terms of animality and generation contribute to a worldview alien to Bloomsbury sophisticates but cognate with Joyce and Lawrence. Second, when this language was written in literary form – MacDiarmid began with short lyric poems, then two extended poem-sequences or 'gallimaufries', *A Drunk Man Looks at the Thistle* (1926) and *To Circumjack Cencrastus* (1930) – it might effect a deliberate strangeness on the page, the desired alienation-effect of Brecht, the forensic intellectual detachment of Eliot, words that stopped you in your tracks. In MacDiarmid's poems, this combination of intimate meaning and weird vocabulary often used conventional poetic forms: based on the ballad-stanza, regular rhymes and rhythms, grammatical syntax, full sentences and linear tonal modulations. This allowed meaning to be decoded quite easily through translation into English. Yet the power of the poems in Scots was intense. 'A Theory of Scots Letters' theorised this.

In 'English Ascendancy in British Literature', the argument opened and compared the status of the literatures written in different languages in the British Isles with the dominance of English-language literature: Scottish Gaelic, Irish Gaelic, Welsh, Scots, English (in its distinctive forms in different regions and nations), all possessed unique qualities and these were being suppressed by the dominance of normative English-language literature. The situation required redress. When this was published by T.S. Eliot in *The Criterion*, MacDiarmid commented that he had taken the war into the enemy's camp. Eliot had situated himself with painstaking work as the central arbiter of poetic authority, his own linguistic idiom of English bringing together his American upbringing with his Anglocentric and Eurocentric ethos, leading to his consolidated position with the prestigious publisher, Faber and Faber in London. The American poet William Carlos Williams considered Eliot's cultural establishment to be confirmed in the publication of *The Waste Land* (1922) and he called it a catastrophe. It was technically brilliant, innovative, magnetic, but culturally élitist and beyond anything Williams was trying to do with a distinctively American idiom. What Williams was attempting in America, MacDiarmid was attempting in Scotland, while Eliot had centred himself in a poetic and cultural position of Anglocentric, Eurocentric authority. Therefore, MacDiarmid's essay against English-language and literary ascendancy was dynamite.

He was betrayed in Scotland by Edwin Muir, erstwhile ally and fellow-fighter in the 1920s, who, in 1936, published a book called *Scott and Scotland*, in which he argued that the only way forward for Scottish writers was to abandon the Scots language and forget about inadequate Gaelic and to write from now on exclusively in English. Muir had already been published by Eliot at Faber and was following Eliot's directive that one nation required one language and one literature to be written in it. MacDiarmid's opposition was to argue the value of plurality, the specifics of multiple strands of history, the coherence that might be found in the diversity of Scotland. He proceeded to edit *The Golden Treasury of Scottish Poetry* (1940), a breakthrough volume including translations from work in Gaelic and Latin, as well as poems in Scots and English (nothing by Muir).

In this context, it is astonishing to read in the present collection Joseph Chiari's letter of 2 September 1978, the last letter in this book and presumably one of the last MacDiarmid read. Chiari, poet, critic, author of numerous books of literary and cultural philosophy, Corsica-born, a professional diplomat based in London and cultural attaché to the French Consulate in Edinburgh, was a close friend of Eliot and knew MacDiarmid well. MacDiarmid wrote a Preface for Chiari's *Collected Poems* (1978) and Chiari wrote a wonderful elegy for MacDiarmid in his subsequent book, *Slanting Lights* (1981): 'Jeremiah'. In the letter, Chiari says: 'I forgot to tell you that I wrote a short memoir on T.S. Eliot in which I said that, in spite of your different social and political attitudes, you were the poet he admired most.' If there is a sense of consolation in the warmth of this letter to a dying man, it does not seem at all like fabrication. That Eliot recognised MacDiarmid's greatness is assured.

The literary arguments raged and intertwined with crises in his personal life. His first wife Peggy left him for a better-off man, a coal merchant William McElroy (letters from both are included in this book), taking their children, Walter and Christine, with her. He met his second wife Valda and with their young son Michael, went to the island of Whalsay in Shetland, the furthest archipelago in the North Sea. Here, physical and mental breakdown followed a period of intense isolation, introspection and psychological anxiety. Yet astonishingly, his greatest poems of the 1930s delivered a way through the crises. 'Lament for the Great Music' reconnects with the deeper traditions of Scottish identity, the classical music of the Highland bagpipe and all that signifies for a multi-layered, complex, tragic, defiant, strengthening, persistent national character. 'On a Raised Beach' begins with the poet utterly alone on a Shetland stone beach but it ends with him lifting a stone, understanding that life is an act of participation in a way the lonely observer never could comprehend. At this time, paramount among MacDiarmid's favoured reading was the English poet and explorer of Arabia, Charles Montagu Doughty (1843-1926). Letters from his wife, from the 1930s, are included in the present book. In his biography of Doughty, *God's Fugitive* (1999), Andrew Taylor comments of his travels in Arabia: 'In [the] contrast between the vulnerability of human achievement and the permanence of human endeavour, Doughty was to find a lifelong inspiration, which he maintained with a religious force and passion.' (p.44) '[H]is imagination was fired by the links between past and present – the continuity imposed by the lives of people on ruins which seemed to speak only of mortality.' (p.56) These perceptions apply exactly to MacDiarmid at this time.

The extended, book-length poems that constitute his later work, *In Memoriam James Joyce* (1955) and *The Kind of Poetry I Want* (1961) largely come from this period too, though they were being worked on right through to their publication. These poems attempt to accommodate as many of all the languages and art-forms of the world by referring to human creativity in all its aspects, as far as he could find out about them, through his own experience, through talking with others, through correspondence in letters, through his reading of books and reviews of books in magazines. He pillaged everywhere and transformed his thefts into verse, amassing page upon page of information about subjects you would never encounter anywhere else between the same covers, turning from a Finnish dialect idiom to the dancing of Fred Astaire, from ancient epic literature in manuscripts dating from five centuries before Shakespeare to Tarzan of the Apes. However, the problem encountered here is exactly that described by Iain Crichton Smith, noted at the beginning of this introduction: selecting from the material the world provides is untrue to life – there it is, unending – but not to select risks extinction, overabundance, mere pluralism, formlessness – and form itself confers power. MacDiarmid knew this as surely as Eliot, so the tension in these long poems comes from the knowledge that art requires form. But the oppressive forms of imperial authority still have to be resisted. Robert Garioch Sutherland (the poet Robert Garioch), in his letter of August 1934, puts it like this:

Our science cannot conceive an acid that can mingle with an alkali to produce something more exciting than either. Life ought not to be reduced to systems: the scientist has a pedagogical desire for things on a plate.

And yet, of course, a poem needs a completeness. Content forms and form contents. But MacDiarmid's great emphasis in his later poetry and political understanding is that form in art also involves movement. It can never be static. One of the most famous utterances of Sir William Thompson, Lord Kelvin (1824-1907), was this:

When you can measure what you are speaking about, and express it in numbers, you know something about it; but when you cannot measure it, when you cannot express it in numbers, your knowledge of it is of a meagre and unsatisfactory kind; it may be the beginning of knowledge, but you have scarcely, in your thoughts, advanced it to the stage of science.

But of course, he was wrong. Some things simply cannot be expressed in numbers. MacDiarmid knew this, but he also learned it, deeply, in his years at the centre of cultural activity in Scotland in the 1920s, then in the years of exile, collapse and recovery in the 1930s, and through the extending correspondence of these and the decades to follow, right through to his death in 1978.

The correspondence gathered in this book is overwhelmingly rich and various. It might help to identify some of the major strands which run through it, and suggest some of the stories that interweave in the course of MacDiarmid's life. The book is a kind of kaleidoscopic biography, and the implicit life-story is visible through the singular forms of address evident in each letter as we read through them all, accumulating a multi-faceted knowledge of their addressee.

Letters from family are primary: his mother, his first wife Peggy and their children Walter and Christine, then his second wife Valda and their son Michael. Letters from friends run parallel, and there are very few people one could name as friends who were not also colleagues or allies in the arts. One who comes out of the book warmly is Charles Nicoll, MacDiarmid's foreman at the copper shell-band factory where he worked during the Second World War, and who kept in touch in later years. Mainly, though, letters from friends are from fellow-poets, artists of different kinds, and confederates and collaborators in the struggle for cultural engagement and revivification to which MacDiarmid was continuously committed. These correspondents are centred in Scotland but extend to figures writing from international locations and provenances. There are also his opponents and a few critics. Of all these men, F.G. Scott is of crucial significance. As the boy Chris Grieve's schoolteacher, he maintained an authority of judgement MacDiarmid was responsive to, although in later years the dynamics of their work and dispositions diverged. The extended letters from Scott carry the weight of his personal authority, but they are characterised by a close supportive quality of friendship as well as a severe and robust critical intensity. This is especially evident in the letters of the 1930s, when MacDiarmid went through his worst times of personal and professional isolation and suffering.

Many letters testify to MacDiarmid's direct political engagement: he was committed to international socialism and to Scotland's independence. He had a checkered relationship with officials of the Communist Party of Great Britain. A series of letters from Peter Kerrigan especially shows the officials' hardline view of what they took to be the liability, provocation and challenge of MacDiarmid's views and publications. The significant dates delineate the story clearly: He was a founder-member of the National Party of Scotland (NPS) in 1928 but not reinstated as a member of the NPS in 1933. After publishing the poem 'John MacLean (1879-1923)' in 1933, in 1934 he joined the Communist Party of Great Britain (CPGB) and in November 1936, he was expelled from the CPGB. In March 1937, he appealed against his expulsion and in May was readmitted to the CPGB. In June 1938, he published the first issue of his journal *The Voice of Scotland*, advocating the John Maclean line of Scottish Workers' Republicanism and again affirming his faith in independence for Scotland. In 1939 he was expelled once again from the CPGB. It was not until 1957 that he was readmitted to the CPGB, publishing his approval of Communism and simultaneously his criticism of the Soviet invasion of Hungary. There are obvious conflicts and contradictions here but there is also a determined unity of purpose. He remained committed to Scotland's independence and the ideals of a socialist society throughout his adult life. The practicality of his engagement with day-to-day politics is evident in his letters to Douglas Young, especially in the 1940s, while the interconnections between personal friendships and political commitments are clear in the correspondence with Barbara Niven and Joan Littlewood, and no doctrinaire limitations curtailed his moving praise in his eulogy for the novelist James Barke.

In all these respects, MacDiarmid is at a far remove from the English socialist poets of his day. There is an exceptional, and to many, exemplary balance between his self-awareness in political commitment and his self-determination as a poet and artist. The aesthetic sense, he knew, was the essential component in art: without it, art has no distinction. Yet equally understood was the fact that art itself, all the arts, take place within the political context. There is no trace of sentimental objectification in MacDiarmid's thinking here. There is rather an implicit abhorrence of the commodification of art and the fetishisation of the exploitative commercial economy so pervasive in western ideology of the early twenty-first century. MacDiarmid's work was predicated on the desire for a better way of living, universally. The given world was never to be merely accepted and used, but celebrated and criticised, built upon or demolished. In this lies his fundamental artistic manifesto: that the function of art is, at the same time, both representation and critique. Mimesis – the representation of reality in art – might present a recognisable scene. But to articulate that scene in an aesthetic form is also to imply a distance from lived reality: the painting has its frame and space from the viewer, the pages of print have their book or magazine covers, the page is held at a space from the understanding of the reader. The reader works to go through it, and takes pleasure in that work. Music performed to be listened to has a different effect from that performed to be danced to. By contrast, the immersion in screen media characteristic of the west in the modern world marks a significant escalation in the degree to which uncritical space is occupied. There is less work, less pleasure and less shock. For this reason alone MacDiarmid remains one of the most valuable writers of the last century. He still has a capacity to shock. He can show humanity at its worst, as well as its best. He remains, thankfully, a stranger to the bland.

Two examples: For generations, to mainlanders and lowlanders and visitors, the islands of Scotland were quintessentially the so-called 'Romantic' Hebrides, with Bonnie Prince Charlie's great escape swirling in impenetrable mist and evidence of a human loyalty incorruptible almost to the point of foolishness. A legacy of romanticising Scottish history had been passing into popular perception over a hundred years. MacDiarmid wrote the first book that shifted the meaning of the term 'The Islands of Scotland' in 1939, on the eve of the Second World War: *The Islands of Scotland*, a revisionary demystification of island life. Over half of it was devoted to Shetland, where he had been living, much to Orkney and relatively little space given to the Hebrides.

And consider the book-length poem *Aniara: A Review of Man in Time and Space* by Harry Martinson (1904-1978), first published in Sweden in 1956, adapted into English by Elspeth Harley Schubert and turned into free verse in 103 'songs' by MacDiarmid, and published in 1963. This is a central work of the Cold War, imagining a post-nuclear apocalyptic earth, polluted by atomic explosions, from which mankind is leaving in swarms of spaceships to colonize other planets, for 'Earth must have a rest / for all her poisons'. The giant spaceship *Aniara*, housing eight thousand people, swerves to avoid an asteroid, is knocked off course, and passes 'the point of no return', heading into deep space beyond known galaxies, through unimaginable time, as the population of the earth dies off and, ultimately, the population on board the spaceship, too, dies off. It is a vast, dreadfully pessimistic dystopian vision, and thus a highly unusual component of MacDiarmid's generally optimistic and affirmative *oeuvre*. That MacDiarmid took on the role of co-translating it says something important about his engagement with the nuclear age and may be considered alongside his anti-nuclear writings elsewhere, such as 'The Unholy Loch'. *Aniara* begins in despair and ends in total annihilation. For Martinson in MacDiarmid's version, moments of lucid memory poignantly evoke the vivid pleasures of an earth that can never be revisited. For example, in Song 72, there are 'glimpses of Karelia' (the landscape made familiar in the orchestral tone-poems of the great Finnish composer Sibelius):

> like a blue streak between tree-trunks, like the paling summer waters
> in the June-translucent twilight when an evening scarcely deepens
> ere the cuckoo sends his flute-like invitation to sweet Aino
> to swathe veils of mist about her, rise above the summer waters,
> go towards the soaring smoke wreaths, come to meet the cheerful cuckoo
> 'midst Karelia's murmuring winds.

The poem is characteristic of MacDiarmid in the sense that it represents the threat of what always encroaches upon us: the terrifying 'empty sterile universe'. If all living things are, like the travellers on the spaceship, destined to become 'transformed once more to blameless dust... / impervious to the sting of bitter stars, / lost and dispersed in oceans of Nirvana', then nevertheless in a poem like this, we can be reminded of the values of the earth we would wish to keep.

In the 1960s and 1970s especially, there are many letters from younger writers and scholars, finding friendship and support from MacDiarmid, as they recognised and responded to his poetry and political stand. There are also, increasingly, letters from scholars and academics, those readers setting out to dive into the archives of work which, at that time, was held in fugitive publications in unexplored depths of the libraries. Letters collected here from David Daiches, Duncan Glen, Kenneth Buthlay, Roderick Watson, T.J. Cribb and others chart the growing and multi-faceted interests that were arising in the universities – from

America to Cambridge – while correspondence from Hamish Henderson, Sorley MacLean, Alexander Trocchi, Compton Mackenzie, Douglas Dunn and Iain Crichton Smith shows different responses to, and feelings about, MacDiarmid, in an incredibly wide range of writers in the Scottish traditions and internationally. Allen Ginsberg, Muriel Rukeyser and Adrienne Rich from the United States, Maurice Shadbolt and Kevin Ireland from New Zealand, Seamus Heaney and John Montague from Ireland, Basil Bunting from England, Yevtushenko from Soviet Russia, visited, wrote about or corresponded with MacDiarmid over the years. Yet his stance with regard to politics and the world at large was never mollified by such breadth of attention but remained consistently edged, shrewd, wry, always carrying the sense that the border was never somewhere else. There would always be value to fight for.

> He either fears his fate too much,
> Or his deserts are small,
> That dares not put it to the touch
> To gain or lose it all.

When James Graham, Marquis of Montrose (1612-1650) wrote those lines, he could not have imagined their resonance in the work of Hugh MacDiarmid, or in the twenty-first century that followed him. Yet they never seemed more necessary, and MacDiarmid's work never more vitalising, than now.

List of Abbreviations

EUL –	Edinburgh University Library
ML –	Mitchell Library
NLS –	National Library of Scotland
SUNYB –	State University of New York at Buffalo
TNA –	The National Archives

Illustrations

Titles of Books Frequently Cited

Particulars of some works relating to MacDiarmid have been abbreviated in the text to avoid repetition and are given below in the order in which they first appear.

Alan Bold, *MacDiarmid,* 1st edn (London: John Murray, 1988).

Hugh MacDiarmid, *The Company I've Kept* (London: Hutchinson, 1966).

Hugh MacDiarmid, *Complete Poems* 1920-1976, Volumes I and II, ed. by Michael Grieve and W.R. Aitken (London: Martin Brian & O'Keeffe, 1978).

Hugh MacDiarmid, *Albyn,* or the Future of Scotland, 1st edn (London: Routledge & Kegan Paul, 1927).

Hugh MacDiarmid, *Albyn: Shorter Books and Monographs* ed. by Alan Riach (Manchester: Carcanet Press Limited, 1996) included the first edition of *Albyn.*

Hugh MacDiarmid, *Lucky Poet, A Self-Study in Literature and Political Ideas* (London: Methuen, 1943).

Hugh MacDiarmid, *The Revolutionary Art of the Future,* ed. by John Manson, Dorian Grieve and Alan Riach (Manchester: Carcanet Press Limited, 2003).

Gordon Wright, *MacDiarmid: An Illustrated Biography* (Edinburgh: Gordon Wright Publishing, 1977).

Hugh MacDiarmid, *Annals of the Five Senses* (Montrose: C.M. Grieve, 1923), 4th edn in *Annals of the Five Senses and Other Stories, Sketches and Plays,* ed. by Roderick Watson and Alan Riach (Manchester: Carcanet Press Limited, 1999).

The Letters of Hugh MacDiarmid, ed. with an Introduction by Alan Bold (London: Hamish Hamilton, 1984).

Hugh MacDiarmid, *New Selected Letters,* ed. by Dorian Grieve, Owen Dudley Edwards and Alan Riach (Manchester: Carcanet Press Limited, 2001).

The Golden Treasury of Scottish Poetry, ed. by Hugh MacDiarmid (London: MacMillan, 1940).

MacDiarmid: a festschrift, ed. by K.D. Duval and Sydney Goodsir Smith (Edinburgh: K.D. Duval, 1962).

Hugh MacDiarmid, *The Raucle Tongue,* Volumes I, II and III, ed. by Angus Calder, Glen Murray and Alan Riach (Manchester: Carcanet Press Limited, 1996, 1997 and 1998 respectively).

Hugh MacDiarmid's Addresses

In their original form some of the letters were formally addressed to Hugh MacDiarmid on the left-hand side of the page. These addresses have not been printed as they were only occasional, and repetitive in the instances where they were inserted. Instead a chronology of his addresses is given below although it has not always been possible to establish precise dates.

16 Links Avenue, Montrose from 17 March 1922 to 9 September 1929.

18 Pyrland Road, Highbury, **London** from 10 September 1929 into September 1931 (home). **10A Soho Square**, **London** (office of *Vox)* from 10 September 1929 to 8 February 1930. From 12 May 1930 into the summer of 1931 he worked as Publicity Officer for the Liverpool Organisation, **357 Royal Liver Building, Liverpool**.

63/64 Chancery Lane, London (home) and **321 High Holborn**, **London** (office of the Unicorn Press) from early September 1931 to mid-March 1932.

'Cootes', Thakeham, West Sussex from 14 March 1932 to the end of August 1932.

A **cottage** behind the derelict limeworks and former **Fruit Farm** outbuildings to the south-east of **Longniddry** (home) and **India Buildings, 1 Victoria Street, Edinburgh** (office of *The Free Man*) from September 1932 into May 1933.

Sudheim, Whalsay, Shetland from 4 May 1933 to 4 February 1942. (From 15 March 1934 into October 1934 MacDiarmid lived mainly at several addresses in London.

The longest stays were at **33 Great James Street, London** - with John Gawsworth - in June, and at **12 Petherton Road, North London** from July into early October. He had also spent a week in Cornwall from 6 to 13 April and had returned to Glasgow and Edinburgh from 3 May to 20 May.)

7 February 1942 into October 1942 MacDiarmid stayed (successively) with his brother Andrew at **70 Grenville Drive, Cambuslang**, F.G. Scott at **44**

Munro Road, Glasgow, and Robin Black at **2 Park Terrace, Glasgow**.

35 Havelock Street, Partick, Glasgow from October 1942 into December 1943.

27 Arundel Drive, Battlefield, Glasgow from December 1943 to August 1946.

32 Victoria Crescent Road, Dowanhill, Glasgow from August 1946 to autumn 1949.
For some months from May 1947 MacDiarmid worked on *The Carlisle Journal*, **60 English Street, Carlisle** (office) and stayed at the **Viaduct Hotel.**

Laundry Cottage, Dungavel House, Lanarkshire from autumn 1949 into January 1951.

Brownsbank, Candymill, by Biggar, Lanarkshire from January 1951 until his death on 9 September 1978.

The information about dates has been taken from

MacDiarmid, The Letters, New Selected Letters, and the editor's biographical papers based on his research in The National Library of Scotland and Edinburgh University Library (Centre for Research Collections).

'After sixty years: once more on the Grieves in Whalsay, 1933-42', in *The New Shetlander,* Lerwick, Voar Issue, No. 223, 2003, pp. 17-21.

'Hugh MacDiarmid in England' in *Markings* 20-21 (Kirkcudbright, 2005), pp.116-125.

'Did Hugh MacDiarmid "Drink the Money"'? in *Weighbauk,* Occasional Paper 2, (Kirkpatrick-Durham, 2010), pp.1-4.

'Hugh MacDiarmid as a Worker' in *Markings* 14 (Kirkcudbright, 2002), pp.10-11, and (extended) in *Weighbauk,* Occasional Paper 2, (Kirkpatrick-Durham, 2010), pp. 5-10.

'The Grieves in Thakeham' in *Times Past* 36, Newsletter of Storrington & District Museum Society, Summer 2010, p.4 (http://www.storringtonmuseum.org/ newsletter. html), and in *Scottish Literary Review 3.1* (Glasgow : Association for Scottish Literary Studies, Spring/Summer 2011).

Note on the Text

In reply to a question from Douglas Young in a review published in *Lines Review* 25, Winter 1967-1968, about F.G. Scott's role in the arrangement of *A Drunk Man looks at the Thistle,* Hugh MacDiarmid showed that he anticipated that letters from his correspondents would be published at a later date. In giving his account of Scott's role in the next issue of *Lines Review*, Summer 1968, MacDiarmid wrote:

'When I was writing the *Drunk Man* I had poured out a great mass of verse. Scott came to Montrose and in an all-night session he helped me to discard a great deal that was inferior, repetitive or not essential. [...] Scott, [Edwin] Muir, my first wife and others who were in touch with me when *A Drunk Man* was being written are all dead now, but I think it is likely that correspondence from them when my letters are finally published will fully bear out what I say.'[1]

No letters relating to the writing of *A Drunk Man* appear to have survived the 'almighty big bonfire' which he made in his garden in Montrose before he left for London in September 1929.[2] However, many thousands of (mostly later) letters from a wide range of correspondents are preserved; mainly in the C.M. Grieve Correspondence in Edinburgh University Library (Special Collections) and in the National Library of Scotland, and these bear on his literary, political and private life.

Sources of Letters to Hugh MacDiarmid:
EUL MSS2942-2978: individual folders of letters mainly from the most frequent correspondents, and from publishing firms, and magazine editors, all arranged alphabetically. The total has not been counted.
EUL GEN. 2094/1-6: over 2,500 letters mainly from less frequent correspondents, arranged alphabetically.
NLS MSS26066, 27148-9, 27150-53, 27155-56, 27166, all passim.
NLS ACC. 7361/1-53: the first 49 folders have each been devoted to one year of MacDiarmid's life from 1929 to 1978, and collect letters, leaflets, brochures, invitations and so on. The contents of the final four boxes are not arranged in chronological order but collect the same kinds of materials. Alan R. Bell, then Curator of Modern Political Manuscripts, Manuscripts Division, NLS, has estimated these accessions at 'c.5,000 letters' in *Scottish Labour History* (Glasgow, 2002), p.81.
SUNYB: Poetry Collection of the University Libraries.

Letters have been selected to express the views of the correspondents and not because the editor identifies with these views.

Ellipses or *points de suspension* are part of the original letter and do not indicate words omitted by the editor. In one instance, indicated by '[...]', a few words have been left out at the request of the copyright holder.

Occasional spelling mistakes have been silently corrected but where the style is unique to the correspondent, that style has been retained and not made to conform to accepted spelling and grammar.

Very famous names have not been referenced in the notes; it will remain a matter of opinion which names are very famous.

1 Young's review is quoted in a note, and MacDiarmid's letter is given in full in *The Letters*, pp. 834-835.
2 In a note in *MacDiarmid*, p.455, Alan Bold gives the source for the phrase, 'almighty big bonfire', as a letter from MacDiarmid to George Malcolm Thomson, 15 December 1954.

Letters

The 1920s

The 1930s

The 1940s

The 1950s

The 1960s

The 1970s

The 1920s

1. From J. S. Muirhead (EUL MS2966)

Baird Smiths, Muirhead and Guthrie Smith
205 St Vincent Street
Glasgow
20 March 1923

Dear Sir,

I must apologise for delaying so long in replying to your letter of 10th inst. I was much surprised to find myself on the front page (with two misprints!) of last month's *Chapbook*.[1] You do me much too great honour. I am rather apprehensive of sending you further verses, as after starting the hunt in this way I shall never maintain the pace, I fear.

I am afraid my finances will only lead to a very humble share in your proposed periodical, but I believe there is room for something of the sort.[2] I should be glad to see a dummy copy, & will speak to one or two people I know who might be interested. I do not imagine you and I see eye to eye on many subjects, but perhaps you will not mind a controversial element occasionally obtruding between us.

I regard, for example, Scottish Home Rule as a clear invention of the Devil, and principally designed to assist the already grievous domination of Scotland by the Irish and the Pole. I am a keen Territorial & served four and a half years in France in the War, and am really a philistine, with a taste for letters. I do not like the bawdy streak in some of your own poems again, e.g., one I think in *Northern Numbers*[3] 'sublimating' (I think that is the word) copulation in a religious guise – preferring art and bawdry (both excellent things in their way) apart, or at least regarding their combination so difficult as to be almost impossible. For example, I know of no artistic presentation of coitus in any kind of art – by artistic I mean one in which the emotion roused is an artistic and not an apolaustic one. However this is not the place for a dissertation.

I shall be interested to hear of your various ventures' successes, & shall, if I have time, submit you more verse.

Meantime accept my thanks for your letter, & for your interesting writing in the *Chapbook*.

Yours sincerely,
J. S. Muirhead.

1   Muirhead contributed two poems to *The Scottish Chapbook,* vol. 1, no. 7 (February 1923); 'Atmospherics' on the front page (p. 179) and 'The Diehards' (p.186) . *The Scottish Chapbook* ran from August 1922 to the end of 1923.
2   The reference here is to *The Scottish Nation* which was launched on 8 May 1923.
3   *Northern Numbers* 1 and 2 were published in Edinburgh in 1920 and 1921 respectively; *Northern Numbers* 3 was published in Montrose in 1922.

2. From George Reston Malloch (EUL MS2962.6 f.29)

St. Enoch Station Hotel
Glasgow C1
8 June 1924

Dear Grieve,

I regret very much to find that it will not be possible for me to get to Montrose on this trip. Various things have interfered with my original plans and I shall have to return south tomorrow or the day after.

I must thank you for placing me in touch with McGill,[1] MacKemmie[2] and Pollock[3] with whom I have had some most enjoyable meetings here. I was much impressed by them all and by the vitality of the Scottish Theatre movement, of which I expect great things under such auspices.

My own movements have been confined to a visit to Oban and to various places on the Clyde; but I think that I have gathered some material to be pondered over and perhaps developed at leisure, when I find any of that too scarce commodity.

In that respect my very brief visit to Scotland has been of great value to me. I am only sorry that it has not included the pleasure of meeting you and Mrs Grieve again. This has not been a real holiday in the sense that I have had to carry on with my ordinary work for the press, a thing I find very difficult to do in hotels which do not supply pens with which one can write. But I am afraid it will have to serve me for another year.

I am looking forward to the new *Northern Review* - if it equals the first issue it will be doing well .[4] Kindest regards to Mrs Grieve and yourself & many regrets at not seeing you both.

Yours sincerely,
George Reston Malloch.

[1]   Alexander McGill was associate editor of MacDiarmid's monthly *The Northern Review* in 1924 and his article 'Hugh MacDiarmid' in *The Glasgow Herald*, 4 April 1925, helped to promote MacDiarmid's reputation.
[2]   D. Glen MacKemmie was Chairman of the Scottish National Theatre Society.
[3]   R. F. Pollock was the subject of an article in *The Scottish Educational Journal*, 13 November 1925.
[4]   The first isssue of *The Northern Review* was published in May 1924; the fourth and fifth issue in September.

3. From George Ogilvie (EUL MS2958.3 ff.1-2)

67 Cluny Gdns
Edinburgh
10 February 1925

My dear Christopher,

You may certainly count on my doing anything I possibly can in support of your application for the post you mention.[1] I am only sorry that at most that will be comparatively little; but once I find out who the trustees are it may turn out that I can get at some of them.

What a pity it is that you have made (as you admit) so many enemies! I especially deplored that superfluous (and for you so crude) attack on Kitchin – in the *Forward*.[2] One of your enemies lost no time in throwing it in my face, and frankly I blushed for you. The mischief is that Kitchin might have been of great use to you now – not to speak of his pal J. C. Stewart who, I fear, has been definitely alienated by the article.[3] You took, or pretended to take, Kitchin's article in *The Scotsman* too seriously. It struck me as kindly enough on the whole.

I hope you have written to Dr Drummond.[4] I am no longer a member of his church, but up to the last time I met him he never forgot to make kind inquiries about you. He is a man of wide influence, & might be of much use.

I shall let you know if I can secure any helpers.

I did not resume work till January. That night I left you at Church Hill to see my doctor was the start of a two months illness – blood pressure and heart trouble. I am not very well yet & am glad to lie 'dormy' by the fire when I creep home from school. The others happily have had only minor ailments. You do not say anything of your household health: I take it that you are all going strong. I do trust that for your own & their sakes you pull off this job or one equally good. It is high time you were out of Montrose.

Kindest regards to all.

Yours sincerely,

Geo. Ogilvie.

[1]   The vacancy was for Keeper of the National Galleries of Scotland.
[2]   George Kitchin (1881-1968) lectured in English at Edinburgh University, 1911-1946. Kitchin's article, 'The "Scottish Renaissance" Group: What it Represents', had appeared in *The Scotsman* on 8 November 1924. MacDiarmid had replied in a letter on 13 November, and in an article in *Forward*, the weekly Socialist newspaper, on 22 November, entitled 'Dr Kitchin, Moscow and the Scottish Renaissance'. Dr Kitchin had referred to the 'Scottish Renaissance' Group as 'intellectual revolutionaries'.
[3]   J. C. Stewart was an Inspector of Schools for the Western Division. He may have been the John Christie Stewart, Classics Master at Broughton prior to 1920.
[4]   Dr Robert Drummond was Minister of Lothian Road Church; he knew MacDiarmid when MacDiarmid was a student at Broughton and later conducted MacDiarmid's first marriage ceremony.

4. From Alexander McGill (EUL MS2966)

37 Bellwood Street
Langside
Glasgow
17 September 1925

Dear C. M.,

I was very glad indeed to hear from you again, and to see that you are full of fight. I have no plans this year except my lecture on the English Trade in Iceland which I want you to hear at all price. The material is accumulating and this evening I had a find in the Calendar of State Papers which surprised even George Insh.[1] Interesting & all as the work is I shall not be sorry to see it finished. The driving force is my desire to get the recognition & if possible the £60 prize in the University as well: as well as my affection for the Icelandic people. So whatever you do for Sn. Jónsson I shall appreciate as a personal kindness.

I shall not go to Edinburgh this Saturday but will go again to the University Library & get into the State Papers again. But I shall spend the Autumn Holiday in the Advocates Library & that with two or three other trips to Edinburgh will finish my research for the present purpose.

The C.M.G.[2] article in the *Herald* would I think not pass the censor as they would suspect me of playing a game. I hardly know what paper would take it. At present I cannot collect my thoughts for our-own-gang-work, but shall do so presently.

I have spoken to O'C regarding your suggestion.[3] He will be writing you directly, but understand clearly that the *Columba* readers are anti-Socialist and strongly pro-English.[4] The paper sells mainly in England, so you'll understand. O'C has a great affection for you and your work, so I think all will go well. In the meantime get started to a good article on the Reformation as I suggested and do your best for O'C.

Insh has just left me. I hope you will do him a good article and speak of his work, not merely of his intentions. I think there is much of interest in his *[Scottish] Colonial Schemes.*[5] He is a very big mind, humble and gentle though he looks.

I shall see Pollock tomorrow and instruct him .[6]

Jónsson & the Icelandic magazine are having a bit of a dispute just now so leave the latter alone in the meantime.

With best wishes to Mrs Grieve and yourself from us both.

Yours sincerely,

Alexander McGill.

---

[1]   MacDiarmid contributed an article on George Pratt Insh to *The Scottish Educational Journal* on 18 December 1925.

[2]   Christopher Murray Grieve. Here it appears that MacDiarmid had asked McGill to contribute his article to *the Herald* under McGill's name.

[3]   'O'C' was Patrick J. O' Callaghan. 'At a meeting held in Glasgow on 5 October 1919, attended by twenty-four Catholic gentlemen, Corkman Patrick J. O' Callaghan asked those present to agree to the formation of a new organisation, which would ultimately be called the Knights of St. Columba.' (http://www.ksc.org.uk/history.htm) .

[4]   *Columba* was 'the official Monthly of the Knights of St Columba'.

[5]   *Scottish Colonial Schemes 1620-1686* (Glasgow, 1922).

[6]   R. F. Pollock's Lennox Players produced McGill's *Pardon in the Morning* among other plays in 1924 and 1925.

5. From Sir Patrick Geddes (EUL MS2948.8 ff.18-19.)

Collège des Ecossais
Plan des Quatre Seigneurs
Montpellier (Herault)
France
19 October 1925

Dear Mr Grieve,

I hoped to see you and Mr Scott again before you left Edinburgh, but I can quite understand that you were too busy – as I also have been since![1] I was to make good (on behalf of our kindred endeavours) your expenses – & so – at a venture – enclose £2. (If any deficit, let me know – if any surplus, you can send me any future paper you find handy.)

And if you come again to France, do not forget this as convenient 'howff' for rest & sunshine, & I trust some conversation too! I have just now my bright old friend Sir Thomas Barclay, whom I hope to rouse to the interest of your movement; & others will be coming in from time to time, though we won't be ready for students this winter beyond the two young *doctorands* now with me and at their theses.

You should know that any active-minded foreigner, ready to produce a good thesis, can present it for D.& C. or D. Litt. in this or other French Univ. with one academic year's residence, & that he need not have taken preliminary degrees – provided he gives indication of studious experience in any form – (for which publications of any reasonable kind are good evidence.)

More & more there is growing on me the possibility of strengthening all our scattered movements of synthetic & constructive & progressive character – whether regional, literary, scientific, artistic, economic or social etc., by trying to bring them together, & thus increasingly present them as each part of a *synthetic movement*, reaching out beyond the chaos-Babel of current action & thought so apparently predominant. The various Regional movements would all gain by this, alike in local appreciation & in mutual aid & impulse, & so for Universities, research institutes, & all sorts of practical endeavours – like the regional and town-planning movement in which my own work has for many years so largely lain. So your suggestions will be valued & I am sure helpful.

Again thanks to yourself & Mr Scott for your visit, which I trust has left an impulse & interest to all who met you; & with cordial regards to both, believe me always,
Yours faithfully,
Pat Geddes.

---

[1] Sir Patrick Geddes's letter was written soon after his meeting with Hugh MacDiarmid and Francis George Scott in Edinburgh. In *MacDiarmid*, Alan Bold writes: 'A month after the publication of *Sangschaw*, Grieve was in Edinburgh at a meeting chaired by Geddes, the sociologist who had, in 1892, established the Outlook Tower, on Castlehill, as an international centre of research into town planning and other of his many interests. As Grieve read MacDiarmid poems and F.G. Scott played MacDiarmid settings the appearance

further undermined the plausibility of his pseudonym.' (London: John Murray, 1988), p 169. In *The Company I've Kept* MacDiarmid quoted a letter of Dr Arthur Geddes, Sir Patrick's son, in which he wrote: 'I well remember the day in Montpellier when in *Les Nouvelles Littéraires*, we first read a few of MacDiarmid's poems and my father wrote to him straightaway; the friendship began with poems and response to them!' (London: Hutchinson, 1966), p.79.

6. From H. J. C. Grierson (EUL MS2976)

12 Regent Terrace
Edinburgh
28 October 1925

Dear Mr Grieve,

I am glad you wrote to me for I was beginning to repent badly of having promised Mr Galsworthy[1] to try to start his club. I had a bad time before over the Spanish Club. The fact is I do not know what authors to apply to. I live so much close. I suppose Buchan[2] shd. be president, if he lives at all in Scotland. Sir George Douglas[3] shd. be approached too. But there my knowledge ends, i.e., I do not know what writers of real interest are living in Scotland except yourself & Neil Munro.[4] The Scottish authors of the creative kind – novelists, poets – tend to drift to London. I know one or two here but they are of no great weight. I spoke to Dixon[5] of Glasgow on Saturday but he was not much interested tho' I think he would come in. If you could give me a list of really good names in and about Glasgow & Edinburgh I would send out an invitation to meet here in the College & create a Committee. Do you think that would be the best way or can you suggest any other? The secretary must send me some more books. I wd. send them out with my letter. Let me have any suggestions & *names* you can, as soon as possible.

Sincerely yours,

H. J. C. Grierson.

[1] John Galsworthy (1867-1933), novelist and playwright. *The Forsyte Saga,* first published togther in 1922, remains his best-known work. The reference is to the foundation of Scottish PEN.
[2] John Buchan (1875-1940), novelist, biographer, historian, essayist, journalist, editor, poet and publisher.
[3] Sir George Douglas (1856-1935), poet and editor of Scottish poets and anthologies of Scottish poetry; author of works linked to the Scottish Borders.
[4] Neil Munro (1864-1930), novelist and journalist.
[5] W. MacNeile Dixon (1866-1945) was Professor of English in the University of Glasgow from 1904 to 1935.

7. From George W. Russell ('AE') (EUL MS2958.21 f.1)

The Irish Statesman
84 Merrion Square

Dublin

3 November 1925

Dear Mr. Grieve,

I find your article on the Scottish Renaissance Movement very interesting, but it is so anti-Protestant in its bias that I would not like to print the article in my own journal where I do my utmost to keep out anything which would hurt the feelings of either my Protestant or my Catholic readers, and indeed this is the policy of every paper in the Free State except one or two small sectarian rags. If you could manage to take the jibes about Protestantism out of your article I would be glad to print it. I do not think anything is to be gained in Ireland at least, by raising the question of Catholic and Protestant in politics. I do not like making any alterations myself so I am returning the article hoping that you yourself will be able to remove the objectionable things in the article which I have indicated with a pencil mark. Perhaps if you could use some word like Calvinism it would not sound so objectionable to my Protestant readers. Protestantism in Ireland has produced many Nationalists, and indeed most of the great figures in the literary movement. I can mention Dr Douglas Hyde[1] and Osborn Bergin[2] among the Gaelic scholars and writers, Yeats, Lady Gregory,[3] Seumas O' Sullivan,[4] James Stephens,[5] Standish O' Grady,[6] and many others among the literary Nationalists who have all based themselves upon Gaelic tradition, so that here my readers would not accept the inference you draw that Protestantism must essentially be antagonistic to the arts and letters. I am sorry for having to make this comment but I hate having in my paper anything that would create an antagonism between the two religions in this country and I am quite certain that it is not necessary to your argument.

Yours sincerely,

Geo. W. Russell.

---

[1] Dr Douglas Hyde (1860-1949), scholar, poet and translator; first President of the Irish Republic (1938-1944).

[2] Osborn Bergin (1873-1950), literary editor and author of works on Irish grammar.

[3] Lady Gregory (1852-1932), playwright.

[4] Seumas O'Sullivan (James Sullivan Starkey) (1879-1958), poet and founder-editor of *The Dublin Magazine* from 1923. Dedicatee of 'Milk-Wort and Bog-Cotton' in *Complete Poems* I, ed. by Michael Grieve and W. R. Aitken (London: Martin Brian and O'Keeffe, 1978), p.331.

[5] James Stephens (1882-1950), poet and novelist.

[6] Standish O'Grady (1846-1928), historian.

8. From Knights of St Columba (EUL MS2970)

COLUMBA

The Official Monthly of the Knights of St. Columba

132 West Nile Street

Glasgow
2 July 1926

My Dear Grieve,

Herewith cheque for one guinea for matter so kindly sent me for 'leader', for which I shall ever be indebted to you.[1] Mr McGill has been telling me of your proposal with regard to a quarterly.[2] I hope this will not interfere with our proposed paper. I am full of hope of the possibilities of your writing, and I am very hopeful of being able to manage the capital necessary to start work about October at the very latest, in fact I did something towards that yesterday in Liverpool, but as all I have in the world would be involved in it, I need scarcely tell you how anxious I am to be on sound lines.

Now, I would be glad to hear from you on this point, and also if you will do something for me that I could make a Leader out of. I would suggest the need for an enlightened Catholic opinion; the necessity for Catholics recognising their responsibility as members of the Church; as citizens, above all as Knights of Saint Columba, getting back to the spirit of the Middle Ages, and a reference to your own pet-hobby; of the tendency of thinking men of today towards neo-Catholicism.[3]

If you can do something like you did last month, I will be able to build upon it.

I would have written you before but owing to our financial year ending on June 30th we held up all payments until after that day.

Perhaps at your leisure you could let me have about two thousand words of Notes and News, or a literary page for the middle of next week. We are going to press on Friday owing to the Glasgow Fair Holidays with our August issue.

I would also like a special article for a special number that we are having in September for the Catholic Congress at Manchester, with coloured plates; you could think out something special for that.

With best wishes and kind regards.

Yours sincerely,

R.W. L [rest of surname illegible].

PS Try and let me have your notes for my Leader not later than Tuesday morning or Monday, if possible.

---

[1] Perhaps it was on the basis of the matter for the leader in June 1926, 'The Order and the Crisis' (on the General Strike), and subsequent leaders, that MacDiarmid claimed to ' [...] have edited [...] a Roman Catholic monthly [...]' in an autobiographical sketch in 1932 (NLS MS27083 f.41). In a letter to George Dott, 1 August 1930, George Malcolm Thomson showed that he regarded MacDiarmid as '[...] the paid agent of the R.C. Church in Scotland [...]' (NLS Acc. 5927/1 unfoliated).

[2] This 'proposal' is not clearly identifiable and was certainly never realised. It may have been 'Scots Art' with William McCance as Art Editor (cf.Tom Normand, *The Modern Scot*, Aldershot and Vermont, 2000, p. 68).

[3] MacDiarmid sent a card to Peggy, his first wife, from Villa de L'Annonciation, Lourdes, 4 June 1919: 'In memory of a year ago. A small souvenir/from the city of Miracles and Prayer. From Chris to Peggy.' The card was of the Virgin Mary with the injunction, 'Vierge

Sainte, priez pour nous' (EUL MS2132/19). In *Scottish Chapbook,* vol.1, no.3 (October 1922), MacDiarmid printed five sonnets under the title 'Scots Catholic Choir' with a note, 'Five sonnets illustrative of neo-Catholic tendencies in contemporary Scottish literature: 1. Jessie Annie Anderson; 11. John Ferguson; 111. C.M. Grieve; 1V. John Ferguson; V. Jessie Annie Anderson.'

9. From Stewart Carmichael (EUL MS2926.1 ff.45-46)

65 Nethergate
Dundee
29 November 1926

My Dear C. M. Grieve,

I was delighted to see Mrs Grieve & her friend on Saturday at my Exhibition & to have the pleasure of introducing her to my wife.

I was sorry her visit was a little rushed as it would have been a great treat to us to have had her a longer time & to have enjoyed a more intimate talk & to have got all her news about your doings.

Your gift to me of *Contemporary Scottish Studies*[1] was most generous & few things could have given me greater pleasure: the dedication so simple & so frank won my heart. Accept my heartiest thanks.

Many of the 'studies' I re-read again yesterday & was delighted with their freshness & fearlessness & the eternal & necessary slogan 'Alba gu Brath'![2] Not that the Gaelic phrase interprets your point of view, but it means something.

You are right in this continual advocacy of the Scottish point of view: you are like unto a Scottish representative of an All Nations' Congress who can think & speak & act as if his country behind him had something inevitable of its own to contribute to the development of mankind in its Art & Life & was determined to express it. You are the mouthpiece of modern Scotland inspiring & invigorating us all.

I hope the book will be greatly read. I shall be surprised if it does not have a big circulation. It is very distinguished in its get-up & excellently printed: there are so few books of this order in Scotland that many will be curious & will say, 'Are there really people in Art, Literature & Education in Scotland who have a point of view that a man can analyse & write upon?'

My friends in Lithuania had hardly heard of Burns & knew nothing whatever of our priceless Celtic heritage in Art & Poetry & less than nothing of our veritable Scots poets. They did know a little of Thackeray, George Eliot & Walter Scott – but our knowledge of their Polish Literature & Art is deplorable! They have great national artists of genius I had not even heard of! We enjoyed Lithuania: it suggested to me what Scotland must have been three centuries ago – moors, lochs & forests with picturesque villages, built of wood, dominated by great white Russo-Byzantine Churches – roads ankle-deep in mud. But when you come to see me, which I hope will be soon, we will talk more of this. Meanwhile let me again express my thanks for your gift of *Contemporary Scottish Studies* & accept from Mrs Carmichael & myself our kindest good wishes to your wife and self.

Denis Saurat - influence on MacDiarmid through his books *The Three Conventions* and *The End Of Fear*.
By permission of Cécile Triat-Saurat.

Yours,
Stewart Carmichael.

1   London: Parsons, 1926.
2   Scotland for ever!

10. From Stewart Carmichael (EUL MS2962.1)

65 Nethergate
Dundee
21 January 1927

My Dear C. M. Grieve,
I am looking forward to travelling to Cupar with you on Tuesday 25th. I will catch the train you come with from Montrose at Dundee T.B. Station at 5.42: keep a lookout for me!

I shall stay the night also at Cupar & leave with the same morning train (8.50) as you propose to do.

I am very pleased to have an opportunity of saying something about you & your work at the Burns dinner. It is the first festival of its kind I have been at & I hope it will go well. I regret Pittendrigh MacGillivray is not to be present – at least his name is not on the toast-list.

Your pamphlet on *The Present Position of Scottish Music* is splendid & I thank you heartily for it.[1] Mrs Carmichael thinks it most admirable & true. Also, for the Augustan *Robert Burns* many thanks.[2] I hope your 'Immortal Memory' will be a triumph.

With kindest remembrances to both.
Yours,
Stewart Carmichael.

I saw your letter in *The Times Literary Supplement*. S. C.

1   Montrose 1927. Reprinted in *Albyn: Shorter Books and Monographs*, ed. by Alan Riach (Manchester: Carcanet, 1996), pp. 40-58.
2   *Robert Burns, 1759-1796*, ed. by C.M. Grieve, London 1926.

11. From Denis Saurat (EUL MS2960.3 f.1)

Institut Français du Royaume Uni
(Universités de Lille et de Paris)
15 March 1927

Dear Friend,
That lazy-bones F.G. Scott writes *now* that you want my essay on Nietzsche. Here it is. *Please send it back*, I have no other copy.

Francis George Scott - twenty letters included here and regarded as MacDiarmid's major
correspondent.
By permission of Lida Moser

That thief – or cattle thief – Mr [Mc]Cance has stolen my copy of the *Thistle*,[1] so that I cannot express fully my admiration for your achievement. I only remember by heart:

    We don't know who the captain is [2]

    But the first mate is a Jew.

That's great. But let me be sorry that you have not put the English on the opposite page, à la Mistral.[3] It will take me years to understand it.

Thank you also for your Scottish worthies.[4] You have been very kind to most of them.

Any chance of seeing you South?

Our wishes to yours, and ever affectionately,

D. Saurat.

1   *A Drunk Man looks at the Thistle* (Blackwood: Edinburgh and London, 1926).
2   ' We've never seen the Captain', *C.P.* I, p.100.
3   Frédéric Mistral (1830-1914), Provençal narrative poet.
4   The book about the 'Scottish worthies' was *Contemporary Scottish Studies* (London: Parsons, 1926).

12. From F. G. Scott (EUL MS2959 f.1)

103 Woodville Gardens
Langside
Glasgow
Sunday 11 December 1927

I'm reading [Percy] Wyndham Lewis's *Time and Western Man*.[1] It's a wonderful corroboration of my thesis! No news from Muir.

My dear Chris,

Just a very hurried note to give you the news of the arrival on Friday night at 10.30 of another son and heir![2] The Mrs and the wee chap are very well indeed – no complications anywhere – and the house is again beginning to settle down. There was too much of a congregation however yesterday morning so I packed off to Edinburgh with Frances and Lovey and deposited the latter with my sister Meg who wants to keep her till the Xmas holidays begin. I hope you observe how well, even in procreation, I am maintaining a perfectly classical balance – two and two – and you can have my assurance, here and now, that I'm not disturbing it – no, never!

The Missus last Monday had a communication from the BBC about giving a recital of my songs (composer at the piano) on 13th Jany – first of a series on 'Living Scottish Composers'. We turned it down for obvious and some not so obvious reasons and I think we did rightly as she's since received a brief acknowledgement of her note, pretty final in tone. They can damned well whistle for all eternity as far as I'm concerned – not even 1st of a series is good enough for me these days! I'll see if I can get the cuttings enclosed with this. Let's hear how you're all doing – and when the 'heluva' turn-up in Scotland takes place.

Ever,
F. G.

1   Percy Wyndham Lewis (1882-1957), novelist and artist; *Time and Western Man* (London and New York, 1927).
2   The children of F. G. Scott and his wife Burges Gray were Francise, b.1914; Lillias ('Lovey'), b.1918; George, b.1925; and Malcolm, b.1927.

13. From George Ogilvie (EUL MS2958.3 ff.3-4)

67 Cluny Gdns
Edinburgh
17 January 1928

Dear *Hugh* (it's shorter than Christopher),
I feel I mustn't let more days of this New Year pass without sending on my sincerest good wishes for the health & happiness of your little household.

I am also anxious to hear how you are getting on, and what you have been, are, and are likely to be, doing – not only to satisfy my own (kindly, I hope) curiosity, but also to appease the (not so kindly, I fear) curiosity of old acquaintances who bombard me often with enquiries about you.

These enquiries, I may say, usually develop into heated arguments about you & your synthetic Scots (particularly). Frankly, I fight a lone hand, tho' young Mackie came to my aid the other night very gallantly & effectively.[1] I hear you are going shortly to break a lance over the wireless. I shall listen in with great interest. By the way, if it is to be from Edinburgh & you have, as on the last occasion, an hour to spare, I shall be glad to spend it with you, & if you have no objection bring Mackie with me. I think you will like him.

How is the sequel to *A Drunk Man* getting on?[2] I do hope satisfactorily. And what else have you on the stocks? I heard of your *Albyn*[3] only the other day & intend to get it.

You will be interested to hear that Cassells is publishing a novel of Albert's[4] next month – *Man's Chief End*: it is a modern novel – a little unequal, I think, but strong in parts.[4] It is difficult to forecast how it will go.

I trust you are keeping fit & that Mrs. Grieve & Christine[5] are well. We are under a cloud at present. Mrs Ogilvie undergoes a major operation for *calculus* on Tuesday first. In the circumstances you will excuse me fobbing you off with this very brief note.

Yours ever,
Geo. Ogilvie.

1   'Mackie' was A. D. Mackie.
2   The 'sequel' was *To Circumjack Cencrastus* (Edinburgh and London: Blackwood, 1930).
3   *Albyn: or the Future of Scotland* (London: Kegan Paul, 1927).
4   'Albert' was Edward Albert.
5   Christine had been born on 4th September 1924.

14. From Oliver St John Gogarty (EUL MS2948.10 ff.1-2)

15 Ely Place
Dublin
4 March 1928

My dear Grieve,

I flew to Paris on last Saturday week back and there I met R.D. Wyndham Lewis the Daily Mail contributor who has lately written a fine book on Villon.[1] When we were talking of Scots Poetry he said of Hugh McDiarmid, 'He is greater than Burns'. Now Wyndham Lewis has for literature 'a nose like a rhinoceros' and a judgment like his is worthy of consideration when one thinks of how 'deep in the general heart of man' Scots lyric poetry was before during and after Burns life, it is unwise to cast the proferred crown aside without thinking. Anyway I thought I'd tell you, for it helps to know that in spite of organised disregard the knowledgeable ones are aware of you. If we find one or two people capable of assessing poetry in their own time, it's enough. 'Tell the minimum size of my audience' said Yeats to a would-be publisher.

AE is being worn out among the choffeurs of America lecturing to their wives just now. Yeats is in Rapallo (not here, O Apollo!) convalescing from high blood-pressure the result of taking no exercise with the body, so I shall not ask you to come here until May. You might make a bolt for Dublin then.

I have a book for the Cuala Press 'Wild Apples' which requires weeding out and I have no one to prune me.[2] I want 50 copies privately printed. If I can get it into type perhaps you would select 20 or so and send them back soon.

Ever cordially yours,
Oliver St J. Gogarty.

[1]   Gogarty refers here to D. B. Wyndham Lewis (1894-1969),Catholic biographer. *François Villon*: a documented survey with a preface by Hilaire Belloc was published in 1928.
[2]   *Wild Apples*, poems with preface by W. B. Yeats (Dublin, 1930).

15. From Compton Mackenzie (EUL MS2954.8 ff.1-3)

Isle of Jethou – Guernsey, C. I.
24 March 1928

Dear Mr Grieve,

Erskine writes to me that you were good enough to express approval of my little paper in his review.[1] I have long meant to write and salute you, but I am always very shy of writing to poets about their work, and I was (and am) particularly shy of writing to you because I have been so deeply moved by your writing. It has been to me like a magic window amid the decorative waste of wallpaper that nearly all contemporary verse has seemed to me. You have said so much of what I could have said if I had had the gift of singing. But it could only have been said in verse, and moreover only in the way you have said it. You have, I venture to think, a great responsibility, and I should much like to meet you and talk over many things. I have not one [one word illegible] politically because I suppose I must be considered an Anglicized Scot, and yet since I was a child of two I have had only one real and enduring passion and that is to see Scotland a nation again. Then again I am a Papist and have thought that I would only do more harm than good. Nor until [four words illegible] has there appeared any practical chance of achieving our object. So little indeed that I had come to find in Ireland the expression of my hopes and latterly in Brittany where the movement for independence grows apace.

I shall be in Scotland in May and June, and if it would not bore you I should like to meet you.

I believe that you are the secretary of the Scottish P.E.N. club, and I am just writing to the English people to say that I want to be transferred to the Scottish branch. I think that there ought to be a Scottish Society of Authors. These things may not seem important, but they have their effect. And I think we ought to have a weekly to be called 'The Scottish Statesman', and with a little self-denial I don't see why we shouldn't have it.[2] However, I mustn't bore you any longer.

I think that at last, at last life is beginning to move again.

Yours most truly,

Compton MacKenzie.

I suppose there is no chance of your being south next month?

[1]   *The Pictish Review*, edited by Ruaraidh Erskine of Mar, ran for eight monthly issues between November 1927 and June 1928. MacDiarmid had contributed an article entitled 'Towards a "Scottish Idea"' to the first issue of the *Review* in November 1927, pp.1-2. Compton MacKenzie supported MacDiarmid's views in his article 'Towards a Scottish Idea' in February 1928, p.40.

[2]   'The Scottish Statesman' would have matched *The Irish Statesman*.

16. From Compton MacKenzie (EUL MS2954.8 f. 4)

Isle of Jethou
Channel Isles
20 April 1928

I go to London on April 27. My address there
will be 7 Sussex Place, Regent's Park, NW[1]
till I go North.

Dear Mr Grieve,

I was very glad indeed to get your letter. Nothing would give me greater pleasure than to visit you at Montrose. But I don't want to be a nuisance and I hope Mrs Grieve will order me to the nearest inn if I'm likely to upset the household!

I heard from Erskine today to say that the National Party is at last taking definite shape and that my name would be useful as a supporter. Of course I should be pleased to have it used.

Between ourselves Ben Shaw[1] wrote to me the other day and asked if I would consider standing as Lab. and H[ome] R[ule] candidate for one of the northern constituencies. I told him that my sympathies are entirely with the Labour Party, but that I could not pledge myself to support the Party if I thought the Party was not doing its best for the country. I dread Nationalism's being used by Labour as Liberalism used it in the [18]80s.

I am glad you are not anti-Irish. I think we can get a good deal of help from Ireland if we take them the right way. They've invited me over again as a guest of the nation for the Tailteann Games[2] and I've always had from Ireland a kindly recognition. Indeed it was through a notice in *The Irish Statesman* that I first came across your work, and found in it the flame for which I had been searching. You mustn't let yourself get bitter, though I cannot understand why you have not had recognition. However, equally, I cannot understand how any Scot can tolerate the position of his nation. And since the great majority do, there's the [one word illegible] why your flame kindles no flame in them.

I will wait on till June 2 for the dinner, & [Gordon] Bottomley. I've never met him, but we correspond and only in his last letter he was saying that he hoped to meet me in Kintail [one word illegible]. I'll try & drag him up to the Isles. I've heard nothing from these wretched P.E.N. Club people about my transference and I'm writing to shake them up. I wish you'd be good enough if you can spare a minute & send me a list of any of the younger Scots poets' work that I can get hold of, and that may have escaped me. I'd like to see you first*. Suppose I get to Scotland by the 10th or 11th and come straight to Montrose for a night before going back to Edinburgh? Would that be all right for you?

Yours,
Compton MacKenzie.
*Before I see Ben Shaw.

[1]   Ben Shaw was Secretary of the Labour Party in Scotland at this time.
[2]   There were three modern Tailteann Games based mainly in Croke Park, Dublin, in 1924, 1928 and 1932. MacDiarmid and Erskine of Mar went to the last fortnight of August 1928 but MacKenzie was unable to go.

17. From Compton Mackenzie (EUL MS2954.8 f.6)

> 7 Sussex Place
> Regent's Park
> NW1
> 29 April [1928]

Dear Mr Grieve,
My plan for going to you on May 10 has been rather upset by my getting a request from the Glasgow University Nationalist Association asking me to introduce Cunninghame Graham as their candidate for the Rectorial election. They have suggested May 10 or 11 for that. But I could come to Montrose on the 12th anyway.

As soon as I hear about [the] date they have fixed I will write and let you know.

It would give me the greatest pleasure to assist at the baptism if I am eligible.[1] But I'm a Roman Catholic and I'm not sure that the Scottish Episcopalian Church would allow me to officiate. You will have to take ecclesiastical advice on this point. But if it is permissible I shall be honoured by the post.

I shan't commit myself to anything in Glasgow till I've had a talk over everything with you.[2] I'm so enormously looking forward to meeting you. I'll let you have a line as soon as I hear from Glasgow what day they settle.

Yours,

Compton MacKenzie.

[1]   The baptism was of MacDiarmid's son Walter, b. 5th April 1928.
[2]   The reference was to the formation of the National Party of Scotland.

18. From George Ogilvie (EUL MS2958.3 ff.5-6)

67 Cluny Gdns
Edinburgh
1 May 1928

My dear Christopher,

I had hoped to write you at decent length in acknowledgement of your gift of pamphlets & in congratulation on your achievement in the oldest creative line of all. But we are still 'in the wood' or 'in the soup' here. Mrs Ogilvie was recovering slowly but surely from her operation, and we risked going to Rothesay for our Easter holiday. Unfortunately both the rooms we were in and the weather outside (it was bitterly cold all the time) did her more harm than good, with the result that she came home with a form of 'flu' on her & has been in bed ever since. Happily there are signs today of the fever abating. You will not wonder at my silence in these circumstances.

We were delighted to hear of the arrival of the son & heir, and of the well-being of Mrs Grieve and the wee one. Christine, I fancy, will be tremendously delighted. We hope to hear of his continued progress. You, of course, with so much on hand in addition to your ordinary work need sympathy. But I have no doubt your energy (always a marvel to me) will carry you through.

I enjoyed your pamphlets & of course I have a copy of your *Albyn*, which in spite of the haste you said it was written in, reads with your accustomed fluency. Indeed I think its prose is an improvement on the involved writing of your *Contemporary Scottish Studies*. Your short note gave you no opening to say how your contemplated vols of poetry &c are getting on. I hope satisfactorily.

I am very glad for Mackie's sake that you are including him in your list of correspondents. I have great hopes of Mackie.... You will have looked into Albert's *Man's Chief End*. It would be interesting to hear what you think of it. However that can wait.

By the way, I have just received from Wm. Kay (an old Brotonian about your time) a vol. of clever doggerel verse. He has been in Hong Kong for a good many years, and has been amusing his friends with parodies &c. They are very clever of their kind. You may not remember him.

Speaking of Broughton, I shall take it as a great personal kindness if you are able to send a contribution, however short, to the Majority Number of the Mag. about which the Editor wrote you the other day. It will – I say this seriously, earnestly – be hopelessly incomplete unless you are represented. I am especially keen on this, as this is likely to be my last year at Broughton. I got on a Headmaster's leet two years ago & it has almost run out.[1] It is hardly worth my while making a change, but I have my pension to think of.[2] (Don't, of course, make any reference to this in your contribution, as even yet I may be shelved.)

Please accept our joint good wishes for the health etc. of your little (tho' now not so little) household.

Yours ever,

Geo. Ogilvie.

[1] That is, he was on a list of candidates accepted for promotion and the Education Committee had used up nearly all the candidates.
[2] Ogilvie became Headmaster of Couper Street Primary School in this year.

19. From Lady Margaret Sackville (EUL MS2960.1 f.6)

Easter Duddington
Midlothian
12 January 1929

Dear Mr Grieve,

I think that you are wise in resigning the Secretary-ship [of Scottish P.E.N.].[1] Except for yourself – Lewis Spence[2] – [William] Jeffrey[3] and a few others – it seems on the *whole* a mediocre affair. Very *pleasant* – but that is hardly enough. Nor do I think there is sufficient material available to make it otherwise? I mean to follow suit and resign also – but, perhaps, I should wait a little.[4]

If you *are* in Edinburgh at any time – I wish you would let me know. I should like to talk over a few ideas?

Yours sincerely,

Margaret Sackville.

[1] MacDiarmid had been instrumental in founding Scottish PEN in 1927 and was Hon. Secretary until 1929.
[2] Lewis Spence (1874-1959), journalist, founder-member of the National Party of Scotland, and poet in English and Scots.
[3] William Jeffrey (1896-1946), poet and journalist.
[4] Lady Margaret Sackville was the Hon. President.

The 1930s

1. From George Blake (EUL MS2967/3)

Faber and Faber Ltd
24 Russell Square
London WC1
6 March 1931

My dear Grieve,

Eliot asked me the other day to read an article of yours on the English Influence in British Literature.[1] I did so and thought it first-rate, and now I am glad to hear that he hopes to use it. A damned good bit of work. I am sometimes tempted to think that this Gaelic tendency of yours is regrettable, if understandable. It seems to me a nostalgic symptom, a running away from what Doctor J. M. Bulloch (whom God preserve!)[2] would call the 'facts', and I'm damned if I see how you can with such assurance pronounce judgment on poetry in a foreign tongue. I do understand the reaction against what there is of Lowland culture – damn it, I'm trying to write a novel *against* the Lowlands just now[3] – but I'd hate to see you of all men running away, whether in disgust or not, from Scots. The Gaelic element is important, but it's only a part of the show, and I hate to see some of the sillinesses it has given rise to. They tell me that young J. H. Whyte[4] goes about St Andrews in a kilt, for instance. That's what I call guying the whole bloody movement. It's no more sensible, and no less funny, than Harry Lauder in a kilt[5]: in fact a damned sight less and more. Surely the job is to break down the artificial barrier between Highlands and Lowlands, not to build a new and still more artificial one and then come down with a dunt on the wrong side of it.

But this is, perhaps, impertinence.

Tuesday

To resume – I fear I owe you an apology. You left a telephone message at my house early in January, and, though I was home late that night, my wife duly delivered it. For the rest, I can only say that I clean forgot it after that until my wife reminded me of it a fortnight later. I was damnably busy with new interests at the time, but I am guilty, and I apologise. I do hope you did not think me discourteous.

Circumjack I have now read three times. It is bloody good. I like the remorseless bits of it particularly: that is what Scotland wants badly – knocked off its complacency and into work. I hope my novel will help in a modest way.

We do a new Marion Angus collection on the 26th – *The Turn of the Day*. And what about our chances of getting your next?[6]

I've joined the National Party.
Yours,
George Blake.

---

[1]   MacDiarmid's essay, 'English Ascendancy in British Literature', was published in *The Criterion*, vol.10, no.41 (July 1931), pp. 593-613.

K. S. Sorabji.
By permission of Edinburgh University Library.

[2]   J. M. Bulloch (1867-1938) contributed to *Scottish Tongue* (1924), a series of lectures on the vernacular language of lowland Scotland delivered to the members of the Vernacular Circle of the Burns Club in London. The other contributors were W.A. Craigie, John Buchan and Peter Giles.

[3]   Blake refers to his novel *Returned Empty* (1931).

[4]   J.H. Whyte was the American proprietor of *The Modern Scot* quarterly (1930-1936).

[5]   Harry Lauder (1870-1950), music hall entertainer whose songs were seen as a caricature of Scottishness.

[6]   Blake and George Malcolm Thomson were then directors of The Porpoise Press which published MacDiarmid's *The Lucky Bag* in 1927 and the second edition of *Annals of the Five Senses* in 1930, both in Edinburgh.

2. From Kaikhosru Sorabji (EUL MS2960.17 ff.1-3)

Societa Anonima
Albergo Pensione Internazionale
Roma (6)

Parva domus Magna Quies
Pensione di 1° Ordine

7 March 1931

Dear Mr Grieve:

Your letter of 3rd has just reached me here where it has been forwarded.

Yes it was a great disappointment to me too not to have the pleasure of seeing you on my Glasgow visit in December.[1] As a part consolation I shall before very long be able to send you a *printed copy* of *Opus Clavicembalisticum* which is in course of being published.

About your suggestion regarding playing in Liverpool. I fear that for the moment it is a [matter] of practical politics as I do not return to London till 18 April and then am off again to Glasgow for the second concert of my works in which I am myself participating. This occurs about 15 April or so. And *Opus Clavicembalisticum* which presumably you would wish me to play will not be get-at-able for 3 months while it is in Vienna being engraved. Perhaps we might arrange something in the autumn of this year if you are then still of the same mind? Perhaps you will let me hear what you think of this suggestion.

On the whole the Glasgow press were not by any means as abjectly and utterly cretinous about the *Opus* as their London confrères would have been and that after all is to say *quite* a lot! I received nothing but the greatest kindness and sympathy in Glasgow and I really enjoy going there to play which is an astonishing state of affairs for one who has the horror and dread of public appearances that *I* usually have!

What a *very* admirable periodical the *Modern Scot* is – what the *New Age ought* to be but isn't!![2] At any rate these are the only periodicals that an intelligent person can read without wanting to scream and stamp with rage at their impotent [one word illegible] as of all the other of our 'high class' 'intellectual' (Holy Christ!!!) periodicals! God *how* I loathe and execrate 'artistic' and 'intellectual' people –

especially when they open the hole in their faces and let out that hollow lugubrious braying they call 'intelligent conversation'!!!

But if once I start railing in this way I shall never end! – So I desist!

All sorts of good wishes.

Yours ever very sincerely,

Kaikhosru Sorabji.

[1] Sorabji performed his work for piano, *Opus Clavicembalisticum*, which lasted over two hours, in Glasgow on 1 December 1930. It was dedicated 'To My Two Friends (E Duobus Unum): Hugh MacDiarmid and C. M. Grieve. Likewise To The Everlasting Glory Of Those Few Men Blessed and Sanctified In The Curses And Execrations Of Those Many Whose Praise Is Eternal Damnation'. MacDiarmid quoted the dedication in his autobiography, *Lucky Poet*, (London: Methuen, 1943), p. 43.

[2] *The New Age*,'A weekly review of politics, literature and art', edited by A. R Orage from 1907-1922.

3. From Ernest Barker (EUL MS2966)

17 Cranmer Road
Cambridge
Easter Sunday 1931

Dear Mr Grieve,

I am a scoundrel not to have written to you for these 6 months and more. I am all the more a scoundrel, as Saurat and McCance and others have told me golden things about you.

I am sending McCance, at Gregynog Press, all the Brown relics I have – only some 20 to 30 pages of letters and one little article – and telling him that he may send them all to you when he is ready.[1] He asked me to let him see them with a view to a possible booklet.

Yours sincerely,

Ernest Barker.

[1] The reference is to George Douglas Brown, whom Barker met at Oxford. Barker's collection of Brown's letters is acknowledged and quoted in James Veitch, *George Douglas Brown* (London: Herbert Jenkins, 1952).

4. From D. S. Mirsky (EUL MS2966)

17 Gower St
London WC1
26 October 1931

Dear Sir,

I feel highly honoured by your letter. Ever since I first heard of your poetry from Edwin Muir & first dipped into *A Drunk Man*, I have been keenly aware that you are one of the small number of poets of the European World. In particular – though this is but a detail – your translations of Blok & Hippius in *Cencrastus* are the only real re-creations of Russian poetry in English (if I may call it English?).[1] So I can only feel highly flattered by your wish to dedicate your hymn to me, and greatly impressed by my unworthiness of both the author & the subject.[2] But that you should write a hymn to Lenin is an indication of what is becoming more & more true, that no strong & sincere mind may any longer fail to recognise Lenin as the one leader of the human race. I am all agog to read the poem when it is out.

Sincerely yours,
D. S. Mirsky.

[1] Mirsky is in error here as the translations are in *A Drunk Man Looks at the Thistle*. This passage is quoted by MacDiarmid in his autobiography, *Lucky Poet*, p.66; the inaccuracies suggest he is quoting from memory: 'Ever since I first encountered your poetry I have recognised you as one of the few living poets of the European world. Your translations from Blok and Hippius are the only real re-creations in English of modern Russian poetry.'

[2] 'First Hymn to Lenin' was first published in Lascelles Abercrombie's *New English Poems* (1931) and collected in *First Hhymn to Lenin and Oother Poems* (London: Unicorn Press, 1931).

5. From W. Kennedy T. D. (EUL Gen.2094/3/1010)

C. M. Grieve Esq.
321 High Holborn[1]
London WC1

Dáil Éireann
Tigh Laighean
(Leinster House)
Baile Átha Cliath
(Dublin)
4 November 1931

A chara[2],
I received your booklet and read it with pleasure.[3]

It is clearly written and very easy for the ordinary person, not conversant with the Social Credit Case, to follow.

I look forward with interest to your other pamphlet.

W. Kennedy T. D.

[1] The office of The Unicorn Press.
[2] Dear Sir.
[3] This booklet may have been *People Versus Bankers*, by Paul Banks (1931). Banks contributed an article to *Vox*, vol.1, no.13 (1 February 1931), pp.444-445, entitled 'Paul Banks discusses "The Radio and Drama"'. The name 'Banks' seems too apt to be a coincidence, raising the possibility that it is a pseudonym for MacDiarmid himself or one of his colleagues. The style of the booklet does not match MacDiarmid's style of the time. Another letter from the Dáil from Patrick J. Little, 29 October 1931, reads: 'Thanks for your latest pamphlet & for the kind thought of sending it to me.' (EUL Gen. 2094/3/1185).

MacDiarmid had gone to London in September 1929 to work on *Vox*, 'The Radio Critic and Broadcasting Review', edited by Compton MacKenzie, which folded after fourteen weekly issues. By the time *People Versus Bankers* was acknowledged MacDiarmid was a director of the Unicorn Press.

6. From D. S. Mirsky (EUL MS2966)

17 Gower Street
London WC1
25 November 1931

Dear Mr Grieve,

I am very glad to be of what use I can be to you. I think the following Jewish writers working in Russian ought to be included in any comprehensive 'Jewish omnibus'.[1]

1) S. Yushkevich (though his best work is a long novel 'The Adventures of Leon Drey').[2]

2) B. Pasternak (a very difficult author, and his masterpiece 'The Childhood of Luvers' rather longish).[3]

3) Isaac Babel, his *Red Cavalry* has been translated into English, but you might see 'The Story of my Pigeon-house', or any one of his stories about the Jewish bandit Benia Krik, which have not yet been translated.[4]

4) Ilya Erenburg.[5]

5) Ovadi Savich.[6]

Yours sincerely,

D. S. Mirsky.

[1]   There is no evidence that the 'Jewish omnibus' was ever more than an idea.
[2]   Semen Solomonovich Yushkevich. 'The Adventures of Leon Drey' translated into English?
[3]   Boris Pasternak (1890-1960). 'The Childhood of Luvers', written in 1918, first appeared in English in *Transformation One*. It is included in Boris Pasternak, *The Collected Prose Works*, arranged with an introduction by Stefan Schimanski (London, 1945), pp. 164-215.
[4]   Isaac Babel (1894-1940), shot, and rehabilitated in 1954. *Red Cavalry* was first published in English in London in 1929. *Red Cavalry and other stories* (London: Penguin Classics, 2005) includes 'The Story of my Dovecot', pp. 27-40, and also the Benya Krik stories in the 'Odessa Stories' section, pp. 237-309.
[5]   Ilya Ehrenburg (1891-1967), novelist and journalist.
[6]   Ovadi Savich (1896-1967), poet.

7. From J. B. Salmond (EUL MS2970)

THE SCOTS MAGAZINE
Published by
THE THOMSON-LENG PUBLICATIONS
D. C. Thomson & Co. Ltd.

7 Bank Street
Dundee
9 February 1932

John Leng & Co. Ltd.

<u>PERSONAL</u>.

My dear Grieve,

I am very sorry that I have to return the short story and the poem you sent to me. My hands are tied in this matter. I have no option. I know you understand things well enough to appreciate that rejection is no adverse criticism of the work.

I am doubly sorry about this at this particular time, when, in all courtesy, I recognise that you must be passing through a difficult period in your own personal life.[1] The whole business of living and thinking is so difficult, that I venture to send you my sincere hope that things will turn out well both for yourself and for those whose lives have been so closely connected with your own.

I am very glad that *First Hymn to Lenin* has been successful. I had a man in here yesterday wanting to borrow my copy. I told him to go buy one for himself.

I have been a victim of the 'flu; and I hope you're quite clear of it now.

Please accept my best wishes for all your work, my regrets for my inability to take the MSS, and my very sincere admiration for the courage with which you pursue your own line of development.

Yours,

J. B. Salmond.

[1]   Salmond, editor of *The Scots Magazine*, refers here to the publisher's antipathy towards MacDiarmid and to MacDiarmid's divorce in the previous month.

8. From F. G. Scott (EUL MS2959 ff.4-5)

<table>
<tr><td>
I've already started my two days
a week in O.H.M.S. and will continue
doing so till well into June. So I'm
in the way of writing reports in any case!
</td><td align="right">
44 Munro Road
Jordanhill
Glasgow W3
7 May 1932
</td></tr>
</table>

My dear Chris,

It's so damned cold today in my own room that I've come downstairs beside the fire –hence the pencil notes on my knee.

The 'Tarras' is alright.[1] Viewing the poem as a whole perhaps the sex-imagery (an illustration after all and not the principal theme of the poem) gets the upper hand in places and leaves the reader wondering whether 'Tarras' is not merely an excuse. You have precedent for this of course in Rozanov[2] who wrote his stuff with his hand on his penis but the results are good material for the Freudians of the future so it really doesn't matter much. I'd have said more on this theme if I hadn't got the 'Water Music' yesterday. This assured me that you are retaining some few notions of objectivity and the concrete in art. Before however leaving the final impression the poem gives, I'd like to warn you in your own words not to revolve too much round your self –

> And O! I canna thole
> Aye yabblin' o' my soul,
> And *fain I wad be free*
> O' my eternal me.

(Scott's emphasis) *Drunk Man* .[3] (Don't you see that you're not *free* as an artist while yet you're in bondage to the flesh! – St. Paul.)

Copulation's a fairly common form of amusement and not much remains to be said on that head! Besides I've a vague notion that in the long run the *impersonal* in art becomes the *most personal*. Coming now to details. A characteristic of a good deal of your work in *Cencrastus et seque* is a sudden flop into the thoroughly prosaic. This of course is rather a matter of diction than of poetry. I see quite clearly that it may on occasion have an effect of downrightness and slapdash that pushes the poem along – but personally I'd avoid the commonplace phrase or give it a slight twist. Samples of what I mean are –

V.(1) 'Naked and unashamed' – I suggest 'skirl-nakit, unashamed'. 'Understanding's ootrun a' talk' – which I won't venture on.

'Wi sensations deeper than ony name' – which could easily be tightened.

In the same verse I have ?'pit' – isn't there a word like 'fosse' (French) more graphic!

1.7   And 'gladly' into it gang back and *last* source instead of *lost* source. (Mere trifles!!)

I've made more question-marks on this stanza than on any other.

Stanza (2) is unpencilled excepting for line 7 where I cut out 'white neck's' and substituted 'paps' instead. The line reads 'Wi' nae paps' howe below' – a short line but somehow it retains the metre. I see all the same that the 'white' is juxtaposed rather nicely to 'black waters' above.

The 3ʳᵈ stanza first two lines beat me altogether if I'm reading what you wrote correctly. 'Beauty is only skin-deep' is another cliché like the 1ˢᵗ stanza specimens. The only contribution I can suggest is in line 6 'find ye' and line 8 'wind ye' which seem to gave an extra 'heich' to the 'jirblin''.

The 4ᵗʰ stanza 'Come pledge her in a horse-punckin' then' is the best o' the lot and up to the best you've ever done. This is what I'm getting at. Just compare this with stanza (1) and note how loose the first is. It's not entirely a matter of words – in the 4ᵗʰ stanza the mind travels farther and moves about quicker. That's what I mean by being intelligent. A hyphen in 'cul-ture' would mark out the pun. In the 4ᵗʰ line I'm sure there's a better word than '*white* to her heather' – but I can't lay my finger on it at the moment.

The second poem beginning 'Gi'e me Scots-room'[4] is quite good. I only pencilled the 'cauldly' in line 9 and the 'callously' in line 10 as being near each other. In the last line your *'tak's* the hill' would have my preference over the 'sweeps' or 'scours'. It's quite clear what you mean – *Mons Veneris*!

'Water Music'[5] in *Scots Observer*.[6]

Primo – I'm rather fond of Anna Livvy – Joyce is an atonal musician who secures relationships amongst his notes. 99.9 [%] of the other atonalists can't do that and the words cease to have meaning – like passing a dictionary through a sausage-machine!

Secundo – Your poem has nothing Joycean about it for me. It's a string of *conceits* – certainly picturesque with a good deal of charm. Extravagant in the latest approved manner.

(I saw a quotation from *Poems* by A. Abrahams this week which describes the clouds as –

'Vast ripped-up bowels that slither
From glist'ning foldings, hither
Thither and everywhere' – and invites us
'To squeeze the udders of the great white cow
That is our world') [7]

The danger in all this is of course that nobody pays the slightest attention or is impressed, much in the same way as nobody stops to listen to a man shouting at a street corner being sure he's got nothing new to say. But I'm not blaming your 'Water Music'. I think on the whole it's a *tour de force* and comes off. The worst of megalomania whether in music or poetry is that so little of it passes into the memory and stays there. You'll be told for your pains that you've been busy among the *bees* and the *pees*. And that's all!

'By Wauchopeside'[8] in *Modern Scot*.

A return to the personal pronoun. It doesn't impress me. The 'blackie' might have done more for *you* or you for the 'blackie'. I'm intensely apathetic to profundities like 'There's mair in birds than men ha'e faddomed yet.' And sheep, nanny-goats and all kinds of things come into my mind. You say you could '[...] gi'e / Wauchope a new course in the minds o' men' – but *do* you? But Hold! Hold! Enough! Enough!

Ever affectionately,
F. G.

Just take a look at the dynamic markings in *Love* by a musician called Scott. *C'est la griffe du lion* [it's the mark of the lion] – as the French understand it!

---

[1]   Scott refers here to an earlier version of 'Tarras' than the published one, *C.P.*I, pp.337-339.

[2]   V. V. Rozanov (1856-1919).

[3]   *C.P.* I, p. 142.

[4]   Titled 'Why I Became a Scots Nationalist', *C.P.* I, p. 339.

[5]   *C.P.*I, pp. 333-337.

6 *Scots Observer*, weekly, Glasgow, 1926-1934.
7 *Poems* (London, 1932).
8 *C.P.* I, pp. 1083-84.

9. From F. G. Scott (EUL MS2959 ff.6-7)

44 Munro Road
Jordanhill
Glasgow W3
15 May 1932

Dear Chris,

I'm endeavouring to work in a reply to both your communications between two doses of inspectorial business, the school reports I've just polished off and the proposed tests I'm giving tomorrow down at an R.C. Secondary School in Paisley. I haven't much to comment on in any case as I take it the 'Second Hymn [to Lenin]' is already beyond praise or blame and has just to be accepted as it stands, and your other communication was chiefly relative to matters that had already been thrashed out. Not quite though! for I think I've hit on one or two improvements even on the new versions of 'Tarras' you sent.

The *new* versions then! Stanza I alright. Stanza II has 'ettled to play' which reappears in the last 'horse-punckin' stanza. In Stanza III 'Ah, woman-fondlin' – you didn't quite get my meaning, 'Wi' nae paps' howe below?' I was really thinking of the omission of the 'white' and the curious slowing down of the line to u---u- rather than uu-(white) u-u-. It's all really a trifle but the whole stanza has an unusual rhythmic quality (unusual even in you) that deserves consideration on that score alone. There's a sense of weariness in it, a kind of alienation from society that Goethe, speaking of Hegel, characterized as one of the diseases of intellectual dexterities and dialectics. So roll along 'The Oon Olympian'[1] – I'm all for Hegel myself – at the moment.

In the next long amorphous stanza beginning 'Her cautelles?' I think I've one or two good suggestions. 'She *turns* to *shine* and *storm* by *turn*' is surely better as 'She *gecks* to storm and shine *in* (by) turn!' And what about this for force of expression –

'Bare to the banes or wi' birds in her hat,
– And has bairns by them a'.
– Bairns!
Bycomes o' bogs and gets o' cairns' etc

and the whole thing's a bit of the heftiest stuff you've ever done.

The last stanza has given me a real find. I felt there was another word instead of *white* in the 4th line but 'waff' isn't it and I had a real thrill when *whey* suddenly flashed on me. Isn't it the one inevitable word in the whole Scottish and English dictionary with all kinds of associations and suggestions about it?

'Their paramuddle is whey to her heather.'

If I get many more finds like that I'll be wanting the Jamieson dictionary back and start off a-making my own poetry!

You're very modest about your dedication of 'An Apprentice Angel'[2] to L.M.W. (Lauchlan MacLean Watt I take it). I like it quite well.

The 'Second Hymn' really makes me *serious*, and compels me to drop matters of diction altogether and think hard on the nature of poetry and art in general.[3] Not only does it make me *serious* – it makes me *suspicious* and I find myself grubbing among lots of queer notions about yourself and Eliot and *The Criterion*. What in hell's name does Eliot want to do with this in *The Criterion* for instance? Is he adding you to his collection of freak writers, letting the young lions roar while he stands pontifically aside and faintly smiles[?] I know nothing about literary gossip, as you well know, but I'm suspicious of a man and his motives when he excises a stanza with one breath and proceeds to flatter it with his next.[4] For fundamentally this particular verse doesn't 'roar' any louder than any other in the poem which is tantamount to a denial that poetry *can* be written at all at the present moment. Why write it then? I really don't believe you've gone right down to the roots of this communism business at all for it ultimately leads to a denial of your own gift and is certainly 'art as communication' (I remember the sneer!) with a vengeance.

'Are my poems spoken in the factories and fields / In the streets o' the toon?'[5] – you ask? Why of course not! I can't at the moment think of anything of yours that will become as familiar as lots of poor, uneducated Rabbie Burns who knew from the beginning by the light of Heaven (just as *I* have always known!) what you are only glimpsing at in your new phase. I'll bet you a thousand pounds that Russia doesn't disown Burns at this moment. But no amount of

Organic constructional work,
Practicality, and work by degrees;[6]
First things first; and poetry in turn
'll be built by these.

will matter a hoot. It remains jargon and not even the arrival of the Socialist Federation of the Whole Cosmos will ever make it anything else.

I'm particularly 'humpy' on this point as you'll see. And I'm particularly sure of myself too for I've made a fairly thorough investigation of the problem as it affects creative work of all kinds. I'm just as anxious as you are to find a way out of the present impasse but my God[!] it's going to be a hellish business. For instance Russia at the moment is little more than Co-operative Stores and Educational propaganda: things we're quite familiar with at our own doors. 'Freein' oor poo'ers for greater things' – *what* greater things? Give me just *one*, s'il vous plaît. Reading 'Hymns to Lenin' – I DON'T THINK!

Affectionately,

F. G.

1 *C.P.* I, pp. 354-361.
2 *C.P.* I, pp. 332-333.
3 'Second Hymn to Lenin' appeared first in *The Criterion,* vol. xi, no. xlv (July 1932).
4 The stanza which Eliot wished to excise but finally retained was: 'Gin I canna win through to the man in the street, / The wife by the hearth, / A' the cleverness on earth'll no' mak' up / For the damnable dearth.'
5 *C.P.* I, p. 323.
6 These two lines have been incorporated from Lenin's own words, '[...] organic constructional work,/ Practicality, and work by degrees', quoted by D. S. Mirsky in *Lenin* (London, 1931), p. 143.

10. From D. Pearson (NLS Acc. 7361/3)

42 Otago Street
Hillhead
4 June 1932

Sir

Your article in *The Times*[1] is typical of that screed's journalism. Any rubbish can get space in its pages whether from self-styled 'Poets', 'Economists' or 'Financiers', but let a Man with brains and wisdom endeavour to utter the *Truth* and it is a different reception altogether. That is the reason I write direct.

You talk about 'Contemporary Poetry' as if the thing were some fetish that had to be worshipped for its wonderful beauty, wisdom, simplicity, and thoughtful understanding, instead of the mere rubbish it is, whether written by Grieve or any of his kidney. The damned upstart impudence of you makes me wild. You get education drummed into you at so much a time and with it some knowledge of 'Poetry'. You then proceed to string a lot of big words, mystical allusions, mythical and Greek lore together and have the damned cheek to call it 'Poetry'.

You don't even seem to have the brain to see that it takes a gifted individual to write it, that Poets *are* born *not* made – à la Grieve.

Who are you to upset, the for all time, accepted truth.

And Tannahill's[2] verse is broken-backed.

And Burns is too much noticed.

And the old Poets have too much public support to leave space for Grieve and his stupid youthful contemporaries who couldn't write a fine simple poem if they tried for a lifetime – that is, one breathing truth, simplicity, depth of understanding and real thought.

Poets are not necessarily meek worms, and as one who has some gift of its powers I consider you are a conceited upstart who, typical of the youth of today, consider yourself superior to any poet that ever lived.

I am open to debate you at any time that suits you, if you have the courage to face a *public audience*, and I shall deliberately compare my own work with yours and that of your so-called highbrows. Your analogy anent Poetry and the Solar System is in keeping with your wonderful mentality which has to stump the country to make itself understood.

Yours etc.

D. Pearson.

---

[1]   not identified –perhaps the *The Evening Times* (Glasgow)?
[2]   Robert Tannahill (1774-1810).

11. From F. G. Scott (EUL MS2959 f.8)

I find this sounds like a Methodist tract   44 Munro Road
when I reread it. Very improving.   Jordanhill
But at any rate my *intention* is subtle enough.   Glasgow W3
                                                                                              5 June 1932

Dear Chris,

You haven't been throwing me much to work my jaws on but all the same I acknowledge *The Free Man* [1] at [the] beginning of the week and, since I've worked off a pile of Leaving Certificate papers, resume joyfully to prog your elbow. The two short things you sent on the 20th, 'The Back o' Beyond'[2] and 'Cheville',[3] were much relished and for different reasons. In the first place I'm glad you can still do such a 'gem' as 'The Back o' Beyond' for it assures me that the vein remains traceable throughout your work right from [the] beginning up till this moment and that your hankering after *fétiches* of any variety is of the moment only. (By the way when is your rejoinder on Bolshevism and culture going to reach me?) You know already how finicky I can get on certain artistic details like this. Don't mistake! It isn't naiveté or mere ingenuousness on my part – not at all! – it's just the very subtlest bit of my brain matter that gets a laugh on cleverness of all kinds, particularly when the clever ones are looking on. The tight-rope walker just does something unheard of and asks the spectators, 'How's that?' You'll then hear a chorus of know-alls telling you, 'Oh, but that's different', 'It isn't in the "game" of how to be very clever' etc. etc. etc. Exactly – it really isn't done, for remember there's no more savagely philistine a gang anywhere than these same knowing ones who just don't know an inch beyond their own smartness. You've gone through your experimental stage by now, you've blustered and hectored in resounding neologisms with the best of them, embraced Dadaism, pragmatism, socialism, Freudism and, latest of all, Bolshevism, and you're still C.M.G. and hardly a seannachie the better for it all. A younger generation is already on your heels eager and able to howl down all your –isms into the dustbin (for we can be certain *their* new fangles won't be what *ours* have been) and you've thought of Bolshevism as the hobby-horse of the future: as big a favourite in fact as last Wednesday's 'Orwell'.[4] And I'm telling you it doesn't matter a damn. You can write pages on pages of Leninism without a glimmer of fundamental brain or creative energy and have it hailed as oracular, colossal or the like and all the time you know as well as I do that 'The Back o' Beyond' is just the tight-rope performer's bit of inexplicable magic and mystery and that it's worth all the rest put together. Most folk for a long time to come will fail to realize that it's happened. That's its inevitable badge of merit. No applause, thank you – just silence!

F.G.

1   *The Free Man* (main series) was published weekly in Edinburgh between 6th February 1932 and 5th May 1934.
2   *C.P.* I, p.331.
3   *C.P.* I, p.353.
4   'Orwell' was a racehorse.

12. From F. G. Scott (EUL MS2959 ff.18-20)

44 Munro Road
Jordanhill
Glasgow W3
19 July 1932

My dear Chris,

I'm a bit late this week – you can blame Glasgow Fair – I'd to take the two girls down to their aunt's in Dunoon yesterday and I've been up to the eyes in work of my own this past week with what is promising to turn out an exhilarating contribution to Scotland's musical achievement. I've not been neglecting all the same your big bundle of stuff and have been turning from notes to words with equal gusto which in itself is a considerable compliment to the quality of what you sent. Let's begin at the beginning.

'The Lost Pigeons'[1] is alright in idea but with a 'hank' in the words. Perhaps the 'I' in [the] 2nd line confuses the 'me' of the 3rd – the 'wise outby' at any rate isn't slick enough. I'm sure you could mend it in a minute or two, & I think it's worth doing.

'The Castle'[2] doesn't tell us anything new – 'fog', 'wi' horrors agog', 'centre o' ilka road', 'counter shapes like God' – well we're just 'nane the better or waur if they do', or don't. So don't!

'The Monument'[3] on Whita [Hill] has something quite good said about it at last. '*Nane* kens' should be '*few* kens' – the truth, sir, is here a matter of importance in the effect you want.

'[...] wha care faur less
For a' the poets and philosophers
Or onybody else o' lasting worth'

– which avoids the trite bit of information about these bloody poets etc. – you really don't seem to realise that you're talking to a musician whose work begins when the poets are obliged to shut up – a much higher being altogether to my mind!

I didn't like at first sight the last rhymes 'wi'' and 'see' and I worked it out rhyming with -

'memorise
In keepin' wi' his fame and o' its emptiness
– The Size!'

I'm not putting this forward as an alternative. This was a first-time emendation. My second thought was much more important: a poem cast in the language of the tombstone, saying exactly what you're saying, here, in even more severely measured terms – the 'Fitly to memorise, in keepin' wi'' kind of thing and in itself taking the shape of Whita monument.

[DIAGRAM]

That would be *one* interesting page more to 'Clann Albainn'.[4] Picture and all! Why not a picture or two in the story?

'On Bare Hill Tops'.[5] A very personal utterance, with rather more emotion in it than is normal with you but since you don't object to everything going into the book there's no reason for you not giving us your apprenticeship (*pace* Wordsworth) and becoming reminiscent. It's a difficult task this, doing an old-fashioned thing in fitting style and you occasionally come perilously near the bathetic when you get 'Yont the last blaeberry' wi' 'a storied landscape at my feet' and 'encompassed by a countless clood o' witnesses' – 'nor trace o' human feelin' – unless in me! (Good God!) What time 'the circling season brings' 'boyish sproutings and the foetal stream' (a new version of the child being father of the man!) which naturally enough 'thrust up my granite gleam' and would have no 'explanation' if not 'a'thing kent at aince – *Totality*'!!! And then come in your old pals 'life and death' like the 'Two Bobs' and the male and female that for the one thousandth millionth time find entrance 'to the sheer secrets o' her being' (body, you mean!) and 'through his onslaught shares his' although you've just said a couple of stanzas back that you in 'the sexual act' are lying doggo, saying nowt among the 'geological processes' (I tell you these old boys knew the things *not* to say even better perhaps than the things to say!) and all for what?

[...]a' that opinion adds
To human existence is likewise dung to blads.
There's nocht in a' the world that we've amassed
But sic a bare cairn o' the lives o' men.'

Well, well! – and the opinions o' bloody 'poets and philosophers' likewise don't matter a damn.

The next stanza 'Death is a physical horror to me nae mair' is better because *truer* and almost (as we musicians say) finds 'expression', viz., is instantly communicated as emotion to the hearer or reader – you see the kind o' subtleties *we* have to deal with – not words, nor meanings but with actual feelings behind notes. 'It is reality that is at stake' means much more than it says. I'm tempted to read you a sermon at this point, namely 'that you can't glorify the spirit within you and at the same time find humanity so despicable'. The antithesis is much too violent and startling to live by and conclude my homily with a phrase of your own, 'the peak o' things / That canna whummle!' And the peak o' things whether in thought, or art or morality has a pretty broad BOTTOM. When you come to realise this more fully that *all* the spirits and brains of the past have put you and me here at this peak of time, well, you'll have had your first lesson in humility and thank God for your privileged position. So please don't try to stand the mountain on its head! It will fall and bury you.

The 2nd poem of this series beginning 'Today I have ascended this high hill / Frae materialism to the mysticism' etc. I don't care for though I note '[...] inspired / to try by active love a' else t'enrich', but The National Messianism and Plato and Christ with their psychological labs. and modern monasteries leave me stone-cold.

'Depth & the Chthonian Image'[6] is almost a 'seamless garment' and very good indeed. You seem in this to have risen to your high theme. There's a lot I could say (and will someday) about the discrepancy between your matter and manner but for the nonce 'there's a manner for every matter' – just say that 3 times and repeat it every morning and night for the rest of your life. So here you seem to have got the *manner* for the *matter* (forget these bloody half-baked Americans!) and it's a poem. I'd cut the reference to [Major C.H.] Douglas,[7] *he's* not in the *manner*.

Mes compliments affectueux.

F. G.

I hope I've praised it enough. I sniffed it out at once. F. G.

---

[1] Lost.

[2] Lost.

[3] *C.P.* I, p.386.

[4] 'Clann Albainn' was MacDiarmid's unfulfilled project for an autobiographical poem in five volumes: *The Muckle Toon, Fier Comme un Ecossais, Dimidium Animae Meae, The Uncanny Scot* and *With a Lifting of the Head* (to be preceded by a Prologue). The project was formulated in the early 1930s and separable parts of the poem appeared *in First Hymn to Lenin and Other Poems* (1931), *Second Hymn to Lenin* (1932) and *Scots Unbound* (1932).

[5] Lost. Patrick Crotty discusses 'On Bare Hill Tops' in his essay 'From Genesis to Revelation', *Scottish Literary Journal*, vol.15, no.2, pp. 5-23 (November 1988). Phrases like 'Yont the last blaeberry' and 'the circling season brings' occur in 'The Last of the Lights' ('Beyond the last of the lights') in *The Revolutionary Art of the Future, Rediscovered Poems by Hugh MacDiarmid*, edited by John Manson, Dorian Grieve and Alan Riach (Manchester: Carcanet, 2003), p.73, and in 'Returning to Scotland' ('the circling year') in *Chapman* 104 (Edinburgh, 2004), p.30 respectively.

[6] *C.P.*I, pp. 346-353.

[7] Major C.H. Douglas (1879-1952) was the founder of Social Credit theories.

13. *From F. G. Scott (EUL MS2959 ff.21-23)*

44 Munro Road
Jordanhill
Glasgow
28 July 1932

My dear Chris,

I feel like sitting down to polish off arrears of some kind before the family sets off to St Andrews for the month of August. And before I forget: Item No 1, during August F.G. Scott, c/o Mrs Henderson, Beethoven Lodge(!), North Street, St Andrews should find me till about the 28th of the month; Item No 2, I've received gratefully *Second Hymn to Lenin*,[1] *The Free Man*, Lamb's 'Head',[2] 'Oon Olympian', for all of which very many thanks. The Lamb's 'Head' is distinctly good; Willie Johnstone's ditto[3] – well, just nothing at all (I hope to God he's not wasting his time on this sort of thing!), 'The Oon Olympian' more likely to do harm to *you* than to Goethe and *Second Hymn to Lenin* much better than I had thought it. Did you alter it much from the proof copy you sent to me? I wanted to compare but must have returned [it] to you. Yes, I did see your long article in *The Criterion* about 'English Ascendancy in British Literature' but I don't think I ever saw a poem of yours on 'Two O'clock in the Morning'.[4]

I think *The Free Man* is distinctly good and intend asking them to forward it weekly. I gave up *New English Weekly*[5] on the score that it wasn't worth (to me) a tanner a week. Am substituting *The Free Man* in its place as serving my purpose equally well.

Now for the poems. 'The Summit', 'The Crown of Rock' and 'The Scott Centenary' are all creditable but not worth bothering about at this time o' day, being more verbal than expressive.[6] If you *must* include any of them then my vote goes to 'The Crown of Rock' which shows at any rate that at one time you *could* write what many folks think *is* poetry. A little bag of sweeties like this may encourage some faint hearts to wrestle with 'The Muckle Toon'.[7]

At a first hurried run through I didn't care much for either of the long ones you sent, 'The Point of Honour' and 'On Coming Home'. I've reread them a few times and admit they have risen. Let's take them separately. 'The Point of Honour' starts off very well.[8] P.56 You'll see I've had a fit of omitting words here and there. Your writing is generally not quite so elliptical as your meaning and I have thought lately that some of your more trite expressions would stand pruning. In verse 1, for example, everybody would understand you weren't exactly bathing in champagne – more's the pity! At the foot of the page 'control – keen' is purely a matter of rhythm. Passim: you've got what I'm hunting for too with your 'Perfection of craft concealed / In effects of pure improvisation'. That's it – only at present there's more of the '*pure* improvisation' than the 'perfection of craft'! in both of us.

P.57 is still exhilarating but I don't like the rhyming 'flesh' and 'enmesh' – too manufactured – 'spend her *nervous energy*' – hence 'quivering' momentum and 'tend' for 'attend' and cutting 'every' keeps the swirl going.

We're getting on famously till p.58 and again you become informative. I've suggested 'rhythms' for 'sound', this being scientific matter-of-fact.

On p.59 you're just continuing the information to which I just barely listen but on p.60 I'd 'blue pencil' the *lyric* -some lyric! 'other' and 'smother' – Holy Mother!!

There's a crossword on page 61

[...] world-free illusion two
Of naught, and they one, [...]

I'd substitute 'like' for 'but' as a clue. I call that real metaphysic. Did you mean it?

Page 62 sounds like Walt Whitman (whom I'm going to reread if you do much of this kind) and the tone persists through p.63. Cutting 'in which' helps, I think (ellipsis). I worried a bit over, 'not revelation; a robin'. What about –

Clear note rings out. Revelation – robin.
Clear note rings out – a robin.

The remainder of the poem is still Walt. You've been remembering his tired Triton manner. All the same the poem's a good one. It's evocative – which is saying a lot.

'On Coming Home' I haven't scrutinised half so carefully.[9] It certainly doesn't evocate anything but C.M. Grieve and the latest tags about Freud, Driesch,[10] Jung, Breyzig[11] and the rest with pituitary glands, adrenals, adenoids etc. etc. thrown in. You should know by this time that your appeal to authorities in psychology is the very worst testimonial you can give yourself for having any savvy of your own. It's all too obvious in the modern style like Willie Johnstone's physog. of you and it's time you were both growing up. You should leave this sort of thing to undergrads at Universities and Art Colleges – it's generally all they ever manage to do. I'd 'blue pencil' as much of the poem as you can or better rewrite it in far more drastic fashion (like 'The Monument' on Whita Hill) in the soberest of language and the most hellish implications imaginable. Words don't hurt anybody - brickfacts do! Must finish – in haste. How's the domesticity faring? F. G.

I've just come across the following. I must have written them after reading 'On Coming Home' earlier in the week.

Pp. 36, 37 Futile excogitation about the future of mankind. The ideas are common property (Shaw etc.) Mankind can't go on! – very romantic and sentimental. Every age has thought itself the *ne plus ultra*.

P. 42 'But not through arguments like this' – No! The whole poem though isn't so bad – a spirited production – like one of my weaker songs played with lots of shouting and noise. You're running out of 'thocht'. You really should go off on a new line of thinking altogether – you're in danger of going stale and most readers will be able to place you without bothering to read you. Practically everybody is thinking just what you're thinking but your friends 'les hommes de bon sens' are looking for solutions, not further conundrums.

By the way, Chris, who in Hell's name is all this poetry meant for – what audience are you addressing? D'ye ever think of *that*! The 'Second Hymn to Lenin' has –

Are my poems spoken in the factories and fields
In the streets o' the toon? etc.

Why not tackle this job? Why not give us some real Bolshie art? Yer behind, man – away in the rear among the romantic decadents still worrying about your soul and religious ecstasies. Even I! – me – I've been worrying your 'The Dead Liebknecht' [12](*Penny Wheep*) for *Brass Band* and *unison for a mob of people*. It's the only thing of yours I can find suitable. And, by God, it takes some doing! Have a go!!

[1]   *Second Hymn to Lenin* was published by Valda Trevlyn (Thakeham, 1932) in an edition of 100 numbered copies signed by the author.

[2]   The "head" was sculpted in bronze by William Lamb A.R.S.A (1893-1951). Only one cast has been made and this is on view at the William Lamb Memorial Studio, Montrose.

[3]   William Johnstone's 'Head' was the drawing used as the frontispiece for *Second Hymn to Lenin*, published by Valda Trevlyn in Thakeham in 1932. It is reproduced in *MacDiarmid:An Illustrated Biography*, edited and published by Gordon Wright, Edinburgh, p. 55.

[4]   'Two O'clock in the Morning' was published in 1933. *C.P.* II, p.1292.

[5]   *New English Weekly* was started by A.R. Orage in 1932 and edited by him until his death in 1934. It was described as 'A review of public affairs, literature and the arts' and continued publication until 1949.

[6]   'The Summit' remains unpublished. The MS is in the University of Delaware Library, MS224, Box 1, Folder 14. 'The Crown of Rock' was published in 1924. *C.P.* II, p. 1241. 'The Scott Centenary' was published in *Scots Unbound* in 1932. *C.P.* I, p. 361.

[7]   The page references below appear to refer to a manuscript of 'The Muckle Toon' as a part of 'Clann Albainn'.

[8]   'The Point of Honour' was published in *Stony Limits and Other Poems*, *C. P.* I, pp. 387 -391.

[9]   A poem 'On Coming Home' was published as the *envoi* to *Scottish Scene* in 1934. *C.P.* I, pp.381-2. It is not clear if this was a part of the 'On Coming Home' MS discussed here.

[10]   Hans Adolf Eduard Driesch (1867-1941), German experimental embryologist and philosopher who was the last great spokesman for vitalism.

[11]   Kurt Breysig (1866-1940), Professor in the University of Berlin who believed in a continuously-improving cultural level of mankind.

[12]   *C.P.* I, p. 57.

14. *From Carmel Haden Guest (NLS Acc. 7361/53)*

27 Victoria Square
London SW1
n.d. [late July/early August 1932]

Dear Comrade,

Please send a letter of protest to the Hungarian Minister, 35 Eaton Place to protest against the execution of F[writing unclear] KARIKAS a proletarian who is accused of actions taken on behalf of the proletarian dictatorship in 1919[1] – I wanted Galsworthy to protest for the PEN but he says he cannot because it is political!!

I hear you have a new little son – good luck to him & his mother – May he also write revolutionary hymns.

I am reading your 'Second Hymn to Lenin'.

Come & see me when you are in London – I haven't told you yet how much I appreciate your poems.

Best wishes.

[form illegible]

Carmel Haden Guest

---

[1]   The Hungarian Soviet Republic of March-August 1919 was led by Béla Kun (1886-1939).

15. From Carmel Haden Guest (NLS Acc. 7361/53)

27 Victoria Square
London SW1
n.d. [late July / early August 1932]

Dear Comrade,

The trial of Karikas has been postponed for three weeks –

Did I ask you to protest against his trial? I wired to you because while I was writing a number of people were talking in the room & I am afraid I may have put execution by mistake. In these countries trial does genuinely mean execution.[1]

It's awfully hot in town – I envy people in country cottages.

Best regards.

[form illegible]

Carmel Haden Guest.

---

[1]   A third letter is dated 12th August 3[2]. The writer notes that H.G. Wells had protested. This letter is incomplete. H.G. Wells (1866-1946); novelist.

16. From Compton Mackenzie (EUL 2954.8 f.15)

Eilean Aigas
Beauly
Inverness-shire
10 October 1932

Dear Grieve:

I enclose a copy of the letter I have just sent to Oliver Brown.[1] I hope you will rejoin the National Party for a conference, if you have to go out of it immediately afterward, possibly in my company.

THE TWO HEADED SCOT
By W. McCANCE.

'Ye Banks and Braes' published in *The Free Man* 1932.
By permission of Mrs McCance.

I will be in Glasgow Wednesday, Thursday, and Friday morning, staying with Rait at the University. We might squeeze in another talk. I have got a lot of interesting gossip which I will keep for our next meeting.

The *Second Hymn to Lenin* is splendid – direct and moving. I was delighted to see you looking so well, and to find you in such evident form.

Yours,

C. M.

---

[1]   Oliver Brown (1903-1976) was a teacher and Scottish Nationalist and socialist speaker and pamphleteer.

17. From William McCance (EUL MS2953.8 f.3)

The Gregynog Press
Montgomeryshire
22 October 1932

My dear Grieve,

I only got back the other day and found your letter.

I was sorry I had passed through Edinburgh before I knew that you were definitely living there for I should have liked to have seen you again.

When I read your letter I sat down to do a drawing with Scottish content and this is what turned out.[1] There is idea in it but it is not exactly a first-rate drawing as I am still a little bit mazed after the holiday and my return to Wales.

The meaning of the drawing is fairly obvious but I shall explain some of the symbols which may be obscure.

(a) The Heid is over an English concern and wears a Rose in his buttonhole.

(b) The sub-title might be 'Never let thy left hand know what thy right hand doeth', for he carries his heart in his left and from it springs a branch of artificial-looking thistle. (The heart, by the way, is, purposely, a bit like a haggis.)

(c) The other hand controls (note wires from fingers) the factories of the South, all of which seem to be smoking, due no doubt to successful Scottish management.

(d) The steps are symbolic of climbing to success and the attitude of the two-headed Scot is one of stepping to a bigger 'heidship', turning his back on the North (marked 'N') and the Braes, while the Banks and the South are well to the fore.

(e) On the 'Braes' side of the design I have placed the Kirk at the foot of the bare and empty Scottish landscape.

(f) The sporran occupying a central position between the two selves has managed to become a receptacle for £.s.d.

Well if anyone wants an explanation you can give them these points and any you care to add.

I do not know how this will reproduce but I think a half-tone should pick up quite a lot. By the way, what happened to the four or five drawings I sent to you when you were at the Unicorn Press? Will they still be there for I should like to have them sometime as they are part of a series which would make a good exhibition later on.

I saw a copy of *The Free Man* and meant to write to you. The article you had written on unemployment was the sanest and most realistic I had read. Having had some experience of the charity in South Wales, and the work for work's sake attitude, I had been thinking along the lines that your articles clarified. Will you let me have a few proofs of this design when you have the block?

Best luck.

W. McCance.

---

1   'Ye Banks and Braes' was first published in *The Free Man*, vol.1, no.48 (31 December 1932) and reproduced as the cover of *Cencrastus* 50, Winter 1994-1995. MacDiarmid wrote to McCance, on 5 January 1933 (NLS Acc. 7361/4), 'Your "Banks and Braes" has delighted all sorts of people, and they are clamouring for more. Can you help again – again, if possible, with something that hits the nails, both of Nationalism and Finance –'.

18. From George Ogilvie (EUL MS2958.3 f.7)

> 67 Cluny Gdns
> Edinburgh
> 31 October 1932

Dear Christopher,

It was with great pleasure my eye fell the other morning on an envelope with your chirography – 'loved long since but lost awhile'.[1] Indeed I had come to think of it as lost altogether, and had added it to a sadly growing list of memories. Of course, as one gets old he is thankful, amid his accumulating losses, that memories at least are left him, and that they brighten as they lengthen. And tho' it appeared I had lost you and your occasional letter, your memory would always be, I knew, among those that 'glow and glitter in my cloudy breast'.[2] Hence my shock of pleasure when your letter made it clear that I had been premature in so coming to think of you.

I would have made an attempt, too, I daresay to get into touch with you after my long illness and convalescence, but I learned you had left the last address of yours I had, & then my wife's long ordeal engrossed all my thought and leisure. And though I have lost her, I have now thanks to that and the dregs of my operation so small a margin of energy left that I had little heart left to search for lost threads.

I ought, of course, to say that I have been following you, with interest, in your poetry, and I was touched by your great kindness in sending me a copy of your *Second Hymn to Lenin*. I am glad to see that you are keeping at it, in spite of the dead set that our mandarins are still making against you, with of course most notable exceptions – so notable indeed that the others don't really count, though one grudges them their spiteful power to detract and damn with at best faint praise.[3]

It was a double pleasure to learn that you are to be so near for a time, and I am looking forward to an occasional chat with you – and with all the goodwill in the world to Mr Lawson[4] – all by ourselves. My time from 3/30 daily & all day Saty & Sunday is yours for the asking. I can meet you somewhere on Princes St. or await you here any evening or any hour on Saty or Sunday.

Ever yours,
Geo. Ogilvie.

1   'And with the morn those Angel faces smile / Which I have loved long since but lost awhile'. – John Henry Newman (1801-1890), '*The Pillar of Cloud*'.
2   'It glows and glitters in my cloudy breast' - Henry Vaughan (1621-1695), 'Friends Departed'.
3   'Damn with faint praise, assent with civil leer', - Alexander Pope (1688-1744), 'An Epistle to Dr Arbuthnot'.
4   Unidentified.

19. From Naomi Mitchison (EUL MS2955.13 f.1)

River Court
Hammersmith Mall
[London] W6
2 November 1932

Dear Mr Grieve,
Very many thanks for your book, which as you can imagine I was delighted to have. It will of course be extremely interesting when the whole thing is put together; in the mean time I find myself happiest with your more lyrical poems in which I feel you are freest to express what is really in your mind. Your poem about the rivers is as good as anything you have ever done and it does not hang one up over words as your other work sometimes does.[1] I confess that my knowledge of Scots is not nearly adequate for a really comfortable reading of most of your present work; compared with a great deal of it, Dunbar is child's play!
    Yours,
    Naomi Mitchison.

1   Naomi Mitchison refers here to 'Water Music' from *Scots Unbound and Other Poems,* (Stirling: Aeneas Mackay, 1932). Her remark about 'the whole thing' must allude to the 'Clann Albainn' project of which *Scots Unbound* was part.

20. From Edwin Muir (EUL MS2955.19 ff.7-8)

7 Downshire Hill
London NW3
6 November 1932

Dear Christopher,
Many warm thanks for your poems.[1] I have read them, some of them many times over, and with increasing admiration. The first three in particular seemed to me absolutely new, fresh and original; nobody but yourself could have written them; they have a unique original quality which has nothing to do, and owes nothing, to conventional poetical magic. I hope you will go on tapping that vein, which in all

the variety of your poetry, seems to me to be the most distinctively your own. In quite a different way I was greatly struck by 'Tarras' with its sustained elaboration of a conceit until the conceit takes on significance after significance, taking me into the heart of a very green world of reality. It is very remarkable, I think. The 'Water Music' is a delightful *tour de force*, marvellously executed; it is the sort of thing that I imagine you can easily throw off; it is all air and fire (as well as water). In 'Scots Unbound' I must say I think you present your reader with too many needless difficulties; also in 'Depth and the Chthonian Image'. I don't deny that they're remarkable; they are; but to me they have not half the significance of the first three poems, which take the mind as deep as it chooses to go. This does not mean that I did not like them, for they're full of power; but I imagine that in writing them you exercised only, comparatively speaking, a surface stratum of your mind, not as in these other poems and 'Tarras', all the deeper levels at the same time. The only poem that I did not much care for was 'The Oon Olympian', not because I've any academic objection to objections against Goethe (I've many myself, and most people have), but because you seem definitely below yourself there; almost absurdly so to me. Especially as this is one of the most striking volumes you've published thus far, so that in the end I can only send you my admiration and congratulations. I feel that a new vein is opening more and more for you, and it seems to me you're on the threshold of a new productive period. All good luck to you and it.

We've had lots of trouble in settling into this house, but have got comparatively in order by this time. Willa has got back to her novel again, which she intends to finish by the end of the year.[2] I've begun, quite unexpectedly, to write a little poetry again, somewhat different from my former stuff. I hope you got *The Sleepwalkers*.[3] I had it sent to *The Free Man*, for I would have found it hard to get a copy for individual recipients. I hope it reached you.

With kind regards.

Edwin Muir.

[1]   Edwin Muir comments here on *Scots Unbound and Other Poems*.
[2]   Willa Muir's novel was *Mrs Ritchie* (1933).
[3]   Willa and Edwin Muir translated *The Sleepwalkers* by Hermann Broch (1886-1951), (London, 1932). It was a trilogy - the romantic; the anarchist ; the realist.

21. From T. Henderson (EUL MS2970)

The Scottish Educational Journal
47 Moray Place
Edinburgh 3
7 November 1932

C.M. Grieve, Esq.
Fruit Farm
Longniddry

Dear Mr Grieve,

I am very sorry indeed to hear of your illness. I wondered why you hadn't managed up, more especially as I heard you had been at the 'Dunbar' Dinner. (I had intended being present but was called out of town.) This week I shall be much away, so perhaps you could manage to come up some forenoon next week.

I got the *Scots Unbound* all right but was waiting until I had seen you before expressing my thanks for so kindly sending it to me and for the dedication, which was thoroughly undeserved and so probably the more gratifying.

Thanks for the articles, which I hope to use soon, and for the Letter to the Editor. I have exercised my blue pencil to the extent of cutting out the last paragraph of the letter. I think you have rubbed it in sufficiently by that time.

Kind regards.

Yours sincerely,

T. Henderson.

22. From James H. Whyte (EUL MS2965.10 f.3)

Little Court
Sunningdale
Berks
12 November 1932

My dear Grieve,

Of course you should be able to get your trunk back from Thakeham: I'm sorry you didn't mention it before. Robbins[1] was in the other day about his poems, as he had had an offer to get them published in America – and naturally I am eager to see what other things you have done while you were in Sussex. 'Water Music' and 'Tarras' are certainly among the very best things you have done, and I should be only too glad to get the opportunity of publishing other poems like it ... The cheque which I am sending herewith should perhaps help to get the trunk up to Longniddry and do for the first two things which we publish of yours. I'll send some more later on when I have the chance of seeing your other work.

I have seen some interesting people in London: the Muirs, who are now in their new house in Hampstead, the Carswells, and 'L.G. Gibbon', whom I like very much. He is coming up to Scotland today for a fortnight, so I hope you will see him in Edinburgh. I am hoping to get some short stories from him for the *M [odern] S[cot]*. On Tuesday someone is insisting that I should meet Hugh Walpole at lunch: it will be curious to see what he has to say in self-defence.[2]

All good wishes to you, Valda[3] and James Michael.[4] I hope it won't be long before we shall meet again.

Yours,

J. H. W.

---

[1] Not identified.

[2] Hugh Walpole (1884-1941), popular novelist.
[3] Valda Trevlyn, MacDiarmid's second wife.
[4] Their son.

23. From Denis Saurat (EUL MS2960.3 f.2)

INSTITUT FRANÇAIS DU ROYAUME-UNI
(Universités de Lille et de Paris)
1-7 Cromwell Gardens
South Kensington SW7
21 November 1932

Mr. Grieve
1 India Buildings
Victoria St
Edinburgh[1]

My dear Grieve,

Thank you very much for your *Second Hymn to Lenin* which I thoroughly enjoyed, and which completes my collection of your works. As you know, I prefer your short poems to your long ones. This doesn't mean that in my opinion you are wrong to write long ones, because possibly the long one is a condition of the production of the short one.

I was particularly elated by your poem about the centenary of Goethe, which said very well some things that are true and on some of which I had insisted in an article in the *Nouvelle Revue Française*.[2]

Your idea of poetry being more important than social reform is a true idea which I hope you will bring out fully. It is, at bottom, a religious idea and I think that there is greatness in the development of it. I hope that however well you may ride the whirlwind of the Scottish National Movement you will apply to it the same test and that poetry will remain uppermost with you. The Scots need a poet much more than they need Home Rule, however badly they may need Home Rule.

My *History of Religion* is practically finished.[3] But it is to be in French. I don't suppose it will be out for a year or two, but you will of course receive a copy.

My wife sends her best wishes.

With kindest regards,

Affectionately,

D. Saurat.

[1] The office of *The Free Man*.
[2] The poem 'about the centenary of Goethe' was 'The Oon Olympian', published in *Scots Unbound and Other Poems* .
[3] *Histoire des religions* (Paris: Danoël, 1933); *A History of Religions* (London: Cape, 1934).

24. From F. Marian MacNeill (EUL MS2955.2 ff.1-3)

38 Royal Terrace
Edinburgh
23 November 1932

Dear Mr Grieve,

It *is* possible that by announcing yourself a Communist and a member of the Communist Party of Great Britain you lost me a few votes – whether a dozen or a hundred who can compute? – but I think we may take it that nothing you said would have alienated any genuine sympathy with the cause. Some of those who were anti-Thomsonites[1] and prepared to give me a purely negative support *may* have refrained from voting, but, good heavens, we were out for something much more vital than mere vote-catching; and no one who had ears to hear what you said that evening could possibly hold that the *vital* issue suffered at your hands. *Bien au contraire.* The feeling was, I think, that you spoke rather over the heads of the people – you know you *do* put on your seven-league boots, whiles, and stride over the continents and the centuries leaving us poor pygmies panting behind! And some, I fear, you unwittingly tread underfoot! So some went away, I was told, with no clear idea in their heads except they were being asked to vote for a Communist – and you know what a bogey the word still is to the generality! But that's all that's to it. Possibly a man who supported me on a previous evening lost me several votes by announcing that he has been a life-long Conservative (I always think it advisable to leave one's personal political sympathies out). And goodness how many I may have lost myself by saying this or that. But what about it? We did jolly well, all things considered, and we've got a good branch going in the ward. (The last thing I wanted, I may say, was to be returned!) And so far from feeling *aggrieved*, I take great pride in the fact that you appeared on my platform. I should willing[ly] have forgone many more votes, if need were, to have had that honour. So that's that!

With kindest regards.
Yours sincerely,
F. Marian McNeill.

[1] Opponents of ex-Bailie William Thomson.

25. From Gordon Bottomley (EUL MS2942.15 f.3)

The Sheiling
Silverdale
nr. Carnforth
Lancs
29 November 1932

My dear Grieve,

It is good and thoughtful and remembering of you to send me the beautifully got-up limited edition of your *Scots Unbound*: I value the gift of so fine a poet, and the thought behind it, deeply – and I thank you with all my heart.

I should have said so sooner, but we have only lately settled down after a Summer of wandering, and I have been swamped by prosy distracting things waiting here. That, however, has given me time to read a good deal of your book much more often than once; so I know all the better that I am privileged in your gift, and all the better how to thank you for it.

It is all transfused with your great gifts in full spate, so I cannot pick and choose among the pieces: but I had better own up that your Goethe piece gave me wicked delight.

I suppose there can't be much doubt that the finest thing of all is 'Depth and the Chthonian Image'. I must be frank and, again, own up that the first two pages floored me handsomely and left me crawling and hobbling: but after that I got into my stride (or was it you?) and enjoyed myself enormously. It is the very essence of you, with everywhere that combination of ingenious thinking and intensely creative imagery that is your sign-manual and passport to Parnassus. I think your imagery there is your very high water-mark.

I have kept myself fairly well up in you lately, for when your book came I had just been reading your 'Second Hymn to Lenin' in *The Criterion* with equal admiration.

I see that people are repeatedly making a triad of you with Burns and Dunbar now: and I like to think that I was one of the first to say so.

I say so still. Your new book makes me think of another fit partner for you: I don't know why I kept thinking of Carlyle as I read, for there is nothing like similarity of writing. I suppose it is simply an indication of the plain fact that Langholm and Ecclefechan are in the same airt.

I am sending you a book in exchange for yours – I fancy you won't care too much about it, for you are hunting a different quarry, and the chase is too hotfoot to turn aside for anybody: but I hope you'll like to have it from another craftsman in admiration and applause, a fellow-craftsman who can hear your music.

You wrote to me last from London: but I have been rejoicing to hear you have come back to Scotland again.

With many, many good wishes, believe me yours most truly,
Gordon Bottomley.

26. From Victor Neuburg (EUL MS2965.10 f.4)

THE VINE PRESS
Publishers
Steyning
Sussex
7 December 1932

O most elusive of poets, why don't you send me a line?
This is about the seventh time of asking.
Are you dead?

Sincerely,
Victor Neuburg.

note:-
send me my original Davidsons[1] back when you're through with them, please.

---

[1] May have been volumes of John Davidson (1857-1909), poet, novelist, dramatist and journalist.

27. From Robin Orr and J. B. Caird (EUL MS Gen. 2094/1/235)

Rutherford's Pub
Edinburgh
n.d. [1932]

Dear Grieve,
We are bloody drunk in a pub, but we realise fully the nonentity of 4 919 000 Scotsmen but you are supreme, the greatest Scot of the generation the only true Scot of this generation; the salvation of the world depends on Scotland, we are drunk, but you are the only man, you have put Scotland on her legs again, damnation to the oughty (?) we are bloody drunk but not drunk enough
Greetings.
Yours,
Robin Orr & J.B. Caird.

In great admiration man. Without you Scotland wouldn't be worth a damn and Major Douglas!

28. From Fredric Grant (EUL MS2966)

The Project Theatre
230 Renfrew St
Glasgow C3
3 January 1933

Dear Mr Grieve,
At last I have found a moment to write to you. First of all, 'A Very Happy and Successful New Year'.
'Nisbet' has jumped its first hurdle.[1] I don't think for one moment you ever expected it to be played. Some of the passages came out very well indeed, but as you may agree there was a lack of theatre. Nevertheless the experiment was interesting.
I wish you had seen it. Our 'Décor' specially painted a 12x8 back-cloth in symbolic design, depicting piles of tenements and everything that is loathsome of Glasgow. The *Daily Record* on the morning afterwards (24th) called it a 'Cerebral Puzzle'. Did you read it?

Now might I ask you have you any more to offer us? We are intent upon doing new plays whenever possible. What a wealth of expression our present time affords, and we like to 'Be Not Too Tame Neither'.

Please don't forget to drop in any time you are in Glasgow.

Yours sincerely,

Fredric Grant.

The officers of the theatre are given in the left margin of the notepaper.

Director.
Fredric Grant.
Producer.
J.D.G. Macrae.
Staging.
J.B. Russell.
Lighting.
W.H. Nicolson.
Decor.
Ian Fleming.
Publicity.
J. Reid Forrest.
Secretary and Treasurer.
J. Hay.

1   MacDiarmid's 'Nisbet, an Interlude in Post War Glasgow' was first published in *The Scottish Chapbook*, vol. 1, nos. 1 and 2 (August and September 1922) and reprinted in *Annals of the Five Senses and other Stories, Sketches and Plays,* edited by Roderick Watson and Alan Riach (Manchester :Carcanet, 1999), pp. 104-113.

29. From Edwin Muir (EUL MS2955.19 ff.9-10)

7 Downshire Hill
London NW3
8 January 1933

My dear Christopher,

I am just struggling out of a rather prolonged bout of flu', so if this letter is dull attribute part of it at least to that. I think, if you don't mind, I would rather choose some less difficult theme for the anniversary number. What Scotland's function is, what it has to contribute to the general wealth of nations, I have no idea: my head is peculiarly empty just now: partly the flu', I think. I should think its real job is to become originative instead of derivative in general: and for that it has to become a nation: so that nationalism is in a way everything at this stage: once a nation Scotland will have a function – at present it has none. If you'll leave me to work out some such idea as this I would be glad to do it. What do you say?[1]

Willa's novel is reaching its end, and would have been finished if it hadn't been for my illness. I think it's going to be very good. I've been writing a few poems –

and expect to write a few more, also another novel, when I'm all right again, and translation allows it. It's a pity *The Free Man* can't be expanded into something bigger in size and more general in scope. Is there any ultimate prospect of that? We've still the intention of returning to Scotland, after a term here in London: we made up our minds to that last April, when we were in St. Andrews. I think a year or two will see a general return: I've met several Scots people here in London who show a definite desire for it.

I hope your poetry is still going on. I envy you your productiveness. All good fortune to Valda and yourself and the family. Except for myself we've all been well, and I'm decidedly on the upgrade now. If you see F. G. Scott give him our greetings and curse him for never writing and thank him for his lovely collection of songs.

Yours,
Edwin.

[1]   Edwin Muir contributed 'The Functionlessness of Scotland' to *The Free Man*, 11 February, 1933, p.6. This article is reproduced in *Modernism and Nationalism,* edited by Margery Palmer McCulloch (Glasgow: Association for Scottish Literary Studies, 2004), pp.254-256.

30. From William McCance (EUL MS2953.8 f.4)

William MacCance
Agnes MacCance
Tregynon
Montgomeryshire
9 January 1933

Dear Chris,

Yes[,] I shall do another drawing. I am glad the last one was liked. The idea I have for this one is this: on the left side will be Montagu Norman[1] holding a gold chain, which is attached to the spoke of the wheel of the abstract machine from one side of which flows a tiny stream into a small pail marked 'PURCHASING POWER'[;] from the other side flows a large stream marked 'SURPLUS'. In the bottom corner are the Houses of Parliament.

Above Norman's head again appear the words 'YE BANKS', while on the House of Commons are the words 'AND BRAYS'. The title will be 'SCOTS! UNITE! YOU HAVE NOTHING TO LOSE BUT HIS CHAIN'[.] This, I think, would hit it off quite nicely.

I haven't time to do the heading just now, but I should like to do one later on.

I have not done the drawing yet, but I have done a caricature of Montagu Norman's head in readiness. The drawing came out rather well in the reproduction [.]

Best wishes and thank Black for his nice letter.[2]

Yours,
Mac.

[1]   1st Baron Montagu Norman (1871-1950) was Governor of the Bank of England from

1066—The Norman Conquest.
1933—Still holding On.

'Scots! Unite! You have nothing to lose but HIS chain' published in *The Free Man* 1933.
By permission of Mrs McCance.

1920 to 1944.

2   Robert MacKelvie Black, the proprietor of *The Free Man*.

31. From Eric Linklater (EUL MS2953.4 f.1)

East Fife Bye-Election[1]
Mr Linklater's Central Committee Rooms

South Street
St Andrew's
20 January 1933

My Dear Grieve,

As one Nationalist to another – as an Individualist to the most individual Communist in the world – may I borrow for my election address the middle passage of the Declaration of Independence quoted by *The Free Man*?

Yours ever,

Eric Linklater.

1   In the by-election of February 1933 Linklater received 1083 votes, the fewest of the five candidates.

32. From James Leslie Mitchell (Lewis Grassic Gibbon) (EUL MS2955.11 f.1)

28, Edgar's Court
Welwyn Garden City
21 January 1933

My dear C. M. Grieve,

The great god Flu has had me enthralled, else I'd have answered your letter before this time. I'm so glad to get in communication with you – I tried once, after that meeting of the Revolutionary Writers' Group,[1] but the telephone wire went wonk. And when *Sunset Song* came out[2] I sent a copy (duly inscribed) to the London address you had given me. A fortnight later it was returned to the publisher, complete with hunting cry 'Gone Away'.

I believe the publisher put that copy back in stock, but I'll make him dig it out and send it to you if you'd like it.

About *The Free Man*: it is very good stuff. But tell me, is communism compatible with nationalism? And what about those Scots Fascists we talked about, abominable breed? I'd like to write something for *The Free Man*, but I'm not much good at political stuff. Or would the pages run to a short short story? Do let me know, and if I'm in time for the next issue.[3]

Kind regards.

Sincerely,

JasLeslieMitchell.

1   Hugh MacDiarmid and Lewis Grassic Gibbon met in London in 1932 at a meeting called to form a British Section of the Revolutionary Writers of the World which had been initiated in Kharkov in 1930.

2   *Sunset Song* (London: Jarrolds, August, 1932).

3   Grassic Gibbon's story 'Sim' was first published in *The Free Man*, vol. 2, no. 19 (10 June 1933), pp. 5-7.

33. From William McCance (EUL MS2953.8 f.5)

Tregynon
Newtown
Montgomeryshire
25 January 1933

Dear Chris,

Here is the drawing, sent in a separate parcel.[1] I have enclosed a piece of paper with the title and sub-title, but in case it is mixed up with the packing, I will give it here.

Title: Scots! Unite! You have nothing to lose but *HIS* chain (and a Country to gain – might be added.)

Sub-title: 1066 The Norman Conquest
              1933 Still holding on

The drawing is a bit dirty, but the truth is I had rather a bad headache when I did it. But you reproduce very well, so it will probably come out all right. You might put in an apology for the drawing of the House of Commons; but it was so bloody boring to do that I got fed up. In a properly organised society, I would get some damned Academic fool, who likes doing that kind of thing, to do it for me.

The idea of Norman holding his hand over his face is two-fold. There was a photograph in the Muck-press of him doing this to hide from the camera – the bloody fool. So I am using this idea partly to suggest the ostrich theme, escaping danger, partly to suggest the mystery-man behind the scenes. The caricature of his nibs is not too good, but it has a suggestion of Uncle Sam about it which is all to the good.

The 'BRAYS' from the House of Commons is obvious, I think, and gives the Scottish Nationalist touch.

Well, I hope your number is a success. It looks as if it would be.

My best wishes.

Mac.

P.S. Be careful when you unpack the drawing, for it is easily smudged.

1   'Scots! Unite! You have nothing to lose but *HIS* chain' was first published in *The Free Man*, vol.2, no.1 (4 February 1933), p.4, and reproduced in *Cencrastus* 50 (Winter 1994-1995).

34. From F. G. Scott (EUL MS2959 ff.29-30)

44 Munro Road
Jordanhill
Glasgow
5 February 1933

My dear Chris,

Let me clear up the concert business first of all. It will take place in Stevenson Hall, National Academy of Music on Wednesday at 8 o'clock. Burnett promised me in Edinburgh that he'd come through and sing on the 9th (Thursday) but fortunately we found the hall was booked for that night and I had much pleasure in regretting his valuable co-operation and would he return at once the MSS in his possession.[1] This he has done so I'm clear of Edin. altogether – and for a long time, I hope. I finished with the lady soloists and handed them over to Chisholm as I'll play for the Bass singer only and conduct the Choir.[2] Chisholm has been compelled by having [been] invited to put on a MacKenzie String Quartet which lasts about half an hour, and some of my songs have been dropped from each group.[3] However, there's enough left to give everyone an inkling as to what I'm doing, though I confess to being pretty near the stage of not caring a damn whether the things are sung or not. I suppose I'm so vitally interested myself in what I'm doing that anything outside me is almost an impertinence and a meddling with my private life. Well here's luck to Wed. in any case and to the chance of seeing the contingent from Edinburgh.

I've been as you'll guess very busy rehearsing with the singers and writing out copies of some of the songs but having finished last night with the women I'm free today to write my comments on the lyrics you sent during the week.

'Verlaine in the Forest' (which I see in *The Free Man*) was the best idea you sent me ('poetic' in the accepted sense) [but] wasn't too well managed I thought. It should have been in English and quite conventional English at that.[4] The *'bright'* accoutrements and the *'starry'* squadrons (the first of these throws 'shadows on the grass' (daylight) and they do it at night-time!) The 3rd stanza rhymes 'pierce' and 'ears' [and] naturally suggested at once 'with a bayonet in my erse'. I think the idea quite a good one – if you rewrite it in usual accepted poetical English it would convince quite a large number of people that you are a poet.

In 'Durscheelte' I didn't like 'adjust itsel'.[5] Could it not be 'coorie', 'huddle', 'bouquet' or something not quite so redolent of the lavatory?

'Breakin' the Ice' is decent enough.[6] Put period after reach.

> reach. It stirred -
> Silently etc.

The ending about the sun isn't quite striking enough to give it a grip on the memory. Perhaps that's only the manner of expression you've given it.

The other bird poem 'Leiderscheinung' is slightly below MacDiarmid.[7] Man as an afterthought doesn't help Man much as a fact. It belongs to the Kingdom of might-have-been – a very prolific people. What about putting the poem into the mouth of the heron soliloquising on 'that afterthought, Man'.

'Riding in the Fog' I see I've annotated so fully that I'll need to return the MS.[8] The change as an address to 'Men of action!' etc. is, I think, very effective, unlike anything else you've done. For safety I'll rewrite it:-

> Men o' action, what's the need
> To set a course afore ye!
> Ye the men wha feel blin' fog
> To poo'ers like God's restore ye.
>   that)
> Ye wha) ride wi' a' forgotten
> Save what ye love best
> Shapeless, like the wind before ye)
> Opens (ing) nae way through the rest.)   pretty dud this.

> Something vaguer, deeper, commoner,
> Than ony form, ye choose;
> And exult that ithers canna
> Guess how deep your views.

N.B. This damned pompous rhetorical style has always had an attraction for me. I detest the thing like blazes but it fascinates me like a snake's coils. I instinctively feel it to be one o' the poo'ers like God's.

In sum, there isn't much in this bunch for me to get my critical apparatus into. I'm grateful of course that you've been thinking over my need for stuff to turn into music and perhaps some of these may go that way later on but I'd remind you that the conventional music-lyric doesn't give me nowadays much room (any more than 'poetical diction' gives you) and I could do more at the moment with a prose 'Milk-wort and Bog-cotton' than with any of the things you sent.[9] I also wish we could put out a volume jointly – 'Six Mystical Songs' – 'Conundrums' or some such title – clean off the earth things for all succeeding generations of Scotsmen to puzzle over and glory in. The 'quintessential of Scottishness' (shall we say following Rabelais) in (a) bawdiness (b) Glasgow filthiness (c) heather & moor (d) herring-fishing (e) the Kirk etc. etc. – six aspects of the Scot with nocht but the smell o' him in them – a kind of film panorama of adjectives only – an *instantanéité* before the eye of the All-Knower. But I'm raving.

See you on Wednesday!

F. G.

---

[1]   George J. Burnett was Director of Studies at Jordanhill.
[2]   Professor Erik Chisholm (1904-1965), composer and professor of Music at the University of Cape Town from 1945.

3   Sir Alexander Mackenzie (1847-1935), composer.
4   Scott's meaning is confused here. 'Verlaine in the Forest', *C.P.* II, p.1267, was first published in *The Free Man*, vol.2, no.1 (4 February 1933), in English.
5   'Durchseelte', *C.P.* II, p.1288. MacDiarmid appears to have substituted 'crowdle' for 'adjust'. It was first published in *The Modern Scot*, vol.4, no.1 (1933) as being 'From Cavaburd and other poems'.
6   'Breaking the Ice', *C. P.* II, p.1289, was also from 'Cavaburd'. MacDiarmid appears to have accepted Scott's suggestion.
7   'Leidercheinung' appears to have been lost.
8   'Riding in a Fog', *C. P.* II, p.1289, from 'The War with England'. It forms part of 'The Dark Whirling Dun' (with variations) first published (in part) in *The Revolutionary Art of the Future*.
9   'Milk-wort and Bog-Cotton', *C.P.*I, p.331.

35. From Herbert Read (EUL MS2958.14 f.5)

9 Tipperlinn Road
[Edinburgh]
5 February 1933

Dear Grieve,

Many thanks for your letter, & for the poems, which my wife & I would feel very honoured to have inscribed to us.[1] Perhaps, as Yorkshire folk, we might have appreciated the *slightly* Scoticised medium. My N. Yorks dialect, at any rate, comes pretty near at times to Burns. But so much depends on accent & intonation. I maintain that Wordsworth's poetry is ruined by an Oxford voice.

I perfectly understand your feeling of isolation here. I even share it. At first I thought I should be too interested in my work & too busy to miss London. But I've been feeling rather despondent lately: there is so little real life stirring here. The miserable audiences we get for the Contemporary Music Society are symptomatic of the rest. The place lives on its past, & does it complacently. It has buried its sensibilities: it is atrophied. I don't think I can do much more than tickle the surface of this inert mass: your revolution must come first.

I was glad to hear that you think of moving into Edinburgh. Then we must foregather in a more congenial evening atmosphere, & try to get over our shyness.

Yours sincerely,
Herbert Read.

1   'Durscheelte' was inscribed 'For Mrs Read' and 'Riding in a Fog' was inscribed 'For Professor Herbert Read'.

36. From Elizabeth Dawson (NLS MS27148 f.4)

Since this letter was largely unpunctuated the convention of showing sentence breaks by capitals only has been adopted.

Laurie's Close
Waterbeck
Lockerbie
20 April 1933

My dear Christy,

I got your letter and I am very sorry to hear that you are so run down and not well at all I don't know if you get your food right I wish I could have been beside you so that I could have looked after you and you seem so worried too I did not see the *Observer* nor any other papers with any article of yours but I hope you are getting things accepted What is Peggy's trouble that she had to go through another operation I take it that the bairns will be in Cupar somewhere Do go and get your warm underwear for now it is very cold again We had some snow showers yesterday Chrissie[1] is keeping better but not quite well yet If you go away from Longniddry what about my furniture Will I have to remove it Let me know Try and take care of yourself We are all fairly well here We have two of [one word illegible] bairns till this weekend then I think the Lochmaben folk are coming their holiday So this is a busy place I do wish you would come down and tell me all about things

    Kind love from mother
    E Dawson

---

[1] 'Chrissie' was her daughter-in-law, first wife of Andrew Graham Grieve (1894-1972), MacDiarmid's younger brother.

---

37. From J. M. MacCormick, National Party of Scotland (EUL MS2962.9 ff.1-2)

THE NATIONAL PARTY OF SCOTLAND
East of Scotland Offices:-   131 WEST REGENT STREET
40 Shandwick Place   GLASGOW C2
Edinburgh

10 May 1933.

C.M. Grieve Esq.
The Scots Free Press
1, India Buildings
Victoria Street
EDINBURGH

Dear Mr Grieve,

Your letter of 21st ultimo was duly placed before the National Council at its meeting held in Perth on Saturday 6th instant.

After giving careful consideration to your letter and taking into account your own often repeated statements of complete disagreement with the Policy of the National Party and also your statements that you had preached from the Nationalist platform Scots Communism, Republicanism etc., and your reported statement that you sought to use the National Party as a means of introducing Communism into Scotland, and considering that all such statements are completely at variance with the Policy of the National Party and that some of them have been made since your application for membership of the Party, the Council resolved to decline to accept your application for membership and to instruct the South Edinburgh Branch of the Party that you are not eligible for membership.

As the Council considers that you are not and have not become a member of the Party since your resignation of some years ago, the Council resolved that it would not be in order for you to make a personal appeal against this decision at the annual Conference.

The Council's decision may, of course, be questioned by any branch of the Party and if you wish to state a case to the Conference you may do so by letter which will be read at the Conference.

Yours faithfully,

J. M. MacCormick.

Hon. National Secretary.

38. From Florence Ann Rowlands (NLS Acc. 7361/4)

CARD FROM CMG's MOTHER-IN-LAW POSTMARKED BUDE 6PM 25 MAY 1933.

24 May 1933

Greetings from Bude Glad to hear you like Whalsay so well – It certainly looks very bare & flat rather different from here It is good to have Valda at home again J. M. is a lovely boy the change is doing them both a lot of good the 31st will come all too quickly.

Love F. A. Rowlands (Florence Ann)

39. From N. C. Jack, National Party of Scotland (NLS Acc. 7361/4)

1 Lochrin Terrace
Edinburgh
31 May 1933

Dear Mr Grieve,

Further to my letter of 11th inst. I held over refunding your membership subscription to the South Edinburgh Branch until something definite was arrived at at the Conference.

Probably you would notice from the press that the matter of your membership was brought up at the Conference and a vote taken, the result of which was 38 for and 55 against. – There is nothing left to do now – except enclose 2/6d paid.[1]

A.R.Orage. Orage was editor of the influential *The New Age*.
(New English Weekly)

Without going into details of the Conference I would say that the 55 people who voted against your reinstatement were influenced by the narrow-minded views expressed by Mr MacCormick. The 38 members who voted for, though determined, could not sway the mob. Again I would take the opportunity of saying how much this is to be regretted, but look forward to the time when a man will not be condemned by fellow-nationalists for holding what moderates call extreme views.

With best wishes.

I am,

Yours sincerely,

N. C. Jack.

(Hon. Sec. for the National Party of Scotland,

South Edinburgh Branch.)

[1]   After Hugh MacDiarmid left Montrose for London in 1929 he either resigned from the National Party of Scotland, or allowed his membership to lapse, some time after 10 May 1930. He was recorded as a member of the Council on that date. (NLS Acc. 5916/3). When he returned to Scotland in August 1932 he attempted to rejoin and paid 2/6 subscription to the South Edinburgh Branch. This was returned to him after the annual Conference. This letter is important in view of the oft-repeated statements by MacDiarmid and others that he had been expelled from the National Party; in fact, he failed to be reinstated.

40. From A. R. Orage (EUL 2958.4 f.11)

The New English Weekly[1]
Edited by
A. R. Orage
27 July 1933

Dear old man,

I couldn't publish your letter without asking for a libel suit & about none of the *N. E. W.*'s real business. You should send a letter to the *T. Lit. Supp.* – I'm delighted to hear you are on good terms with your genius again. Damn it all. You're the only man's poet even England – let alone Scotland – has had since Byron! I'm sorry to say Black is too optimistic about the *N. E. W.* The fall of the dollar has just about ruined any hope of our life ... However ... Best wishes to the family.

Yours ever,

A. R. Orage.

[1]   *The New English Weekly* was started by Orage after his return to London from the US. It was described as ' A review of public affairs, literature and the arts'and was edited by him from 1932 until his death in 1934. It ceased publication in 1949.

41. From James Leslie Mitchell (Lewis Grassic Gibbon) (EUL MS2955.11 f.6)

107 Handside Lane
Welwyn Garden City
11 August 1933

My dear Grieve,

It was very nice of you to give me that notice[1] in the FREE MAN; I should have thanked you before, but that I've been too damn busy earning a living.[1] I hope that the Scots Republic, when it comes, will put deserving authors on the dole.

What I wanted to ask is: Will you let me dedicate GREY GRANITE to you? And if so, shall it be to C.M.G. or H. M'D?[2]

Do let me know.

Kind regards.

J.L.M.

[1] MacDiarmid's 'notice' was 'Lewis Grassic Gibbon', the first of his series of 'Contemporary Scottish Studies' in *The Free Man*, vol.2, no.26 (29 July 1933), p.7.
[2] It was dedicated to Hugh MacDiarmid.

42. From James Leslie Mitchell (Lewis Grassic Gibbon) (EUL MS2955.11 f.8)

107 Handside Lane
Welwyn Garden City
31 August 1933

My dear Grieve,

Let's write a book together. The notion came into my head this morning while I was shaving . ... A unique book about Scotland by Hugh MacDiarmid and Lewis Grassic Gibbon. We'll call it 'The Scottish Scene',[1] and it will be interwoven so:

Verse (by H. M'D.)
Short story (by L.G.G.)
Short biography of a living Scot (by either of us)
Newsreel (quotations from contemp. journals showing up the state of Scotland)

Let's say five pieces of poetry, five short stories, five short biographies, and five newsreels. That would produce something unique, wouldn't it? Besides, you could use spare verse and I spare short stories that have seen only magazine publication so far.

This is a hasty first note on the subject. Tell me what you think – and give additional proposals.

Sincerely,

JasLeslieMitchell.

[1] *Scottish Scene* (London: Jarrolds, 1934).

43. From Edwin Muir (EUL MS 2955.19 f.14)

THREE
SOUTH STREET
ST ANDREWS
9 September 1933

My dear Christopher,

Forgive me for being so long in replying to your letter and the poems you've so generously put at Janko's disposition and my own.[1] It's partly that I could not make up my mind about them, and partly that I was so busy absorbing impressions – I haven't been in Orkney since 1912. I think I would like best to print the two English poems you sent me first – both of which in their different ways I like very much. But will you wait until I see Lavrin first? My choice has nothing to do with the poems' being in English, I needn't say: but the one is so lovely and the other so witty that I got more from them than from the Scottish or the synthetic – which are also remarkable, but did not ring the bell so clearly in my case. So I think it will be the two English, but it might be either of the other two. I shall write you again in a few days about them.

I'm more glad than I can say to hear the news of your fresh [one word illegible] of energy. I've been reading 'Harry Semen' and I should have to use the wildest superlatives to give any idea of my admiration for it.[2] I do sincerely hope that nothing will interfere with your new and magnificent productive vein – and I'm sure that you will take this as absolutely sincere and quite untinged with the literary envy that writing people so often have for one another. All good luck and success of the kind you deserve and want and will have in greater and greater measure.

Yours,

Edwin.

---

[1] In May 1934 *The European Quarterly,* vol. 1, no. 1, edited by Edwin Muir and Janko Lavrin and published by Stanley Nott, included MacDiarmid's poem 'First Love', *C.P.* I, pp.434. Janko Lavrin (1887-1986) was a Slovenian who spent most of his life abroad, first in Russia then in Great Britain. Originally a journalist, he became a literary historian, essayist and translator of Slavic Literature. He was Professor of Modern Russian Literature at The University of Nottingham (1923-1953).

[2] In a later letter, 3 October 1933 (EUL MS2955.19 f.15), Muir wrote, 'I saw "Harry Semen", as I said, in St Andrews, and it still remains in my memory as the chief literary event of the past months. I don't think you've ever produced anything more astonishing or more absolutely original.' 'Harry Semen', *C.P.* I, pp.483-485.

44. From W. R. Aitken (EUL MS2942.2 f.1)

The Student
Edinburgh University
Students' Representative Council
Edinburgh 1

25 September 1933

C.M. Grieve, Esq.

Dear Sir,

As Editor of the above magazine – the official student organ of Edinburgh University – I have been asked to produce a special 'celebrations' number in connection with the University's 350th anniversary. For this number messages have been asked and articles invited from many 'great' Scotsmen of today. All with one accord, from Dr Watt to the Prime Minister, write of the PROGRESS made during these years. They do not seem to realise that for the last 100 or 150 years Edinburgh has fallen from a place of mediocre reputation to one of no reputation at all as far as general culture and artistic life is concerned.

Knowing your views on such subjects and as a devout worshipper of your work I am sending you this letter to invite you to contribute either a message, or if you have time a short article, to readjust to some extent the scale of values that these fatuous noodles have set up. As *The Student* is an amateur production I can offer you no other payment than my hearty thanks.

Yours faithfully,

W. R. Aitken.

45. From William McElroy (NLS MS 27148 f.13)

Iddesleigh House
Caxton Street
Westminster SW1
4 October 1933

My dear Chris,

I should have replied to your letter (not the letter red. today) & intended to do so but pure carelessness etc & you ken – Todays letter contains good news – Your first letter also contained good news ÷ Health, good air – getting fit to fight & the knowledge that *you* yourself knew and feel that the power was returning, for Chris it had become intermittent & false, My opinion Chris rightly or wrongly, My God Chris it is good news I have sent for the magazines. *New Britain*[1] & *New English Weekly* – Sean[2] is not too well. Altho I speak to him on phone regularly have not been out to see him – Will write you again when read – 'Song of the New Economics'[3] Peggy keeping well.[4] We had two weeks in Scotland. Children [but] for usual infantile complaints quite well.

Yours,

Billy.

---

[1] *New Britain* 1933-1936, weekly.
[2] Sean O'Casey.
[3] 'Song of the New Economics', *C.P.* I, pp. 396-401.
[4] William McElroy was living with Peggy, Hugh MacDiarmid's first wife, at this time. McElroy was the dedicatee of 'Charisma and My Relatives', *C. P.* I, pp.301-302.

46. From William Duff McHardy (NLS Acc.7361/4)

King's College
Aberdeen
13 November 1933

Dear Mr. Grieve,

I do not feel unduly depressed. Analyse it thus: about 20% of the total number of votes were cast for you.[1] We were 2nd in two nations and 3rd in another. That in itself would be fairly satisfactory in view of the fact that we entered the lists to challenge two other non-political parties who had by this time considerable ground advantage – and were run by the 'best people' in our midst & by students who had large personal followings in various societies.

But further, in two nations at least, Buchan & Moray, the Grieve procurator had a clear advantage in Arts, Divinity, Law & Science, which was lost solely because Medicine voted solidly for Elliot. This is at once consolation for us & a condemnation of the mentality of the medical student. In fairness I should add that I consider they have chosen the one candidate whose Rectorial address they may follow.

On behalf of my committee I would like to thank you very warmly for consenting to stand at this Election & for the interest you showed in forwarding articles & in addressing our meeting. But for your assistance we had not been able to break through tradition so violently nor inaugurate so impressively our campaign against humbug as represented in our 'Varsity by dotage-authority' & the 'Grammar School–Girls' High' outlook.

Personally I would thank you for evoking in me a latent fanaticism!!

I regret we have been unable to fix up our spree for Thursday as various other functions take place on that date, but if you have time to drop us a note I shall be very pleased to convey to the company any message you may send, & I trust we may soon have an opportunity of meeting you again.

Kindest regards.
Yours sincerely,
William Duff McHardy.

[1]   Emslie, another supporter, sent a telegram, 10 November 1933: 'Elliott elected Grieve third beating Huxley Quite satisfactory'. David Murison was also a supporter. A photo in *Letters* (1984) shows MacDiarmid addressing students. The results were, Walter Elliott, 307; G. K. Chesterton, 220; C. M. Grieve, 158; Aldous Huxley, 117.

47. From Graham MacGibbon (EUL MS2954.4 ff.1-2)

45 Dinmont Rd
Waverley Road
Glasgow S1
5 December 1933

A Charaid,[1]
Your reply to my letter delighted me, we may yet do something for Scotland![2]

I hope you did not misunderstand my remark about 'credit', you are articulate where we are not, you would be listened to, where we would not be listened to.

Please write your man in the South as soon as possible and let me know the result of his report. As I am an engineer I may be of some use in solving any problems of removal etcetera with which he may present us.

Being a wage slave I do not finish until 5.30 pm which does not allow me sufficient time to dress, feed and make a return journey to Edinburgh by train, so I will be unable to see you this time. Saturdays and Sundays are really the only days I could manage through to the Capital.

Some points – Get from London a suggestion as to the most suitable period of the year for the carrying out of the coup. My friend is available anytime, but I may be only available during the summer holidays or on occasional long weekends. If I cannot take part in the actual expedition, I would, of course, await at this end and give financial support.

Transport – we have a fairly good light lorry at our disposal, but two cars would reduce the chance of a hold-up in the event of mechanical trouble. Transport by road is best, I think?

Finance – each participant paying his own expenses is the most logical arrangement. Do you agree?

There must be a 'rightness' about the place chosen as the destination of the symbol. I am sure you will be able to think of the proper spot with due regard to dramatic effect. When chosen, this spot will also require surveying.

Everyone taking part must be of Scots birth and parentage. We cannot let the English press use the 'English origin' jibe.

I expect you to lead this plan to a successful conclusion and anxiously await the news from London.

I think I could enlist one more trustworthy Scot later, if needed.

Is mise,[3]

Graham MacGibbon.

[1]   'Dear Sir'.
[2]   The reference is to the developing plan to bring back the Stone of Destiny to Scotland in 1934.
[3]   'I am'.

48. From Neil M. Gunn (EUL MS2948.15 ff.12-13)

Larachan
Dochfour Drive
Inverness
21 December 1933

My dear Christopher,

The season's greetings to you & the best of luck in the New Year! May your poetic power & prestige increase!

As you say, a talk would be necessary to make up the leeway, though even at that you are hardly warranted in misinterpreting a few remarks of mine into meaning: yourself v. Nat. Party![1] I know you're modest, but don't overdo it, or I'll take you seriously! Your remark that the N.P. has done nothing or less than nothing is merely – I was going to say absurd, but let us say contrary to ascertainable facts. Take Inverness itself. In a matter of a few weeks' intensive propaganda, some of it pretty extreme, over 4 000 folk voted Nat. Of these, let us say modestly that 100 are game for *anything*, & of these 100 let us say that not one has heard of C.M. Grieve, the poet, or for that matter, N.M.G., the so-called novelist. Let that be repeated all over Scotland – increased – intensified, and *then* you have a magnetic field upon which *you* may work or any other with clear-sighted, definite views, aims, revolutions, dreams or ideals. Without that potential magnetic field, there ain't no use shoving in any extremist armature. My point was the very simple one that it's bad business to have interference amongst different groups honestly preparing (& the more they feel themselves God's anointed the better) different sections or levels of the body politic. But possibly to your fine fervour that savours of cynicism! Ah well, I'm merely trying to look at the millions (whom you dub nitwits, though how you think nitwits are to be roused by your philosophy, God knows) and get a sort of all-round realisable glimpse so that it may be possible to estimate exactly how long it will take for that mass to be moved by possibly the sudden emergence of certain measures. Certain things have to be done to 'em before then. I am prepared now to forecast, however, fairly accurately, I believe.

But we can't begin to write about it. So here's good health to you and cheers!
Ever yours,
Neil Gunn.

[1] The National Party of Scotland, established in 1928, merged with the Scottish Party in 1934 to form the Scottish National Party.

49. From F. G. Scott (NLS MS27155 f.113)

[1933]
[THE ONLY SURVIVING PART OF A LETTER FROM F.G. SCOTT TO HUGH MACDIARMID CONCERNING SCOTT'S IRISH VISIT IN 1933]

successive nights, one of which included Yeats, and took to him as to a long-lost brother. Gogarty is a great chap, how I envy him his mere physical fearlessness, and speaks of you (as did Yeats) with the liveliest appreciation. I put some of the essential Scott across them and I fancy added another white stone to Scottish reputation. (*Sotto voce* – I think we could and will ultimately leave the Irish contingent well in the rear!) We seem to be operating on a very much more advanced and modern plane altogether. Yeats, for instance, I found rather dully ruminative, he spoke in soliloquising fashion about 'visions in deep sleep' and 'ghosts' etc. till I was inclined to pull his leg by a discussion on Yoga. He seemed to think nobody had heard about it before. – My hat!

But if I go on I'll not get this away today. 'Ho! My Little Sparrow' has a nice kind of shimmer on it – it twitters in quite sparrow fashion [about] nothing in particular but is likeable for all that.[1] 'Bracken Hills' I take it is one of your efforts to make poetry out of anything.[2] I prefer poetry out of something e.g. 'The Caledonian Forest'.[3] What about turning your hand to an operatic libretto. [Erik] Chisholm keeps telling me that the Glasgow Grand Opera Soc. would produce anything of the kind I did – humorous, tragic or what you will.

Meanwhile glad to have your collaboration in a hefty writer's correspondence. Scotland is resting heavily on our shoulders. I sold Bayley & Ferguson other *two* part-songs last Wednesday (for nothing!)

Ever affectionately to Valda & youngster.

F.G.

---

[1] 'Ho! My Little Sparrow', *C.P.* I, p.385.
[2] 'Bracken Hills in Autumn' was first published by Colin H. Hamilton, 112 Rose Street, Edinburgh on 4 June 1962 in an edition of twenty-five copies. *C.P.* II, pp.1151-2 .
[3] ' In the Caledonian Forest', *C.P.* I, pp. 391-2.

50. From Graham MacGibbon (EUL MS2954.4 ff.3-4)

45 Dinmont Park
Waverley Park
Glasgow
15 January 1934

A Charaid,

I am delighted to hear that things are moving, and can almost visualise the symbol being borne along Princes Street in the glare of thousands of torches. What a scene!

Remember, we are with you to the bitter end, and absolutely at your command as far as our present state of economic slavery permits.

When the time is almost ripe, you could let me have the dimensions, and we will have a suitable container made, with rope handles etcetera.

I believe it is a kind of red sandstone, and we could calculate the weight from its volume.

We can also make a rubber-tyred trolley to facilitate handling.

At the risk of annoying you by repetition I think that a convoy of at least three cars is desirable. We cannot risk a breakdown or mishap holding us back.

Transport by train is, I think, impracticable and undesirable. Perhaps London could help with this?

I was sorry to hear that you had been unwell, but wish you happiness and prosperity in the New Year and more power to your pen.

May 'Scotland's Luck' return to her before the year has passed.

Is mise,

Graham MacGibbon.

51. From Aonghas Cleireach (Angus Clark) (EUL MS2954.4 f.9)

26 Claremont Grove
Woodford Green
Essex
17 January 1934

A Charaid,

Your letter via the *Free Man* office arrived last night. My wife joins with me in sending you greetings & all good wishes for the New Year. To refresh my memory & to make more careful observations I propose to visit the haunt you refer to early next week. Unfortunately I cannot do it earlier, but if all goes well my report should be in your hands about Friday the 26th or at latest the 27th.

So far as the weight of 'the goods' is concerned they could be handled by one man. Unless arrangements have been altered in recent years I believe cement & Iron are not in use. Meantime I will defer further comment till I see the whole situation after which I will report.

Your stipulation about the contract is carefully noted.

Le Beannachdan agus meas.[2]

Aonghas Cleireach.

[1] 'With blessing and respect'.

52. From Edwin Muir (EUL MS2955.19 f.18)

7 Downshire Hill
London NW3
17 January 1934

Dear Christopher,

The Epoch is coming out at last, and you will have a copy in a few days' time. I think it is quite an interesting venture. Thanks more than I can say for your exquisite poem.

I have not managed to do anything yet about your poems, unless you are prepared to appear in Stanley Nott's list; he has set up as a publisher and is anxious to have you, and also seems to have an excellent list, including a book by Soloviev on Plato. I saw him the other day and he said he was going to write to you; but I have written too to make sure. I've tried Cape's, Secker's, Methuen's, Wishart's and Dent's (who are bringing out a small volume of mine in March or April). The Scottishness of your poetry is the one insuperable drawback. Wishart seemed promising for a time, but I doubt whether they could be brought to the scratch without a great loss of time – and even then it is doubtful. I think, on the other hand, that Nott is more or less a certainty if you will take him: he seemed eager to have you. And I really think it might be all to the good to be brought out by a new publisher.

Nothing much happening here, except that we see a great number of more people than usual. I do hope the Nott proposition will be satisfactory. I hope Valda and you

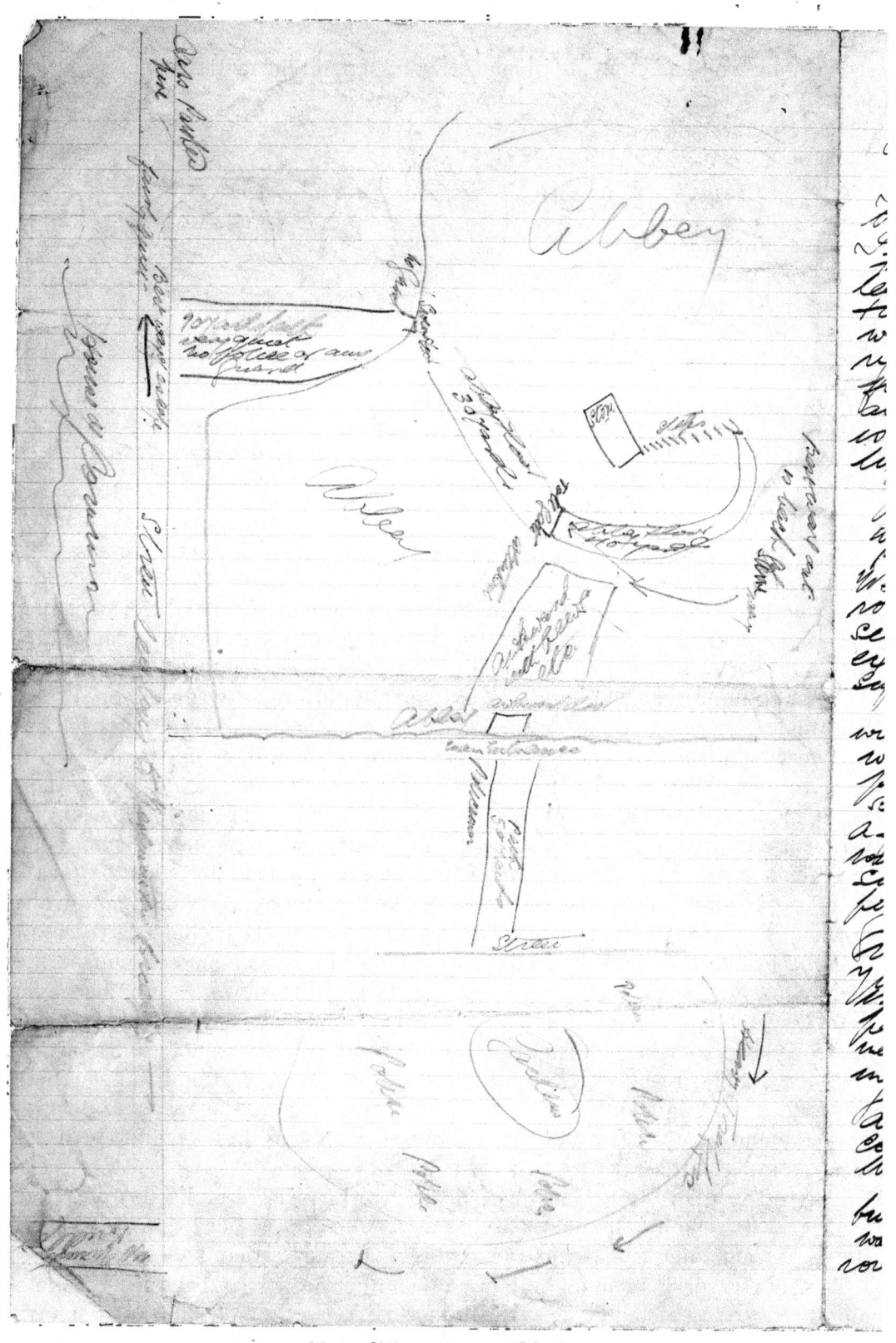

Map of Westminster Abbey.
By permission of the National Library of Scotland and Duncan Clark.

are keeping well and enjoying the novelty of Shetland life, and that poetry is still smiling on you.

Love from us both.

Yours,

Edwin.

Nott's address is
Sentinel House
46 Southampton Row
W.C. 1.

53. From George W. Russell ('AE') (SUNY B)

41 Sussex Gardens
Hyde Park
London
22 January 1934

Dear Grieve,

I got your letter this morning and went to MacMillan's where I saw Daniel MacMillan & told him your idea of a companion volume to Lennox Robinson's.[1] I said all the things proper to say about your ability as a poet and your special competence. He seemed impressed, got your address and said he would write to you. I think MacMillan would like to have a Golden Treasury of Scottish Verse. The Irish one sold very well, and as it was I who suggested it to them they may be inclined to trust me about the one you have in mind. So it is up to you For the Glory of Scotland to get an anthology as good or better than the Irish. You can go further back in the vernacular than we can. Even if you had not in our time quite such a clan of poets with Yeats at the head. I imagine you would have to supply a short glossary for the non-Scottish reader. I suppose you know all the literature and it would not involve much new research. And you have probably already made your choice as you read.

If you bring the anthology up to contemporary poets as Lennox Robinson did, what about yourself? With you out it would be a thin show. I remember some anthology of English lyrics compiled by an English poet who added to his preface a sentence saying that his publishers thought he should be represented, and to escape from the dubious position of including his own verses a selection had been made by another writer. I mention this as it might relieve you of the awkward position of seeming to choose a fair number of your own poems as these ought to be in any representative anthology of Scottish poetry.

Is Byron Scottish?[2] Is William Sharp Scottish or English?[3] Stevenson is, of course, Scottish. I don't know the dual heredity about the others. But I think even since Burns you could find true things by persons of Scottish birth or ancestry.

Pamela [Travers] is coming to London from her Sussex cottage for a couple of months.[4] I am interested much at the prospect of a new book from you. I hope you are well. You find a refuge in Shetland. I hope by the summer to find a refuge in Donegal.

Yours ever,

AE.

1   Lennox Robinson (1886-1958) edited *The Golden Treasury of Irish Verse* (London, 1925).
2   Lord Byron (1788-1824) wrote, ' But I am half a Scot by birth, and bred/ A whole one.'
3   William Sharp (1855-1905) was a Scottish writer of poetry and literary biography in particular, who from 1893 wrote also as 'Fiona MacLeod'.
4   MacDiarmid writes, 'The lady with the pheasant-coloured hair is quite a figure in Bloomsbury circles'. (*Letters*, p.386).

54. From Aonghas Cleireach (NLS Acc. 7361/52)

Tuesday night [23 January 1934]

A Charaid,

Today I visited the premises as I promised. There are two entrances, one I will call the Main, the other the Side entrance. The latter I think is the most favourable for the work. From the Street there is a quiet path at least 60 yards long, leading through a wide gate & into a double-sided swinging door of average width. Immediately on entering, you turn half right & go forward about 25 yards, all plain wide floor. You are then confronted by a large gate and allowed to pass through on payment of 6d.The gate is attended to by a Church official dressed something like a priest; he takes the money & passes you in.

You walk along a plain wide passage for about 30 yards, which brings you to the foot of twelve wide steps. On the top of these is situated the Stone. Picture a very ancient kind of armchair all intact. Wedged in under between the seat and a wooden baton round the legs of the Chair is the Stone. It is not secured as far as I could see in any way except that it fits pretty closely between the supporting batons and the Chair's bottom.

Its approximate size is 24 inches long by 18 inches wide + 12 inches deep, and I imagine it must weigh at least 150 lbs. (The estimate in my previous note was too light.) This particular part seems to me to have few visitors. Today I was a full ten minutes all alone examining the Stone without a soul coming near. In that time I am sure the Stone would be removed from its present position, ready for action. There is no special guard as far as I could ascertain, the nearest official being the man who takes your 6d. when you enter this area in which is placed not only the Coronation Chair, but other paraphernalia of that nature. From this position near the entrance gate he could not see anyone in the vicinity of the Stone, and as far as I could judge the position is not overlooked from any angle. There are no awkward doors, corners or narrow passages. In that respect there should be no difficulty whatever.

I am sorry I cannot give you a sketch, but let me sum the position as I see it. By the way there is a very ordinary bit of wooden fencing round the chair, but that presents no difficulty.

(1) You get to the required spot without any difficulty, and you stand a very good chance of removing the Stone without being disturbed. Once this was done, it would have to be placed in a sack or some suitable receptacle, and placed on the back of one man who would have to carry it just like a sack of cement or something of that kind.

Assuming now the Stone is on someone's back, he would immediately walk down twelve easy steps, he is then on the floor of the building. He turns to the right, walks about 30-40 yds & will have to pass through the tollgate where one or two priests will be loitering round, sitting or standing in a lazy, dreamy fashion.

If this gate is passed safely, he continues straight ahead about 40 yards, making for the swinging door above referred to and which is on his left. This door is ordinary size and swings in the usual way & once through he is then outside the Abbey on to the quiet path to which I refer in the earlier part of the letter. This is about 70 yards long leading to the street. He would altogether have to cover about 140 yards from where the Stone is to the street, & run the gauntlet of the toll-gate & get out by the side door.

Assuming a car is waiting the parking ground is some distance to his right once he reaches the street. This would increase the strain of carrying it, but if the driver of the car was of [one word illegible], he could by keeping his eye on the exit, time himself so that he could be waiting at the nearest spot so saving time & energy. The only policeman I could see in this area was away on the opposite side of the street half-asleep, standing against one of the entrances to the H. of Commons.

(1) The Stone is not secured in any way as far as I could see. It has a rusty, very old iron link in each end. I examined these carefully & I don't think they are used for securing purposes, they seem to be quite free.

(2) It is fairly well wedged in between the bottom of the Chair, & the underneath supporting batons, but apart from that I could see no fixture of any kind.

(3) Its size and weight I have described.

(4) I could not see or detect a guard of any kind except one or two attendants loitering about the toll-gate.

(5) At 1.30 o/c today only one attendant was there & he was sitting ten yards to the left of the gate.

(6) Looking from outside the side door to the street 70 yards away, there was only one man walking on the path leading to the door, & not a policeman, nor any other official in sight anywhere.

(7) I cannot say it is always like this, but on ordinary weekdays I imagine it is more or less the same, with an odd visitor here and there looking round the Abbey.

(8) There are many workmen repairing the building in various parts & to pose as workmen might be worth considering.

(9) I would suggest 3 men (if possible) apart from the driver. One could act as sentry while the other two were working.

(10) If the heroes can spare the time, it would help them a lot to spend two days visiting the place, surveying the position in & out beforehand. As you know the traffic round this area is very heavy & it would be necessary to decide beforehand

which course to steer to avoid the one-way traffic area in the vicinity. In such spots they are liable to be held up. These points, I think, are quite easy to solve once they see the place. I hope this report may be helpful but if there is any point not clear please let me know & I shall endeavour to give you the necessary information.

(11) I imagine from about 1 o/c – 2.30 p.m. is about the quietest time; at dusk one might be kept more under supervision.

(12) I am not discussing the Main entrance, the difficulties of getting out all more the distances are longer. A policeman is at the door & several others not far away directing traffic etc. The Side entrance is quicker & in every way freer from observation.

Buaidh leis a chuis.[1]

A.C.

---

[1] 'Success to the project'.

55. From Watson Thomson (EUL MS2970)

THE
NEW ATLANTIS
FOR WESTERN RENAISSANCE AND WORLD SOCIALISM[1]
55 Gower Street
London WC1
27 January 1934

Dear Grieve,

This joint letter is to make as impressively as possible an invitation which we believe is also a great opportunity – for you as for all us concerned.

Some people here in London believe that the moment has arrived for New Scotland to come into being. It may seem odd to some that this impetus should come from London, but you are aware that what we live in the birth-throes of, is not any local revival, but a new order of things for Western civilisation and eventually for the world. We believe that Britain can and should take the lead for the establishment of this new order. We believe also that *we* are now sufficiently imbued with, and personally orientated towards, this conception (i.e., as to spirit and as to structure) to dare to begin.

Tentative beginnings have been made already. The *New Britain Weekly*, the *New Atlantis Quarterly*, the New Europe Group, and the New Britain movement as it is up till now (some 50 or 60 groups throughout England) have been our experiments in expressing this same conception. And, however inadequate, they have had their reality and their effect, and a few have made great sacrifices for them,

But now we want a great drive, a crusade to rouse men with that 'violence of the spirit' which is the only answer to the physical violence of Fascism.

In terms of 'programme' we have all that the New Scotland wants.

1. Nationalisation of credit.
2. Socialisation of industry – Workers' control.
3. Devolution -i.e., regional autonomy and separation of politics from economics.
4. Federation as the necessary correlative to devolution.

Our principles of method are equally simple and inclusive:-
1. From the heart.
2. By individual initiative.
3. From personal alliance.
4. Towards the Absolute Collective.

This, we are convinced, is what Scotland needs. Within this formula there is room for nationalist and communist aspirations and for the money change which is such a crucial point of the necessary revolution. On such a basis, there is the possibility of reconciling all existing dissensions in the Scottish parties.

We are already in touch with a number of people in Scottish Nationalism, including the Geddeses. Geddes sociology would, of course, be an integral part of the New Scotland ideology.

It is all absolutely possible. It is also urgent (do you realise in Whalsay how Fascism grows?). The time is ripe now.

We have many plans but we need you here to discuss them. Will you come down – sooner than you planned? We'll help with the expenses, etc.[2] Do come.

Watson Thomson.

PS You may be interested to know that the first signatory is also a Scot, born and bred. On the evidence here, it would seem that Scots or Irish or Welsh are less hard material for the personal change than the English.

[1]   The *New Atlantis Quarterly* published two issues (October 1933 and January 1934). It then appeared as *New Albion* (April 1934). Subsequently it was incorporated into *New Britain.*
[2]   On 9 February 1934 Thomson wrote to MacDiarmid, 'If we can't raise say £30 in the next fortnight out of London Scots, then there's something wrong with us, and you'd better not come.' On 15th March, when MacDiarmid had just arrived in London, Thomson wrote, 'I shall phone you Monday to fix time & place of our meeting.' (EUL).

56. From F. G. Scott (EUL MS2959 f.45)

44 Munro Road
Jordanhill
Glasgow
5 February 1934

My dear Chris,
I can't lay my hands on your questionnaire about Rilke's *Duineser Elegies* which I

have now got a copy of in the original. Will you please state your requirements once more and I'll get the combined intelligences of two Germans and one Scot to read your riddles as best they can?[1] I'll have some news for you soon but in the meantime I want to get this note away. It's been held up by Naomi Mitchison's visit here this weekend. I've enjoyed seeing so much of her. She's due for tea here at any moment. So I'll get this off before another evening's gone.

Love to everybody – all well here.

Ever

F. G.

[1] The two Germans were Fraulein Dr Dörken and Dr Reinald Hoops. F. G. Scott's Rilke notes are preserved in EUL MS2959 ff.158-9 recto and verso.

57. From Graham MacGibbon (EUL MS2954.4 ff.5-6)

45, Dinmont Road
Waverley Park
Glasgow
12 February 1934

A Charaid,

I received your letter this evening and immediately held a consultation with my friend.

His father is extremely busy just now, and the longest period he could manage away from business during the next two or three months is from Friday night until Monday morning. This knocks him out completely if the project is to be carried out before the days lengthen.

All my Nationalist friends, no matter how sincere or enthusiastic, have jobs to lose. Even the Free Scots in Glasgow are all in the same boat as myself so that I am afraid your only hope is Edinburgh. Mr Black should be able to help.

I give you my word of honour that no mention of this project has [crossed] or shall cross my lips until you give the word. My friend has made the same promise.

We will give you any help we can at this end such as transporting the stone any reasonable distance around Glasgow on its arrival in Scotland or later. We will also assist in concealing the stone if necessary and ask no questions.

If you wish to make any arrangements you could call on me or I could meet you on your way south. I am at home all day on Sundays, after 2 pm on Saturdays and after 6 pm on other days.

If your visit proves that the scheme is impracticable just now, we may still be able to make the attack in the summer.

I can only close by wishing you the very best of luck for Scotland's sake and hoping that I may be able, some day, to vindicate myself in your eyes.

Is mise,

Le meas,[1]

Graham MacGibbon.

[1]   With respect.

58. From James Malcolm (NLS 7361/5)

19 Fettes Row
Edinburgh
14 February 1934

My Dear Grieve,
I had your letter on Saturday, but delayed replying in the hope that I would be able to write to you more fully on the Racial Destiny idea. I find however that the heavy nature of the work I am doing makes it beyond my powers to do more than rest in the evenings and the weekends, so I shall have to do it by portions, but will send on the result of the attempt to simplify the matter.

I was surprised and delighted by your letter, and thank you for your kindness, the first I may say I have had as being for the work and not for myself. I should have made contact with Black long ago, but being unable to endure the S[ocial] C[redit] meetings at India Buildings stayed away, and thus missed the opportunity of a talk. I have thus been out of touch with what you have been doing. On the occasion of the debate on Communism at Coates Crescent at the time of the Aberdeen Rectorial I went up as I heard you were to be there, but was disappointed. On expressing my disappointment to Mrs Robertson I was told you had gone to the University to decide some question in dispute.

I can believe that you are feeling ever so much the better of your sojourn in the north, for it has been evident in your work of late. I enjoyed and agreed with the 'telling off' you gave Compton MacKenzie, and I was very interested in your experiment in language in the short verse 'In the Caledonian Forest' – even if you were pulling the woman's leg – printed in that letter to *The Free Man*, and in my opinion it is by some such means that we shall have to break the spell of English upon what we hope will be a very different consciousness, the Scottish consciousness.[1] There is no doubt that a language different to one's immediate racial neighbour is much to be preferred as an isolating medium for the development of a distinct culture – especially if that neighbour is of a dominating character – to being under different rulers. However in Scotland's case a different dynasty to that of England is an absolute essential, and it must be a dynasty of native origin.

I am enclosing herewith the only Hindoo books worth while left to me. As I am sure you will go to the root of the matter in Hindoo thought I will not apologise for sending Kapila[2], for although he is a renegade as it were, from the general monism of the Upanishads[3], the *Baghavad Gita*[4], and Patangali[5], etc., he is yet a figure of some importance, although the thought is hard. All Hindoo thought is difficult, as is to be expected of a race of speculative thinkers who had surpassed the idea of God to formulate the conception of its origin in the neuter Brahmin.[6]

There are many books in English on Hindoo thought, but to understand its reality one I think should read the translations of the originals, for our commentators distort most of what they touch. A year or so after the War one of the booksellers in George IV Bridge had a copy of Protap Chundra Ray's translation[7] of the *Mahabharata*[8] for sale. The price was four guineas, and as I had the money then, I have cursed myself ever since that I didn't buy. It might however be possible to cajole the Carnegie Library people to procure a copy, for I understand there is now a pooling system whereby the student can procure any book he wants since all the libraries are at his service, both at home and abroad. Max Müller[9] has several works on the speculative and religious literature of India. A Hindoo once told me that Müller was the most trustworthy of the commentators; but for my part I would trust nobody's opinion on the matter. It is worth while I think to read S. Radhakrisnan's[10] *The Philosophy of the Upanishads*. The publisher is Allen and Unwin. It may be that he is a time-server; but he is quite modern, the copy in the Edinburgh Central Library being dated 1924. This I am sure could also be procured from Dunfermline. It is so long since I read the Upanishads I cannot remember the author of the translation, although I have been puzzling my mind to do so. Many of my books were abandoned at my mother's death ten years ago, and at the best I have a vile memory. I will however make an endeavour for more information for you.

Meanwhile kindest regards.

Yours,

James Malcolm.

---

[1] Compton MacKenzie had contributed three articles to *The Free Man* vol.2 in 1933. They were published in no.35 (30 September), no.36 (7 October) and no.38 (21 October). MacDiarmid included 'In Reply to Compton MacKenzie' parts I and II in his series 'At the Sign of the Thistle', in *The Free Man* no.39 (28 October) and no.41 (11 November) respectively. Dr Mary Ramsay's letter 'Nationalism & Vernacular' appeared in *The Free Man*, vol.2, no.43 (25 November). MacDiarmid's reply to this, in *The Free Man*, no.45 (9 December), quoted the first part of 'In the Caledonian Forest' which he had written that summer.

[2] Vedic sage.

[3] Sanskrit theosophic or philosophical treatises.

[4] Hindu scripture.

[5] Hindu author, mystic and philosopher.

[6] In a note on the writing of *In Memoriam James Joyce* MacDiarmid said, 'I was moved to indite this poem in homage to James Joyce because of my disgust at the tone of the special obituary article on him which appeared in *The Times Literary Supplement* (London), 15 January 1941. I only touch in this book on a few points in this connection, since the whole subject is the theme of an immense poem, "The Song of India", on which I am now at work'. (NLS MS27116 f.14r.).

[7] Protap Chundra Ray (1842-1895); the actual translation was by Mohan Ganguli Kisari.

[8] One of the two major Sanskrit epics of ancient India, the other being Ramayana.

[9] Friedrich Max Müller (1823-1900), German philosopher and Orientalist.

[10] Sarvepalli Radhakrishnan (1885-1975), Indian philosopher and statesman.

59. *From William Soutar (EUL MS2960.18 f.4-5)*

27 Wilson St
Perth
25 February 1934

My dear Grieve,

It was good of you to write at length when you were so busy. I have forwarded the article to Morrison so you ought to hear from him in a few days – if he intends to make anything of the thing.[1]

I was very glad to see from *The Free Man* & from your letter that you are about to come along strong – & in diverse fashion. I can picture our visitors from abroad in June sitting over their Gibbon & MacDiarmid[2] in innumerable hotel bedrooms and buying Valentine's postcards in lieu of the conducted tours.

I'm afraid I seemed biased in my remarks on intellectualism; but I can't admit that it is only pseudo-intellectuality that one must guard against. One can be most damnably intellectual, most honestly intellectual, & yet be working *in vacuo*: & this danger is most evident, I feel, in men who *are* creators but have no national roots. Imagine Joyce, for example, without these long attenuated roots which still retain some health by feeding on the Dublin of his youth. And in spite of your appreciation of Pound and Eliot, would you not admit that both – whether aware of over-intellectualism or not – are aware of an unrootedness, compensated for in Eliot by his reversal to a more or less orthodoxy in religion & in Pound by a classical architectonic[?] This too, by the way, in Joyce's *Ulysses* – where the parallel minutiae of the symbolism etc. confesses to that linking of intellectualism with mechanistic concepts. That is why I lumped orthodox economics, behaviourism & (that blasted phrase) endocrinal philosophy together – merely as representative words of mechanised thinking & blasphemous because fundamentally inhuman. I think you'll agree that the advent of Lawrence was timely & that, apart from his art, his significance as an anti-'intellectual' force can barely be overstressed. And what about yourself? If you aren't content to hobnob with Goethe's 'pure phenomenon' isn't it because you are so sensible of the black matrix of creative force out of which the lighted world of sense lifts – the very pulse of feeling rather than the echo of it which is ultimately at its most rarified – our old friend – intellectualism *in vacuo*.

But I'd better come off my high horse before it coups.

I had a visit a week ago from Whyte, Cunninghame[3] & two of their lady friends. I expect Whyte will be making a big splash in the June issue of *The M.S.* What did you think of Montgomerie's *The Mountain*?[4] I have seen the proofs of his new book entitled *Squared Circle* [5]– some of it good – but I think he has over-revised it. A bit staccato & wooden in places, though you'll like his use of native symbol: the book is Scottish all right.

I've got the Moray Press practically persuaded to have a selection of verse *The Solitary Way* in English out before June but there isn't anything exciting in it.[6] However I wanted to have something to heave at the [PEN] Congress[7] – & I haven't a solid enough book of Scots yet.[8]

Hope that wintry blast has left your far awa Isle – & that you were able to hang onto your proofs. All join with me in the good wishes to all.

Yours aye,

W. S.

1 'Morrison' was editor of *Scots Observer*.
2 The reference is to *Scottish Scene* which Gibbon and MacDiarmid were writing together.
3 'A. T. Cunninghame' was the pseudonym of John Tonge.
4 William Montgomerie published *A Vision of the Cairngorms* (London, 1933).
5 *Squared Circle* (London, 1934).
6 *The Solitary Way* was published in Edinburgh in 1934.
7 The PEN Congress took place in Edinburgh in 1934.
8 *Poems in Scots* was published in Edinburgh in 1935.

60. From Catherine Carswell (EUL MS2946.1 f.5)

[POST CARD]

> 17 Keats Grove
> London NW3
> 28 February [1934]

I've only now come across your Burns item in the January *Modern Scot*.[1] Congratulations! Now why didn't I think of that? Anyhow it's good that somebody did & best of all that you did.

It's good about Dimitroff & his pals, isn't it?[2]

Cold here – snowing hard today.

Yours,

Catherine Carswell.

1 'The Last Great Burns Discovery' was first published in *The Modern Scot*, vol.4, no.4 (January 1934), pp.316-319.
2 In the immediately previous letter, dated 17 February 1934, and written on headed notepaper, 'Berlin Central Hotel, Berlin NW7', Catherine Carswell had written, in ink, 'I was so glad to get your letter, and just as I was going to answer was swept out here. [...] Here it has been queer & something of an experience. I was sent out to take a turn at holding the Dimitroff ladies hands. Will be coming home tonight if alls well.' The reference is to the Reichstag Fire trial in which Georgi Dimitrov and others were accused of burning down the Reichstag and acquitted (EUL MS 2946.1 ff.3-4).

61. From Robin M. Black (EUL MS2942.11 f.16)

> 1 India Buildings
> [Edinburgh]
> 1 March 1934

Catherine Carswell.
By permission of the Carswell Estate.

Robin Black, proprietor of *The Free Man*, first series, 1932-1934, and of *Alba Nuadh*, 1935-1936.
By permission of Rona Taylor.

My Dear C. M.

I have made judicious enquiries & can get you the men. The trouble is expenses. I take it from your letter they pay their own & that is a real stumbling block as the fellows of the right stuff are needy. I await your further word on this.

About *F. M.* I have squeezed out a few quids for a guarantee enough for about 4 weeks & I'm going to try & get advts: not much time to do the job but it has to be tried in any event: the larger size & the chance of bigger circulation should, of course, help. Pray for me!

Now I have but to say I hope your scheme fructifies & that you & the gallant David dinna ding the bit chuckie on your fingers! By the way I hear your friends of *New Britain* are planning to bring oot a *New Scotland*.[1] Have ye heard?

How are resources with you? & how about J. M. & Valda?

Does the young scamp *ever* remember the words we had?

I know this is just a hell of a letter but I'm in the thick of so many troubles that even this is about the best I can do. If you have any spare stuff to send please do.

My thoughts are often with you all.

Yours aye,

R. M. B.

---

[1]   This did not appear. However, R.M. Black used the title for his own periodical *Alba Nuadh* (*New Scotland*), 1935-6.

62. From W. B. Yeats (EUL MS2961.17 f.1)

> Riversdale
> Willbrook
> Rathfarnham
> Dublin
> 4 March 1934

Dear Mr MacDiarmid,

I am sorry, for you have done lovely and passionate things, but I cannot do what you wish.[1] I am entirely absorbed in a book about my friend Lady Gregory and the movement that centred on her house. It is slow, difficult work, and with the exception of one broadcast of old work upon St Patrick's day I have refused every extraneous activity.

Yours,

W. B. Yeats.

---

[1]   MacDiarmid quoted this passage in *Lucky Poet,* on p.66: '"You have done many lovely and passionate things" – W. B. Yeats'. The nature of MacDiarmid's request at this time is not known.

63. *From J. L. Grant (NLS Acc. 7361/5)*

Quiet-Ways
Chatham Road
Worthing
Sussex
5 March 1934

My dear Grieves,

I was over at Storrington yesterday, Sunday, and saw Roy Armstrong, who has been ill. I have paid Mrs Henson the £5, that you sent, and enclose the receipt that I got for it.[1] She handed me a small card-board box which contained a few letters, and says that this is all that she has belonging to you, as Michael took everything else away from there which belonged to you.[2]

Now Roy Armstrong says that when Michael brought your stuff to his garage, Roy did not himself see what was brought, it was all left in the garage together with some things of other people's that was stored there, and as Roy has been ill, he has not had time to go through and look out what is your stuff there. So Roy suggests that as all your things are now at his garage, he will himself make out a list of them and send to you asking you to tick off the things that you want sent on to you.[3] He says that he will do this in a day or so. And he says that you are not to send any more money until you hear from him about the whole thing. He has some pieces of furniture of yours and says that they balance anything you might owe to him on the money he paid to De Montalk for rent.[4] Norman and Joan [Suddaby] are come back to the Common for a while, although Norman says that they are going to move again shortly. Norman showed me the box of Valda's, and has given it to Roy to be sent on with the things that he sends to you. Norman says that the box was broken open when Michael handed it to him to keep. Further, Norman states that when Michael took charge of your affairs and things, he broke up a lot of things anyway as being of no use, and gave a lot of things away, such as dishes, etc., books, etc., and these are now scattered all over the place to different people, and in many cases none of us know the people to whom these things were given. As Norman says, perhaps Grieves does not realize how these things were freely distributed by Michael to all kinds of people in Thakeham, and elsewhere, and that as Michael told people that he was in charge of your affairs no one could do anything in the matter, and indeed many of us did not know until too late what was happening to your goods.

However, you will be hearing from Roy in the course of a few days as all the things of yours that are at his place, some of the books I gathered from Roy yesterday, are scattered all over the place, and will have to be collected together again what remains of them.

Mrs Henson has nothing further of yours, and says that Michael took away with him a few small things of yours before he disappeared. The letters have been put in the box that Joan had of Valda's. About the sewing machine, Roy will mention it when he writes to you. Roy thought it best for everything to be sent from his place since it is all there, and to save it being sent into Worthing and then sent off by

Peggy Grieve, MacDiarmid's first wife, c.1934.
By permission of Christine MacIntosh.

rail. So do not send any more money on the rent business until you hear from Roy himself this week. Let me know if there is anything else you wish done. Hope that you are all well. I have got a bit more work to do thank goodness.

Yours ever,

J. L. Grant.

Receipt enclosed:

Received from J. L. Grant, the sum of £5-0-0, being payment for the debt of £5 on cheque owing to me by Mr C. M. Grieve when he left Thakeham. The payment being made on behalf of Mr. Grieve by Mr Grant. Mrs Henson. 24 February 1934.

[1] In a letter to Valda MacDiarmid says that J. L. Grant had forged the receipt. (*Hugh MacDiarmid: New Selected Letters*, edited by Dorian Grieve, Owen Dudley Edwards and Alan Riach, (Manchester:Carcanet, 2001), p.74.

[2] 'Michael' was A. R. Duy Vinycomt who was left in charge of the Grieves' affairs when they hurriedly left Thakeham in Sussex in August 1932.

[3] This list still exists (NLS MS27214 f.98).

[4] MacDiarmid had rented the cottage of Count Geoffrey de Montalk when the latter was in Wormwood Scrubs for seeking to publish 'obscene' literature. Stephanie de Montalk, *Unquiet World : The Life of Count Geoffrey de Montalk* (Wellington:Victoria University Press, 2001).

64. From Peggy Grieve (NLS MS27148 f.23)

The Priory
Laleham-on-Thames
Middlesex
12 March 1934

Dear Chris,

Many thanks for your letters. I will certainly help in any way I can but I think I had better make no definite promises about a car until I hear the plans.[1] There are all sorts of difficulties about registrations and things, you see. However, there's no need to climb unnecessary hurdles.

My movements this week are inclined to be uncertain but as you arrive on Thursday perhaps the best thing to do would be to arrange to meet you at Antoine's restaurant in Charlotte Street (upstairs) at 1pm on Friday, i.e., 16th inst. If there is any change in this arrangement I will wire you to c/o Mrs Wells. If you want to get in touch with me you can get me at Victoria 1796. If I am not in, ask for Miss Watts who will take any message or you can send me a note to Iddesleigh House, Caxton Street, SW1.[2]

I hope you have had a pleasant journey. Without presuming to interfere I frankly think you are bartering the substance for the shadow if you leave your island for any city. Till Friday – au revoir!

Peggy.

1   'A car' would have been needed to take the Stone of Destiny out of London but the plan did not materialise. On this visit to London MacDiarmid stayed initially with Mrs N. Katharin Wells with whom he was writing the unpublished 'The Wolfe of Badenoch'.

2   At this time Iddesleigh House was the Head Office of W. McElroy & Company Ltd. Peggy, i.e., Margaret Grieve, was a director. Victoria 1796 was one of the lines.

65. From Aonghas Cleireach (NLS Acc.7361/8)

'Glenfinnan'
Worcester Crescent
Woodford Green
19 March 1934

A Charaid,

On my arrival home tonight, was pleased to find your note awaiting me.

I can meet you Wednesday afternoon [1] Oxford St Tott–ham Ct Rd Corner at 3.30 pm till 6. I hope this suits you. At 6.30 onwards I have a meeting on in the White Heather Tea Rooms (opposite Charing X) hence my reason for wishing to see you earlier. You are very welcome to attend the meeting if you feel inclined to do so.

Now if Wed. afternoon is unsuitable, I could arrange for Thursday. I am hoping you will have this note sometime tomorrow (Tuesday) and if my time does not suit you, phone Albert Dock 1307 & ask for me anytime up to 5 pm & anytime on Wednesday up till 1 pm.

If I do not hear by then I shall conclude you are free to meet me at 3.30 pm & will act accordingly.

Quite looking forward to our meeting.

Yours,

AC.

PS Having recently moved into this room I have no phone.

1   21 March.

66. From Graham MacGibbon (EUL MS2954.4 ff.7-8)

Graham MacGibbon
45 Dinmont Road
Glasgow S1
19 March 1934

A Charaid,

In your last letter you said that you hoped to carry out the exploit within the next five weeks. The time is up and I have seen nothing in the press, but in the meantime I have a piece of news which forces me to ask for my release from my promise of silence which I gave you.

I have made contact with a sincere extremist who is looking for a scheme of this kind. He has time, money and brains and is not of the Ex-Bailie Thomson or Wendy Wood[1] calibre. His character is spotless and his personal history is open to the most searching examination. I am not at liberty to divulge his name.

I have also available ten extreme nationalists who are unemployed and are willing to take part in any direct action involving prison. We are in a position to keep the expedition in the big city for a month if necessary and they will stop at nothing. Lorries and cars are available. This [is] a chance in a million.

If you will release me from my promise of silence I will explain the scheme to him, after exacting an oath of secrecy, and may then be in a position to give you fuller details.

Is mise,

le meas mor,[2]

Graham MacGibbon.

[1] Wendy Wood was the leader of Nationalist groups, e.g., Democratic Scottish Self-Government Organisation (DSSO) (founded 1932) and Scottish Patriots (founded 1947).
[2] With great respect.

67. From Robin Black (EUL MS2942.11 f.47)

Publishers of	The	The Publishers of
THE FREE MAN	Scots Free Press	BOOKS AND PAMPHLETS
an Independent	1 India Buildings	on Scottish Affairs
Journal	Victoria Street	
	Edinburgh	

Monday [March 1934]

My Dear C. M. G.,

Both men are O.K. for Sat. Leave here by day bus. C. can drive but would want car taken out of London – for traffic reasons – first. Licence for him in name of 'John Calder', as this he will use throughout in case of snags. Now we are all set at this end. Waiting cash, & your final instructions. Both C. & D. game & eager.

All the best.

For Scotland,

Yours,

Robin.

68. From Brian Campbell (NLS Acc. 7361/5)

YMCA

South St Andrews St

Edinburgh

Sunday [before 10 April 1934][1]

Dear Grieve,

I've just seen [Robin] Black and am proposing to travel down on Monday evening and look forward to seeing you. I don't, of course, know anything of the plans, but will see you about them when I arrive, for I can suggest one alteration as a result of the little I heard from Black.

I had intended to write a proper letter, but started arguing in a pub and have nearly lost the post. I owe you a letter of thanks in any case for *Sangschaw*. I enjoyed having it exceedingly. You may be amused to hear that I was sent *To Circumjack Cencrastus* the other day from a friend in Canada of all places. Having it already, I passed it on – to France.

Till Tuesday!

Yours,

Brian Campbell.

[1] Brian Campbell's Letter Card was addressed to MacDiarmid c/o Mrs [N.K.] Wells at 6 Acacia Place, St John's Wood, London, N.W.8. The Edinburgh postmark is illegible in parts. The 'H' of 'MCH'can be read. The Card was re-addressed to MacDiarmid by Mrs Wells on '10 AP 34'.

69. From Mrs Dyke White (EUL Gen.2094/6/2417)

Merchiston
Lenzie
Glasgow
14 April 1934

Mr C.M. Grieve

Dear Sir

At the early part of the year I had a request from the *Daily Record* – Glasgow – on your behalf – for a selection of Scottish Cartoons by my late husband 'Dyke White'. These cartoons were specially taken from his portfolio in the Glasgow Art Club – where there was at that time a Memorial Exhibition of my late husband's work & sent off to you & I have not up to date had an acknowledgement of these.[1] I shall be pleased to hear from you.

Yours faithfully,

Mrs Dyke White.

[1] MacDiarmid had failed to collect the cartoons from Jarrolds' office after the publishers had decided that *Scottish Scene* was unsuitable for illustration. Grassic Gibbon undertook to return the cartoons to John MacNair Reid, the go-between, with the comment, ' Had I been collaborating with any normal being this mess would not have happened. All I can do is to attempt to clear it up and present my apologies to Mrs Dyke White & yourself.' (12th April 1934, NLS Acc. 5561).

70. From Peggy Grieve (NLS MS27148 ff.26-27)

Iddesleigh House
Caxton Street
Westminster SW1
4 May 1934

My dear Chris,

Many thanks for your letter. I think Whyte will help you get back to the Shetlands and he can be repaid when you collect your money. I agree that you don't want to stay in Glasgow any longer than need be.

I have been in communication with Watson Thomson and he states that he has sent a cheque to somewhere – did you not give him instructions to send the money to Valda? – but we are looking into the matter and will get a settlement of some kind – the more to your benefit the better and with as pleasant a manner as possible. He is to meet me in the beginning of the week and I gather that he had not intended to meet you that night if he could have got out of it.

Gollancz I expect to see on Monday and will use all the influence I can bring to bear to get some sort of definite arrangement with him, even if it is a monthly series of payments.

With regard to your debts in Shetland, I think you must exaggerating the extent of these because I used peat last winter in two fires and it didn't cost me £10. I couldn't afford that amount. The flooring must have been necessary but surely that can be paid at so much per month. Then as to Valda, I wonder sometimes just how much value you put on her – it seems out of all proportion to what you receive, in all fairness to her. She may want this and she may want that – well, let her earn it. I had to work hard – work in this office as it is most days of the week till 7 and 8 pm from 10 in the morning without even a lunch hour – so that I can keep Christine and Walter fed and clothed. Valda never seems to think of my children – or your children. If she hates Shetland let her stay in Cornwall. You'd be better off with a housekeeper except for one thing. If she wants you then let her carry part of the load – she can't have all the fun. I never get to a Cinema unless a 1/- newsreel now and then. I buy my clothes in Berwick Market, I haven't had a holiday for eight months. I do my own washing and cleaning before I come here in the morning. She may be the most fascinating girl in the world but she is older than I was when I started out and infinitely more sophisticated and world-wise.

You have got one duty and one duty only and that is to yourself and the genius which you have given you to guard and develop. If you pledge that for a mess of pottage you will be the most miserable soul on God's earth. Why should we break our hearts for you as we did the other night, as if you were a Christ, and you spending your energy and vitality on things which are as shadows. Far better go to the fishing grounds with the fishermen for they have souls if they haven't got intellects, and they haven't got notions, but the fear of God is on them.

You can depend on us doing all we can and making the best settlement for your own interests. On the other hand, it will give us only bitterness if you persist in being untrue to yourself.

Our blessings on you anyhow.
Peggy.

PS. We are arranging to get your luggage from Mrs Carswell and when McElroy was phoning her she told him how hard poor Valda had tried to keep you off the booze and how she had never wanted to leave the Shetlands and never wanted to come to London and all she wanted was to get back to Whalsay, and so on and on. All this makes one wonder really whether the world is still right side up. You said you were a fool the other night but I must be an even greater one.

71. From Peggy Grieve (NLS MS27148 f.31)

66 Victoria Street
London SW1
12 May 1934

Dear Chris,

Thanks for your letter. Things yesterday were a repetition of what had happened on the previous occasion with some additional evidence. It didn't seem too good. However, it comes on again on Monday and again on Friday and then there will be a committal.[1]

I have made some efforts to get in touch with Gollancz but he is elusive. However, Robert Lynd[2] has promised to help me to see him. The New Britain people are difficult. I got a small cheque from them which I sent to Whyte as I understood he was financing your passage to Whalsay. He is in Skye at the moment but will be in St Andrews next week and will get in touch with you. The New Britain people say you have no claim against them but I have only accepted their cheque as a payment to account.[3]

With regard to Valda, of course, what you give her is a matter for yourself. I would simply point out this to you that you are bartering the only thing that matters for a chit of a girl who doesn't matter a damn. You may find that by drinking and poisoning your body you get certain reliefs but at the same time it is the cup which holds the wine and not the wine the cup, and therefore the cup must be handled carefully, because it contains the value. Had I been you I would have sought the seclusion of a monastery somewhere where the things of the mind and the spirit are predominant, and where silk stockings and cinemas are the last thing one thinks about.

We are very tired. Sick in mind and weary in body. It is difficult fighting the world and still more difficult fighting oneself. It would be an immense comfort to me if I knew that you had conquered your inclinations and were fighting your corner, and helping yourself. You have many friends but they now see that by helping you financially they are helping you to damn yourself.

Anyhow. Blessings!
Peggy.

[1] In a letter to his brother Andrew Graham Grieve, [12 April 1934], MacDiarmid notes: 'I found that Peggy's husband – who is extremely wealthy – had not only been suddenly beggared but that the papers in an intricate civil case had been passed on to the Public Prosecutor. I saw him & Peggy last Friday – the Public Prosecutor had just given his fiat – and the upshot is a criminal case on a fraud charge due for hearing on 22nd inst. I like the man – I am as fond of Peggy as ever – and there are my two children to consider'.(*New Selected Letters*, p.70) In the event the trial was postponed. McElroy was acquitted.

[2] Robert Lynd (1879-1949), journalist and essayist.

[3] On NLS MS27148 f.30 Peggy has typed, 'Have accepted this sum without prejudice as a payment to account. Amount owing was £42 which less £15, leaves a balance of £27 still due to C.M. Grieve. Have requested payment of this sum at their earliest convenience'. She sent the cheque to J. H. Whyte but F. G. Scott noted that Whyte wasn't prepared to act as accountant.

72. From Edgell Rickword (NLS Acc. 7361/53)

16 Amwell St
[London] EC1
Sunday [May 1934]

Dear Grieve,

I passed you in a bus the other day, but by the time I had got off and walked back to meet you, you had disappeared.

Can you come and have something to eat on Tuesday evening – say about 7 o'clock? I think two people on the committee of the W.I. will be here and it would be a good opportunity to talk things over.[1]

I hope you will be able to come, but if not will you tell me what evening you have free, as I very much want to talk to you before you leave London again.

Amwell St is just near Finsbury Town Hall, a penny bus – 19 or 38 – from Gt James St. This place is about 300 yds up Rosomon St, to the left as you get off bus, by the post office. Ring the bell marked BACK.

Yours,
Edgell Rickword.

[1] 'W. I.' was the Writers' International.

73. From George W. Russell ('AE') (SUNY B)

c/o Mrs Margaret O'Donnell
Parkmore
Ballymore
Co. Donegal
19 June 1934

My dear MacDiarmid,

I have had your book by me for some days but could not get at it because there were visitors here and these are very distracting eating up one's evenings & the time for reverie in wild talking.[1] But they went on Sunday and I could put your book in my pocket & carry it out to the shore & test it as Whitman said philosophies could be tested by the flowing sea, and if philosophies, why not poetry? All your scientific things faded out for me, but the pure poetry glowed as it had a right to with other elemental things.

I think 'Lament for the Great Music' extraordinary, passionate, fine & sustained.[2] It is your soul going not so much into its subject as into yourself & all pure poetry comes of going deep into oneself no matter how much we are deluded into saying we have gone into something else. You have more of an elemental volcanic quality about your poetry than any other living poet. Others have tamed & harnessed their fires to turn out artwork of a high quality. But somehow artwork even of very high quality seems remote from central depths and we admire it more than we are excited by it; and you excite me as if I saw somebody perilously on the edge of a crater which was spitting out its lava. I think you feel like this about yourself as I surmise from reading 'The Point of Honour'.[3]

I hope that agonised crying over a lost Scotland or rather a Scotland that has lost itself will stir some of your countrymen to their deeps if they have any left. I had that agony over an Ireland spiritually dead & now as I am old I have become a futurist & think no country worth lamenting over, only that we should look for the return of the Golden Age for all life. So I try to get a planetary consciousness even though the Brahmanical cycle will have it that we have 420 000 years of the Iron Age before the spirit floods life anew & we lose the heresy of separateness & feel we are part of the Great Being.

I'm a small party of one in this island, and I think you are tending to be a party of one in your own country. I will have time now to really sink myself into the best of your writing. I can't read a book right through. I have to take a poem at a time as the Japanese take a picture at a time. A man who reads a whole book of poetry through at a sitting can get nothing out of it except surfaces. But if you really get to the bottom of one poem you have almost got to the bottom of the man.

I took this cottage in three months, must clear out of it end of July, God knows where I will go then but MacMillan's will know. I keep them acquainted with my address to forward any letters. I will try to find another place here but I am afraid the few places where one can stay are let. I have almost finished a new book of verse. I can't be volcanic like you, I am too old. But such as I have in me I will send you if the book seems worth publication. I did not go to the PEN club in Scotland & escaped your ironic welcome.[4]

With best wishes.

Yours ever,

AE.

[1]   The book was *Stony Limits* (London:Gollancz, 1934).
[2]   'Lament for the Great Music', *C.P.* I, pp. 462-482.
[3]   'The Point of Honour', *C.P.* I, pp. 387-391.
[4]   MacDiarmid's 'ironic welcome' was 'Welcome to the PEN Delegates', *C.P.* II, pp. 1299-1302.

74. From D. S. Mirsky (NLS Acc. 7361/5)

Moscow
ul. Gorkogo 68, KB.68
25 June 1934

Dear Hugh MacDiarmid,

Please excuse me for answering you with such delay. The *Moscow News* forwarded your letter to an obsolete address, & I only received *Spartacus* [1]yesterday. I have only just looked into it: it looks the genuine article. Thank you very much for sending it to me. I shall probably have occasion to write about it soon. Have there been any new books of your own?

    Sincerely yours,
    D. Mirsky.

In my lectures on contemporary English literature I often have to speak about you. I have to do it from memory as there are no copies of your books in Moscow (except the *First Hymn* which you sent me). Do you think you could send some or all of your poems (especially the *Drunk Man*) to the Central Library for Foreign Literature here? They would greatly appreciate this, as their 'valuta' budget is too small to buy anything but textbooks & that sort of thing.

    D. M.

I have put a few lines about you in the article on Scottish Literature in the Great Soviet Encyclopedia.

[1]   By James Leslie Mitchell (Lewis Grassic Gibbon), London, 1933.

75. From T. H. Wintringham (NLS Acc. 7361/5)

WRITERS' INTERNATIONAL
British Section,
c/o Collet's Bookshop
66 Charing Cross Road, W.C.2
Provisional Committee
John Strachey
Ralph Fox
Michael Davidson
Treasurer
Edgell Rickword
Secretary
T. H. Wintringham

5 July 1934

Dear Grieve,

Now that you have got your load of half-bricks[1] well unloaded on your unhappy country, it's time for you to weigh in with something for us.[2] What of it?

Yours sincerely,

T. H. Wintringham.

[1]   The 'load of half bricks' was MacDiarmid's share of *Scottish Scene* (London: Jarrolds, 1934) which had just been published in London.

[2]   T. H. Wintringham here requests a contribution from MacDiarmid to *Left Review* which was published monthly from October 1934 to May 1938. At this time Wintringham was co-editor with Amabel Williams-Ellis and Montagu Slater. MacDiarmid contributed 'Killing No Murder' to the first issue, *C.P.* I, pp. 536-537.

76. From the Communist Party of Great Britain (NLS Acc. 7361/5)

THE COMMUNIST PARTY OF GREAT BRITAIN
NORTH LONDON SUB-DISTRICT

157 Seven Sisters Road
London N7
15 August 1934

C. M. Grieve
12 Petherton Road
N. 5.

Dear Comrade,

Your letter, applying for membership of the Communist Party, has been passed to the North London Sub-District Secretariat for attention.

Could you come for an interview with the Secretariat at this office on the evening of Monday, the 20th of August, at 8.30 p.m.?

Yours fraternally,

THE SECRETARIAT.

77. From Robert Garioch Sutherland (NLS Acc. 7361/5)

109 Bellevue Road
Edinburgh
August 1934

Dear Mr Grieve,

I have just got to Page 49 of *At the Sign of the Thistle.*[1]

I have the beginning of a short story that was to have a man and [a] woman making love in a back lane in Edinburgh for lack of a better place: they were to be scanned by a passing bobby, and the man, naturally priggish in any case, was to save the situation by talking loud-voiced philosophy incomprehensible to the bobby, who would scratch his head under his helmet and pass on, leaving them to it. The whole to pass before a background of Edinburgh's Romance and so on, which made the start.

Now I think the man's cerebration could be shown up against the woman's clear muddle of mind for the rubbish that it is. This would come out especially in the talk on the approach of the bobby. Copulation could be represented by a jumble of thoughts and impressions of the whole thing, Edinburgh and history and philosophy and different attitudes to love with none of the connections of thought on which collected people so prided themselves. Then it could finish with a prosaic rattle going home in the cold with the rain coming on, with the usual thoughts and clear fears and all that. Must try to overcome my laziness to do this as well as I can.

Perhaps this is the way to use my muddleheadedness and priggish attempts at thinking that I have always felt must turn up sometime. This is somewhat done, ignorantly, in the teaching story that I am going to try and get a copy of from the *S[cots] O[bserver]*.[2] I have been wondering all my life about boring banality of order and the life that lies in muddle; hence the glamour of Soho, of which I know so little. Am afraid of the thought of the order of Fascism or of Communism. Yet sometimes envy the Trappist monks. Must read Gertrude Stein[3] properly: what should I read? Must read simultaneously the Bible and Gertrude and *Ulysses*: have suddenly recognised these are complementary, not mutually destructive.

Our science cannot conceive an acid that can mingle with an alkali to produce something more exciting than either. Life ought not to be reduced to systems: the scientist has a pedagogical desire for things on a plate. Education, Montessori and so on teaches children to sort colours, weights, so on into categories. We do this sort of thing therefore in everything. Realists, naturalists, idealists damned and otherwise, humanists, Tories, fools, the intelligentsia, Bloomsbuggers, all the shades of buggery even: how we delight in spotting a 'good' Lesbian, i.e., one which is unusually complete and free from nuances. Churchill is a pigheaded fool, but he is id at least complete. Dr Johnson would be better. Nebulousness is a far, far better thing than any such completeness. Oh how pleased I am becoming with myself: I am almost completely nebulous ..... so we are back in the scientific again, I have, God wot, a large field to ere. Should I try my hardest to ere it?

Sutherland.

---

[1] *At The Sign of The Thistle* (London: Nott, 1934).
[2] *The Scots Observer* ceased publication on 29 June 1934.
[3] Gertrude Stein (1874-1946), American author who settled in Paris.

78. From Andrew Graham Grieve (EUL MS2948.13 ff.4-6)

Arkinholme
2 Beauchamp Rd
Liberton
Edinburgh 9
3 September 1934

My dear C.
I got home from Orkney early on Saturday morning (23 hours late) & of the many

things awaiting my attention this letter to you claims priority & must open with an apology & an explanation. The apology is of course on account of the long delay in writing you & the explanation is that, harassed up to the last minute I did not get you written before leaving for the North & took your last letter with me (& a note of certain figures) to deal with at my leisure. You can judge of my horror when I found a day or two later that your last letter to me bore no address & while I recollected that the one previous gave a *changed* address, I hadn't any earthly idea as to how or where to locate you. Also I was not any easier in my mind when I reflected that I could have come to a settlement which would have let you have the balance of money due to you early in August when you were I knew in serious need of it. I am most sorry about the whole incident which is just one of the exasperating type sent to try us from time to time – wholly fortuitous & unlucky. The same trouble accounts for the absence of a p.c. to let you know how we fared on holiday.

I am enclosing now a copy of an account showing how Mother's estate fell to be divided & a note of income & expenditure. I have also made out a form of discharge & acknowledgement & if you will return this to me I shall send you a cheque for £9.10/1at once. I will just mention again that I have not entered any charge for train fares for Executry business, for legal advice I had to take, for the cost of remittance by wire to you & for sundry other small items. Also I did not adopt Mother's suggestion of equalizing regarding which I spoke to you. So I trust you will feel that I have done the best I can for you.

We had a good holiday in Orkney in very indifferent weather – which, however stormy, was not so wet as to keep us indoors. Unfortunately we had to keep on the move most of the time as it was not warm enough for sitting about & this defeated to some extent the ideal for Chryssie of a restful rather than a strenuous holiday. But she is very well & tanned & I hope lasting benefit will accrue. We bathed a lot & saw everything worth seeing on the Mainland of Orkney.

I contrived to read *Scottish Scene* & *Stony Limits* & had much enjoyment from them both. There is something I find in your work which other people miss due to my knowledge of you & of our locality & it is pleasant to find for instance a rehash of the old tale about Staplegortoun Churchyard & the exodus over Sorbie Hass on the last day – the best illustration of my meaning![1]

I derived a lot of amusement from both Gibbon's work & yours in *Scottish Scene*. The best of the work was very good indeed & much of the propaganda (which destroyed here & there the standard) was subtly & skilfully introduced. As regards *Stony Limits* the lyrical work was certainly beautiful & powerful & in no way inferior to the best of your previous work but the propagandist poems would, for many bleak stretches, have been better written in prose. I have never disguised my opinion that your best work is lyrical poetry & that time spent by you on anything else however important or interesting or successful or the reverse is misspent and a matter for regret. There is a limit to the worlds any man can conquer & the truth that there's nothing but a limit for most of us leaves us still regretting the neglect of the realm of achievement for another or other realms which may not prove so greatly worthwhile if & when gained.

However you've given me a deal of pleasure & of something more important & I'm grateful for this last lot. *At the Sign of the Thistle* has not reached me although it was reviewed more than a month ago. Has the publisher overlooked me? I'm thus brazen on your assurance that the cost to you is Nil.

I hope things are prospering with you & that they will continue to do so. I doubt if you'll ever be induced to husband your resources as you should do & I hate like hell to think of your many enemies rubbing their hands in glee at the thought that you are playing into their hands & damaging yourself irreparably by living wildly. If you believe in your work & in the gospel you preach you should not let the things you stand for suffer the setback of losing you a minute sooner than you can help.

As your sole surviving near mature relative I'd delight to intern you somewhere & let you work to your heart's content on your many lines – whipping & lashing your indolent & careless compatriots today & stirring them with lovely lyrics tomorrow. Besides you might get on then with that half-promised autobiography. I do believe I could fill in nearly as many blanks in *your* story as you could in a biography I could write of you.

Now I hope this letter reaches you soon & safely & I'll be expecting to hear from you before long.

All kind regards from us all.

Yours very sincerely,

A. G. G.

---

1   In his remark about 'a rehash of the old tale' Andrew Graham Grieve refers to the play 'Some Day' which was first published in *The Scottish Nation* on 30 October 1923, and reprinted in *Hugh MacDiarmid: Annals of the Five Senses*, ed. by Roderick Watson and Alan Riach (Manchester: Carcanet, 1999), pp. 121-127.

79. From James Leslie Mitchell (Lewis Grassic Gibbon) (EUL MS2955.11 f.26)

107 Handside Lane
Welwyn Garden City
10 September 1934

My dear Grieve,

My thanks and apologies. The Journey to Scotland made me mislay your letter.

The Eccentric Scots: I can't see any time to tackle these chaps. Why not do it yourself? So far as it's my idea I present it to you lock, stock and barrel. But why not come out for a day and a night (bringing Valda if possible, says my wife) and we'll discuss things?[1]

Yes, *Grey Granite* is finished at last and being printed.[2] Don't know how the dedicatee will like it – you never can tell about Hugh MacD!

I've lots of *Scottish Scene* reviews – you'll feel tickled to read them.

All the best to both of you.

Yours,

JasLeslieMitchell.

Do come both of you – soon, and stay a night or so ere returning to the Shetlands. Regards. Ray.

[1] The Grieves stayed with the Mitchells, 15/16 September, 1934.
[2] *Grey Granite* (London: Jarrolds, 1934).

80. From John Grierson (EUL MS2946 f.15)

General Post Office
LONDON
21 Soho Sq.
5 October 1934

Dear Grieve,

Yes please, if you are in town on the 15th [October] & before you go north, will you call in. I am not sure myself to what extent the material you have given us can be fitted in, - but you have set us the problem we wanted. [1] Whether it is a question of using the full form of poetry, or only giving it in snatches i.e. as something overheard and apprehended accidentally. The question is to make poetry perform as one instrument with others. That is why one feels *a priori* that the vers libres quality may be the right one. But as I say, I don't know, & unfortunately this Savings Bank film is not the right one for a proper experiment.

I wish I had chosen the Ceylon film instead which has a Buddhist theme (Buddhism behind the Imperialists) going through it. There we have taken our words in solid snatches from Robert Knox's account of Ceylon written in 1680. The 17th century English, spoken by a half-caste, seems to hit the right quality for a supporting factor. More of this when I see you. We can look over one or two examples, & consider how it works!

Yours sincerely,
John Grierson.

[1] MacDiarmid submitted poetry for the GPO Unit promotional film *Savings Bank* (1934) and was paid eight guineas (NLS MS27152 f.12r). It has not been possible so far to find this poem in an archive or to discover what use, if any, was made of it. Whether MacDiarmid met Grierson before he went north is not known. He was in London on 5 October and wrote to Catherine Carswell on that date, 'I am sorry I won't see Donald & you before we go off.' (*Letters,* p.422) MacDiarmid had contributed an article 'Poetry and Film', headlined 'A Poet Looks at the Cinema', to *Cinema Quarterly,* edited by Norman Wilson, vol. 2, no. 3 (Spring 1934), pp.146-149.

81. From Ezra Pound (EUL MS2958.10 ff.3-4)

Via Marsala 12-5
Rapallo

7 Dec.

anno XII

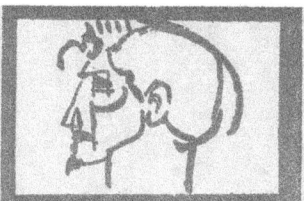

E. POUND   RAPALLO

VIA MARSALA 12-5

My Dear Mac Diarmid

I dont know quite how complete an ex=
ception you are trying to make me. I don't think the
passages   in XIX and XXII are in any way isolated
from the mass of the Cantos. Though the more specific locus
of economics in in Cantos XXXI/XLI ,

                                        can't write everything
all at once on the same page.
Also I am probably a more boycotted , trimmed , excluded
author than you apparently think.
AND the question how far an economic concern (by a
writer of verse) can be or shd/ be confined to
lyric or metric expression ...seems to me a variant.

                When in a canto not yet printed , I got
round to Doug's A plus B. I thought for a few hours
I had committed a species of innovation. But within
the day's length I found Dante before me. (as cited now
at start of XXXVIII.)

/ I shd/ think however that (with the brief exception of
Oppens few lines) all the contributers to "Active Anthology"
HAD a very definite economic " concern " ; and to my
mind there is sign of it in the metrical work of all of them

either smack on the top in specific phrases , or
underlying.

                After all the pubr/ deleted a lot of Bunting
AFTER B/ and I had seen the proofs , simply to avoid

Letter from Ezra Pound, 7 December 1934.
By permission of Edinburgh University Library.

danger of lible on specific grounds. Even Marianne seems
to have thought of at least social bearings.

I was able to use quite a good deal of even earlier Cantos
in my Milan lectures on economics. I mean AS the briefest
and clearest statement I knew. That, I dont expect anyone
yet to lap off the page . personal supervision of econ/
by Malatesta and the Este/ etc... Kublai etc... not absolutely
separate , or mere barroque decoration of theme.

Nor has even the spiritual state of Englad in 1919
(specifically the hell/shit cantos) a merely isolated
sealed up etc...etc.... status.

When even forrard looking economists write to me that the
forrard looking WONT (editors) let 'em express opinion or print
questions...etc....

          Why bother with detail... ? I mean about this .
Do you know how far I AM excluded and kept from
print ?

I grant you are dead right about the general swill ...etc...
Do you see New Democracy ?
Yet again // quia poetry can one be expected to
falsify one's language for the sake of a dogma ?
          I dont think so.

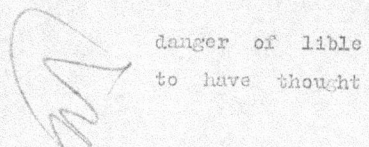
This note mainly to suggest possibility of diffusion of thought
via that blithering and shitten system (that tolerates Audleton
Murray and gets him STILL into the N.E.W.) the discussion
of the philosophic trend and other Pewk in poetry. Activ Anth.
shows conscience economique , not merely conscience sociale.

My dear MacDiarmid,

I don't know quite how complete an exception you are trying to make me. I don't think the passages in XIX and XXII are in any way isolated from the mass of the Cantos. Though the more specific locus of economics is in Cantos XXXI/XLI, can't write everything all at once on the same page. Also I am probably a more boycotted, trimmed, excluded author than you apparently think. *And* the question how far an economic concern (by a writer of verse) can be or shd be confined to lyric or metric expression seems to me variant.

When in a Canto not yet printed, I got round to Doug.'s A plus B,[1] I thought for a few hours I had committed a species of innovation. But within the day's length I found Dante before me (as cited now at start of XXXVIII).

I shd think however that (with the brief exception of Oppen's[2] few lines) all the contributors to *Active Anthology had* a very definite economic 'concern'; and to my mind there is sign of it in the metrical work of all of them either smack on the top in specific phrases, or underlying.

After all the pubr deleted a lot of Bunting[3] *after* B. and I had seen the proofs, simply to avoid danger of libel on *specific* grounds. Even Marianne[4] seems to have thought of at least social bearings.

I was able to use quite a good deal of even earlier Cantos in my Milan lectures on economics. I mean *as* the briefest and clearest statement I knew. I don't expect anyone yet to lap that off the page. Personal supervision of econ. by Malatesta and the Este etc.[5] Kublai etc.[6] not absolutely separate, or mere baroque decoration of theme.

Nor has even the spiritual state of England in 1919 (specifically the hell/shit Cantos) a merely isolated sealed-up etc. etc. status. When even forrard-looking economists write to me that the forrard-looking editors *won't* let 'em express opinion or print questions etc? Why bother with detail? I mean about this. Do you know how far I *am* excluded and kept from print?

I grant you are dead right about the general swill etc. Do you see *New Democracy*?[7]

Yet again *quia* poetry can one be expected to falsify one's language for the sake of a dogma? I don't think so.

This note mainly to suggest possibility of diffusion of thought via that blithering and shitten system (that tolerates Mudleton Murry[8] and gets him *still* into the *N. E. W.*), the discussion of the philosophic trend and other pewk in poetry. *Activ. Anth.* shows *conscience économique*, not merely *conscience sociale*.

E. P.

---

[1] In the economic theories of Major C.H. Douglas (1879-1952) Group A comprised all payments made by a factory to individuals in wages, salaries and dividends, and Group B consisted of all payments made for raw materials, bank charges and other external costs. C.H. Douglas, *Credit Power and Democracy* (London:Cecil Palmer, 1920), p.21.

[2] George Oppen b.1908. *New Collected Poems*, edited with an introduction and notes by Michael Davidson, and preface by Eliot Weinberger, Manchester, 2003.

3   Basil Bunting (1900-1985), poet.

4   Marianne Moore (1887-1972), poet, prose writer and editor of *The Dial* 1925-1929 (monthly).

5   Sigismondo Pandolfo Malatesta (1417-1468), Italian nobleman and condottiero, poet and patron of the arts, was the subject of Cantos VIII-XI. His first wife was his niece Ginevra d'Este.

6   Kublai Khan (1216-1294). The beginning of Canto XVIII quotes Marco Polo's account of Kublai Khan's paper money.

7   *New Democracy*, New York, 1933.

8   J. Middleton Murry (1889-1957), journalist and critic and editor.

82. From John Drummond (EUL MS2948.10 f.16)

Albergo Rapallo
Rapallo
Italy
14 December 1934

Dear 'Hugh MacDiarmid',

I have been expecting to hear from you for a long time, but nothing seems to have reached me since your letter of August 7th in which you promised to have a copy of *Stony Limits* sent to me so that I could select something for Mr Pound's forthcoming Anthology. I replied on August 27th, and sent a further postcard on October 27th, both addressed to C.M. Grieve in London. I am sending duplicates of this letter both to London and the Shetland Islands so as to make sure you get one or the other.

The Anthology is now nearly ready for final editing by Mr Pound, and from what I have seen of the American section I do not think that England will show up at all badly. It must be admitted, however, that so far there is very little first-rate stuff from either country. All I have of your work so far for inclusion is 'At the Cenotaph'[1] and 'One of the Principal Causes of War' (the latter of which I would prefer to keep in the original Scots+ as it appeared in the *New English Weekly*, though retaining the above title),[2] and the Anthology badly needs more.[3]

Please let me hear from you soon as time is getting short now, and I should be very glad to have a copy of *Stony Limits*, as well as some more of your work if you have any. If the book got lost in the post, let me know and I'll be very glad to get another copy myself.

Yours sincerely,
John Drummond.

+Unless you would rather keep it in English

1   *C.P.* I, p.358.

2   *C.P.* I, pp. 538-9 in English; p.496 in Scots.

3   On 18 July 1934 Drummond asked MacDiarmid for poems for an anthology number of the American *The Westminster Review*, a kind of continuation of *Active Anthology* which had been edited by Ezra Pound and published by Faber and Faber in London in 1933. 'It does not matter if it has already appeared in print, but should be contemporary and

should have "economic awareness" etc. You will know the sort of thing he wants.' 'The Westminster Magazine/ A Quarterly Review / Edited by Robert England / Oglethorpe University / Georgia. *The Westminster Magazine* edited by Robert England announces its Spring issue, an anthology of British and American verse, devoted principally to the work of younger poets. The British editor is Mr John Drummond, the American editor is Mr T.C. Wilson; and the whole number is under the general editorship of Mr Ezra Pound.' (EUL MS 2966 unfoliated).

83. From Neil M. Gunn (EUL MS2948.15 f.14)

Larachan
Dochfour Drive
Inverness
26 December 1934

A Good New Year to you and those
who may be with you!

My dear Christopher,
I was delighted to hear from you & had indeed been wondering in what part of the world you were sojourning. When this season's rush is over, I must get down to a hefty epistle to you so that you may gather the inwardness of much that may not appear properly reflected on the surface. There are all ways of going about a business – even about Scottish Nationalism, though you're aye itching to have a wallop there! Your belief in the ideal in humanity is superb. I should like a long ceilidh! No chance of you passing down this way? I believe we might quietly get down to something. I have lost all hope in the mere talkers & egoists. *Doing* is the only thing that attracts me now. You can slash the Scottish Nationalists, if you like. But that doesn't excite me: it's too easy. The only thing I've ever doubted about Nationalism is the capacity of the Scots to govern themselves. On the whole – the long view – it rather looks as if we are fated to die out. No sense of cohesion anywhere. No sense of subduing ourselves to one conjoint heave. We stick to our little points though the heavens fall. Though that is unfair to a fairly large body that has stuck together – & that accordingly you must beat up! Cheers.

No, I'm not doing another novel. I'm a bit tired with overwork, official & otherwise. I have fallen out of liking for writing. So I'm letting it slide, for a year or so anyway. I'm not prepared to give sixpence for any man's genius at the moment!

Though, talking of genius, I've been rereading the *Drunk Man*: no doubt about it: the real stuff is there. Some of your superb strokes made me roar with laughter and feel the old warmth of – how many years ago? Noble fellow. I'll quote from it – if you don't mind – in my whisky book: which I must not forget I have to do.[1] What a title! Enough to condemn me in every decent Scots home. That was the extra enticement. And, by God, I'll tell them what good whisky is. And show them how to consume it, I hope, in considerable quantity & with the continental manner! I'm delighted to hear you're busy. And particularly interested about Lenin book in series.[2] The real stuff. I'll send you a *Butcher's Broom*, if you've nothing better to read.[3]

Yours ever,
Neil.

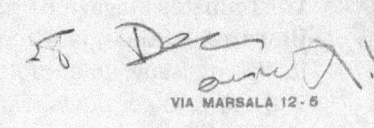

VIA MARSALA 12-5

E. POUND   RAPALLO

Dear McDiarmid

      I am asking Faber to send you some books
(Includin' Act/ Anth) But they dont like to have their stuff
in circulation. If you dont hear from 'em ask for an Ac/ Anth
on plea that you want to answer that ass Beavers.

As a suppressed and boycotted author... I dont feel my
lack of immediate contact with the great is completely me
own fault.
      I have interjected unwelcome ideas into every
crevice that I cd. see ; smell or feel..
                            howver , no use
arguing on personal and individual case.
                I have no use for the god damn present
avoiders (95% of the poETs and pros/asses ... who will
not look at the world, and who have NO conception of and
no curiosity re. the relations between the ideas of
Lenin, Mussolini, C.H.Doug. + Gesell .

(supposing that by now some aroma of Fraser, Fabre , Gourmont
       and in very rare cases Fenollosa's CHINESE (as distinct
from Jap.) studies (Written Charcter)

I think quite a number of American independent magazines wd/ send
you review copies if they knew you WANTED to review them
... even if you cant place the reviews/ you cd. promise to do
note in N.E... ???

Munson and A.R.O. are economic... they are NOT so to speak
crits/ of licherchoor... Munsons American notes ignore the
items of interest// besides he is now so busy editing New
Democarcy that he hasnt time to watch what goes on in Am/
lit.

You aren't missing much by not seeing the continong.. not cert.
in poesy...
Frobenius on Africa/ and Cocteau surviving FROM the age of
D Aurevilly ... Londres' rapportage (no stopped)
young Crevel's " es Pieds dans le Plat "...

                apart from which damnd if I know
anything I cd. recommend to you..
                Simenon's first set of detective
takes... waaal.. not ezzakly superior to Ed/ Wallace but
more lecturrery...

American PUBLISHING system is pewk// they cd/ have taken over
lead from Eng/ in 1917/19.... but I think we gord dam
yanks have now a marginal lead in poetic technique...

If any frog except Cocteau can WRITE... lead me to it. relative
The rest simply dont KNOW.... which is the reverse of stat's
                          in 1912

Marginal note (left): Mat Ernst's engravings + ours Freudian word slingers. are licherchor.

Marginal note (right): tohave higher penetrated the litist since

Letter from Ezra Pound, 28 December 1934.
By permission of Edinburgh University Library.

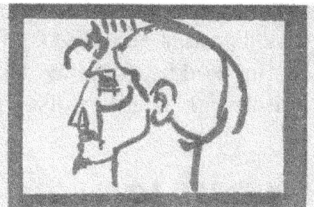

VIA MARSALA 12-5

E. POUND   RAPALLO

They havent even a critical machinery. a poop like Valery

can make a good showing against some american college prof/
but apart ça....

                How the hell YOU are ever to find out
anything in Ucter Isles.. with nothing but the shit of Fleet
street and to poohng of McZarty and co... governing 96 % of
british printing... kzrrrist alone xknoze...

I think J.Drummond (Queels College . Cambridge)) wd/ send you
Cambridge Left.

and "ut ante dic/" various american pubctns/ wd. send you rev/ copies
if you showed an interest...

     apply ^as/ Loughlin. Eliot House   E.41   Cambridge. Mass. U.S.A.

Robt. England. Westminster Review / Oglethorpe University. Georgia
                              U.S.A.

          (stranded and FAR from contemporary...)

T.C.Wilson   I625 Geddes Ave. Ann Arbour . Michigan U.S.A.

               (not on any mag/ but contemporary.. and
you cd/ get details from him.. thus sparing yr/ present aged
correspondent .. an puttin th woik on somen un yunger.

L.Zukofsky. co/ W.C.Williams   9 Ridge Rd. Rutherford. N.J. USA

   (new publishing venture.. books; not mag. but Williams
    in touch , and more or less white haired boy of a group
of transient left wing attempts...

Bunting has gone to the Canaries/// no more central than you are.

Uh guy at Oxon has just asked me to restart a peereeyodicl... I
dunno what he can DO... I have said I wd. edit an annual
anthology IF....
           Have you any valoobl suggestions..along this line...
my idea wd be NOT to uses same group year after year...
or at least to vary the proportion VERY greatly if one
exhibited or retained some of the same components.

There are 9 or IO possibilities , excluding those in present A/A/
or "over and above" present components . Counting H McD.
                              The ? ariz. after my letter to you
I dunno that it(ll come to anything.

1   Neil Gunn's 'whisky book' was *Whisky and Scotland* (London: Routledge, 1935).
2   MacDiarmid's 'Lenin book' became 'Red Scotland' which was never published.
3   Neil Gunn, *Butcher's Broom* (Edinburgh:The Porpoise Press,1934).

84. From Ezra Pound (EUL MS2958.10 ff.1-2)

Via Marsala 12-5

Rapallo

28 December anno XII [1934]

Dear MacDiarmid,

I am asking Faber to send you some books (includin' *Act. Anth.*). But they don't like to have their stuff in circulation. If you don't hear from 'em ask for *Act. Anth.* on plea that you want to answer that ass Beavers.[1]

As a suppressed and boycotted author I don't feel my lack of immediate contact with the great is completely me own fault. I have interjected unwelcome ideas into every crevice that I cd see, smell or feel; however, no use arguing on personal and individual case.

I have no use for the goddam present avoiders, 95% of the *poETs* and pros/asses who will not look at the world, and who have *no* conception of and no curiosity *re* the relations between the ideas of Lenin, Mussolini, C. H. Doug & Gesell[2] (supposing that by now some aroma of Fraser,[3] Fabre,[4] Gourmont[5] and in very rare cases Fenollosa's[6] *Chinese* – as distinct from Jap. – studies (Written Character) to have penetrated the higher lit. circs.).

I think quite a number of American independent magazines wd send you review copies if they knew you *wanted* to review them; even if you cdn't place the reviews you cd promise to do notes in *N. E. W.*?

Munson[7] and A. R. O.[8] are economic. They are *not* so to speak critics of licherchoor. Munson's American notes ignore the items of interest. Besides he is now so busy editing *New Democracy* that he hasn't time to watch what goes on in Am. Lit.

You aren't missing much by not seeing the continong, not cert. in poesy. Frobenius[9] on Africa and Cocteau[10] surviving *from* the age of D. Aurevilly,[11] Londres'[12] rapportage (no stopped), young Crevel's *Les Pieds dans le plat* [13]– apart from which damned if I know anything I cd recommend to you, Simenon's[14] first set of detective tales, waaal, not ezzakly superior to Ed Wallace[15] but more leeturrery. Max Ernst's[16] engravings *are* licherchoor & oust the Freudian word-slingers.

American *publishing* system is pewk. They cd have taken over lead from Eng. in 1917-19 but I think we goddam Yanks have now a marginal lead in poetic technique.

If any frog except Cocteau can *write* lead me to it. The rest simply don't *know*, which is the reverse of relative status in 1912. They haven't even a critical machinery. A poop like Valéry[17] can make a good showing against some American college prof. but apart *ça*.

How the hell *you* are ever to find out anything in Outer Isles with nothing but the shit of Fleet Street and the Pooping of McFarty and Co. governing 96% of British printing kzrrrist alone xknoze.

I think J. Drummond, Queen's College, Cambridge, England wd send you *Cambridge Left* and *ut ante dic* various American pubctns wd send you rev. copies if you showed an interest.

Apply Jas Loughlin,[18] Eliot House, E41, Cambridge, Mass., USA.

Robt England, *Westminster Review*, Oglethorpe University, Georgia, USA (stranded and *far* from contemporary).

T. C. Wilson, 1825 Geddes Ave, Ann Arbour, Michigan, USA (not on any mag. but contemporary and you cd get details from him thus sparing yr present aged correspondent and puttin the woik on some un yunger.

L. Zukofsky,[19] c/o W. C. Williams,[20] 9 Ridge Rd, Rutherford, N. J., USA (new publishing venture, books not mag. but Williams in touch, and more or less white-haired boy of a group of transient left wing attempts.

Bunting has gone to the Canaries, no more central than you are.

Uh guy at Oxon has just asked me to restart a peereeyodicl. I dunno what he can DO. I have said I wd. edit an annual anthology *if* ... Have you any valooble suggestions along this line. My idea wd be *not* to use the same group year after year or at least to vary the proportion *very* greatly if one exhibited or retained some of the same components. There are 9 or 10 possibilities, excluding those in present *A. A.* or 'over and above' present components. Counting H. MacD. The ? ariz after my letter to you. I dunno that it'll come to anything.

    E. P.

[1] 'Beavers' was Lord Beaverbrook (1879-1964), press baron and member of Churchill's wartime Cabinet.

[2] Silvio Gesell (1862-1930). *Natural Economic Order,* translated by Philip Pye (London, 1958).

[3] Sir James George Frazer (1854-1941), social anthropologist and classical scholar. *The Golden Bough,* first edition, 1890.

[4] Antoine Fabre d'Olivet (1768-1825), playwright who diversified late into the study of the languages and cosmogonies of the ancient world.

[5] Rémy de Gourmont (1858-1915) was described by T.S. Eliot as 'the critical conscience of his generation'. (*New Oxford Companion to Literature in French,* 1995).

[6] Ernest Francisco Fenollosa (1853-1908), poet and student of oriental art. Pound wrote *The Chinese Written Character as a Medium for Poetry,* 1920.

[7] Gorham [Bert] Munson (1896-1969), literary and social critic, interested in Social Credit theories (among others).

[8] A. R. Orage.

[9] Leo Frobenius (1873-1938), ethnologist and archaeologist and major figure in German ethnography. Pound corresponded with Frobenius from the 1920s, initially on economic topics.

[10] Jean Cocteau (1889-1963), poet, novelist, playwright and film director.

[11] Jules Amédée Barbey d'Aurevilly (1808-1889), novelist and short story writer.

[12] Albert Londres wrote *The Road to Buenos Ayres,* London, 1928, and *Terror in the Balkans,* London, 1935.

[13] René Crevel (1900-1935), Surrealist novelist. *Les Pieds dans le plat* (1933).

14   Georges Simenon (1903-1989), prolific Belgian-born author of detective and other fiction and autobiography.
15   Edgar Wallace (1875-1932), English journalist, dramatist and prolific writer of 'thrillers'.
16   Max Ernst (1891-1976), German painter, printmaker and sculptor, naturalized American in 1948 and French in 1958.
17   Paul Valéry (1871-1945), poet, essayist and critic.
18   James Loughlin, publisher, New Directions.
19   Louis Zukofsky (1904-1978), born of Russian immigrant parents on New York's Lower East Side. In 1927 he began his great poem 'A', presenting in diverse forms his experience of art and life, of personal and public events, that began in 'A' 1-12 (1959) and 'A'13-21 (1969) and was finally completed with the publication in 832 pages of 'A' (1979).
20   William Carlos Williams (1883-1963) practised medicine as a pediatrician. *Paterson* in five volumes, 1946-1958, is his best-known major work.

85. From James Leslie Mitchell (Lewis Grassic Gibbon) (NLS MS26066 f.37)

107 Handside Lane
WGC
12 January 1935

My dear Chris,

It's a long [time] since I heard from you. How are you and what are you doing? I hope Lenin on Scotland is going strong.

We've collected 8 out of the 10 for the series, including Linklater and Mackenzie. You and I, alas, are the only communists. I tried to foist James Barke upon them, but they wouldn't have it.[1]

However, I imagine we'll keep the red flag flying pretty efficaciously.

Have you received the copy of *Earth Conquerors* I sent you?[2] It's going with a fair boom in America – selling at a steady 400 a week. (Here, of course, it's quite dead.) Specimen American notice enclosed for your delectation.

I hope Valda and the Son are flourishing, and that the winter isn't too severe on your lone shieling in the distant island.

Regards.

Yours,

JasLeslieMitchell.

1   James Barke (1905-1958), novelist and friend.
2   *Earth Conquerors* was the title of the American edition of *Nine Against the Unknown* (London:Jarrolds, 1934).

86. From John Drummond (EUL Gen.2094/.1/444)

CARD.

Albergo Rapallo

Rapallo

Italy

16 January 1935

Many thanks for your letter of Dec. 21st. *Stony Limits* has not arrived, but the stuff for the Anthology has already gone to America. Your poems included are: 'At the Cenotaph', 'One of the Principal Causes of War' (Scots & English versions, as Pound wanted to show that, tho' better in Scots, the poem didn't depend on that for its effect), 'Nemertes',[1] 'The Skeleton of the Future'[2] and 'In a Neglected Graveyard'.[3] The last 2, I take it, are from *Stony Limits* and I will write them for permission to reprint.[4] Let me know if you want the rest of your MSS returning.

The Anthology ought to be out about March and be on sale in the Charing Cross Road shops.[5] It has turned out much better than I expected.

Yours sincerely,

John Drummond.

---

1   *C. P.* I, p. 303.
2   *C. P.* I, p. 386.
3   *C. P.* I, p. 462.
4   'The Skeleton of the Future' and 'In a Neglected Graveyard' *were* from *Stony Limits.*
5   In Spring 1935 *The Westminster Magazine* merged with the poetry review *Bozart* to become *Bozart-Westminster.* 'The Anthology' was Issue 9.1/24.1 (Spring-Summer 1935).

87. From F. G. Scott (NLS MS27155 f.112)

[early 1935]

THE ONLY SURVIVING PART OF A LETTER FROM F.G. SCOTT TO HUGH MACDIARMID IN INK.

Neither [W. & R.] Holmes' nor [John] Smith's had the books and held out little hope of getting copies, an advert some couple of years ago not raising a single reply. I picked up in Holmes' a book of notices which included one on [Sir Thomas] Urquhart and had it sent on to you as something to show you that I was on the hunt. On Friday I received notification from Smith's (who were to advertise) that they'd located both the books, so you should have them in a few days.

You'll probably wonder why I didn't borrow the things from the University Library. Well, [George Pratt] Insh was very hesitant about the plan and excused himself on the grounds that the University were very particular about sending books out of Glasgow and that they 'had been very good to him' etc.[1] Damned annoyed you can guess I got at this and went off on my own. So you needn't return the copies when they reach you – I'm making you a present of them.

Very interested in your many other activities and only sorry you have so much hack-work ahead of you. What are the '40 Songs' like?[2] You don't seem to have tackled the dramatic lyrics I spoke about and which I'm so badly in need of. Glad to see 'The Birlinn of Clanranald' in the last *Modern Scot*.[3] Curiously enough I had [J.H.] Whyte staying overnight just before your last long letter came and he was enquiring about your 'In Praise of Ben Dorain' etc. of which I could give him no information.[4] I think he is quite anxious about your work at present and wanting as much of it as possible for his magazine, which, in your absence, is a pretty thin affair. Why not strike out on the new dramatic lyric idea and kill two birds at once?

Before I forget I'm enclosing a P.O. for 5/- from *The Bulletin*[5] which came here after you had gone off to London. It got mislaid (in an old suit) for some months and now I can't cash it. Perhaps you had best explain to *The Herald* folk about it and say it has just come to you after your wanderings.

Sorry to hear about Valda's chest trouble. I do hope she's not really ill. We hear on our new Marconiphone (6 valves) about gale warnings in Orkneys and Shetlands – seems like every night for the past 2 or 3 months and we picture you right in it, filling reams of paper amid the howling blasts.

You can console yourself at any rate that you're not a bit more solitary than I am in the heart of Glasgow for I see nobody nowadays. I don't want to – I just want some stuff out of you that will keep me working. I'm sending Dunbar's 'The Twa Kimmers' for next *Modern Scot*[6] and turning a critical eye to his 'Resurrection' poem.[7]

Ever affectionately,

F.G.

---

[1] George Pratt Insh (1883-1956) was the author of *Scotland and the Modern World* (1932). MacDiarmid wrote about his work in one of the additional essays which he added to the MS of 'Red Scotland' (NLS MS27035 ff.118-152). He had previously written about him in *Contemporary Scottish Studies*; and contributed an obituary as editor of *The Voice of Scotland* in April 1956.

[2] 'Forty Songs' was dropped as a title and 'Second Hymn to Lenin' included to make *Second Hymn to Lenin and Other Poems* (London: Nott, 1935).

[3] The 'last *Modern* Scot' had been published in January 1935, vol. 5, no. 4, and contained MacDiarmid's translation into English of ' Birlinn Chlann-Raghnaill' by Alasdair MacMhaighster Alasdair (c.1695-1770), i.e., Alexander MacDonald, pp. 230-247. In a note MacDiarmid wrote, ' This is one of a series of English verse translations of the principal Scottish Gaelic poems, in making which I have had the invaluable collaboration of Mr Sam MacLean of the Island of Raasay'(p. 247). 'Birlinn Chlann-Raghnaill' was later included in *The Golden Treasury of Scottish Poetry* which MacDiarmid edited (London:MacMillan, 1940), pp.65-85.

[4] 'The Praise of Ben Dorain' in MacDiarmid's translation from the Gaelic of Donnchadh Ban Mac an-t-saoir (1724-1808), i.e., Duncan Ban MacIntyre, was published in *The Golden Treasury*, pp. 43-58. MacDiarmid again acknowledged MacLean's contribution in his introduction, p. x.

[5] *The Bulletin and Scots Pictorial* was a tabloid daily published in Glasgow from 1924 to 1960.

[6] Vol. vi, no.1 (April 1935), pp. 30-34.

[7] Scott did not set Dunbar's 'On the Resurrection of Christ'.

88. From John Tonge (NLS Acc. 7361/6)

36 East Haddon Rd
Ddee
29 January 1935

Dear C.M.,

James [Whyte] has handed your note to me. I'm sending the Christopher North book,[1] but am sorry I don't have the Cruden.[2] I don't have anything of much use about Ossian Macpherson:[3] the enclosed is just the sort of thing you'd get out of any encyclopaedia. John Lorne Campbell (who is at the Tartan Hotel, Rothesay Place, Edinburgh for a few days) has been working on Macpherson with a view to bringing out a book, & could no doubt elucidate any difficult points.[4] I've been trying for ages to get something new about Urquhart,[5] but the intro to the Maitland Club volume[6] & Willcock's essay are all the known facts.[7] There is something in the B. M., apparently, if one could get at it: Jean Plattard, the great Rabelais scholar, who was here last week, tells me he has come across nothing in Paris.[8] I'm sending a précis of the article in the D.N.B. Not knowing precisely the sort of thing you want, I've just copied down all the facts, omitting the comments. The phrases quoted from U., as you'll probably recollect, are from the 'Logo'.[9] I'll post a copy of M'Gonigle tomorrow.[10]

I hear good news of you from Scott & Whyte, and was delighted to read the 'Birlinn'. With best wishes to Valda & yourself.

Yours as ever,
John Tonge.

[1] 'Christopher North' (John Wilson) (1785-1854). *Noctes Ambrosianae* selected and arranged by John Skelton, Edinburgh, 1876.
[2] Alexander Cruden (1699-1770) published *A Complete Concordance to the Holy Scriptures of the Old and New Testaments,* London, 1738. Many other editions followed.
[3] James MacPherson (1736-1796) was known as 'Ossian' because he 'translated' Ossian's legends in *Fingal: an Ancient Epic Poem* (1761).
[4] John Lorne Campbell (1906-1996), author of works on Canna, Barra and the Hebrides in general. He was married to Margaret Fay Shaw.
[5] Sir Thomas Urquhart (1611-1660) is best known for his translation into English of François Rabelais' *Pantagruel* and *Gargantua* (1653).
[6] *The Works of Sir Thomas Urquhart of Cromartie, Knight.,* edited by Thomas Maitland, Maitland Club, 30, Edinburgh, 1834; introduction pp. i -xxii.
[7] Rev. John Willcock (1853-1931), *Sir Thomas Urquhart of Cromartie. Knight.* (1899).
[8] Jean Plattard (1873-1939), scholar of Rabelais and Montaigne.
[9] *Logopandecteision* (1653) was reprinted by The Scholar Press, Menston, Yorkshire in 1953.
[10] William McGonagall (1830-1902), 'poet and tragedian'.

89. From James Leslie Mitchell (Lewis Grassic Gibbon) (EUL MS2955.11 f.29)

107 Handside Lane
Welwyn Garden City
30 January 1935

My dear Christopher,

Nice to hear from you again, though not so nice to hear of Valda's condition. We do hope she's on the road to recovery. After all, Spring is coming, even in the Shetlands.

How is the son?

Here we are all in good health – including even myself. For I've had a couple of months, more or less, in bed and on the sick list with acute gastritis: a feeling as though I'd swallowed and inadequately digested a boa constrictor.[1] Result: no work, and I'm miles behind with everything I'm contracted for. You and I are in the same boat.

How goes the 'Lenin'? You're the man to make a good job of this, though, reflecting on the subject, I've wondered how you're going to bring it to 35 000 words. No doubt it's going to be 'Lenin' in a general sense – i.e., a survey of rebel and revolutionary movements in Scotland since early times? Let me know.

Both you and I figure in the current *Left Review*.[2] Swashbuckling devils. The 'Left' has asked me to nominate someone to do a survey of this 'Communist-Anarchist-Nationalist-Credit-Reform-epidemic' in modern Scots letters; and I've nominated James Barke. He'll probably go for both of us with a spiked club. Hope so!

Most *Grey Granite* [3]notices, *T. L. S.* (Aggie the Whore)[4] and *Observer* (Fat Gerald with the pawky paws)[5] excepted, have been pretty good – sometimes enthusing, and sometimes horrified. The explorers book in this country is a flop, but in America selling a steady 400 a week, which is passable, at $3.50. The Americans have given it an immense press – specimen (for burning) attached.

Have you seen *The Scottish Standard*?[6] Nine out of the ten in our series are fixed.[7]

Now I must do some work.

All the best to all of you from all of us.

Yours,

JasLeslieMitchell.

[1]   Grassic Gibbon died as a result of peritonitis on 7 February 1935.
[2]   Grassic Gibbon and MacDiarmid both contributed to 'Controversy' in *Left Review*, vol. 1, no.5 (February 1935), pp. 179-180 and p. 182 respectively.
[3]   *Grey Granite* was published in London in 1934.
[4]   'Aggie the Whore' was Agnes Mure Mackenzie (1891-1955), historian and novelist.
[5]   'Fat Gerald with the pawky paws' was Gerald Gould (1885-1936).
[6]   The monthly *Scottish Standard* began publication in February 1935. It was later incorporated with *The Modern Scot* into *Outlook* which first appeared in April 1936.
[7]   Gibbon was editing *Meanings in Scotland* for Routledge. After his death MacDiarmid became editorial advisor on the series which was renamed *Meanings for Scotland.*

90. From Sorley MacLean (EUL MS2954.13 ff.8-9)

c/o Mackay
Wentworth Street
Portree
Skye
16 February 1935

Dear Mr Grieve,

I am sorry for being so long in sending you any stuff. I hope that the packet reaches you without delay. I have been dreadfully busy for the last fortnight or so and troubled by the imminence of inspectors and other evils. I hope that my delay has caused you no inconvenience. I have seen your translation of 'The Birlinn [of Clanranald]' in *The Modern Scot* and I consider it wonderfully good. It is certainly far nearer the spirit of [Alexander] MacDonald than any translation of Gaelic poetry is to the spirit of the work translated, and as a poem there is of course no translation from Gaelic to be compared with it. All the Gaelic-speaking people to whom I have shown it have expressed great approval. Knowing well the great difficulty of your task, I am really astonished at your success. I received a few days ago an enthusiastic letter from [George Elder] Davie, who declares himself greatly stirred by a reading of it.

With regard to the poems I have sent this time I hope you will approve of them. 'Inverlochy' and the MacKinnon poem are very striking in their difference but both very characteristic of the two sides of Iain Lom. There is a great musical quality about the MacKinnon poem which will be very difficult to reproduce in English. Perhaps the poems from [William] Livingston are not so characteristic as a passage from a longer poem might be but I will look up some of his longer poems and try to hit on another passage as well.[1] I am really sorry that I have not been all winter working for you but since I did not hear from you in autumn (when you promised to send some of Sinclair) I judged that you would have no further time to do translations. But now I shall be extremely delighted to send you stuff as long as you have time to make use of it.[2]

Yours sincerely,

Sam MacLean.

P.S. I shall be delighted if you could send any MSS of Sinclair's or Caimbeul's.[3] I have read only one poem of Sinclair's – 'Ros Aluinn' in the *Voices from the Hills*. I shall send you a translation of it in a day or two.[4] I have read nothing of Caimbeul.

---

[1] *The Golden Treasury of Scottish Poetry* includes translations from Gaelic of 'The Day of Inverlochy' and 'To MacKinnon of Strath' by Iain Lom (John MacDonald)(1620?-1716?), pp. 32-35 and pp.97-99, and of 'Ireland Weeping' and 'Message to the Bard' by William Livingston (1808-1870), pp. 63-65 and pp.327-331, which are referred to directly or indirectly in the letter but no attributions are made in respect of the translations.

[2] *The Golden Treasury* also includes translations from Gaelic of 'Omnia Vanitas' and 'The Day of Judgment' by Dugald Buchanan (1716-1768), pp.113-114 and pp. 304-305, 'Last

Leave of the Hills' by Duncan Ban MacIntyre, pp. 221-233, 'Another Song' by William Ross (1762-1790), pp. 155-156, and 'The Path of the Old Spells' by Donald Sinclair (1886-1932), pp. 18-19.

3 Aonghas Caimbeul (1908-1949) published *Gaelic Songs* in 1943.

4 Sorley MacLean's translation of Sinclair's 'Ros Aluinn' still exists in MS. (NLS Acc. 7361/52).

91. From John Gawsworth [Terence Ian Fytton Armstrong] (EUL MS2948.7 f.2)

33 Great James Street
Bedford Row
London WC
14 March 1935

My dear Chris,

As no doubt you have heard Lahr got six months after I had bailed him out, and has still 5 months to go.[1] Esther who is trying to keep the shop open has just found the MS of your *Forbidden Poems* (left with Charles to print) and is deathly afraid of the police (who still watch the place) finding them.[2] She is in a bad way for money (as we all are) but if she can regard the *MS* as *her* property would sell it to me if I offer a fair price. This price I named at £1 or 30/- as you are *not* collected *widely* here in London and I would only put the 50 odd pages of it in my despatch box at the bank out of harm's way. She wants to see a note from you to me giving her permission to sell and saying whether you agree to £1 or 30/- being a suitable sum: and on receipt of a reply from you she will act. I have all the text in my proof of *Stony Limits* with the exception of two poems [:] 4 lines entitled *His Majesty All Dolled Up* beginning 'Ours is a constitutional king, you say'and one of 12 lines *To Oswald Mosley* beginning 'Fascism will create...'.[3] But *The Ode to All Rebels* looks different (i.e. shorter) and *O Love it is a lovely thing* appears to have 16 lines instead of 23.[4]

For these facts (if none others) I would like to acquire the MS. Perhaps when you write you will let me know if you[5]

1 Charles Lahr, secondhand bookseller, had been jailed for reset.

2 There are letterheads in the name of E[sther] Lahr for both 68 and 69 Red Lion St, London WC1. The 'Forbidden Poems' were the poems deleted from the first edition of *Stony Limits* on legal advice.

3 These two poems have never been found .

4 As printed in *C.P.* I, pp. 490-1, the italicized lyric beginning ' O love it is a lovely thing' has 43 lines.

5 The letter breaks off here.

92. From Rhea Mitchell (NLS MS27152 ff.22-26)

107 Handside Lane
Welwyn Garden City
3 April 1935

NOTE

After 8th April
34 Attimore Road, Welwyn Garden City.

My dear Valda and Chris,

Do forgive me not writing ere this and please accept my sincere thanks for your most kind letter.

Leslie's sudden death was and is a terrible blow to me. It's such a pity for his own sake to have been cut off so young, so full of vigour and power. Is there any meaning in anything? All our efforts and ambitions simply shattered and what was sure to have been a glorious life for the children now passes to one of *comparative* want. Rhea[1] especially has had such opportunities and complete happiness and she is feeling all this strangeness & cannot understand why daddy doesn't come back & why we are moving to a small house. Maybe she was growing a wee bit of a snob but I hardly think so. I tried to explain to her about life & death & told her Leslie would not come back but she just doesn't understand. Time will, I hope, help her.

How are you both and Michael? I do hope you are fit. Write to me soon & tell me about yourselves.

Yes! that was a glorious & unforgettable weekend we all had together. It is something to treasure with other happy memories of our-almost-10 years together. He joked about our 'leather wedding' which, he said, was the 10th anniversary & he threatened to write to everyone we knew to inform them that we expected gifts of leather goods. I told him we were almost sure to collect a good supply of leather bootlaces or maybe braces.

On Monday 8th April I am moving to a small house – I've given you the address. It's the best I could find but it's not much cheaper than this. The Garden City is full at the moment & so houses are scarce. My difficulty is, of course, that I dare not take a year's lease in case I find a job to take me away from here. The monthly tenancy is the only possible & this house is on a monthly basis. I shall not get all my furniture in it but there's a garage & I shall put my surplus in it. There's a great lack of outside sheds here – they are supposed to spoil the beauty of the place but one does need something & this garage was the only thing I could find possible. The rent is 26/6 per week inclusive & I must find a lodger to help pay the rent. It's a worrying business & the baby is such a handicap no matter how I plan – he is so young & at the stage of crawling a bit & trying to walk.[2] (He has been ill the last 2 days – the 2nd bout since Leslie died & I think I'll have to have his adenoids removed.)

Have you heard that the Royal Lit. Fund granted me £300? I never expected such a sum and the generosity moved me to tears. If only it could have brought back Leslie. Priestley[3] did his utmost for me – he is on the Committee – & Ivor Brown,[4] Linklater, Edwin Muir, Compton Mackenzie & James Bridie gave their support to my application.

Leslie was not able to finish his book for Heinemann – it's half-done I should say & after I get my letters of administration I shall send what there is of it to Evans & we'll hope that something can be done.[5] Of course they will do what they can in order to get back the £500 paid in advance of royalties. It was to have been published here, & in America by Doubleday, Doran [and Company, New York]. I do hope it can be published altho' I can hope for nothing after such a big advance. The Wallace book which he was doing for Faber cannot be found.[6] I think he must have destroyed it for I cannot trace it. There seems nothing of any importance (unpublished) left & the publishers (Jarrolds) say that his books will drop out now. I don't see why that should be for Galsworthy still sells & I'm sure the *Scots Quair* is as important – to Scotland at least – as *The Forsythe Saga*. Maybe I'm wrong. Anyway Hall gave me no hope at all. So I'm just relying solely on the £300 & a job to keep me going. He had a small insurance but I have had to pay over £100 in debts – funeral, stores, etc. etc. I get quite frantic at times – it's the children I worry so much for.

I'm trying to get reinstatement to the Civil Service but I find the wage is as low as £2.6.9 a week & that would just pay fares, rent, & a meagre lunch a day. Still it'd be something to pay one's rent. Again there's the children & unless I can trust Catherine[7] (I'm taking her from school at Easter – she's 14) with Daryll & can rely on her cooking them a meal it's going to be a lot paying someone to look after them. I've thought of going to Hampstead & looking around for a house (buying it on the deposit system) & taking lodgers. It might work & [George] Malcolm Thomson advises me to try.[8] Mrs Ivor Brown says I might be able to get Daryll in a crèche but he'd have to be resident & Catherine in the same crèche to train as a nurse. Still there's Rhea, &, poor little mite, she keeps saying that she has nasty thoughts about me leaving her. I don't want to have to part with the children but then I didn't want to part with Leslie.

This letter is full of nothing but myself. Forgive me going on at such length.

Thank you so much for your kind offer of help. I don't know what I could ask of you except it be your influence in getting either *Spartacus* [9]or *Sunset Song* filmed. Both are being considered by Korda[10] at the moment but I've no hope. Did you hear from Mirsky when you wrote to him about *Spartacus*?[11] A film might help considerably. Then there's *Three Go Back* [12]which could equal *King Kong*[13] I imagine. I wish I could write but I would fail miserably.

Now that's all. Do write soon & tell me lots & come to see me whenever possible, won't you? We had hoped to visit you this year –

My warmest love to both of you & a kiss to Michael. Keep fit.

As ever,

Rhea.

PS I have omitted to say that Leslie died 3 days after an operation for gastric ulcers and the peritonitis had already set in prior to the operation. He must have been suffering greatly & had not said. On Monday (4th Feb.) morning at 2 o'clock I was awakened – he was in terrible pain but it passed off & I phoned the Dr at 7 am. He came at 11.30 *after I'd told him the symptoms*. I have accused him of slackness, & rightly so, for maybe he could have saved Leslie even then. Of course Leslie ought to have been X-rayed before Xmas when the Dr was called in but even then the seriousness of gastric ulcers was not considered by that clown – maybe he did not even suspect ulcers. Anyway the mixture of powders he prescribed must only have soothed the ulcer & was no cure. Leslie had not had the pain after taking the mixture but, of course, its effects worked off with the result – this sudden attack which ended so fatally. It's all ghastly & one desires so much to go back the few months and do the right thing. If this is the plan of life which so many seem to believe in, then I consider it a damned awful plan – a wasteful, nonsensical hurtful plan. Forgive again. R.

[1] b. 1930.
[2] Daryll b.1934.
[3] J.B. Priestley (1894-1984), novelist and playwright.
[4] Ivor Brown (1891-1974), theatre critic.
[5] The 'book for Heinemann' was a novel based on the Covenanters, cf. *Smeddum* ed. by Valentina Bold, (Edinburgh: Canongate Classics, 2001), pp. 807-9.
[6] The only existing fragment of 'the Wallace book' was published in *Cencrastus* 61 under the title 'William Wallace Knight of Scotland' which was the title advertised in the Faber catalogue for Autumn, 1934. It was introduced by a brief article 'Braveheart in Kinraddie' by John Manson.
[7] Catherine Middleton, Rhea's half-sister.
[8] George Malcolm Thomson (1899-1996), journalist.
[9] London, 1933.
[10] Alexander Korda, film producer.
[11] MacDiarmid wrote to Rhea Mitchell, 14 May 1937, 'I wrote Mirskii twice at least, after I heard from him, re *Spartacus* etc. But I had no reply to either of these letters. I will make another effort straightaway.' (NLS MS26078 f.20)
[12] London, 1932.
[13] US, 1933. A film producer on safari brings back a giant ape which terrorizes New York.

93. From Stanley Nott (EUL MS2955.23 f.16)

Stanley Nott Ltd
Publishers
69 Grafton Street
Fitzroy Square
London W1
19 May 1935

Directors
S.C. Nott
M.S. Stephens

Dear Chris,

We've been waiting for Will Dyson's drawing, to include it in 'Forty New Songs'.[1] At last he has promised to let us have it not later than 14 June. It is going to be a frontispiece, which will also, we hope, be reproduced on the jacket.

I want to ask you if you will include 'Second Hymn to Lenin' in the collection – if it is not already included in a collection. It would go very well & would help the signed edition. Will you let me know by return. If not that, perhaps you have one or two other things. We have several blank pages; & to make an even working we ought either to include something or to take something out – which of course I don't want to do.

Things are beginning to move at last. Douglas books are selling well. I'm lunching with Saurat on Thursday.

These pamphlets are for you – a little light reading.

Kind regards to you both.

Stanley.

[1] Will Dyson's drawing appears to show MacDiarmid as an angel, holding a bowler hat. Two stout men in tails and butterfly collars gaze up at him, tight-lipped. The caption reads, 'The Fellow's Scarcely Human!'

94. From Barker Fairley (EUL MS2948.1 ff.10-11)

The University
Manchester 13

29 May 1935

Dear Grieve,

It was nice to get your letter from Lerwick. We have been thinking & talking of you ever since you left and are somehow changed by your visit.[1] But I think now you ought to send on those teeth & spectacles so that we can bring our mental picture of you up to date!

The pamphlets I sent you are neither here nor there, I haven't written much anyway. And the little remark about Heine and Scots was made before I knew your work. I should modify it now. The Wordsworth analysis is one I think of extending. What John Davidson says of him throws more light on Davidson than on Wordsworth, though the germ of a truth is there. Don't waste your time on these small papers. But if some day you can spare time to follow my analysis right through I should like your reactions. But again, it is much more important that you should write than read.

You will be amused to learn that Charlton, the professor of English who met you at tea & ran off not very graciously, met me a day or two later with shouts of enthusiasm for your verse, which he had just sampled. He is a very negative reader of modern things, but you have penetrated his defence. I shall put him on to the *Drunk Man* & gradually educate him! The students were all stirred up by your talk & if you come again you can be sure of a great welcome.

Anne Treneer will send you a copy of her Doughty book.[2] She says fine things about Doughty's words & she knows his words, as I didn't. I don't suppose her book or my *Extracts*,[3] which you will also get, will be out before autumn.

My wife sends best wishes with mine to yourself & family & lasting thanks for a great weekend.

Yours sincerely,
Barker Fairley.

1   Fairley had invited MacDiarmid to address a meeting at Manchester University on 10 May 1935.
2   Anne Treneer (1891-1966) published *Charles Doughty : a Study of his prose and verse* (London, 1935).
3   Fairley's *Extracts* was *Selected Passages from The Dawn in Britain*, arranged with an introduction (London, 1935).

95. From Fredric J. Warburg (EUL MS2969)

Broadway House
68-74 Carter Lane
London EC4
29th May 1935

C.M. Grieve, Esq.
Whalsay
Shetland Isles

Dear Mr Grieve,

It is a delicate task I have to undertake in this letter, but I do hope you will let me off as lightly as possible. The fact is that we are so keen to make the greatest possible success of your book on Scottish Eccentrics that we want to recommend certain changes which would in our opinion make it a much more marketable proposition. In view of the vitality which you have infused into the writing and your style, which is not imitable anywhere else, the changes which we suggest are minor, but they are important nevertheless from the point of view of general sales organisation.

First, and most essential, we must ask you to cut as much as possible of your introduction, which is far too specialised for the rest of the book, and to allow us to print it at the end rather than at the beginning. If you could cut it by as much as half, it would be excellent. It is not only the reader who may be put off, but more important to you and to us, it will be the reviewer, and bad reviews, or unintelligent reviews, of a book of this type will not be helpful.

Second, some of the sentences are so long that the ordinary reader will be hard put to follow them through to their logical conclusion, although no doubt they read logically for someone who is used to coping with long sentences. This is really a matter of using more full stops, and involves practically no alteration to the wording. It will save you trouble, and it would be quite easy for us, if you would allow us to put on a thoroughly competent editor to see this done.

This, I think, covers what we want done. It is difficult always to approach an author of your standing in this way, but we are anxious to do as much as we can for the book, and we think that the alterations we suggest will greatly improve the book's chance of success without in any way spoiling your conception of the way the book should be done. If you agree, will you let us know at once, and we will put

Sorley MacLean and Hugh MacDiarmid on Whalsay in 1935. The two poets met for the first time in early 1934 when Sorley MacLean was still completing his studies at Moray House Teachers' Training College. By 1934 MacDiarmid was already interested in Gaelic poetry and in particular that of the 18th-century Jacobite poet Alasdair Mac Mhaighstir Alasdair (Alexander MacDonald). By permission of The MacLean family.

on our best man to shorten the sentences where necessary in the way indicated, and to shorten the introduction. When this is done, we shall, of course, send it to you for final approval.

Yours sincerely,

Fredric J. Warburg (Junior Managing Director [Routledge]) .

96. From Sorley MacLean (EUL MS2954.13 f.14)

Churchton
Raasay
Skye
17 July 1935

Dear Mr Grieve,

I expect to leave Raasay for Shetland next Monday. I don't know yet when I shall arrive or whether I better go by Aberdeen or Wick but I shall find out when I get to Kyle of Lochalsh. At any rate I shall wire you when I found out when the boat arrives at Lerwick. I shall bring all the Gaelic books that I have suitable.

Yours sincerely,

Sam MacLean.

97. From Fredric J. Warburg (EUL MS2969)

Broadway House
68-74 Carter Lane
London EC4
25 July 1935

Dear Mr Grieve,

We have given very careful consideration to your long, reasonable, and reasoned letter of July 21st, in connection with the revision of 'Scottish Eccentrics'.

I have not yet myself found time to read any of your book and cannot therefore speak with that assurance which comes from personal knowledge. I asked Mr Paterson,[1] however, to look carefully into the points raised by our editor, in the light of your reply to them. His view is – and it is one which I provisionally agree with – that the book should be sent to press as it stands. It is clear that our editor and you yourself look at books in general, and this book in particular, from such poles apart, that by no conceivable conjunction of circumstances could you write a book which would satisfy him. As you say, however, you have written the book that is in you to write, and I do not think we can reasonably ask for more, even though the book you have written is by no means the book we envisaged when we commissioned it.

I have therefore given instructions for your book to be sent to press and proofs will be sent to you as soon as they are available. We are adopting your suggestion for order and hope there will be no further trouble about this worrying affair – worrying both to you and to ourselves.

As for your book 'Red Scotland', I think Mr Paterson has already written you telling you that this is twice the length required for the series and will therefore have to be drastically cut if it is meant for the series. This, of course, means delay, but if 'Scottish Eccentrics' comes out towards the end of October, we should aim, I think, at publishing 'Red Scotland' in January of 1936.

With kind regards.

Yours sincerely,

Fredric J. Warburg (Junior Managing Director).

---

1   A.J.B. Paterson was Sales Manager.

98. From Rich & Cowan, Publishers (EUL MS2968)

RICH & COWAN LIMITED
Publishers
25 Soho Square
London W1
21 August 1935

Dear Mr Grieve,

We have now had our reader's report on 'The Wolf of Badenoch', and I regret that we cannot accept the manuscript as fulfilling the provisions of the contract.[1]

In addition to the fact that the manuscript did not arrive until about eleven months after the date contracted for delivery, it is also more than 10 000 words short of the agreed contract length, being less than 50 000 words.

Also, in our view, the manuscript does not come out as the 'popular biography' for which we contracted; nor does it fulfil the expectation aroused by your letter of December 14th, 1934 in which you said you were 'certain that the story of the Wolf lends itself to very effective treatment along vivid popular lines'.

Further, of the 162 pages which the manuscript contains, all but 51 pages are Mrs Wells's original script, practically untouched by you.

In the circumstances we must return the manuscript to you with very much regret, as not fulfilling the terms of our contract, with the request that you will refund to us the £15 already advanced to you on account.[2]

Yours very truly,

[signature illegible].

---

1   'The Wolfe of Badenoch' is included in ' Notes on our Forerunners', *The Voice of Scotland*, vol.1, no.4 (March-May 1939), pp. 7-11. There are also references to him in *Lucky Poet*, pp. 210-217 and 365-6.
2   Rich & Cowan had advanced £15 to Hugh MacDiarmid on 12 April 1934. The MS of 'The Wolf(e) of Badenoch' had been received by Rich and Cowan on 16 July 1935 (EUL MS2968).

99. *From Valda Grieve (NLS MS27149 ff.76-78)*

Isle of Whalsay
Tuesday evening
[10 September 1935]

My dearest Christopher,

How awfully glad I was to get your letter – but so sorry you've had such a wretched week – poor darling – I do hope you'll soon be better – I hear the News – is fairly satisfactory – a general infection – which can be cured with arsenic injections – I note you said the Dr could not tell when you contracted it – I hardly expected him to do that – Did you? – You're the only person, old dear, who can have a rough sort of idea of that – Why don't you speak up – it would certainly give Dr Chambers a better idea of things – every little helps in these matters, you know – Quite frankly – I think you knew about it & that Peggy did also – otherwise it seems very strange – that two people living in close proximity to each other could go as long – as you & Peggy without any sexual relations at all – the last time I saw you – you said you'd asked Peggy last year 'if Christine had Hutchison's teeth'[1] – why on earth should you do that – if you had never been affected – ? Of course if you deny it – that's that – the only other thing is – last year – if you choose to waste your substance on such women as Annie Neel Duff & etc – it is your own look out – I suppose – but you should also remember your responsibilities – your work – James Michael & myself –.

I've had two very kind letters from your brother – he is holidaying in the Isle of Mull – but coming back next week – but then, you'll have got his note by now – I expect.

I think he wants to come up & see you – you should let him – after all – he's your brother & it is nice to be friendly with one another.

I glad you did not see Helen – I had a letter from her – saying 'She'd stayed the night in Perth & had rung up the Hospital – but as the Matron who knew all about you was out – she did not go up.'[2] Ha! Ha!

I meant to write you a long newsy letter – but I'm decidedly tired – Have hurled 30 bags of peat home to day – my back feels as if its permanently bent – neck sore & aching of the skin of the palm of my hands – What a life.

JM & I are managing 'no sae bad' – I find I can live on 10/- week – which is something – .

I miss the 'Mails' these days – only one by the last Mail & that from your brother – none for you – Routledges are getting on with 'Scottish Eccentrics' – so you need not – worry about that –

Now – Christopher dear – is there anything you want –? or would like? – do let me know – if it is possible we'll get it for you – I'm enclosing a few papers –nothing exciting – still they may pass the time a bit for you.

All love – JM sends kisses & hugs

Valda

---

[1]   'Hutchison's teeth' is the term applied to the narrowed and notched permanent incisor teeth which occur in congenital syphilis. They are so named after Sir Jonathan Hutchison

(1828-1913), the London physician who first described them. *Black's Medical Dictionary*, London, 1999, p.258.

2 'Helen' was Helen Cruickshank (1886-1975).

3 At this time MacDiarmid was in The Gilgal hospital, Perth.

100. From Robin Black (EUL MS2942.11 ff.39-40)

The Scots Free Press
1 India Buildings
Victoria Street
Edinburgh
17 September 1935

My Dear Chris,

Even as you were writing to me on Friday I was busy in Oban over our project, & I got your letter on my return.[1] I have made some headway, but my plans want some readjustment in view of one interview which took place just a few minutes before train-time.

Here's the problem. I've no doubt a positively 'left' paper is wanted, & will get support, but it must start small & grow slowly. For that I worked out £750-£950 capital & see no serious obstacle to getting it. What arose at interview in question was a scheme for big thing with plant etc & a capital of £7000 or so. The man in question has dough & moves where dough is in tankfuls! But for the fact that he has an axe to grind I'd be chary of his optimism – but he has an axe! Likewise he's a grinder! Now, we could have & hold a sweeping proposition I fancy, but not of the left! Neither would it be of the right – *but tending there*! Query, can we use them & ultimately hold the grip or –? The one spells power from the word go, & the other – well you understand. Again I'm torn by a subtle pull. The proposed premises under the big scheme occupy the site my father held! It is so easy to fool ourselves! However, meantime I ponder the quandary but will drive with developments before deciding. For the present, as it will take a wee while for things to mature, what about you & Valda coming to Edinburgh? You certainly cannot trek north again. 'Sides which, you deil, I'm needing & wanting you.

Esh! it was good to see your fist again & to hear of progress. Keep it up, for Alba's sake – it's all that matters to us anyway.

Margaret's address is 2 Park Terrace & she'll be prood to see you.[2] Just above Kelvingrove Park, & drop a p.c. so's she'll be in.

Now, dear man, I maun gang, as I have 192 ½ things that all want to be done at once – & how fervently whiles I wish they didn't! 'New Scotland' & other projects are moving, & I'm getting some guid folk – unsullied by nituritism about me – & the more the better.[3]

I have a long tale to unfold but wait to get near your lugs. How soon?

Say when, & let it be quickest possible. I might see you in Glasgow?

My love to you.

Robin.

1   Correspondence about 'the Oban project' continued into 1936 but the venture was never realised. Black's attempt to start a paper to be called 'Pro Patria' also foundered.
2   'Margaret' was Robin Black's wife.
3   *New Scotland* commenced publication weekly on 12 October 1935, sub-titled '*Alba Nuadh* with which is incorporated *The Free Man*'. It ran until June-July 1936. Later Black revived *The Free Man* in reduced form from 1938 to 1947. On 17 July 1933 Black had founded groups of Free Scots to advocate Douglas economics. In *Scottish Scene* Lewis Grassic Gibbon wrote, 'And I like the thought of Mr R. M. Black and his mysterious Free Scots, that modern Mafia, assassinating the Bankers (which is what bankers are for)....' (The National Book Association edn, n.d., London and Melbourne, p.118). He also founded *Scottish Cycling News* on 1 February 1934. He seems to have coined the word 'nituritism'.

101. From Peggy Grieve (NLS MS27148 f.40)

66 Victoria Street
Westminster SW1
20 September 1935

My dear Chris,

I am vastly sorry you have been so ill & that you are still in need of rest. I telephoned Dr Valentine[1] when I was home – I only came back here on Monday – & he had not returned – otherwise I should have seen you. I did see Scott the day I took the bairns to St. Andrews – crossing the Links – but I did not risk a snub.

The 'case' is dormant at the moment – no news.[2] I wrote you some time ago telling you this & also asking what was wrong with you & if I could help in any way. At the same time I told you that I left McElroy in May or thereabouts & had been living in the Cora Hotel. The letter would be lost, I expect.

Please don't worry your poor head about my troubles. If you are to be at Gilgal some time longer I will take a weekend at home & bring Christine to see you.[3] She is still very fond of you – I tell her that you live away in Shetland & that you work very hard. She sent you a postcard for your birthday I think. She said she had. If I bring her to see you – don't upset her. She is very emotional & the Dr says she mustn't be excited.

Let me know how you are & if I can send you anything or help in any way. You know I will if I can. Meantime the enclosed photographs may interest & please you.[4]

Take care of yourself.

Love.

Peggy.

1   Dr Valentine (1906-2007) was one of the founder-members of the National Party of Scotland. His career was in mental health.
2   The 'case' was the enticement case which Mrs McElroy brought against Peggy in April 1936.
3   Peggy visited Gilgal on 28th September but did not bring Christine. F. G. Scott was there at the same time.
4   'The enclosed photographs' were photographs of Christine and Walter.

141

102. From Peggy Grieve (NLS MS27148 f.41)

66 Victoria Street
Westminster SW1
1 October 1935

My dear Chris,

Many thanks for your letter and for the kindly thought which prompted it. Please do not worry about my train fare to Scotland – that is a matter for myself only. I have never said I was desperate for money. I'm not. I have simply told the truth which is that I have no funds behind me – only my salary and if I lose my job here will have nothing at all. That is the simple truth. Whatever has been said in Scotland has been said spitefully.

With regard to your other letter – I got a terrific shock. All I can do now is to have the children's blood tested – likewise my own.

So far as you yourself are concerned, take the advice of a friend and stay where you are for a month more. You are not yet fit to fight the everyday things especially under the conditions depicted to me. You will be being unfair not only to yourself but to Valda – who must have a fund of courage beyond comprehension. As a friend, please consider this and stay where you are getting well. You will hold the Oban job down all the better for it. If you like, I will pay Valda's expenses down to her people in Cornwall. She would be among her own people and you would not have the feeling that she was alone. Consider it as a loan if you like. Meantime, we will look around and see what else can be got for you somewhere or other, if the Oban scheme falls through. I'm not trying to persuade you against your will – simply putting the case to you as I am sure you would do to me under similar circumstances. I got a terrific shock when I saw you – give yourself a chance now. You aren't fit to battle with with cold and wet and discomfort yet. If you agree to this, let me know at once and I'll wire Valda the money. Only, please do not let anyone know I have done anything. They think I am bad – let them think it.

I am very busy and very tired. So much to do and only one pair of hands to do it.

Blessings!

Peggy.

103. From George Elder Davie (EUL MS2946.12 ff.1-2)

37 Albany Terrace
Dundee
1 October 1935

Dear Mr Grieve,

I am very glad to learn that you are on the road to recovery, and am deeply indebted to you for putting yourself at such a time to the trouble of writing so full a letter. But speed, as you say, is essential. You shall therefore, when you board the Lerwick boat at Leith on Thursday, receive a sort of prolegomena to your campaign, including vital facts and accurate references as well as my tentative suggestions for the details of the programme, which, once criticised, corrected and augmented by yourself, will supply the topics for the manifesto. On Wednesday, I am to be in Edinburgh, where I will complete my researches into the Rectorial problem and get in touch with Douglas Stewart, and I will probably remain till Thursday.

Without knowing your requirements, I worked on Buchanan in August, and was turning my attention to Boyd and Johnston when news of your illness made me postpone translation. You will see my renderings of Buchanan on your return to Whalsay, and, since you need but one poem, I think you will agree that a complete version of the 'Epithalamium' is the best choice. I will therefore send up in translation the parts I left untranslated, if you so request, within a week's time. Boyd's and/or Johnston's representative poetry will follow about a week later.[1]

As I have managed to secure *Towards a New Scotland* [2] for reviewing in *The Student*, I will take the opportunity of making clear your literary stature to the University. In this connection, would you be so good as to let me know the 'source' where I can find the context of Mirsky's weighty pronunciation on the covers of *Scottish Scene*?[3]

I am sure that with your health restored and with the aid of a congenial climate you will soon be crowning your excellent translations from the Gaelic with original masterpieces whose splendour will astonish and delight more than Scotland.

I am,

Yours very respectfully,

G.E. Davie.

---

[1] 'Epithalamium for Mary Stuart and the Dauphin of France' and 'Of the Sad Lot of the Humanists in Paris', translated into English from the Latin of George Buchanan (1506-1582), and 'A Fisher's Apology', translated into English from the Latin of Arthur Johnstone (1587-1641), were published in *Golden Treasury of Scottish Poetry*, pp. 3-9, 25-29 and 217-230. Although MacDiarmid acknowledges George Davie's 'assistance' in his Introduction, he does not claim that he (MacDiarmid) translated the poems himself in the text. Parts of Davie's translations still exist in the National Library of Scotland: MS27077 f.29r. and ff.30-31(both r. and v.) for 'Of the Sad Lot of the Humanists in Paris', and MS 27077 ff.32-35(rectos) for 'A Fisher's Apology'.

[2] *Towards a New Scotland* was a selection from *The Modern Scot,* edited by J.H. Whyte with music by F.G. Scott, and four illustrations (London, 1935).

[3] 'Ever since I encountered Hugh MacDiarmid's poetry, I have recognised him as one of the few living poets of the European world' was a paraphrase of the first sentence of Mirsky's letter of 26 October 1931.

104. From I. J. C. Rankin (EUL Gen. 2094/5/1875)

Post card from I.G.C. Rankin in Gilgal, Perth

23 October 1935

Many thanks for p.c. Glad to hear you survived the stormy passage, & are progressing favourably. 4 new patients, but our Bridge 4 has broken up! yours v. sincerely

Yours v. sincerely,
I.J.C. Rankin.

105. From W. Ballingall (EUL Gen. 2094/1/62)

CARD

23 October 1935

Many thanks for P.C. Very glad you reached home. *Mens sana in corpore sano.* Weather here climatic but not too bad. Snow on Grampians. Several changes here – one or two have left while others arrive. – Enjoyed a card party down below in Matron's Room. I am very well. Business at home going very well. Kind regards from those you met here including Sister Duff and myself. Yrs W. Ballingall

106. From John G. Anderson (EUL MS2966)

East Hamister
Whalsay
4 November 1935

Dear Mr Grieve,

I would be very much obliged if you would settle up with me for the remaining part of the payment on the house at Sodom viz £15.

If you could manage it at any time in the near future it would much oblige
Yours faithfully,
John G. Anderson.

P.S. I will get you a proper receipt for the full amount, when the payment is complete. J.G.A.

107. From J. U. Bruce (NLS Acc. 7361/6)

Gilgal
Perth
15 December 1935

Dear Mr Grieve,

I have to thank you ever so much for your kind letter and for being so kind as to remember my jumper.

I would like one with a fawn background, square neck and the sleeves would need to be extra long.[1]

There is nothing new here. All the people that were here during your stay are away with the exception of Mr Rankin and Mr Stewart.

With that recent frost the gentlemen had several days curling which spared them going to the verandah in am.

I must now close trusting this finds you well & fit and enjoying good health. Once again thanking you for your kindness.

Wishing you all a very happy Xmas & a bright & prosperous 1936.

Yrs sincerely,

J.U. Bruce.

[1]   MacDiarmid must have mentioned his wife's Shetland knitting.

108. From Roderick Watson Kerr (EUL MS2951.12 f.4)

8 Buckingham Avenue
Sefton Park
Liverpool
6 January 1936

Dear Chris,

Your exceedingly kind letter awoke many memories in us, we have one of you sitting by the fireside in our front room with our little boy standing between your knees, gazing, fascinated, at your face. You put your hand on his head and he is so pleased. I also see myself on the first day of my Broughton School days gazing, fascinated, across the road at a shining personality among a group of shadows: you. And I have never forgotten that picture.

Yes, Chris, my wife and I are deeply touched, and we both feel grateful that you wish to pay a tribute to our little boy or to his memory in a poem.[1] We shall treasure it and feel it to be ours in a peculiar sense.

Hamish Kerr   Born 28 June 1928
Died 20 November 1931

There's a bitter-sweet short story for you, Chris.

Kindest greetings to you and your wife from my wife and myself and a Happy New Year.

R. Watson Kerr.

[1]   In an earlier letter R. Watson Kerr, 17 December 1935, had written, 'We lost our little boy some years ago: acute appendicitis: a terrible experience for us.' (EUL MS2951.12 f.2r.). It is not clear whether such a poem was written.

109. From A. J. B. Paterson, Routledge (EUL MS2969)

Broadway House
68-74 Carter Lane
London EC4
15 January 1936

My dear Chris,

This is one of those letters which should be worded with the delicacy of a diplomat. But as I am incapable of any such subtleties, I ask you to take all this for granted.

'Red Scotland' has arrived safely and has been read and returned here with a most discouraging report. It is apparently our reader's considered opinion that in its form it lacks sufficient appeal to return the cost of its preparation for publication. My directors feel it is only fair to acquaint you with this reaction and to express their doubt as to the advisability of publishing the book. Of course, there remains the fact that we have agreed to do so, but, in view of their lack of enthusiasm, you might prefer to offer it elsewhere, a course to which my directors have agreed. On their part they would pay you the balance of advance due, and any money you received from another publisher by way of advance on 'Red Scotland' could be refunded to Routledge. Here is the reader's report to which I refer:

Report for Mr Paterson on 'Red Scotland'

'My criticisms of the above manuscript are as follows:

1) That the theme in itself can only have a limited public unless it is developed and written with real poetic fervour and enthusiasm, in a style that would hypnotise the general public, even against its will, into reading it. While MacDiarmid is undoubtedly capable of producing such a book, he has certainly not done so here. Here and there there are passages which show what he might and could have done, but he makes all his points and develops his whole theme almost by the use of lengthy quotations from other people's works. Well over fifty per cent of the book consists of quotations, not all of them apt, and none of them, I think, written with the fervour and power which the author himself could have instilled into the argument, had he chosen to state it in his own words.

2) That there are passages here and there which are definitely libellous, and would inevitably lead to prosecution and / or the suppression of the book were they published – notably references to the King and Queen and the Royal Family, the Duke of Kent / Princess Marina wedding, and the Queen and the new giant Cunarder.

The latter criticism could be dealt with simply by excision, but the former is a much more serious criticism. Quite frankly, I can see no sale for this book at all. Whether the author has deliberately used the method of quotation I don't know, but this method would undoubtedly be an insuperable handicap to the success of the book. It is a pity, because there is not the slightest doubt that MacDiarmid could write a first-class book on this subject, which would galvanise people into thought and life, if he only would write it out of his own mind.'

I am truly sorry about this development but I know you will appreciate my predicament. Perhaps you would think over my suggestion and let me have your reactions.

Hope you are feeling fitter and experiencing no ill effects from this wretched weather.

Yours aye,

Pat.

110. From John Purves (EUL Gen. 2094/4/1865)

The University
Edinburgh
17 February1936

Dear Mr Grieve,

It is a pleasure to give you the information for which you ask.

Folengo's dates are 1496 to 1544; and his chief works are the *Moschaea* (a poem in three books in macaronic verse, telling of a war between the Ants and the Flies); the *Zanitonella* (a parody, also in macaronic verse, of the Virgilian-Petrarcan eclogue); the *Baldus* (in 17 cantos, 1516: a parody in macaronic verse of the romantic (Carolingian) epic); the *Orlandino* (1526), in Italian octaves, a kind of vernacular *Baldus*; and several minor works: *Il Caos del Triferuno* (1527), an allegorical hotchpotch in prose and verse, Italian, Latin & Macaronic; an *Alto della Pinta* (1539), a 'rappresentazione drammatica', or miracle play, written for a church in Palermo, dealing with the Creation of the World & the Incarnation; and *L'Umanità del Figlinol di Dio* in Italian octaves.[1]

There is an interesting account of Folengo, with specimens of his macaronic verse, in De Sanctis' *History of Italian Literature*, Chap. XIV; and a still fuller account in Giuseppe Toffanin's *Il Cinquecento* (pp.310-331). If you would care to have extracts from either of these, I shall be glad to let you have them. There is something about him in J.A. Symonds's *Renaissance*.

With kind regards,

Yours sincerely,

John Purves.

---

[1] *In Memoriam James Joyce* (Glasgow, MacLellan 1955) was originally conceived as 'In Memoriam Teofilo Folengo'.

111. From Caroline Doughty (EUL MS2962.3 f.21)

Merriecroft
Cranbrook
Kent
8 March [1936]

Dear Mr MacDiarmid,

Thank you very much for sending me your article on my husband's poetry,[1] you are wonderfully generous in your praise but I must say my breath was quite taken away by the first sentence!! The U.S.S.R. was anathema to my husband! & how you can think of Lenin and C.M.D. at the same time passes my comprehension. I think if you had *known* my husband you would have thought differently.

You are one of the *very* few who really enter into his poetry. I hope your article may open some people's eyes. I hope Mr Robbin's book will not be very much longer before it is ready.[2] Mrs Treener's and Prof. Fairley's were delightful; of course, you know that *Adam Cast Forth* is being translated in Germany.[3]

With kind regards & many thanks.

Yours sincerely,

C. A. Doughty.

1   *Charles Doughty and the need for Heroic Poetry* (St Andrews, 1936) was a reprint of an article in *The Modern Scot,* vol. 6, no. 4 (January 1936).
2   Not identified.
3   *Adam Cast Forth* (London, 1908).

112. From John MacNair Reid (EUL MS2958.15 ff.4-6)

Woodside
Thorntonhall
Lanarkshire
9 March 1936

My Dear Grieve,

I have just read *Scottish Eccentrics,*[1] and I'd like to be numbered among those who as your admirers think the thing a real triumph in polemical writing. I haven't enjoyed any book on Scotland so much for a long while, and I thought I'd drop you a note to say so.

Although not hearing from you or writing you, I've known roughly of your movements from mutual friends & I was genuinely distressed to hear of your illness. I hope you are completely recovered now. I see you are broadcasting soon. That's an important date for my humble wireless set! Are you coming to Edinburgh? And if so, will there be a chance of your visiting Glasgow?

I have gone some way in emulating you in one thing – my health has petered out. According to doctors, including my wife,[2] I have little chance of continuing my present rush – & – tumble life. A spell – of a year at least – of rather quiet rest is ordered.

It's a blow, and a great worry. But I suppose it must be faced.

The boys here, in Glasgow, are having some lively meetings.[3] It's just possible that in a year or so Glasgow may be an interesting – and vital – place. I hope so indeed; it's been dead long enough.

James Barke, the writer of some three novels of the Highlands (he was, I believe, born in Galloway) is a Communist with a punch.[4] He's after blood all the time – a long time before the official revolution. He is one who makes Glasgow more promising; and there are others. But I may have to leave it all.

Meantime, is it too much to hope that I may see you on your visit south? Please do let me know.

Yours very warmly,

[John] MacNair Reid

1   London: Routledge, 1936.
2   His wife was Josephine Shepherd.
3   'The boys' were MacNair Reid's journalist colleagues.
4   James Barke (1905-58) was not born in Galloway, his parents were. His first three novels were *The World His Pillow* (1933), *The Wild Macraes* (1934), and *The End of the High Bridge* (1935).
     He supported the policies of the Communist Party in the 1930s but whether or not he joined the Party cannot be established.

113. From Pittendrigh MacGillivray (EUL MS2954.5 f.20)

Ravelston Elms
Murrayfield Road
Edinburgh
12 March 1936

Well, my dear C.M.G. ...

I have been hearing about you lately – and I have just written a letter to Montrose to [William] Lamb – and of course Montrose brings you to mind.[1] ... And, lately I got your address – quite out of the common world!! ... As things go with me, I am practically out of the world too – 'brothers in misfortune'!!

I wish we could turn back to that Sunday morning up on Corstorphine, when wandering along among the trees and in sight of vistas of land and sea, we got a psychic glimpse of each other. – Neither of us have gone back on that quiet Sunday morning contact – so far as I know. I am writing because I have heard that affairs do not go well with you – and to express a hope that circumstance will yet take a turn for the better with you.

Whatever I may hear of you I do not forget our contact and that in speaking of me – quite with[out] any *arrière-pensée* – you gave me courage – and something of spiritual understanding serious, and far removed from empty puffery!

If you feel in the mood to write to me, I shall be glad to hear ... .

With kind wishes,

Sincerely yours,

Pittendrigh MacGillivray.

I reach my four score on the 30th of May next – ending in material circumstances – as I began – with nothing! Spiritually, of course, that is as it ought to be!

1   MacGillivray's punctuation has been retained here. The ellipses do not indicate omissions.

114. From Pittendrigh MacGillivray (EUL MS2976)

Ravelston Elms
Murrayfield Road
Edinburgh

29 March 1936

My dear Grieve,

I am glad to have yours of the 23rd inst: and to find it, in mood and temper as I, confidently, expected it. I am old enough in experience of life to understand much, and to look without anger or blame on much that seems faulty and unpardonable ... I have only to look within and remember. If I have not been so unfortunately bad or blameworthy as I might have been, I must thank the stars of my inheritance rather than my native impulses... ... Nowadays, I do not blame any human ... I know that wherever there is fault, there shall surely be punishment – somewhere, sometime – . That law is inexorable; and, no doubt, in your recent illness you have had ample time to worry over it:- that you have come out top dog with your *mea culpa* is all to the good .... Many times I have thought of *you* .... without forgetting your, true as steel, honest, wee Peggy. ....And, as you know, have regretted your leaving poor, bare Scotland for that lee shore of hell! – London.

. . . . . .

Often I wish I were away on some far lone isle – as you are now. – from what I feel to be very evil conditions. – where the tumour of wrongness is fast swelling to a burst.... The Russians were lucky to get through.. but now, I feel, they are heading for the curse of machinery ... maybe – meantime – in self-defence.

. . . . . .

I note that you hope to be in Edinburgh in the summer and shall look forward to seeing you. I think you will like my Exhibition... And there will be a lingering walk on Corstorphine hill-wood, where things fundamental may become articulate.

With all kind wishes.

Yours as ever.

Pittendrigh MacGillivray.

115. From William Power (EUL MS2958.11 f.13)

Associated Scottish Newspapers Ltd
67 Hope Street
Glasgow C2
3 April 1936

My dear Grieve,

I have to-day remitted £111-2-9 to the Commercial Bank of Scotland Ltd, Lerwick, to be placed to the credit, in a joint account, of yourself and Mrs Grieve. This is the total sum subscribed to date, less expenses of postages and printing and the album.[1] I wish it had been more, but I hope it may be of use to you.

I enclose another signature for affixing on the last page of the album.

I think it would be an excellent idea for you to establish a regular journalistic connection that would bring you in a steady four pounds a week, without compromising you poetically or philosophically in any way. Lewis Grassic Gibbon ought to have done this. Mr William Will[2] would advise you as to this. It would leave you absolutely free on the creative side.

With best wishes.
Yours aye,
Wm. Power.

---

[1]   Power refers to the Testimonial presented to MacDiarmid (cf. *Lucky Poet*, pp. 41-43).
[2]   Author and journalist. Burns scholar.

116. From Mlle H. A. Valette (EUL MS2970)

Blace
Rhône
Monday 6 April 1936

Dear Mr MacDiarmid,
It was a great relief and joy to hear that you liked your lyrics in their new French dress[1] – though I am afraid Mr Scott will say they don't match his music at all. I tried to render the meaning & spirit and so had to leave the rhythm untranslated. I don't think a compromise between the two would be satisfactory. But it would be rather exciting to do a special French version to fit the settings. I don't know them so will have to get at a few people to let me hear them when I am back in Manchester after April 23rd. I hope your visit will not be before that date as I should much like to meet you. If you come in June I shall have had more time to consider & attempt further translations. The new French poetry review you are to appear in is not out yet but ought to be shortly.
   Yours sincerely,
   A. Valette.

[1]   EUL MS2954.16 ff.160 and 161 has H.A. Valette's translations of 'The Bonnie Broukit Bairn', 'The Eemis Stane', 'Crowdieknowe', 'O Jesu Parvule', 'Hungry Waters' and 'Moonstruck'. As these two folios are pages 1 and 3 of the TS, page 2 appears to have been lost or misplaced. They were found in the file of William MacLellan's letters to MacDiarmid. 'Moonstruck' ('Luné') appeared in *Adam*, September 1948.

117. From Pittendrigh MacGillivray (EUL MS2976)

Ravelston Elms
14 April 1936

My dear Grieve,
I have your kind letter – and am pleased anent what you express about Spence[1] ... I have just written to him asking that the hatchet between you should be buried.... I think you have written handsomely; and that, between you, there should be no more playing at impossible French and German games! – nae mair flightin's! in the Auld Menner:- makin' yersel's a kind o' scandle to the young scribes!.....
   It is very good and kind of you to think of something to mark my eightieth birthday but I have no idea of what it might be – only I do not want anything in the

way of money. – I have, in pensions, £230 a year, and I sit here rent-free at the hands of Lord Bute! But, alas! I have to keep a man – £75 – taxes £33. Housekeeper £43 – leave me too bare for upkeep, personal and household.

I have sold nothing through the last two years – and *somehow* – however unwilling! – I must get out of here or risk getting into *debt*: ... I am busy with that idea at present.....

I look forward to seeing you at the end of the week – some time. Would Sunday forenoon or afternoon suit you? – you'll write and let me know.

With all kind wishes.

Yours ever,

Pittendrigh MacGillivray.

I wish I could go to Cunninghame Graham's funeral[2] – quite a historic event. I suppose I am now 'the faither' of the PEN ... I would deem it a great honour to follow him: if that might be.

[1]   MacDiarmid had lampooned him as 'the bald-faced Spence' in 'Welcome to the PEN delegates', *C.P.* II, pp. 1299-1302.
[2]   R. B. Cunninghame Graham (1852-1936) had been a radical Liberal (elected to Parliament in 1886), then militant socialist, and finally founder-member of the National Party of Scotland. He had estates in Scotland and Argentina and was the author of a variety of literary works.

118. From Catherine Carswell (EUL MS2946.1 f.22)

International Association of Writers for the
Defence of Culture
(British Section)
ROMNEY'S HOUSE, HOLLYBUSH HILL, LONDON, N.W.3
English Members of International Committee:
E. M. FORSTER, ALDOUS HUXLEY, VIRGINIA WOOLF
Executive Committee:
LASCELLES ABERCROMBIE, JAMES HANLEY, GERALD HEARD, CECIL
DAY LEWIS, SIEGFRIED SASSOON, HUGH WALPOLE, AMABEL
WILLIAMS-ELLIS

17 Keats Grove
London NW3
17 May 1936

My dear Christopher,

I never thanked you your letters giving the required references (the sources *were* a disappointment, but never mind).

This, among other things [,] is to suggest that you cough up 10/- (yes, I know, but we are all Jock Tamson's bairns there) and join the above Association if you haven't already done so. I felt I had to as there is nothing else of the sort except the P.E.N., which, being strictly non-political, is different. This means out & out anti-fascism for members. All the most distinguished French writers of the Left are members & the Conference in Paris was a great success last summer I understand. I was asked to go & to speak, but couldn't rise to it financially or otherwise. Now, Chris think about this, & if you decide to come in, write direct to Amabel Williams-Ellis. They will welcome suggestions from members.

So far Valda has not given tongue, but I daresay she hadn't time. I hope she's well now, & the boy, and you.

This has been a tough winter, but we have made another spring.

'Another spring, the heart exulting cries', as the bad poet Bloomfield says.[1] But how much better the Italian proverb for which we have no equivalent – the blackbird is supposed to utter it – 'Now the winter is past, I fear thee no longer, oh Lord!'

Anyhow I seem to have lots of work, if most of it is very ill paid. Don[2] has had a slack time, but is thinking of another book, playing with the notion of another play & building on a fortune from the one that is to be produced – D.V. – in August. May he be right! John[3] is well & working hard & happily.

I wonder if you saw also my review of your *Eccentrics* in *The Spectator*? I hope the book is going as well as can be expected. The proofs of our Week-End book [4] --interminably held up – have not yet come home, & now the book won't be out till late autumn or even Christmas. Blast all publishers! I suppose you heard that Paterson has given up this calling to keep a pub. in Wilts or Berks or somewhere truly rural?

I'm moving surely & rapidly toward the Left – & by that I mean Communism. It has taken me some time.

Ever yours,
Cathie.

[1] ' "Another SPRING!" his heart exulting cries', is a line from 'The Farmer's Boy' by Robert Bloomfield (1766-1823). In *Wiltshire Essays* (1921) Maurice Henry Hewlett said, 'Bloomfield was a bad poet, Clare was a good one.'
[2] Donald Carswell, her husband.
[3] John Carswell, their son.
[4] *The Scots Week-End*, edited by Donald and Catherine Carswell (London, 1936), had five MacDiarmid items.

119. From Helen Cruickshank (EUL MS2946.9 ff.16-18)

Office
18 June 1936

Dear Chris,

'Mountains between us and the waste of seas' – but I re-awake from a gardening dream to say 'how d'ye do' again. One reason for my non-writing is that I had a communication from Peggy, enclosing a letter for *you* which she wished me to hand you – to which I replied, truthfully, that I did not know your whereabouts, & thought

I'd better return the letter to her. Which I did. Since then I had a note from you, wishing me a happy half-century, thank you.

I'm gardening furiously & deliciously every night, have erected my sleeping tent again under the protection of the rowan tree, & sleep peacefully every night. Only once has a cat cried near me, but it was a low mournful 'intimate' cry-in-the-night, as from one woman to another, & I did not resent it. The garden is lovely just now: masses of fat old-fashioned red paeonies & pink & blue lupins.

I haven't heard from V. for weeks, & hope things are going well, or at least, better.

Saw Davey,[1] Caird[2] & Livingstone[3] at WGBM's[4] garden party. About a hundred turned up altho' only seventy accepted! Mary Litchfield in a sensationally-wide scarlet Cardinal hat, with gloves & lips to match; & cloaked in black silk.[5] Tonge[6] brought her over from St A. JHW[7] was then in Barra with the Lorne Campbells.

Attended Grierson's presentation last week & he was in good form, (but Mrs G. was ill with bronchitis). Flora[8] was up with Joan Shelmerdine.[9] They've bought an old car now & find it most useful for their work, which seems to be going well. F. has finished her tome on Aeneas Sylvius.[10] ('Who the dooce was he?' as a sailor uncle of mine always used to say.)

I don't think I've much news, except that I'm having a week's holiday 21st-29th of this month. Spending a weekend in a railway caravan near Benderloch, then ferrying over to the Isle of Lismore (mouth of Loch Linnhe) to complete the week.

I think you expected to be about Langholm near end of this month, or is it July? Let me know. I shall write Valda when I get to Lismore. (Address 'Kilchurn House, Isle of Lismore, Argyll.')

How are the sketches going? And the poems? And your digestion?

Hope all are well.

Love.

Helen.

I don't expect to be away from home all July & August.

You will be sorry to know Mother F.A. Forbes died last week. I am so sorry you never met her. A grand woman & a fine intellect.

[1] George Elder Davie.
[2] James B. Caird.
[3] David Livingstone, contemporary student.
[4] W.G. Burn-Murdoch (1862-1939), artist and explorer.
[5] Communist ex-teacher who played a social role in writers' lives.
[6] John Tonge.
[7] James H. Whyte.
[8] Flora Marian, not identified.
[9] Published *Introduction to Woodstock* (with drawings by Ian MacNab, Woodstock, 1951).
[10] Pope Pius II (1405-1464) was Pope from 1458-1464. He was known in literature as Aeneas Sylvius or Silvius.

120. From James H. Whyte (EUL MS2941.14 ff.42-43)

OUTLOO[1]

6 Old Gloucester St
London WC1
25 June [1936]

My dear Grieve,

I am hastening to reply to your letter of the 22nd which has just reached me here in order to put an end to a very unfortunate misunderstanding which seems to have arisen between us. It is quite true that I am not anxious to publish your letter to OUTLOOK, but my reasons for not wishing to do so are very different from what you imagine.

Edwin Muir's article is, in the first place, a chapter from his forthcoming book on Scott in the *Voice of Scotland* series and was not specially commissioned.[2] It was certainly never published in order to cast any aspersions upon your reputation, only to state a thesis which, however misguided you may consider it, is at any rate an interesting one. I think you do Muir a grave injustice by interpreting in a personal manner what is only part of a much wider issue – as well as to me by identifying me with all of Muir's opinions. I showed your letter to various mutual friends – Mary Ramsay[3] and George Scott-Montcrieff [4]– and they were quite unanimous that such a letter would do far more harm than good to the ideas for which you stand. Mary Ramsay is writing a letter which we shall print in our July issue stating her own objections to Muir's attitude and if you like to continue the discussion further in our following number I should be very happy.[5] I must, however, make it clear that I cannot undertake to publish indiscriminate abuse of Muir himself or complete denigration of his critical abilities in other spheres for which you have had so much admiration in the past. What I want is an objective article dealing with the issues involved in a dispassionate fashion.

I am well aware of the shortcomings of *Outlook*, but still confident that it has a future and that it is getting in touch with a new and more varied public, which has hitherto taken no interest in the Scottish Movement. I know that in the process many of our old interests have to be curtailed but there is still room for the good stuff as well. It is a pity if Mr. G.E. Davie thinks that he has been 'snubbed' – that is another example of making the wish father to the thought. We are willing to give expression in *Outlook* to every point of view and every topic provided that it is of some general interest and not the ventilation of some purely personal grievance.

With best wishes to you all,

Yours sincerely,

James H. Whyte.

---

[1] The spirit of the times is shown by the removal of the 'K' from the letterhead leaving 'OUTLOO' or 'outside toilet' - presumably by Valda. *Outlook* had been formed by the union of *The Modern Scot* with *Scottish Standard*. J. H. Whyte was the literary editor. It ran for ten monthly issues – April 1936 to January 1937- and was published in Glasgow.

²   *Outlook* had published 'A Literature Without a Language', by Edwin Muir, in its third issue (June 1936), pp. 84-89. MacDiarmid was not mentioned in this excerpt, although he is discussed elsewhere in Muir's *Scott and Scotland* (London, 1936). The June issue of *Outlook* also contained MacDiarmid's story, 'Aince There, Aye There: A Shetland Story'.

³   Dr Mary Ramsay, secretary of the independent nationalist 1935 Group, at this time.

⁴   George Scott-Moncrieff (1910-1974) edited *Scottish Country: fifteen essays by Scottish Authors* (London, 1935) . MacDiarmid's contribution was ' In the Shetland Islands', pp. 119-137.

⁵   Mary Ramsay's letter in the July issue of *Outlook* was dated 11 June 1936.

121. From Caroline Doughty (EUL MS2962.3 f.22)

Merriecroft
Cranbrook
Kent
26 June [1936]

Dear Mr MacDiarmid,

I thank you very much for your kind letter & for the book¹ that soon followed it; I think it so extraordinarily kind of you to have taken the trouble to write an explanation of the difficult passages in your charming memorial poem for my husband. I thank you writing such delightful things about him, 'the supreme human serenity' *does* delight me, also the last four lines of the poem. I have so often *felt* that, & now you have put it into words!

When I read the 'Raised Beach' too, although I do not understand the geological terms, still, I see so much in it that he loved & wondered about, I wish you could have met him.

With very many thanks for giving me so much pleasure.

Yours sincerely,

Caroline Doughty.

¹   It appears that MacDiarmid had sent a copy of *Stony Limits and Other Poems* which included 'Stony Limits (In Memoriam : Charles Doughty, 1843-1926)', *C.P.* I, pp. 419-422, and ' On a Raised Beach', *C.P.* I, pp.422-433.

122. From Lawrence & Wishart (EUL MS2968)

LAWRENCE AND WISHART LTD.
Publishers

2 Parton Street
London WCl

C.M. Grieve Esq.
The Shetland Islands

14 July 1936

Dear Sir,

We thank you for the offer of your manuscript 'Red Scotland' and are sorry to have to say that after full consideration we are not able to accept it for publication.

Whilst recognising the brilliance of the book as a polemical work, we feel that a book on such a great and urgent subject should begin on a simpler plane of exposition. We appreciate the fact that the book will be keenly debated in Scotland but we do not feel that in its present form it would reach a large public in England.

We are therefore returning the manuscript to you under separate cover by registered post.

Yours faithfully,

LAWRENCE AND WISHART LTD.[1]

---

[1]   The letter appears to have been signed by D. J. F. Parsons, one of the six directors.

123. From Thomas Douglas MacDonald [Fionn MacColla] (EUL MS2954.3ff.7-8)

Montrose
20 July 1936

A Charaid,

I am returning at once the batch of MSS which has just reached me here as I gather you are anxious that it be sent out as soon as possible & I cannot undertake to despatch it. Mamie[1] is not now able to do more than a very little typing – not more than an hour or so per day – & as we must have the extra income from the N.U.S.[2] this means that I have to do the work myself after my own is over. You will understand therefore that I have neither the time nor the inclination to begin further heavy typing work after all that – it would mean about an 18-20 hour day, & I am not capable of it. So that I fear there is nothing for it but to call off the arrangement we made.

This is our second week here, & to all appearance the weather has completely broken. We have little to complain of, however, & expect to return to Edinburgh much the better of the change. Montrose is much as you left it & quite a number of your old friends & enemies are still to be observed about the streets – Foreman,[3] Christison,[4] Mary Grieve,[5] etc. One damnable thing – the aerodrome has been taken over by the Government as a Flying School & day & night are rendered hideous by the continuous droning of engines. Worst of all, this has meant a huge influx of Sasunnachs & the offensive accent is everywhere to be heard about the streets.

I suppose that by now Valda will have rejoined you & I hope that the trying time she must have had in Cornwall has not prevented her from having in many respects benefited by the change. Please give her my kindest regards.

I am sorry that circumstances should have rendered necessary this abrupt termination of an arrangement that I had hoped would have been helpful. But there is no help for it; as things are it cannot be gone on with. By the way I have 40 pages in duplicate of the Autobiography; do you wish them sent on, or shall I hang on to them yet awhile?

Now to get this off before the post office closes –

With kindest regards from us both to you all,

Tom and Mary MacDonald. 'Tom' was 'Fionn MacColla'.
By permission of the MacDiarmid Estate.

Yours aye,
T. Douglas MacDonald.

[1]   Mary MacDonald, his wife.
[2]   He worked for The New University Society from 1935 to 1938 as a literary advisor.
[3]   James Foreman, proprietor of *Montrose Review*.
[4]   James Christison, Librarian.
[5]   Not identified.

124. From Nan Mercer (EUL MS2954.12 ff.4-5)

42 Auldhouse Rd
Newlands
Glasgow S3
6 August 1936

Dear Mr Grieve,

I received your letter of the 1st inst., and am very interested in what you tell me.

I had heard about your book 'Red Scotland' some time ago, and was very disappointed when it was not published last spring.

Naturally I am very pleased to hear you are contemplating writing about father.[1] We were very disappointed when Mr Maxton's attempt failed, and we have several times been disappointed in other directions.[2] He seems to be a difficult subject! As a matter of fact, I decided several months ago to write a biography myself if I could get nobody else to do so, and since then have been gathering material.

I shall be only too glad to send you anything I have. However, as you already have material, perhaps you will let me know either what sort of material you would like, or give me an idea of what you have. This is because I intend making duplicates of what I send you, as I know already to my cost how easily these things go astray, and naturally I do not want to trouble about anything you already have.

For instance, have you full newspaper accounts of his trials and dismissal? I mean particularly the 1915, 1916 & 1920 trials, as I expect you will have a copy of 'Condemned from the Dock' containing his speech at the 1918 trial. Of course the latter trial was the most important, but there are very interesting points in the others. I have full court reports of the lot, and full newspaper reports of the first three; I am at present going through the files of *The Glasgow Herald*, and have only reached 1917 so far. Mr Maxton did not send me much material, and most of it was about pre-War days. I have pretty full data about that time, as I have just returned from London after making an examination of the files of the old SDF[3] organ, *Justice*, and also several other papers. I shall make copies of my notes for you, if you like.

I have quite a lot of data now, except for the last years of his life. He was writing then in *The Socialist* and I have not yet been able to see the files, and I expect to get something from *The Glasgow Herald* files also. This means that the material I shall be able to send on immediately will be practically limited to pre-War and War years.

I expect you will have all his pamphlets – *Co-operation and the Rise in Prices*, *The Greenock Jungle*, *The Coming War with America*, *The Irish Tragedy: Scotland's Disgrace*, and his Election Addresses.[4] I have quite a few cuttings from newspapers of varied Socialist & other opinions containing obituary appreciations, also letters from organisations and individuals. Then there are his letters from prison, and his letters to my sister and myself just before he died, all giving insight into his personal qualities. Would you like that sort of thing? Or do you intend writing something purely political?

As you say, even if I go on with my own project, as I would like to do, I do not suppose it will clash with yours. My intention is to write a book with the historical side predominant over the personal as much as possible; that is, as much from the Marxist point of view as I can. Thus a lot of the material I have gathered may be quite irrelevant for your purpose.

I hope I have made the position clear, and that you will let me know the sort of things you wish.

Assuring you of my earnest desire to help you,

Yours sincerely,

Nan Mercer.[5]

---

[1]   John MacLean (1879-1923).

[2]   James Maxton (1885-1946) was ILP MP for Bridgeton (Glasgow) from 1922 until his death.

[3]   SDF = Socialist Democratic Federation.

[4]   With the exception of 'The Greenock Jungle' these pamphlets are reprinted in *John MacLean :In the Rapids of Revolution*, edited by Nan Milton (London: Allison & Busby, 1978).

[5]   Nan Mercer (née MacLean) was John MacLean's younger daughter, born in 1913. She later married Ellice Milton.

125. From Mary Ramsay (EUL MS2958.12 ff.73-4)

11 Saxe-Coburg Pl.
Edinburgh 3
7 August [1936]

Dear Christopher,

I have been asked to get your signature if possible for the enclosed letter on the subject of a National Peace Congress. There is to be an International one in Sept. in Brussels to which I hope to go as a delegate: the DSSO is co-operating & the Anti-Conscription League[1] & we are anxious to take the opportunity of showing the Scottish demand for independence – the right to refuse an English War. Wendy Wood & I hope both to be there & a number of Scots are going who will we hope be ready to insist on that *right* at least, even if they are not pledged to Nationalism. The fact that a *National* Congress is to be called thereafter (in spite of some indignation in London I am told, on the grounds that it can't be 'National') is in itself encouraging.

I have been put recently on the Central Committee & was asked to get your name (along with some others, one being Mrs Burnett-Smith, 'Annie Swan').[2] I don't know if you will feel this in or out of harmony with your projected campaign. I see no reason on earth why it should not bear your name myself & I hope it will.

I had the circular[3] by the bye & I have not felt it possible to write on the matter. You know I am to a great extent at least of Communist tendency. I feel Communism can allow full play to the true expression of the National principle, indeed as no other form I know of can. You know also that I feel there must always be 'many mansions' & that I'd rather see yours perfected than some others pulled down! You know too that I feel you have a message, & most of all the voice to utter it which none of the rest of us has. Also that I don't expect always to agree in everything with even my best friends!

I hope you are all keeping fit. I fear the wee boy has not been well from what Helen told me she had heard from Valda, but I hope it was a passing trouble. (I am writing under difficulties – our active & most beloved kitten is rampaging over my desk. I am holding the ink bottle in one hand to prevent an overturn & have just poured some on my own dress & my pen is a special attraction to pussy's paw as it moves over the paper. Do excuse incoherency.) Greetings to [Donald] Gordon[4] if he's still with you.

Love to you all.
Yours for Scotland,
Mary Ramsay.

[PS] I'm not responsible for the headings on the lines for names. They remind me of my eldest nephew's remark at his grandparents' – my parents' – table when (aged about 4) he was told once by his grandmother that he could go & play if he wished & replied, 'I'd rather stay please & hear the conversation – if there *is* to be any!'

[1]   Several organisations opposed conscription at this time.
[2]   Writer of popular romantic fiction (1859-1943).
[3]   The 'circular' was an open letter to J. H. Whyte, printed in *The Letters of Hugh MacDiarmid*, pp.851-4.
[4]   Donald J. Gordon contributed 'Some aspects of Stephen Spender's Poetry' to *Essays in Literature*, edited by John Murray and introduced by Harvey Wood (Edinburgh and London: Oliver & Boyd, 1936), pp.114-128.

126. From Catherine Carswell (EUL MS2946.1 ff.25-29)

Hotel Sauvage
Calais
8 August 1936

My dear Christopher,
I know I have been an unforgivable time in replying to your letter, but I've been on

the move & excessively occupied with keeping going from day to day between work & worries. You will have heard, perhaps, that Brandon Thomas has let Don down badly over the play, going right back on his signed contract & calmly postponing production 'till May' – without any suggestion of compensation, without even so much as an apology. But the theatre is like this, & publishers are angels of punctuality etc. beside producers. It knocked all our summer plans sideways & at first Don was all for going to law with a very good case for damages. But after much discussion it is judged wiser to wait & give the play its chance of being put on in May. It is not likely to be placed elsewhere & even though our confidence in B.T. is badly shaken he still insists that the postponement is due to nothing but his desire to do it justice with the right cast, most of the suitable actors being engaged in two big Scottish films at the moment. Anyhow, that's that.

Now about your anti-white-mouse-faction letter. I sympathise with you about the refusal of *Outlook* to publish your letter. The same happened once to me with *Time and Tide*, only it was in some respects worse because I sent a letter elicited by a letter attacking me & full of erroneous statements. Also my reply was polite if also – as I hoped – cogent. When it didn't appear, I wrote to ask Naomi Mitchison if she could use the influence she has there. She merely replied that having just returned from Russia, she could not see that such small & personal matters were of any account! I told her to think hard about Russia next time she got a grit in her eye. All the same she was right in so far as the unimportance of quarrels that have anything personal in them, by comparison with the furthering of things as a whole. I can hear just what you'll reply to this & your reply is true. *But* there's no doubt that Moscow reading your letter & an account of the whole thing would find not a great deal left when the personal elements on both sides were removed. All it comes to is that Whyte & Muir are of the stuff of which reactionaries are made. But allowing for this Whyte, I suppose, has a right to print or refuse to print what he likes in his own magazine. But there is nothing to prevent you from attacking him elsewhere. I can't see what Moscow has to do with it.

Remember also that I did not read Muir's article, so I don't know what he said by way of attack – but as it was an extract from his Scott book, it doesn't rank as a 'letter' attack, & might be best replied to in a book of your own. Communists are too much absorbed just now with things in Spain, France, Greece, etc. to be much interested in Scotland. We hope that Scotland's time will come. Meanwhile can we collect any money there to help the Spanish workers?[1] By the way, the fact that Muir contributes to 'capitalist' papers is surely beside the point. So do you when you get the chance. And what harm in that? It is not that that is wrong with Muir.

It comes to this. I don't understand what you expect me to do about your letter, or what you expect to achieve by it. Sorry, Chris, if this sounds stupid. It is true. I don't see any point in it apart from its being a relief to your feelings with which I sympathise. Surely you'll get your chance to say what you want at the University election in October?[2]

As to invective. Anybody can call names (tho' some people are cleverer at inventing nastily appropriate ones than others!) but as a rule mere invective falls flat unless backed with wit. Your letter strikes me as far too long, too angry, & – yes – too much concerned with the personal nature of Muir's criticisms, whatever these may have been. If I had been an editor I doubt if I should have wanted to put it in & my doubts would have had nothing to do with politics. I'd have asked you to think it over & condense it.

I must read your 'Red Scotland' when it comes out. Good luck to it & you & don't waste too much energy on the White moor mice.[3] They are not worth your energy except by way of a flip now & again.

I'm in France by myself, but it is too dear. When I finish Boccaccio[4] (which is for Martin Lawrence) I'm hoping to do some political reading & Left writing. Also I'm helping with a new woman's paper that *The Daily Worker* people are contemplating. But I must rest a bit first. I'm awfully tired.

That Conference was very interesting, especially from the disgraceful behaviour of H.G. Wells which disgusted both the Russian delegate (Ehrenburg) and the French (André Malraux)[5] – both excellent men, Malraux particularly fine. Did you hear of their great scheme for a new international Encyclopedia? Scotland ought to be able to contribute to that *and* to find the money for the Scottish section. England has been pretty feeble so far, but may buck up. The French are well on with their scheme. The idea is that each section should be written by the writers of each country, seeing everything from the effect it had on the consciousness of the people of that country. Then translations will be made *for every other country taking part in the scheme*. A number of countries are in the scheme & it should promote unity & understanding if only it can be carried out.

Enough for now. I regret very much if my reply to your letter is disappointing. But I can't for the life of me see a menace in a white mouse compared with all the powerful white crocodiles that are about.

Ever yours,
Cathie.

[1] General Franco had commenced his rebellion against the Spanish Republican Government on 17 July 1936.
[2] MacDiarmid was a candidate for Lord Rector of Edinburgh University on 10 October 1936.
[3] MacDiarmid's term 'the white mouse faction' was a pun on the name of J.H. Whyte.
[4] *The Tranquil Heart*, a life of Boccaccio, was published in London in 1937.
[5] André Malraux (1901-1976), novelist, politician and art critic.

127. From George Elder Davie (EUL MS2946.12 ff.7-10)

c/o Robertson
Hawthorn Cottage
West Haven
Carnoustie
Angus

Dear Grieve,

Not until yesterday did I receive your letter accompanying the copy of the appeal for funds which I am to despatch to [W.R.] Aitken this afternoon that it may be circularised. I am just back from Raasay where I was hospitably entertained by the MacLeans for a fortnight after the conclusion of my hike. It was a great experience to get in touch from the inside with what must be one of the liveliest families in all the Gaeltacht both in its firm grasp on all that is good in tradition and in its keen concern with contemporary issues. I may add that the advent of your wife and yourself is eagerly awaited – Sam was disappointed not to have had word from you already to that effect – and that especially for Mrs Grieve an acquaintance with this novel side of Scottish life will prove a wonderful and exciting holiday. Friendship of the MacLeans is a passport to the kindest treatment all through Skye as I myself found. When on Raasay, suggest privately to John who is glad of any excuse to go that he take you to Edinbane: verb. sap.[1]

It is a pity about the delay in the issue of the circular letter; however there is time yet, and it will be on its way next week. I hope that Lawrence & Wishart have by this time accepted 'Red Scotland'. I wish of course to get the 'Survey of Scottish Politics'[2] into my hands again in order to add a page or two in the light of what Gallacher says, so that the relationship of MacLean to the Scottish Secretariat may be fully & fairly set forth, and that Gallacher's charges of (or rather innuendoes of) softening of the brain may be exposed.[3] Further, a paragraph must be inserted on the significance of Murdoch, and the politics of rural Scotland, where his policy, completely at one with MacLean's, ought to prevail.[4] Then, too, I should be glad if you could send me the appendix dealing with Kerrigan's denial of Scottish nationality,[5] since this is the core of the whole question, and since I have some matter in Dundee which I wish to incorporate in it, either with a view to publication in 'Red Scotland' or else for subsequent issue. Then there is Hood's article on the Lennox Kerr question,[6] which I will get hold of & send up, that its matter may be used to strengthen the 'Scots Culture & War' essay.[7]

I am to be meeting Hood tomorrow when we will discuss the line that our issue of the 'Hammer & Thistle' will take.[8] The results of our conference I will submit to you when I send up the Hood articles next week. Hood is having a nasty time this summer: his father nearly banished him from their sober chaste & bourgeois ménage; and so apart from short stories he has not been able to write anything. He is busy at the canning factory, and among the Montrosian CPers. Whyte (whom in Raasay, in view of his ownership of land & property on the neighbouring island, they call 'MacGuggenheim Ronae') of course refused to publish the article in question.

Caird is occupied with short stories too – but of a more subjective & pessimistic type by far than Hood. Both are disgusted with *Outlook* and Hood is almost equally annoyed with the so-called *Left Review*. I will be writing to you next week, by which time I hope to have visited Scott at St Andrews, and to have investigated the Whyte-mouse faction's tactics from close at hand.

I am,

Yours respectfully,
G. E. Davie.

1   *verbum sapienti sat est* - a word is enough for a wise man.
2   'A Brief Survey of Modern Scottish Politics in the Light of Dialectical Materialism' was seized from Harry Miller, editor of *Scots Socialist,* on 3 May 1941, at the time of police raids on Nationalist premises, and never recovered.
3   William Gallacher (1881-1965) was Communist M.P. for West Fife 1935-1950. In his *Revolt on the Clyde* (London, Spring 1936) Gallacher claimed that John MacLean '[...] was suffering from hallucinations [...]' as a result of his imprisonment for sedition in 1918 (p.215). MacLean declined to join the Communist Party when it was formed in 1920 and refused Lenin's invitation to go to the Soviet Union for recuperation. He would have had to travel illegally (which Gallacher had done).
4   John Murdoch (1818-1903) founded *The Highlander* newspaper (1873-1881) to promote the crofters' cause during the Land Agitation.
5   Peter Kerrigan, Secretary to the Scottish Secretariat of the Communist Party, published a letter in *Alba Nuadh* (New Scotland), 1 February 1936, which was headlined 'The Errors of Mr C.M.Grieve/Scotland is not a nation'.
6   Stuart C. Hood, b.1915, was then a student at Edinburgh University. Lennox Kerr, the Paisley novelist, had opened a debate in *Outlook,* June 1936, under the title, 'Literature: Class or National?' Neil Gunn and Edward Scouller also took part in the July and August issues.
7   MacDiarmid's essay, 'Scottish Culture and Imperialist War', was contributed to *Eleventh Hour Questions* (Edinburgh and London, 1937), pp. 105-111.
8   This appears to be a reference to 'Hammer and Thistle' which was to be issued by the Hugh MacDiarmid Book Club.

128. From Nan Mercer (EUL MS2954.12 ff.6-7 and EUL Gen. 2094/6)

42 Auldhouse Rd
Newlands
Glasgow S3
22 August 1936

Dear Mr Grieve,

I was very pleased indeed to have your letter of the 15th inst. and your suggestion that we should collaborate to produce a really good biography of my father.

If it could be worked – and the great difficulty is that it would have to be worked by correspondence – it is a splendid idea and would simplify matters greatly for me, as I have no literary experience and my leisure is limited.

Although I think the three points you make regarding publishing, royalties, and the leaving of the final decision to me on any point except politics, are very fair and sound, as is also your suggestions about method of work, I would like to have a try-out before deciding definitely.

For this purpose I am sending all the data I have up to 1914, and also all the material that Mr Maxton handed on to me. I would have sent you everything, but that is the only part I have quite ready, and I think you could write something on the basis of these facts without the later material.

In my opinion his life falls naturally into three phases, pre-war, war-time and post-war, and I think you know sufficient of the last two to estimate the importance of the first. If you would do this and send me what you have written, I think that would give us an idea as to whether our opinions would clash too much. I would have waited until I had more material ready, but I gather that you are eager to make a start.

Maxton's material includes the remnants of what he wrote for his proposed biography (he said he had destroyed the rest as being very poor stuff), and a copy of the banned *Forward* which describes Lloyd George's famous Glasgow meeting. These are the most interesting items.

I have written nothing myself yet. I was waiting until I had obtained the stuff from *Justice*, and I could get to London only during my husband's summer holidays; we had just returned when your first letter came. I have strung together for you in a disjointed fashion, I am afraid, all the facts I have been able to gather about his childhood and youth. There is sufficient, I believe, to give an idea of the forces of heredity and environment operating to make the man he became – the sturdy peasant stock not yet devitalised by city life, the struggle of his widowed mother to provide for her children, the extremely narrow religious upbringing, and later on the contact with advanced thinkers.

When I first started gathering this material, I did so with the intention of getting James D. MacDougall,[1] who was father's closest friend and colleague until a few years before his death, to write the book. He was very enthusiastic and dictated some stuff to me with the intention of improving and elaborating upon it later. However, his interest waned, partly due to ill health (he has been a nervous wreck since his imprisonment during the war) and partly due to his hope that Gallacher's *Revolt on the Clyde* and your 'Red Scotland' would do enough justice to MacLean without a biography being written. However, 'Red Scotland' did not come out then and Gallacher's book was rather disappointing, so I determined to carry on myself. So I hand on to you MacDougall's stuff just as he gave it to me. On the whole I think it is quite accurate, although a bit gushing. MacDougall, by the way, has a very great admiration for your work.

This has nothing to do with the subject, but I mention it just as a matter of interest. One of the men MacDougall mentions, at whose house MacLean was first introduced to *Capital*, is MacDougall's uncle, Daniel MacDougall, who has just published a novel *Savage Conflict*, the first of a long series.[2] It has been having pretty good reviews. It was he who sent to the *Pollokshaws Review* the letter about MacLean's likes and dislikes when a young fellow of twenty-four.

I enclose *Co-operation and the Rise in Prices*. It is not very important but it does show how tremendously father was interested in the Co-operative Movement in these days. Also I understand from MacDougall that it was the only bit of writing that he ever took pains with – so that his style and expression is much better than his usual, which was pretty poor, due, MacDougall says, to being pressed for time.

Then last but not least are the notes my husband and myself took from *Justice* up to 1914. These mainly consist of extracts from branch reports and notices from 'Scottish Notes', with occasional letters and articles by himself. He was never well-known in England, although during these years his reputation in Scotland was steadily growing. Using the pseudonym 'Gael' he wrote 'Scottish Notes', which was always a full column, from 1911 till the beginning of the war, when he was completely boycotted in *Justice*. I took his articles and letters in full, as we have so little of his writing. MacDougall says that he was one of Hyndman's most vigorous opponents at the annual conferences, but I find no mention of him in the reports. He had a great admiration for the 'grand old man' even after he began to disagree with him on the big navy question.[3]

The outstanding fact about these early years is his tremendous activity. He must have had a remarkable amount of vitality. Remarkable, too, is the fact that he never suffered from periods of reaction, of depression and fedupness, according to my mother. He must have been living at a very high pitch, as also was MacDougall, and that, together with their similarity of outlook, explains their reaction to prison. Gallacher's explanation of Petroff's influence is sheer grovelling to Moscow, for Petroff is a Trotskyist now.[4]

He was a bit of a Puritan, perhaps a relic of his Calvinist upbringing. He was a strict teetotaller, he never smoked, he had stern ideas about duty, and although his opinions about marriage relationships were of course enlightened he always considered that a Socialist propagandist should be conventional in order to trail no red herrings across the Socialist path.

These pre-war days were gloriously happy ones. He was the soul of generosity and hospitality; there were always people staying or being entertained. Mother never knew when he would bring in hosts of people to be fed or even to sleep. When there were conferences, they were even sleeping on the floor. In these days he was easy-going and very pleasant to live with, always jolly and joking. It has been said that he had no sense of humour; he certainly had, but I think what is meant was his great sense of responsibility to society, his fanatical devotion to the socialist cause.

I note you would like the book published by autumn. I quite agree with you that the time is ripening for its issue, but another few months will not make much difference, and will make all the difference to making a thorough piece of work. I have not yet obtained nearly all the material I would like – most of it in the nature of historical detail. I do think it is absolutely necessary to have the historical background as accurate and as much in perspective as possible. Of course, perhaps you are well versed in that. I consider Gallacher's analysis of the situation at that time to be very poor, and would like something much better done.

I shall be delighted to see 'Red Scotland', and am eagerly awaiting it; your additional essays sound interesting.

I am sorry you have been so ill, and hope you are well enough now to tackle this job without harm to your health.

I expect to have more material ready in a week's time, and hope you are pleased with this lot.

Yours sincerely,
Nan Mercer.

PS I am sending the material under separate cover.

1   James D. MacDougall was a member of The Tramp Trust Unlimited, John MacLean's group of socialist speakers which also included Peter Marshall, Sandy Ross and Harry MacShane. It was formed in 1920; the name was jocular.

2   Daniel MacDougall's *Savage Conflict* was published in London in 1936. *Ian of the Burdens* by the same author was published in London in 1937.

3   H.M. Hyndman was the founder of the Social Democratic Federation in London in 1881. In the years before the First World War he advocated a 'Big Navy for Britain'.

4   Peter Petroff escaped from prison in Siberia in 1907 and came to Scotland where he was befriended by John MacLean. He was deported back to Russia in 1918. Gallacher thought Petroff influenced John MacLean to be over-critical of his comrades and of prison conditions.

129. From Dr M. C. (NLS MS27148 f.96)

14 Endsleigh Gardens
London WC1
23 August [1936]

Dear C. M. G.,

Yes I have read all this egoism. But it doesn't impress me. So long as you cannot see nor hear of your two children, in whose upbringing you ought to have a say, I don't see how you are going to be particularly gratified by anything that is said in your praise from here to China.

If you can afford it, I'd stop publishing for a year & turn your wits to this other problem. I don't suppose you'll want to see me: London or anywhere else, after this dig. I'm glad you are better. I thought you looked very poor when I saw you last. Yes I'm all for correlation, but it must be of the will as well as of the mind.

I'm glad you've found a wife who doesn't care about money. At the same time, I think it's very nice to give one's children the advantages one wishes one had had for oneself.

Yours ever
Dr M. C. [illegible][1]

1   Not identified

130. From Kenneth Patchen (EUL MS2962.7 f.9)

Reproduced by permission of Pollinger Limited and the proprietor

3 Placita Rafaela
Santa Fe
New Mexico

August 1936

Dear Hugh MacDiarmid,
This is to say that I think you a fine poet.
Respectfully,
Kenneth Patchen.

131. From F. G. Scott (EUL MS2959 ff.65-68)

44 Munro Road
Glasgow W3
1 September 1936

My dear Chris,

We arrived back from St Andrews late last night, all of us in very fine fettle and brown as berries after the extraordinary fine weather of last weekend. I had as you'll have already guessed some hesitations before I went off as to how things would turn out, having of course received the 'circular letter' and smelt the smoke of battle. Even before we left Glasgow, Whyte had stayed here and shown me all the correspondence he had had with you. He had told me too that Willa, in particular, was very wroth about it all and was thundering about the 'blether-skyte', 'play-boy', 'exhibitionist', 'charlatan', who was devoid of 'integrity' and 'decency' in his dealings with either friends or rivals. The Muirs who had been holidaying in the West Highlands came back to St Andrews a week after our arrival there and weren't long in paying us a visit on the usual friendly terms, viz., pretending to be vastly amused with everything and everybody, especially 'Christopher'. The ridiculous nature of the 'circular letter' was the chief point of interest at this stage and both of them expressed regret that you were likely to do yourself more harm than anybody else. In short they were quite sorry for you.

By the second week I was conscious of a division in the happy band of St Andrews intelligentsia. The Muirs threw a big party one Sunday night which included Dr and Mrs Oeser, psychologist at the university,[1] Mary Litchfield, then staying with the Muirs, Whyte and Tonge and all the Scott family excepting the two boys. We had a very intellectual time indeed doing games of a psychological character that depressed me almost beyond words and showed me up as a real sulky brute. I told Willa next day the school-room yarn about 'the bloody-coont' but she repelled this as a description of her party. It was clear enough however that the Oesers, the Muirs and Whyte were on exceptionally friendly terms continually 'phoning and arranging matters so I kept out of the way and saw very little of them. Whyte by this time was spending most of his time with his family up at Braemar (the whole family is going off with him to America about the 20th of this month) and coming back to St Andrews only for a day or two at a time. Tonge has obviously been treated to some 'freezing' out and I think it would be correct to say that although he and Whyte look as friendly as ever, Whyte is definitely anxious to break with Tonge. At any rate Tonge spent almost all his leisure time with Francise and Lovey and my nephew Alan [Furness] from Edinburgh who stayed with us during the whole month. This quartet had a terrific time of it every night in Tonge's house drinking sherry & smoking cigarettes, so much so that I was left wondering whether his inclinations were towards the masculine or feminine.

You'll have to work in here Dr Orr's visit. He's a very decent fellow and I quite enjoyed his 'size', a kind of big unspoiled country lad on the side of the angels all the time, too big to take a small view of anything. He's a very good friend indeed and his judgment deserves respect. Orr was the first of a long list of visitors. During the 3rd week we had Willie Johnstone, wife and kiddy for three days. Willie's full of his new book which comes out in October from Stanley Nott.[2] I learned quite a bit about you and London from him. He thinks there's a bit of a 'set' against you up-by, that you're finished (I'll tone it down to 'in the meantime') as far as poetry goes but that Butchart[3] thinks your autobiography should be a best-seller both in America and here if you'll put off the prophet's mantle, for God's sake don't take yourself seriously as Saviour of Mankind, Europe or even Scotland, but do your damnedest to view the human scene with a sense of detachment and a measure of fun – I'm putting as briefly as possible the gist of what Johnstone said although he told me all this confidentially. In the present circumstances I will add that I think this good advice. It's no use being pig-headed – if the whole affair is a 'ramp' – well then, take a hand in it, it's one of the few chances for 'ramping' you'll ever have and you'll be able to fulminate thereafter quite as effectively as you are doing now on an empty stomach. Whether you like it or not Hugh MacDiarmid as a world-beater is cutting no ice, not even here in Scotland. I think myself you should try (if for this occasion only) a change of clothes and turn gay like the rest of us. It's a chance, Christopher, and I'd take it. What a grin you could have at your detractors. A cool £1000 or 2 or 3 would rehabilitate you like nothing else! You'd be coming down to St Andrews then to see how the Muirs were getting on!

During the fourth week we had the whole Burt family[4] for three days. The Muirs were equally occupied with visitors, Whyte away in Braemar and not much doing between the lot of us. From a chance confab. with Mary Litchfield (à deux) on the beach I gathered that she is a very bitter enemy of yours, being also a member of the C.P. and hoping to God the Party will at long last settle your account when you come up for court martial in November, or whenever you come south. This hope was on several occasions repeated by the Muirs. You are evidently not aware that *they* are members of the 'United Front' established recently in London, that they're in touch with *good* Communists like Rickword, who by the way turned down your 'Red Scotland' etc., etc., – in other words the Litchfield bitch and the Muirs have you 'taped off' all along the line and you're simply putting up a bluff amongst those who don't know any better. Even Edwin, who can generally be astute, found hilarious laughter in somebody's 'Whalsay front', the MacDiarmid Club's weekly, monthly, quarterly and Xmas Annual. So you'd better mind your step! They're at present finding heaps of amusement to see you wriggling in the net you've set for them. The Whalsay Press working overtime is a good joke to Willa and Edwin rubs on the salt by adding that he's 'sorry for you, but what else can you expect'.

I've been doing a little music to 'The Dance of the Sevin Deidly Synnis' No. 2, *Ire*.[5] I tell you this to help you understand what follows. Last Saturday Edwin called round when I was out with his new volume on Scott (advance copies just to hand). The dedication on the flyleaf will interest you – 'To F.G. Scott. Hoping to turn aside Ire from Edwin Muir'. I read most of the volume on Saturday night (we'd had George Bruce[6] and his wife from Dundee and Stuart Hood from Largo but Davie failed to keep his appointment to come to St Andrews, though I wired to Dundee and gave phone number). Stuart Hood seemed a bit puzzled about how things are going (as a C.P. member and as a person sitting his finals this next session). I hadn't opportunity to talk much to him (the Bruces being in the conversation) but I'll swear the band of Edin. students are feeling a bit disrupted already at the way you're splashing about. However let's get on with the story. We (the Scott family) were away all day at Gleneagles with Whyte & Tonge in the motor car. I had a long talk with Whyte about Muir's book and *proved* to him that the pair of you are diametrically opposed to each other not on mere personal grounds but on fundamentals. I convinced him so much (he's not exactly unintelligent is Whyte) that he said that if you hadn't made such a hash with the 'circular letter' business you'd have been the ideal person to write a review of the 'Scott' book. Tonge is also of this opinion, he's been repeating to me all the month that Christopher is quite right, so you can count on Tonge's support for what it's worth (remember that the buggers are not happy in their present contacts!)

Late on Sunday night the Muirs phoned over that they'd like to come over to see us before we left on Monday and would come late bringing with them a big bottle of claret (as a peace offering?) I had a long and very exciting talk with the pair of them, told them that I disagreed with everything in the book, proved that in 'The Eemis Stane' you had written a metaphysical poem of the first water, asked Edwin to put anything in English beside it (which he couldn't do), made him confess Burns a *major* poet especially in dialect, pointed out that any strictures on *your* work were equally applicable to *mine* ('I suppose I should be writing string quartets for lounge lizards'), told him that the book was a justification of himself, that he was only finding out what he was looking for etc., etc., etc. Willa turned extremely grave and *silent*, asked timorously if I was prepared to become 'the spiritual father' of Christopher in this conflict. I said I was. My only alternative was to deny myself as a creative artist. Then Whyte and Tonge blew in about 1.30 am and the tension eased a little. I hurried round to shake hands just before we left yesterday but I'm pretty sure the 'little bit of London in Ecosse' as I phrased it on one occasion is not so sure of itself, let's call it 'in a state of unstable equilibrium'.

To sum up – you shouldn't have been in such a hurry about the 'circular letter' business. Your case would have been 100 times more effectively put if you'd kept the personal bits out altogether, had made no mention of your latest activities, 'Red Scotland' etc. (the Muirs immediately wrote to Rickword about it and got satisfaction) and in general had kept to principles instead of personalities and what looked like puff pars. on your own behalf. I can assure you that both Whyte and Tonge are prepared to go a good long way to give publication to your work but you mustn't make it impossible. Tonge was asking me who should review the 'Scott' book – he suggested Willie Soutar in the absence of anybody else. I agreed to this, but of course that's nothing to go on. But I needn't get into further details. Willie Johnstone has this morning sent me the whole caboodle of galley proofs of this book and I'm to return them by Thursday to London.

I'm very glad you're so fit. I'll keep you informed about everything if you'll gang cannily and mind your step.

F. G.

[1]   Oscar Oeser was head of the Psychology Department at the University of St Andrews, and his wife was Dr Drury Oeser.

[2]   *Creative Art in England* (London, 1936) which was republished as *Creative Art in Britain* (1950).

[3]   Montgomery Butchart, literary agent for Gilbert Wright (London) Ltd.

[4]   William Burt (d.1949) was an English teacher at Langholm Academy when MacDiarmid was a pupil. 'Hungry Waters', *C.P.* I, p.52, was written for Burt's son who was killed in the Second World War.

[5]   William Dunbar's poem.

[6]   George Bruce, teacher, poet and BBC producer.

132. From James H. Whyte (EUL MS2961.14 ff.24-5)

North Bay
Isle of Barra
10 September 1936

My dear Grieve,

I had not answered your letter of August 11th because I thought that my own position in your controversy with Edwin Muir had been made sufficiently clear, but your second letter makes it necessary to reply to your allegations point by point.

(1)While I naturally appreciate the extent of your disagreement with Muir and agree that your attitudes are fundamentally irreconcilable now, I am surprised that in the not-so-distant past you should have written so enthusiastically on Muir's literary achievements in *Contemporary Scottish Studies* and still more recently. You can scarcely blame me for 'falling under his influence' in view of what you wrote and that it was in your own house that I first met him, and it seems to me that your own attitude to Muir has been extremely equivocal, if what you say in your first letter is true.

(2) I cannot under any circumstances agree that you were placed in a subordinate position in *The Modern Scot*: a glance through the 23 copies which appeared in all will show you that your work appeared far more regularly than that of any other contributor. In my desire to put your name forward I published many articles and poems which I now realize to have been unworthy of your pen and seriously compromised the future of the magazine by your 'Welcome to the PEN Delegates' which was published in spite of all my friends' exhortations to the contrary. If

latterly I refused any work which you sent me to see it was because I realized that publishing work of inferior quality was doing no good either to *The Modern Scot* or to your own reputation – a view reinforced by F. G. Scott and John Tonge, whose opinions and criticisms I knew you yourself valued.

(3) As far as the publication of 'Red Scotland' is concerned I have an absolutely clear conscience, being informed by Messrs Lawrence and Wishart that they had already decided not to publish the book before my writing to them. In view of the hysterical tone of your circular letter and the many mis-statements which it contained, Muir and I considered ourselves perfectly justified in writing to see a copy of 'Red Scotland' [in order to prevent] any further dissemination of such inaccuracies. It may not have been the usual practice to do so – but I fail to be impressed by your tone of outraged virtue when you pride yourself openly on your ability to break every rule of literary controversy in the name of 'Marxian dialectic'.

(4) I have, in conclusion, no wish to discuss Muir's personal quarrels with you, especially in regard to financial matters, as I have no knowledge of the allegation concerning the publication of 'Red Scotland' to which you refer. I can only say, out of my own personal experiences and those of mutual friends, that you would be wiser not to mention your financial transactions in public if you wish to enlist support and sympathy. As I have said before and repeat now: if you think Muir's arguments so pathetic it is up to you to argue with him in intellectual terms and not in those of a spoilt schoolgirl. If you wish to substantiate your claim to be Scotland's greatest man of letters that is the only course which lies open to you.

Yours truly,

J. H. Whyte.

P.S. I am keeping a copy of this letter should the occasion arise when it must be published in full.

133. From Edgell Rickword (EUL MS2968)

LAWRENCE AND WISHART LTD.
Publishers

2 Parton Street
London WCl
19 September 1936

Dear Mr Grieve,

I have now returned from my holiday and read your letter with regard to our decision not to publish your book 'Red Scotland'.[1]

You will no doubt understand that the decision of a firm as to the publication or otherwise of a book is determined by a general consideration of its chance of success. The author's estimate of this is of course a factor to be taken into account, but cannot be expected to determine that decision. And the publishers' recognition of certain particular qualities in the book may be outweighed in their opinion by the form of presentation of the material as a whole.

Your suggestion that our decision was influenced by any individual outside the firm is completely unfounded and we are confident that you will accept our assurance of this.

Yours sincerely,
Edgell Rickword.
LAWRENCE & WISHART LTD.

---

[1] The directors of Lawrence and Wishart at this time are given as E. E. Wishart, R. T. H. Bishop, A. L. Bacharach, D. J. F. Parsons, D. M. Garman and J. E. Rickword. Parsons had written earlier rejecting the book (14 July 1936). However, MacDiarmid believed that Edwin Muir had influenced the rejection. Cf. F. G. Scott's letter of 1 September 1936 where he writes, '[...] the Muirs immediately wrote to Rickword about it and got satisfaction [...]'. But on 2 October 1936 Scott wrote, '"Red Scotland" was turned down by Parsons (Rickword had nothing to do with that part of it[...]').

134. From Guy A. Aldred (EUL MS2942.4)

GUY ALDRED
ADVICE, LEGAL AID AND SECRETARIAL AGENCY
145, Queen Street, Glasgow C1.
Office Hours – 10 a.m. – 1 p.m.
3 p.m – 5.30 p.m.

23 September 1936

Dear Comrade Grieve –

I have just heard from Barcelona this morning – Confederación Regional del Trabajo de Cataluña[1] – with the request that I get certain experts to the French side of the Pyrenees, & the Barcelona administration will do the rest. Time is everything. Do you know of anyone who will help us – not to send charity or just medical units – but this practical delegation? In the end, those who help, apart from the reward of helping freedom, will be compensated fully, if freedom wins.

Re press. The press I mentioned is sold. But I can get the option on an Arab & motor, with some type. All we need is a good Arab or (*for preference*) a flatbed. I will secure *Exchange & Mart* to-morrow.

New leaflet on Spain later. Arranging for the CNT to circulate your article in all languages throughout the world.[2]

Best wishes,
Guy A. Aldred.

P.S. We have been instructed to send 4 delegates.

---

[1] Regional Federation of Labour of Catalonia.
[2] CNT – Confederación Nacional del Trabajo (National Federation of Labour). With regard to MacDiarmid's article, Willeke Tijssen of the International Institute of Social History in Amsterdam wrote to the present editor, 22 October 2004, 'About two years ago you

wrote to the IISH about an article by Hugh MacDiarmid. On and off we have been looking for it in the papers you suggested, but we have not found it. This may be because of the article's not being signed or its not having been published, we do not know.'

135. From James H. Whyte (EUL MS2961.14 f.26)

French Line
S.S. Normandie
27 September 1936

My dear Grieve,

I am sorry not to be able to answer your letter sooner, but it arrived as I was on the point of leaving London and I wished to consider my reply carefully.

You will naturally appreciate that the attitude which you have adopted towards Edwin Muir places me in a difficult position if I wish to retain the co-operation and friendship of both of you. While I do not agree with Muir's recent pronouncements any more than you, my personal friendship with him makes me resent violently the remarks which you have made about his character in your circular letter, in which you made completely false and malicious charges – such as that his criticism of your work was due to his antipathy to you as a Communist, that he was a Scott-adulator (merely because he discussed Scott's work at all) and finally that 'he was a well-known connoisseur of buttered bread'. I do not consider that there is any valid excuse for making such allegations outside a pub. – and my regard for your judgment has naturally been seriously affected.

As I do not have a copy of the circular letter with me I do not propose to discuss its other inaccuracies in detail – though it seems to me that by stating so categorically its inclusion in 'Red Scotland' you gave Muir and me a misleading conception of the book. We wrote to Messrs Lawrence and Wishart under the impression that the rest of the book would be similar in tone and we naturally wished to save the publishers the onus of a possible libel action in consequence. You are perfectly at liberty, as far as I am concerned, to see a copy of my letter to Edgell Rickword – I have, as I have said before, a perfectly clear conscience in the matter, since the decision not to publish the book had already been taken by the publishers.

I still continue to think that you would be ill-advised to wash still more dirty linen in public and particularly in the circular letter form, and those friends who have your best interests at heart have been quite unanimous in their disapproval. Your refusal to reply to Muir in the pages of *Outlook* must appear a weakness to those who know your feelings – and there is no other paper in Scotland which would give you an opportunity. If you do not trust yourself to reply without introducing the personal element I should be quite prepared to consider an article by Davie or any other of your friends. This is my last offer – and perhaps the last time you may hear from me again.

Yours truly,
J.H. Whyte.

136. From F. G. Scott (EUL MS2959 ff.69-70)

44 Munro Road
Jordanhill
Glasgow W3
2 October 1936

My dear Chris,

I went to bed last night saying, 'I *must* write Christopher tomorrow', and this morning I've a note from Dr Hyslop[1] saying he had been to Whalsay recently, had seen you and that you were looking very fit. The real reason for my delay in replying has been that after the purchase of a new piano all the books in my study have been transferred to various parts of the establishment and I couldn't lay hands on Hubert anywhere.[2] The Mrs has just succeeded in digging them out from a press under the stair.

Your letter at the beginning of the month was a very good indication that I had jolted you out of your 'dogmatic slumber'. I meant to! I was very pleased all the same with the spirit you put into it – the assurance that the matter is really serious and should be dealt with seriously. This damned Scottish Nationalist business has been so messed up with spinsters and dilettanti of all kinds that any self-respecting person must think twice about his appearance in it, e.g., I thank God that I hadn't after all to address a weekend hen-party down at Ardentinny Hydro last weekend, because of lack of numbers. The handiwork of Power and others of like kidney has also been very detrimental – they have given the thing a purely sentimental appeal that attracts all those folks who attend lectures on this and that, and in fact fill up their leisure talking about something intellectual – but not too much so. It is clear that this won't work with the communists and perhaps it is just as well to allow the conflicting principles to get to grips – it can only clarify the issue.

I was speaking to [Peter] Brody,[3] an Aberdonian, head of Collet's shop in High Street, [Glasgow], during the week. He's a great friend of 'the Litchfield bitch' (but no names were mentioned). As a further bouquet to the posy I made you in my last list, he thinks you're a washout, both in literature and politics. Evidently he's the person who engineered the forthcoming number of *Left Review* – Mary Litchfield, Whyte, Brody. In reply to my query about you he says that Whyte gave him your address, that he wrote to you and that you didn't reply. 'Red Scotland' was turned down by Parsons (Rickword had nothing to do with that part of it) as being disappointing on both the literary and the political sides. He says Martin Lawrence's firm isn't making money but rather losing it & ditto with Gollancz. I ventured to doubt the latter! They've 22 000 members of their Left Book Club. What's that? 22 000 x 2/6? About £300 per month. Well, it's something at any rate!

I haven't heard a word of any kind from St Andrews since we left. Willa Muir wrote through to Lovey about something or other and invited her through for a farewell party they were giving Jimmy before he went off to America. I think things had been messed up a bit at the time – Tonge's brother in RAF was killed about the middle of Sept. and Whyte was leaving on 23rd. At any rate he didn't write to me about our proposed golf game at Gleneagles so he went away without any blessings from Glasgow.

I've just remembered about the *Outlook* and the review of Muir's book. It should be out now, I'll get a copy when I go out to post this.

Have had quite a correspondence with Willie Johnstone about his *Creative Art in England*, which I read over for him and made suggestions about. The creative principle he seemed to be discussing I suggested was the Celtic element – he hadn't a word about Celtic in the whole fit-up – and rather went off the deep end to get something in about it. He tried to do this in a preface but the whole preface was so badly written that I took it upon myself to blue pencil the thing from beginning to end. He writes to say that I've greatly improved it! He's a terrible mix-up of a chap, Willie. I haven't read so much bad English for very many years – I don't know what sort of reception the book will have – but the reproductions will be alright at any rate. You'll be glad to hear that he has been appointed Head of Hackney Art School – began duties in Sept. – and is in ever so much better position financially. I've made half a promise to stay with him at Xmas. He's in tow with Nott, of course, and, indirectly, with Saurat (who finds the book 'most delightful'). By the way Saurat is due in Glasgow next weekend for Honours Grads examination at the 'Varsity so I'll hear some news from him about metropolitan matters.

I'm doing away with the 'Sevin Synnis' fairly well – going very slowly – trying to be both as simple and as vital as I can – not straining the originality business but just depending on my native originality to come through – being in other words an 'original' in every sense. I don't know exactly what you're busy with, but I'm pretty sure you're doing your damnedest. We *must* make a big effort, Chris. *Now* – no bloody nonsense – or we'll be listed with all the others who retired from the battle – defeated.

F. G.

PS. What about the MacD. Club?[4] Have you got it going? I want my name to be included and Tonge assured me he would certainly want to be in it. Let's hear all about it. Remember me and all here to Valda and my regards to the Doctor. (Capitals please!) Burt is doing fairly well – the family stayed with us in St Andrews for nearly a week. He'll also want to join you.

---

1 Dr A.F. Hyslop was an H.M.I..
2 Henri Hubert, *The Greatness and Decline of the Celts* (London, 1934).
3 Scott wrote 'Boddie'.
4 The Hugh MacDiarmid Book Club was announced in *The Bulletin*, 27 August 1936, in 'Pertinent and Otherwise'. To quote from the Prospectus: 'SEND NO MONEY, but sign this form and post it to the Secretary, Hugh MacDiarmid Book Club, Whalsay, via Lerwick, Shetland Islands:– I agree for one year from this date to accept on publication the four or five books to be issued during the ensuing twelve months, at preferential rates to Club members, by the Hugh MacDiarmid Book Club, also the weekly paper, *Red Scotland*, and the monthly *Hammer and Thistle*, at a total inclusive rate, including postage, of 40/–'. *MacDiarmid: An Ilustrated Biography*, p.62.

137. From Catherine Carswell (EUL MS2946.1 f.32)

2 November 1936

My dear Chris,

Thank you for sending along the leaflets,[1] and good luck to you. As to Muir and Whyte having any influence with Lawrence and Wishart, I simply don't believe it and I wish you wouldn't either. I know Garman pretty well. Also I think I should have heard something of it if it were true. I know nothing of what happened about your 'Red Scotland'. But surely it will eventually come out? Anyhow I'm sure that merely attacking people is almost always waste of one's energy, besides doing them no harm. However we must all do as seems to us best, and you may get stimulation that way, which is all right.

Good that you are all three well. John has just won an annual school competition for writing on prose, poetry and plays. I hope this augurs well for his scholarship exam which he sits in the middle of this month. He is in good form and developing well I think. Don is as usual. I am overworking but well. Once I see John fairly launched I hope to make some changes in my own régime. At present I have to grind out far too much journalism and to shoulder too many domestic worries. But one can do much so long as one has a purpose and sets a term to conditions that ought to be changed – I mean one can do much without undermining one's nerves. And it is satisfactory to see a thing through.

The other day I went to a meeting of that Defence of Culture Association to hear Day Lewis, Spender, etc. talk about culture. And they all seemed to me unlicked puppies. Malraux knocks them into nothing, while they criticise him. I think of resigning as there doesn't seem much sense in the affair so far as I'm concerned anyhow.

This is a hurried scrawl. I get hardly any time for letter-writing.

Our love to you all.

Cathie.

---

[1]   The 'leaflets' were copies of 'Scotland; and the Question of a Popular Front against Fascism and War' which had been published at the time of the 1936 Rectorial at Edinburgh University for the Hugh MacDiarmid Book Club and has been reprinted in *Albyn: Shorter Books and Monographs*, pp.352-5.

138. From the Communist Party of Great Britain (NLS Acc. 7361/7)

The Communist Party of Great Britain
Scottish District Committee
83 Ingram Street
Glasgow C1
30 November 1936

Dear Mr. Grieve,

The Scottish District Committee at its meeting on Saturday unanimously decided to expel you from the Communist Party.

The grounds for this decision were political irresponsibility and failure to conform to the discipline of the Party.

As you are aware from correspondence received from the District Office, for a long time we have been desirous of meeting you in order to discuss with you your position in the Party. On the 26/9/36 we received a letter from you in which you explained how difficult it was for you to comply with our request because of the heavy cost of travelling and the fact that you were under doctor's orders and he refused to allow you to travel at that period. As a matter of fact, you offered to supply a certificate to this effect.

Since then, a matter of only a few weeks later, you were in Glasgow for a period of one week and made no effort to get in touch with the Party District.

The latest example of your political line which we were desirous of taking up with you and which was considered by the District Committee on Saturday is contained in the pamphlet issued over your name, headed 'Scotland; and the Question of a Popular Front against Fascism and War'. It is an impossible position for us to be in that you should be claiming to be a member of the Communist Party and making in this pamphlet such a statement as 'The betrayal of John MacLean's line by the Communist Party of Great Britain has resulted in a loss to Scottish Socialism beyond all reckoning. Even William Gallacher, M.P., who was primarily responsible for it, admits this in his autobiography, *Revolt on the Clyde*'.[1]

In conveying our decision to expel you for the reasons given in the first part of this letter, I want to draw your attention to the fact that you have the same rights as any other individual who is expelled from the Party, i.e., the right to appeal to the Central Committee, etc.[2]

Yours fraternally,
THE DISTRICT SECRETARIAT.

[1]   Gallacher praised MacLean in *Revolt on the Clyde* but did not say that 'The betrayal of John MacLean's line by the Communist Party of Great Britain has resulted in a loss to Scottish Socialism beyond all reckoning'.

[2]   In his reply on 4 December 1936 MacDiarmid wrote:
'I shall, of course, exercise my right of appeal to the Central Committee, etc. All I wish to say in the meantime is
1) that I regard what you say of my being in Glasgow for a week and making no effort to get in touch with the Party District as a typical example of the sort of misinformation upon which you are in the habit of acting – since I have not been in Glasgow or in Scotland at all since the Spring and am in a position to prove that I have been continuously on this island from May to the present date.
2) that the statement you quote from my leaflet on 'Scotland; and the Question of a Popular Front against Fascism and War' is not an expression of opinion, but a statement of fact which brooks no denial, and which I am in a position to demonstrate in an absolutely unanswerable fashion. I am in possession of the full facts and intend to thresh the whole question of John MacLean out against William Gallacher and show that 'betrayal' is by no means too strong a word for the way in which the latter acted to the former. The whole C.P. line in regard to Scotland was based on that diabolical bit of trickery, and must be –

and will be – altered in the direction I suggest. I will publish the whole story shortly and the Scottish workers who gave MacLean his great following will then be in a position to measure Gallacher and his present associates correctly on the basis of the indisputable facts (though the slow progress of the C.P. in Scotland suggests that, in the absence of these facts to date, the Scottish workers have instinctively distrusted the individuals in question and refused to follow their corrupt anti-Scottish and non-Communist leading.)' (TNA KV 2/2010, 21G.).

139. From George Elder Davie (EUL MS2946.12 ff.89-97)

c/o Whiteford
10 Parkside Terrace
Edinburgh
Thursday [December 1936]

Dear Grieve,
Tonight, going in to Princes Street district for a few beers, I ran across Brian Campbell. I heard from him about your expulsion from the CPGB about which previously I knew nothing. Campbell, as usual, avowed his sympathy with your fate but his entire agreement with the Party's action, and was undoubedly genuine in what he said. So far as I could gather, the cause of your condemnation was the Muir circular letter. He told me that someone in the Party who received a copy brought the matter up. Its recipients were Fred Douglas,[1] the Glasgow centre and Campbell himself, who can be ruled out. So it must likely have been one of the former pair. He said he had met enemies of yours in the Party, hating you with that furious bitterness which your work often evokes in Scotland – for instance, a woman whose eyes almost shot out of her head at the mention of your name etc. I did not learn their names.

It is rather difficult to harmonise his various statements. Apparently, however, one charge was your total misjudgement of the Muirs who, he averred, are moving further & further to the Left. I mentioned Muir's ventures into mysticism. He admitted Muir needed talking to about that, but said they were fundamentally sound. I then suggested that the anti-Scottish cultural line propounded by Muir in *Scott and Scotland* justified your attack on Muir. He said that there was right on both sides – that Muir's denial of the possibility or advisability of a Scottish cultural renaissance, and exhortations toward the total assimilation by Scotland of English culture seemed certainly wrong – but that, on the other side, it was an open question whether the assimilation of Scotland to English had not gone so far as to make the line Muir advocated the proper path along which the future culture in Scotland must proceed. As confirmation of the pro-Muir view, he instanced two facts (i) that your definitely Scottish work had had neither following among the public nor the support of a crowd of writers i.e., that it looked like a flash in the pan (F.G. Scott's work is outside his orbit; the apparent abandonment by Hood & Co. of interest in Scottish culture on Scottish lines serves as further confirmation) (ii) in any case, your own work has of late in poetry been in English, and has in effect been a denial of your synthetic line. As far as Scots is concerned, Campbell said that tho'

180

at one time you looked like succeeding in your aim of rehabilitating it, the present development of your work seems to show a confession that you have given up the fight. The conclusion is that Muir may well be right.

On the political issue, I think that he said that your 'Red Scotland' line contradicts and hampers the whole present Party line. It was really difficult to guage Campbell's real views since he swithered in his positions. For example, when I cited MacLean's authority for the 'Red Scotland' line, he first cited Gallacher to the effect that, in MacLean's later days, he said anything that anybody, however irresponsible, put into his head, that he surrounded himself with a group of spongers, that he was unbalanced as the result of sufferings in prison. Then after I said – this was one of my few interjections intended for any other purpose than to learn from him – that I disagreed with Gallacher's reading of Maclean's life, he changed his tune, and said that what MacLean said may have been relevant seventeen years ago, and that in twenty years' time it may again be proper to recall his teaching, but that just now his line is quite out of place. I did not push him farther in his admissions.

What he went on to say was that you ought to have mingled with the Scottish comrades, argued your line with them etc. instead of issuing in a circular letter a quite separate line for all and sundry to see; and a line at that likely to do the CPGB harm i.e., lose it a little support. He proceeded to tell the old story that Scotland and England were so closely knit that only after the revolution could separatism be considered and to say much else to the same effect very much in keeping with the bourgeois English predominance view of Scots history. The upshot of his conversation was to say what Barke says – that all the intelligent & virile people in the Scots Nationalist movement ought to abandon Scots nationalism for work in the CPGB. I told him that the virile and intelligent Caird,[2] the virile and intelligent Hood[3] – not to mention others – had followed this very path already. For myself, I explained that recognising that it was out of the question to work up a Scots separatist movement just now, but being still in agreement with Maclean's line, I was following the opposite path to Hood & Caird and concentrating on private study.

I then said that there was surely no objection at least to political thought, and to the production of books on the Scottish question. I referred to your 'Red Scotland', your book on MacLean etc. but I was thinking about my own aim of following these up with other stuff on similar lines. I had no intention of letting Campbell know what I wanted to do. He said first that scarcely a left wing publisher would take such deviationist work. I then asked (with my tongue in my cheek) if it was not possible that the right-wing publishers would be ready to sponsor 'Red Scotland' books, since they were deviationist and therefore in essence pro-reactionary or Social Fascist. He was candid enough to say that he didn't think they would. I asked if he thought the publication of such books harmful. He declared it was, in that it might distract some people from the CP line. He went on to say that he didn't think that you would get much published besides poetry for a long time. I sounded him enough to be able to say quite definitely that Campbell has given the most cursory attention to what Marx, Lenin & Stalin have to say about the National Question. As I have said, his views on nationalism in general are such as you would expect from an English petty bourgeois.

One point I ought to have mentioned earlier is that, so far as I could gather, one of the charges against you was Douglasitism, or, more precisely, your claim that Douglasitism, Communism & Scots nationalism were consistent. I pointed out that you disavowed Douglasitism in 'Red Scotland' and that on an examination of your writings it would be found that what appealed to you in Douglasitism for the most part – what you meant by Douglasitism – were precisely the elements in it that John Strachey commended.[4] He admitted that perhaps I was right, but that they hadn't seen 'Red Scotland' – for the good reason that they themselves were indirectly responsible for preventing its publication.

I might mention at this point a striking thing Comrade MacIntyre told me.[5] He said that he had always been puzzled as to why, in *The Free Man* days, Black and yourself called yourselves Douglasites since the substance of your writings was quite Marxist and by no means what was generally called Douglasitism. I admired much McIntyre's open-minded eagerness to comprehend the *substance* of your position, its content; and his refusal to be put off by its non-Marxian form or name. But Campbell & Co. are men of a different stamp – legalistic Party-liners.

Well, after that, Campbell tried to urge me to join the YCL. He was quite a persuasive Jesuit: he admitted readily enough that Kerrigan's denial of Scottish nationality was ignorant nonsense despite the fact that from Kerrigan's position alone can the CP line towards Scotland be defended. As a matter of fact Comrade MacIntyre told me that Kerrigan was the straightest and most honest of the Glasgow CPers. He agreed that the University Communist Group had been wrong – not backing our Rectorial campaign which apparently found some favour in the eyes of the CP. His positive arguments were not to the point or else based on what seems to me a mere smattering of Leninism or else concerned with points I had already thought out e.g., he suggested that my nationalism was a species of religious fixation in that it was based on mere self-hypnotising repetitions of word-incantations, as if I had been engaged of late both in theorising and in practical work at the Rectorial Election time etc. etc. Our conversation was abruptly terminated by his having to catch a last tram.

He reiterated often his sympathy with you, said he wished that like Day Lewis & Spender, poets, he said, of only half your capacity, you were doing useful work for the Party, hoped that your treatment by the Party would not embitter you, pointedly stated that if his sentiments were accurately conveyed to you you would see in him a friend, which doubtless you have etc., etc.

I must apologise for always forgetting to send up the leaflets. Calum Maclean[6] is to distribute some in Skye in the vacation, others in other parts.

'And unbreakable spirit, MacLean, of you'.[7] I suppose that I who stand in relation to you similar to that in which MacIntyre stood to MacLean am being likewise accused of being a cause of your ill-health, and deviations. I hope, however, that your health is keeping up: history will answer the hurlers of the charge of deviation yet.

My regards to Mrs Grieve and yourself.

Yours,

G. E. Davie.

PS. Campbell said that the best plan for you would have been to resign your Party membership if you wished to put across the 'Red Scotland' line. He also, by the way, said that he had recently met the Muirs, found them very friendly & sympathetic towards you etc. He even went as far as to suggest that surely the reason for the absence of the Muirs' signatures on your Testimonial was that they had never been asked to sign. For my part, I regard Edwin as deserving only assassination. Please pardon this disjointed record, which I send up simply because it is likely to interest you, and clear the air.

Yours,

G. E. D.

1   Fred Douglas (1900-1971), Edinburgh Communist. One of the five editors of *Eleventh Hour Questions* (Edinburgh and London, 1937).
2   There is no evidence that Caird supported CP policies.
3   Hood was a member of the CP at the end of the 1930s; he subsequently lapsed his membership.
4   John Strachey (1901-1963), Left Socialist in the 1930s. Later Minister for War in Attlee's second government 1950-1. M.P. 1945-1963.
5   'Comrade MacIntyre' was Peter MacIntyre of the Scottish Workers Republican Party.
6   Calum MacLean (1915-1960) collected Gaelic folklore in Ireland and Scotland. Published *The Highlands* (1959).
7   Cf. 'John MacLean (1879-1923)', *C.P.* I, pp. 485-487.

140. From A. R. Duy Vinycomt (EUL Gen. 2904/5/2358 a&b)

Arno Ward
Princess Alice Hosp
Eastbourne
[1936]

Dear Chris

This will be a bit of a surprise for you.

How are you & James Michael & Valda getting on

Lots have happened since I last heard from you all of which has ended in nothing

I have spent the last few years being sick with periodic stays in the various hospitals here & elsewhere

I had an operation for my tummy trouble 3 years ago but derived no real benefit from it so have been more or less sick ever since

This is my fourth trip into hosp to get rid of incessant sickness I have seen at various times that you have been keeping your pen busy & have had the good luck to have been given a copy of your *Scottish Scene* & I would like to send it to you to get your moniker on it. I am enjoying it very much indeed & even in my ignorant way can appreciate it

It would be impossible to tell you in a letter how I have lived for the last few years. Casual wards, odd work & odd coppers sleeping when possible in barns & ditches totally alone most of the time tho' I have met one or two interesting people

I came into this hospital after a breakdown about 11 days ago & expect to be here another fortnight if they don't operate again

I would be glad to hear from you & am sending this to you through your publishers as it is the only address I have

Write & let me know how you are getting on before I leave here

Seasons wishes & kindest regards to Valda self & James Michael

Ever yours

(Michael)

A. R. Duy Vinycomt

141. From Ed Scouller (EUL MS2954.12 f.3)

47 Alcraig Road
Mosspark
Glasgow SW2
10 February 1937

From Edward Scouller, M.A.

Dear Grieve,

You are really very amusing.[1]

Yours faithfully,

Ed Scouller.

[1]   In his previous letter Edward Scouller had asked MacDiarmid to demit the task of writing a biography of John MacLean in his favour since he had known MacLean and heard him speak as early as 1910. He refers, in the earlier letter, to his unpublished novel 'Sons of Halleluiah', which features MacLean and other leaders in one section (EUL MS2954.12).

142. From Douglas MacKillop (NLS Acc. 7361/8)

9 Ulitza Vakhtangova
Moscow
20 March 1937

Dear Mr MacDiarmid,

I apologize for usurping the privileges of your friends in writing to you: I was so moved by *Scottish Eccentrics*, by the philosophy underlying the whole book and nobly expressed in the dedication that I have not been able to resist the temptation to do so. You can always tear up an impertinent letter and scatter it to the winds of your island.

Why are great tines especially a danger and a drawback to the Scottish stag? because he lives in a zoological garden, not in a forest and wire-netting is a special risk for the antlers. As I take you to say, the model of the conforming Scot with his materialist preoccupations, his yes-man humour, his frugality and fortitude (all admirable qualities in a conquered race, from the point of view of the conqueror) was first created as a figment of English propaganda and subsequently adopted in self-preservation by a conquered nation that accepted its own conquest and its own death. I have always felt that.

And it *is* dead. Everything *distinctively* Scottish is separated from the life of men of today by centuries of complete cessation of national existence *and growth* and is completely anachronistic. The feudal savagery of clan and tartan is absurd in the Europe of today: its real home in this century is the Congo. Scots and Gaelic in their present, that is fossilized, form are artificial survivals too, except in peasant speech which (like patriotism) is 'not enough', because the real, distinctive, and very rich life of the Scottish nation in which its languages and institutions were rooted, and in which alone they could live and develop nationally and harmoniously, ceased when we were wiped out or sold out.

What is Scotland today? a museum, a grouse moor, and a slum. You can't make a nation out of that (or so at least it seems to me: you as a real Scotsman must know.) And what ought to be the population of Scotland today consists too largely of men like myself, exiled from our own country two or three generations before we were born.

Please forgive my bad manners in writing to you and of course please do not bother to reply. You must receive hundreds of these tiresome letters and this one has served its purpose, which was to clear my mind of the painful toxins which your book was bound to create, and I am sure was meant to create, in any normally constituted man of Scottish blood.

Yours sincerely,
Douglas MacKillop.

143. From Kenneth Patchen (EUL MS2962.7 f.10)

Reproduced by permission of Pollinger Limited and the proprietor

April 1937

Dear Hugh MacDiarmid,
I have delayed the extension of my thanks (for *Second Hymn to Lenin*) and my greetings (for first word from you: an event in my life). I have been in Hollywood, golden-idiocy centre of the world. Desire for money brought me here; longing for peace is taking me away to New York. I own several of your books. Wonderful things. Also, I have been press-agenting for you: two bookshops in California have promised to get works by you.

My first book of poems, *Before the Brave*, was published in 1936 by Random House. I was awarded a Guggenheim Fellowship in that year. A lack of health induced me to spend some time in Arizona and New Mexico. I have been married 3 years and have reached my 25th year. My second book (unpublished as yet) is better than my first. But I am not worried about writing; I like living. I shall send you some of my new poems after I get settled a bit in New York. And write you further then.

Respectfully,
Kenneth Patchen.

144. From the Communist Party of Great Britain (TNA KV2/2010)[1]

4 June 1937

Dear Comrade Grieve,

With reference to your appeal against expulsion from the Party, which came before the Party Congress last weekend, we are pleased to inform you that the Congress decided to allow your appeal. At the same time, Congress expressed the most strong condemnation of your whole attitude towards the Party, as implied in the publication of articles and expression of opinion contrary to the policy of the Party, without first consulting with the leadership of the Party in the Scottish District. However, the Congress was impressed by the pledges made in your appeal, to submit all such material to the Party in future, and to carry out the line of the Party as decided from time to time at Congress; this being the duty of all members of the Communist Party, without exception. Therefore, the comrades decided to allow your appeal on the following conditions:-

1. That you be on probation as a member of the Party for the next six months i.e., that at the end of this period the views of the Scottish leadership shall be requested by the Central Committee regarding your attitude as a member of the Party at the end of the six months probation.

2. That you play an active part in carrying out work amongst Scottish writers for the Party loyally co-operating with the Scottish District leadership in this activity.

3. That a discussion be arranged between the Scottish District Committee and yourself on the question of Scottish Nationalism, and the differences of opinion which exist between yourself and the D.P.C. on this matter, with the object of arriving at a satisfactory understanding between yourself and the D.P.C.

We hope that the decision of the Congress is acceptable to you, as we believe it will be, and that you will feel that you are in a position to carry through the conditions which the Congress made, with regard to your appeal against expulsion, successfully.

Yours fraternally,
The Secretariat.

[1]   TNA KV 2/2010, 23A.

145. From George Elder Davie (EUL MS2946.12 f.50)

Letter Card from George Davie
postmarked 'Dundee Angus 6pm 15 JNE [1937]'.

Dear Grieve,

Many thanks for the 3/- A rather nasty time is in store for me. I've been ordered by the doctor to take three months of a complete rest, and have been permitted to finish my philosophy degree only on condition of leaving Edinburgh, and studying in Germany.[1] I have also been told that I can count on academic promotion in my career only if I cut loose from politics & cease to give you aid. Thus ends in temporary defeat & surrender a very worrying conflict. But I am submitting only because I myself must have a rest, a change & peace to study & because the opposition forces (esp. the Muir-Communist alliance) are far too numerous & in point of influence powerful to dish with my present resources. On the advice of my professors, I think my mother is to write to you, telling you to withhold your 'corrupting influences' etc.[2] That ought to be amusing. I'm reading Balzac thro' just now, & going abroad presently. Don't please write. Regards to Mrs G. and yourself. More power to your elbow.

Yours ever,

G. E. Davie.

---

[1] The Senatus of Edinburgh University later allowed George Davie to study elsewhere than Germany and he chose Montpellier. However he wrote to MacDiarmid from Freiburg, 15.02.1938. (EUL MS2964.12 f.56).

[2] In a letter to Alan Bold, 7 October 1983, Dr George Davie wrote: 'Briefly, [Professor] Kemp Smith had been reported as saying that he would not give backing to my career as a student unless I ceased my association (writing etc.) with Chris, who was in Shetland at that time. I told Chris about this before I spoke to Kemp Smith who emphatically and unembarrassedly denied that what he had said bore any such construction and there for me that matter ended.' (*Letters*, p.574).

146. From George Blake (NLS Acc. 7361/8)

The Glenan
Helensburgh
Dunbartonshire
3 July 1937

My dear Grieve,

I thought I had that cutting beside me but looking through a bundle of such things, I suddenly remembered I had given all the articles in that lifeboat series to the Lifeboat Institution. And now it is too late to get a cutting out of the *Express* pics.

Actually, I got the facts out of an R.N.L.I. magazine they publish monthly, and I am sure you could get them by writing to the Hon. Secretary, Royal Naval Lifeboat Institution, Aberdeen. The episode took place on Christmas Day, 1936, – and it was a very queer affair. There seems little doubt that the men lost their lives through their own fear of taking the jump.[1]

If you have difficulty in getting what you want, let me know, and I'll try the R.N.L.I. in Glasgow. Just at the moment I am hopelessly tangled in a mass of obligations & engagements.

You are certainly far removed from the world these days, but I most sincerely hope that you are happy, well & productive.

All kind regards.
Yours sincerely,
George Blake.

1   MacDiarmid describes this tragedy in 'The Wreck of the *Swan*', *C.P.*, I, pp.728-734.

147. From Kenneth Patchen (EUL MS2962.7 f.14)

Reproduced by permission of Pollinger Limited and the proprietor

2163 ½ Beechwood Terrace
Hollywood
California
23 July [1937]

Dear Hugh MacDiarmid:
It was my intention to write you before now, but the press of work of one kind and another has delayed me.

Have you seen my poems as yet? I should like to send you some of the things from my new manuscript. Would that be of interest to you?

I am making a short visit to New York shortly, and I hope to get further work of yours there. It is my desire to acquire all things from your pen.

Are all of your books available through Stanley Nott?

Could you suggest an English publisher who might be receptive to my work – I'd like to publish there.

I am very fond of your 'In the Slums of Glasgow'.[1]

Forgive me this aimless note: but accept the poem.[2]

Respectfully,
Kenneth Patchen.

1   *C.P.* I, pp. 562-565.
2   Kenneth Patchen sent 'The Fox', which was published in *The Voice of Scotland*, vol.1, no.3 (December 1938-February 1939), p.22.

148. From William Soutar (EUL MS2960.18 ff.20-21)

27 Wilson St
Perth
23 July 1937

Dear C.M.G.,
If I hadn't had ample evidence of what sort of verse I produce to order I might have agreed to become the Jonah for your whale of an idea; but I have already written something like twenty thousand lines of set verse and if the most generous critic can find 20 lines of poetry in the lot I'll be greatly surprised.[1] Not that your idea isn't an excellent one – but such an anthology as you propose cannot, in my opinion, be

anticipated. I know well enough what sort of work you are after as I have seen a few Russian anthologies; and I think you posit the problem yourself when you assert that your ideal poem for such a collection would be one such as a worker might have written himself. That's the crux – can the worker have his poems written for him? So baldly stated I think the answer is obvious. Hence my own conviction that lyrics such as your 'Seamless Garment'[2] are about as near as one can get to proletarian poetry while the worker is yet an exploited member of an imperialism. Going deeper into the psychology of the contemporary embarrassment of poetry – any attempt to anticipate what can be done only by the communalised proletarian poet is a kind of inverted exploitation; out of an over-anxiety to help comes the assumption of responsibility for – an attitude I believe which has its origin not only in the one-sidedness of the theological interpretation of vicariousness but in the capitalistic presumption of taking it for granted that the common man is not to be trusted with full self-responsibility. I need hardly add that an approximation to full self-responsibility can come only within a true socialism, & with it the capabilities of complete self-expression. If however I am convinced of the futility of forcing experience I am as thoroughly convinced that you are right in maintaining that the present necessity for Scottish (or any) poets is to achieve simplicity; and it is because of this persuasion that the ballad tradition means so much to the contemporary Scottish poet & will be ultimately the jumping-off ground for poetic drama in Scotland. And such a simplicity seems to be the natural concomitant to communistic faith: as you wrote in the 'Second Hymn':-

A' the cleverness on earth'll no' mak' up
For the damnable dearth.

Nor is it stressing the dialectic to see that the growing need for simplicity is not only a necessary communal preparation but a natural revulsion from the excessive intellectualisation of the post-war years; the movement from the 'ideal coterie of one' to the audience of all. Joyce, for example, seems to me to manifest a Nazification of genius – the private (introverted) polarisation of what in public we subsume under Hitlerism; the worship of the one.

I hope you keep exceptionally fit in spite of your phenomenal productiveness, may it not be long before we see the first of the 'vingtuplets' yelling from the publishers' lists. All join in sending every good wish to yourself, Mrs Grieve & Michael.

Ever yours,
W. S.

---

[1]   In his letter to Soutar, 31 May 1937, MacDiarmid had suggested 'A book of 400 or thereby lyrics (lyrics = short poems in this connection, not necessarily songs) - title *The Commons of Scotland* poems to be in Scots and for most part, to average 12 to 20 lines'. (*Letters,* p.157).

[2]   'The Seamless Garment', *C. P.* I, pp.311-314.

149. From W. D. MacColl / Dùghall MacColla (EUL MS2953.9 f.3)

Am Baile nan Dorchadas[1]
18 August 1937

Dear Chris,

This is good news and I'm delighted to have your letter and to know that all is well with yours and you – thank God for that – and that your activities, purposes and work are unimpaired. Physically separated as you are in some respects from your fellows in far-off Whalsay, you are not divorced from Nature there, and that is less isolating perhaps than some of us in the midst of a 'cloud of witnesses', but who bear *quelle témoignage*! [2]

I rejoice at the prospect of our meeting, but as I have allowed myself to get too tired to plan anything very clearly, would some itinerary of this sort suit you, – say, meeting at Arisaig in Morar about the 7th [September], with visits round about and to Eigg and Canna; thence to Loch Scavaig and over An Cuilithionn Sgitheanach (the Coolin of Skye) to Dunvegan, – I'd like to visit Boreraig for the sake of the MacCrimmons, for I don't know these parts at all and so to Uist, where I have a cousin who I hope will be at home. From there we could get back to Strome Ferry or Wester Ross?

Alternatively, we could go the other way round; but I fancy the first makes a better progression of interest, – from the quieter to the more lively, from the tourist, the deer-shoot, the babies on the sand (heaven bless 'em, if they are Scots) to the Native? And if that date suited you, it would enable me to recover some native sense and spirit en route before meeting you?[3]

Shure, I'm plaised to hear you'll be wearing the fine dress, Uisdein Mhic Dhairmaid, for it's what I'll be doing myself, with only a gaberlunzie wallet and a waterproof forbye (unless for a change of clothing in a kitbag sent on before). So if the natives don't welcome us with, Haf you come alone or is this *the* General Rising? I'll be disappointed.

I'll not attempt to answer your interesting literary news now, even if I thought myself able; for in anticipation of our meeting will you sometimes remember how Nature in her playfulness has created higher and lower organisms, through all the atomic numbers and their combinations, yet not haphazardly perhaps but for the better exciting and combining them?

It was stupid of me to write Wanda for Valda and you must both excuse me. Dr. A.[4] I well remember if only for his too early rising after a late night and his seeming sense of regret to have spent it, if not among dishonest or ill-intentioned, at least (as events have shown) among somewhat self-flattering bums. But hope and humour are great redressers of our human foibles..

Will you remember me very kindly to him, and warmly.

Buaidh leat agus leibh, a charaid,[5]

U. Dùghall MacColla.

---

[1] In the town of darkness (i.e. London).
[2] What witness!
[3] MacColl refers here to his plans for his journey through the Highlands and Islands with

MacDiarmid in September 1937. In his next letter, 6 October 1937, MacColl estimated that they had travelled 750-800 miles between Arisaig and Perth of which less than a third had probably been by water. MacDiarmid commemorated the journey in 'A Golden Wine in the Gaidhealtachd' which was addressed 'To W. D. MacColl and our hosts and hostesses in Arisaig, Eigg, South Uist, Raasay, Skye, Barra, and Mull', *C.P.*, I, pp.721-722.

4   Possibly Dr Orr.
5   Literally, 'May success be with you (singular) and you (plural), my friend'. In other words, 'May success be with you all, my friend'.

150. From Ruth Pitter (EUL MS2958.8 ff.3-4)

55A Church Street
Chelsea SW3
20 August 1937

Dear Kit Grieve,

Many thanks for your letter and for the curious poem, the parallel of which with our painful art is so exact: I wonder where you find your material?[1] I could wish you had trimmed it a little: the first line, for example, where you write,

It is with the poet as it is with the guinea-worm

– couldn't it be,

As with the poet so with the guinea-worm – ?

The intensity of the whole thing makes me ashamed that I don't suffer as I suppose you do: I have many tricks of avoiding it, and no doubt my work is worth the less in consequence.

I don't mind wormy material in the least, having long since got over the nice-and-nasty classification of ideas, and indeed being rather partial to these our innocent enemies, who are flowers of Paradise compared with some of our gifted contemporaries. I can well believe that Scott-James[2] could not stomach it: perhaps if I were an editor I might feel obliged to reject it myself. I hope not.

Did you get the copy of my last book which I sent you?

Yours,
Ruth Pitter.

1   Ruth Pitter here refers to the poem, 'To my Friend, Miss Ruth Pitter', which was first published in *The Voice of Scotland* (January 1955), with 'Winner of the Hawthornden Prize, 1937' in brackets under the title and a starred footnote, 'The macabre detail of many of whose poems in *A Mad Lady's Garland* (1934) perhaps excuses my helminthological figure here'. In *Complete Poems* (1978), the title has become 'To a Friend and Fellow-Poet' and a footnote gives her name. The notes in the first publication have been omitted.
2   Rolfe Arnold Scott-James (1878-1959) was editor of *the London Mercury* from 1934 to 1939.

151. From F. G. Scott (EUL MS2959 ff.76-78)

44 Munro Road
Jordanhill
Glasgow W3
6 September 1937

My dear Chris

Another letter from you this morning, making altogether *three* I've to reply to – how has it to be done? Let me say right away that I very much welcome this spate of correspondence. In St Andrews one of the few serious conversations I had (with Tonge) was about the absurdity and the pity of your being cut off so drastically from the genuine support and supporters you still have in Scotland. They don't amount to much in some ways but all the same a little assurance from them now and then helps the wheels to go round. I went up to see Soutar before I left – he's another anxious enquirer about all your concerns – genuine to the core and proud of all your work. What a pleasure to find such disinterestedness and self-effacement!

Now to business. You're having a pretty hellish time of it I can see what with this publisher and that and the uncertainty of how things are going to turn out. I honestly wish to God you could somehow or other get shot of all this donkey-work. I know all right that you like messing about in all kinds of strange waters – *vide* your letter this week in *Times Lit.* – but what after all is it going to amount to? Why should you bother your backside about *The Chronicles of Eri*?[1] You must realize at your time of life that your *own* work is sufficient evil for the day and be content to push aside lots of interests as being outside your immediate range. I have of course nothing to say against books you are committed to write, but I myself would reduce as far as possible the number of these and get on with *your own job*. Think for a moment of C.M.G. finishing off as one of yon bespectacled literary cranks that haunt the British Museum and public libraries digging up dead worms of information – dead maggots on dead carcases! I hope the prospect frightens you! To hell with everything that distracts you from the business of writing poetry. If needs must, then write pot-boilers that will give you the leisure you require, not these recondite tomes that are taking up so much of your time and energy!

So that's grouse No. 1 off my chest! No.2 is about the Autobiography –who's this Edwin Muir that requires 20-30 000 words, the excerpt you refer to? For the love of Mike, have some sense of proportion. If it's a history of your opinions you're writing, well and good, but even then I'd think Muir could be dismissed in a mere 500 or so. You wouldn't like to admit that he (Muir) has been so important as all that in your life story? I'm sure he'll feel flattered! It's all rather curious, Christopher – but if you take *my* outlook for a moment you'll perhaps see in *your* attitude a sign of your own nervousness with regard to Muir – which means a want of real confidence in yourself. Recalling my advice to you to remember that you're not a world-beater you say that you've 'very carefully neglected that advice', and go on to give a publisher's statement about what he had read of your auto.: 'I could criticise it endlessly. MacDiarmid's arrogance is an amazing phenomenon, etc., etc.'.[2] But that's just it! My whole point regarding the 'world-beater', taking into account *my* view of things, is that you *think* you are. I pay you a higher tribute than that – I know that you *can* be when you come to terms with yourself and your own destiny, in other words, when you find the confidence in yourself necessary for the accomplishment of your work. You will then stop playing at hide-and-seek with yourself, cut out the arrogance and get on quietly with the job. It's difficult, I know, but it's got to be done. Perhaps you won't then *think* yourself a 'world-beater' but I'm pretty sure you *will* be! And don't be so very careful to neglect my advice – mister!!!

The 'Ceol Mhor'[3] book is still in the land of maybe. I'd still like to write it but everything pertaining to Gaelic culture is a hellish morass of contradictions and I sometimes feel compelled to leave the Gaels to finish the fight amongst themselves – the contradictions being in Gaelic and arising out of the language itself. They're quite happy about it all – they have the finest language in the world, the finest poetry, the finest music – and the finest lack of common sense about everything else under the sun.

Turner's essay on 'Words and Music' is quite a reasonable statement from *his* point of view.[4] If you're thinking of controverting him I warn you to beware. Musically he's sound enough – you confuse his meaning when you quote as damned nonsense his 'music speaks solely to the ear' – not the mind, but the ear! He's not thinking about the mental repercussions, he's merely referring to music as an auditory experience, just as painting etc. comes to us via the eye. So give the devil his due. If you can recall an essay of mine on 'Poetry and Music' which I think you read when in Glasgow you will see that I dealt with the whole thing far more fundamentally than Turner by taking as a basis for both arts, *RHYTHM*. I showed there that both arts have shown corresponding changes, now markedly rhythmical as in lyric metres and dances, now less regularly rhythmical as in blank verse, free verse etc., the musical equivalent being the song of an expressive kind. To schematize the argument:

	Poetry	Music	Life as
(A) Simple regular rhythm –	lyric stanzas	dances	ACTION
(B) Complex irregular rhythm –	loose metres like blank verse etc. songs of slow tempo	chants, church music, pibrochs,	CONTEMP-LATION

This isn't very good after all! I'm going on with my explanation all the same – it may be useful to your own work. First of all it must be understood that the two categories are continually running into each other and there are countless cases where it would be difficult to decide which category a poem or song belonged to. What Turner is trying to say is that a poem in Class A shouldn't be set to music of Class B type, and vice versa. He thinks (and I agree with him) that Wagner, Strauss (and I may add all the moderns) have made the mistake of confusing the classes so that the simple rhythm of a lyrical poem is often treated to the countertones of a musical rhythm at complete variance with the poetic rhythm. But that's elementary. If you poets, I'm including Hugh MacD along with Yeats, the whole bunch of you in fact, want your songs to be sung

[...] in the factories and fields,
In the streets o' the toon?
Gin they're no', then I'm failin' to dae
What I ocht to ha' dune.

– I say if you're really wanting to be *sung* in the *communist* sense of 'the people' singing – then you'll have to forswear free irregular rhythm and stick to plain-Jane stanza poems with plenty of swing and energy in the rhythm. That's elementary too! Well, but here's one for you. You and I are both lyricists of no mean order. For some years you have been anxious to appear as a major poet (this is in class B – the philosophical, contemplative etc.) and you have pushed the irregularity of your rhythms so far that many have described your poetry as *PROSE*! It's inevitable, it's a matter of degree. If there's *no* regularity in the metre (poetic or musical) the thing becomes prose, just prose. I haven't seen enough of the 'Heroic Song'[5] but *Cencrastus* shows the evolution of your muse, large lumps of prose, let's call it for the moment, with snatches of poetry you printed generally in italics. The warning finger points out to you that no matter what the content of your latest stuff may be it will in the end be styled 'prosy', 'prosaic poetry'. For good or ill, it won't stand as poetry and worst fate of all, the 'content' you were so proud of will have become stale and outmoded like the opinions in yesterday's *Glasgow Herald* or better, yesterday's *Daily Worker*.

Mind you, I'm not saying that you're wrong. In fact I finished my lecture aforesaid by saying that the problems of the day could not be expressed in simple lyrical stanzas and that the poetry of the future would necessitate the use of a complex rhythmical kind of verse. The more complex it is will not hinder it from being poetry but the complete absence of any kind of rhythm will undoubtedly land us in a prose epoch. That of course may be the communistic millenium, which certainly looks prosy enough from many points of view; still, I imagine there will always be folks wanting to sing songs of some kind instead of reading the report of the last International – so it's up to you, my boy, to be doing something for *them*, to give me the (communist) songs of the day after tomorrow and let me get busy putting them to singable music. I want you to *anticipate* the era of communism.[6]

1   In his letter to the *TLS*, 4 September 1937, MacDiarmid asked for information about Arthur O'Connor (1763-1852), and Roger O'Connor (1762-1834) who wrote *Chronicles of Eri* published in 1832. (*Letters*, 778).

2   Victor Gollanz was the publisher who wrote the statement (NLS MS27152 f.44r.).

3   *Ceol Mohr* - Great Music.

4   H. Sandiford Turner (1869-1928).

5   'Cornish Heroic Song for Valda Trevlyn' became the First Appendix to 'Mature Art' and was published in *The Criterion* vol. xviii, no.lxxi (January 1939). *C.P.* I, pp.704-712.

6   F.G. Scott goes on to quote Blake's 'Jerusalem' in full and the letter breaks off.

152. From Valda Grieve (NLS MS27149 f.140)

17 September 1937
12:30pm

Dear Christopher –

Many thanks for postcards & wires – if I realised you were staying longer – I would have sent these on before – I hope it is not too late & that you will get them before you leave Lochboisdale –

I am glad you are having a good & interesting time – this holiday should really do you the world of good & there will really be no excuse when you come back to say you're on the brink of a nervous breakdown.

I've enclosed letter which came from [Donald] Gordon day with a couple of books – I am very surprised & annoyed to know that you have been borrowing money from him – surely £19.15 – was enough to last you a fortnight in Edinburgh – I'm tired & fed-up with unexpected bills coming in – surely you have some control over yourself If it is not too much to ask you – I would be grateful – if on the homeward voyage – you would spend as little as possible – after posting this – I will have 7 ½ left – it is the regatta to morrow & I'm afraid Michael will have to go without the usual 6d he expects & should have – I'm afraid now I have little patience with your concern for Christine & Walter – at least they are well clothed & have the things that make a child's life worth living – M was wet through several times last week – his Mac is too short & tight & his rubber boots leak water – After the Gilgal business – you led me to expect a straight deal & it is evident you're not man enough to keep your word or control yourself. Because you have brains – you think, I believe, that you can do anything – & expect everything from me – Expect on, laddie – as Gay Taylor say's Even a worm will turn[1] – Cheerio Valda.

---

[1] Gay Taylor was a member of Charles Lahr's circle in London.
  A note at the end of the letter says 'the 'tec books are in at Symbister – have got – the enclosed'. In the margin at the beginning of the letter Valda has listed six books. Perhaps these books came from Mr W. A. Bruce, the laird of Whalsay, who lived at Symbister House.

153. From John G. Anderson (NLS MS27166 f.9)

East Hamister
Whalsay
16 October 1937

Dear Mr Grieves,

I wrote you a letter about a year ago requesting the payment, or part payment of the debt you still owe me for the house and I never received any answer.

I have received from you £40 and there is still another £15 due. I would be much obliged if you would settle up for the amount mentioned, or part of it, at your earliest.

Attention to the above would much oblige

Valda Grieve with their son Michael.
By permission of the MacDiarmid Estate.

Yours faithfully,
John G. Anderson.
E. Hamister
Whalsay

154. From Ruaraidh Erskine of Mar (EUL MS2946.16 f.10)

Carlton
Biarritz
France

21 October 1937

Dear Mr Grieve,

I was very pleased to get yours, forwarded from London, and to hear that your health is improved, and to this good news you add what I regard with a peculiar satisfaction, that you are now seeking to draw to a head the men in parties in Scotland of whom something may with reason be expected in a true national way. Needless to say I am entirely at one with you in this, and if I can be of any help you have but to let me know.

My own opinion is that much time and energy have been wasted by reason of bunglers who have no sense of politics at all & vainly beat from post to post, uncertain even as to their primal objectives, thus reproducing the kind of vain futile conduct that prevailed at the time of the parliamentary union. What I should like to see is a complete cutaway from all these futilities (persons & principles), and a bold start made with an essentially Celtic policy suitable to modern conditions and above all antagonistic to the Germanic ideology. It would take me a long time to explain all that I think, more especially as to the current international situation, and the grave need there is for a *really* Celtic *resorgimento* in the West, to save the world from 'democracy' or Germanic Liberalism on one hand and Communism on the other, but some at least of the notions I have I hope to set forth in a book on which I am at present engaged that deals with modern Europe & the racial content. There are men in Ireland who might be got to join a serious move having for its object the re-assertion of the Celtic West; & in Wales & Brittany also I think a group might be formed on the same lines, and clear of all imputation of 'Pan-Celticism' and suchlike fantasies of the 'limelight' spirit. I have approached some, & found them willing enough; but now that I am come abroad for a time at least I doubt if I could or can do more at the moment than help to form the groups I speak of. Feeling this, I wrote to you to find out if *you* have anything in the same way on the anvil, and I'm glad to learn you have; and I wonder if *your* lines are in any sort of correspondence with my own.

The flat we had in London my wife & I have given up, so we'll not return to. The bad London atmosphere and the rough habits of the Londoners have driven us forth, & though poor France is manifestly much decayed, and decaying, still one ceases here to breathe the poisonous airs of the great Germanic ideology and that at least is some gain! Next spring I hope to return to Scotland & there to be of some use to put things into shape, but meanwhile I think that you & I – you in your Shetland & I in my French retreat – might do something to mend our common country.

Always v. sincerely yours,

Ruaraidh Erskine of Mar.

155. From Catherine Carswell (NLS MS27152 ff.45-47)

Don has had no further word either from C.F.[1]

35 Gloucester Crescent
[London] NW1
1 November 1937

Dear Chris,

I give you the address of my 2-room London flat, where I spend more than half my time, though I am writing this from Essex. By the same post I'm asking your friend, Miss Robertson, to ring me up and come one evening after I get back in a few days from now. You don't say what her post is, & neither does she, but I'll hear all that when I see her, & she will be very welcome as a friend of yours.

I sympathise more & more with all disinclination to work, i.e. for a living! But other means of livelihood are apparently even more irksome, so I see nothing for it but to go on. My Boccaccio book is not going well, though it had warm reviews in *The Times Lit Supp*, *Observer*, *Manchester Guardian*, & some other papers, while it met with lengthy hostility in *The New Statesman*, *Spectator* & *Time & Tide*. Not that I feel I care much. I know it is pretty good. It is, however, a bit of bad luck that the publishers, Lawrence & Wishart, are being, they tell me, banned by the booksellers for their Leftishness which has gravely affected my sales as, though strongly Left, *The Tranquil Heart* is not very saleable by Left Bookshops who deal chiefly in political books inexpensively produced. Well, there it is.

We are all well & John writes in great spirits from Oxford where he seems to be thoroughly himself. He says one can have a rich social life there in spite of being a hard-up scholar.

Don prefers to live mostly in the country & comes to London only for the day as a rule every 10 days or so. I like being on my own in my flat without having to run a household after more than 20 years of that over-rated activity. We are both on our own now, financially, and if only we could pay off past bills, we could sail along in a quiet way without too much worry. But the bills are not yet paid off, & freelance journalism is an uncertain business.

Don, after long postponement, will probably visit Scotland shortly, both to see editors in Glasgow & Edinburgh & to try & screw something out of Thomas for failing to produce his play. I may go up in February as I have been offered fares & hotel bill there if I speak at the Soroptomists (whoever they may be!) annual dinner there. I usually have to sing for my supper, though my hosts don't always seem to enjoy my singing.

Both Don & I have dates with the B.B.C. Don is to give a Book Talk on Dec. 5 from London. (Have you anything 'recent' enough for him to include?) I am to pot a serial for the Scottish Children's Hour, I think, running from Jan. to March, but not to do the talking.

It is good to know that Valda & the boy are well. I hope you have got rid of your chill by now. Did the kilt play you false for once?

Any chance of seeing you in Glasgow, Edinburgh or London? I doubt if either of us will get as far as Shetland on a winter trip.

Here's hoping for us all.

When are you going to give us some more poems?

Love to Valda & Mike.

from

Cathie.

[1]   Covici Friede, US publishers.

156. From Ruaraidh Erskine of Mar (EUL MS2946.16 ff.8-9)

The Carlton Hotel
Biarritz
France
13 November 1937

Dear Grieve,

I think that now that the anti-Communist Pact[1] is *une chose accomplie* a general racial alignment will take place on ideological lines, and continue till 'the day' comes, & the biggest struggle of the centuries is begun. *In these circumstances I think that we should be moving.* No doubt the Pact will in course of time split up (as England & the rest of the Brit. Isles) into factions. Some will be for & some against it, and some, taking their cue from the English government, be neither, but neutrals or pretend to be so. Now therefore is our chance to come forward with an alternative policy – one neither specifically Communist nor anti-Communist nor yet midway policy, but *designed for Scotland first and last*, and if it could be rendered so as to put it into shape with Irish and Welsh aspirations & conditions we should thereby come at what I think is necessary at the present time – *namely, an all-embracing union & pro-Celtic policy*.

Our natural ally & friend on the Continent is France; but France at present is merely England's echo, and we can do nothing with her so long as this state of affairs prevails. France (as representing old Gaul) is the natural ally of Scotland, Ireland & Wales (which countries are Celtic) but I repeat that so long as the mind of France remains attached to England we can make but little progress here. On this reasoning, it is obvious that the need is a Celtic policy which in its broad features at least will appeal to the Celtic parts of the British Isles and at the same time interest France. I think this might be done – 'wild' though the idea may sound at the present moment; and I think that the best way to prepare the way for it is to show France and the rest of the Continent that the Celts of the British Isles are at long last again 'on their elbow'. I think the treatise I am now preparing for the press might go some way towards calling attention to our – the Celtic – continued existence, and thus prepare the way for such a pro-Celtic policy as these remarks indicate. It would not be difficult I think to take Celtic principles of government, of culture, and social organisation, and from them evolve a way or mode of life and living that would suit ourselves as well as the French.

I am strongly persuaded that the next few years will be devoted to the alignment spoken of above. The world is small nowadays, and I see no room in it for the ideologies of Communism and Dictatorship: inevitably, they must clash, and fight it out for mastery; but I see no good reason why either Hebrewism (Communism) or Germanism (Dictatorship) should rule the Celts; and if we and the French stand firm at the coming crisis together we might 'save' Europe (and the world generally) far more effectually than the English have ever done, assuming that their boast that they have 'saved' Europe once or twice already is not mere bluff & swank, which for my part I think it is. Let me know what you think.

Sincerely yours,
Ruaraidh Erskine of Mar.

---

[1]   The anti-Comintern Pact was concluded on 25 November 1936, between Germany and Japan. Italy joined the Pact on 6 November 1937.

157. From Henry Grant Taylor (EUL MS2966)

Bridgend
Southwick
Dumfries
20 November 1937

Dear Sir,
I have received a letter from Mr Montgomery Butchart of Gilbert Wright Ltd., in which he suggests that I might be of assistance to you in the capacity of secretary-typist. My name had been passed on to him by Mr Robert Sutherland of Edinburgh.

The proposition has been put to me very clearly, and at the outset I must state that I am only too willing to come north and do my best to be of some assistance to you.

I have only one misgiving. I can lay no claim to being an expert shorthand-typist. I type accurately and at a fair speed, but my shorthand is not up to the same standard. It is some time since I used it, but I am confident that in the course of, say, a month, I could bring it up to a standard sufficient for your needs.

At the same time, I think you might find that this temporary disadvantage would be offset by the keen interest I would take in your work, and the qualifications I have for handling it. I have done a small amount of literary work, and it is my intention to make my living as a journalist, and perhaps one day as an author. The work of preparing MSS is quite familiar to me. As for keeping your literary work in order, handling correspondence, and relieving you of tasks of lesser importance, I feel confident that I could deal with these competently.

I hope that I have given sufficient detail to enable you to form an impression of the person who would be working for you. I shall be only too glad to furnish further information if it is desired. If you do ask me to come, you may be assured that the interest I would take in your work would be more than a merely academic one. And I would give you every ounce of help of which I am capable.

Should you decide to engage me on trial, I am ready to travel whenever you wish. I await your decision.

Yours truly,

Henry G. Taylor.

158. From Norman Kemp Smith (EUL Gen. 2094/5/2136)

Braid Hills Hotel
Edinburgh
22 December 1937

Dear Mr Grieve,

I am very glad to have your letter – & have had it in mind to reply to it long before this. But I must not delay longer in acknowledging it, & of telling you how glad I am that the misunderstanding has been cleared up.

I had a letter recently from our mutual friend Davie. He rejoices in Freiburg; & I trust will be able to put in a winter of good work, with much else thrown in, and return with renewed health. All good wishes of the season to you.

Sincerely yours,

Norman Kemp Smith.

159. From T. S. Eliot (EUL MS2967/3)

8 February 1938

Dear Mr Grieve,

I am very glad to hear from you after this long time, and shall be very glad indeed if you will let me see your long poem. It sounds to me very interesting, though I must say the title MATURE ART is somewhat forbidding! I look forward also to reading your essay.

With best wishes,

Yours very sincerely,

T. S. Eliot.

160. From Vincent Flynn (NLS Acc.7361/9)

c/o Duncan
22 Hayburn Cres.
Glasgow W2
19 May 1938

My Dear Comrade MacDiarmid,

You must forgive me for my long silence which has been caused by having to run back and forth on trade union business. This is just a scribble; I shall reply to your lovely letter tomorrow, but I want you to cast your eye over the enclosed manuscript.

The editor of *Scots Independent*, whom I interviewed, sent it me for my views, but I feel that your views are more important than mine. You wrote the article explaining why you were associating with us and I feel that you alone have the right to say what should be cut.[1]

Frankly, I am opposed to sub-editing of material of political substance; and this man provides an excellent example of how to edit the word and mutilate the idea. It is an old trick to set up shies to knock them down again. I am not saying this man had any deliberate intent to misrepresent, but I do feel that his effort is a travesty.

It was suggested to me that I should let it go and then we could all start a good correspondence, but I feel we'd be so busy explaining what really was written that we'd never get anywhere with the real matter. And a controversy confined to long explanations gives uninformed people the impression that someone is trying to hide something.

Anyway, I am sending the *Scots Independent* version for your view.

I think the man is in a hurry to go to press so if you wish you may send in the article, when finished, to 28 Elmbank Crescent, Glasgow. But it is as you wish, comrade. I have no fear that you will let anyone peg something into you. I think you can look after yourself.

I must hurry for the mail.

Best wishes.

Yours ever,

Vincent Flynn.

---

[1]   Flynn's letter here refers to an article which MacDiarmid sent to the *Scots Independent* headed 'The force of necessity versus the Pernicious Anaemia of Capitalist Culture' and from which the *S.I.* only had space for some extracts. These extracts included: 'I am proud to associate myself with the Glasgow Workers' Theatre Movement ... it represents by far the most important cultural development Scotland has witnessed since the death of Robert Burns'; 'It is of supreme importance that an increasing number of the younger writers of Scotland to-day belong to the working class, and have seized upon the key importance of proletarian drama, and established the Glasgow Workers' Theatre Group. It becomes at once the principal focus of all creative art in Scotland. Any writer who fails to realise its importance ... writes himself down either as a dunderhead, a lackey of the old order, or both'; 'It is a great task to which the Glasgow Workers' Theatre Group has addressed itself ... It will speedily become a splendid radiating core of Scottish Realism

throughout the whole body of Scottish culture. All the other cultural movements in Scotland to-day are hopelessly corrupt and anaemic.' – *Scots Independent*, August 1938. In January 1941 Glasgow Unity was formed by five companies – Glasgow Workers' Theatre Group, Clarion Players, Glasgow Players, Transport Players and the Jewish Institute Players. James Barke was the first Chair. This article was the first indication of MacDiarmid's support for working-class theatre which continued with his support of Theatre Union (Manchester) and Theatre Workshop of which he became a director.

161. From Neil M. Gunn (EUL MS2948.15 ff.33-36)

Braefarm House
Dingwall
Ross-shire
19 May 1938

My dear Christopher,

I am delighted you liked our news in *Off in a Boat.*[1] A lot of the most piquant stuff had to be cut out – the whole record, e.g., of the pinching of the oars by a General + Baronet – because of the curious law of libel. I fought my publishers stubbornly on this. But no use. Truth can be a most damning form of libel apparently. However, I think my conception of the landlords that inhabit – & have inhabited – the West comes through. Which is the main point. And Daisy is pleased you like her photographs.

I see your point about preferring this to fiction. But fiction is merely a vehicle for what one imagines one has to say about things – much as your poetry is to you. No comparison of content intended!

The success of a travel book of this sort is quite another kettle of fish. It gets a bit too near the marrow of conditions on the West, & in Gaeldom for that matter, to satisfy the leisured money class, I'm afraid, I always spoil poor old success by some silly cantrips of that kind.

Though *Highland River* has just been awarded the James Tait Black Memorial Prize as the 'best novel or literary work of that kind' published in 1937. And as a cheque accompanied the reward, I'm not complaining. As we are leaving on Monday for Munich, the cheque comes in very handy anyway. We hope to be away for a month or more. I have publishers in Munich who have been selling my stuff pretty well. They started off with *Butcher's Broom* last year. And I had a very long article in a German literary monthly on Modern Scot. letters (translated by some German in London Univ.) in which I gave your all-importance its due. So I – we, Daisy & I – are taking a turn over to see what it's all about. One of the fellows in the firm I met in this country & am getting him to show me all that's to be seen. You'll be amused at this connection! But you're not the only one who may smile.

So we're not cruising this year. In fact we're selling our boat. As you'll have gathered, she was hardly fit for rough seas. But I have made arrangements for the use of a bigger more seaworthy craft for the following year. Starting from Stornoway, the Shetlands shouldn't be impossible. And if this book squares the publishers, then by heavens I ought to get a decent chapter out of Whalsay! After I write the chapter I'd submit it to you to get your written promise not to pursue me for libel! I saw a book by Louis MacNeice about the West Coast. He called on Compton Mac. 'the sage of Barra', and found him like 'Lionel Barrymore (film-actor) about to turn into a bird' – or, at least, so says a review lying before me. But at least I'll be honest. If we'll both get drunk, we'll both get drunk!

However, that's fantasy – compared with the splendid news of your great poem.[2] By heaven, I hope she'll steer right into magnificent print. It's high time something was being produced in our land. The times lately have been arid & life is short. The thought of such a work from you excites me. There's so much niggling & so little in the grand generous manner that I'm looking forward to your opus, notes and all. You'll be a damned pundit & pedant yet! Being upsides with Eliot & that ilk, I suppose. Why not – and cheers anyway.

Yours,
Neil.

[1]   London, 1938.
[2]   'Mature Art'.

162. From Wendy Wood (EUL MS2966)

CAIRT PHOSTAIL TO MACDIARMID FROM WENDY WOOD POSTMARKED EDINBURGH 7.15 PM 25 MAY 1938. IT SHOWS A SPEAR THROWER IN KILT AND PLAID STANDING BARE-FOOTED ON A CLIFF.

Gaelic 'Failte's Furan'[1]

Many thanks. I cannot think of any particular way at the moment to take advantage of your kind offer. Hope to see you at Bannockburn. Think you will find it particularly interesting this year. This is one of five designs of un-English P.C.'s I am issuing. All the best. W.W.

[1]   Welcome and Hospitality.

163. From Kaikhosru Shapurji Sorabji (EUL MS2960.17 f.8)

175 Clarence Gate Gardens
London NW1
29 May 1938

My dear Grieve,

Is there any need to ask me whether I am gratified or not by your 'intarsiating' my name into your big new work?[1] Although not a literary person, and finding it necessary, both from inclination as well as time, to read ever less and less and exercise an ever-more ferocious Nazi-like exclusiveness in what I *do* read, nevertheless, you know what I know of you and your work to realise at how high a level I appreciate that immense compliment!

Have I ever, I wonder, come across Mr. [Dugald] MacColl in Glasgow? I seem to remember his presence somewhere where I was, some years since.

How is your health, for which sake you retired to the Hyperborean Islands? I myself have just returned from Italy and Sicily where I and my mother spent Easter, and the return to the blear-eyed climate of England has not proved at all welcome to us! Do you know Sicily at all? It is by far the most wonderful part of Italy, which it isn't a part of at all by the way, being as distinct as Scotland from England, and there is a sanity in its air that there is not in this air here! Each visit to Italy shows me new and admirable aspects, as far as the condition of the mass of the people is concerned, of the present regime, and no one who knew what Italy *was*, and I have known it since a child, can form any conception for the transformation; and there are not wanting indications that, although lip-service is still paid to the crazy and pestilent superstition of Sound Finance, that institution is being strained, in many particulars to breaking-point, particularly when it comes to providing settlers on the reclaimed Pontine Marshes with a house, furniture, agricultural implements, and as much land as they can manage *gratis*, this with a scale of taxation that is, as far as I could gauge, less than one quarter of what it is here, with a cost of living that varies from one-eighth to one-tenth, with preferential and very substantially reduced rates upon the railways, sports organisations, cinemas, theatres, opera houses etc. for workers organised in the *dopo lavoro* [2]organisations which give them these privileges. In fact, what it all amounts to is a Socialistic form of Government of greater humanity and thoroughness than any of our 'Left' crew over here either dream of or *dare to admit the existence of*. But this is not a dissertation upon Fascist Italy but a reply to your letter!

Yes, much new work exists, a number of immense works since *Clavicembalisticum*, which I now consider quite outclassed by some of its successors. I am hopelessly out of practice of it in these latter days, but if and when I do work at it again, I'll remember to let Mr. MacColl come along and hear it. But you will understand that both the time involved in working it up, and the titanic effort involved in its performance are things that I wriggle out of if I possibly can. After all, it's bad enough to have written the bloody thing let alone play it as well!

Most cordial regards and good wishes from yours ever,

Kaikhosru Shapurji Sorabji.

[1]   Sorabji was one of the intended dedicatees of 'Mature Art'. MacDiarmid wrote in 'Author's Note' that this dedication was '[...] partly in poor return for his dedication to me of his magnificent "Opus Clavicembalisticum" [...]'. (NLS Acc. 12074/1, ff. 9-13B [9]).

[2]   *dopo lavoro*- after work.

164. From T. S. Eliot (EUL MS2967/3)

THE
CRITERION
A QUARTERLY REVIEW
EDITED BY T. S. ELIOT

24 Russell Square
London WC1
8 June 1938

Dear Mr. Grieve,

You will have understood that my delay in writing to you about 'Mature Art' was due to my absence abroad. I tackled it on my return, and I must say that it seems to me an extremely interesting, individual, and indeed very remarkable piece of work. There can be no doubt that it is something that ought to be published, but the question is how, and by whom. For in the first place, any publisher who undertook it ought to have the courage and conviction to be prepared to publish the whole poem when it is complete.

I am sorry that I cannot get my colleagues to consider undertaking a work in verse of this size. I cannot afford to lose much money for them on poetry. You will understand that to say frankly that a book of poetry is going to make a considerable loss for its publisher is no criticism of its value: it may even be a compliment. But while I can sometimes urge them to publish a small book of verse which I know will lose money, I cannot ask them to tie up so much capital in anything so monumental as this. I would like to see it published, and I would be willing to give my personal support, for what it is worth, if you approached some other firm. Until hearing from you, as the manuscript is large and the distance great, I will keep it here for further orders.

Yours very sincerely,

T. S. Eliot.

165. From F. G. Scott (EUL MS2959 ff.83-85)

44 Munro Road
Jordanhill
Glasgow W3
12 June 1938

My dear Chris,

You've been on my conscience, you know what *that* means, for a very long time. The extenuating circumstances, you'll maybe remember, include the fact that this time o' the year is just the very busiest for me, inspection of schools, correction of exam. papers and general derangement of the routine of college. I've been particularly busy with the school visits, three and even four per week and have still other seven to do before the 24th of the month, but the reason I'm getting down to letter-writing today is that I've finished off this weekend the 200 odd final exam. papers, the correction of which is the one veritable nightmare of the year. I feel in consequence rather better able to support a hefty talk on all kinds of interests and of being able to hold my end up.

Replying to your last letter first of all – the information I've received about Whyte's books is that the great bulk of them went to Henderson, Bookseller in Church Street, St Andrews but whether Whyte at that time disposed of his own publications, first editions, etc. is not known to anyone. Tonge *may* know but I've still to write him on the matter. He stayed here one night and then two nights a week later on his return from Naomi Mitchison's house in Carradale where he'd been on holiday. You know, of course, that he's chucked his job in Dundee and is living on – I don't know what! – his friends – he says! But this visit of Tonge's was before your letter and I've to thank Mary Litchfield (who also has slept a night here) for what information I'm able to give you. If you're very anxious to know why Tonge has quitted you can have her opinion that he did *not* give up but was *told* to go and had no option in the matter. And that's nice and mysterious enough to keep tongues wagging for quite a long time!

And now for 'Mature Art'. Well I confess I didn't give it half a chance. You asked me to give it the *once*-over, but as a matter of fact I gave it the *twice*-over and a bit and even then couldn't feel sure that any opinions I had come by were worthy of putting before you. If I could convince *myself* that I knew exactly where the world is going at this moment I might be emboldened to tell you straight that *your* reading of the situation is a correct or a totally absurd one. But I *don't* know. And to tell you anything less than that is to miss the whole *raison d'être* of the work, isn't it? To deal with this or that aspect of the poem is to deal with something you either know already or else don't want to know. I have already and often sworn and taken a solemn oath on my conviction that no art known to me can afford to be in the nature of an improvisation, a thing dashed off extempore, and at the same time be a great or memorable or lasting contribution. I can't deny the possibility of such a thing (since anything is possible) but *all* evidence from the past goes to show how little store is set on work too idiosyncratic, original, diverse. You'll no doubt reply that this is exactly the kind of aim you have set yourself, an idiosyncrasy, an antisyzygy to all the stars in heaven – but this doesn't affect my statement one little bit. You're taking a risk, a chance maybe, but all the fates are against you. That's any rate how I see it.

Idiosyncrasy! – that's the word I'd like to harp on – but how does that sound in a world swung between Hitlerism and Stalinism? You said in one place I remember 'I am a Communist', and had to add a little later that you'd have none of it when all the world would accept it.[1] So why say you're a Communist? Why not say, 'I am an Anarchist?' It would certainly be nearer the truth than the other. Your trouble then comes from how you're going to equate Anarchical Art with dialectical materialism à la Stalin and not find yourself at a Moscow trial. And, mind you, I don't object to your Anarchical Art – indeed I can see a large lump of sense in such a purely irrational point of view but I'd advise you to forswear politics altogether in that case and sing the glorification of chaos. Why waste sympathy on Spain, Ethiopia or China – why not join Hitler and Musso. and have an everlasting conflagration? Strange how extremes meet!

Thus much for the general import (or thesis) of the poem. The various sections of the book show the same inconsistencies. Just what in Hell's name does it matter to Anarchy what all the languages of the world have thrown up by way of curiosities? strange how much of a throwback you are in these philological matters, a phenomenon which I've noted elsewhere, in Pound for instance, and which might be called 'the new academical', in a way just as bad as Royal Academy pictures of 50 years ago. A very pernicious disease this, mighty akin to pernicious anaemia and a sure sign of low vitality. The recipe *for* the complaint (not *against* the complaint) seems to be to throw into a witch's cauldron all the funny bits of philosophy, psychology, theology and all the other –ologies together with the facetiae of linguistics, ballistics, mathematics and all the other –tics, stir the hodgepodge well round and present it in reams and cantos to a public so damnably stupid as to think it a masterpiece. On this count the scissors-and-paste man wins everytime, 99 of the ignorant will think him for a short time omniscient and I will know him to be a complete ignoramus. To know so much is to know nothing at all.

And it's all been tried before, the Greeks had a name for it, the 13th century and the 18th century both had overdoses of it – how to be clever and nae bother at a'. Any history of literature, music, painting will give you the names of hundreds who figured high in the world's esteem and who are now dead as mutton, men who must have had eyes but who unfortunately couldn't see, and see far enough. It makes one wonder quite seriously if art is any more an experiment than life, if there are not bounds set up beyond which neither of them can pass without falling into the ridiculous.

So that's off my chest. I've said already you're taking a risk and I mean by that that there's a very marked dichotomy in your nature (as in most people's) which is persistently pulling you not one way and then another (as for instance in Flaubert) but which is pulling you both ways at once, *all* ways at once. As I have said there's no great art known to me which shows such a lack of unity, harmony, equilibrium. If you're going to achieve immortality you'll have to start from somewhere and go somewhere – not everywhere. If it's to be Anarchy – well let it be. To me it would seem your best objective – but for God's sake a serious and directed anarchy.

There were as you'll guess not a few other issues in the poem that raised my bile. I've spoken about them before so now I prefer to mention one thing that *did* satisfy me in rather a remarkable way – I mean the versification, the flow of the language, the readableness of the whole thing. Curiously enough the Scots bits ran very awkwardly, sprigs of heather, very naive and commonplace, generally marking a fall in the temperature. And I can't forbear one more girn: why in Heaven's name all the paraphernalia of introductions, dedications, and quotations – the thing in places looked like a summary of all your recent reading – can't you stand on your *own legs*? Props, I call them!

So, there, Christopher, I've done the best I can for 'Mature Art'. Mind you, I hadn't much of a chance with it – I kept it for little over a week and posted it to Barker Fairley who has since replied (19th May) and assured me he'd return it to Whalsay. I need hardly say that I didn't discuss the poem with him nor with Tonge nor anybody else. In your letter you say that Eliot hasn't sent you any word yet. I'll be interested, of course, to know what Fairley and Eliot have to say though I'm not likely to be much influenced by either of their opinions. It's probable that I'm hardening in old age – but somehow I don't feel it. I find myself on the contrary more concerned with the future of my own work than with the merit of anything I've done in the past. I believe like you that everything, life, literature, morality and everything else is in the melting-pot, that there are no standards of criticism, no rules of composition etc., etc. but maybe I'm more conscious than you of the need to keep swimming even against the stream. I can't credit, being a real sceptic, that Communism or any other -ism is going to transform life so much that the art of the next hundred years will obliterate all we today know as art, or create life of such a kind that ours will look flat, stale and unprofitable. In my gloomier moments I can foresee a human society that has reached a veritable heaven (or hell) of mediocrity and uniformity, with bread and circuses, picture-houses, wireless, television, aeroplanes, clinics, tractors with nae bother at a', all free, gratis, and for nothing, trying to figure out what kind of lunatics the Beethovens and Grieves and Scotts were, who had such fantastic notions about life, and who in reality knew so little about how to live. Art will then be purely utilitarian, something to amuse and entertain. It's some notion this Marxism – I can see whiles that it places value only on the living present – and unfortunately you and I are both getting old and older. Never mind – keep up your pecker – we'll hae munelicht again![2]

Ever,

F. G.

---

[1]   Scott appears to refer here to some lines from 'Talking with Five Thousand People in Edinburgh', viz., 'For I am like Zamyatin. I must be a Bolshevik/ Before the Revolution, but I'll cease to be one quick / When Communism comes to rule the roost,' *C.P.* I, p.1158. Yevgeny Zamyatin (1884-1937) wrote *We* in 1920-21. It has been called the archetype of the modern dystopia.

[2]   'There will be moonlight again' is the refrain of 'The Blades of Harden' by Will H. Ogilvie (1869-1963), included by MacDiarmid in his *Golden Treasury of Scottish Poetry* (1940).

166. From Lancelot Hogben (NLS Acc. 7361/9)

Regius Professor of Natural History:
Lancelot Hogben F.R.S.

University of Aberdeen
Natural History Department
Marischal College
Aberdeen
22 June 1938

Dear Hugh MacDiarmid,

As I see it constructive social proposals are at present obstructed equally by militaristic nationalism on the one hand and diffuse cosmopolitanism on the

The

Vol. I, No. I
June - August, 1938

Voice of
Scotland

A Quarterly Magazine of Scottish Arts and Affairs

Edited by HUGH MacDIARMID

CONTENTS

QUARTERLY   ONE SHILLING

Cover of *Voice of Scotland*. June to August 1938.
By permission of the National Library of Scotland.

other. If therefore your new Scottish quarterly proposes to direct Scottish national sentiment – the proper concern and regard which decent and modest people have for those who are nearest and dearest to them – into the task of implementing the Age of Plenty, I welcome the venture from the bottom of my heart.[1] Scotland has had a nationalism which sentimentalised about its honest modesty. It needs a nationalism which will denounce poverty as a survival of barbarism, and waken the conscience of Scotland to a sense of shame concerning its slums and pride in the efforts of men like John Orr[2] who are taking their part in doing so. Above all constructive nationalism should set itself to rescue the Scottish universities from their complacent self-satisfaction and rehabilitate Scottish education as a force for democratic enlightenment, and an instrument for carrying into effect the cultural tasks to which the age of potential plenty invites us.

Yours sincerely,

Lancelot Hogben.

[1]   The first issue of *The Voice of Scotland* was dated June-August 1938. MacDiarmid printed this letter on the first page of the second issue.

[2]   Sir John Boyd-Orr (1880-1971), authority on nutrition and Nobel Peace Prize winner in 1949 for his work as director of the UN Food and Agricultural Organisation (1945-8).

167. From F. G. Scott (EUL MS2959 ff.86-90)

44 Munro Rd
Jordanhill
Glasgow W3

5 July 1938

My dear Chris,

My last letter certainly drew from you a spirited response, I won't be nasty and say *too* spirited because I think it good for both of us to rub each other, it will sure be advantageous to both in the long run. First of all – wasn't I pleased to discover that I'd jumped ('oot o' my ain heid'!)[1] on the latest shibboleth 'anarchism'? It was real clever for one who never sees the magazines and weeklies of the intellectuals: I must just have felt it in the air and then on the Friday following the writing of my letter to discover the *Times Lit.* review of Herbert Read's *Poetry and Anarchy* (I beg your pardon!) *Anarchism* to be followed by your letter pointing out that Anarchism is 'the fine flower of integrated communism'! After that I couldn't do anything else but put down my 6 bob for Read's book – I was so pleased with myself! And so, of course, I had to refer to my authorities, such as I have, e.g., 'The Programme of the Communist International' Section VI under the No. 1 heading, 'Ideologies among the working class inimical to Communism':

'But Communism has to contend also against a number of petty-bourgeois tendencies, which reflect and express the vacillation of the unstable strata of society (the urban petty bourgeoisie, the degenerate city middle class, the lumpen proletariat, the declassed Bohemian intellectuals, the pauperised artisans etc.) These tendencies which are distinguishable by their extreme political instability often cover up a right-wing policy with left-wing phraseology, or drop into adventurism, substitute noisy political gesticulation for objective estimation of forces. They often tumble from astounding heights of revolutionary bombast to profound depths of pessimism and downright capitulation before the enemy.'

But I can't quote the whole long paragraph; let's get to the point –

'Anarchism [...] denies the necessity for wide [...] proletarian organisations and thus leaves the proletariat powerless before the powerful organisations of capital. By its advocacy of individual terror it distracts the proletariat [...]. By repudiating the dictatorship of the proletariat in the name of 'abstract' liberty, *anarchism deprives the proletariat of its most important and sharpest weapon against the bourgeoisie* [...]. Being remote from mass movements of any kind [...] *anarchism is steadily being reduced to a sect which*, by its tactics and actions, including its opposition to the dictatorship of the working class in the USSR *has objectively joined the united front of the anti-revolutionary forces.*' [2]

Now there's a nice pickle of bother for you to explain, especially when you tell me you are 'quite untainted with any Trotskyist or other heresies'. I've a good mind to send you *Left-wing Communism, an Infantile Disorder.*[3] If you cotton on to 'Anarcho-syndicalism'[4] which seems the very latest (*vide* Read) let me tell you the Communist Intern. Prog. is just as drastic in its next par on 'Revolutionary Syndicalism'. Not that this whole business of terminology matters a hoot to *me*. I don't intend following a paper chase! And it's nothing more than paper – it's given Read another opportunity for a book! (Now for dinner!)

And now being well-fed let me continue. I remember Muir having a great word in favour of Read as critic, poet, artist etc. and I remember too how severe I was and how confidently I affirmed that he was neither the one nor the other – none of them; that he was just a Jack-of-all-trades, a mere tinkerer, a dilettante of the worst type ready to discuss and make books about anything under the sun, in fact a journalist who fancies himself as an authority. And his latest effort *Poetry and Anarchism* corroborates my point of view. Note his egregious self-satisfaction, complacency, and omniscience – his 'Am't I a wonderful chap to know so much', just 'bring all your troubles to me' sort of attitude, 'you silly gowks that are painting pictures, writing music, poetry, knocking marble about etc., etc. just come round and I'll tell you the whys and the wherefores of anything you're doing'. And I wasn't thinking of Read only as I thought and said this – there was Muir himself for instance and all the other literati that read each other's effusions in the aforesaid journals. No, no, no – it won't wash! the journalists aren't artists at all except in the sense that they drivel on about it and keep themselves in the forefront of about 90% of the printed matter in the country. Yes, I'll have to get it off my chest – in so far as you poets, novelists, literary critics etc. continue to gasbag about art, you're just so much less artists. When I remember that paint is paint, sound is sound, and marble just marble – by God, I've to ask myself if there's any art in *words* at all. I'm certain at any rate that all real artists (I mean the painters, musicians, sculptors) have a far better and far better-grounded knowledge and understanding of their respective jobs (that's why they don't jabber about it!) than you others. Think of Willie Power as a painter, composer etc. and you'll see what I mean. He just couldn't get a start at all, couldn't begin – but by the Lord Harry can't he talk and give advice!

So I'm going to send you Read's *Poetry and Anarchism* – in my opinion he knows nothing about either and I can thank God for Monsieur Stalin (this once) that he has the power to choke poets like Mayakovsky (isn't that a hellish sample of sentimentality on p.21?) and Herbert Read along with composers like Shostakowitch (who incidentally is of ditto importance).[5]

But the worminess of Read is what worries me – how he manipulates the mask of know-all – now trotting out Mayakowsky, and then Shostakowitch and then the Chinaman Lin Yutang [6](whose book is reviewed only *this* week!) and a bit of Proust, another bit of Freud etc., etc. till all the 6d readers of *The Spectator*, *The New Statesman*, *The Listener* think an oracle is speaking to them and are hurrying on picking up tittle-tattle of the Read variety wherever it can be found in the hope that *they* too will some day pose as artists or (better still) art critics. I tell you it's a *RAMP*!

And don't think I'm digressing on the Read tack – not at all – I'm being very much to the point and replying to *your* letter. I had expressed the opinion that I thought 'Mature Art' too idiosyncratic, miscellaneous, and original, too amorphous, too heterogeneous, too personal etc., etc. and I gave it as my opinion that *no* great work of art had these faults. I'm not saying that work of this kind hasn't been *done* – as a matter of fact most (or all) *bad* art could be recognised by these same characteristics, what I am saying is that such work has small chance of being accounted a masterpiece for long. *Time crumbles it to bits*! But I've gone into this business often and often with you. It's been one of the few things I can say I've learned in my pilgrimage on earth – that these buggers wi' the style (that's my own natural reaction to the phenomenon) *are the only artists that matter in the long run*. 'Our little systems have their day', our little petty prejudices, our notions, our opinions (political or other) – but just you take any masterpiece you can think of, whether in paint, poetry, sculpture or music and you'll find it makes faces at your idiosyncratic, disjointed, over-original or over-personal specimens. And I'm not thinking only, or at all, of long poems – the thing holds even with the shortest lyric.

Isn't your 'Eemis Stane'[7] (wonderful poem though it is) just about spoilt with the 'history's hazelraw' bit at the end? Don't you feel a slight effort as of something as they say dragged in by the hair o' the heid – something that just doesn't *belong* – due to a moment of inattention or lack of technique on the poet's part? And I've been looking at my setting of 'Empty Vessel'[8] quite lately – (wonderful music) that nearly brought the tears to my eyes when I reflected on your springtide of creative activity, when we ran about from Glasgow to Montrose at weekends and jogged along country roads ready to make a masterpiece at a moment's notice. I ask you, can you do it *now*? For myself, I believe I can answer 'yes' – 'maybe' – just because I've maintained, held on to, the certain knowledge that I can't add one inch to my stature, that I am what I am, and that that's enough for the job I've to do. And above all, no hanky-panky with myself, no playing at hide-and-seek with myself, no shooting out my neck, no personalities, as little of myself as possible, and *everything for the work in hand.*

Which all means that what I call *art* is the *work of art itself* with as little admixture of the person who made it as possible (e.g. 'Empty Vessel', 'Perfect').[9] If this dictum seems to you obscurantist I can assure you it is a truism in music – in Bach, Handel, Mozart, Beethoven and even in Wagner – in plainsong. Of course, there's no feeling of authorship at all, just as there's none in Gothic cathedrals, or in Shakespeare, Milton, Spenser, Chaucer, even Doughty. I find that the stupider my students are the more ready they are to think music is what they can make associations with, e.g., Wagner's 'Fire Music', anything indeed *they* can understand, waterfalls, aeroplanes, power stations, locomotives that are as far removed from *musical* intelligence as possible. And it's much the same with the personal factor in art – the reader or hearer gets away from the work itself to its accessories, its accompaniments, its queer bits, eccentricities, its oddities – anything but the subject matter in hand. I've been amazed over and over again to discover that students had (evidently) completely mistaken the whole meaning of a lecture but that they could recall & refer to an anecdote, an odd phrase etc., etc. that had nothing whatever to do with the point under discussion.

And that's my charge against the heterogeneous in art – mature art and immature art – the creator hasn't seen his work completely, he hasn't realized it completely, it's half-baked, undigested, full of shreds and patches, padding, digressions in all directions and irrelevances, your 'paraphernalia of references' in short.

And your preoccupation with linguistics, semantics and quotations of all kinds are in much the same case. You have taken on the job of telling me about Scotland today and its relationship to the rest of the world, in politics, culture and everything else. I read the poem – but I'm sorry to say I'd have had difficulty in saying what it was you were really getting at, what exactly was the tenor of your song – not, mark you, what *you* think it's about but what *I* as a fairly intelligent reader think of it. If you imagine that you can put tags of Greek, Gaelic, Russian, Spanish, German etc. into a poem and then claim you're keeping your eye on the work of art, well, I can only admonish you that you're doing anything but that. Like our friend, Mr Read, you're trying to astonish me with your cleverness and it's ten to one that where I can match you with my own specialized information I can catch you out every time. Whenever you quote for instance German or French I find myself asking, 'Now what in hell's name has that done for the poem?' 'Why in heaven's name have I been fobbed off with *'fehlt charakteristischerweise hier'*, *'atemberaubend* pace'[10] like a little prig talking about 'jardin' for 'garden'. The point, however, is this: that when I *can* translate I think they're silly and when I *can't* (the Gaelic, Russian, Greek etc.) I pay no attention to them at all – I skip the passages feeling pretty confident that if you'd really something excellent to say about the matter you'd be only too glad to say it in English, something understandable (that's to say) *if you want to be understood* and *if you're really concerned with the theme of your poem.*

The effect of the whole thing is just the same as in the case of Read – you're not caring a dump about anarchism or poetry either, they're matters of no importance –

214

'*Che la facesse di menzogna rea!*'[11] You see I can generally manage the Italian bits too.

'But', you'll say, 'surely to God my poetry isn't nothing but a series of quotations – it's *you* who's making all the song about the purely subsidiary things!' And of course this is quite true, and just the very reason why I'm making all the fuss. I *do believe* that you can write a first-class poem on practically anything you set your mind to – if you'll rid yourself of all idea of being clever, modern, up to date, experimental, omniscient, aye and anarchist, communist and all the rest of it, too. You say America thinks you're the greatest Communistic poet ever – whatever *that* means: the greatest 'evolutionary' poet ever – try it with any qualification you like – it's just my old reference back again – the greatest Jew's harp composer, the greatest composer for the concertina, etc. I tell you for the 1001th time your theories won't in the long run matter a cuss (for they'll be out of date), and only the poetic significance, the style, the quality of the poem as poetry will survive. I know that's difficult, but 'the poetry of the thing' shouldn't be any more difficult than the music of a musical work, just as we now say there's far more *music* in Mozart than in Wagner for instance, more detachment, more of a quality less conditioned by things not musical, more in fact of a creation and less of a mechanism.

> '[...] it is impossible,
>> [...]
>> [...]
>> [...]
> Not to fall ultimately,
> As into a heresy
> Into an unheard-of simplicity.'[12]

as you quote in your 'Glasgow' Appendix. So don't flyte me with my declension from experimentalism – or I'll retort that I'm coming to think *experimental art* not *art at all* or at best just *bad* art. The hallmarks of it are that heaps of explanations are served out along with it, footnotes galore, – all, just attempts to explain why the thing is poetry, music etc. *when it isn't anything of the kind.* I tell you *it's too easy!* You should leave it to the Herbert Reads and Ezra Pounds, the latter being, according to one of my Honours students, 'an old bagman'. What an age to live in! What posturing, what gesticulation, what advertising, what mad efforts to attract notice by any means whatever and how difficult to sift the sugar from the sand, the true from the false. Your experimentalism has certainly done one thing – it's allowed every kind of charlatan, nincompoop and nitwit to gatecrash into 'the garden of art', (that's just for annoyance!) and trample through the rosebeds. And don't you tell me there ain't no rosebeds. There are – there's a lovely rose just outside below me in the garden. I'd like to send you it just for remembrance and assurance and hope and beauty.

But I'll have to get down to particulars: indeed I thought at first I'd say nothing of a general nature at all but delve right into your Appendices. Well here goes: Ist Appendix, 'Choosing Red Again'.[13] Yes, quite as good as anything I've seen lately, a bit *drawn* in places as on p.3 – resipiscence, xenomorphic, stasimorphic, sarmentous toils, sarothrum, reptant, thalline hyphae, unrabbetable lands – p. 6 – moliminous, red moccado, locram, skiascoped, prepotent, protoparentally, proseuchae, *ionraic* etc. All the same the leading motive *survives* – but you've got to work the 'I sing of Cornwall' pretty hard to keep tally with your researches in the dictionary.

2ⁿᵈ Appendix (Glasgow).[14] If you're Fr Rolfe who wrote *Hadrian the Seventh*[15] I'd give you full marks for your quotation.

The bit on Venice[16] pp.3 & 4 a throwback to the feudal period. I've no doubt the poor Venetian devils had and still have a rottener time than we Glaswegians.

On p.5 in walks Virginia Woolf. I thought you didn't make use of your latest reading – Society of Outsiders etc.

Pp.9, 10, 11 begin to be journalism in verse, bad temper, disappointment.

There's a bit of magnificent nonsense on p.12 about 'the Kneipen at Heidelberg', 'Zuppa di peoci', 'Aryballoi', 'hero saga of Gesser Khan' that sounds very childish coming after the topmost line on 'nothing but words, high-sounding impotent words'.

The paragraph at the foot beginning 'The face that launched a thousand ships' is very near to poetry as the *Forward* might think of it and the genius with the bicycle spokes doesn't impress me in the slightest.

Heine's syllogism about 'every man has the right to eat' is a far-off cry today, everybody wants picture-houses, motor cars, holidays with pay, and (most important) the bestlooking women.

Towards the end you begin to speak of 'my kind of poetry', 'Bolshie art' and the charming Utopia of 'iridescent glass, windows for walls', (see 'The Programme of the Communist International'.)

The last 2 pages pretty thin, back to *Forward* notions of poetry, and self-pity, 'I too am heard […]' and right on to 'I look through my all-observing and half-shut eyes', finally plunging into 'WE HAVE WHAT IT TAKES',[17] which is just the very opposite of the truth, '*You just have not got what it takes*'. You can consult on this matter Chamberlain, Hitler, and the majority in every country.

The 3ʳᵈ Appendix is the poorest of the three:[18] you've evidently been far more occupied about making a catalogue of (a) colours, flowers (a nice line on p.3 'flutter their cuffs like a great bird in flight') . So *you* too can recognize poetry even in Chang Hang. Then a whole page of geological terminology which I can assure you nobody will even read. The next page again full of information having nothing to do with Cornwall or anything else. You seem to think you can discuss point A in terms of point B and then point C, point D and so on down the alphabet – a kind of digression on a digression on a digression to infinity. I could imagine it being successful in a novel for instance, where a story could be manipulated from a thousand points of view – but as a form of poem I fear it is pretty near boredom, you'll confess yourself there's nothing on earth so boring as having to listen to somebody telling you how much *he* knows. Think of Blake (not George, but William) when he gets going in his prophecies and even *that* has the merit of being at any rate imaginative. But no, you're trying to commit yourself to a kind of poetry you call communistic, a poetry of facts, when I've told you, and the students at the Varsity, that poetry doesn't deal ever with facts of any kind, that facts can never become poetry. To speak the truth, Chris, I think you're trying to put yourself in a strait waistcoat, I don't see why with your gifts you should find it necessary to compete with the incompetent. How I wish to God you'd go away to Arabia, cancel your interest in politics, communist, anarchist or whatever else, get down to the business of facing *your* destiny and Scotland's destiny too for that matter, and make a serious, genuine masterpiece of it. These frills and falderals would slip off your back at once if you had real confidence in yourself, for I'm sure you have the ability to do it. 'Just as I am, without one plea' and I'll guarantee you'll discover very soon in the process all that I've been trying to say in both my last letter and in this, i.e., that the adage is 'Ars longa, vita brevis' and not 'Vita longa, ars brevis'.

But there's enough here to keep you thinking for a bit at any rate. I'm now on holiday; we're *all* of us on holiday; haven't fixed up a single bed for our annual holiday anywhere; am beginning to hedge and hesitate about applying for the Professorship (before 31st August). What the devil do *I* want with £1 300 a year and three times the work; money never meant anything to me and my wife feels the same about it. Item, Willie Johnstone has been appointed Principal of Camberwell School of Arts & Crafts, one of the largest in London, 1 250 students and 80 teachers, and he's coming up to see me in his new car. Did you know that the four of us (Johnstones and Scotts) would have been in South France all this summer if Willie's father hadn't died in May and Willie had to cancel let of house etc.? I'm lecturing (summer class) between July 11th and 22nd and getting still more money for it too. There won't be any St Andrews for us this year – there's nobody there but the Muirs and I'm not having any. Of course I've all the parts of my Overture to write out for performance, it's already on the prospectus I have heard but I'm too lazy to get begun to that form of drudgery. I'm going to enclose [Ramón] Sender's *Seven Red Sundays* [19]and beg to give you the information that there's only *one* Communist in the Negrín Government at this moment.

Ever affectionately,

F. G.

[1] 'Oot o' my ain heid' is a line from 'By Wauchopeside' (*C.P.*, II, p.1084).

[2] Emphases Scott's.

[3] *Left-Wing Communism, An Infantile Disorder*, sub-titled ' A Popular Essay in Marxian Strategy and Tactics', was written by Lenin and dated 27 April 1920.

[4] 'Anarcho-syndicalism' – a development of trade unionism which aimed to put the means of production in the hands of unions of workers.

[5] Sir Herbert Read (1893-1968) published *Poetry and Anarchism* in 1938. The 'hellish sample of sentimentality on p.21' occurs in the second chapter, 'Poets and Politicians': 'On the 14th April, 1930, Vladimir Mayakovsky, then acknowledged as the greatest poet in modern Russia, committed suicide. He is not the only modern Russian poet who has taken his own life: Yessenin and Bagritsky did the same, and they were not inconsiderable poets. But Mayakovsky, by all accounts, was exceptional - the inspiration of the revolutionary movement in Russian literature, a man of great intelligence and

of inspired utterance. The circumstances leading to his death are obscure, but he left behind him a piece of paper on which he had written this poem: 'As they say / "the incident is closed". / Love boat / smashed against mores. / I'm quits with life. / No need itemizing / mutual griefs / woes / offences. / Good luck and good-bye'. – Translated by Max Eastman, *Artists in Uniform* (Allen & Unwin, 1934). The reason for Mayakovsky's suicide is still debated. Scott's low opinion of the work of Mayakovsky (b.1893) and Shostakovich would now find little support. Dimitri Shostakovich (1906-1975) was the most important Russian composer whose musical education and career took place entirely in the Soviet Union.

6   Lin, Yu-T'ang (1895-1976), Chinese-US essayist and author of best-sellers *My Country and My People* (1935) and *The Importance of Living* (1937).
7   *C.P.* I, p.27.
8   *C.P.* I, p.66.
9   *C.P.* I, p.573.
10 *'fehlt charakteristischerweise heir'* does not occur in MacDiarmid's published poetry; *'atemberaubend'* appears in 'Glasgow', *C. P.* II, p.1335.
11 *'Che la facesse di menzogna rea'* – 'As plainly manifested it was a lie' (Ariosto). MacDiarmid's note in Delaware MS of 'Glasgow 1938'. Not included in MacDiarmid's published poems.
12 Included in 'Glasgow', *C.P.* II, p.1338.
13 The 1st Appendix to 'Mature Art', 'Choosing Red Again' was published as 'Cornish Heroic Song for Valda Trevlyn', *C.P.* I, pp.704-712. The original title refers to 'Why I Choose Red', *C.P.* I, pp.603-4. Another poem, 'Of Red, the Socialist Colour', remains unpublished, NLS Acc. 12074/1, ff.117-118. The groups of words which Scott quotes are on *C.P.* I, pp.707 and 710 respectively.
14 The 2nd Appendix, 'Glasgow 1938'. MacDiarmid used the title 'Glasgow 1938' because the Empire Exhibition was held from May to September in Glasgow that year. Parts of this poem are to be found in 'Glasgow', *C. P.* II, pp.1048-52, and in 'Glasgow', *C.P.* II, pp. 1333-39. 'Glasgow 1938' exists in full in the Delaware MS. Scott's references to the poem are all contained in the published parts, *C.P.* II, pp.1048-52 and 1333-9, with the exceptions of the comments on 'The bit on Venice', 'Virginia Woolf', 'the face that launched a thousand ships'.
15 Frederick William Rolfe (1860-1913), novelist and short story writer, also styled himself Baron Corvo and Fr. (i.e. Father) Rolfe. *Hadrian the Seventh* (1904) is the story of George Arthur Rose, a failed priest, clearly modelled on the author, who is elected Pope.
16 'The bit on Venice' refers to the contrast MacDiarmid makes between the stones of Venice and the stones of Glasgow in an unpublished section of 'Glasgow 1938' (Cf. NLS MS27029 ff.41-51, [44-47]). 'The bit on Venice' is a section of 22 lines based on Adrian Stokes, *The Stones of Rimini* (London: Faber, 1934), pp.16-18.
17 The last line of the Delaware MS of 'Glasgow 1938', *C. P.* II, p.1339.
18 The 3rd Appendix was published as 'Once in a Cornish Garden', *C.P.* II, pp. 1102-1109.
19 Ramón J Sender, *Seven Red Sundays,* translated with an introduction by Peter Chalmers-Mitchell (London, 1936).

168. From Neil M. Gunn (EUL MS MS2948.15 f.29)

Braefarm House
Dingwall
Ross-shire

My dear Christopher,

Glad to get your letter & see you are on the warpath with new quarterlies & what not. We are just on our way to Thurso for salmon fishing (the troubles of this free life!) and shan't be back before the 21st but I shall get your new periodical then. How long ago since I used to look you up about the old periodicals, *inter alia*?

And many thanks for your congrats. over James Tait Black. Came on me as a bolt from heaven. But cheque marvellous handy!

I'll never get that telegram from you about a satisfying book. Should think something had gone wrong with you if I did! Or with me?! Cheers. Reading Catherine Carswell, I see she says that, expecting something really worthy from him, she was always disappointed with each new book of D.H. Lawrence's. What a pity Lawrence never brought it off! Joking apart, I hope MacMillan comes up to scratch. Eliot is really a sincere kind fellow. All the same, Faber is now a pretty big concern. Might have risked it, hang 'em. But I know enough to know that you can't quite blame Eliot there. (Eliot is working hard on a new play).

We had a very pleasant & extremely interesting holiday in Germany, as we met all sorts of folk. But of that, some time again. Meantime, tell Marjory & Elma[2] that if they feel like coming here for a look around, duly accompanied by their guides, we'd be glad to have them. Apart from having to give me my breakfast in bed, they could do as they liked. I trust you will see to it that they behave in a respectable & conventional manner & not let their uncle down.

Greetings from us both.

Neil.

In the left margin – 'We didn't manage to get to Eigg, but still hope to do so'.[3]

[1]   Gunn dated this letter 1937 which must be a mistake. *The Voice of Scotland* was launched in June 1938, 'Mature Art' had just been rejected by Eliot (letter of 8 June 1938) and the Gunns had visited Germany earlier that year.
[2]   'Marjory & Elma', Neil Gunn's nieces and their boy-friends, one of whom was John Brough, visited Whalsay in 1938.
[3]   The Gunns might have hoped to visit John MacNair Reid and his wife, Josephine Shepherd, on Eigg.

169. From Barbara Niven (EUL MS2976)

Tuesday 2 August [1938]

Dear Christopher,

I wrote you a very scrappy letter the other day, under difficulties – there were people talking in the room at the time and they would talk to me. I meant to tell you something about Ernest Brooks, who is coming with me. He is a young man of 26 who had to earn his own living early so that it is only for the last few years that he has been painting seriously, though first of all saving enough to have a short period at the Art School here and then getting a scholarship. Because of this approach perhaps he has a directness and scope that are something new and I'm certain will just go on developing.

Of course, he has also a directness of attitude to things that makes the other – in painting – inclusive; otherwise the word would not mean very much.

He was deeply interested in hearing about you, and in your poetry which I lent him and when I suggested the possibility of coming up to see you he was enthusiastic and I think had thought of it himself.

I am looking forward to coming with excitement and am anxious to be off. But a committee who may be induced to give Ernest a grant of £100 to go to London (or somewhere) for a short time has recently sent him a notice to go on Friday of this week to see them with work; so we shall definitely catch a boat leaving Aberdeen at 8 p.m. on Monday Aug 8, the *St. Sunniva*. I can't find out exactly when it arrives, but we will get the next boat to Whalsay.[1]

With love and best wishes.

Barbara.

[1]   EUL MS2976 Fri Aug 3 [1967] BN to CMG, 'How lovely that you'll meet us at the station to go to your book-launching party – the wrong way round, but lovely. I think (as I often do) of the time when you stood to welcome us on the tiny Whalsay quay and we practically floated off the boat treading on air.'

170. From Muriel Rukeyser (NLS Acc. 7361/9)[1]

Yaddo
Saratoga Springs
New York
5 August 1938

Dear Hugh MacDiarmid,

The magnificent *Third Hymn [to Lenin]* followed me for a while, reaching me after a little delay, or you would long ago have had my thanks for it, for the chance of reading it now and for its naming of me.[2] It is fine; knotty and subtle and far above what anyone writes about cities, and with Lenin as Virgil, picture, image, and statistics come through in one clap of poem. I cannot tell you how excellently glad and ambitious it makes me to have you associate me with the poem.

I have shown it to Horace Gregory, who likes it tremendously, and wishes to have it stand as the final poem in your American edition.[3] But he is ill now in Wisconsin, and a letter came today from Covici[4] to let me know that he has gone under financially. While the firm itself will be dissolved, he is taking his own place with the Viking Press; I'll ask him to let you know immediately what will become of the arrangement for your book. I can't understand the laxness of so many people as you mentioned: I've tried to reach all of them – Selden Rodman[5] published one poem in an anthology that has just appeared; Gregory you know about; I don't know what [Philip] Rahv[6] plans to do, and I don't know how to reach Kenneth Patchen at the moment. His permanent address is care of Random House, 20 East 57th St., New York City (at least, they have published him, and he may be reached through them). I hope you've heard by now from these people. If you wish, I'll be glad to remind anyone else; all that is an unnecessary and extra difficulty.

Your first issue of *Voice of Scotland* has come, as I type;[7] it's a rousing, exciting magazine, I wish the Communist press here were publishing something like it. I haven't read it through yet, yet I have been very stirred by 'The Red Scotland Thesis' and 'The Glen of Silence'. Are you doing anything about distribution of it here? May I help?

I have been here for the past month, and shall stay until the end of August. Saratoga itself is a horse-racing, mineral-spring, parasite town, ghostly with the white wrought-iron buildings of 1870, living for August and the races and the month's splurge each year. Yaddo is a 600-acre estate whose house is patterned after the palace of Carmen Sylva.[8] It was built by a Wall Street family whose four children died before they resolved to give the place to the arts. And now its artificial lakes, its plush, its thrones and formal rose gardens are turned over, during the summer, to people working in creative arts who come here by invitation. It is, in its nature, oppressive, a Magic Mountain carried a step farther, into the arts; but this summer the people are good, and it is all working very well. I am going ahead with 'US1' here, working out problems of biography in poems – I mean to have interludes of individual lives – and getting down to a prose book that started to be a novel about the beginning of the war in Spain and is changing from that first draft to a book about a train of tourists caught by any war, civil war.

How marvellous the opening of the *Hymn* is, the sea and weather and myriadmindedness parts! And the blazing end. I am so glad to have it.

I shall be glad to see Dr Orr; he has not tried to reach me.[9]

With all thanks, and best wishes,

Yours,

Muriel Rukeyser.

---

[1]   MacDiarmid knew Muriel Rukeyser's work in the American *Nation* but he did not meet her until 1963 in Newcastle.

[2]   'Third Hymn to Lenin' was first published in full in *The Voice of Scotland,* vol. vi, no. 1, in April 1955 although about a third of it had appeared in *Lucky Poet* (1943).

[3]   Horace Gregory (1898-1982), poet and critic. This edition did not appear.

[4]   Covici Friede, Publishers, New York.

[5]   Selden Rodman (1909-2002), poet, editor and translator.

[6]   Philip Rahv (1908-1973), editor and critic.

[7]   *The Voice of Scotland,* vol. 1, no. 1, (June-August 1938).

[8]   i.e., Elizabeth, Queen Consort of Charles 1, King of Romania.

[9]   At this time Dr Orr had given up his job on Whalsay and had gone to see the operation of the Social Credit scheme in Alberta where he took up another appointment.

171. From Ruaraidh Erskine of Mar (EUL MS2946.16 f.24)

San Veremundo
24 Rue de la Frégate
Biarritz
7 August [1938]

Dear Mr Grieve,

I wrote you some few weeks ago, but so far have had no reply. I will give you a sure address. Write to me c/o The Westminster Bank, Carlos Place, Mayfair, London W.1. Letters sent there will always be forwarded – *no matter where I may be.*

I hope your new quarterly does well. I have not seen it, nor know where I might get a copy, which I'd like to do, of course. Let me know about this, & also if you would like a short piece from me.

I think Browne & Nolan of Dublin will publish my racial piece. I am hopeful of concluding negotiations with them. They have quickened their interest considerably since Racialism (whose coming I have long prophesied) has appeared in the forefront of European affairs. What are you doing? Let me know – I'm a bit of an exile here.

The articles in *The Times Lit. Supp.* about the decay of letters rather amuse me. Of course, the bottom has fallen out of the whole thing, and anyone not hopelessly bemused with Democracy can see the cause i.e., Democracy itself, its standards & tastes which necessarily are beastly. I shall be curious to see what remedy is proposed, but for my part I can see none short of educating 'the people' up to a level of aristocracy, & that will take centuries to do. So personally I find myself turning ever more & more away from English letters – a damned & ruined cause in the meantime at all events – & thinking to myself how needful it is for us who are Scots & *have a literature of our own* (though we neglect it) to return to it, and in a body do our damnedest to put it on its legs again. I should like to put this point of view before your quarterly readers, to the end that it may be followed up, not by action on Comunn Gaidhealach lines (rustic, futile, crude for the most part) but intellectually, in company of men such as yourself. Tell me what you think as to the possibilities of this crusade. I hope you are well. Very hot here at times but a cool wind from the sea blows almost daily.

Mise le meas[1]

Ruaraidh Erskine of Mar.

[1]   I am with respect, The standard form is 'Is mise, le meas'.

172. From Norman MacCaig (EUL MS2953.7 f.1)

c/o Munro
8 Boswall Road
Edinburgh

Dear Mr. Grieve,

I have been lost to the post for three weeks, and have only just received your letter, so please do not blame me for this long delay in replying.

If an anatomist were to map my brain in the manner of the old cartographers the Political Regions would be left blank. This fails to worry me (in spite of everybody) because it seems to me that this same cartographer would fill such regions in the minds of other people with diversely impossible monsters. None of my verses then are of deliberately political origin; but on examination I find there are some which may come within a stone's throw of your object. I shall not be surprised if the stone is thrown. If any of these is suitable I shall, of course, be pleased if you can use it.

Yours sincerely,

Norman MacCaig.

P.S. Are you tired of praise? – I am sure you are not yet tired of 'Cwa' een like milk-wort'.[1]

---

[1]   The reference is to the first line of 'Milk-Wort and Bog-Cotton', *C.P.I*, p.331.

173. From Catherine Carswell (EUL MS2946.1 f.34)

From
Black House
Toppesfield
Essex
28 August [or September] 1938

THERE IS STILL TIME

Please sign this card and post it immediately.

Then write 10 more cards and 10 letters identical with this one and send to friends on whom you can rely to respond.

Halifax will have half a million in a few days.[1]

A few minutes of your time will help to preserve peace.

---

[1]   This card demonstrates Carswell's opposition to the Munich Agreement. Lord Halifax was then Foreign Secretary from 1938 to 1940. The agreement was signed on 30 September 1938.

174. From T. S. Eliot (EUL MS2967/3)

24 Russell Square
London WC1
n.d. [before 17 September 1938][1]

Dear Mr Grieve,

I must apologise humbly for my unpardonable delay in dealing with your manuscripts, for which I can only give the excuse of the disorganisation of life and work which overtakes me every year during the summer months. I have sent the 'Mature Art' to Macmillan & Co with my warm recommendation, and I should like to accept your suggestion of publishing the first Appendix (on Cornwall) in *The Criterion*. As I have sent this on with the rest of the poem, could you, at your convenience, provide me with another copy?

I must say that I think this Appendix will be very much more impressive and effective in *The Criterion*[2] than your article on Scottish Politics in its present form.

For one thing, the article is about twice as long as is convenient to publish. For a second point, I had much rather have a contribution which you could sign with your own name, than a manifesto from the Red Scotland Committee. Third, I feel that for the purpose of *The Criterion* your article covers far too much ground. There is no objection to your slanging the English, but I think it could be made more effective in a different form, and in more minute particulars. In this essay you seem to me to make too many charges to be able to convince the reader of the force of all of them, and a detailed forensic on one point might be more effective than making too many points which you have not the space to justify in detail. For my purpose an essay like this includes the germs of a number of single articles, such as one on MacLean, although I do not suggest that as one particularly suitable for *The Criterion*.

Yours very sincerely,

T. S. Eliot.

[1]   MacDiarmid replied to this letter on 17 September 1938.
[2]   The article was 'Brief Survey of Modern Scottish Politics in the light of Dialectical Materialism' which appears to have been lost at the time of the police raids on Nationalist premises in May 1941.

175. From L. L. Johnson (NLS MS27152 f.48)

Gulberwick
Lerwick
26 September 1938

Dear Comrade Grieve,

Many thanks for your letter of 14th inst., and acceptance on the part of yourself and Mr Taylor *re* standing for the forthcoming County Council elections; also for circular in which members evinced the keenest interest.[1]

We have to thank you also for offer to address a meeting. Our Labour Party meetings are held fortnightly on alternate Thursdays (next meeting Thursday week, October 6th). If any evening rather than a Thursday is more suitable we shall endeavour to get you an audience; only let us know a little beforehand when it is convenient for you to be in Lerwick.

With regards.

Yours sincerely & fraternally,

L. L. Johnson.

1   Although MacDiarmid and Grant Taylor, his honorary private secretary, agreed to stand
    for Whalsay and Fetlar respectively in the forthcoming County Council Elections, they
    did not do so.

176. From Archie Lamont (EUL MS2952 ff.1-2)

> The Geology Department
> The University
> Edgbaston
> Birmingham 15
> Sasana
> 14 October 1938

Dear Grieve,

I've just been reading the first issue of *The Voice of Scotland*, and I like it very much. In fact I think it should develop into the Quarterly, which I always said was necessary to complete the trio of *Forward*, weekly, *Scots Independent*, monthly, and ? each quarter. This does not mean that I agree that it is intelligible (except for Wendy Wood's article)[1] to the 'workers' it is alleged to be written for, or that any of it has the remotest resemblance to the factual propagandist style followed by men like Marx and Lenin. It is also much too dear for the 'workers'. But its sentiments and direction are splendid. And Oh! how nobly you walked away from the A.R.P.[2] and war-mongering policy of the Communist Party by ignoring them! You seem to be just my kind of Marxist altogether.

Now, Grieve, let me say a few things about your allegation about being expelled *in absentia* from the old National Party of Scotland, of which I was assistant secretary. In the first place you tied my own hands as well as Muirhead's[3] by wanting to be a member of Council, but not by popular vote,[4] and then some of your enemies managed to prove a *prima facie* case that you had joined the C.P. Finally you applied for readmission at the annual conference of that year. I moved that you be again admitted, I think Dr Muirhead[5] seconded but the motion was lost by a narrow margin. I didn't worry much about that, as I knew things were touch and go, and that everything being equal the next Conference could be trusted. However, before that, [George] Dott,[6] and [Fred] Robertson,[7] and Douglas MacDonald,[8] and Mary Fraser,[9] and a huge crowd of others had all resigned. And since then as you know I have been left with the baby to hold all by myself; while the only effect of the resignations, of which I never approved, was to put the stupider and less go-ahead section of the Nationalist Movement in the saddle for the past four years...

The moral of this letter is that the only way to get the Scottish Nationalist Movement on its feet is to recapture the Party which, after all, has some organisation and some funds, and a paper *The Scots Independent* which is in Muirhead's private hands and of a price and policy to appeal to 'workers' and 'bourgeoisie' alike. Your subjective, and shall I say 'sentimental' appeal, might make a nice supplement to my factual, Leninist style. What about it? You talk about yourself as oil which can't mix with water. The truth I think would be that you are like pure Scotch whisky – very stimulating but with damned little food value. My own *S.I.* work is I know a bit like a haggis, but nutritional! and you're only a bloody literary gent after all if you turn up your nose at it. I shall expect to be hearing from Muirhead very soon that he is publishing an article of yours.

Yours fraternally,

Archie Lamont.

1   'We Will Fight No More in England's Wars', vol. 1, no. 1 (June-August 1938), pp.15-17, has been reprinted in *Modernism and Nationalism*, pp.374-5.
2   Air Raid Precautions.
3   R.E. Muirhead.
4   The present editor has seen no evidence of this.
5   Dr R.F. Muirhead (d.1941) was the brother of R.E. Muirhead.
6   George Dott published *Early Scottish colliery wagonways* etc., with illustrations and maps (London, 1947); and *Save Scottish shale oil*, (Musselburgh, 1959).
7   Dr Fred Robertson became County Librarian of Caithness.
8   T. Douglas MacDonald ('Fionn MacColla').
9   Mary C. Fraser married George Dott and became National Secretary of the Scottish National Party.

177. From T. E. Nicholas (NLS Acc. 7361/9)

Glasynys
Aberystwyth
18 October 1938

Dear Comrade,

The Voice of Scotland to hand through Mr Griffiths c/o Foyles.[1] Thanks very much, I shall treasure it. The point of view expressed in it is about the same as mine. The freedom of Wales and Scotland will be, when it comes, the gift of the united working class of Great Britain. The exploiters of our class will never agree to give us national freedom. I wish you every success in you[r] venture. I am not an expert in the English language, but I enclose a Sonnet composed to a comrade that I knew, who fell in Spain. Since then a few others have fallen. I composed the Sonnet in Welsh and then I tried to put it in a 'foreign language'. If it will be of any use to you, you are welcome to it.[2] Send me a copy of you[r] next issue again, and I will send a subscription for a year when it comes. I am very busy at the time, and [getting] stuff for a volume of poems ready if I can get a publisher. I am afraid it will shock the 'saints' when it appears. Their pet ideas and their gods are satir[is]ed and made fun of. I have been inventing new swear words for the last month but I have failed to get them strong enough to describe the stand made by the 'saints' during the crisis.[3] Well, best luck with your *Voice of Scotland* [.] It is bound to do a lot of good.

Yours in the great cause.

T. E. Nicholas.

¹   At the time of writing Nicholas might have received either of the first two issues of *Voice of Scotland*.

²   *The Voice of Scotland*, vol.1, no.4 (March-May 1939) carried Nicholas's poem in Welsh, 'I Gofio Cymro'. The poem was also included in *Wales*, vol.8, no.9 (August 1939).

³   He refers to the Munich crisis.

178. From J. F. Hendry (EUL MS2951.4 f.11)

20 Vernon Rd
Leeds 1
22 October 1938

Dear Mr MacDiarmid:

Congratulations on the second issue of *The Voice*. It's better, I think, than the first; but that may only be because it's newer to me.

I'm looking forward to the Celtic Front No., & enclose a few poems which Norman MacLeod[1] & C. J. Russell[2] have asked me to send. Return what you can't use, won't you? Of course you may publish only *sections* if you like, especially of Russell! He's just beginning!

About the incident in Spain. I'm afraid it might prove libellous. All I really heard was that the Celtic section of the British battalion – which had never got on well with the English, because of the lack of revolutionary enthusiasm in the latter – became completely sick when Spender came looking for his boy-friend Toni,[3] so they left in a body & joined up with the Americans. This is confidential of course. I shouldn't print it; I certainly shouldn't mention any *names* as it isn't absolutely certain it's true.[4] However I'd mention the 'break' for what it's worth.

I hope things are going well with you? The story in *Seven* seems to have been generally appreciated. Philip O'Connor[5] wrote me about it; & John Goodland, the Editor etc.

I may have a novel, 'The Eye in the Triangle', out in Spring probably by Faber.[6] It's already finished.

With best wishes.

Yours sincerely,

J. F. Hendry.

¹   Norman MacLeod's poem 'The Eyes on the Potatoes' appeared in *The Voice of Scotland* vol. 1, no. 3 (December 1938-February 1939), p. 7.

²   J. F. Hendry and C.J. Russell co-edited *Albannach: A little Anthology of 1938 Scots Poetry* (Dingwall, 1938).

³   'Toni' was Thomas Arthur Rowett Hyndman (1911-1982). Note 8 to letter 191 refers in more detail.

⁴   It was on the basis of this letter that Hugh MacDiarmid wrote inside the front cover of *The Voice of Scotland* vol. 1, no.3 (December 1938 –February 1939), under the headline 'Spain and the Celtic Volunteers': 'One of the most interesting facts in relation to the Spanish struggle is that the Celtic members – Scottish, Irish and Welsh - of the

International Brigade found it impossible to work hand in hand with their English comrades and had to break away and join up in a body with the Americans instead.' However, it is now clear that only some of the Irish Brigaders had joined the Americans. In *A Soldier of Liberty* (1996), Peter O' Connor wrote: 'All the Irish comrades were summoned to a special meeting to decide whether to remain a section of the British Battalion or join the Lincoln Battalion. I believe that such a meeting should never have been called. About 45 comrades attended and decided by a majority of 5 to join the Lincoln Battalion, the main reason given was the wrongs done to Ireland by the English in the past ...' (Quoted in *You are history You are legend*, a brochure published in memory of the eleven Waterford volunteers in 2004). The 45 Brigaders who attended the special meeting formed less than a quarter of the 200 Irishmen who fought in Spain (though they might not all have been in Spain at the same time). Donald Renton, an Edinburgh Brigader, recalled to Professor Victor Kiernan: 'There had been brought into being an Irish Company. In the light of the struggle of the Irish people for their own national independence this company should have been, in my view, quite a separate organisation, even though attached to the British Battalion and part of the International Brigade. In practice, however, the Irish national struggle as a related factor to the Spanish fight was not in my opinion concretely enough recognised. So it brought about one or two ugly situations at Madrigueras during the training period.' (*Voices From the Spanish War*, ed. by Ian MacDougall (Edinburgh, 1986), p.24). In 1998 William Herrick, a member of the Lincoln Battalion in Spain, seemed to confirm that an Irish company (only) had joined the Americans. Herrick wrote: ' A new group arrived one day, this one not from the States but from the Brittish Battalion training camp – an Irish company. Though so far as we knew no bullets had been fired, the Irish troubles had broken out among the British, and the Irish company transferred to us.' (*Jumping the Line: The Adventures and Misadventures of an American Radical* (University of Wisconsin Press, 1998) p.149.

5   Philip O'Connor (1916-1998) was a contributor to *Wales* 5 and 11. *Selected Poems 1936-1998*, chosen and introduced by Patrick B. de Maré, 2003.

6   Unpublished.

179. From Dylan Thomas (EUL MS2966)

Sea View
Laugharne
Carmarthenshire
[Dated 'October 1938' in MacDiarmid's hand in pencil]

Dear Hugh MacDiarmid:
Thank you for writing. Afterwards, I regretted my uppish letter. I'd just been talking to Keidrych Rhys, and his arguments against the English – a lousy lot, I agree, and I can no more get money out of them than I can out of Wales – made me suddenly angry against what I was foolish enough to call the Celtic set-up; & your letter, the first circular, came as a godsend for a grievance in which I really put hardly any feeling at all. Of course you should be allowed to ask for, roughly, what sort of contributions you want; though, actually, who, of the people you wrote to would have sent a hymn to Chamberlain?[1] I'm enclosing a few short poems; if they don't

suit, let me know & I'll post along some more. I'm very busy these days, & very hungry too. Thanks again, & best wishes for the Celtic Front number.[2] I hope very much that one day we shall meet.

Yours sincerely,

Dylan Thomas.

PS As you see, the poems I enclose have been printed before: the little ones in *Poetry* (Chicago). And the longer one in *Life & Letters Today*.

PPS Also one other poem – the typed one, which hasn't been printed anywhere.

[1] Neville Chamberlain, Prime Minister 1937-1940.
[2] The Celtic Front Number was vol.1 no. 3 of *The Voice of Scotland* (December 1938-February 1939). Dylan Thomas was represented by 'Poem' of which the first line was, 'The tombstone told me when she died', p.12.

180. From Jack Kahane, The Obelisk Press (EUL MS2968)

THE OBELISK PRESS
John Kahane

16 Place Vendôme
Paris 1er
2 November 1938

Dear Sir,

I was very interested to have your letter on the subject of your poem 'Mature Art'.

The length of it makes it an extremely difficult proposition; 20 000 lines representing, I suppose, about 10 times as many words or perhaps somewhat less. Mine is not a rich firm and I am rather frightened at the production costs that would be involved, while fully recognising the advantage of prestige.

Would it not be possible for you to get a hundred subscribers at a guinea? Supposing I were to draw out a circular do you think we would get extra subscribers in that way? In any case I would like to see your manuscript and in sending it you might be kind enough to give me your opinion on my queries.[1]

Very truly yours,

Jack Kahane.

[1] On the death of Jack Kahane the following year, his son, Maurice J. Kahane, took over the business. 1500 'Mature Art' circulars were printed of which only three were returned at one point. Andrew Graham Grieve, MacDiarmid's brother, and Prof. Herbert F. West each ordered one copy, and Prof. Barker Fairley ordered two copies. By the time the circulars had been printed the price had been provisionally fixed at two guineas.

MATURE ART

An Exercise in Schlabone, Bordatini, and Scordattura

by

HUGH MACDIARMID

THE OBELISK PRESS invites subscriptions for the above work by the famous Scottish poet. The price has been provisionally fixed at Two Guineas. This is his first long poem since he published « *To Circumjack Cencrastus* » in 1930. It is an enormous poem of over 20,000 lines, dealing with the interrelated themes of the evolution of world literature and world consciousness, the problems of linguistics, the place and potentialities of the Gaelic genius, from its origin in Georgia to its modern expressions in Scotland, Ireland, Wales, Cornwall, Galicia and the Pays Basque, the synthesis of East and West, and the future of civilisation.

It is a very learned poem involving a stupendous range of reference, especially to Gaelic,

FRÈRE - TOURCOING

Prospectus for 'Mature Art' from The Obelisk Press, Paris, 1939.

181. From George Waters (EUL MS2970)

JOHN RITCHIE & CO.
John E. Ritchie Findlay
George H. Law
Peter Findlay

Office of
THE SCOTSMAN
Edinburgh
8 November 1938

Dear Sir,

I have to acknowledge your letters of 10ᵗʰ October (received when I was taking my belated summer holiday) and of 4th November with reference to Mr. Charles Cammell's obituary tribute to the late Dr. Pittendreigh MacGillivray. I note your statement that Mr. Cammell quoted in his article from your copyright writings without acknowledgement and that you expect suitable compensation for this unauthorised use of your work. So far as my recollection serves, there was no indication in Mr. Cammell's manuscript of the source of the quotations, but the article was received long before it was used and I have now only my memory to go by. At the same time, I think it most unlikely that I or any member of my staff made any editorial deletion of your name. I presume that Mr. Cammell thought that the small use he was making of your writings did not necessitate acknowledgement, although I think it would have been better if he had mentioned the source. At the same time I cannot agree with you that the incidental use of a few borrowed phrases in a long and original estimate of Dr. MacGillivray's work entitles you to compensation.

I notice, with surprise, the statement in your letter of October 10 that *The Scotsman* has, over many years, persistently attacked you in the most unscrupulous fashion. There is not a word of truth in this allegation. You have never been attacked by *The Scotsman*, and it was only when your persistent abuse of *The Scotsman* had become too obvious to be ignored that we ceased to review your books. Prior to that we published adequate and favourable notices of your publications, and I myself went out of my way to see that your books were placed in the hands of a sympathetic reviewer. Moreover, many years ago, when you were beginning your career as a poet under the name of Hugh MacDiarmid, *The Scotsman* published a long and favourable article on you which ought to have been welcome and should have been helpful to a young, rising poet. You will remember yourself how you treated this attempt to bring you to the notice of the Scottish public.[1] You have only yourself to blame for *The Scotsman*'s later attitude to your books, and I must again deny with the utmost vigour that *The Scotsman* has ever attacked or abused you.

Yours faithfully,
George A. Waters
Editor.

---

[1] Possibly a reference to Dr Kitchin's article on 8 November 1924 and to MacDiarmid's reply of 13 November (already noted).

George Campbell Hay - Gaelic poet.
By permission of Gordon Wright.

182. From George Campbell Hay (EUL MS2951.2 f.1)

14 Carlton St
Edinburgh
14 November 1938

The Editor
The Voice of Scotland
Dear Sir,

I am sending you this mixed bag in the hope that you will find something of use or interest in it. It is mostly in Gaelic, I'm afraid, and of course the number of people who want to see Gaelic is small, while the number of those who flush with anger when they see it is increasing. Is truagh nach urrainn dhuinn cur as daibh.[1]

There are enclosed some Gaelic and one English original poem, translations from the Gaelic into English, and translations from Modern Greek, Welsh (Cywydd), and English into Gaelic. I have two Gaelic things satirising Jehovah and the clerics, but they are too long, one being of 122 lines.

The Gaelic of my home place, Tarbert Loch Fyne, diverges very widely from the so-called 'standard' Gaelic, wherever *that* may be spoken, but I think the things which I enclose conform fairly well to the literary norm. 'À' for 'è' (he) is an exception, but it is to be heard from The Mull to Cape Wrath, and in printed books the rhyme demands it hundreds of times.

I only hope that these things may be of help to you, for I wish your magazine well – the only one of a type which Scotland needs so much.[2]

Yours faithfully,
George Campbell Hay.

[1] Is truagh nach urrainn dhuinn cur as daibh – *it's a pity we can't do away with them.*
[2] MacDiarmid published 'Seven Poems' by George Campbell Hay in *The Voice of Scotland*, vol.1, no. 4 (March-May 1939), and gives the third paragraph of this letter in a note. The 'English original poem' was 'To a certain Loch Fyne Fisherman who keeps to the Old Ways'. There were also two original Gaelic poems, one translation from Gaelic into English, two translations from modern Greek into Gaelic, and one translation from Welsh into Gaelic. The latter was placed and dated 'An Tairbeart' 28 October 1938. MacDiarmid also published Hay's essay, 'Gaelic and Literary Form', in *The Voice of Scotland*, vol.2, no.1 (June-August 1939).

183. From Helen B. Cruickshank (EUL MS2946.9 f.22)

From
Helen B. Cruickshank
4 Hillview Terrace
Corstorphine
Edinburgh 12
23 November 1938

Dear Chris,

This will be a brief note, as I hope to see you in Glasgow on 3rd [December], but I want to know what Valda & you want done about the December instalment of the RLF money?[1] Will one or other of you please drop me a note? You may be wanting it split between you (like splitting a pea, I'm afraid – but I don't propose to increase the pea, despite Xmas etc., as the balance is growing perilously small.)

I dislike intensely the tack you are on about the Muirs. Instead of pulling that beard for you, I now want you to grow it as long as you possibly can, so that I can gag you with it. I really think you're wasting your time – quite apart from the ethics or justice of your attack – but ye're a thrawn de'il & the mair I tell ye ye're wrang, the mair ye'll ging intillt said she, in her worst Scotch.

I'm to be Bessie MacArthur's[2] guest at the Central Hotel on Dec. 3rd & return to Edin. on the Sunday, as I want to attend a discussion at 4.30 on the 'teaching of Scots literature'. Harvey Wood is the speaker.[3]

I hear there will be over 200 at Willie's dinner.[4]

I don't know whether you'll be in Edin. If so, I hope to see you again, but am sorry I can't ask you to stay. I rarely ever have visitors now, but if you're about, we'll fix up something. Anyone you particularly want to see? But I'm afraid I'm rather a back number as a hostess now.

Love to all.

Helen.

PS By the way I never told Power about your RLF award. Gossip runs round in Scotland so quickly that I kept as mum as possible about your affairs except to the few people whom Mary R[amsay] & I 'tapped' before the RLF came forward.

---

[1] MacDiarmid had been awarded £125 from the Royal Literary Fund. He received a cheque for £75 to pay off bills at shops on Whalsay and the remainder was to be paid to Valda at the rate of £5 a month by Helen Cruickshank. On this letter Valda has noted, 'Asked Helen to send it on here – as it's all we have to live on for the month & nothing else seems to be coming in. You'd better 'tap' Peter.? V.' [Peter MacCallum Smith, Secretary and Treasurer of Scottish PEN.]
[2] Scots poet whose publications ranged from *The Clan of Lochlann:two celtic plays* (1928) to the poems in *From Daer Water* (1962).
[3] H. Harvey Wood was Scottish representative of the British Council in Edinburgh at this time.
[4] The dinner in honour of William Power, retiring president of Scottish PEN, was held in the Grosvenor Restaurant, Glasgow on 3 December 1938.

184. From Monica Campbell (NLS Acc. 7361/9)

SCOTTISH JOINT COMMITTEE FOR SPANISH RELIEF

Broomfield Crescent
Edinburgh 12
6 December 1938

Caricature of Willa and Edwin Muir by Barbara Niven, first published in *The Voice of Scotland* vol. 1, no. 2, September-November 1938 with Willa's head cut off. By permission of Rosemary Sutcliffe.

Dear Mr Grieve,

Some time ago you were good enough to sign a Scottish authors' appeal on behalf of the Spanish people. May I trouble you once more?

This Edinburgh committee is holding a big Spanish bazaar on the 16th and 17th of this month, to be opened by the Spanish ambassador, and I have undertaken to help in collecting books for their book stall. We should be most grateful if you could let us have a signed copy of one of your books, or more, and/or anything else of interest, not necessarily autographed, which you think you could spare. I think we shall have no difficulty in selling all we are given, and a contribution from you would certainly be of enormous help.

We are both terribly busy these days, and Brian is out all and every day. However, we are both hoping to see you when next you come to Edinburgh.

Yours sincerely,

Monica Campbell.

185. From Elizabeth Skinner (EUL Gen.2094/5/2011a&b)

South Road
Cupar
22 December [1938]

Dear Chris

I received a second letter to-day I hope its the last one of that kind I dont know what Ive ever done to you that you should try to threaten me or mine you are laying yourself open for a very serious charge I only wish to say that the next one of that kind that you write me I will just hand it into the Police As regards the children you are taking a sudden interest in them after shirking your responsibility so long We have lived here quite openly for over 6 years & you could have found us out as easily as you seem to have done now the children have never been kept from you or anyone & you could have seen them any time

They are very well & happy & have been well looked after as any one in Cupar or Methil would tell you Peggy has never once failed in providing for them & has had to work very hard indeed to do same they have had everything reasonable they have wanted & are considered very lucky children they have been told no ill of you Christine knows you are married again & she is old enough to judge for herself she has already chosen who she wants to be with she has done & is doing very well at school she was 2nd Dux girl at Castlehill of course she is at Bell Baxter now Walter too is getting on all right but you never had much interest in him

Now as you have nothing whatever to do with Peggy you will let her alone also Ina who never did you any harm though I'm left alone I have plenty of friends & I am quite able to look after myself & my family I dont set myself up to be your judge what you have done & what you are doing lies between you & your Maker people who try to do harm to others gets it returned on themselves Peggy doesnt need your pity she can always work for herself & is not without brains she was always too good for you

About your papers you had them yourself & left them at Chancery Lane when you left there now hoping you will think before writing me a letter like the two you sent the first is in other hands in safe keeping wishing you well

E Skinner

PS. I gave Christine your letter to her she is not much of a letter writer you may get an answer sometime

186. From F. R. Leavis (EUL MS2970)

SCRUTINY [1]
A Quarterly Review

Editors
D. W. Harding
L. C. Knights
F. R. Leavis
Denys Thompson

Offices
6 Chesterton Hall Crescent
Cambridge
England

9 January 1939

Dear Mr MacDiarmid

I ought to say first that we differ from *The Criterion* in having no financial backing & being unable to pay contributors. I believe you live by the pen (our connexion lives mainly by teaching) & so I can't assume that you can give your work away.

That said, I add at once that we should be extremely interested to see your essay (I like your Burns review very much).[2] Length *would* be a difficulty, though one that, as you suggest, could probably be overcome (the space problem bothers us more & more – again we differ from *The Criterion*). I have long been convinced myself that Scott stands in need of a radical revaluation.[3]

All good wishes.
Yours sincerely,
F. R. Leavis.

[1] *Scrutiny* was published quarterly from 1932-1953. It was reprinted in full by Cambridge University Press in 1963.
[2] MacDiarmid had reviewed Keith Henderson's *Burns – By Himself* (London, 1938) in *The Criterion*, vol. xviii, no. lxxi (January 1939).
[3] MacDiarmid was not published in *Scrutiny*.

187. From Peter Kerrigan (NLS Acc. 7361/10)

Communist Party of Great Britain
Scottish District Committee
83 Ingram Street

Glasgow C1

25 January 1939

Dear Comrade,

I wish to direct your attention to the previous letters which I have sent to you, to which, up to the moment, you have made no reply.

In view of the fact that in *The Voice of Scotland* which I have received today[1] there is a declaration that a thorough analysis is going to be made of A. Ferguson's pamphlet[2] and as from previous notices on this matter it is likely to be controversial, I wish to insist on you honouring the arrangement made on your re-admission into the Party, i.e. that all controversial matter be submitted to the District before printing.

I also want to object in the strongest possible fashion to the complete travesty of facts regarding the British Battalion of the International Brigade which is printed in the inside page of the cover. Surely, before you make such declarations, you ought to consult the Party as this, in my opinion, is something of an exceptionally serious character and one which the Party would never have agreed to being printed if it had known in advance. I say this because I know, personally, the statement to be untrue and obviously based on wrong information in relation to some of our Irish comrades in the Brigade.[3]

I am also convinced that your Editorial 'A Reply to T. A. Jackson' comes into the category of an article which should have been previously discussed with the Party. Can I have a reply at an early date?

Yours fraternally,

Peter Kerrigan.

Scottish District Organiser.

[1] Peter Kerrigan had just received *The Voice of Scotland*, vol.1, no. 3.

[2] Aitken Ferguson's pamphlet was *Scotland* (Glasgow, 1938). In 'Scottish Nationalism: The Communist Report' in *The Voice of Scotland,* vol.1, no. 4 (March-May 1939), pp.27-33, MacDiarmid notes that copies of *Scotland* had been sent out to subscribers to the previous issue.

[3] In a letter to the Scottish District Committee, recovered from his M I 5 file, MacDiarmid wrote in postscript, 6 February 1939:'If you care to write to *The Voice of Scotland* denying what has been said in the last issue regarding the Celtic elements in the International Brigade, I will be glad to print your communication –and reply to it. No matter what you do I am perfectly confident that I will have no difficulty in carrying the matter over your heads and vindicating my socialist integrity all right and at the same time exposing your mean machinations and your moral and intellectual bankruptcy.' (TNA KV 2/2010, 29A). No such denial appeared in *The Voice of Scotand.*

188. From the Communist Party of Great Britain (NLS Acc. 7361/10)

The Communist Party of Great Britain

Central Committee

16 King Street

Covent Garden
London WC2
23 February 1939

Correspondence between yourself and the Scottish District Party Committee, particularly with Peter Kerrigan, also copies of *The Voice of Scotland* edited by yourself, and a request from the Scottish D.P.C. for your expulsion from the Party in consequence of your failure to comply with the conditions of your re-instatement, were remitted to the Central Control Commission for consideration.

The following were the conclusions and decisions arrived at by the Control Commission.

1.   To write to the Scottish D.P.C. and yourself intimating that your failure to comply with the conditions of your re-instatement had been established.

2.   In that you had failed not only to submit controversial material to the D.P.C. before publication, but also to keep the appointment with the Scottish D.P.C. which had been asked for in your letter of 7 November 1938.

3.   You had also failed to consult the D.P.C. before undertaking the editorship of *The Voice of Scotland*.

4.   That in your capacity as editor and writer you had allowed *The Voice of Scotland* to be utilised to attack the Communist Party of Great Britain, its policy and certain of its leaders.

5.   The completely arrogant and undisciplined tone of your postscript to your letter of 6 February 1939 was also noted.

After careful consideration of all these facts, the Control Commission decided that the request of the Scottish D.P.C. for your expulsion from the C.P.G.B. was fully justified and is endorsed herewith.

CENTRAL CONTROL COMMISSION

189. From R. E. Muirhead (NLS Acc.7361/10)

Scots Independent
28 Elmbank Crescent
Glasgow C2
Scotland
25 February 1939

Dear Mr Grieve,

It is sometime since I had your letter enclosing the typescript with certain explanatory paragraphs. Many thanks for same. You will by this mail, I hope, receive the half-dozen copies of the March issue in which your article is printed. Should you desire any further copies I shall be very glad to have them posted to you.[1]

I have noted with interest all you say about fighting the enemy inside as well as outside our own ranks. To my mind it is sometimes a little difficult to define an enemy in the Scottish National movement. I am certainly more inclined to give those attempting to work for Scottish Self-government the benefit of any doubt as compared with enemies either declared or not.

To my opinion one of the chief reasons why we lack Self-government in Scotland is the difficulty of getting individual Scots to sink sufficient of their personal ideas to enable them to line up with other citizens in a concentrated demand for Self-government. My strong belief is that every individual day that Scotland lacks Self-government she becomes more and more entangled with the English Government and people. We Scots cannot afford to fight amongst ourselves at present unless there is some very serious difference.

Trusting you are enjoying the best of health.

Yours sincerely,

R.E. Muirhead.

---

[1]   MacDiarmid's article in the March *Scots Independent* was the first part of 'The Press and Scotland'.

190. From Gilbert Wright (EUL MS2969)

105 Great Russell Street
London WC1
29 March 1939

Dear Mr Grieve,

Thank you for your letter of the 24th instant enclosing 'The Flaming Poetaster'.[1] We share your view that it may be somewhat difficult to place owing to its slashing nature.

However we will try all the English publishers you suggest and then go on to the USA firms.

We will even try Longman's although what sort of reception we will get remains to be seen.

Yours sincerely,

Gilbert Wright (London) Ltd.

pp. A. F. Braydon.

---

[1]   'The Flaming Poetaster' was re-titled 'The Battle Continues' and published in full by Castle Wynd Printers Ltd in 1957. The original title was a reference to Roy Campbell's *The Flaming Terrapin* (1924). *The Battle Continues* forms an attack on Roy Campbell (1901-1957), South African poet and satirist, who attended Franco's victory parade in Madrid, 19 May 1939.

191. From Keidrych Rhys (EUL MS2970)

Penybont Farm

F'Annwyl[1] MacDiarmid:

This is to say how very glad I was to receive 'Canu Aneurin'. I'm afraid I can't promise definitely to print it because as yet I don't know whether I'll be able to keep *Wales* going.[2] So far I've been able to collect odd sums from friends besides what I get from my people, but now there's *The Welsh Review* [3]which is wealthy & financed by most of the Welsh bureaucrats & coalowners, who hope to send us all to sleep by doling out fivers. Strangely enough *Wales* created a stir, & sold & woke everybody up: it would be in a safe position now but my Left distributers rooked me – no money in at all yet, although the bookshops say they paid them. Then I'm being persecuted – my father has been warned against me by Sir David Hughes-Morgan! (a director of our only morning paper *The Western Mail*, whose sister used to own the farm) & others, which is beginning to make life more of a hell than it was before. I don't know what to do quite. Pretty hopeless trying to get a job, I suppose.

Hendry told me you were going to attack the English literary Left. I hope you do – as it is long overdue. It was bad enough having the *Left Review* run by a clique, always drinking double brandies in New Books. (That's where the proceeds of Dylan's *18 Poems* went!),[4] but I think the *New Writing*[5] clique is far worse, & personally hope you deal it its death-blow. I respect Spender somewhat, & was pleased to see him debunking Goronwy Rees[6] in *New Verse*[7] commitments No., but when one of his boyfriends Tony Heinemann[8] (a Welshman & the T.A.R. of the poems) tells me in the B.M. that Auden doesn't think much of MacD & says his stories etc. 'are lots of things lying on the ground' it makes me sick. Heinemann was a Private in the Army & got picked up by Spender in Trafalgar Sq., & deserted from Spain & Spender got the *New Statesman* lot to petition Del Vayo etc.[9] That doesn't much matter except in so far that a hermaphrodite can never get anywhere near Truth in his verse. But now this boy & 2 others who deserted are being put across in *Poems for Spain*, etc. Heinemann has been given a £100 advance by the Hogarth Press to write something, & has gone to the US & will probably become 'The Welsh Poet', no doubt due to what K.J. Raine[10] called John Lehmann's dilly-dallying with blonde proletarians. But Lehmann's attitude in itself is also harmful: his group 'The Yellow Book of the Thirties'[11] (it's sufficiently decadent) – I don't know who is their Oscar Wilde [12]– swamp the younger writers, the younger Group since *New Signatures*,[13] who naturally enough take up a Wyndham Lewis stance: they are too Left for these nice wealthy neurotics.

The thing seems to be to include the *New Signatures* group, Tom Harrisson because he wrote Auden, Spender, & Madge[14] up in 'Letter to Oxford', & the Lehmann family – Rosamund,[15] Rosamund's ex-hubby (Wogan Phillips)[16] whose father Kylesant ruined hundreds of farmers in Carmarthen, Beatrix Lehmann's[17] boyfriend Goronwy Rees & so on. Heinemann was quite open & said that there weren't any Scots, Irish & Welsh writers nowadays.Nothing I suppose outside the Gordon Square literary aristocrats & Lehmann's own manufactured proletarians – 4 Jewish writers, whom Lehmann dragged out of an East End Boys' Club – Willy Goldman,[18] Julius Lipton (Lipschitz),[19] Abraham Fagan (who was sent out to Russia & ran the YCL) Simon Blumenfeld.[20] It's disgusting this buggering – & making proletarians out of petit-bourgeois Jews, nearly as disgusting as the 'proletarian accent' of Calder-Marshal1[21] & others who contributed to 'The Old School'.

There has been some uneasiness in Wales over this lately. The miners are beginning to see through the Gollancz racket, which with the Penguins, has spoilt the chance of any younger writer ever getting a novel out. George Ewart Evans,[22] who's had stories in *Left Review, New Masses* [23] etc. can't find a publisher – 3 years now – they're damned good. There seems to be a conspiracy. Gwyn Jones, a loud Gollancz author who sexes up long-dead literary bohemians like Grieve,[24] seems determined to smash up my group. The capitalists here come to terms with the Communists, ask [Arthur] Horner[25] to shoot grouse, but spend time & money attacking Nationalists. They stooped as low as to say Saunders Lewis had piles when he was in prison, which is of course a typical trick. They even give the Left publicity (only recently though) & review Lawrence & Wishart books. Nationalists get neither.

Still! I feel, however, that something on the lines advocated by *The Voice of Scotland* is bound to come pretty soon. The public (the middle classes) won't always be satisfied with Auden & racketeering & lies & Public School men with large private incomes ... educated solely for Culture. Edgell Rickword is about the only person with some idea of Nationalism, but even he was in the Black and Tans.[26] Wintringham, I hear, was expelled for living with someone.[27] True bourgeois morality! & the time will come when contributors to *Wales* will be allowed to write plays & scenarios for our Miners' May Day pageant instead of Montagu Slater![28] So you deserve all our thanks.

But so far no one has dared attack them except perhaps Dupee[29] in an article 'The English Literary Left' in the *Partisan Review* [30] & Herbert Read, indirectly, & myself (in a letter) v. indirectly in this week's *Time and Tide* & Savage's[31] rather brilliant 'Poetry Politics in London' in *Poetry* (Chicago) Jan. 1939. Trotsky now seems to give more hope for nationalism than Georgia's Stalin! I can't see how one can possibly hope to build any militant organ upon a Clique of Public School pansies, all of whom are making a comfortable living out of it, & know nothing whatever of the lives of workers.

It will be a difficult job. I think one of the first essentials to create a new group in opposition & get them publicized. *New Writing* of course won't print George Barker,[32] Dylan Thomas, because they'd only show up Auden, & Lehmann, Spender, MacNeice seem to have got around *Poetry* (London):[33] that has possibilities & in its circular advertised all the younger poets – O'Connor, Savage, Hendry, Niall Montgomery,[34] besides the Symons lot.[35] It's no good looking for support in the weeklies: Verschoyle[36] of *The Spectator* has issued a writ on Savage already: he really is one of the lowest of the low. Savage visualised his home being broken up & his books sold. Or in *The Listener*. Or in *The London Mercury*. Robert Herring[37] is the only editor who prints the younger people: he is also tied up with *New Writing* & the old *Left Review* clique though.

I don't know if you understand Welsh: anyway I shall send you a copy of *Tir Newydd* [38]& *Heddiw* [39] again. Meanwhile v best wishes to *The Voice* – it's unique & it's got fight.

Yours ever,
Keidrych Rhys.

PS The *Newydd* has a good article on the Left attitude to the Welsh language & culture (says their Welsh branches haven't shown any interest yet, even after promises in their Report: also on the difference between the Welsh 'People' and England's proletariat.) Really excellent piece of work.

I believe I owe you an advert too.

1   My dear.
2   *Wales* was founded in August 1937 by Keidrych Rhys who edited the first issues, and 6/7 with Dylan Thomas. Nigel Heseltine edited 8/9, 10 and 11 and these completed the first series in 1939/40. No. 8/9, August 1939, included 'On Reading Professor Ifor Williams's "Canu Aneurin" in Difficult Days', pp. 232-234. (*C.P.* I, pp. 689-691).
3   *The Welsh Review* vol. 1, nos 1-6 and vol. 2, nos 1-4 (February to November 1939) was edited by Gwyn Jones.
4   Dylan Thomas, *18 Poems, Sunday Referee* poets, vol. 2 (London, 1934).
5   John Lehmann (1907-1987), poet, edited *New Writing* 1936-1939, *Penguin New Writing* 1940-1950 (in association with Roy Fuller), and *London Magazine* 1954-1961.
6   Goronwy Rees (1909-1979) later translated *Conversations with Kafka*, notes and reminiscences by Gustav Janouch, with an introduction by Max Brod (London, 1953 and 1971).
7   Geoffrey Grigson (1905-1985) edited *New Verse* (1933-1939).
8   'Tony Heinemann' was Thomas Arthur Rowett Hyndman (1911-1982). He was the dedicatee of Spender's *The Trial of a Judge* in 1938 with the sonnet 'The world wears your image on the surface', and joint dedicatee with Auden of *The Burning Cactus* in 1936. One of his poems was included in *Poems for Spain* in 1939. There is no evidence that he was '[...] given £100 by the Hogarth Press to write something [...]'. He did not go to the US because of immigration problems. Tony's poem was 'Jarama Front'. The anthology was edited by Spender and John Lehmann, London, 1939.
9   Julio Alvarez del Vayo (1891-1974) was minister for foreign affairs in the Spanish Republican Governments of Largo Caballero from September 1936- 17 May 1937 and of Juan Negrín from April 1938 to the end of the Spanish Civil War. He then emigrated to the US and died in New York. According to John Sutherland's biography of Spender (London, 2004), Barry Thomas, the First Secretary of the British Embassy in Valencia, offered to refer Tony's case to Del Vayo (p.219).
10 Kathleen Jessie Raine (1908-2003), poet and critic.
11 The reference is to *The Yellow Book* of the 1890s, published between 1894 and 1897.
12 Oscar Wilde (1854-1900), poet and playwright, novelist and short story writer.
13 *New Signatures* was a collection edited by John Lehmann and published by the Hogarth Press in 1932.
14 Tom Harrisson (1911-1976) and Charles Madge (1912-1996) are remembered for their work for 'mass observation'. *War begins at home.* By Mass Observation, edited and arranged by Tom Harrisson and Charles Madge, London, 1940.
15 Rosamund Lehmann (1901-1990), novelist, biographer and short story writer.
16 Beatrix Lehmann (1903-1979), novelist.
17 Wogan Phillips(1902-1993) was wounded while driving for Medical Aid to Spain in

the Spanish Civil War. He became the second Baron Milford in 1962 and was the only member of the Communist Party to sit in the House of Lords.

18 Willy Goldman wrote the novel *A Tent of Blue,* London, 1946.

19 Julius Lipton (Lipschitz) published four titles in the 1930s. *Poems of Strife,* London, 1936.

20 Simon Blumenfeld, novelist, published four titles in the 1930s.

21 Arthur Calder-Marshall (1908-1992), novelist, short story writer, and author of a variety of literary works, including autobiography.

22 George Ewart Evans (1909-1988), author of a variety of prose works related to country life and traditions. Autobiography: *The Strength of the Hills,* London, 1983.

23 *The New Masses* (1926-1948) was a prominent American Marxist publication edited by Michael Gold.

24 This perhaps suggests that Rhys did not, at least at this stage, realise that MacDiarmid was Grieve. MacDiarmid did not include this reference to 'Grieve' in his quotations from Rhys's letter.

25 Arthur Horner(1894-1968) was a Welsh miners' leader.

26 A good deal of the material of this letter was used by MacDiarmid with and without quotation marks in his editorial 'The English Literary Left' in *The Voice of Scotland*, vol.2, no.1 (June-August 1939), pp. 5-6, and subsequently in *Lucky Poet* (Methuen, 1943), pp.171-173. *Lucky Poet* had to be withdrawn from sale until the reference to Edgell Rickword's having been in the Black and Tans in Ireland was removed.

27 Tom Wintringham was expelled from the Communist Party in 1938 for living with Kitty Bowler, an American freelance journalist whom he had met in Spain and whom he married in 1941. This may have been because she was thought to be a Trotskyist.

28 Montagu Slater (1902-1956), poet, novelist, playwright, and librettist of the opera *Peter Grimes* for which Benjamin Britten wrote the music.

29 Frederick Wilcox Dupee, US critic and editor.

30 *Partisan Review* (1934-2003), quarterly magazine, originally a partisan of the Communist Party, but independent since 1938.

31 Derek S. Savage, poet and critic.

32 George Barker (1913-1991), poet and essayist.

33 *Poetry* (London) was edited by Meary James Thurairajah Tambimuttu (1915-1983), Tamil poet, editor, critic and publisher, from February 1939 to Winter 1951 (with Anthony Dickens from 1939-May 1949).

34 Niall Montgomery, (1914-1987), poet and architect.

35 Julian Symons (1912-1995), poet, novelist and journalist; founded the magazine *Twentieth Century Verse* in 1937 and edited it for two years.

36 Derek Verschoyle (d. 1973) was literary editor of *The Spectator* from 1932 to 1940, and, later, a publisher.

37 Robert Herring (1903-1975) was a Scottish (and Welsh) poet and author of a variety of literary works. He was an early film critic. Assistant editor *The London Mercury* 1925-1934 and editor of *Life and Letters* 1935-1950. *Westward Look :* Poems 1922-1945, Glasgow [1947].

38 *New Ground .*

39 *Today .*

192. From Arthur Donaldson (NLS Acc.7361/10)

North Halket
Lugton
Kilmarnock
6 April 1939

A charaid:

Thanks for your letter of the 4th and the P.O. for 2/- We particularly welcome your joining us.

The League is continuing to attract members, not yet in large numbers but steadily and of a good quality.[1] Nor can our work be measured only by the number of actual members for our influence extends over a far wider circle than those who have joined up. The Scots people are not good 'joiners', as you know, and their experience with Nationalism (from an organisation point of view) has not helped. But we have already put out over 30 000 leaflets into all parts of Scotland and there is no saying how much we have done to stiffen the people in their resistance to National Service. Most remarkable of all for a Nationalist organisation, we are paying our way as we go.

At the moment we are trying to organise the live elements in the SNP for the forthcoming Annual Conference. Whether or not we can gain control over the SNP is very doubtful but we can make a start and shake up the MacCormick gang. Until we are able to throw them out, organised Nationalism will not be of much importance. Don't mention this matter to anyone of whom you are not completely sure – we don't want to warn the 'enemy'.

I am glad you are finding the NYT useful.[2] It always seemed wrong that I should just burn it or give it to a bunch of boors who looked at the photographs.

Gu dileas,[3]
Arthur Donaldson.

[1] The 'League' was the Scottish Neutrality League which had been formed in 1938. Arthur Donaldson was Secretary.
[2] *New York Times.*
[3] Yours faithfully.

193. From Kenneth Patchen (EUL MS2962.7 f.11)

Concord
Massachusetts
20 May 1939

Dear Hugh MacDiarmid:

You must try to forgive this long long silence: I have been very ill for an awful time. The magazine had to be abandoned (I have your poems – shall I return them you? – Many people have seen them).

My new book, *First Will and Testament*, will be published in October by New Directions. Will send you a copy.

I am working on a little farm here – and getting well.
California was poison.

Saw Ezra Pound yesterday: like him.
I should greatly like to hear from you again.
Sincerely yours,
Kenneth Patchen.

194. From Glyn Jones (EUL MS2951.10 ff.12-13)

Traws Coed
Heol y Bryn
Rhiwbina
Glam.
[June 1939]

Dear Hugh MacDiarmid,

Thank you for sending on the lastest number of *The Voice of Scotland*. I liked very much your editorial on the 'English Literary Left'.[1] I agree with nearly everything you have to say there – although I appear to get more *amusement* out of the antics of our puplic-school communists than you do.[2] They seem so funny to me, absolutely out of touch with the working class – could you imagine the *orchidaceous* Spender enjoying a meal with a railwayman? But there is one point in your article upon which I believe your information is not quite accurate. You say (page 5) 'In Wales, there is now the *Welsh Review*, which is wealthy and financed by the crowd of Welsh bureaucrats & coalowners –'. Now I don't think that is true. Gwyn Jones, the editor of the *Welsh Review* is well known to me, and his integrity cannot for a moment be questioned. Yet in the July issue of the 'Review' he says that unless he can get a larger number of subscribers the magazine would have to cease publication – and what he has told me privately leaves me in no doubt that this is absolutely true. So the support of 'Welsh bureaucrats & coalowners' seems to me illusory. I know that this class is capable of doing almost anything to maintain its position – my point is that they don't apppear to have done anything *here*. This may be a small point but I feel that the *Welsh Review* should not be needlessly damaged – after all Gwyn Jones has achieved one remarkable feat – he has persuaded W.J. Gruffydd[3] & Iorwerth Peate[4] to contribute to an Anglo-Welsh journal. I think he deserved credit for that.

I seem to have pleaded at such length for the *Welsh Review* that you must be beginning to wonder what interest I have in it! Well, I make the usual disclaimer.

I'm only a contributor, as Keidrych is.

If you care to suggest a Welsh topic for an article I would be very glad to help you.
Yours sincerely,
Glyn Jones.

---

[1] 'The English Literary Left' appeared in *The Voice of Scotland*, vol.2, no. 1 (June-August, 1939), pp.1-6.

2 Glyn Jones appears to have used 'lastest' and 'puplic-school' deliberately here.
3 William John Gruffydd (1881-1954), poet, scholar and critic, editor of *Y Llenor (Man of Letters)*.
4 Iorwerth Peate (1901-1982), poet and scholar.

195. From Stuart Hood (EUL Gen. 2094/2/904-5)

> Jubilee House
> Coverack
> Helston
> Cornwall
> 28 July 1939

Dear Grieve,

Many thanks for your offer to lend me your material on MacLean. At present I am having a rest from work but shall be glad to have the pamphlets etc. after 27 August.

I know more about Scottish history than I did, but not as much as I should. Some person – or persons – unknown has very carefully removed all the footprints on the sands of time that would give the least clues to our mystery. Only a damned inscrutable Providence could account for some phenomena – e.g., the support given by the Liberal capitalists to Home Rule. What did they hope to get out of it? Was it merely a disinterested application of the laissez-faire principle? I think not.

Again what on earth caused *The Daily Express* & the *Record* to adopt Nationalism in 1932? I have read *The Free Man* carefully but find no exact or convincing analysis of this. Your own article pre-supposes knowledge of a *Record* leader,[1] and doesn't help much at this distance. Perhaps when I see you next or when you send the stuff down you might be able to give me some data on the actual history of the Nationalist Party.

My wife & myself will be very pleased to give you hospitality on your Edinburgh visit and are looking forward to it very much.

Yours sincerely,
Stuart C. Hood.

1 The Daily Record published 'A Plan for Scotland' in its issue of 30 June,1932, pp.1-2 (not a leader). This 'Plan' was followed by other articles and correspondence throughout July 1932. MacDiarmid referred to this 'Plan' in his article on 9 July 1932 in his 'At the Sign of The Thistle' series in *The Free Man* (and in subsequent articles on 16, 23 and 30 July). These have all been reprinted in *The Raucle Tongue* II, pp.401-411.

196. From Gwyn Jones (EUL MS2970)

> 3 Lon-y-Dail
> Rhiwhina
> Glam.
> 31 August 1939

Dear Mr Hugh MacDiarmid,

I have just received from Glyn Jones a poem of yours: 'Diamond Body In a Cave of the Sea', and with it a letter telling me it is submitted for publication in *The Welsh Review*. He received it, he tells me, from Mr Keidrych Rhys. My opinion of your work has always been such, and my opinion of this poem now is, that in normal circumstances I should think it a privilege to print it.

You will not be surprised if I refer for a moment to your editorial attack on *The Welsh Review* in the June-August number of *The Voice of Scotland*. I thought at the time of writing to you, but it was so apparent you had not seen a single copy of the *Review* and had allowed yourself to be completely deceived by your 'correspondent' that there seemed no ground for argument between us. An adverse but studied opinion of our contents list would be one thing, but your fantastic misstatement of facts known to everyone who takes *The Welsh Review* seemed best left unanswered.

There must be some, like your correspondent, who would find pleasure in an editorial combat. I believe we both have something better to do with our time.

I hope I shall hear from you soon. Meantime, may I hold your poem?

Yours sincerely,

Gwyn Jones.

197. From George Campbell Hay (EUL MS2951.2 f.2)

14 Carlton Street
Edinburgh
7 September 1939

Dear Mr Grieve,

I am sending you this very mixed bunch of things, in case you might find any of them useful. I realise now that the Gaelic translations I sent you were pretty hellish, in that they illustrate the very Rob Roy MacGreigor characteristics which have already been fantastically overstressed. They are 'not safe for infants' (i.e., the public).

I hope that you manage to keep *The Voice* going in spite of this awful outburst of civilisation, for things of spirit will be more neglected than ever, and this war of cardboard tickets and conscript khaki hordes will have a dangerously levelling effect. A great trust lies in the hands of those who will not be snatched into the machine.

When I saw the Islay Territorials marching through Tarbert I could have bitten out my tongue with vexation, that the whole Highlands were not valued at the price of a submarine. Yet I have played a weak part, for I have let myself in for service with the RNVR[1] or the RN[2] already, should they choose to take me. As Scotland has lived up to her traditions as a province there was nothing else to do, except starve on the hills.

I am not afraid at all, but damned vexed on account of a lot of might-have-beens.

I have met John Tonge, who is good company & a man with a great appreciative and critical faculty, and Scott, which is a privilege.

Do you still mean to visit Edinburgh in October? I am going to Tarbert next week, but if you still do I will try and come through. However, it looks as if Göring's pets

will get there before you.
Yours sincerely,
George Campbell Hay.

1   Royal Naval Volunteer Reserve.
2   Royal Navy.

198. From Gwyn Jones (EUL MS2970)

3 Lon-y-Dail
Rhiwhina
Glam.
12 September 1939

Dear Mr Hugh MacDiarmid,

I was more than pleased to get your letter this morning. It was most generous and leaves me with nothing to say further, except that I want you to believe I meet it in the same spirit. Your personal apology I accept willingly, and I look forward to seeing the next issue of *The Voice of Scotland*.[1]

I am sending you today, under separate cover, copies of all numbers of *The Welsh Review*. I'll see too that your name goes on our mailing list. Do send along the copies of *The Voice of Scotland*.

You will see from the Editorials of the July and August numbers that we have not been without our crises, even before the present catastrophe. A desperate shortage of money has been our normal state of existence, and in July things were so bad that I had to guarantee the cost of publication to the printer personally. Our appeal then brought in a moderate response, and we seemed all set till next January. I've worked like a galley-slave this last week to ensure that we don't go under without a struggle, despite the probable shrinkage of circulation and the sharp increase of overhead costs. The prospects are now fairly good again. Since June we have not paid our contributors, save for a couple of items briefed in advance. The Editor throughout has been unpaid. You will guess how my eyebrows lifted at finding the *Review* described as monied. Still, that is by the way.

I should very much like to use your poem.[2] I regret I cannot offer you a fee for it, but such pocket-picking is inevitable, and no new experience I daresay for poets. I should like it for November or December, I'm not sure which. If you have a paid market, don't hesitate to ask for it back.

I think you know Glyn Jones. He is my near neighbour and friend. Jack Jones lives within a hundred yards.

This looks to me like a nasty time for literary periodicals. I hope you keep the flag flying (the editorial flag, I mean), nonetheless. I hope we do, too.

With good wishes,
Yours sincerely,
Gwyn Jones.

Barbara Niven, artist, and friend of Hugh MacDiarmid who visited him with her husband
Ern Brooks on Whalsay in 1938 and 1939.
By permission of Rosemary Sutcliffe.

1 MacDiarmid intended to print an apology to Gwyn Jones. However *The Voice of Scotland* didn't appear again until 1945.

2 'Diamond Body In a Cave of the Sea' was published in *The Welsh Review*, vol. 2, no. 4 (November 1939). *C.P.* II, pp. 1034-1038.

199. From Sir Alexander MacEwen (NLS Acc.7361/10)

Old National Bank Buildings
Inverness
12 September 1939

Dear Mr Grieve,

Your letter of 5th inst only reached me yesterday morning, and it was quite impossible for either my son or myself to reach Lerwick in time for the Appeal Court today. I telegraphed both to you and to the County Assessor, and I hope you have been able to get someone else to appear on behalf of these cottars.[1] In any case, we are so short-handed as a result of the War, that it would have been very difficult for either of us to have got away.

Yours sincerely,
Alexander MacEwen.

1 MacDiarmid had dictated letters on behalf of crofters and others who were appealing against the proposed increase in rates.

200. From Barbara Niven (EUL MS2957)

Lerwick
Tuesday
[12 September 1939]

Dear Christopher and Valda,

So you see we got stuck in Lerwick after all and that lasts till tomorrow noon at the earliest. Can you imagine – ! First, when we arrived after a bit of a tossing, we found there was a cargo boat only going in the evening but we thought we'd certainly go on that. However when we went back later as they said we must we found the 12 places were taken by naval reserves or such and we couldn't go on it. What was the use even of getting angry? – tho' we did. Then we started looking for reasonable rooms in Lerwick (which is all of what you, Christopher, say of it) and at the 8th house found a room not filled with Air Force guys. However it serves, and we thought we should at any rate be off today: but though the *St. Clair* came in early this morning she doesn't go till tomorrow probably afternoon. And we might have been pestering you for two days more, if we had only known. That is infuriating, to us.

A woman fell off the pavement this morning, looking at Ernest's beard, and dropped her shopping. Nothing else has happened. We're not used to that now.

Nothing else to say now. We just feel suspended and the knowledge that you're not far off is bad not good at all.

Love from us both to all.

Barbara & Ern.

To think now of that mad rush to Symbister!

Love to Mary[1]

Have enquired at the 2 hotels and on the *St Clair* to see if McEwen came but apparently not. B.

[1]   Mary Shearer was a neighbour of the Grieves at Sudheim, Whalsay. Barbara and Ern may have lodged with her.

201. From Barbara Niven (EUL MS2957)

27 September [1939]

Ernest will be writing shortly.

He sends love to all.

Dear Christopher,

There's so much to say and yet all I can think stupidly is how I would like to be talking to you instead. It seems so long since that day we watched you disappear over the hill at Symbister, and yet between that and saying goodbye was already long. I wish that could be done without: there is a sudden politeness about it that is very distancing and stays in one's mind like a discomfort. Can you think of a cure for it? – And do you know what I did, that morning? I came away leaving the poem behind,[1] in a roll of brown paper on the bookcase: and now and as soon as we got back it seemed to me quite impossible that I should have forgotten that: because now I don't want to read anything else. Can you understand it? (I can) and will you send it to me?

We keep wondering, knowing the time that boats take, what is happening about mails: whether you get them regularly if seldom, or what. And I would like to know all sorts of things that seem, from the time, as if they must have happened and yet since it's only a fortnight – I suppose, – may not have: whether you've heard from Paris yet, or heard any more about the effect of the *Voice* in London, or even heard of anything from newspapers in Scotland. I just have to think about how difficult things may be for you, and to hope that they won't. In any case apart from other things, the annoyance of the mails must be very bad.

Last year I told you how it was, coming back. But now this time there was so much, I feel secure and don't mind the place but rather through some understanding not so completely felt before I am glad to be here and only want to find some direct way in which it can come out. Apart I mean from painting where it certainly will: and perhaps writing, which I mention since you suggested it but with a kind of apology all the same. I would like – I feel I must – find some direct and practical way to work for communism. I will write in a day or two again about this because it must be at some length and I can see that already I am being led into what look like impersonal issues when what I want most to say ought to stay near the delight of being such a long time up there with you. But it's only in effects I can start to tell you what you've given me: if it was exciting and marvellous last year I know from what I have now that was just a surface thing, necessary in order to cut deeper. (It must be the peat I am thinking of – no suggestion of knifing was intended, though perhaps surgery wouldn't be so out of place.)

I can see there's no way of saying what I would like to and perhaps even the desire to try is stupid and slightly insulting to you, as if you don't know already what it is that you're giving. But it comes from this, that there are things that can't be made clear and it's against those I am struggling: and all the more because you accuse me here of a kind of clarity that isn't in my possession.

I wonder if you are still going over to the office morning and afternoon – if so you must just be about returning for dinner, perhaps in one of those unfamiliar winter aspects of the voe that we haven't seen. Here it is cold and dull which makes me think of winter anyway. I have just been scouring the library for books on mosses and lichens but any good ones must be in the reference section so I must spend time in that hothouse, it seems. People here – the Millers most of all – are very enthusiastic about the possibility of your weekend here.[2] I do hope the Glasgow meeting holds and that you can come.[3] We would like to arrange a big meeting with more than Theatre Union to listen to your poetry.

I badly want 2 dozen poetry sheets to sell to people here but though I wrote to Potts as soon as I got back (10 days ago now) none have come yet.[4] Could you give him a reminder when you are writing? There were none here when I got back either. I think they, and others that may come, couldn't be published at a better time. I believe they will go deeper and be more easily accepted too.

About Theatre Union and other things I must write again in 2 or 3 days.

Best wishes and love.

Barbara.

---

1   The poem which she left behind may have been a carbon copy of 'The Flaming Poetaster'.
2   'The Millers' were Jimmy Miller (later 'Ewan McColl') and Joan Littlewood.
3   The 'Glasgow meeting' may have been the dinner in honour of William Power on 3 December 1938. MacDiarmid did not go to Manchester at this time.
4   Paul Potts had published 'Speaking for Scotland', six poems by Hugh MacDiarmid, as broadsheet No.3 in August 1939.

202. From Glyn Jones (NLS Acc.7361/10)

Traws Coed
Manor Way
Cardiff
9 October 1939

Dear Hugh MacDiarmid,

I am enclosing the little article on the Welsh literary scene you asked me to write for *The Voice of Scotland*. Do you still need it, or is it too late?[1] I haven't gone very deeply into the subject as you will notice, I have treated the thing broadly as I ought to do in an article whose chief function, as I see it, is to give information. The interpretation I leave to more experienced & skilful critics than myself. Don't you agree that notes, something sketchy, are more suitable at this stage than anything more involved?

Please tell me if the notes will do. And will you please check up on my French –I've got a bad memory for languages.

Kind regards & all good wishes.

Yours sincerely,

Glyn Jones.

[1] This article was 'too late' as the last number of the first series of was vol.2, no.1 (June-August 1939).

203. From Nigel Heseltine (NLS Acc.7361/1)

Cefu-Bryntalch
Abermule
Montgomeryshire
10 October 1939

Dear Mr MacDiarmid,

In sending you the current number of *Wales* I must apologise for the absence of your advertisement: I hope you will understand when I explain that I enlisted in the RAF on the outbreak of war, and so was unable to direct the printers, who left out several things. I will put an advertisement of *The Voice of Scotland* in the Christmas no. Incidentally, Rhys gave me a long poem of yours about Yeats which I am anxious to print in the next number if you have not already disposed of it.

I see you are billed to appear in the next *Welsh Review*! Evidently they believe in buying over the enemy. I do not fear any competition from *them*!

I have just finished reading 'Cornish Heroic Song', I don't think there is anyone else who could write a poem of similar length of such sustained excellence. (It also enriched my vocabulary by five words!)

I have had an accident and smashed my pelvis so am out of the War for some months.[1] This war, necessary though it is, pushes on the ruin of Wales: we are faced either with fascist extinction or attrition in continual capitalist wars. None protests here: none act.

Yours sincerely,

Nigel Heseltine.

Am looking forward to the next *Voice of Scotland*.

In a note in the left margin Heseltine wrote 'Poetry Like the Hawthorn' which appeared in *Wales* 11 (Winter 1939-1940). This poem is now part of *In Memoriam James Joyce*, C.P. II, pp.756-759.

204. From R. E. Muirhead (NLS Acc.7321 Box3 File 42)

23 October 1939

Dear Mr. Grieve,

Since the last article from your pen came to hand, that was the one on Wm. Power,¹ a change has taken place with regard to the control of the *S[cots] I[ndependent]*. As you would probably see in the September issue the Annual Conference having requested that the Journal should again become a Party organ, that has been acceded to and the October issue was the first paper sent out under the new series, that is a Scottish National Party organ. The group of Scottish Nationalists who have been carrying on the paper for the past four years are not now associated with the new editorial staff. It is hoped, however, that the new Editors will continue to accept articles from independent Scottish writers such as yourself. A member of the new editorial staff is a trained journalist and therefore it is possible that the paper will be published in a more acceptable form.

The war has very much interfered with Scottish National activities here. The manifesto sent out to the press is not in my opinion satisfactory. I am hoping that an extraordinary conference of the Party may be held in order to consider the whole situation which has been created by the coming of the war. Scotland was not consulted as to whether or not she favoured a war policy, therefore Scotsmen are not rightly entitled to be conscripted to fight [for] English Imperialism.

Yours sincerely,

[R.E. Muirhead].

¹   MacDiarmid's article on Power was published in *Scots Independent*, September 1939, p. 6.

205. From Wendy Wood (NLS Acc.7361/1)

Samalaman
Glen Uig
Moidart
Inverness-shire
October ? [1939]¹

A Charaid,

We were delighted to get your letter – it means a lot to us. I must first of all express regret at so tardy a reply. Moe [MacAndreis] & I have joined issues for good² & are taking 3 crofts to make into one in this spot which can only be reached by 5 or 8 miles of broken pathway. In spite of that fact, it is utterly Gaelic & being pre-Reformation, quite unspoilt – full of young lads & girls, people who are unrepressed & national in the real sense.

It may seem to many that we are avoiding issues by thus burying ourselves, but that is not the case. We are realizing that the reason that even good men fail Scotland at any issue is because they are not distinctly and consciously 'foreign' to the English. Here, where the English are complete 'outsiders', where people never use a word of English except to such outsiders & who hold a wholesome despising of them as Scotland's everlasting enemies, only here, from such places, we feel we can rebuild. All round us are empty crofts. It is our hope to fill them with Gaelic-speaking people, to create ever-growing communities, and we are sure that the increasing need for food, scarcity of food, will create a land drive. That drive must find places such as these already settled with Gaels, that they do not become semi-English from Town influence. Our position, here also, leaves us free with our belongings in a safe place, to stravaig the country at will – Edinburgh became untenable, with CID and police raids and every contact under surveillance – nor was it of any value to go to gaol for the period of the war, instead of carrying on propaganda on a wide circuit as we are doing. Our advice to our members has been the same and we offer glen retreats to those who might be victimised. I am working hard at my art, – a thing to have kept away from eyes which would not have understood, but which I believe would please you – & I am aiming at having an exhibition in Dublin sometime tho' I have not mentioned it to anyone yet. *In fact, please treat all this letter as confidential meantime.* The crofts business is in the hands of the Land Court still. Naturally we are having a difficult time, starting in the winter & more on intentions than immediate work. But anyway, England's goddam war has brought happiness to one under a thatched roof, even tho', at the beginning I just felt incredulous at the collapse of all Scottish sentiment. If ever we had a chance to knock hell out of England, – ! We are walking down to Glasgow or Edinburgh this week, but letters will be kept for us here, tho I'm afraid yours will not be one of approval, – (expect that's just my own restlessness expressed).

All good wishes,
Wendy.

1 '?' Wendy Wood's.
2 Her first husband was Walter Cuthbert.

206. From W. R. Aitken (EUL MS2942.2 ff.102-103)

Edwin Muir & Sir Donald Pollock are Edinburgh's two candidates for the Lord Rectorship!

Arthur Askey (B.B.C. comedian) and Admiral Sir E.R.G.R Evans and Dame Sybil Thorndyke are Aberdeen's!

Churchmont
Lochgelly
Fife

Dear Chris,

I can only apologise once again for my long silence. I have been extremely busy – the Library is operating almost at normal pressure – and I have been spending a large amount of time house-hunting. Betty and I have come to the decision that – War and all – we must have a place of our own.[...] It's going to be a squeeze on £2 a week, but we have prospect of a house (2-roomed) with a rental of £11 (+ taxes = £15).

I'm sending herewith a batch of letters, MSS, etc.

About *The Voice of Scotland*. Financially we have £8.7.2 ½ in hand, but our account with Mackie stands at £40.1.6. – consisting of

£13	.15		for no.3
13	.10		for no.4
12	. 3		for Vol.2, no.1
	.13	.6	for subscription leaflets
£40	. 1	.6	

and in April I advanced £8.10 to clear off the cost of no.2. I'm afraid I may need to recover that if I get a house and have to buy some furniture, i.e. roughly there is an adverse balance of £40, and some people are expecting three other issues at least of *The Voice*, having paid 4/6 for v.2.

Mackie's are adamant and refuse to handle vol.2, no.2 until something is paid towards that £40.

But a grave difficulty is this. Vol. 1 was supported by some 80 subscribers, all of whom were asked – urged – to renew their support. Copies of vol.2, no.1 were sent to all previous subscribers – those who had renewed their sub., and, with a reminder, to those who had not. But the roll of subscribers to vol.2 has not reached nearly half of our former number: only 31 have paid up. We are printing 300 copies and distribute about 80 copies free. But 80 + 31 = only 111 and that leaves us with 200 copies nearly on our hands. *Can* we carry on under these circumstances?

I'll be glad to hear what you're thinking and planning. As long as I'm available I'll continue the Managership and sub-editing and proof correction, etc., of *The Voice* but I'm afraid we're at a standstill with Mackie's until Dr Orr can be persuaded to advance something. I regret too that they are unwilling to handle Paul Potts' pamphlet.[1] Would you like me to return it and let you try another printer? Or would you like me to get an estimate from another firm in Dunfermline?

How is the War going to affect Whalsay? and in particular, yourself? I remember how in June you foresaw that a War situation would probably make your position untenable. Are you finding it possible to make ends meet? What prospects? Are your food supplies becoming scarce and dear?

Prices here are rising. Rosyth is the target for enemy aircraft almost daily. In Dunfermline we hear anti-aircraft guns booming frequently. The place is crawling with soldiers and sailors. And of course we're 'blacked out'. (That won't be unfamiliar to you in Whalsay!) There are many accidents on the darkened roads: and (perhaps not entirely unconnected with the War) there has been a large pit accident (an explosion) at Valleyfield.

The years 20-22 have been called up, and locally there have been only a handful of conscientious objectors. All acquiesce – half-heartedly certainly – but there is no revolt. Sir John is hated particularly after last Tuesday's performance, when he attempted to curtail our Freedom so drastically that one M.P. suggested it was high time one of the propaganda bills, 'Freedom is in danger: Defend it with all your might', should be hung in the House of Commons. He wished to impose curfew, search and apprehend anyone on the slightest suspicion, prohibit processions and protest meetings, and demand the suspension of newspapers publishing articles inciting to disaffection.

By the way one of the most common propaganda posters reads:

YOUR COURAGE
YOUR CHEERFULNESS
YOUR RESOLUTION
WILL BRING US VICTORY

Several people have pointed out the significant change from 2nd to 1st person!

Please give my regards to Valda, Mike, the Doctor, Mrs Roe[2] (if she's still with you), Grant, etc...

I *will* try to write soon again.

Thanks for returning Mackenzie so promptly.

Yours,

Bill.

Encl.

1. 1 MS from G.S. Fraser
2. 1 copy of 'Seven'
3. 1 copy of 'Townsman'
4. 1 pithead letter issued by Cowdenbeath group C.P.G.B.
5. Review of DeLancey Ferguson's *Burns*
6. Article on Landsmål
7. Review of Edwin Muir's Engl. lit.
8. *Glasgow Herald* review of your *Islands* book
9. News about conscription – n.b. high proportion of C.O.'s in Wales
10. Poem (and stamped addressed envelope) from Miss R. Blackadder.

[1]   Canadian Poet.
[2]   Mrs Roe was housekeeper to Dr MacCrimmon who had succeeded Dr Orr. W. R. Aitken visited Whalsay on three occasions.

207. From Henry Treece (EUL MS2961.6 f.4)

55 Ferriby Rd

Dear Mr MacDiarmid,

This is a covering letter to my last covering letter. Since writing a month ago I've been too ill, too overworked, too debt-ridden to pack up the stuff I mention. Even now I have not got it all to hand, but if you'll be kind enough to answer the following questions I'll send it during the next few days.

(1)   Would you be interested in an article called 'Notes on Celts and Poets'? About as long as my last lot of Notes which appeared in *The Voice*.[1]

(2)   Would *New Alliance* be interested in a very fine, statuesque head, in black & white, by John Melville?[2]

(3)   The most difficult question of the lot to ask you – and one which will need some preliminary explanation: J.F. Hendry and I have co-edited an Apocalyptic anthology – which (with the exception of Picasso) is Celtic, and which we intend to produce twice yearly if possible. The second volume would contain, we hope, some of your own work, poems & criticism by Rhys, Glyn Jones, Heseltine, Porteous. We are publishing this book at our own expense and will have to work like fiends to make other volumes possible. In all confidence, our publisher is not making our job easy since he insists on our consent not to approach London booksellers – he wishes to do that himself. Therefore, our only contacts must be provincial ones. I am, therefore, asking three magazines (*The Voice*, *Wales* & *Seven*) to help us in this way:- I hope that each magazine will allow us a small announcement, saying that this book may be obtained through the editor. All orders would then be passed on to me & I would deal with them. Each magazine concerned would receive 1/3rd of money orders for the books it sold. (1/8 in 5/-) We are only being allowed 90 copies – the rest of the issue goes to the publisher, who will sell it through his usual channels in London, leaving us the rest of the islands – and we must sell them to cover our costs.

If we sell out our 90 copies I shall insist that a second impression is produced, or buy up more copies from the publisher.

I feel you'll forgive this request for help. There's ruin & rottenness all round: I hear that Symons' paper has passed out – it is symptomatic. Soon we will be the only writers left – the anti-Grigsonites, the Nationalists, the Apocalyptics. It would be criminal to my conception of culture to let the moment go without stamping it with our imprint. It will never come again, and if we hold it, it might stay.

Please help me to hold on to this moment and we'll soon have the game in our hands.

I've enclosed a leaflet – I think Hendry told me he'd sent you one before he left England – which might interest you.[3]

I shall look forward with interest to your reply.

Yours sincerely,

Henry Treece.

1   *The Voice of Scotland* had ceased publication before Treece's letter arrived. Henry Treece's 'Some Notes on Poetry Now' appeared in *The Voice of Scotland*, vol. 2, no. 1 (June-August 1939), pp.7-10.

2   MacDiarmid had no direct connection with *The New Alliance* although he advertised it on the back page of *The Voice of Scotland*, vol.2, no. 1, as a new quarterly due to appear on 1 September 1939. The intention to include reproductions of works by outstanding artists of the younger school was stated there.

3   The leaflet was the announcement of *The New Apocalypse*, a Guide to Modern Chaos, Critical prose, Poems, and Stories, etc., by Dylan Thomas, Pablo Picasso, J.F. Hendry, Henry Treece, Norman MacCaig, Dorian Cooke and Robert Melville.

208. From Douglas Young (EUL MS2961.18 f.1)

106 Don Street
Old Aberdeen
23 November 1939

Dear Mr Grieve,

Since I wrote you last in June, I have had discussions of some length with George Davie on certain matters, but I have not obtained from him a satisfactory answer to the question I put to you in my letter of June, 'Are you primarily a Communist or primarily a Nationalist, or do you hold the two positions are fundamentally one?' As Davie tells me there is some hope of *The Voice* being heard again soon, may I ask for a pronouncement on this, now even more important, topic?

I do not know whether you, in Whalsay, are aware that the conversion of the Scottish Communists to Nationalism is very superficial. The average CP worker in Aberdeen for example does not even know that Home Rule is a CP plank, and is against it.

You yourself have given more attention to these matters than anyone else; that is why a good many people have been waiting for some time to hear your views on the new situation caused by the Nazi-Soviet Pact and the War.[1] The present time offers an opportunity to Nationalists to do something radical, it seems to be being not taken.

I hope you are continuing to be missed by the explosive missiles which are reported to be hurtling through the air in your neighbourhood.

Yours compatriotically,
Douglas Young.

1   The German-Soviet Non-aggression Pact was signed on 23 August 1939. The Soviet Union had been repeatedly ignored in its attempt to enter into a collective security agreement with Britain and France against Nazi Germany, most noticeably at the time of the Munich Conference (September 1938).

209. From Norman Suddaby (EUL MS2965.10 f.17)

Old Heathfield
East Sussex
29 November 1939

Dear Chris Grieve,

What dim and distant past your letter revives .... It seems another life, since I took Valda and the then new baby to you at Horsham. And now you are in the much-sought-by-bombers Shetlands; we in Sussex (after much roaming in Dorset and many odd places).

To answer your query. I regret that we have no trace of the box you ask about. When we left Storrington I know we handed a few things over to Roy Armstrong and we believe that Valda's box was almost certainly left there. No doubt it went into his 'garage' along with all sorts of things. Michael was with us for some time and I seem to remember his saying that it would be best to leave the box on the Common (that was, at Roy's). Had we not done so it would be with us now; for I remember Joan being very fussy about the box. Perhaps you will ask Roy if he can find it (tho' I doubt his safe-keeping efficiency in a life like theirs).

We also have a child, a very nice little daughter named Karen, 5 years old. Storrington was left behind immediately she was born and we went to live in a desolate Coastguard Cottage on a Dorset headland. After a brief return to Storrington, then to two addresses further east in Sussex. So we, too, have wandered around a bit; and not always easy (as you say about yourselves). Michael is still seen from time to time. A lone bloke, doing odd jobs. He is now to be addressed at Berwick, East Sussex. I fixed him having an operation for his duodenal, and since then he has been fit. If I see Michael Vinnycomb I will ask him about the box. Perhaps he has it, and you might drop him a line.

The Shetlands to London is a far cry; yet I have heard of your being in Town since you left Storrington, and if you come up enquire for me at The Kenilworth Hotel, Gt. Russell Street W.C.l, where I am often to be found. Reg. Reynolds is in Town too.[1] He married Ethel Mannin,[2] and is still politically active. Glass[3] and Montalk are also in London and seem to be pursuing their usual ways and keeping to character.... But it is long since we saw the old crowd; so I can give you little real news. I expect that Hugh MacDiarmid still issues forth from time to time.... I hope so, anyhow.

Joan joins me in wishing you all happiness. It was pleasant to meet and talk as we did, and we hope it may be so again.

Yours sincerely,
Norman Suddaby.

[1]   Reginald Reynolds was a W.E.A lecturer who later became General Secretary of the No More War Movement. *My Life and Crimes* (London, 1956).
[2]   Ethel Mannin (1880-1984) had already published several works at this time.
[3]   Douglas Glass was a New Zealand friend of de Montalk and later became a photographer.

The 1940s

c/o Scott
Lyndhurst
Langlands Road
Hawick
Wednesday 10 January [1940]

My dear Christopher,

I have great difficulty in writing you now as I am so terribly ashamed of myself for not answering your two last letters and for not doing anything for *The Voice of Scotland* except reading it and for not acknowledging the terribly kind words you had to say of the poem of mine which you published in the first number.[1] I think the real reason is that I have gone through over a year of sluggish depression when I had nothing poetical to send you of which I thought you might approve and when I felt I had nothing to say in prose which others could not say better. But for the last month or two I have been more active. I have now about 3 000 lines of Gaelic verse on my hands which I would publish if I could. It includes a medley of some 1 700 lines in 7 parts called 'The Cuillin' and dedicated to yourself and to the memory of Alexander MacDonald.[2] It varies from the most direct political utterance to varying degrees of symbolism. It works out from the history of Skye to a sort of contemplation of Scotland and the rest of Europe. When I get the whole of an English translation of it typed I shall send it you. There are about 100 lines of it in the booklet I am sending you.[3] Since the war started I have confined myself to writing verse. I have been in Hawick with evacuees since October and find it a good place to work in.

How are things with you now? If you manage any more numbers of *The Voice* I shall send you all I have to do what you like with it. I am glad you published Campbell Hay's stuff. He is a fine chap and I would like to recommend to you to publish anything he sends you in Gaelic. Nowadays I am more and more worried and ashamed of the way Scotland has treated yourself whom I, at least, recognise as one of the great European poets of all time. I find that all the people whose opinions I value are now certain that this century has seen two major poets in the British Islands, yourself and Yeats, and they are all agreed that in lyric intensity your poetry is far above Yeats's. It is amazing to find how many subscribe to that view without doing anything about it in public. I shall send you translations of my own stuff very soon. I hope you will like Garioch's poems. Though temperamentally he is poles apart from you, you will easily see how much his poetry owes to you though he is so very different from you.

The booklet is so very small because Garioch underwent the labour of printing it himself.[3] I add a translation of the poem for you on page 5.[4] It is a slight thing but technically it satisfies me. It is really one of 40 poems I have written for a woman whom I call Eimhir in the booklet.

I wish I had the past year over again so that I could have a chance of pulling my weight for *The Voice* which owing merely to my sluggish depression I have badly let down.

How are Mrs Grieve and Mike? I expect Mike will be a big fellow by now. Give them both my very best regards. Also give my regards to David Orr who I suppose is now in Whalsay again.

I have spent a year in Mull, which depressed me. I left it last New Year and have been in Edinburgh until last October but I expect to get back to Edinburgh in February. It is a pity you are so far away and isolated from us all just now. I have been seeing very much of George Davie for the last while. Hood, by the way, is with me in Hawick. Caird is teaching evacuees in Banff. At the end of January I am going to Glasgow to give a paper to the Gaelic Society there and I hope to see Scott. In March I am to give the Gaelic Society of Inverness a paper on the poetry of Livingston. I have not yet decided what to give the paper on in Glasgow but I think it will be on certain aspects of MacDonald and MacIntyre.

I shall write you again very soon. At the moment I am in a hurry as I have great arrears of work owing to having been down a week or two with a very bad throat. Calum, my brother, is doing research in Dublin. He hopes to get into touch with Higgins as soon as possible. John is now married to Morag MacDonald of Edinbane and is teaching in the Royal High, Edinburgh.

All the best just now.
Somhairle MacGhill-Eathan.

---

[1] 'Ban-ghaidheal' ('A Highland Woman'), vol.1 no.1 (June-August 1938), pp.4-5.
[2] Somhairle MacGill-Eain / Sorley MacLean, *An Cuilithionn 1939 / The Cuillin 1939 and Unpublished Poems*, ed. by Christopher Whyte (Glasgow, The Association for Scottish Literary Studies, 2011).
[3] The booklet was *17 Poems for 6d: poems in Gaelic, Scots and English* by Robert Garioch and Somhairle MacGill Eathain, (Edinburgh: Chalmers Press, 1940). It included 110 lines of 'Opening of Part II 'of 'The Cuillin', pp. 6-8 .
[4] The poem was 'Tri Slighean' ('Three Paths'), now 'xv' in *Dàin do Eimhir (Poems to Eimhir)*, ed. by Christopher Whyte (Edinburgh: Polygon, 2007), pp. 60-61.

2. From John R. Scott (EUL Gen. 2094/5/2053)

Skerryvore Lighthouse
Earraid
Fionphort
Oban
Argyll
13 January 1940

Hugh MacDiarmid,
Author of *The Islands of Scotland*.

Dear Sir,
Recently I had the pleasure of reading your new book, as above. I got it as a Christmas present.

Please forgive the liberty, but I would like to draw your attention to a few errors. Perhaps you have already detected them, in which case no harm done.

On page 53:-'The present position of the old Norn or Shetland language is just as Dr Jakobsen, the great Faroese philologist, described it in 1807'. Should that not have been 1907? I remember Dr Jakobsen very well, and I am not a centenarian yet.

On page 108:- Re Sweyn Asliefson, 'For when he died, in 1711, the viking age was already long dead'.[1] I doubt 1711 was not the year of Sweyn's death, and readers unacquainted with the history of the Islands are apt to get wrong impressions.

On page 110 you write of Mr D. J. Robinson, OBE. That is not how he usually spells his name. The name is Robertson. I have heard that he can trace his ancestry back to the time of Malcolm Canmore, which is more than most can. I feel sure he would not like to be called Robinson.

Your bald statement that the cultural condition of the Shetlands is wholly zoistic could be questioned. However, I must say that for a ferrylouper you have done very well in your effort to describe the intimacies of Shetland courtship and marriage. Your knowledge of same is far from complete; but it never will be now, at your age.

When writing of the Scottish Islands next time do not forget Earraid off the Ross of Mull. It is a curious island, where the Skerryvore and Dhuheartach lightkeepers have their homes and families; why? God knows.

Thanking you for the pleasure of reading *The Islands of Scotland* and other writings.

Yours respectfully,

John R. Scott.

---

[1] The sentence on page 108 was a quotation from Eric Linklater (wrote MacDiarmid, without giving the reference).

3. From Henry Grant Taylor (EUL Gen.2094/6)

Hawick

22 January 1940

Dear Folk,

My apologies for failing to write all this long while. Little excuse to offer – I've done precious little with my time. An enjoyable holiday, nevertheless, though it hasn't been exciting. At present, as you see, I am in Hawick, where I am spending a few days with Cathie.[1] She is very much better now and able to carry on with her work, but has to take great care of herself. I'm afraid it will be a long time before she is as strong and healthy as she used to be.

How are things with you? I hope you had a good Christmas and New Year, and that the weather hasn't been too hard on you. I expect you will have some pretty severe frost as we have had here, and snow as well. Temperatures in some parts of Europe are almost unbelievably low.

I've been wondering if there is any news of the autobiography. Meantime, I'm getting rid of one or two of the 'Mature Art' subscription forms. Wattie's little artist friend (she is due in Dumfries for a holiday) is friendly with Seumas O' Sullivan, and one of the leaflets is going to him.[2] I think I'm getting another planted here in Hawick. The chap I'm staying with, a near-Communist who runs a Left Book Club group, has a friend called David Hill[3] who writes poetry in Synthetic Scots, if you please, and is a fervent admirer of Hugh MacDiarmid. I haven't met this Hill, but it seems that he is fairly comfortably off and almost certain to subscribe to 'Mature Art'. Incidentally, there's quite a nest of Leftists in Hawick. Stuart Hood has been down from Edinburgh with the evacuees, and created a great impression at one of the Left Book Club meetings when he took part in the discussion.

I've just discovered that Cathie used to be friendly with George Davie – used to go to Martin's for morning coffee with him and so on.

You will notice that conscription goes on apace. I'm due for registration in August at the present rate – perhaps sooner if things start happening before then.[4]

Another sin of omission is that I have never sent on the bundle of magazines etc. that I promised you, but I am going to make that my first task when I get back to Dumfries, and you should get them very soon after this. I am enclosing with this letter the butcher meat counterfoil from my ration book. Actually registration was supposed to be completed some time ago but I think you will still manage to get it done if you consider it necessary; the actual rationing of butcher meat doesn't start for a week or so yet, and no doubt Johnnie Shearer[5] will be able to handle this all right.

Such news as I have gathered I will give you when I come – though I have learned nothing startling so far. But you will get another communication from me in the shape of a parcel of light literature.

Here's hoping you are all in the best of health and spirits. I'll be with you again soon.

Yours,
Grant [Taylor].

---

[1] Cathie Tait.
[2] 'Wattie' was Walter K. Hunter, Dumfries.
[3] David Hill (1911-1977) also contributed a story to *Penguin New Writing* in 1944 and a programme to Radio Scotland's Scottish Heritage series. Duncan Macrae took the leading part in Hill's full-length play broadcast by Radio Scotland.
[4] In *MacDiarmid* Alan Bold writes, 'As for Taylor, he was summoned that summer [1940] to a tribunal in Aberdeen where his case, as a conscientious objector, was turned down. An Appeals Tribunal in Edinburgh confirmed the Aberdeen decision [...]' (p.379). In a note Bold wrote, 'After his appeal had been turned down in Aberdeen and Edinburgh, Taylor got a job with the Forestry Commission near Southwick.' (p.462). In a letter to Harry Miller MacDiarmid wrote, on the 17 February 1941, 'My friend, Grant Taylor, who for 2 or 3 years lived with me here and did the typing etc. was on the 11th inst. for refusing to be medically examined, sentenced by Sheriff Johnson in Dumfries Sheriff Court to pay £2 fine, or go to prison for 10 days, and be detained in custody till arrangements be made for his attendance before a medical board. He refused to pay the fine of course and will at each successive step under civil and martial law go the whole distance in resistance.' (TNA KV 2/2010 39A). However, Bold records that Grant Taylor was later '[...]drafted into the Royal Corps of Signals. He served for five years, including eighteen months in

Persia and Iraq.' (*MacDiarmid*, p. 462).
5   Johnnie Shearer was the butcher on Whalsay at this time.

4. From Barbara Niven (EUL MS2957)

Friday 26 January [1940]

Dear Christopher,

All this time since the Spain poem came, and because I have been trying vainly to find a space to write properly in, I haven't said anything about it at all. (Now I am writing at Stockport, because the studio for the last week has not been my own: different people have been coming to help me to do big streamers of lettering for a congress and meeting.) It seems a long time since it came because I have read it so much and so often since, to myself and to others, that I am really getting to know it. It is tremendous stuff, full of all the strongest personal and impersonal feelings, so strongly linked that they make into something like a bomb of thought. I can't say strongly enough how deeply it has made me think and feel or how many times something I have apprehended is there fully stated and clothed in words and related with a fierce sanity to all of the objective facts.

I left the poem last night at the house of some people where I went to read some passages to them, just because I can't keep it to myself; and I need it to describe some of the passages where I feel you diagnose whole areas of contemporary disease in a transparent way. But I will write more fully about these when I have it back. Jimmy Miller & his wife, to whom I want particularly to show it, have been ill with colds etc. & I have not been able to see them since it came.

The satire is magnificent. I like its anatomical knocks. [Roy] Campbell comes out by the end pretty well described from head to foot and the word 'beetle' might well be a worse one – except for Gorky.[1]

There are many passages where you speak directly that are so moving that they are hard to read aloud at all; yet I experience very strongly in doing this that your poetry must be spoken aloud to get its full import; things that are just there in reading it to oneself possess one entirely in reading aloud and run away with one's understanding and even one's voice. That passage for instance in 'The International Brigade' section starting, 'Fascists, you have killed my comrades',[2] a short separate poem with a rhythm and mounting feeling that is like a Hebrew psalm and has everything – anger, irony, grief and something white-hot that makes these be one thing. The long poem too starting with the address to the men of the field is very beautiful, with a note of triumph like trumpets.[3] What's the use of trying to say what I like specially because in your poetry it is really impossible to unlink one passage from the next.

When it came, the first free day I had I spent reading and re-reading it and it was just as it was with the big poem when you were reading it, – nothing else will do, all that is necessary is to have more and more of it till the experience (which is a very complex one in this poem too) is complete. The feeling of *necessity* is a very compelling one.

I wish it were possible to talk to you about it and about many other things. Sometimes this amounts to a necessity too.

Tell me how long it took you to write. People seem interested to know this and won't believe that you wrote it rapidly. All to whom I have shown it – one or two journalists and three or four artists in my group, and Ernest of course, feel it tremendously strongly.

There are comparisons – as where you use the pressure of the hand, or the slow tears, and others, that I feel are poetry at its very highest, so high that they are at the same time entirely natural and to be at home with.

I can't write more now and will write next week answering your letter and telling you other news when this meeting etc. for which you are working is over.

But it was getting a weight on my mind that I hadn't said something of what I thought about the poem. Thank you *very* much for sending it.

My love.

Barbara.

Love to Valda, and everybody.

I think it is very likely we shall get other subscribers for 'Mature Art'.

---

1   Maxim Gorky (Alexei Peshkov, 1868-1936) wrote novels and plays of which *Mother* and *The Lower Depths* are best known respectively; and an autobiographical trilogy, *My Childhood*, *My Apprenticeship* and *My Universities*.
2   'Fascists, you have killed my comrades' is not in 'The International Brigade' section as published. It is in 'Part 1'.
3   'The long poem too starting with the address to the men of the field' is 'Major Road Ahead', *C.P.* II, pp.992-999.

5. From George Woodcock (NLS Acc.7361/11)

82 Station Road
Bucks.
8 February 1940

Dear Mr Grieve,

I am writing to ask if you would care to contribute a poem (or poems) to a paper I hope to start in the near future.[1] Our common friend, Charles Lahr, who will be my London agent, thought you might be interested.

The paper will be devoted to good writing, clear thought and the freedom of the individual conscience. Anti-war and anti-British Empire (coming from the Welsh Marches I am largely Celtic in blood and sympathy). Each issue will contain a large quantity of poetry, together with one or two short stories and two or three articles, political, sociological or literary.

There are two snags to the idea. Firstly, I shall be unable to pay for contributions. Secondly, as I have only small funds but consider something should be done to keep good writing circulating, the paper will probably have to be duplicated instead of printed. But, if these disadvantages do not prejudice you against the idea, I should very much like a contribution from you. I hope to bring out the first issue early in March.

Yours faithfully,
George Woodcock.

1   In 'Note to Readers' in NOW 1 (London : Freedom Press, 1943), p. 2, George Woodcock, editor, wrote 'The magazine, *NOW*, appeared in Spring of 1940 as a cyclostyled sheet[...]. Two further numbers, printed, appeared in the autumn of 1940[...]' . Another series of seven issues started in March 1941 and yet another series in 1943. MacDiarmid did not contribute.

6. From Harold MacMillan (EUL MS2969)

MacMillan & Co. Ltd
St Martin's Street
London WC2
28 March 1940

Dear Mr Grieve,

I write personally to acknowledge the receipt of your letters of March 15th and 20th and of the corrected slip-proofs of the text of your *Golden Treasury of Scottish Poetry*, and the MS. of further material for the Notes. You will receive proofs of the Dedication, Preface, Indexes, etc., quite soon now, but these are always the last parts to go into type.

I am sending you under separate cover the proofs and typescript of your Introduction, which I have read with a great deal of interest. I am sure, that, in view of the origins of my family, you will acquit me of being a thin-skinned Englishman if I suggest that some of your observations on England and her literature are rather sweeping and uncharitable, and hardly likely to be to the best advantage of the book. I know that in *Who's Who* you put your recreation as 'Anglophobia', and it would be very far from my wishes to interfere with the expression of your views, but I feel that one ought to bear in mind the special character of the Golden Treasury series. It has had a long and successful history, and several of its Introductions have been famous for their scholarship and literary value. They have never, I think, been strongly controversial, and this to some extent accounts for their very wide popularity. I should wish your book to find the same wide circle of readers, sound Englishmen as well as ardent Scots, and not to endanger its *general* appeal in any way. I am sure that you will not mind considering if anything ought to be done to modify some passages of your Introduction with this end in view. It could be done without a great deal of cost or difficulty while the material is still in slip-proof, and I think that the Introduction would then harmonise better with the contents of the book since its abridgement.

I have ventured to make a few comments in the margin of the proofs where it struck me that sentences were either incomplete or were rather difficult to follow by reason of their somewhat unusual length. I feel certain that you will receive these

and my other suggestions in the spirit in which they are offered.[1]
    I am,
    Yours sincerely,
    Harold MacMillan.

[1]   On returning the proofs on 6 April 1940, MacDiarmid wrote, 'You will see that I have done my best to eliminate or modify the personal elements to which my attention was drawn on the margins of the slip-proofs, and I have broken up the longer sentences to which objection was taken [...]', and concluded his letter, ' In this difficult position I have been happy to accept your suggestions in the spirit in which you set them out [...]'.(NLS MS27077 ff.58-63 all rectos, carbon copy).

7. From Joan Littlewood and Ewan MacColl (NLS Acc.7361/52)

377 Oxford Road
Manchester
[March 1940]

Dear Hugh MacDiarmid

I am writing to you for Jimmie Miller and myself. We have wanted to write to you for some time but there were all kinds of difficulties and it isn't so easy to write to someone you've never met and yet feel you know something about. You see we have read a good deal of your work – and there was the letter you wrote to Theatre Union when we produced 'Fuente Ovejuna'[1] – and now your Spanish poem.[2] We must thank you for that, better than thanks – we must tell you how your poem is going down with the people who come to see our Living Newspaper. At the moment, the show is being done in a place called 'The Round House' in Ancoats – a hall where the Chartists used to hold their meetings. It is playing to the right audiences and will go on playing to them for some time, as we will later be taking the show to Durham and N.E. Lancashire, to mining towns and weaving villages, places where no theatre has as yet ever had any influence. It is a long time since people clapped and stamped their feet at poetry – well that is what is happening to yours. Passages such as 'It is impossible that Franco can win',[3] 'Honour forever to the International Brigade',[4] 'Wonderful days, so General Mola had to stop the advance on Madrid'[5] etc. have even been cheered at some performances. The Spanish episodes in the Living Newspaper consist of passages from your poem interrupted here and there by scenes like – Pasionaria addressing a crowd of women[6] – at another point, four men stand with rucksacks by their sides on a long platform encircling the audience and as their names are called passing singly across the stage ... expressing the way the International Brigaders went off to fight. At another point, refugees move along the same platform carrying heavy bundles and are machine-gunned as they go. There is a scene on the Jarama Front and another where a group of 'Friends of National Spain' play dice and deliver themselves of such statements as 'I recognise General Franco to be a gallant Christian Gentleman.' – 'Franco is leading a crusade for all that we in England hold dear.' etc. The final scene is of desolate battlefield with the declamation of 'Fascists you have killed my comrades.'[7] Many of the scenes are in mime and do not so much 'cut across' the poem as move with it.

We wish you could see this Living Newspaper. It is extremely mobile and capable of assimilating any new form or idea. It is an exciting medium and we do hope that later perhaps you can get down to see it. In telling you about the show I have omitted to say what we thought of the poem. With Lorca's poem on the bullfighter it stands as the finest work of our time [8]... the first great poetic statement of the modern proletariat.

I am enclosing Jimmie's novel.[9] He has tried three publishers – Gollancz, Longmans Green and Secker & Warburg. Longmans said quite nice things about it but gave no reason for turning it down. The other two firms just sent it back with ordinary publishers' notes. It is not a book which would be quickly accepted, we know that, and having it returned has not been a surprise altogether. Jimmie is aware of its many faults but is not too sure of its real value. We should be pleased if you could give us your opinion and advice.

Hoping to hear from you.

Sincerely,

Joan & Jimmie Miller.

[Joan Littlewood and Ewan MacColl]

[1] *Fuente Ovejuna* (1619) by Lope de Vega (1562-1635). The villagers of Fuenteovejuna united to oppose and kill a tyrannical ruler, vowing never to reveal the identity of the actual assassins but to assert instead that 'Fuenteovejuna did it'.

[2] The reference is to a Theatre Union show in March 1940. Joan Littlewood writes, 'Passages from MacDiarmid's *Flaming Poetaster* linked the Spanish Civil War scenes.' (*Joan's Book*, London: Methuen, 2003, p.108). Joan's account here is headlined 'AT LAST. MARCH 1940. WE'RE READY / LAST EDITION / at / THE ROUND HOUSE'. The show was closed by police on the night Hitler invaded France, 12 May 1940. Joan Littlewood and Jimmie Miller were bound over for twelve months and fined five guineas each. (*Joan's Book*, pp.112-114). 'The Flaming Poetaster' was published as *The Battle Continues* in 1957.

[3] The lines beginning, 'It is impossible that Franco can win', *C.P.*, II, p.914.

[4] The lines beginning, 'Honour forever to the International Brigade!', *C.P.*, II, p.970.

[5] The lines beginning, 'Wonderful days! / "So General Mola had to stop the advance on Madrid./ For Why?"', *C.P.*, II, p.961. Mola was a Fascist General.

[6] 'La Pasionaria' was Dolores Ibarruri (1895-1989), leader of the Spanish Communist Party.

[7] The lines beginning, 'Fascists, you have killed my comrades', *C.P.*, II, p.920.

[8] 'Llanto por Ignacio Sánchez Mejías' by Federico García Lorca (1899-1936).

[9] The unpublished novel was 'The Damnable Town'.

8. From F. G. Scott (EUL MS2959 ff.109-112)

44 Munro Road
Jordanhill
Glasgow W3
20 April 1940

My dear Chris,

I seem to have so much to discuss with you that I hardly know where to begin so let us take as read the contents of your letter *re* 'Golden Treasury', 'The Autobiography', 'Mature Art' and even your influenza and domestic mishaps of one kind or another. Yesterday I received from Douglas Young the proof-sheets of the 'Treasury' introduction so I'll begin with them. I sent Young a p.c. last night asking him where you wanted them sent from Glasgow, whether to Whalsay or London if by so doing time might be saved – but perhaps I'll return them to you and you may want to make some alterations in the light of what I say, so I'll have to hurry up.

I have no fault to find with the ideas expressed in the Introd. but on D42 you open out on Muir and continue to use his name no fewer than 14 times, its last appearance being on D48. I think this is a serious mistake. It gives an importance to Muir's opinions on the subject of Scottish poetry which they don't deserve and, what is more important, it gives the reader the feeling that you are carrying into the Introd. a personal feud and even perhaps that Muir's attitude may not be so far mistaken after all, since you think it requires so much criticism to destroy it. Couldn't you state in brief the things Muir is supporting and go on to demolish them one by one without reference to Muir by name? I know you'll say that it is very necessary to controvert what Muir stands for but why in Heaven's name give *him* all the credit? A reading of the Introd. as it stands makes out Muir to be the *diabolus in poetica Scotorum* and, whatever his views, the constant repetition of his name shows that you attach considerable weight to them. Personally I'd restrict you to one 'Muir' and all the rest to the kind of things such deracinated Scots and Orcadians stand for. I am stressing this point about Muir appearing in a Scottish 'Golden Treasury' because I feel it is out of place in a book ostensibly 'Golden' – the best Scotland can do – a book likely to remain for a long time authoritative. I wonder if you'll like (ten years after this) to read 'Muir', 'Muir', 'Muir' all over the Introduction? To hell with his opinions – now! – and give the book a chance to speak for itself and in your behalf.

For somewhat similar reasons I regret your assiduity in notes, footnotes and footnotes to footnotes. You really can't keep anything informative to yourself. But that's a mystery to me – I just can't understand why the whole paraphernalia of cogitation should be dragged out into the sunshine like the old musty carpets and furniture during a spring-cleaning. To continue the analogy there's more dust than anything else in both operations and here again I think the introduction to an anthology isn't the place for carpet beating any more than, say, a social gathering among friends would be.

On the whole I find your pencilled extensions more interesting than some of the matter in the proof-sheets. The poem of Dr Longmuir for instance is a hellish poor poem whether written in Scots, English or Urdu: if it can't find a place for itself in the body of the book I'd cut it out of the introduction no matter what point you seek to prove by it.[1]

In conclusion, it occurred to me a strange thing that neither you nor Muir had stopped to ask what *my* opinion of the vernacular versus English controversy was. Much as I'd like to give you my whole 'paraphernalia of cogitation' (as above) I'll say just this that the language question has nothing to do with the poetry – *given a poet*, he can write poetry in any language he's familiar with but he always writes his *best* poetry in the *speech rhythm* he is *most* familiar with. You and Muir can both chew on this sentence till you understand it. The oracle has spoken! – 'and requires some food' my wife has just added.

And now to continue in 'after-dinner' fashion. The Michael Bruce Trust (in Kinross) asked me through a third party to write music for Michael Bruce's 'Ode to the Cuckoo' and this I have done in schoolroom song fashion with piano accompaniment. Is the poem in your 'Treasury'?[2] I hope so. I have been through the Bruce-Logan controversy and give Bruce the honour, though some of the emendations in the Logan version are small improvements on the Bruce original.[3]

You will, of course, have had copies of Soutar's new *In the Time of Tyrants* and his portrait done by somebody Gilchrist.[4] I found a lot to admire in both especially some of the longer things like the sonnets; the shortest lyrics I thought very good indeed but on the whole resembling hand-grenades rather than big bombs – the size counts when something big has to be shifted. And Soutar leads me on to speak in prophecy.

I herewith give warning that George Campbell Hay will be the next star in the Scottish firmament and unite in himself both Gaelic and Scots traditions. I have been in the closest touch with him for the past month and he has spent two different days with me in Glasgow discussing his and other folks' poetry. I am finding something completely new in his *rhythm* sense (no doubt Gaelic) and in less than a week I had finished music to three of his lyrics – one at any rate as good as 'Calum thonder'.[5] He went back to Edinburgh last Sunday night well posted up (by me!) in what his mission should be so I'm hopeful we'll all see results that will surprise and delight us. For a lad of twenty-four he amazes me by the maturity of his judgments on people and literature. I like him immensely as a person and his work, though tentative at times, has a real classical sanity about it and, as I've said, a rhythm that stirs me right over into music – by which I mean that I *feel* what he is saying and that what he is saying is true. If he continues working with me and develops along the lines we have agreed upon I am certain he'll outdistance any of his immediate contemporaries – yes, Sam included!

And now for Kierkegaard. I don't know much of his own writing; what I have seen has been review notices like the ones in this week's *Times Lit.* but I can thank God that his influence is making itself felt in Whalsay. The 'Farewell to Eros' is the best thing you have done for years – again, just because it is real and true. Since this War began I've been rapidly drifting away from all forms of materialism – the dialectical and all others – and although I can't yet say what I'm drifting *to*, I can feel

275

in my bones the absurdity of maintaining that I have sprung from mere muck up to my present consciousness. Can it matter a rap to me what I began as in comparison with what I now am? And, my dear Christopher, you are in the same boat – both of us have waged a lifelong spiritual war and this war will continue to occupy all our interest whatever the past history of man has been. You deceive yourself – the materialists of this world, the butchers, bakers and candlestick-makers are our deadly enemies whether they call themselves Communists or Fascists and they will continue to be our enemies under every political system one can envisage.

And this is where Kierkegaard comes in.[6] His unfortunate love story and your own both left wounds on the spirit, impossible to be healed, and from those wounds the spirit speaks – 'Spirit is just this – Not to be like the others'.[7] And further on: '"Nay, nay, thou infinite love'"[8]– I endure to be a sacrifice.[9]

By way of criticism (which really means how I would have written it) I quote the devil against himself: 'The Buddhist style of composition, *prose* for explanations, verse for all that is suggestive, and all that is to be pronounced with clearness, directness and force'.[10] I find the manner of expression (not the ideas) parenthetical and periphrastic, too prosily explanatory where love is concerned, too much of Kierkegaard and too little of Grieve the poet. For instance your opening stanza should read something like:

O time of love
When at every encounter, every glance of the eye,
One brings something home,
Just as a bird in its busy season etc.

The second paragraph 'And I loved her so much' will do, but the first six lines of the next paragraph 'What are all gloomy thoughts' (poor); 'Thou blind God of love' (very good); lower down the bit 'like the lily of the valley' is very involved (nine lines of it).

On page three the thirteen lines beginning 'Everywhere, in the countenance of every girl' is far from being direct and forceful. Almost all the rest of the poem is quite all right but I can't reconcile myself to such colloquial phrases as, 'One is fearful on one's own account'; 'One is fearful on account of the thing one loves'; 'May appear perhaps less perfect'; 'Without being painfully reminded'; 'One can, it is true, by the most frightful efforts, / Endeavour to conceal what one at that age / Regards as his disgrace'; 'This may perhaps succeed up to a certain point / But nevertheless [...] / And the success is assured / Only up to a certain point'.

On page six you have 'almost maltreated one'; 'While yet the mass of men will certainly beg / To be excused'. All such phrases give a very flat-footed effect, a plain prosy effect in fact with their qualifications of 'perhaps'; 'it is true'; 'but nevertheless'.[11] What poet ever spoke of 'My love is like a red, red rose (perhaps)'. This is just the kind of poetry Muir can write – a series of little thinks in the shape of verse. I'd like to see the directness of affirmation and a good deal of exclamation brought into the poem but maybe you'll say I'm thinking musically rather than verbally. In reply I can only say that if poetry isn't musical it's just prose. I'm quite in earnest when I say this for I've often wanted to ask you how you came to switch over to your irregular rhythm of recent years. Quite recently I went through *Sangschaw*, *Penny Wheep* and *A Drunk Man* for some explanation but what came out most clearly was that the success of these books was largely the natural forcefulness of the poetic rhythms they contained. How you came to lose or throw away this sense of rhythm is a mystery to me. You may not think so but I can assure you not much of your stuff since these books has had any musical vitality. Forceful and exaggerated statement is a different thing altogether.

Lastly: I've been asked to go to Aberdeen Training Centre as Principal music lecturer at a salary over £100 more than I have in Jordanhill. The generous Aberdonians have figured it out that they'll give me half of the increase *now* and pay up the rest in yearly increments till my retiral in 1945. I had the momentous decision to take this week that I'd only go to Aberdeen for the *whole* increase now or not accept the transfer at all. This weekend there's a solemn silence which can almost be felt for the issue will affect my own and the family's future financial resources. I've told Aberdeen 'All or nothing' and am awaiting their deliberations. The girls have been saying that if we went to Aberdeen you'd be able almost to come for a weekend now and again – but can you imagine me finishing my days in such a God-forsaken place, a place I've cursed all my life.

All the best to Valda and Michael and let's keep the pot boiling about the matters I've discussed herein.

Ever,

F. G.

---

[1] MacDiarmid gives ten stanzas in 'Standart Habbie' form of a poem by Dr John Longmuir who was the editor of the works of Alexander Ross (1699-1784).(*Golden Treasury of Scottish Poetry*, London, 1940, pp. xxxiii-xxxv). He indicates a break after the fourth stanza. In the MS of 'Mature Art' (NLS Acc. 12074/1) MacDiarmid titles stanzas five to ten of the above as 'The Inn at Drousty' without attribution (f.35). Drousty is in the parish of Langlee where Alexander Ross was schoolmaster.

[2] Michael Bruce (1746-1767). His 'Ode to the Cuckoo' was not in MacDiarmid's *Golden Treasury* which was abridged to half the length of the MS before publication.

[3] John Logan (1748-1788), a college friend, claimed that 'Ode to the Cuckoo' was his own after Bruce's death.

[4] This portrait was painted by Soutar's friend Jack Gilchrist at the end of November 1939.

[5] 'Calum Thonder' - the first two words of 'To a Loch Fyne Fisherman' in *Collected Poems and Songs of George Campbell Hay*, ed. by Michel Byrne (Edinburgh: Edinburgh University Press, 2003), p. 19. Scott's setting was included in Book 5 of his *Scottish Lyrics set to music* (London and Glasgow: Bayley & Ferguson, 1939).

[6] Scott refers here to MacDiarmid's poem 'Farewell to Eros' which was published in Zed_2O *Magazine*, no.22, pp. 13-19, edited by Duncan Glen (Autumn 2007). In NLS MS27008 f.38 MacDiarmid wrote '(After Søren Kierkegaard)*', under the title and added a footnote, 'Pieced together by the present author from scattered passages in Kierkegaard's writings.' Søren Kierkegaard (1813-1855).

[7.] Zed_2O *Magazine*, no.22, p.18.

8   Ibid., p. 19.
9   Scott has adapted MacDiarmid's lines, 'It is by such torments indeed/ That a man is educated to endure/To be a sacrifice.' Ibid. p19.
10 MacDiarmid quoted this sentence from a lecture by Prof. Meiller in 1925 in his Introduction to *The Golden Treasury of Scottish Poetry*, p. xxiii. The emphasis on 'prose' is Scott's. The full sentence reads, 'The Buddhist style of composition, prose for explanations, verse for all that is suggestive and all that is to be pronounced with clearness, distinctness, and force, is not an isolated thing in the Indo-European world'.
11 Clearly Scott saw the six-page MS now NLS MS27008 ff.38-43, published in *Zed$_2$O Magazine*. NLS MS 27301 ff. 19-26 is another MS.

9. From F. G. Scott (EUL MS2959 f.113)

I think that after reading this supplementary note you should re-read your Kierkegaard poem – the first [paragraph] should be enough!

Sunday Forenoon 21 April 1940

Dear Chris,

I finished the foregoing yesterday and find myself on a wet Sunday with nothing to interest me, so I'm going to continue my already long letter. This business of rhythm and speech-rhythm is a most important one and I've had my interest in it stimulated recently by a very careful study of Wagner's 'Opera and Drama', a book I showed you at one time and from which you got some ideas on the subject of 'the heroic' in art. I have always known in the writing of my own songs that for some types of lyric I had to keep very strictly to the dum-di-dum scansion of the metre if I wanted to put across the directness and force of the words, that is to say, I had to observe the musical patterns (rhythm, rhyme etc.) and give less attention to the purely verbal ideas of the poem. This type of lyric is the purely lyrical and as I say the musical elements carry the burden of words and meaning with a directness that stays for neither question nor analysis. (The best songs of Burns are examples as good as any in any language.) When on the other hand 'THOUGHT' or 'KNOWLEDGE' come on the scene, these manifestations of direct, forceful Rhythms which to Kierkegaard is 'LOVE'

> appear now before Thought
> Even as those enigmatical creatures
> In tales of olden time
> Come up from the bottom of the ocean,
> Clothed in seaweed.[1]

And further down the page

To make answer to the many questions
[…]

The enchantment vanishes,
And never more can it be produced.[2]

Irregularity of Rhythm is accounted for by the intermittent nature of Thought, which has always to stop and take account of the next step in the argument. 'One step enough for me' might be its motto: but here I'll remind you of Goethe, 'Gray is all knowledge but green is the tree of life', or put it into the most crude language – when your balls run dry, shoot yourself! The trouble with our age, as D.H. Lawrence hinted, is that (what with masturbation, contraceptives and the like) it can get no thrill out of anything but sits, in the figures of Ezra Pound, T.S. Eliot and Hugh MacD. looking at its navel and tells the rest of us how curious we or they are. Well, we've all got navels and can examine them at our own leisure. That this is an exact description of what is (or rather has been) taking place is proved by the fact that none of you can make head or tail of said navel but have to read up from all the ends o' the earth, and all the languages and, worst of all, from each other what has been said or thought or conjectured on the subject of navels. Meanwhile the Muse of Poetry being a female inquires whether there still lives a too-bald man. She will recognise him by the clearness, directness and force of his speech-rhythm – sure sign that his sexual members are functioning. This I believe is the truth behind the masks of Hitler and Mussolini. They deny the 'tragic view', they deny Christianity for the same reason and the miserably defeatist music and poetry of the democracies, who look like getting the thrill they've been asking for.
    F. G.

[1.] *Zed ₂O Magazine,* no.22, p.16. Scott adapts the line '– *That* appears now before thought'- to suit his syntax.
[2] ibid. p.17.

10. From Sorley MacLean (EUL MS2954.13 ff.37-38)

Lyndhurst
Langlands Road
Hawick
12 May 1940

My dear Christopher,
Again I have to apologise for my very long delay in answering your letter of February. A few days ago I sent you a translation of 'the Cuillin' and I hope it has reached you. It is a crude declamatory poem but certain passages manage to sound fairly well in Gaelic. In the very rough translation which I made for Davie and which Jessie Scott[1] typed the crudity is painfully apparent and such few graces as it has in the Gaelic are conspicuously absent but there is in Gaelic some crude effective noise in parts of it. I have a fair amount of lyrical stuff of which I shall send you versions when I can. They please me more. At present I have begun what I hope will be a fairly long thing but quieter, more introspective and more imaged than 'the Cuillin'.

I did long ago send the subscription form for 'Mature Art' to Paris but I have had no word of it from the Obelisk Press. I hope my letter got them. I was very glad to meet Taylor but having to go to Edinburgh on the weekend when he was in Hawick I saw far less of him than I should have wished. Perhaps he told you that John's wife died about the middle of February. You remember her at Edinbane. She had been really unwell for about 10 years having TB. John himself is very well and is still teaching in Edinburgh in the Royal High School. Calum is enjoying himself immensely in Dublin and has met [F.R.] Higgins[2] a few times but, as far as I know, he has not yet met [Frank] O'Connor[3] who, I believe, now lives in Wicklow. I have not seen Davie for about three weeks but expect to see him in Edinburgh next weekend. Hood, of course, has been in the Army since February. When I was in Edinburgh last I saw [George] Campbell Hay but what happened to him since I don't know. He has given all his Gaelic verse to my safe-keeping and the English he has given, as far as I know, to [Douglas] Young. I think Hay is about the finest young Scotsman of our day. He is at least the finest young Highlander I have ever come across but I am afraid he is in for a bad time. The Cairds have been in Banff since September last. I saw Caird at Easter in Edinburgh and his account of life at Banff and its cultural side was devastating and sombre.

I look forward greatly to the appearance of your autobiography and of *The Golden Treasury* which I hope will be out soon. This is a bad time for such but all the same there are some people who now cling more than ever to that in view of the apparent hopelessness of the political scene. Perhaps I should have said that the political scene is rather terrifying than hopeless for, whatever happens, I suppose capitalism and imperialism are doomed; and I can imagine that ten or twenty or perhaps even five years hence may be times of great hope.

Give my very best regards to Valda, Mike, and Dr Orr if he is still in Whalsay.

Yours,

Sam MacLean.

---

[1]   Jessie Scott (later Kocmanová) was a recent graduate of Edinburgh University.
[2]   F.R. Higgins (1896-1941), poet.
[3]   'Frank O'Connor' (Michael O'Donovan) (1903-1966), short story writer.

11. From Sorley MacLean (EUL MS2954.13 ff.39-40)

Lyndhurst
Langlands Road
Hawick
Saturday 25 May [1940]

My dear Christopher,

I got your letter some days ago and I here enclose English versions of 19 or 20 of my shorter pieces. You may do what you want with any of them you choose and with the 'Highland Woman' too. I am not very concerned as to which of them you choose because it may be right to take one that sounds better in English even if others are really better in the original.[1] For example George Campbell Hay thinks 'Dàin do Eimhir IV' the best poem in the little book. I agree and yet it sounds pretty awful in English. My stuff like most Gaelic verse has a sensuousness chiefly for the ear. Now, as far as I can see, recent English poetry concentrates on a jungle of bristling, more or less surrealist imagery which strikes the eye. To me it is bad because I like rhythmic line or whatever you call it most in poetry. For that reason Dylan Thomas etc leaves me impressed but really unmoved. My antecedents are Gaelic and, quite sure that I could never approach the under-the-skin awareness and auditory magic of your own lyrics, which I consider as quite unrivalled and unapproached in the British Isles at present, I sometimes imagine that I could be a humble follower of the School of Yeats, who essentially is a very mundane poet compared with you. I am especially interested in Yeats because I am certain a sense of inferiority is one of the main dynamics of his poetry though this sense of inferiority frequently, as in his Anglo-Irish ascendency aristocratic sense, is an inferiority complex. I don't think I have the complex but I have the inferiority feeling quite clearly. Names like Lenin, Connolly, John MacLean etc. are more to me than the names of any poets.

Whatever is deficient in my verse it has in Gaelic a rhythm and auditory sensuousness that pleases myself. This, of course, cannot be translated. I do not strive after imagery. Usually a lyric comes to me quite spontaneously as a whole and then I don't blot a line. I fail to see how the jungle of poorly-defined imagery that you have e.g. in Dylan Thomas can have any spontaneity. At any rate Dylan Thomas to me does not achieve significant form in his whole poem. As for Auden, Spender etc. they are beneath contempt. I shall not be unduly perturbed if you do not accept any of my pieces for the anthology. If you think any part of 'The Cuillin' will do you can use it provided you tell me beforehand as a good deal of it is libellous and I can't afford a libel action.

How are things with yourself at present? I myself expect to be in the Army sometime in Autumn, as our reservation age is being raised from 25 to 30. If Hitler does win what can Scotland expect? Slovakian status, at the very best! That is my opinion and the prospect does not cheer me sufficiently to make me object to serving in the British Army. I may be totally wrong and the best men I know, like Hay, do not agree. And would Russian communism survive a Nazi domination of Europe for very long? I think our fate would be ultimately to cooperate with Hitler in the destruction of Russian communism. I think the Nazis would make a thorough job of a domination of Europe which the English and French could not do. Therefore I cannot but think a Nazi victory the very worst possible. Of course the possibilities of a long war of exhaustion are infinite. That would ultimately be the best conclusion but what if the Nazis are going to have a rapid victory? They would get a ready welcome from hosts of English gauleiters and their power would be very difficult to break, far more difficult than the power of the ramshackle British Empire.

At present I am studying Rilke. I am fascinated by the complete antithesis in his attitude to life to all my own instinctive feelings. To me his attitude is completely unreal but I suppose no modern poet has at all expressed the whatever-is-is-right feeling with anything like his subtlety and consistency and poignancy.

I shall write you soon again. If you have time and do choose any of these pieces perhaps you might tell me which so that I could spend more time over those selected in order to improve the version.

Kindest regards to Valda, Mike and Orr.

Yours,

Sam.

---

[1]   MacDiarmid had proposed a selection from six contemporary Scottish Poets to Hogarth Press. They were Sorley MacLean, George Campbell Hay, William Soutar, Douglas Young, Sydney Goodsir Smith and himself.

12. From Roy Armstrong (EUL MS2965.10 f.18)

Highover
Heath Common
Storrington
West Sussex
5 June 1940

Dear Grieve,

At last I have had an opportunity of getting at your stuff. The two packets of personal letters you wrote about I am enclosing herewith. The rest of the stuff seems to be a litter of hundreds of odd letters, manuscripts, bills, etc., together with quarterlies and magazines, newspaper cuttings and so on. It is not the kind of material I can possibly go through systematically or evaluate, so the only thing I can do is just to leave it where it is, for the present at any rate, but I must disclaim all responsibility for its safe keeping from now onwards, although there is no reason why it shouldn't remain intact for you if you ever are this way again. But I can't guarantee it from the mildew or damp. About the books, – apart from a set of George Eliot, mildewed, a translation of Homer, some French verse, a book on Scottish literature, a series of 'Half Moon Press' verses,[1] and a few other odd volumes, some uncut, there seems to be nothing worth sending on; but as all of these are in poor condition and the postage high I will not forward them unless you especially wish it.

Best wishes to yourself and Valda.

Yours,

Roy Armstrong.

---

[1]   Probably Charles Lahr's 'The Blue Moon Press'.

13. From Esther Amall (EUL MS2969)

44 St John's Wood Road
London NW8
3 July 1940

Dear Mr Grieve,

Thank you so much for your letter. I delayed answering it until I had had further word with Methuen. They are much interested in the autobiography, but they do feel that for present conditions it is [a] rather vast and un-coordinated mass, but on the other hand they are prepared to be helpful about it. I don't want to raise your hopes unduly, but the position at the moment is that they are considering most seriously how they can pick out the really important parts, so that a readily saleable volume will result. If they find that this can be done, they are going to write out a rough outline with details of what they would like you to do, and let you have it back.

This is very much more helpful than Gollancz who left everything vaguely to you, and did not give you any lines on which to work. I should be very pleased to get the American copy typed for you as soon as we get a definite word from Methuen. They tell me they would like till Monday to consider it further.

Meanwhile, before the cheque for the Faroese book comes through they are waiting to hear about your passport etc., and as to whether it is going to be possible to get to the Faroes. Do let me know as soon as you can, and believe me that I shall do everything in your interests.[1]

Yours very sincerely,
Esther Amall.
p.p. Margaret A. Watson [Director].

---

[1] Gilbert Wright sent MacDiarmid a cheque for £30 on 16 January 1941 – the first half of the advance on *Lucky Poet*. He was sent a cheque for £30 on 8 July 1940 – advance for a book on the Faroes. Methuen were still expecting the MS of 'Faroese Holiday' in 1945 but the book was never written.

14. From George Campbell Hay (EUL MS2951.2 f.3)

14 Carlton Street
Embro
4 August 1940

Dear Hugh MacDiarmid,

Douglas Young – sometimes known as Dia – told me you wanted to know what was doing with regard to the Gaelic poems of Sam and myself. I ought to have written you long ago, especially after the very great honour of the poem you addressed to the two of us.[1]

Sam thought that Gaelic MSS are likely to be seized by the censors because of their, to them, cypherlike appearance. When it was found they were Gaelic the English would not treat them with much care, and it would take their Gaelic experts (*if* they have any) months to read through such a bulk of verse. In reading them through they would find plenty to jib at. Again Sam's Communism and his accurate but hot comments on the late Vicar of Christ would not commend him to men like Hyde.[2] These considerations weighed with us and caused us to do nothing. (The Rev. John MacKechnie sent the second vol. of his Iain Lom to the Irish Texts Society a while since, and it was seized, while he was visited by various heavy-footed men in soft hats. The MS was in Gaelic, it was going to Dublin, and it had an apparatus where abbreviations like IRA (Royal Irish Ac.) might be found. A correspondent of the IRA, of course. They haven't released his MS yet, a work of some years' scholarship.)

But if you think we should go ahead, and I would be ashamed to throw away the trouble you seem to have taken for us, you will have to persuade Sam. He is in Raasay just now, I don't know his address, and he has typed versions of all my Gaelic stuff.

Our military geniuses bid me appear and be medically examined tomorrow, but deil the bit o me they'll see. So Whitehall and myself are like to disagree very soon. I am already defending my country (Scotland) in the L.D.V.,[3] and I refuse to shed my blood in East Anglia, Iraq or any other foreign clime – I have no desire to gift myself body and soul to those doubtful gentry and suddenly find myself shooting down Arabs, Indians, Russians, Irish – (all possibilities). Anyway, I may not be at liberty for long, so Sam will look after the matter. He has carte blanche to do what he likes with my Gaelic verse, he can burn it, dance on it, twist it into spills, roll it into rolls, make cocked hats or paper darts of it, or publish it – direach a thoil mhaith fhein.[4]

I enclose two productions, which are pretty slight, and three renderings of Gaelic songs, homely and of a kind that touches the heart – tho not, of course, the British heart which can only be touched by the destruction of a bank or the loss of investments.

With all good wishes.
Yours sincerely,
G. C. Hay.

---

[1]   'On receiving the Gaelic Poems of Somhairle Maclean and George Campbell Hay (1940)' is titled 'The Gaelic Muse' in *C.P.* I, pp. 657-662.
[2]   'Hyde' was Dr Douglas Hyde. MacDiarmid quotes his own pamphlet on Charles Doughty in *Lucky Poet*, 'How the English Ascendancy policy treated Irish Gaelic literature, Dr Douglas Hyde shows us'. (1943 edition, p.290).
[3]   'L.D.V.' were Local Defence Volunteers which became the Home Guard. On 14 May 1940 Sir Anthony Eden, Secretary of State for War, broadcast a call for Local Defence Volunteers.
[4]   direach a thoil mhaith fhein – just as he likes.

15. From F. G. Scott (EUL MS2659 ff.116-119)

Brolas Farm
Taynuilt
Tuesday Forenoon
21 August 1940

Send me anything you can – Speirs' book[1],
your Spain poem etc. I'm trying to send
you Saurat's *Christ at Chartres*[2], his
latest spooky bit of philosophy but

haven't a large-sized envelope. I'll send
along anything of interest in a day or two.
F. G.

My dear Chris,

I received your letter this morning while still in bed and had at any rate one good laugh from your description of birthday celebrations and your own easy movement and good wind while passing the 48th milestone. That your physical fit-up continues unimpaired is further testimony to the highly moral life you have always lived but I feel something like regret that you have passed 48 milestones and are on the way to an Old Age Pension. Speaking of ages lets me give you the final word on Aberdeen. A member of the Committee who was present at the meeting wrote: 'The only reason why Mr Scott's appointment was negatived was that his age (60) proved an insuperable barrier as the college here would have his services for 4 or 5 years at most. There was no other reason'. *This*, after the very grounds on which I appealed for maximum salary were that in view of my 15 years of honourable (!) service and early retiral my appointment was the only decent thing possible. The selected candidate is music master in Glasgow Academy, about 35 years old, was inspected by me and given lots of good advice on how to proceed and belongs either to Aberdeen or Banffshire. At the age of 35 he begins with £25 a year more than I've had all the time I've been in Jordanhill, and goes on to maximum while I stick where I am. It makes me wonder whether any form of totalitarian government could be so inept and unjust. – But enough of this: I'm sick to hear more of the 'granite city' and hope it continues to have the consideration it so richly deserves from the Nazi bombers.

I went to London on 8th August in reply to S.O.S. calls from the Saurats, especially Madame, who signalled that many things with them were in a bad way, e.g., their only son Harold had been missing since 2nd June (with the French Army); their eldest daughter seduced, abducted and bairned by a hack-journalist, kind of lawyer body of no means, repute and sense of decency; that since the downfall of France, Saurat has gone 'potty' about Jesus Christ, has been dreaming dreams, seeing visions and having confabs with poltergeists, spirits and God knows what else. (Muir by the way wrote to me in Glasgow that he was reading the New Testament and St. Augustine's *Confessions*, and T.S. Eliot and Middleton Murry, as you already know, are well on the way to a padded cell. T.S. Eliot was lunching with Saurat while I was in London; we didn't meet, Saurat thinking it wasn't likely to be a success). To continue Saurat has two Catholic nuns on the night-watch with his invalid mother and one ditto by day. The others of the domestic circle – Madame and the remaining two girls are flirting about in good old fashion, Cécile, a lass of eighteen can inform the whole lunch-table that she had 'a hell of a time last night at the Spanish Restaurant'. A pretty confused sort of world and what is really more important, a kind of hopeless confusion I felt everywhere I went in London. My thoughts frequently wandered back to the douce, canny folk up in Scotland who are honestly fighting this latest war to end war.

And now for de Gaulle.[3] He's another honest-to-God individual who as you know still preaches that France 'n'a pas perdu la guerre', 'elle retrouvera sa liberté et sa grandeur', 'tel est mon but, mon seul but'! (I quote from his proclamation stuck up everywhere). For about a week after his arrival in London there was a possibility that the English government would declare him head of the French government (with Saurat, prime minister) but since then the English Foreign Office has taken a different view of the situation. A Pétain government having already betrayed France may prove good for other kinds of betrayal.[4] Hitler might one of these days sprawl up against Italy, Spain and France (a nice Latin bloc) and wouldn't England like to be in on the right side. Meanwhile de Gaulle has been supplied with cash for food, clothes etc. and told not to upset the manoeuvres of the Foreign Office. So Saurat (as de Gaulle's spokesman) has been sadly neglected of late, his phone hardly tinkles once a week nowadays and neither he nor any other real son of France can explain what wangle, expedient or manoeuvre is afoot. What is fairly clear is that de Gaulle is being made a tool of, on *this* side by Jews financing his propaganda, on *that* side by Catholics who are fighting to preserve their *rentes* and property and authority in both France and London. Complete, absolute demoralization has blasted the French everywhere; 'what can we save from the ruins'?, 'how can we hold on to what we still have'?, 'don't bother about *honneur* or anything of that kind', 'let Pétain or Laval[5] or anybody else agree to anything they like if we can keep "un peu d'argent"'. Even the French in London (with funds in France no doubt) have no use for de Gaulle's 'Vive la France' slogan. I can almost swear they'd not be too disappointed if England went down too if the 'peu d'argent' were made more get-at-able. The intellectuals in Saurat's opinion were cowards to a man – [André] Maurois[6], Jules Romains[7] and hosts of others started looking for a boat as soon as they landed here and most of them have reached America by this time.

I leave to your own judgement the proper conclusion to be drawn from all this. Neither Saurat nor [William] Burt will agree with you but I will. I kept advising Saurat to come straight out with a statement of the position but he was afraid Goebbels[8] would be too too delighted. He says Halifax and Churchill know; Attlee[9] is 'acquainted with the facts and the Labour Party is maintaining a careful watch on the situation', and so on and on. The best I could do was to phone Dick Mitchison[10] and put him wise. Saurat and he were to have lunch together after I left London.

I saw Willie Johnstone and heaps of other folk including Ruth Pitter who heard some of my recent Campbell Hay songs and the 'Cumha na Laoch' ('Lament for the Heroes' to you!)[11] originally written and played by Horace Fellowes[12] this past winter, 'a noble theme' she called it. Willie Johnstone was leaving for Scotland on the following morning but I spent lunch and the afternoon with him, going round his Art School at Camberwell and delighted with his latest pictures. The school is now continuously in session, although some of his students are in Northampton or Nottingham and Willie is in Scotland for only a fortnight. He expressed the idea that maybe you weren't pleased with him about some blocks he sent you but I was able to correct any misapprehension on his part. If you have occasion to write, Camberwell School of Arts and Crafts, Camberwell, London will find him.

I can't remember if I ever referred to Erik Chisholm's Competition for Scottish Composers, the results of which competition were announced about Eastertime with Chisholm himself as First Prize-winner with a symphony which secured 95% in the way of marks. Another hellish wangle that was. My reason for referring to the business now is that the Association of which Chisholm is head, front, backside and all has a publication fund, he tells me, of some two or three hundred pounds. Whether as mark of his genuine appreciation or of his fear of incurring my indignant opposition to his manoeuvres, he suggested about June that the Association would like to publish a sixth volume of my songs with the Oxford Univ. Press as medium. I didn't exactly fall for the proposal but before I left Glasgow for Taynuilt wrote out fair copies of thirteen songs: four of yours, i.e., 'The Auld Men o' the Sea' (with Curwen's permission to reprint);[13] 'Grey sand is churnin' in my lugs';[14] 'I wha aince in Heaven's height';[15] and a real, vital, brand-new setting of 'The Sauchs in the Reuch Heuch Hauch'.[16] The volume would also contain settings of Soutar's sonnet 'Samson',[17] Muir's 'Merlin'[18] and two of Hay's, 'Alba'[19] and 'The Old Fisherman'[20]. The others I can't recall at the moment but 'Whistle, whistle, auld wife'[21] originally published by Curwen is one of them and Montrose's poem on the death of Charles I is another[22] and Dora Sigerson's dramatic 'The sea hounds' is still another.[23]

If the Dunedin is genuinely anxious to print the volume I'll let it go on but I've more than a notion that Chisholm hopes to push through some symphony of his own eating up a good £150 of the fund and is prepared to spend a paltry £50 on me as a blind. He's a real snake in the grass is Erik and I get on guard whenever he makes a move in any direction.

The night before Francise, Lovey and I left Glasgow Tonge, who has been working for Reid and Lefevre in London,[24] brought along J.D. Fergusson and Margaret Morris of the Margaret Morris Movement – the M.M.M. as it's familiarly called. This M.M.M. has settled on Glasgow as its last refuge and abiding city, has linked up with the Saltire Socy and the Dunedin Assoc., kicking off with a Celtic Ballet Club and looking all round the horizon for pupils. Willa Muir I learn attended a meeting of all three movements in Glasgow and said she would write a scenario on 'Hunting the Bawbee' (you'll remember something of this in the Montrose days) and expressed the hope that she'd get F.G.S. to write music for it! J.D. Fergusson, living in unlawful conjugal relationship with Margaret Morris, has left Paris for good and settled down in Glasgow. He's also, as needs must, highly interested in Celtic this and that as something quite new in the way of culture so I send you warning of a new epidemic – a veritable sandstorm from three airts at once – farts by the M.M.M., the Saltire Serpent and the Dunedin Demiurge. So look to your rigging, Christopher, the Kennedy-Fraser 'Hi, ho, horo' was nothing to what's coming; I reckon you'd better move off to the Faroes before it strikes you in Whalsay.

As for life in Taynuilt now I'm back from the disillusionment of London, it's just plain dumb I am – eating, sleeping and *no* fishing in the wretched weather of the past week. I've been doing some orchestration and in the intervals trying to read Lenin's Volume II on *Materialism and Empirio-Criticism*, surely the dullest thing in the whole range of philosophical writing.[25] You'll see from all this that I'm in rare fettle for quarelling with everybody. I'm finding the panorama of existence hardly worth bothering about and am inclined to throw the tow after the bucket. In my present mood I see the people of every state as the galoots who slave, save, fight and shite for some tin god or other. Every now and again some devil behind the scenes sends plague, pestilence, fire, sword, brimstone, bombs and damnation in an effort to teach the fools some sense – all in vain! You should rewrite Burns' ode to stupidity – it wants amending and bringing up to date.

To end on a somewhat cheerier note, we've had two nephews already here staying at Brolas, may be visited one of the days by Tonge who is 'working his way up the West Coast' and are digging ourselves in here till end of *September*. Why be bombed in Glasgow when you can admire the grandest of Scottish scenery in Taynuilt? Love to Valda & Michael and a real 'heeze up' to yourself. Wha's like us?

Ever,

F. G.

1   John Speirs, *The Scots Literary Tradition,* (London:Chatto & Windus, 1940).
2   Denis Saurat, *The Christ at Chartres,* (London, 1940).
3   General de Gaulle (1890-1970), soldier and statesman, broadcast his appeal to the French people from London on 18 June 1940. France 'has not lost the war', 'she will regain her freedom and her greatness', 'that is my aim, my sole aim!'. He became President of the post-war provisional government from 1944 to early 1946 and first President of the Fifth Republic from 1958 to 1969.
4   Marshal Philippe Pétain (1856-1951) headed the collaborationist regime at Vichy from the fall of France in June, 1940 until the end of the War in August, 1944.
5   Pierre Laval (1883-1945) was Prime Minister of the Vichy government during 1940 and again from 1942-1944. Executed.
6   André Maurois (1885-1967), popular biographer.
7   Jules Romains (1885-1972), novelist, dramatist, poet and essayist.
8   Josef Goebbels was Hitler's Minister of Propaganda.
9   Clement Attlee (1883-1967) was Leader of the Labour Party (1935-1955), Lord Privy Seal in Churchill's coalition government from 1940 to 1942, Deputy Prime Minister from 1942 to 1945, and than Prime Minister from 1945 to 1951.
10   Dick Mitchison, Labour M.P., husband of Naomi Mitchison.
11   'Cumha na Laoch' ('Lament for the Heroes') was Scott's own composition.
12   Horace Fellowes (1870-1951), editor, scholar and cathedral musician. *Music in the Heart*, Edinburgh, 1958.
13   C.P.1, p.52.
14   C.P.1, p.129.
15   C.P.1, p.234.
16   C.P.1, p.18.
17   *Poems of William Soutar*, ed. by W.R.Aitken (Edinburgh: Scottish Academic Press, 1988), p.30.
18   *The Complete Poems of Edwin Muir*, An Annotated Edition ed. by Peter H. Butter (Aberdeen: The Association for Scottish Literary Studies, 1991), p.80.
19   *Collected Poems and Songs of George Campbell Hay*, ed. by Michael Byrne (Edinburgh: Edinburgh University Press, 2003), p.57.
20   Ibid. p.64.
21   anon.
22   *Golden Treasury of Scottish Poetry*, p.35.

[23] Dora Sigerson (1866-1918), Irish poet, born in Dublin.
[24] Reid and Lefevre, art gallery.
[25] *Materialism and Empirio-Criticism* was written in Geneva in 1908 and published in Moscow in 1909.

16. From F. G. Scott (EUL MS2959 f.120)

Brolas Farm
Taynuilt
Argyllshire
14 September 1940

My dear Chris

Just a short note on returning Speirs' book and to congratulate you on the placing of the autobiography on what looks like very promising terms in these confused times. You're evidently bucked by the prospect of having the auto. in print soon and though I've never seen the manuscript I heartily rejoice with you and look forward to its success from every point of view.

I am enclosing with this the Penguin edition of Shaw's *Back to Methuselah*[1] which I picked up in Oban and was glad to re-read in the absence of any literature on the farm. As you know I never was a 'Shawite' in the days when these were as common as gooseberries but of late I've been veering a little to the old fellow as one of the few really sane people now living and I have to confess that this *Methuselah* production has fitted in with my present mood much better than I'd have thought probable. I'm not discussing Shaw as artist but he's certainly a masterly thinker and writer, and I literally revelled in his prose style. At any rate he made it quite impossible for me to read *The Scots Literary Tradition* as anything but the laboured effort of [a] schoolboy. Speirs obviously can neither think nor write and though he basks at Grieve to draw attention to himself if he can, you'd be well advised to take no notice whatever of him. You can't waste paper and ink explaining the alphabet when the world rocks on its axis.

Still another reason for writing is that you needn't return the Saurat typescript. He sent me this week the published book itself (with the corrections we together made over in the park opposite the 'Institut Français'). These don't alter in any way the thought-matter but only the turn of the phrases, so you have by you all you will want. I've twice re-read it since the book came and I must say it improves in the reading as everything by Saurat does. *Verbum sapiens* – have a good look into it! One can't serve up Shaw or Saurat a nostrum like 'dialectical materialism' or shout at them 'fascist', 'opium-eater', or the like, (even George Davie is already tainted with academicism enough to tell me that there is *no philosophy at all* in Marxism!) This just brings you back to the position of Speirs with his idiotic book of the 'Scottish Tradition' or Lenin's *Empirio-Criticism* with its amateurish wonderment about whether matter produced spirit or vice versa. The whole point of the matter is that spirit *does* exist (and has always existed) and that you as an artist are dealing with *things of the spirit*. The quibble doesn't matter a damn!

So I prefer my science in a textbook and my art in a work of art. Now it must be conceded that the medium for *fact* is prose, just as the medium for the subtler rhythms of imaginative writing is verse. The *force* of a statement of fact requires as a counterpart in poetry the subtle variations of *stress* which verse alone can give (and here I would ask you to reflect that free verse *weakens* the stress-tension). So your 'Auld Reekie' to me is handicapped in several directions.[2] The theme is essential[ly] 'factual' (I have yet to learn that 'politics' is an *art*) and you, correctly enough, express it in a kind of verse little distinguishable from prose. (I had Lovey to read it through aloud just to listen to its effect in this direction. Her opinion *en passant* was that it was 'quite interesting, useful, but just like prose').

Perhaps the most interesting touches in the whole thing were your phrases like 'the mighty impetus of creative force'; 'justifying faith'; 'primal power'; 'the miraculous achievements of men of the past'; 'the primal indispensable power'; 'our deeds are evil'. If you go on like this you'll be invoking the Almighty very soon and find yourself where I am, maintaining that evidently the *'purely human'* is a *wash-out*! And Saurat's quotations should help in confirming you in *this* faith. What vision! What a canvas both Blake, and Hugo paint on! Go and do likewise! The times have need of it and you!

Ever,

F.G.

¹   George Bernard Shaw (1856-1950). *Back to Methuselah* (1921).
²   'Auld Reekie' was published as 'Edinburgh', *C.P.* I, pp.644-646.

17. From J. H. Miller (EUL MS2955.8 ff.2-3)

54 Arrowsmith Ave
Glasgow W3
20 September 1940

A Charaid,

Many thanks for your letter and MSS. I will take good care of them. I will print the poem in the forthcoming issue. You have dealt with the situation in a hard-hitting and forthright manner and I am glad to see that you have differentiated between the English state and the English people. So often we are accused by Socialists of Anglophobia. Our Scottish Socialists are such thorough 'British Nationalists' that at times I feel nothing will shift them, and I become filled [with] a hatred of the word 'British'.

I have read with considerable enjoyment and complete agreement your 'Brief Survey of Modern Scottish Politics'. I am inclined to agree with you re the length of survey and, much as I would like to print it, I don't think the mag. in its present form could carry it, even by instalments. I would like to see it published as booklet with the necessary alterations and additions to bring it right up to present betrayal of the Scottish workers. What are the chances?

What is the present position of the Red Scotland Committee?[1] I am afraid that

I am badly informed, as, while I knew of its existence, I never contacted it, except thro' *The Voice*, believing it chiefly to be a literary group. For some time now I have been trying to create an active propagandist organisation that would carry on the [John] MacLean line by the normal political means, but so far have not had much success. I have gathered together a handful of people for this purpose but with the exception of Oliver Brown the others are very ordinary people without experience although useful as workers. We have taken the name of the Scottish Socialist Party, the old one now being defunct.[2] We have no money and no premises and unless we can attract some more people, particularly experienced ones and some speakers, the project may be stillborn. We have been holding open-air meetings with good audiences and good reception, and I have no doubt that progress can be made if we can get properly founded. We have no propaganda as yet other than the mag. and have been using [Thomas] Burns' *Real Rulers of Scotland*,[3] now sold out, and Brown's *Scotland and Westminster.*[4]

I feel that we must do something to prepare for the revolutionary situation which the war will bring about and, as it is, the CP have the field to themselves. I am convinced that in addition to independent action our hopes lie in convincing the CP of the necessity for Independent Scottish Action and that can only be brought about by the creation and building up of an organisation such as we are attempting. If we don't, then the chance will once again slip away, diverted in the British angle.

The main weapon is, of course, the printed word and my hopes are that sooner or later the *Scots Socialist* can be printed as a monthly or weekly for which purpose money is needed, and which as the war develops will become scarcer.[5]

I will be pleased if you can put me in touch with any people likely to be interested in working in this direction, particularly in the Glasgow area, and your observations or suggestions as [to] how we can cooperate with the Red Scotland Committee if still in existence or any groups of Scottish Socialist Republicans.

November [30] is the anniversary of John MacLean's death and I intend the November issue to be a commemorative one. Can you do me an article which, while paying tribute, will briefly bring out his policy. I haven't space to do it justice, but could handle about 1 500 words, roughly three pages of typescript.

Please excuse this scrawl but I wrote most of it during an air-raid. Again many thanks for your cooperation.

Yours sincerely,

J. H. Miller.

P.S. A Scottish People's Convention is being held in Glasgow next month, sponsored by the People's Vigilance Committee (Pritt's outfit)[6] and I intend attempting to influence the proceedings to the extent of securing support for the self-determination of Scotland and a Scottish People's Government. I am nothing if not an optimist.

---

[1] MacDiarmid wrote that 'The Red Scotland Thesis', published in *The Voice of Scotland*, vol.1, no.1, in 1938, ' [...] was drafted at my house in the Shetlands in 1936 by a group

of friends constituting themselves "The Red Scotland Committee"' (NLS MS27037 f.52). This 'committee' probably consisted of MacDiarmid himself, Dr G. E. Davie, a visitor, and Dr David Orr, the resident Doctor.

2   The foundation meeting of the Scottish Socialist (Republican) Party was held on 16 May 1940. The secretary was J. H. Miller-Wheeler, usually referred to as Harry Miller, who also edited *The Scots Socialist*.

3   *The Real Rulers of Scotland*, issued by the London Scots Self-Government Committee, Glasgow, 1940.

4   *Scotland and Westminster*, issued by the Labour Council for Scottish Self Government, Glasgow, 1939.

5   *The Scots Socialist* no.5 (November-December 1940) included the first past of MacDiarmid's article, 'John MacLean, Scotland, and the Communist Party', which was concluded in nos. 6/7 (January-February 1941) and 9/10 (April-May 1941).The poem 'England is our Enemy' was printed as a supplement to no.4 (September 1940) and has not been reprinted. It is not the same poem as the section of *In Memoriam James Joyce* with the same title.

6   D. N. Pritt, a Labour M. P. and lawyer who had been expelled from the Labour Party, was figurehead of the People's Vigilance Committee, which had been set up on 7 July 1940 to campaign for 'a people's Government' and 'a people's peace'. The U.K. People's Convention assembled in Manchester on 12 January 1941.

18. From Barbara Niven (NLS MS27152 ff.65-66)

25 November [1940]

Dear Chris,

I am very sorry the 3rd Hymn didn't reveal itself.[1] But, if you haven't given up the search in despair, there is a far better use for it – or for anything else you might consider even more suitable – at the People's Convention for which preliminary meetings are now being held all over the country, and which will be in Manchester on January 12. It is practically certain that T[heatre] Union will do a 'declamation' then and I have already been asked to undertake the decorations & publicity in the way of leaflets, posters, etc. The choice fell on Manchester partly because it has not yet been badly attacked from the air and because also, among other cities in this fortunate condition, it is the centre of an industrial area.[2] It would be such a grand occasion to use your poetry that I can't really bear the thought of not doing so.

Also, and forgive me for asking this again but I want and even need it so very badly – will you let me have the flimsies of Mature Art for a bit?[3] You don't know what a difference it would make to me, now even more than any other time. It needn't be any parts that you can't find easily, just any that I could get into order myself. Life here just now is divided into many small jobs, a great many involving skill and energy and some of an organisational kind, and tho' they are necessary and seem important now, they only touch indirectly those other more creative and slower things which are increasingly difficult under these circumstances. So you can see how much I need it. I don't want to read anything else.

As far as painting goes I have done none for months, tho' I have used my own past (as it were) for designing for all kinds of things like Theatre Union and meetings. I am planning to go to London for a few days if they will pay my fare – still planning, since this practical step hasn't come to anything yet – to see the shelters and Tubes and devastation and do something in the way of pen drawings, if I can, that touches on the horror of it. I saw a rescue squad worker back from Coventry on Saturday and the understatement of the murder and devastation there is so gross that it is like a final insult just thrown in the face of the people, even to have mentioned it at all. According to them – sent from as far as here because there was no equipment in the place – thousands are nearer the mark.

You'll know of course about the Scottish D[aily] W[orker], hastened by the imminent danger to the London offices, but also I believe planned for some time in relation to this slow and partial and belated understanding of the Scottish position. I have been wondering whether to write to the Editor in London, whom I know, about your position again, but would like to know first what you think. Because imagine even speaking of Burns and MacLean and not reckoning with the voice they could use if they wanted to. Let me know soon whether you would like me to do this and what you would like me to say. It seems stupid for me to be suggesting such a thing to you, in one way; but we are so little developed yet that enmity to great power seems inherent in every undeveloped person whatever their beliefs (of course they are also suffering from incomplete beliefs along with all the rest of their outfit), so that if someone, like me, less to be suspected by them can be used – well, let it.

How are you going on? Has the Scottish Treasury come out yet? How is Valda, and you yourself? Please tell me this, and what you are working on, when you write. I am looking forward to your letter a lot.

Love to Valda.

My love

Barbara

1   There was no copy of the 'Third Hymn to Lenin' in the manuscript of 'Mature Art' to which Niven refers in this letter (NLS Acc. 12074/1).
2   Manchester did suffer an air raid in December after this letter was written.
3   MacDiarmid did send the 'flimsies' or carbons of 'Mature Art' as they were among Barbara Niven's papers when they were sold to the National Library of Scotland in 2002.

19. From William Soutar (EUL MS2960 ff.37-38)

27 Wilson St
Perth
19 December 1940

Dear Chris,

Very glad to have news of you – I was just about to write H.B.C. for confirmation of your existence when your lifey letter arrived. Judging by the accumulation of MSS now surrounding you I should fancy that you, at least, have the consolation of a more than adequate shelter – so it's the long-nose to time and Hitler. Naturally I was delighted to learn that

[Soutar here sketches an air-raid shelter of MSS with 'Heroic poem' as the lintel and five blocks on either side marked (left) 'Auto. Vol. 1', 'vol.2', 'vol. 3', 'etc.', 'etc.' and (right) 'Poems', 'Essays', 'Docs', 'Short Stories' and 'Plays'. 'Docs' is a reference to MacDiarmid's book on Scottish Doctors which was unpublished. MacDiarmid sits between the jambs smoking a cigarette.]

you had brought Gollancz to an arrangement about your autobiography;[1] and in present conditions I should think that its appearance in sections could hardly be avoided: it will also make your initial volume a clean-cut introduction to your work & thought; and I think this is all to the good. I was also pleased to note that the anthology had come out in time for Christmas sales. I can't speak about it yet as my copy hasn't been handed in to date; nor have I seen any notice, with the exception of a colonial one which had no significance: there must have been some reviews already in the home papers but, like everything else, the delivery of cuttings is greatly delayed.

Do you hear of anybody breaking the Caledonian silence these days? Incidentally my latest collection of verse in English is entitled 'The Signature of Silence' – and I doubt it holds implications more comprehensive than I had intended for it remains in MS. Since bundling these together last June I have been writing only Scots verse, & have a fair gathering, but see little likelihood of shoving it into book form. As regards your enquiry; you would note that *In the Time of Tyrants* was limited to only 100 copies.[2] This works out most expensively for individual copies – something like 7/6. A more suitable arrangement for sale, with about £10 extra on initial outlay, would be a format similar to my *Poems in Scots*. This would work out at somewhere near £40 for 500 copies; so, on a 50/50 agreement your expenses shouldn't exceed £20. Priced at 3/6 your royalty would be ½, & you would clear your outlay by selling 400 copies. But if you have a small book of this type in mind why not approach Oliver & Boyd? They might be prepared to add a modern to their series of Saltire Books; & naturally you are the first obvious choice. Anyhow I should think it a possible chance – so you'd better act on it right now before I begin to wale out a bouquet for St. Andrew.

I've met (about six weeks ago) your (?) latest protégé, Douglas Young. An altitudinous lad of 6ft 6 with a jutting black beard – & a fluent Oxfordian utterance. Since then a flutter of MSS has descended from Aberdeen at intervals. No doubt, like myself, you found a certain liveliness in the work, but most of the Scots has a library smell about it. However, it's fine to come on an enthusiast recruit to an orchestra which now appears to be reduced to a first and second fiddler. My only other literary caller in the last six months or so has been Fred Urquhart.[3] An exceptionally decent chap of 27. I read his latest novel in MSS which has a Galloway setting; but I thought he overworked the rochness. There is a kick in his stuff tho', & something of Gibbon's directness – but he has, as yet, little of Gibbon's sense of background.

I've bundled up some Penguins, & odds & ends, to go with this post – I hope they arrive to be our Christmas knock on your door; & find you all in good health. The household here joins in the greetings to yourself, Mrs Grieve and Michael.

All the best,
Yours Aye,
Willie.

[1] Methuen published *Lucky Poet* in 1943, not Gollancz.
[2] Perth, 1939.
[3] Fred Urquhart (1912-1995), short story writer and novelist.

20. From J. H. Miller (EUL MS2955.8 ff.9-10)

54 Arrowsmith Ave
Glasgow W3
4 January 1941

A Charaid,

Bliadhna mhath ur duibh.[1] Now that I have time to answer your letters let me thank you for all the stuff you sent me and to offer my congratulations on the publication of your *Golden Treasury*. I have not seen it yet but Collets are getting some, which reminds me, they wanted to know if you would autograph a few copies. You can let me know how you feel on this. I have not contacted all the addresses you sent as I thought I'd wait until the new issue appears, 'twill make a better impression.

I have had a letter, a donation and an article from Tom Burns, he is very pleased and will support well: one or two other donations have come in, not nearly enough but [I] will with a bit of luck manage this issue and hope for the best.

The Memorial meeting was not a great success, the turnout was poor, due no doubt to [the] large number of people working, the weather and the omission of *Forward* to insert the second advert the Friday before the meeting. Brown and Nicholson[2] both spoke very well indeed and were well received, especially Brown.

Re the Convention – its transference to London makes it difficult to attend, and it may be cancelled again. We have reconsidered the matter and feel that our best policy is to use the Scottish Convention rather than run the risk of getting a Self-Government resolution thrown out by a gathering largely composed of Englishmen.

I have got the memo to Pritt drafted but have had so much stuff to get typed that the poor lassie that churns it out in her spare time is buried in it. However, I will get it away within the next few days. I don't think [it] will have much effect, but it will be a protest.

I will be calling a meeting soon for the purpose of creating a Scottish Council of Civil Liberties. Meantime do you know a Scottish lawyer or advocate who is sufficiently aware of his nationality to do an article on Scots law, how it is being undermined and Anglicised, and the private rights of Scots according to their own law.

A meeting of the proposed Prisoners Aid Committee will be held within the next week[3]. R.E. Muirhead has agreed to be chairman and I shall inform the meeting of your willingness to join.

Re your Socialist poetry I will be very pleased to publish the collection as a supplement, but as we now go over to print and a different size, it may be worthwhile waiting for the first issue in order that you can consider the layout and if all the poems could be contained on an extra page. I could then go into the matter of cost.

I could use one short poem per month on a topical subject, either satire or parody.

I haven't seen a copy of *Eleventh Hour Questions* but will get one. My series of *The Voice* is now complete. When do you intend re-issuing it?

I sent Douglas a copy of the *Scots Socialist* but it was returned by the censor.[4] [We] need a permit to send printed matter to Eire. Will write him however.

You will have heard about the Glen Affric Power racket.[5] Fortunately Inverness-shire and Ross-shire are opposing it. Balfour Beatty Ltd must not get their provisional order. Even Lochiel has drawn his claymore.

The latest racket is in sending Scots girls to Coventry, refusal means their dole is stopped while English wenches are arriving in droves and walking into jobs.[6] Glasgow is crawling with prostitutes from London, Birmingham and Coventry. The same thing applies to men, there seems to be a deliberate transference of population.

In Glasgow although there are about 20 000 names on the Corporation waiting list, English arrive in hundreds and walk right into houses.

Yet people apparently lie down to it all and the press yells its head off about the Irish, but never a word about the droves of English.

Will write you soon when [I] have more news.

Is mise an sgath Alba Nuadh[7]

J. H. Miller

PS Who is behind *The New Alliance*?[8]

[1] Happy New Year.
[2] Not identified.
[3] Prisoners Aid Committee became Mutual Aid Committee.
[4] 'Douglas' was Ronald MacDonald Douglas (1896-1984) who lived in Eire during the Second World War.
[5] At this time a great deal of criticism was expressed about the plans for hydro-electricity in the Highlands cf. Douglas Young's pamphlet *Fascism for the Highlands?* [1943].
[6] Criticism was also expressed about Scots girls being directed to work in England.
[7] An sgath Alba Nuadh - for the sake of New Scotland.
[8] *The New Alliance* was first published in Autumn 1939. In a letter to Alan Bold, Sorley MacLean wrote, 'Johnstone-Stewart [was] a Galloway laird associated with [George] Scott-Moncrieff in *The New Alliance*, and, as I remember, associated with *The Free Man*, a Scottish Nationalist then [and] a very likeable man.' (*Letters*, p.610).

21. From Joan Littlewood (EUL MS2965.11 ff.101-102)

Oak Cottage
Higham Lane
Hyde

Dear Hugh

Have you still got the copy of 'The Damnable Town', which we sent you a while ago? We don't feel there is much chance of getting it published but Jimmie has asked me to write you for it as it's the only copy he has. At the moment he has very little opportunity for work, army life is as deadly as a concentration camp. We have kept our theatre group alive – and while he was home on sick leave Jimmie got down to work with us for a short while and wrote some of our new show.

I hope you are able to work as you did before – in spite of being cut off more than ever.

We have been faced with a big problem in our work here. For years now we have worked to form a group of people capable of making a revolutionary theatre. You know about this. It has meant years of patient work, constant struggle against the diehards & the phoneys whose common line – is – the bowdlerisation of art, they can never cheapen the theatre, literature, painting enough. They constantly attempt to vulgarise and distort in order to reach that abysmal level of ignorance which is their assessment of proletarian understanding. As working-class artists we have treated this stuff with the contempt it deserves. We have constantly tried to raise the standards of the work in the theatre. Every moment that our people can give has been spent in study and training. Every play that we have done has been worthy of a revolutionary theatre.

Our last show *Lysistrata*[1] – rewritten with passages of Thucydides[2] dramatized – and given new stress in the light of today's events – has been labelled an academic exercise, while an audience of cotton-workers in the Rossendale valley rocked with laughter at it and thought it a better show than the living newspaper. Our people did a great deal of work on the Greek theatre before and during rehearsals. That work has still been going on. We have also been studying the *commedia dell'arte*[3] – and a small group of us are working on the translation of Molière's *Flying Doctor*,[4] an understanding of improvisation is absolutely necessary in our theatre – & the Molière should help them a great deal. We have never stopped our work on the Elizabethans, we feel that such writing can come back to the theatre. We feel that a play must be written on a great human problem today. We must dramatize this struggle for life. We thought of a play on love – with war devastating all that is fine and beautiful in love, marriage. We have been taking *Romeo and Juliet* to pieces in much the same way as we did Aristophanes' *Lysistrata*. We have already got parts of the new play in our minds. Simultaneously we are studying *The Origin of the Family*[5] and Balzac's *Catherine de Medici*[6] as political background to our *commedia dell'arte* work.

This has been done in spite of the bombing of our premises – and of many of our homes.

We feel that it is vital that our work should go on – we are the only group who are working for understanding and knowledge. We are the only group in this country which is capable of building a new proletarian aesthetic. Others are singing 'Roll out the barrel' in air-raid shelters -saying that now is not the time for 'propaganda'. We feel that such behaviour is insulting – apart from its banality. Many people who used to think as we did have been unable to survive the raids on Manchester, they at once felt that they must abandon everything & go from shelter to shelter, giving comfort to the people in the way of jolly songs to keep their spirits up. The people do not want pity and we are not philanthropists. Again we say that we must go to the organized workers with our plays and that these productions must be the best we are capable of.

If we cannot survive 2 bad raids[7] what will happen as the struggle gets even more intense – everything that we have worked for will disappear. And if our work goes we might as well be dead.

We have been faced with a frontal attack on the theatre – we have been practically ordered to give up this 'monastic striving after technical perfection'. We have been asked to abandon ourselves to day-to-day struggle. Sing in shelters, during a blitz.

Actually it is only thro' the standard of our work that we have won any support from the workers. Also people trained for theatre work are seldom capable of going off on their own and singing comic songs about 'the disappearing onion'.

So you see we are fighting for survival as a theatre as desperately as we've ever done – and against some who were formerly with us.

I think this problem is not only ours, but yours, it is the problem of anyone who is concerned about creative work. I think that we have to fight this thing out. Fundamentally these people despise those that they are supposed to lead else how could [they] lash out such rubbish? How could they talk about their nonsense – being 'above the workers' heads'?

Maybe all this seems a remote problem to you – perhaps you have solved it for yourself. It seems to me that the understanding of many of these so-called leaders lags far behind that of ordinary working people.

I started out to ask you to send the novel back – but this Theatre business obsesses me at the moment.

Sincerely,

Joan Littlewood.

---

[1] Aristophanes (?445-?385BC) wrote *Lysistrata* in 411BC. He was the greatest ancient Greek writer in comedy and wrote over forty plays of which eleven have survived.

[2] Thucydides, Greek historian of the 400s BC, is famous for his history of the Peleponnesian War.

[3] Italian Renaissance comedy, mainly improvised and with stock characters.

[4] Molière (Jean-Baptiste Poquelin) (1622-1673) was considered to be the greatest comic actor of his day and one of the greatest comic playwrights of all time. *Le Médecin Volant* (1645).

[5] Friedrich Engels (1820-1895), *The Origin of the Family, Private Property and the State* (1884).

[6] Honoré de Balzac (1799-1850), novelist.

[7] Manchester had suffered air raids in December 1940 and January 1941.

22. From Douglas Young (EUL MS2961.18 ff.5-7)

Auld Aberdeen
11 February 1941

A Charaid,

Ye'll nae dout hae seen my owerluikan o the *Gowden Treasorie* in the current *Scots Independent*; a silly eneuch bit article for the readers o that blad. Thir last twa moneths I hae ettlet aye to scrieve ye a richt critique, but have na had the time, forbye beean sick wi a flu and a laryngitis causeit by threepan ower lang on a cauld nicht at a Nationalist convene to a bourach o North Britons that were nae warth the bother.

I haena had access to Colonel Waddell's buik,[1] albeid I hae assayit it mair nor yince; but I hae read L. Albert's furthset o Roger O' Connor's *Cornikillis of Eri*, whas 'essential historical veracity' I dinna credit.[2] I am bumbazeit that ye can, eftir readan Hubert's twa buiks,[3] still gie credit to O' Connor. I winna deny that there are elements o truth and o plausibility in O' Connor but ye canna pit it doun for History. I dout the Celts were gey sma beer till about 500 B.C. In 1 500 B.C. their culture was, relative til the Mediterranean and Near Aist cultures, about as far ahint as the Aist Europeans Slavs are yet ahint the mair *kulturtragende Voelker*[4] o the Wast. I wad agree that the Celtic ingyne is mair humane and cultural than the Germanic or the Latin, but I maun quarrel ye anent the 'Ur-Gaelic impulse to civilization'; '6 000 years of Gaelic grandeur' is ower monie, sae far onie wey. In 4 000 B.C. they werena verra far forrit in the Fertile Crescent, the Nile, Euphrates and Indus straths, (and aiblins Yemen forbye, that's nou dessicate throu the recession o the ice-caps), and the evolution o civilisation in thir parts doesna manifest Celtic northern impulses. I dout gin there are Celtic influences in the Mediterranean afore 1 500 B.C. and then mainly in spiral decoration and the like. I dinna think the reivan folk ye read o in the Tel-El-Àmarna epistils and the tablets o Boghaz-Keui are onie kind o Celts.

Kenspeckle is that the Celts were nae empire-biggers. Ye speak o the 'vast Celtic empire' in the 4th yearhunder B.C. It was richtlie nae empire, but a diaspora o independent nations, wi nae subordination amang them; unless aiblins the Belgae had something like an empire i the modern sense, as Caesar maks ye jalouse. There was indeed a certain Pan-Celtic internationalism amang the Celts frae the Atlantic richt ower to Asia Minor, and the leids were mutually intelligible til Jerome's day;[5] but an empire, in the sense o Dareios, the Ptolemies, or the Antonines, na.

Exaggeration is better nor understatement, especiallie gin the thesis is novel and important; but there suld be a merch til exaggeration, whan the truth is guid eneuch onie wey. As Celts, the Scots hae a langer and better cultural tradition nor the English, little as the maist o us ken it. Ye maun be thankit for sayan it again.

I jotted doun a wheen corrigenda, but there may be mair.

p.22, 5th stanza. 'Art, magicianis ...': is that sense? Even tho Mackay Mackenzie[6] has it, that's nae guarantee. Is it no 'Art-magicianis ...' practitioners o *Ars magica*?

p.78, [line 10]: 'in *time* of need' [for 'in till of need']

p.120, 2nd stanza, 2nd line: 'the only a per se'. Naebody has tellt me exactly what that means. Siccar it suld be in italics. I jalouse 'per se' is 'sui generis', and it suld read 'a' (i.e. alltogether) per se', the anerly ane that's aathegither 'sui generis'.

p.122, line 5 gangs a wee thing halt. Micht it be 'secure' for 'sure'? Aiblins the second syllable o 'luve' is voiced, and the accent gaes on the first o 'suppois'. The present standard o scholartis i the Lallans, as ye richtlie observe, is sic that ye canna find out sic matters verra conveniently as ye can for ither leids, sic as auld Latin or medieval French. That's a thing we maun redd up in the New Scotland.

p. 133, LX [note]. I haena a copie o *The Gude and Godlie Ballatis*,[7] but I dout there's naething omittit here, and I dout this isna an owerset frae Luther. Isna there a muddle?

p.246, XCV, 2nd line: I hae heard this sung about Aberdeen, 'And a *gey* time it was then' (as ye also hear 'gey Gordons'). In sic cases nae dout the English has replaceit the Scots. In Greek textual criticism we hae a principle *Praestet lectio difficilior* (Let the mair difficult reading be preferred) as the mair likely to be pitten out by anither. The same micht apply in Lallans.

p. 385, 2nd line: 'suspicor' [for 'suspicior'].

I understand the *Treasorie* has had a guid reception aa ower; Donaldson has issued a directive that aabody maun buy it, but that's ower sair for the maist o the patriots I ken.

Monie are sayan that ye arena a richt judge o your ain poetry, to luik at the outwale ye gie here. Houever that may be, we suld walcome anither anthology frae yersel, this time o makars anerly o the last half-yearhunder, in aa leids, sae's ye micht schaw what ye think maist significant.

I hae typeit out and band thegither, in a braw buik by a skeely binder-chiel, the hale warks o Somhairle and Deorsa, baith for my ain use and delyte and edification in the Gaelic, and also because the mair exemplars there are the mair chance they will hae o survivan in the imminent chaos. Somhairle has gien me his leave to attempt to get his *Dàin* and *Cuilthionn* furthset throu the McCaig Trust; but I dout the Communism and religious backslitheran will connach that enterprise, as it did wi Deorsa's twa years syne. I hae just nou heard a repercussion o your flytan wi the Revd Kenneth[8] anent this. Somhairle had leave last sennicht, but misgogglit the scryvan o his military pass, sae's he culdna travel ayont Embro, and I didna see him; but he scryves he is gyaun on wi the 'Coilltean Ratharsair',[9] the quhilk is a lang screed eftir the manner o *An Cuilthionn*; the first three hundred lines, that I saw, are gey guid. Deorsa lippens til the Epicurean precept, liggan laigh awa frae the steer, and sends an antrin epistil wi a bit sang or owerset frae the Gaelic. The Revd. John MacKechnie has a protick for anither buikie o the type o *The Owl Remembers*[10] and I hae gotten thegither a wheen owersets intil Lallans, amang them ane by a chiel in the royal artillery o Donncha Ban's 'Fareweel til Ben Dorain', guid eneuch.

I was in Glesga a while back and visited the sang-scriever, whas sangs are to be sung sune at a special Scots concert we are organizan here; but we fell intil a political langamachie whaurin he permittit an auld-farrant subjectivism to enter in, and I dinna think he enjoyed the visit ower muckle.

In Embro I hae seen George Davie, far ben in German philosophy o the last bairntime, and nae muckle interestit in onie ither maitters. Verra richt. He got a postponement o sax moneths frae gangin intil the khaki mengie. I am masel deavit frae time to time wi official inquisitions, but sae far havena been molestit; albeid I jalouse I'm gey near the end o the towie nou. Ye'll hae seen the secretar o the Welsh Nationalist Party was brocht afore a sheriff or some sic cratur and gaed aff wi a sma fine; aiblins the heid yins will ca canny likewise; the mair sae wi Tammas Johnston at the tap.[11] But I dinna fash masel avaa, and conserve my neutrality with scrupulous integrity, albeid I bide in a hous (umquhile John Stuart Blackie's,[12] when Humanist here) wi twa refugee Jews, a Cornubio-Britannic naval officer, twa militant Sassenachs and an international-socialist Scotsman of the Ramsay MacDonald order.

That minds me, I was blyth to see the second part o your article on in the *Scots Socialist*. I agreed with it, a thing I dinna aften do wi a political article. There is nae political activity warth speaken o hereabout; the SNP does a devolutionary propaganda, unnoticed; the maist active are the Communists, haudin an antrin demonstration, and an endless series o sma doctrinaire langamachies amang thersels. The masses are dozent and apathetic mair nor ever I mind; and as naebody is in a hurry to finish the war, Hitler also not, we are livean in an orra kind o limbo meantime. The maist hopefu place is the Clydeside, and the maist hopefu movement the Scots Socialist Party (1940), albeid I dout it may get shuntit into the cul-de-sac o pacifism, wi Oliver Brown, the Duke of Bedford[13] and the like. But it is aye gey sma, as is the Donaldson group.

I was blyth to meet Dr Orr at a convene I harangued in Embro a moneth syne, but we had nae lang speak thegither, I luik forrit til anither. I heard tell o anither pronouncement o *The Voice o Scotland* sune, lang bideit for and lang thocht til.

I hope ye got the twa *Spasmodicals* I sent afore the New Year,[14] in spite of the hazards o the route. I ettle to furthset anither sune. A wheen fowk gied me siller for the Scots in Germanie, the quhilk I intend to expend on Gaelic buiks for the Red Cross camp library, an appeal was made in *The Scotsman* for siclike. It intrigues me to think o Gaelic buiks makin a way to Scots captives throu Lisbon, Geneva etc.

I dinna scrieve onie political observes; onie wise man kens the probabilities, but nane kens exactly hou and exactly when things will happen. At the moment I am sweir to pit out ma ain notions sin I hae scryvit three articles recently for Black, the *S.I.* and the Embro student patriots, mair or less anent the same *Kerngedanken*.[15]

I suld be blyth to receive a word frae ye, gin ye're nae ower thrang. And I hope ye're aye crouse and canty baith in Ultima Thule:

with you for us
Douglas Young

[1]   Dr L.A. Waddell (1854-1938). *The British Edda* (1930).
[2]   Roger O'Connor (1762-1834).*Cornikillis of Eri* (London, 1822).
       Dr L. Albert's edition was entitled *Six Thousand Years of Gaelic Grandeur Unearthed* (London, 1936).
[3]   Henri Hubert, *The Rise of the Celts* and *The Greatness and Decline of the Celts*, both London, 1934.

4   *kulturtragende Voelker* — culture-carrying people.

5   Saint Jerome (about AD 340-420) was a great Biblical scholar of the Christian Church. His most important achievement was his Latin edition of the Bible, known as 'The Vulgate'.

6   Ed. W. Mackay MacKenzie, *The Poems of William Dunbar* (London: Faber and Faber, 1932), p.21.

7   *The Gude and Godlie Ballatis* was written and compiled by the brothers James, John and Robert Wedderburn and published in 1567. It is the earliest known metrical treatment in Scots to reflect the aspiration of the Reformation movement in Scotland.

8   Rev. Kenneth MacLeod was Gaelic editor of *Songs of the Hebrides: and other songs from the Highlands of Scotland*, some collected and all arranged by Marjorie Kennedy-Fraser (London, 1909).

9   *Coilltean Ratharsair* —'The Woods of Raasay' in *O Choille gu Bearradh* (*From Wood to Ridge) Collected Poems*, in Gaelic and English translation (Manchester: Carcanet and Edinburgh: Birlinn, 1999), pp. [169]-183.

10   *The Owl Remembers*, Gaelic poems, selected and edited with notes by John MacKechnie. Introduction and English versions by Patrick McGlynn, 1933.

11   Thomas Johnston (1881-1965), Secretary of State for Scotland, 1941-1945.

12   John Stuart Blackie (1809-1895), author of essays and lectures on Gaelic, Greek and German literature.

13   Hastings Russell, 12th Duke of Bedford, a longstanding anti-war campaigner, held public meetings six times in Glasgow.

14   'the twa *Spasmodicals*' were copies of *The Auld Aberdeen Courant and Neo-Caledonian Spasmodical* which Douglas Young produced.

15   *Kerngedanken* - core of ideas.

23. From William Soutar (EUL MS2960.18 f.39)

27 Wilson St
Perth
18 February 1941

Dear Chris,

I ought to have replied to your letters before now, but I had hoped to have a number of notices for you, and delayed in expectation; however only one or two have come my way and, no doubt, you have already seen them by now. It is good news to hear that the run of English reviews is so favourable; and I am not surprised to know that they are in bright contrast to the home breed which in general seems to be always biased by some private grudge or meanness. You would be astonished to find that the *T.L.S.* had been so generous; and had concentrated on the unique elements in your collection – though the reviewer has overlooked that your own contributions are not limited to translation. I have been going through the anthology with much interest and have missed very few items which I had expected to meet; and these few are among the moderns which you had to curtail. Spence and Muir might have had a poem each rather than Ainslie[1] and Ogilvie,[2] & Marion Angus something in the vernacular; and if space had permitted I'd have liked to have seen Montgomerie there too. Incidentally you have been generous to myself and I thought your choice an excellent one.

I am very pleased to learn that the first volume of your autobiography is so far forward, & need hardly say how keenly I await its publication. Many thanks for the promise of a copy; but do not hesitate to drop me from the complimentary list when the time comes should you discover that you have overlooked some other friend who might not be able to get one for himself.

I am sending two copies of *Labour Monthly* with this post.[3] If you are not already in receipt of it please let me know and I'll continue to forward my copy – though, alas, there is every likelihood that before so long it will follow *The Daily Worker*[4] and *The Week*[5] into silence.

I had another visit from Douglas Young who was as peppy as ever, & now contributing to *Scots Socialist* and *Scots Independent*. My only other contact for many months has been a reintroduction to Robin Black through the resurrected *Free Man*. I think R.B. runs it as a kind of mutual friend and memento of times past – for I hear that he prints off only about 100 copies.

What of the lumbago? I trust that it cleared with the snow and has not threatened to return. My mother has been indoors with sciatica for six months – but the rest of us thrive. All the best from the household to Mrs Grieve & yourself; also Michael to whom I'm sending an answering limerick. Cheerio.

Yours aye,
Willie.

---

[1]   Douglas Ainslie (1865-1948) was represented by 'The Stirrup Cup', pp. 16-17. He was a poet, translator, critic and diplomat.
[2]   Will H. Ogilvie was represented by 'The Blades of Harden', pp. 30-31.
[3]   *Labour Monthly* was edited by R. Palme Dutt, Communist theoretician.
[4]   *The Daily Worker* was banned between 21 January 1941 and 26 August 1942.
[5]   *The Week* was a duplicated paper written by Claud Cockburn.

24. From Sorley MacLean (EUL MS2954.13 ff.41-42)

2331381 Sig. S. MacLean
33 Squad, 2 Coy, 1st O. T. B.
Le Cateau Lines,[1] Catterick camp
Yorks
8 March 1941

My dear Chris,

Again I have to apologise for my long long delay in answering your letter of December but here I have practically no time myself, no time to read and very little even to think or write letters. As for writing verse I just cannot because I can't get the simmering time that is necessary for me. That is my chief personal quarrel with the Army life and especially with the Signals training which is excessively technical requiring almost continuous concentration on the most boring of things. In the interval I have had leave, at the very beginning of January. The snow prevented my getting home to Raasay and I had to spend my seven days in Edinburgh with

John who is still teaching there and with Norman who is now a medical student there. I saw much of Caird and of Davie. Caird is in the Searchlights and was then at Dreghorn but I think he has since been moved to Duns or thereabouts. Garioch too is still in Edinburgh as he is over 30 which is still the teachers' reservation age. I have seen *The Golden Treasury [of Scottish Poetry]* and at present I am still waiting for a copy I ordered by post but it should be here any day now. With it I have one quarrel namely that you did not include nearly enough of yourself and perhaps of Soutar. I cannot thank you enough for your over-generous mention of myself and Hay. I hear much from Young and from him I get news of Hay but I don't hear from Hay directly. I am very much looking forward to the appearance of *Lucky Poet* which I hope will be out very soon.

How are things with you? With Orr away and Taylor too Whalsay will now be rather lonely for you but I hope you are getting much work done. I have seen various numbers of the *Scots Socialist* which appears to me the kind of political paper that was very much needed. I hope its circulation will increase but conditions are so difficult and there is so much perplexity as to immediate policy, especially on the war, among left-wingers in general that it will obviously be very difficult for it to get a proper audience. As to general revolutionary influence it or any paper can have at present I don't know. I can only go on my personal feelings which are at sixes and sevens, my personal hatred of the Nazis being even more than my hatred of the English Empire. My own only hope is the one which I had from the beginning, namely that the British and German Empires will exhaust each other and leave the Soviet the dominating influence on the oppressed peoples of all Europe including Britain and Germany and my experience of the Army has only confirmed my long conviction that the only real war is the class war and I see my own little part merely as one that contributes to the mutual exhaustion of the German and British Empires. I support the British just because I think it the weaker and therefore not as great a danger to Europe and European socialism as a German victory would be. I cannot therefore go the whole hog with yourself and Young and Hay though I must confess I find my present position involving me in very bad company politically. I cannot share the belief that Britain is likely to win and, as a result, the fear of a long Nazi domination of Europe is an obsession with me and at any rate I cannot see what the Nazis would give Scotland when they have given Vichy[2] to France and Franco to Spain and Antonescu[3] to Romania and Quisling[4] to Norway. Everywhere their victory has meant the erection to power of the most hateful and reactionary of capitalist thugs. Scotland I suppose would get Maule Ramsay[5] and Ireland O' Duffy[6] and the rule of the Lithgows,[7] Warrens etc.[8] would be made even more permanent. And I am afraid that if they knock out Britain they will knock out the Soviet later and thereby extinguish the greatest, perhaps the only hope of Europe's working classes. I cannot therefore view this war as I would have done the last war when Germany was more hopeful from the working class point of view than Britain was. I know hundreds of so-called Socialists are advancing this viewpoint merely to put a face on their own cowardice and fear of any real Socialist activity but the certain fact that all the Dollans[9] etc. are doing this cannot really alter my own obsessing fear and hatred of the Nazis. God knows my course is indirect and unsatisfactory and based on a very pessimistic outlook whereas at the beginning of the war I was full of hope expecting Germany and Britain and France to knock each [other] out and leave a clear field for the Soviet. This hope was chiefly responsible for the hopefulness that I sometimes expressed in the 'Cuilithionn' but Germany's great victories have done much to dissipate that hope, which was very real, notwithstanding my realisation of the terrible suffering it would all involve.

Forgive my long silence. I shall try to write more often in the near future but here I am so cut off from most of my friends that I have little news of any kind. Give my best regards to Valda and to Michael who will now be getting a big fellow and if you can write me sometime and let me know how things are with [you] I shall be more than grateful. Meanwhile all the best.

Somhairle

1   'Le Cateau Lines' is a reference to Le Cateau-Cambrésis.
2   The collaborationist government in France during the Second World War was known by the place of its headquarters, Vichy.
3   General Ion Antonescu (1882-1946) was the fascist military dictator of Rumania from 1940 to 1944; executed in 1946.
4   Vidkun Quisling (1887-1945) was a Norwegian Army officer whose collaboration with the Germans in their occupation of Norway established his name as a synonym for 'traitor'. Executed.
5   Captain Archibald Maule Ramsay, then Conservative M.P. for Peebles, was interned for four years on account of his pro-Fascist activities and beliefs.
6   Eoin O'Duffy was the leader of the Irish Fascists who fought for General Franco in the Spanish Civil War.
7   Sir James Lithgow (1883-1952) was a leading Scottish industrialist. A chart of his enterprises is given in *The Real Rulers of Scotland*, inset.
8   Sir Victor Warren (1903-1953) was Lord Provost of Glasgow from 1949 to 1952.
9   Sir Patrick J. Dollan (1885-1963) was Lord Provost of Glasgow, 1938-1941.

25. From T. S. Eliot (EUL MS2967/3)

[Faber headed notepaper]
Faber & Faber Ltd Publishers
24 Russell Square
London WC1
24 April 1941

Dear Mr Grieve,

I have read with great interest the part of your long poem which you sent me and wish that we could publish it. It is, incidentally, a very fine monument to Joyce though I am afraid that it gains no advantage from the association until such time as Joyce's later work is properly appreciated. I not only enjoyed the poem but there is a great deal in it that has my sympathy and agreement as well as admiration, but in this time when we are really being starved for paper, it is works like this which must suffer. I hope that you can find a publisher who will venture on it and I am sorry to relinquish it, but it is works which could gain only slow appreciation that must suffer during this immediate crisis.

With best wishes and cordial regards,

Yours sincerely,

T.S. Eliot.

26. From Harry Miller (EUL MS2955.8 ff.16-18)

SCOTS SOCIALIST
FOR A SCOTTISH SOCIALIST REPUBLIC

Editorial Board:-
J. H. MILLER.
OLIVER BROWN.
JOHN MACLEAN.
LAURENCE SELLAR.

Business and Editorial Office:

63 BURNSIDE STREET
GLASGOW C4

18 May 1941

A charaid,

Your letter to hand two days ago: no doubt you will have received my last letter ere now and be in possession of latest actions of the C.I.D.

I regret that among the effects seized from me were some of your MSS including your essay 'A Brief Survey of Modern Scottish Politics in the Light of Dialectical Materialism'. However I am trying to get them back, and Mary Ramsay has reported the theft to PEN.

Just cannot remember how much I told you in last letter but will give a few more details. In all 17 people were raided and all papers, books, lit. etc seized and the people arrested for questioning and subsequently released. Glasgow, Aberdeen, Edinburgh were the main centres of activity. Donaldson is in Barlinnie under 18B and is receiving political rights. [Graham] MacGibbon was arrested and spent 10 days in jail awaiting trial on an arms charge – a miniature arsenal was discovered when police raided him. He was tried last Wednesday and fined £20 to everyone's surprise (who expected a heavy sentence). There is evidence to indicate that London put screws on locally, and the case was rushed thro quietly, no doubt they had good reason to do so.

Three papers were raided and seized, *Scottish News and Comment*,[1] *Free Man* and *Scots Socialist.* They stripped the offices and pulled in the editors whose homes were also raided and all personal effects in books, literature, letters etc taken.

The offices of The Scots Secretariat were raided and two vanloads of stuff removed. R.E. Muirhead was arrested at Bridge of Weir and brought to Glasgow for interrogation. Meikle Cloak was searched and stuff removed, including some powder & shot dating from the Boer War.

Rev. John MacKechnie was likewise treated and both his houses in Glasgow and

Lochgoilhead searched and much stuff removed, including Gaelic literature. Here is a job for PEN: this is twice he has had Gaelic MSS stolen, including priceless stuff by [Alexander] MacDonald.

In Glasgow the following people were pulled in with their effects: R. M. Black, R. E. Muirhead, Liam Smith, Betty Logan, Muriel Gibson, Isa Hillhouse, Graham MacGibbon, Bill Fisher, Rev. John MacKechnie. In Edinburgh: Tom Maxwell, Iain Haig, Walter Ross, and Mrs Hay, mother of George Campbell Hay. Aberdeen saw Douglas Young and Bruce Watson involved.

Donaldson was arrested by some 14 CID men and 3 armed soldiers. He is interned not because of what he had done, but because of what he may do.

Questions by police concerned a large number of people – in fact, everyone active in the National and Republican movements. They were trying to discover pro-Naziism and subsidisation by that outfit, and, of course, the extent of the Independence movement. They were also concerned with our contacts with the Irish and Indian movements, and the various other autonomist movements, Breton, Cymric, Catalonian etc. This only the beginning, I fear, and there are already indications that this is quite big and mixed up in the international situation.

[Tom] Johnston[2] in his recent broadcast laboured the point about near-unity in Scotland but has to admit the presence of what he termed a minority opposition. Questions have also been asked in Westminster about stories of Scotland being ready to make a separate peace with Germany. 'Haw Haw'[3] has also made references to the position in Scotland. Needless to say there is not [a] chance for that outfit doing a deal with Nationalists and Republicans in Scotland. Funny that Hess should fly to see a member of the ruling class, the only bunch who are likely to do a deal with Hitler, and who probably will.[4]

The [Mutual] Aid Committee was also raided and all documents & records seized. Your PO was returned to Muirhead as it had not been paid over to the Treasurer.

Steps have been taken to rouse the people and if you can do anything with your pen to help, please do so. We want the whole business plastered all over the place, so if you can do anything thro' your contacts it will be valuable. The challenge has been made and the fight is on and it is up to everyone to rally to the fight.

We need funds and every kind of help. Support is to hand from ILP,[5] CP,[6] PPU,[7] NCL,[8] University Clubs, [Scottish Council of] Civil Liberties, but it must be pursued and quickened.

I am glad that you have accepted Vice-President of the Scottish Council of Civil Liberties. Will you use your influence on all bodies you are a member of with a view to securing support? Communications, donations, and copies of resolutions should be sent to me meantime.

Thanks for the MSS. I haven't had time yet to consider how best it can be used but the next issue will be devoted to this business and to stuff already on hand. Will write you later in the week.

I am back in Glasgow at my home which has been temporarily made habitable.

Will be glad to hear from [you] soon.

Please excuse hasty scrawl but have written so many letters that I can hardly hold a pen.

Is mise an sgath Alba.

Harry Miller.

PS My mail is examined.

1 *Scotland News and Comment* was edited by Arthur Donaldson.
2 Tom Johnston was Secretary of State for Scotland from 1941to 1945.
3 'Haw Haw' was William Joyce who was tried and executed at the end of the Second World War for making seditious broadcasts for Nazi Germany.
4 Rudolf Hess, Hitler's deputy, crash-landed on a farm in Renfrewshire on 13 May 1941 in an attempt to meet the Duke of Hamilton.
5 Independent Labour Party.
6 Communist Party.
7 Peace Pledge Union.
8 No Conscription League.

27. From Sorley MacLean (EUL MS2954.13 ff.43-47)

Sig. S. MacLean 2331381
Room 7, 2 Coy, 1st Holding Battn
Loos Lines
Catterick Camp
Yorks
15 June 1941

My dear Chris,

I have not written to you for a very long time because for the last seven weeks or so I have been on draft for abroad, somewhere tropical and I have been expecting to leave here any day for that period. That I have not yet gone, however, makes me think that I may be in the country for a while yet, but I may be leaving any day.

How are things with you? Here I am so cut off from Scottish things that I hear little. I am very glad to hear that in America you are getting some recognition of a tangible kind. That *Times Lit.* review of *The Golden Treasury* was pretty good in many ways. I wonder who did it. I did not see any references in the Scottish Press but of course I never see any of the Scottish papers. I did, however, see Douglas Young's review in the *Scots Independent.* As to my own stuff Young and [John] MacDonald, Gaelic Reader in Aberdeen, are trying to get some of it published. What the chances are I don't know but I have left revised and corrected copies with them. The news that I was going abroad stirred me to some activity that I would not otherwise have been stirred to.

You may have heard that Hay has had at least ten days in Saughton jail. I have not heard what has happened to him since as there has been a recent break in my correspondence with Young. I hope he is not too badly treated and I hope that Young himself is still untouched. I know he has been officially visited but that did not at all disturb him, but Young never fusses and is never disturbed. I have never met one of such an aristocratic mind and temperament as Young's.

Give my best regards to Valda and Mike. I hope they are both well. How I wish I could see you all sometime in the not too distant future! Calum is still in Ireland having had now almost two years there – and from all his accounts a very great two years. He will be very sorry ever to leave it but I expect he will come home in September or October. John is still teaching in Edinburgh and Alasdair is finishing his medical course in Dundee while Norman has just finished his first year in medicine in Edinburgh. The two girls are at Portree School and don't get home much now with the curtailment of the steamer services. I have been at home twice in the last two months – the second time, five weeks ago, on embarkation leave. The woods are being rapidly cut down in Raasay, which has changed the look of the place considerably.

Having sent all the books I had with me to Edinburgh when I was put on draft I do not [do] much reading now as anything worth reading is pretty difficult to get here but I do find time to go over most of my ideas on poetry and clarify them somewhat without, however, writing them down, but poetry itself is not coming now but then it comes with me only in bursts and very occasionally. I cannot imagine anything more calculated to exasperate me with boredom and sense of futility and countless minor irritations than the British army. Whatever the political and industrial and journalist rulers of Britain are as psychologists, the army authorities are unbelievable fools who do almost everything that can annoy the army and lower its morale. Their sheer stupidity is in itself a powerful Fifth Column.

I hope to hear from you sometime before I go abroad if I am here some time yet. When I am definitely going to leave Catterick I shall try to let you know. Of course once I leave Catterick my movements will be totally unknown beforehand to myself but I think the chances are that I shall be here some time yet.

Meanwhile all the best.

Somhairle.

28. From Charles Lahr (EUL Gen. 2094/3/1100)

12 Little Newport Street
London WC2
17 June 1941

E. LAHR
Bookseller

Dear Chris & Valda,

I was glad to get your letter and appreciate your kind thoughts. But most of the people we used to know in the old days ([John] Brophy,[1] [Liam] O'Flaherty,[2] [H.E.] Bates[3] etc.) have got on too well and don't need me any more. Brophy edits *John O' London's Books of the Month* I believe. I haven't seen him for years. Bates is and always has been mean. The only two I care for are you and Rhys Davies,[4] mainly because you are both like me and our motto is: 'Take no thought for to-morrow'.

We got £25/-/- from the Public Assistance when the shop went. Most of that was spent on the next place which lasted three weeks. Then we got another £40/-/-which started me here. Esther is looking for a job. The children are evacuated to Welwyn Garden City. Alec Bristow has a £450/-/- a year job at the BBC but he has four kids and never a penny.[5] I am busy digging a ten-pole allotment and am growing all our food, so we won't starve.[6]

I've got a nice shop at the back of the Hippodrome and facing Leicester Sq. Tube Station. Plenty of life and I think I'll do alright.

I expect you have heard the story of the Scotsman who came to London to get a Free Frenchwoman?

I am looking forward to your autobiography.

Excuse this disjointed letter. After every line someone comes in and I have to attend to them.

Will write again soon.

Best wishes to you all.

Yours,

Charles.

[1]   John Brophy (1899-1965), novelist.
[2]   Liam O'Flaherty (1896-1984), novelist.
[3]   H. E. Bates (1905-1974), novelist and short story writer.
[4]   Rhys Davies (1903-1978), short story writer.
[5]   The Grieves had stayed with Alec Bristow at The Hermitage, Cerne Abbas, near Dorchester on their way home from London in October 1934.
[6]   A ten-pole allotment would have extended to c. 300 square yards.

29. From John Gawsworth (NLS Acc.7361/53)

> 1246619 AC2 T.I.F. Armstrong
> SHQ, Central Registry. R.A.F. Station
> West Freugh
> Stranraer
> Wigtownshire
> 28 July 1941

Well, I'm on the right side of the Border at last, and have been these 2 months! Can you spare a proof or copy of the G.T. of S.P. from which you rightly dropped me? If you can't – write all the same. I am exceptionally lonely 500 miles from a friend of culture, from a book, and 15/- a week hardly alleviates the lot. I'm in Crockett's[1] grey Galloway and not *our* Dumfries.Write (and I'll forgie you 30/- you owe!) Love to Valda. John.

[1]   S R. Crockett (1859-1914), minister and Kailyard novelist.

30. From Richard Church (EUL MS2962.1 f.48)

> Curtisden Green
> Goudhurst
> Kent
> 10 August 1941

Dear Mr Grieve:

Thank you for your letter, in which you explain how this wretched misunderstanding has arisen.[1] I realise the position, and I think that you may have imagined in me a symbol of the indifference & ignorance which exist in England toward the Scottish movement, of which you are one of the leading figures. It is a pardonable mistake; for it is a mistake. I am no English tough. I am full of misgivings and uncertainties about political influences on poetry; that is all. I believe *absolutely* in local influences; in roots. Therefore I respect the work which you are doing in re-asserting the traditions of such Scottish geniuses as Dunbar, Hogg and Burns, and in finding a contemporary expression of their spirit.

But in criticism, a man has – so I believe – to judge finally not by his intellectual sympathy, but by the effect of verse upon his very vitals, his instincts. It may be that you and I cannot find points of contact in this way; so our verse is mutually antipathetic. But there is nothing personal in all this, and I should not dream of accusing you of such animosity. There is enough evil of that kind in the world without writers venting it on each other.

So I wish you success, and the vindication of that faith which so many critics have in your work. I shall stick to my own views, but I believe that you will not respect me the less for that. In the long run, it is the only solid ground on which one stands – one's *own* feelings about a work of art.

I hope, therefore, that this clears the air, and assures you again that there is no reality in the suspicion which has tormented you. I am sorry – if it is my fault – that you have had this distress.

Yours sincerely.
Richard Church.

[1] MacDiarmid may have written to Church regarding his review of J. G. Southworth's *Sowing the Spring* (1940) which had a chapter on MacDiarmid. His letter to Soutar refers to this (*Letters* p.182).

31. From F. G. Scott (EUL MS2959 ff.130-131)

> 44 Munro Road
> Jordanhill
> Glasgow W3
> 7 October 1941

Well, well, Christopher!
I plead extenuating circumstances! I've just come across a letter dated 12/7/41

which I believe is the last I heard of you – nearly four months ago – makes me feel tonight like giving a handshake to an old friend just returned from a trip to America. And how'r'e doin'? What's going on? How's the autobio. and the publishers and the other books farin'? God! I hardly know the sound of my own voice.

The extenuation? Well, the Scott family, that's to say all five of us, returned last week to Glasgow from Taynuilt, with hay growing out of our ear-holes (I said *ear*); knees like those of rugby scrummagers; eyes showing the yokel's bewilderment at being in a huge town and lastly my nanesel with the complete orchestral full score of 'The Dance of the Sevin Deidly Synnis' – 215 pages of it, that's to say of some of the best music I ever have written or ever will write – 215 pages of manuscript looking as if put down by the point of a needle, every dot and dash in place – a miracle in calligraphy and expression. You'll see how proud I am of my 'Sevin Deidly Synnis', even the manuscript of it, not to mention the music of it. As you already know the actual composition was completed some months ago but my job all summer (most of it by the way more like mid-November) was to get the damned thing down to the least significant semiquaver exactly in place. I became indeed at times almost fanatical in my pursuit of the absolute, in expressing my ideas. May this be an example to you of how a masterpiece is brought about – a combination of one's finest ideas and one's finest calligraphy. (I'm now thinking of the streamlined dramatic poem you promised me. How's it progressing?)

The only bit of literary contact I had during the summer months was with Willie Soutar who sent me the manuscripts of three volumes of poetry with a request that I'd give him an opinion of them. I think they were called 'Theme and Variation', 'Poems (Lyrics) in Scots' and 'Whigmaleeries', and I believe he intended sending them on to you after I had returned them. Well, I went into Willie's performances when I'd nothing doing or was having a breather off my own concerns and managed to give him a pretty decided verdict that I wasn't much impressed by most of the pieces. The things to me seemed very facile and competent but at the same time void of significance and I just told him so. Willie seems from a subsequent letter to have imbibed from you or somebody a good deal of nonsense of a dialectical kind about the poet being the product of the society he lives in and failed to realize that the real poet *makes* society as well as being made by it. He thinks the contemporary poet just can't possibly produce lyrical poetry in this year of chaos – to which of course I reply, 'Of course not if he isn't enough of a poet'.

I refer to this because I've been thinking a good deal about your own case and my own too, more acutely perhaps after dabbling in Eliot, Spender, Auden and the *New Writing* gang. I've come to the positive conclusion that these contemporaries of ours are certainly the products of the society they've lived in and are bad poets just because of the badness of the society they really reflect and represent. Has it ever occurred to you, Chris, to ask yourself if anything great *could* be done in such a world as the present with its rampant corruption, black markets, gangsters (big and little) and complete lack of idealism of any kind. As I told Dr Rusk, our lecturer on education, I'm beginning to believe there must be a divinity of some kind after all seeing what a hellish mess of things the mere human can make. Three months among the cocks and hens have made me realize as never before that man is an animal – just an animal who can't get far away from the beast and its limitations. Yes, the cocks and hens reminded me of a lot I had for a long time forgotten, and above all that as an artist I had no alternative to an idealistic philosophy. And this goes for you too – on the materialist plane you'll never write anything that matters. If you doubt this, well just cast your eye back over your, is it fifty years of life? and ask and find the answers to a few questions.

Before beginning this letter I wrote a long epistle to Saurat relative to the recent marriage of his daughter Cécile to a Free French soldier who has come all the way from Chile to fight in the French cause. No doubt you'll have seen a notice of Saurat's next book dealing with his mission to Brazzaville in the Congo in support of de Gaulle.[1] I don't know that Saurat has much idea of where he is in the general confusion. He's certainly pretty shaky on the political side of things and like his own Milton is probably on the Devil's side without knowing it. Burt *per contra* has sent his eldest boy into the R.A.F. to train as an air-pilot. Francise continues to enjoy WAAF-ing[2] at the Air Ministry and Lovey started today to do her teacher's training up at Jordanhill, having graduated last June. Willie Johnstone came up all the way to Taynuilt and stayed for only a few days. He's not making much in the way of recovery and seemed anxious to get back to the quiet life he's been having in Selkirk for the past nine months – has had his salary from the L.C.C.[3] stopped since April and worrying about Flora and Elizabeth[4] in America where he has perhaps a remote hope of finding himself if circumstances were a little better. I was real sorry about Willie and a bit put out that he seemed to get it into his head that I was too busy to be bothered with him. His sensitivity about being a bit of a nuisance during his stay made it all rather awkward and I'm hoping to make amends soon by insisting on his coming to Glasgow soon.

To return to 'The Deidly Synnis'. I'm in touch with [Warwick]Braithwaite in Manchester who is conducting the Scottish Orchestra during the winter series of concerts and there's a possibility, even a probability, that he'll give the 'Synnis' its first performance or, what is more likely, play some of the dances. The whole score would take up half an hour to perform and the Glasgow Committee of Management may (they haven't yet) object to F.G.S. taking up as much room on a programme as Beethoven. I'm just at the moment awaiting news from Braithwaite what he thinks about it and the subject is also to be broached at a Committee meeting on Friday. I haven't left much room for Valda & Michael but tell her I've read all about the peats and the days on the hillsides. I hope you're all healthy and happy. Now, Chris, your news per return. I've been missing you.

Ever,

F. G.

---

[1]   *Watch over Africa* (London, 1941).
[2]   Women's Auxiliary Air Force.
[3]   London County Council.
[4]   William Johnstone's wife and daughter.

32. From Sydney Goodsir Smith (EUL MS2960.16 f.23)

40 Warrender Park Terrace
Edinburgh
1 November 1941

Dear Mr Grieve,

It is long since I sent you any poems, but here is a copy of my first collection,[1] together with some more recent ones written since the printing commenced.

I hope you will like some of them, and I should be so grateful if you could perhaps spare the time to offer any criticisms you may think fit.

Anent the recent correspondence in the *New Alliance* I might mention that though born in New Zealand of a Scottish mother and a New Zealand (English descent) father the first words I remember being spoken to me were 'Haud yir wheesht' by my mother. Praps that is why I gave up English for Scots in my poetry; though I myself put it down to the cataclysmic effect of my first reading of *A Drunk Man Looks at the Thistle*, an effect similar to my discovery of the existence of poetry at the age of 13 with *Childe Harold*. I shall never go back to English now, Scots is without any doubt in my opinion the greatest language for poetry in the world.

But enough of this; please accept this small book as the first instalment of my debt to Hugh MacDiarmid.

Yours sincerely,
Sydney [Goodsir] Smith.

[1] *The Skail Wind*, Edinburgh, 1941.

33. From William Soutar (EUL 2960.18 ff.46-47)

27 Wilson St
Perth
16 December 1941

Dear Chris,

It was a pleasant surprise to get your extra note, which puts me a couple of letters down, so I'd better hustle along in time for Christmas & hope that favourable weather will allow the boat to come in. You sturdy islanders – native or adopted – seem to have a weak spot for flu'; but no doubt that 85 mph hurricane swept off the lingering bugs, & I am hoping this scribble finds you all in high fettle, with Michael on top gear in every meaning of the phrase.

You'll be quite exasperated over the autobiography postponements – & I am becoming increasingly impatient too; all the more so now that I know you have set out your conclusions in vol. 1 about 'difficult' art, & have amplified them in vol. 2. I don't believe we shall be so far apart in our final analysis when this is related to social structure. Actually the phase of difficult art which we have had in the west – barring Russia – is bourgeois, though it necessarily contains emancipatory elements. Could you give me chap. & verse for Lenin's and Plekhanov's comments – I am eager

314

to learn out of what social implications they arose. It is this correlatedness of the social moment and its expression which so many of the English university wits have overlooked; they appear to have got quite a lot of Marx *in vacuo* – & never learned his basic teaching on necessity. What M. gave in philosophy & Lenin embodied in social opportunity ought to have been ample instruction against the fallacy that any amount of manipulation with the deracinated technique of Hopkins, Pound and Joyce could possibly evolve the timeous mode – by circumstance & generation they were faced with a fresh necessity. This cuts across F.G. [Scott]'s hankering for the restitution of the Burnsian lyric – just as it eliminates the hope of anybody (outwith the USSR) to write like Mayakovsky. Within the social chaos of a transitional period now *in extremis* I can see no better centre from which to reconstruct a poetic technique than the ballad form which, though traditional, is undated, impersonal, unbourgeois. However, I shan't elaborate in theory but will let you see later on what I have endeavoured to put into practice.

I am sorry Rodgers was a disappointment;[1] and trust you weren't confronted by a triple flop when you turned to the Scots manuscript – though, so far as I can recall, I said nothing that would awaken undue anticipation. Indeed, I shan't be surprised to hear that the lightest of the lot (whigmaleeries) has more of the Scottish spirit in it than either of the other two.

I had an offer the other week from Williams & Norgate *re* the latest bunch of English verse I've collected – a sort of epilogue to the *Tyrants*. Their reader has written a most enthusiastic report of four pages which they enclosed along with their proposals. The two documents were an excellent commentary on what Faber calls 'the government of money values' – in short, these warblings of the Holy Ghost (according to reader) elicited a monetary faith of £27 which, translated into publication, meant no publicity and no library sales and a paper-covered brochure about the size of a glorified temperance tract – and, just in case I should fail to assess the enormity of the risk – could I guarantee 300-400 sales; finally, how many would I purchase myself? It's an old story, of course, but the first time I've had it repeated to me so naively. So it looks as if Geoffrey F[aber] has asked to be put to the test – but perhaps, by that time, the returns on his own collected edition will have had a temporising effect.

I hope you have word about your American issues soon, & that the extension of the war will mean no further delay. What a soss! Anyhow, whatever good fortune there be in 1942, may it come your way. My salutes to Mrs Grieve and Michael, & with them the affection of our house.

All the best,
Yours aye,
Willie.

P.S. Many thanks for the offer of Jones' book which I'd be very pleased to have on loan.[2]

W. S.

1   Soutar had loaned MacDiarmid W. R. Rodgers' *Awake and Other Poems* (1941).
2   MacDiarmid had offered to loan Soutar David Jones' *In Parenthesis* (1937).

34. From L. W. Arthur (EUL MS2966)

MINISTRY OF LABOUR AND NATIONAL SERVICE
EMPLOYMENT OFFICE
LERWICK
7 January 1942

Dear Sir,

I am now advised that you have been accepted for the Course of Training at Thornliebank, Glasgow, and that you should travel in order to reach the Centre not later than 5p.m. on Thursday 15th January, 1942.[1]

Please therefore arrange to travel with the S.S. *Earl of Zetland* on Tuesday 13th January, 1942.

A travelling warrant for the journey from Whalsay to Lerwick is enclosed, and you should call here on arrival when warrants from Lerwick to Glasgow will be issued to you.

Yours faithfully,
L.W. Arthur (in ink)
Officer in charge.

C.M. Grieve, Esq.,
Sudheim,
WHALSAY.

1   MacDiarmid's letter to his wife shows that he didn't leave Whalsay until 4 February 1942 (*New Selected Letters*, p.200).

35. From Valda Grieve (NLS MS27149 ff. 145-147)

Sudheim
Whalsay
Monday 9 February [1942]

My dearest Christopher,

Thank God for the wire – I was dreadfully worried – wondering what on earth had happened to you – Wednesday till Monday afternoon seemed a devil of a time –. What an awful journey you must have had – I hope you had enough money – to see you through – longing to hear all news – this is only a short scrawl – have had a hectic time today – G and I twice to the hill – haircut for Mike & self – & it's now passing 11 o'clock & I've a shirt to iron for G & my dishes to wash –. Haven't been anywhere since you left.

The two airmen came up on Wednesday night – they couldn't find the house &

had to get old Johnnie Eunson to bring them around – had quite a pleasant evening – played darts most of the time – left at 25 minutes to 2 –.

The next night the two Laurenson boys came up & played darts with Mike – finally managed to push them out at the back of eleven.

Friday night Babbie came up – Sat. clear – Sunday afternoon, Mary came in –. Today Titch came in just when we were finishing dinner – nice fried haddock –.

Sent JM down to the pier today to see if he could buy some fish – Jimmie Williamson gave him three beauties – and when he asked the cost said – 'These are to wish your faither luck' –. Very nice of him, wasn't it.

On Saturday JM got some roes & four scallops – gosh they were good – the scallops I mean –.

Longing to get a letter & to hear all news – do take care of yourself –. Give my love to the Scott family.

All my love, dear Christopher, the house seems very empty without you. Valda

P.S. Enclosing U.E. form – letters from B. Fairley – V. Stewart & C. Liberties

It's been snowing heavily since 2.30 pm – quite a few inches of snow – now I hear the wind rising – probably G. [will] not be able to get to-morrow.

36. From Sorley MacLean (EUL MS2954.13 ff.48-55)

Sig. S. MacLean 2331381
No 1 Squadron
7th Armoured Divisional Signals
Middle East Forces
23 February [1942]

Dear Chris,

It is now a very long time since I had direct news of you, but I always wonder how you are and hope that things are going well with yourself and Valda and Mike. I did write you last June but perhaps the letter failed to reach you. At any rate I have had no reply from you and between June and December my movements were so uncertain that I stopped writing almost everybody because I did not know when I was to leave. When I was in London in July and early August I had news of you from MacColl with whom I had some very pleasant meetings. I hope your American publications have come off or will shortly if they haven't already, and I hope that you are working as well as ever.

I am now in Egypt in a tank division and my movements are such that I can take very few books along with me but I have as yet managed to cling to the *Drunk Man* and MacMillan's *Selected Poems*[1] and on the strength of those two I manage to persuade any intelligent Scots I fall in with that there is living in Scotland a greater than Burns. In my sojourn in the army I have come across one remarkable man, a Glasgow cattle salesman called Keith, who has been a professional singer in opera and a member of Sir Hugh [Roberton]'s choir.[2] He had not known your poetry before I met him but now he quotes whole lyrics from the *Selected* in letters to his wife and he goes for the best too. He has shown me many things in them that I had not noticed and in short is about the most fervent devotee of your lyrics that I have known. Incidentally he has as striking an ear for what is best in Yeats and Shakespeare. He is still with me and brightens life for me very much.

As for my own stuff, I have not done anything since September or October and I know now that, if I am ever to write any more verse, it will be very different from what I have written, that it must be less subjective, more thoughtful, less content with its own music, and above all that I must transcend the shameful weaknesses of petty egoism and doubts and lack of single-mindedness that now disgusts me in much of my own stuff. Terrible things happened to me between 1939 and 1941 and my own poetry was a desperate effort to overcome them and that left its marks. But now I think I have overcome all that and, if I survive this fracas, I will certainly cut away everything that deters me from a complete devotion to Scottish poetry and, if I have no longer anything to give to that, it will have to be for me complete devotion to my political beliefs, which are now more uncompromising and far more single-minded than ever. I shall try to do what I can to follow as closely after your single-mindedness and disinterestedness in those two things as I can.

Why I did not write you again between June and Dec., although I did not get a reply to my June letter, I don't very well know. I did expect you to write me in answer but now I sometimes think that I may have promised to write you again and tell you of any changes in my address before I expected you to write me, and when I went to London I had always fresh news of you from MacColl. But all the same I am terribly sorry I did not myself keep in touch with you. I have also lost touch with Davie, who has not answered my last letter and of whom Douglas Young and Sydney Smith had heard nothing when I saw them in November. I wonder where he is. Caird is in Scotland in the educational corps and Hood, I hear, is in Persia. I have, of course, heard nothing from anyone since I left Britain in December but I expect to hear from Young and John, my brother, any day now. Incidentally, I met David Orr for a few minutes in Edinburgh in November but I was in a hurry at the time and saw little of him, to my great regret.

I have read Sydney's book *Skail Wind* and have been much attracted by his more recent pieces in Scots and some of his shorter things in English or Scots-tipped English. I thought they marked a very great advance on his earlier stuff which was so influenced by the contemptible verse of the Auden clique and the (to me) unsuccessful aspirations of Dylan Thomas and his followers of the surrealist or near-surrealist type.

I learned much from my delightful meetings with MacColl whom I got to know properly. My friendship with him I consider, along with my friendship with you, as one of the two or three greatest things in my life. Just now I am bitterly sorry that my own carelessness since last June (or May) has interrupted my hearing from you.

I am afraid this will have to suffice or the letter will be too heavy for the regulations but I'll write you again very shortly and hope you will find time sometime to write me. Meanwhile kindest regards to Valda and Mike and all the best to you all three.

Yours sincerely,
Sam.

[1]   Hugh MacDiarmid, *Selected Poems* (by himself), London, 1934 (in Contemporary Poets series).
[2]   Glasgow Orpheus Choir.

37. From Michael Grieve (NLS MS27151 f.4)

Whalsay
27 March 1942

Dear Daddy I hope you are well. We are having dreadful weather yet, a fresh fall of snow fell to-day. I have been expecting my Westerns for a long time. Our stack is fast disappearing so we are waiting for a fine day to come so we can go to the hill. I hope you will soon get my bell, my bike is still O.K. And our holidays have started and I am enjoying myself very much indeed.

So cheerio Daddy
your loving Michael
[followed by 53 kisses and mini-drawings of 'cow', 'ship', 'hen egg' etc.]

38. From Valda Grieve (NLS MS27149 f.178)

Whalsay
1 June [1942]

My dearest Christopher,
The weather here is hellish – cant get on with any thing – Today received letter from Dugald – & he says you are looking extremely well – I'm glad – he was also particular to stress re. your talk in the Central Hotel – that you drank three gingers – hells teeth – I won't know you – Was going to have a big night tonight – packing – with the assistance of an ex Welsh miner[1] – he's a driver in the R.A.F. camp – & hates it like hell – you know they rather look down him – but at about 7pm it started to rain & its rained & is still pouring cats & dogs – Bad luck!

The weather has really been awful for the past month – When next you write please give me the address of the Scotts laundry – I will have to send the clothes on the bed there – for I'll be needing it up to the last minute.

Despite the fact Mikes been away such a lot – he was top again in the exams 147 marks – against Mary Jeans 128. – he only had 8/50 for sums – none right – but 2 marks for each one attempted.

Enclosing two letters. – Fraid there isn't much news & I don't seem to have made much progress with the packing – when the muddle is cleared up a bit – I expect I'll find I've done quite a bit – if we could only get a nice warm day – I'd be able to wash the mats & get them dried & packed away –. I managed to do the wool rug & one of the upstairs one's between the showers – but its so much easier when one can just

Hugh MacDiarmid during Industrial Conscription 1942-1944.
Photo Charles Nicoll by permission of the MacDiarmid Estate.

go ahead slog at it –.

Good night my darling Sorry for this unsatisfactory letter – but I'm almost asleep – wish to God I was on the boat.

All love

Valda

[1]   Charles Davies.

39. From William Johnstone (NLS MS27155 f.119)

William Johnstone
Camberwell School of Arts and Crafts
Peckham Road
London
7 July [1942]

Dear Chris,

Please forgive my being so long in answering your letter. Francis came to London [,] my mother died and so on. First let me say how sorry I am to hear about you losing your job.[1] It all seemed so promising. If there was anything I could do to help you may be sure I would do it but at the moment there is absolutely nothing. In every direction I am tied hand & foot by Govt. control. I hope that something will develop. Give my good wishes to Valda.

Have posted you a copy of my new book.

With good wishes, Chris, as you know I am all for you. This putting of this new all this is damned pest.

yr sincerely,

William Johnstone.

P.S. I hate to give advice but don't you think some reconciliation with Edwin Muir should be undertaken. He is in a strong position with this British Council. I know how you feel about it all but consider the thing. Muir would be helpful.

again good wishes,

W. J.

You should be at the bloody British Council.

[1]   Johnstone refers to the job MacDiarmid had with Messrs Mond Nickel Coy Ltd when he first came to Glasgow in 1942 (*MacDiarmid*, p.461). MacDiarmid lost the job because women had been called up to do the job at a lower rate.

40. From John Singer (EUL MS2960.11 ff.2-4)

c/o W. MacLellan

240 Hope Street
Glasgow
6 October 1942

Dear Chris,

I feel I haven't thanked you properly for all the trouble you went to about my book, and your encouragement generally. I'm afraid I haven't been very helpful about your flat, but here the plain fact is that try as I could (in the time available) I drew a blank every time. Simply couldn't find a place at all – not even a room for myself, and am still living at a nightly hostel, and I'm beginning to really dislike it. But will keep on trying.

How's your leg?[1] Are you back at work and if so, what does it feel like?

I received a copy of *Cage Without Grievance* from Graham the other day (I've agreed to give him *The Fury of the Living* in return) together with your *Free Man* article.[2] He had reacted rather bitterly to your opinions and appended some scathing remarks.

You've definitely alienated that group, but on the whole I think rightly and inevitably so (for the time being) but if they've got any spunk they should get over it and begin really thinking, experiencing and creating.

The Fury of the Living appears in about two weeks. Am hard at work on 'Journey to Triumph' and further poems, and a collection of thirty short stories (I hope!).

Am reading *San Michele*.[3] David Martin sent me a nice letter from Hampstead full of good cheer and compliments. He thinks the poems are much more revolutionary than they seemed on a first reading.

Have you heard from your family and when are they coming down? I do hope things work out smoothly.

Have you seen MacLellan since he returned from London? I believe he met quite a few interesting people down there, and your contacts were useful. Martin isn't doing too badly apparently. He hasn't managed the *Evening Standard* post, but is making up nicely by heaps of freelancing and now a B.B.C. script.

When is your next 'quarterly' out? What about David Archer's publishing ideas [?] Will the *Free Man* article affect your connection (and [Robin]Black's[?])

Writing is the grandest and most satisfying trade in creation.

Yours sincerely,

John.

---

[1]   The medical Certificate stated, 'Mr Christopher Grieve is unfit for work following an accident sustained, during the course of his employment on 2nd Sept. 1942'. (NLS MS 27214 f. 16).

[2]   *Cage without Grievance* (Glasgow: Parton Press, 1942) and *The Fury of the Living* (Glasgow: MacLellan, 1942) were the first books of W. S. Graham and John Singer. MacDiarmid's *Free Man* article cannot be traced in the NLS.

[3]   *The Story of San Michele* by Axel Munthe (1857-1949) was first published in London in 1929.

41. From Douglas Young (EUL MS2961.18 ff.9-10)

[H.M. Prison, Saughton]
14 January 1943

Dear Christopher,[1] I have long wanted to thank your Bardship personally for joining the cortège of July 18th to this hydropathic, but my allowance of correspondence is exiguous & even in this I must devote space to chores of writing I ask you to do for me. Sometimes I look at your photograph at Elderslie among the Scots Worthies (*quantum mutati ab illis*,[2] how different from Lochgoin's), & often read in your *Treasury*, so you are as they say with me in spirit. Indeed, just as all Russian prose-writers 'flew out of Gogol's "cloak"' & all Latin Alexandrians were 'cantores Euphorionis' (Euphorio's songsters), so all Lallans makars from now will be of Clan MacUisdean (though I note the dodo J. W. Oliver[3] telling Soroptimists that Scots poetry stops with Violet Jacob). And the Gaels too. I have three wonderful letters from Somhairle, the last Oct. 6th, and on Dec. 18th, I think, I had a vivid sensation of his being present & impelling me to get ahead with work on his poems. Please write him by airgraph (Sig. S.M. 2331381, Signal Troop, 1st R.H.A., M.E.F.) that in the last 5 days I have drafted a near-literal assonantal projection into English of the First part of *An Cuilthionn*, & hope to have the whole done before I emerge (8 weeks).[4] I choose English, not Lallans, to reach a wider public, but it is like transliquidating whisky into ditch-water. I wrote Hay, urging him to collect & publish his pieces forthwith & hope you will give him a preface. Please write my parents (Ardlogie, Leuchars) thanking them for Dwelly's dictionary & the reading-glass, & say I have a warm comfortable job & survive quite well, & wish my mother many happy returns of her birthday. Give Wintringham[5] my *personal* good wishes for his campaign, & say that, while I can see no use in Scots folk sending 'representatives' to the Duma, if he thinks it worthwhile to go, I hope they will send a non-British English democrat rather than an anti-Scottish North Briton. Tell Murison[6] (Laurelhill nursery, Stirling) I invite him & Hilda for Jan. 28th or after, and defend my Gesserant = metallically flashing (as you & Soutar also have used it, I think) by analogy with Magenta = (1) a battlefield (2) a synthetic dye, (3) a colour. Cf. also such usages as 'a peach complexion'. I was glad to read Muir arranged a concert for F.G. Scott. What news of MacColl & Davie? And Sydney Smith? Robin Black owes me an answer to mine of 5th Nov. which I don't even know if he got. Seeing the photographs of Dwelly printing his dictionary I think of RM's long devoted work on *The Free Man*, which I trust will yet find its way in here. The *S.I.* advertises MacLellan's edition of S.M.[7] with [William] Crosbie's[8] illustrations, – 500 years hence at the Sotheby's of the day the millionaires, or the commissars, will scramble for it. A housebreaker here, bred in the slums off the High St., makes poems with all the verve & some of the vocabulary of 'Twa Mariit Wemen',[9] – what's bred in the bone will come out on the tongue. I am looking forward to seeing the new work by you which R.M. was thinking of putting out every so often. I hope you are in good vein & have got comfortably settled with your family somewhere around the doubtless erubescent Clydeside. Yours aye. Douglas Young.

1. This letter has been copied as written – without paragraphs in order to make the maximum use of the three pages allowed.

2. 'quantum mutati ab illis' – 'how much changed from what they were'.

3. J. W. Oliver edited (with J.C. Smith) *A Scots Anthology Verse in Scots from 14th Century to present day* (Edinburgh, 1949).

4. Douglas Young had been sentenced to a year's imprisonment in 1942 for refusing '[...] compliance with any British Conscription proposal on the grounds of Scottish patriotism [...]'. (*A Scot's Free Fight*, The Scottish Secretariat, Glasgow, n.d.).

5. Tom Wintringham (1898-1949) contested North Midlothian for Common Wealth on 5 February 1943 and lost by 869 votes.

6. David Murison, later editor of the Scottish National Dictionary, accepted alternative service.

7. The first edition of Sorley MacLean's *Dàin do Eimhir agus Dàin Eile* (Glasgow, 1943).

8. William Crosbie (1915-1999), painter.

9. William Dunbar's ' The Tretis of the Twa Mariit Wemen and the Wedo'.

42. From O. H. Mavor (James Bridie) (NLS Acc. 7361/14)

3 Camstradden Drive East
Bearsden
Dumbartonshire
Bearsden
4 March 1943

My dear Grieve

Thank you indeed for your most generous-hearted letter & for the 'Cornish Heroic Song'.[1] It is a strange song, with its twisted, writhing, cacophonic, jungle-growths of dictionary tricks & the sudden burst through of magnificent marching & ringing verse. I hadn't read it before.

I wonder why your prose is so bloody. Power told me the other day that it used to be clear & logical & shapely & indeed, I've a vague remembrance of some of it in the early days ... Anyhow, who the Hell am I to talk about prose? Or verse either for that matter.

Could we meet sometime? We have never talked to each other at all. I'd probably bore & irritate you, but it might be worth while trying – 'As I had taken sour John Knox into an opera house at Munich, fastened him into a front row box & danced off the ballet in trousers and tunic'. But perhaps your austerity relaxes from time to time. When are your free times, if any? I'm more or less a masterless man just now.

Who is publishing the new book? I'd like to order it early.

Again many thanks & forgive me.

Yours sincerely,

O. H. Mavor.

(James Bridie)

1. Caledonian Press, Glasgow, 1943.

43. From A. S. Neill (NLS Acc.7361/14)

Summerhill School Ltd
Festiniog
N Wales
8 March 1943

My dear Grieve,

Fine, man, to hear from you again. Aye, pity we didna meet at Kil[quhanity] House. I had a good time around Ochiltree and got a lot of good stuff, but much more by letters. I don't know Bruce's book[1] (delighted if you will lend it to me) but I think I have seen most of the matter printed about B[rown]. What I can't get is the truth about his father. Some say the vivid phrases in *[The] House [with the Green Shutters]* spring from his dad's racy vitality in speech, but there is also evidence that he never met his dad till he went to Oxford. I want to view his life from a psychological point, wondering (so far in vain) what gave him such a hell of a hate to express in his bodies,[2] and indeed he was touchy and quick of temper with his pals, but apparently a likeable bloke.[3] Barbie isn't Ochiltree.[4] It is nowhere. When I wrote that silly rubbishy book *The Booming of Bunkie* nearly 30 yrs ago Bunkie was nowhere, just vaguely situated at Lunan Bay.[5] You mention his girl. Accounts differ. Some say it was a bad match, others the opposite. But interesting that the book is *The House with the Sex Shutters*. No passion, no love, his women are inferior fowk ... Mrs Gy the sick fool,[6] the daughter dying,[7] Wilson's wife a masculine woman. [8] B[rown] must have been most repressed. He wrote a schoolboy book *Love and a Sword* with hardly a sign of his genius in language; in it his love passages are stilted and artificial.[9] Must have been scared of sex.

God only knows when I'll get down to the book. Am on one on education of tomorrow, and must get it out soon to try to counteract the bloody fools who are planning for tomorrow ... TUC, CP, NUT, all planning outward things like schools and subjects, ignoring the psychology of the kid all the time.

Saw the Muirs in Edinr in Jany. Willa after a long illness looked better but not herself. Edwin as ever. I often see J. B. Salmond when I go north. He also is in bad health. Dreadful thing time, forcing a man to be aware of his kidneys and prostate and sapping his work.

Man, Grieve, I have a complex that handicaps me. Fowk say that you are a great poet, but I simply canna appreciate poetry, never could much, and 4 yrs under [George] Saintsbury[10] may have killed any embryonic ability to love it. I got badly mauled the other night when in a conversation I said that there shd be a new division with new names, claiming that if 'The Hound of Heaven'[11] is poetry, 'Lochinvar'[12] and most of Pope's verse are something else.

Aye, it's a long cry back to one night in Montrose Muir and you and I sat over a dram. Luckily I never look back with emotion, although I do forward, wanting to live 1000 yrs to see what will happen. I guess I'll live long enough to see the hell of a class war which began in 1939.

All the best, laddie, and if you send me that book you'll have it back safe and sound.

Yours,
A.S. Neill.

1   *Twilight in Scotland* (1934) by Norman Bruce.
2   'His bodies' are the village gossips who stand at the Cross.
3   Neill refers here to his plan to write a biography of George Douglas Brown, the author of *The House with the Green Shutters* (London, 1901). This plan did not come to fruition.
4   The scene of the novel is the fictional village of Barbie.
5   *The Booming of Bunkie* was published in 1919.
6   'Mrs Gy' is Mrs Gourlay who is married to the master carter, John Gourlay.
7   Janet.
8   'Wilson's wife' was the wife of James Wilson, Gourlay's competitor.
9   *Love and a Sword* by 'Kennedy King', London, 1899.
10 Professor of English at Edinburgh University from 1895 to 1915.11Francis Thomson's *The Hound of Heaven* was published in 1908.
12 By Sir Walter Scott.

44. From William Johnstone (EUL MS2951.9 f.2)

London County Council
Camberwell School of Arts and Crafts
Peckham Road
London SE5
17 March [1943]

Dear Chris,
Excuse short note as I am terribly busy. Thank you for your letter. Had tea with M. Saurat yesterday. He said the reading of your poems was the 'highlight' of the poetry reading. He said the French were so interested in the *sound* and were all on edge, then the *sense* from Saurat's reading just struck home. We agreed that the brevity was the thing as all were left feeling they wanted more. They shall have it!
    With much affection to Valda & yourself and the son.
    William.

45. From T. I. F. Armstrong (John Gawsworth) (EUL MS2948.7 f.17)

1246619 T.I.F. Armstrong
242 Squadron R.A.F.
B.N.A.F.
2 April 1943

Dear Chris,
How flourishes the literature of Alba? I add little to it I fear, now or at any time, but I keep a journal, full of curious stuff, for this is a curious and interesting part of the world.
    Has a copy of my selected poems *Legacy to Love* reached you from Collins?[1] I gave your address ere I left.

I fear your *Golden Treasury* never reached me. Could you spare one? It would be an absolute life-saver out here where we have no books whatever, and there's much in that vol. that I desire to study and learn. Proofs will do: but send, send, I pray and also a decent longish letter with news of new books, and of Valda, and your health and general well-being.

It's 9 years since Great James St, and I've only heard a handful of times from you since. Comfort my mud, and mosquitos, and snow, and sand with Alba's best, and I'll drink you down when I return.

Thine, yearning for intelligent conversation,
John (Gawsworth)[2]

1   *Legacy to Love :Selected Poems 1931-1941*, London, 1943.
2   This letter was countersigned 'L. W. Coulthard' probably to comply with wartime regulations.

46. From John Singer (NLS Acc.7361/53)

Million[1]
New Left Writing
c/o MacLellan
240 Hope Street
Glasgow
30 June [1943]

Dear Chris,

Thanks a lot for your welcome letter. To deal with the most important matter right away – I know you will understand what has happened when I tell you that I erred rather badly in estimating the size of the quarterly, 64 pages, in relation to the MSS in hand. The fact is that MacLellan[2] and I have more than enough to pack the thing, and this excludes a number of plates. But I'll be honoured to include 'Scottish Proletarian Literature' and some more of your poetry in the second collection which will appear late this year, I hope.[3] You are, of course, already represented by 'A Poet Rejects a Right-Wing Plea'.[4]

I really believe *Million* 1 is not too bad. There are contributions by Winifred Horrabin,[5] yourself, Sean O'Casey, Langston Hughes,[6] Reg Moore,[7] John Atkins,[8] S. D. Tremayne,[9] Mulk Raj Anand,[10] George Borodin,[11] Sydney [Goodsir] Smith, some left-wing poets, and an article with two colour plates on the painting of George Hannah,[12] an article with illustrations on 'Soviet War Cartoons' by the English editor of *Soviet War News*, and a long article by myself on 'Literature and War' – which I believe will make them sit up! The price will be 1/9d, and publication date about the third week of Aug.

I'm chairman on Sunday 4th [July] (I believe) at the New Art Club, when MacColl recites and discusses your poetry. My first visit for a month. I've also been inveigled into giving another talk – on 11 July – subject, 'The effect of historical development

Cover of *Million* 1.
By permission of the National Library of Scotland.

on art' ... Whoohh ...

I hope your talks are successful. How's the heavy industry? Sorley's book is on the way. I've given Bill your new address, and he'll pass it on to [Maurice] Lindsay.

Thanks for your good wishes – they are heartily returned. Regards to Valda (tell her her bookshop manner is in the best tradition – if I were a customer I'd be awed).

Yours,

John.

1   There were three issues of *Million* 1943-1946.
2   William MacLellan, the publisher.
3   'Scottish Proletarian Literature' appeared in two parts in the second and third issues; pp. 14-24 and pp. 53-59 respectively. MacDiarmid's poetry was not represented again.
4   *C.P.* II, pp. 1317-1319.
5   Co-author (with J.F. Horrabin) of *Working-Class Education*, London, 1924.
6   Langston Hughes (1902-1967), US poet, novelist and playwright.
7   Reginald Moore (1914-1990), joint editor (with Jack Aistrop) of *Bugle Blast, an anthology from the services*, London, 1943.
8   John Atkins (1916-2009), former literary editor of *Tribune* (before Orwell), teacher, creative writer and critic.
9   Sydney D. Tremayne (1912-1986), born in Ayr, worked for 43 years as a journalist, published six volumes of poetry including *The Turning Sky*, (London, 1969).
10 Mulk Raj Anand (1905-2004), novelist. *Untouchable* (London, 1935), and *Coolie* (London, 1936).
11 George Borodin (1903-1996), consulting surgeon and author.
12 George Hannah (1896-1947), founder-member of New Art Club and The New Scottish Group. *The Charwoman* (1943) and *Street Scene* (1943) were reproduced in *Million* 1. Although John Singer's death was reported in *Scottish Art and Letters* 5 (Glasgow, 1950), he wrote to MacDiarmid on 11 November 1965. (EUL2960.11 f.3).

47. From F. G. Scott (EUL Gen.887/77 f.77)

Willie brought back MacMillan's
Selection of Poems: I had given him
the book for Saurat's poetry reading!

BROLAS
TAYNUILT
Argyll
8 August 1943

My dear Christopher

I sent you on Friday copies of the *Studio* and the *New English Weekly* which I knew would buck you up. Willie Johnstone arrived here the day after Lovey and I left Glasgow, and he stayed on till last Tuesday going on to Galashiels and Midlem (Selkirk) and returning to London about the middle of the month. The Sorabji you can keep a hold of (I managed to get half-a-dozen copies from London) and the Saurat [you] can keep till I return. I'm specifically writing now because of a proposition I made to Willie that the three of us should make a 3-pronged volume of poetry, painting and music fit to challenge the best producible anywhere in Europe.

Cover of *Poetry Scotland* 1.
By permission of the National Library of Scotland.

We discussed the idea from many points of view and agreed that six to ten of your lyrics taking up twenty to forty pages would be the most convenient size of volume. The question of whether your lyrics would be new ones or old is a more ticklish point to settle – it being problematic whether either you or I could produce to order either ten or even six items to rival our very best. On the other hand I reckon I could get together half-a-dozen settings like 'Lourd on my heart';[1] 'Sunny Gale';[2] 'The Man in the Moon';[3] 'Country Life'[4] which are perhaps 'good enough' for the occasion and would have a kind of semi-novelty as music at any rate. The big task would of course be to start with a clean slate, everybody that's to say starting from scratch (which suggests a 'slate'!) and doing something better than our former best. I'm game, Willie's game – are you? It's time Scotland, and England too, wakened up to the fact that three Borderers constitute a force that can't be damned with faint praise and just 'negleckit'. I expatiated largely on the Border aspect of the business to William – we're neither Glasgow, Edinburgh, Aberdeen, Orkney nor West Highland – What are we but just Borderers in our tenacity to win through against the opposition? It may be quite a fanciful misconception but I really did feel something in London very like what Burns must have felt when he appeared before the Edinburgh intelligentsia – a David living, up against a Goliath dead. And you'd have felt the same had you been in my shoes! Willie Johnstone is sick to death over the painting racket in London too – so what have you to say about it all?

Ever

F. G.

---

1   *C.P.* I, pp. 204-5.
2   *C.P.* I, pp. 67-8 .
3   *C.P.* I, pp. 24-5.
4   *C.P.* I, p. 31.

48. From Mary Baird Aitken (EUL MS2942.1 f.1)

11 Hillside Street
Edinburgh 7
24 October 1943

Dear Christopher Grieve,

May an old Broughtonian – another of those who came out of George Ogilvie's loins, send you thanks for your continued fidelity to your Scots spirit of intellectual beauty; your 'intervening as a Scot in the European debate' at all points; & your being an 'unrepentant highbrow'?

I have laughed at you a good deal in *Lucky Poet* – 'your flyting'! Just the way you used to speak at 'The Lit'. You enjoyed yourself then too. I have a bone to pick, however. So far as I can see, no mention of George Ogilvie. Is the memory of that opal mind perhaps too precious?

I am glad you have managed to keep your contact with the folk, & that you are finding satisfaction among them on Clydeside.

When I have felt the Scots spirit of intellectual beauty growing woolly, I have many a time taken a dose of you in Prose or Poetry.

With best wishes.

Yrs sincerely,

Mary Baird Aitken.

49. From Maurice Lindsay (EUL MS2953.3 f.147)

32, Athole Gardens
Hilhead
Glasgow W2
[1943]

Dear Mr Grieve,

Yesterday, William MacLellan and I founded 'Poetry – Scotland'.[1] Its going to be for Scotland what Tambimuttu's 'Poetry London' is for England, we hope all that's best in the corpus of Scottish verse will be represented.

I hope you'll agree with the scheme, and contribute some of your new work. At present by law, we're only allowed [to] envisage one number, which we hope to get out soon.

You'll get our official letter, and I will be talking to you about it next week, but he thinks it might be a good plan if I came to visit you whilst still on leave.

By way of a calling card I leave the MSS of my book of poems at present in the press.[2]

I'd like to visit you on Sunday morning if you don't mind.

Sincerely,

Maurice Lindsay.

[1]   *Poetry Scotland* Number One, was published by MacLellan in 1943 with a cover design by William Crosbie and an introduction by Compton Mackenzie. MacDiarmid contributed 'Two Memories', *C.P.* I, p. 671, 'The Glass of Pure Water', *C.P.* II, pp. 1041-3, and an article 'Poetry in Scotland Today'.

[2]   *No Crown for Laughter*, London, 1943.

50. From J. A. White (EUL MS2967/10)

Methuen & Co. Ltd
Publishers
36 Essex Street
Strand
London WC2
26 January 1944

C. M. Grieve, Esq.

27 Arundel Drive
Battlefield
Glasgow 3

Dear Mr Grieve,
We have now considered with our Solicitors the question of Mr. Rickword's claim in respect of your reference to him on page 172 of *Lucky Poet*.[1] The sentence seems probably to contain a misstatement on a matter of fact. We must therefore alter it, and we propose to do so by substituting a fresh printing of pages 171 and 172. Would you be kind enough to let me have 'copy' for two lines of unexceptionable matter which can be substituted for the two offending lines on page 172.[2]

We do not propose to take any further steps, and as soon as the new page has been printed and substituted we shall resume the sale of the book. Our Solicitor is writing to Messrs Spiro to that effect today.

The claim is a fantastic one, but there is just that justification for it that you have, it seems, made a misstatement of facts.

The sooner you can let me have the new 'copy' the sooner the page can be cancelled and the book placed on sale again.

With kind regards,
Yours sincerely,
J. A. White.

[1] The lines which Rickword complained about are, 'Edgell Rickword is about the only person with some idea of Nationalism, but even he was in the Black-and-Tans.'
[2] MacDiarmid agreed to substitute, 'Hardly any of the London *literati* has any idea of nationalism or does not aid and abet imperialism in one way or another.'

51. From J. D. Fergusson (EUL MS2948.2 f.1)

4 Clouston Street
Glasgow NW
8 February 1944

My Dear Grieve
I expected to see you at the Party's[1] Burns night and thank you for your most sympathetic letter about my book,[2] I didn't get to the meeting, and should have written before now for I appreciate your letter which makes me feel with you in what you have fought so courageously for, that we don't see each other often isn't so bad if we're in sympathy. I'm sorry you can't get at your work but there seems to be always something. You needn't worry you've already done so well and you can make something of the present state of affairs.

My very best wishes to you both.
Yours very sincerely,
J. D. Fergusson.

[1]   The 'Party' here is presumably the Scottish National Party of which MacDiarmid was a member at the time. MacDiarmid was then working in Mechan's on Clydeside during industrial conscription.

[2]   *Modern Scottish Painting*, Glasgow, 1943.

52. From M. F. Somerville (NLS Acc. 7361/15)

R. MELVILLE, Chairman
J BROWN, Secretary
TELFER. Treasurer
C. M. GRIEVE. J.P. Publicity
H. ANDERSON. Convener
M. F. SOMERVILLE. Organiser

SCOTTISH UNION OF EX-SERVICE MEN AND WOMEN
205 BUCHANAN STREET, GLASGOW C.1
(REGISTERED UNDER WAR
CHARITIES ACT, 1941)

Bankers:
ROYAL BANK OF SCOTLAND
(Hope Street Branch)

14 March 1944

Dear Sir,
A meeting will be held in the office of Mr W. P. Jones, Solicitor, 217 Buchanan St, on Friday 17 March at 8p.m.[1]
Business – Reorganisation
Please make a special effort to attend.
Yours faithfully,
M. F. Somerville.
Organiser

[1]   The Association asked Guy Aldred to stand as a candidate for Peace in Glasgow Central in the 1945 General Election. He stood as an Independent Socialist and received 300 votes on 5 July that year.

53. From Nancy Cunard (EUL MS2946.10 f.5)

Permanent Forwarding Address:
C/o National-Provincial
97 Tottenham Court Rd
London
26 March [1944]

Dear Hugh MacDiarmid

Thank you so much for your good letter and here is a copy of my translation of your poem (which I like even better now, after closest acquaintance with it).[1] I have sent it to the French friend I mentioned to you, the one who okays for literary exactness, but I don't think he will find many things to change. I'll let you have the final version, the one that goes to the French Delegation for distribution. I wish they could pay us, but they say that in the present conditions it is impossible to do this, and were apologetic.

What to do about adding the amplification of the lines you sent me – I mean, the extra four lines around the image of the compass in its binnacle? I like them very much. Should I *add* them to the end; why not? Yes, do let us do that. Here you have a copy of the part I took from the longer poem; it is the *end* of it, you remember? And to add these lines would be good. It might be too late, I think *not*, though, to add them to your poem sent in Anthology to the publishers.

I will await your answer on this latter point.

I read your letter to Sylvia and Val yesterday.[2] We then rushed to Sylvia's copy of *Lucky Poet*, found the reference to Edgell ...[3] Well, I do think, even without knowing any of the detail, that it is a bit thick asking for damages, etc. on that score. Of course Edgell was was in the B[lack] and T[ans], and he hated it bitterly and was aghast at being in all that; I remember well his telling me of it many times in the days I used to see him a lot, in 1933-4. I should have thought that an explanatory note in the next edition, or a rectification etc. 'tipped in' to the present edition would have been far more to the point than these 'measures', solicitors, etc. I hope it comes out alright though for you.

Don't bother to answer this. I can see how madly busy you are, and appreciate your letter. Just send a card, please, saying if I AM to add the four lines as I would like to, to the typescript of your poem that is finished long ago, I mean with the publishers. I'll add them in any case to the French translation.

And now the coastal ban affects me – all those not regularly domiciled here have to leave ... I go to near Yeovil for a while, and will write from there giving you new address. But I AM here till Friday next.

Anyway if you address me care of Sylvia Warner From Vauchurch, Maiden Newton, Nr Dorchester I shall get it next day. Am posting you to-morrow the *Our Time* with her review of you. Keep it.

All best greetings, hoping to meet again,
Nancy Cunard.

---

[1]   The poem referred to is 'The Fall of France' *C. P.* II, pp.1320-1321. It was included in *Poems for France written by British Poets on France since the War* Collected by Nancy Cunard Published by La France Libre, London, 1944. The translation was included in *Poèmes à la France*, 1939-1944 Réunis et Traduits de L'anglais par Nancy Cunard avec une préface, des notes biographiques et le portrait des auteurs and published by Pierre Seghers in Paris in 1947. The French title was 'La Chute de la France'.

[2]   Sylvia Townsend Warner (1893-1978), novelist, poet and short story writer, lived with Valentine Ackland from the early 1930s until her death in 1969.

³   In this letter Nancy Cunard supports the view that Rickword was in the Black and Tans. However, in *Edgell Rickword: A Poet at War* (Manchester, 1989), Charles Hobday writes: 'The story that Rickword had been a member of the Black and Tans (the force of British ex-servicemen employed on police duties in Ireland during the War of Independence in 1920-1921, who became notorious for atrocities against the civilian population) seems to have circulated quite widely at this time. [...] His sympathies with Irish republicanism, developed as early as 1916, would have made him the last man to volunteer for the Black and Tans; even if he had, a one-eyed man invalided out of the Army would not have been accepted; and in 1920-1921 he was fully occupied, first in keeping his terms at Oxford, then in supporting his family by contributing to the *Daily Herald* and the *New Statesman*. The only foundation for the story seems to have been the fact that he had been stationed in Dublin with his regiment for two short periods in 1917-1918.' (p.203).

54. From J. A. White (EUL MS2967/10)

Methuen & Co. Ltd
Publishers
36 Essex Street
Strand
London WC2
3 April 1944

Dear Mr Grieve,

Your letter of March 31, with the corroborative evidence which it contains of the correctness of your statement in *Lucky Poet* about Mr. Rickword, is very interesting. But I think that things having gone as far as they have – the book has been back on sale for some time – we had better leave them as they stand.

Incidentally, Mr Rickword's Solicitors at one stage augmented the original denial of Rickword's membership of the Black-and-Tans by saying he was never in Ireland at any relevant time.

I should say that in any case it would be a very difficult matter to establish, and certainly not worth while making a legal fight to do so, if it can be avoided without dishonour.

Nothing further has, so far as I know, been heard from Rickword's Solicitors, so I imagine that they simply propose to let the matter drop.

With kind regards,
Yours sincerely,
J. A. White.

55. From Charles Nicoll (EUL MS2956 f.1)

120 Shakespeare St
Glasgow NW
9 November 1944

Dear Mr Grieve,

I was delighted to receive your letter on Tuesday.[1] It was indeed an agreeable surprise to have it handed to me at the gatehouse when I entered the work that morning.

I am very glad to know your change of occupation has proved a successful and pleasant one.[2] Life, to you now, must be much fuller compared to the monotony of copper shellband production.

You give me nostalgia with your account of Loch Long, Gareloch and Holy Loch. Many happy days have I spent on these same waters in the irredeemable past.

I wonder how you fared on Saturday of last week when the storm was raging. I read of gales of 80 m.p.h. on the Firth of Clyde.

How I would have enjoyed that. I like rough waters when the ship under me is sound and seaworthy. Wonder where this love of the sea comes from in a Glasgow-born landlubber like myself.

I remember when I used to go to the East Coast of Scotland I would wander along to a secluded cranny in the cliffs and there lie and listen to the call of the gulls and the sound of the surging seas below. These sounds to me were music.

Mrs Nicoll and baby are doing fine and as for myself I'm O.K. in health but still as disgusted with Mechans. Same old troubles still.

I miss the 'cracks' we used to have in the mornings although I fear I must have bored you horribly at times. It is, indeed, with some amusement that I look back and think how I used to pester you with some of my dud poetry.

These, however, are the evils you must be called upon to suffer. Rabbie Burns had to thole this to some extent from his own friends.

You were saying you might call in some day on a visit. We would be very glad to see you and hear you again. Remember there is always a welcome for you at 120 Shakespeare Street as well.

Regarding photographs I would really be delighted to oblige. I struck a little seam since you left and I have both film and paper. If you can get it fixed let me know and I'll be down pronto and glad to oblige.

I have made up a string of poems (?) or songs (?) for Watson's competition in connection with Young Scotland so you just got out in time to miss this lot.

I hope you'll let me know when Soutar's work, which you are compiling, can be obtained.

I am really anxious to have a copy when it is published.

By the way I had Douglas Young's portrait entered in a portrait competition, in connection with the Club,[3] and it received a very creditable commendation.

Well, I hope I shall be seeing you in person in the very near future.

Yours,

Charles Nicoll.

---

[1] Nicoll replies here to MacDiarmid's letter of 1 November 1944 (*New Selected Letters*, pp.244-245).

[2] MacDiarmid had joined the National Union of General & Municipal Workers on 6 November 1943 (NLS MS 27214 f.17) and paid dues weekly until 30 September 1944 (ibid. f.19). The inference must be that he left Mechans at the end of this week and

transferred to the Merchant Navy.
3   Partick Camera Club.

56. From William MacLellan (EUL MS2976)

240 Hope Street
Glasgow C2
n.d [1944]

My dear Chris,

I wonder if you could possibly be at the New Art Club next Wed. (11ᵗʰ). Dr Silver, head of the Research Department at Weirs, is talking on 'Symbolism in Art and Poetry' and I think you may find some of his ideas interesting. He writes some poetry of which h/with is a sample but in this practical sphere he has some way to travel and I thought you may be able to help him by criticism and discussion.[1] He is, I feel, a helpful contact with the scientific world which would be useful to the movement generally, for we must come to terms with our future masters!

Have been thinking over your Smoking Concert idea and it seems that it wd be a grand type of affair to launch the Scottish Society at.[2] We could have a private room at the Lit. Club & keep the numbers fairly small; Bridie, Carroll,[3] Honeyman,[4] Fergusson, Crosbie, Barke, F. G., Crombie,[5] Chisholm (if in town), Farmer,[6] you & me. Can you think of any others? I cd send them copies of that draft of aims & ask them all to speak on the subject of a Scottish Cultural Centre for 5 mins or so. Somebody would have to lead off with a longer statement – Who?

If you can be up early on Wed. we are having tea at Lit. Club 6-8 p.m. So perhaps may see you there first.

Yrs aye.

Bill.

1   The 'sample' of Robert Silver's poetry which MacLellan enclosed was called 'Conflict'. Many years later Silver published *Conflict and Contexts: Selected Poems of the Quarter Century 1930-1955* (Edinburgh, 1991).
2   This 'Scottish Society' may have been seen as an alternative to the Saltire Society. The last paragraph of Charles Nicoll's letter of 11 July 1977 appears to refer to it.
3   Paul Vincent Carroll (1900-1968), Irish playwright.
4   T. J. Honeyman (1891-1971), Director of Glasgow Art Galleries (1939-1954).
5   R. Crombie Saunders (1914-1991), teacher, poet and editor.
6   H. G. Farmer (1882-1965), musicologist, orientalist and conductor.

57. From Valda Grieve (NLS MS27150 ff.28-29)

[January 1945]

Whats happened to you – I was expecting you home last night & had the tea waiting for you – I'm enclosing this note in with Anders instead of enclosing Anders in with yours as I should do in case you come home before this reaches Rothesay – (I've no idea how the mail is there –) and I want Olsen[1] to get my note – as there is a Picture I would like to see 'A Cornish Rhapsody'.

I am wondering if the reason you did not come home was because I did not send you any money I was going to – but it would run me very short and Anders said you could ask him for it – after all there was a lot to do with the money this pay day – Mike going away – the electric Bill to pay etc – You may be sure I hav'nt blown it in – the extent to which I have spent on myself amounts to 5/3 – So what!

There are a few letters for you – one from Dakers[2] & one from Maurice Lindsay – Douglas Young's father is dead –. The calendars will be ready definitely this weekend, Robin is bringing them out[3] – Letter from America trusting your MSS hasn't gone in the deep sea & that is all – I'm glad you did not come home at the beginning of the week for my boiler burst & I had to have the whole range taken out & no fire for 3 days.

All the best
Love
Valda

[1] Anders Olsen was the skipper of the M. F. V. *Gurli*, based at Greenock, on which MacDiarmid worked from 1944 to 1946.
[2] MacDiarmid was editing *Complete Poems of William Soutar* for Andrew Dakers Ltd – finally published in 1948.
[3] 'The calendars' were *Scots Makars Calendars: Selections from the works of Hugh MacDiarmid* (a poem a month), Glasgow, 1945. The frontspiece photograph of MacDiarmid smoking a pipe was by Charles Nicoll.

58. From Denis Saurat (EUL MS2960.3 f.7)

Institut Français du Royaume Uni
5 February 1945

My dear Grieve

It is a great treat to have a long letter from you, and news, on the whole good. I do not wonder at your reticence about *Le Soldat*:[1] I feel myself to be on tiptoe when I venture to re-read it, and hardly to reach the level.

I shall look forward to your next volumes. I feel most grateful to you for your kind and shrewd references to F. G. and myself in your *Lucky Poet*, which is one of your most successful Encyclopaedias.

Excuse this brief note – I am as yet rather under pressure from the health point of view.

Affectionately,
D. Saurat.

[1] Denis Saurat, *Le Soldat romain: poème épique en vers blancs* (Hyperion Press: London, 1944).

59. From Charles Nicoll (EUL MS2956 f.6)

120 Shakespeare St
Glasgow NW
6 February 1945

Dear Chris,

Was very pleased to meet your friend and skipper Mr Olsen. I think I got some nice pictures of him and also one of Mrs Grieve. I shall know to-night as I intend to develop the plates after I finish this little note. Among the prints I am sending you now you will see one of the double exposure negative taken in Mechans.

I think it is quite hopeless and useless for the purpose you had in mind. Very sorry to disappoint you, Chris, but maybe the next time you are up here, which I hope won't be very far away, we can have a shot at staging an unusual photograph.

Many thanks for that very original calendar, the possession of which I am very proud of.

Perhaps I shall hear from you soon but I am hoping to see you before hearing from you.

Yours,

Charles Nicoll.

60. From Marie de Banzie (EUL Gen.2094/1/62)

The New Scottish Group
299 West George St
Glasgow

Treasurer   Secretary

Anne Cornock-Taylor   Marie de Banzie

Monday 12 March [1945]

Dear Mr McDiarmid,

On behalf of the New Scottish Group I am writing to ask you if you would be so kind as to open our Exhibition in McClure's Gallery in Wellington St on Sat. 5 May at 3 p.m. This will be our third public Exhibition and we feel it is time we had someone with some sympathy to perform this ceremony. You will understand that we must start organising this Exhibition now as there is much work to be done especially publicity.

We really would be honoured if you would do this for us and I do hope your answer will be in the affirmative.

Yours sincerely

Marie de Banzie

Sec.

61. From Valda Grieve (NLS MS27150 ff.26-27)

27 Arundel Drive
Battlefield
Glasgow S2
15 March 1945

Dear Christopher,

Thank you for your letter – What is done, can't be helped – so the less said about it the better –. I know you're not having an easy time – I'm sorry for you – very sorry – only you make it so difficult for me to give you the help & sympathy I would like too –. When you have been drinking – I hate it – and can you blame me – for I know exactly what is going to happen – you are going to say all sorts of nasty things – I am quite prepared to face up to things with you – when you are sober – but not otherwise – I've always been fond of you & have always done my best for you – under trying circumstances for a young girl – now I am older I just can't 'take it' – that is all –. I think that is easily explainable & reasonable –

My lack of interest is untrue – it is true that I cannot agree with you on all subjects I do on the main ones – so I do not see you have anything to grumble about –

I'm going down to see Bill today as so far nothing has arrived from him or from Dakers –. Mike won't be home for another fortnight at the least & will be home for a month so you will have plenty of chance of seeing him –.

Now cheer up – pull yourself together –
Love
Valda

62. From Sadie F. McLellan (EUL MS2954.15 f.16)

Sadie F. McLellan, D.A. (Glas.), N.R.D.
14 Ferguson Avenue
Milngavie
(Mrs. Walter Pritchard)
Artist in Stained, Engraved, and Sand Blasted Glass
Saturday [5 May1945]

Studios
45 Queen Street, Edinburgh
The School of Art, Glasgow

My dear Chris,

I feel I let you down as a friend today – not by criticising you but in criticising you at the Exhibition before people. Doubly so since I knew you wouldn't retaliate & hurt me – for some reason known only to yourself you indulge me, in fact you treat me like a child.

Well I'm not a child. I'm a full-grown (!) woman & an artist – and you let me down as an artist – you let yourself down as an artist. I have little or no sympathy for the

New Art Group but they did ask you in all seriousness to open their show & first you got tight & then blethered.

If Rembrandt etc don't matter in Art, why then are you anxious to bridge the gulf between the present day & the Scots poets of the past? Why do you go back to 15th C. Scots to evolve your new Scots which you have written so magnificently in if you have no feeling for tradition or national Art? And why are you considering standing for the Scottish National Party if you feel Scotland has contributed so little culturally? Upon my word I'm mixed-up. I nearly wept this afternoon – I was so unhappy for you.

I wish I could have come to tea with you – it was nice of you to ask me but J.A.[1] was at a house in town being kept for me & I had to return for her. *And* I am prudish or Calvinistic & I don't like being in public with someone not quite himself no matter how fond I am of him!!

Love.

Sadie.

PS I find it queer too that you should be prepared to go and open an Ex. like that & you won't even bother to look at my glass.

[1]   'J. A.' was her daughter, Judith Anne.

63. From Joan Littlewood (EUL MS2965.11 f.1)

228 Higham Lane
Hyde
Cheshire
England
17 May 1945

Dear Hugh MacDiarmid,

You may remember Barbara Niven telling you of the theatre work Jimmie Miller and I have done. We have always wanted to have your interest and support but, of course, you don't know enough about us. The war changed the form of our work, after a time we found it impossible to mount productions, those of us who were left went on training and studying – as best we could. We are now preparing to put on plays again, full-time training and rehearsal will begin before the end of this month.

I must tell you that our idea is not just to make a good theatre group, but to create a new aesthetic through the theatre – we have always believed that theatre is a synthesis of all the arts. We find ourselves faced with the problem of creating a new dramaturgy, as well as a new conception of production and acting. The CP is content with a J.B. Priestley music hall act, war has seen the glorification of mediocrity, even in the Party. This contempt for the greatness of the ordinary people angers me more than anything. I wish you could have been at some of our shows, seen the Lancashire cotton workers watching our *Lysistrata* and *Fuente Ovejuna* and Molière and our documentary plays on cotton and coal. You may remember that we incorporated passages of your 'Flaming Poetaster' into our living newspaper on the National Government [in 1940]. Your poetry ran right through the play – you should have been there to hear the people respond to it. We have always said that if the theatre fails we will solve the problem by going on the road and taking poems and songs to the people – direct.

As for our re-opening – we need people. Two members of the group – an actor and a sculptor – have been killed, some of the others who trained and worked with us won't be back for a long time. We need about eight more people – and would like to draw them from different places like Wales, Scotland and the West of England. You see they can bring the language and background of their own place into the group and this will help later when we develop *commedia dell'arte* methods for some of our work. Of course it will be full-time work, we have lighting equipment and other useful gear like turntables and wood and curtains – we have also got some money together – enough to give us all £3 a week at the beginning. We shall not stay in one place when the productions are ready, but tour the Durham coalfields, the Rhondda, N. Lancashire and parts of Scotland.

Do you know any young artists interested in any aspect of theatre work who would like to join us? I am coming to Scotland very soon to meet one or two people who may come in with us and I thought you might be able to put me in touch with others. Some productions are planned so I will list them.

1. *Rogues' Gallery* – by Ewan MacColl – satire.
2. *The Flying Doctor* – from the early Molière and the Italian script with 3.
3. A ballad opera – using the genuine folk-songs of the N.E. coast of England & Northumberland. Sung narration, in ballad form – telling story of a young man & woman from the days of unemployment till this war. Dramatic scenes, inset, crowd scenes mimed on wide plane.
4. A Lorca play – either *The Shoemaker's Prodigious Wife*[1] or *Don Perlimlín*.[2]
5. *Hell is what you make it.* Ewan MacColl – satire.
6. *The Birds* – Aristophanes – retranslated & adapted.
7. Documentary play on the fishing industry – research by the group as for previous living newspapers.

I hope you will be able to help us.
Yours sincerely,
Joan Littlewood.

[1]   (1930).

[2]   *The Love of Don Perlimplín for Belisa in the Garden* (1931).

64. From O. H. Mavor (James Bridie) (EUL MS2955.5 f.1)

16 Roman Road
Bearsden
Dumbartonshire

Dear Christopher,

After I saw you at the New Art Club I asked MacLellan to let me have a proof of my 'attack' on you in the *New Scot*.[1] I had honestly forgotten all about it.

I was thus quite objectively delighted at the fun of the little piece and at its absence of real offence – for (God knows why) I hold you in affectionate regard.

What I really wanted to ask you was whether you could bring yourself – after the election is over – to harness the most neglected of your Seven Devils and set him to a job of work. I refer to your sense of humour, the ugly duckling of your large mare's nest, the crult of the litter.

I want a play for the Citizens' Theatre and that is the only one of your Devils to whom I can appeal. The poet Johnson,[2] whom you resemble in many ways, did not despise the Theatre of Marlowe[3] and Burbage[4] and its discipline did him a lot of good. He also wrote comedies, very salubrious to his own soul. Anyhow, how is the best dramaturgist in Scotland ever to make anything of his Theatre (in his own way, mind you) if the best poet in Scotland contents himself with crazy and ill-informed abuse of his venture?

The Theatre, observe, is a branch of rhetoric in which I am somewhat expert and you are not. I may be a bad expert, but I am the only one who is prepared to give you an intelligible showing. I have seen your verse very badly printed and very well printed and half and between. I like it best when it is set up by people who have learned their job.

I have now extended to you an invitation as it was my clear duty to do. I keep in mind that you are as capable of writing a thoroughly bad play as you are capable of writing a masterpiece. Even if you write the former, I shall treat it with respect. That is to say, I shall tell you that, in my opinion – the only opinion in Scotland that is worth a row of Soya beans – it is unworthy of you and we shall part friends or enemies, whichever you like.

If you say that you wouldn't be seen dead in the Citizens' Theatre, I shall know you for a Snob-Nazi, power-maniacal, sacerdotal, narrow-minded literary Wee Free and reflect sadly that it is possible to be that and a memorable artist at the same time.

Yours ever,

O. H.

[1]   Bridie appears to refer here to a very brief reply (in *The New Scot*) to MacDiarmid's article 'Post-War Prospects of Scottish Arts and Letters' in the first issue of the magazine. Both issues were in 1945.

[2]   Ben Jonson (1572/3-1637), dramatist, poet, scholar and writer of court masques.

[3]   Christopher Marlowe (1564-1593), dramatist.

[4]   Richard Burbage (?1567-1619), actor and painter in oil colours.

65. From William MacLellan (EUL MS2954.16 f.7)

The Dunedin Association

For the encouragement of the Scottish creative arts[1]
Founded 1911

240 Hope Street
Glasgow C2
22 August 1945

National Organiser
William MacLellan

My Dear Chris,

Thanks for your note. I wrote Connelly[2] ref. money but he has not replied so far; however am glad to hear it will be possible to repay soon.

I am also deeply troubled about *The Kist*[3] & *The Cock*[4] along with a dozen others which lie in type at the bottleneck in the caseroom. I have had to stand blow after blow to my staff in the last year & the low ebb was reached (I hope) last week when my fourth comp. left me. There is a general reshuffle going on now & these temporary war men are all drifting back to old jobs. With a fifth of my staff I cannot move but the signs are all pointing to improvement. Douglas's book we start imposing next week so I may be able to keep my September promise if the binder plays.[5] *The Kist* I think can follow. I aim to have the next six in the *P.S.* series out in October. I feel my wings hopelessly clipped. There is so much to be done & could be done if I could only find the men to do it; however three or four out of the million releases may come our way.

I can quite understand yr reluctance to talk of new things as things are & I would rather it was that way until I am out of the jam.

The urgent need for the Dunedin [Association] is an up-to-date constitution & I wd like to talk over the Object Clause before submitting it to the meeting. I will try to stay up an evening next week & come out to see you. Would Tuesday be O.K.? We could meet in town & eat if it wd give us more time.

Let me know.

Yrs,

Bill.

---

[1]   The Advisory Council was Dr Erik Chisholm, Dr Henry G. Farmer, J. D. Fergusson, C. M. Grieve, John MacKechnie, and Compton Mackenzie.
[2]   Not identified.
[3]   MacDiarmid's *A Kist of Whistles* became the tenth book in the Poetry Scotland series in September 1947.
[4]   Fionn MacColla's *And the Cock Crew* was published in 1945.
[5]   Douglas Young's *A Braird o Thristles* was the twelfth book in the Poetry Scotland series, also in 1947.

66. From T. S. Eliot (EUL MS2967/3)

[Faber headed notepaper]
Faber and Faber Ltd Publishers
24 Russell Square
London WC1
28 August 1945

Dear Mr MacDiarmid

I was interested to get your letter of the 23rd. I am afraid the paper situation is not appreciably better now but if you are willing to take the trouble to send me the poem again on such chilly encouragement, I should like *very much* to have an opportunity of reading it again now!

Yours sincerely,

T. S. Eliot.

67. From Edward Gaitens (EUL MS2948.6 ff.9-10)

A.A. Hutments
Yetholm
Kelso
Roxburghshire
17 September 1945

Dear Christopher,

At last I am voluntarily bringing my unmentalist existence here to a close and I am looking forward to some hours of mental adventure with you. Though I have another week to go I have decided to leave here on Thursday. In any case I must be in Glasgow for the 24th to broadcast my story. Yes, after all I decided to read my story myself as I felt it was weak of me to allow some young man with an anglified Scottish voice to pipe it nicely or some elderly prurient Scot to locute it lugubriously. The public can be damned if they don't like my reading. I am not so enamoured of the B.B.C. as to desire to shine in their eyes.

I suppose my stay here has done me some physical good though the damnable headaches persist. My only recourse now is to think and work as if the latter did not exist.

I cannot say I have enjoyed camp life much. It is sadly astonishing to live for a month in a company of fifty youths and men and not meet with a single original idea or a moment's virile conversation. I have hung on here only because of the beauty of the Border country to which I shall often return in memory and as often as possible in person.

Charles[1] came here for two week-ends and we went a week last Sunday in search of your birthplace. But we could get no further than Hawick. It was a shining day and we tried to hire cycles but failed so we spent the day in Hawick. The bus ride from Kelso to Hawick is one of the loveliest I know.

Charles was at the first night of the new 'Citizens'. He met Bridie, during one of the intervals on the stairs. Bridie asked him if he was enjoying himself and Charles flatly said 'No!', at which B. was taken aback.

As a commercial venture the 'Citizens' may prosper, as an artistic one it does not exist.

May I ask Valda and yourself if you'd both care to put me up on Thursday night, provided you have no one else staying. Then I may try to find lodgings in your neighbourhood. I hope Valda is very well and has had some treatment for that occasional anaemia.

Yours sincerely,
Edward.

1   'Charles' was Charles Turner who contributed 'Gaelic Pantomime', a short polemical article, to *The Voice of Scotland,* vol. 3, no.4 (June 1947), pp. 1-2, and a story, 'Ruins', to *New Short Stories* 1945-6, edited by John Singer, pp.189-191.

68. From Ruaraidh Erskine of Mar (EUL MS2946.16 ff.11-13)

Hotel Lefevre
Biarritz
24 September [1945]

[No address]
You will see by this that we have not yet left here: there is a great crowd to cross the Channel & we have to wait our turn. However, I hope we shall leave Biarritz this weekend, or early next week. I'll write you as soon as I reach London.

You will have seen doubtless in the papers about the movement of [Stanley M.] Bruce (High Commissioner for Australia) to form a confederation of British nations. This might well suit *us*, so I have written him a few lines, & hope thus to get in touch with him. If he is still in London when I get there I will go and see what he has to say. I'm inclined to think that [William Lyon] Mackenzie King[1] might take up the Bruce plan if he is not already too dipped with the Yanks. I know from letters to me that in principle at least he favours the Scots cause. Him too I might see when he goes to London a few months hence. My idea is (and I hope Bruce will agree to it) that there should be an inner British circle, consisting of *all* the nationalities of the British Isles – that is Scots, English, Irish & Welsh – *besides* this outer ring of the confederated peoples, Canadians, Australians, New Zealanders, etc. And I have pointed out to Bruce that his plan must break down unless he gets in the *Irish*. In this way he might solve the Irish problem altogether: make good Eire's unity, and restore her to the circle of the British Nations. If Bruce agrees to this I suggest you & I might go to Dublin & put the matter before [Eamon] de Valera.[2]

Of course I have not dropped the idea of the supercession of the Militarist State as the sole means to bring about lasting peace. The more one contemplates the fearful mess the 'statesmanship' of Churchill & his sort has got us into the more clear it seems to me that the *forbidding arms to each & every nation is the sole true remedy.*

Fear of the Atomic Bomb should help much to bring home this idea to the popular mind. In my letter to Bruce I told him that there were others besides the Scottish Nationalists afoot at this present conjuncture, & who intend to work to rouse the nation to a sense of the seriousness of its position unless the existing political relations with England are revised, not in the direction of 'separatism' but of union for each & all on an *independent* basis. It is just as well to put Bruce 'wise' at once to our views: the colonial statesman or politician is not always as understanding as he should be. Slàn leat an an àm, is piseach oirt.[3]

R. A. M.

PS My idea is of course that Bruce should work through *us and our friends & political sympathisers through the country*. With what should be a big move like this behind us we should go *fast & far with our nation*.

[1] MacKenzie King (1874-1950) was Liberal Prime Minister of Canada 1921-1926, 1926-1930 and 1935-1948.

[2] Eamon de Valera (1882-1975) was then Prime Minister of the Irish Free State which became the Republic of Ireland in 1949. He was elected President in 1959 and 1966.

[3] 'Farewell to you, and may you be making progress soon'.

69. From David Martin (EUL MS2968)

Musarts Limited
48 South Molton St
London W1

Directors:
P. Fishman (Russian)
Herbert Marshall

9 October 1945

My dear Grieve,

Many thanks for your letter of the 4th. I shall, after all, not be able to see you in Glasgow this week, because I am absolutely inundated with work and, among other things, continuing my labours on an interrupted and long overdue book. Instead I shall try to clarify my own ideas about your proposed books in the following few paragraphs. I shall simply try and tell you what was in my mind when I first wrote to you.

I feel that a novel by Hugh MacDiarmid on a Scottish theme would be of great literary value. You are famed as a poet and an essayist, and your autobiography or what appeared of it, has been tremendously interesting. But you have never written a real novel as far as I know, a genuine novel, and that is what I would like to see. When using the word 'genuine', I mean a novel which is not autobiographical or too concretely political, but one which is great enough to swallow up its own author and one in which fact is only used as the mortar of imagination.

In contemporary Scottish literature there have been only two genuine and fine novels, *The House With Green Shutters* and *A Scots Quair*. Most else has, at best, been only dramatized reportage.

You are the living embodiment of Scotland's tomorrow and what is more, you consciously experience this strange and unique position. If this awareness transcends your novel like light falling from a window on to a large and independent canvas, all will be well. But if it causes the writing of a polemic book or a fictionalised argument all will not be well, may the work be yet so brilliant.

Thus, we are looking to you for a novel in the classic sense. A classic sense interpreted by a revolutionary spirit.

I can, of course, make no useful concrete suggestion to you. I feel you will understand what I have in mind when I lay such stress on the need for a novel, a *real* novel.

I do feel that the Highland story which you outlined is exceedingly full of promise and should perhaps precede the Clydeside book. Its action takes place at an earlier date, and in certain ways I feel that it forms the foundation of the other story. It is the sort of theme, I believe, in which you could let yourself most freely go, allowing your readers to participate in the movement of history as it resounds in the heartbeats of human beings, your characters.

We have never had a Highland novel which was more than fragmentary. Your late friend, Grassic Gibbon, was, I think, a genius, but he consciously narrowed down his range. Yours, I feel, should and would be an historic novel in the strongest sense of the term.

Now to come to finance. Musarts Ltd. would like to commission one novel of 120,000 words with an option on the second. This firm offers an advance payment of two hundred pounds, to be paid when you commence writing the script which I suppose will be when you are released from the Merchant Navy. The advance payment to be made on account of royalties which would commence at a rate of 12 ½ % up to 10,000 copies sold and rise to 15% of the published price for any sale exceeding 10,000 copies. The price of the book to be not less than 15/- net, so that your royalties would be substantial.[1]

We would look forward to delivery of the first book next summer. If these terms suit, perhaps you will let us know, or otherwise make some proposal of your own. If you wish us to deal with an agent on your behalf, let us know who he is and we will contact him. This is rather a bread and butter letter, but at this stage bread and butter letters are indicated. I am looking forward to hearing from you in the near future. I do not feel that with a writer of your calibre a synopsis would be of much use, as long as you can indicate in what way your approach differs from these few points I have made.

Yours fraternally,
David Martin.
(Manager).

---

[1] MacDiarmid signed Musarts contract. 'Returned signed 1 November 1945' he wrote on David Martin's letter of 30 October 1945. Subsequently Musarts decided to suspend all publication. Martin tried to interest Pilot Press Ltd, 45, Great Russell St., London W.C. l. Mr Charles Madge wanted a test chapter.

70. From John L. Kinloch (NLS Acc.7361/16)

The Scottish National Party
59 Elmbank Street
Glasgow C2
14 October 1945

Dear Christopher,

Personal

With regard to your personal note to me in your letter to the Council, I would point out that I was not present when you walked out of the Council, and had nothing whatever to do with extruding you.[1]

In my many years of Council work I have never once supported the expulsion of any member, and there have been many expulsions.

It is true that I did say to several members that I was glad you had walked out. It is not true to say that I hoped Dr Lamont would come to share this opinion. What I did say, when I heard that Dr Lamont proposed to propose that you be asked to return, was to the effect that I hoped Dr Lamont would not create a scene and raise the feelings of the Council to fighting pitch.

You like plain speaking, so I will speak plainly. Frankly I am glad you have left the Council, for the simple reason that your methods and the majority of the Council's methods were opposed. Your letter frankly admits that. Every schoolboy knows that you can't have an effective football team when every time it meets, instead of practising the game, it fights as to whether it should play according to association or rugby rules. This is even more true in politics. For months we have fought every Council meeting as to methods of advance. Neither side converted the other. So long as your strong personality was in the Council, we would have gone on fighting. The Party has been wasting valuable time and opportunity. Now you can work efficiently outside the Party, and I hope we will do some efficient work within the Party.

All this is clear to me without any personal feeling in the matter. I could even enjoy the vigour of your style and admire your choice of words. The use of 'extrude' was very clever – vigorous but non-committal. 'Thrust out of life altogether' has all the vigour of 'bumped off' and yet is excellent English!

Thus, in spite of your vigorous abuse of me and my colleagues, I continue to admire your work for the cause of Scotland and wish you all success in it. I, for my part, can only continue to work in the way that seems to me best. Personally I should like to continue friends on a personal basis while differing on political questions and methods. I sincerely hope that time will heal the present sores, and that you can come to think kindly of me again.

Yours sincerely,
John L. Kinloch.

[1] MacDiarmid had been elected to the SNP National Council at the Conference on 29 May 1943 (letter to him from Douglas Young EUL MS2961.18 f.12). He attended seventeen out of the twenty-three Council meetings between 5 June 1943 and 28 July 1945. On

the latter occasion he resigned from the Council and from the Party and walked out. (NLS Acc. 7295/14) MacDiarmid then wrote a letter to the Council on 3 October 1945 which the members found offensive: this letter has not been preserved. In the spring of 1946 he applied to rejoin the SNP through Glasgow Central Branch and withdrew the offensive remarks. (NLS Acc. 10090/6 and 7) Precisely how long this renewed period of membership lasted is unclear. John L. Kinloch was National Secretary of the SNP at the time he wrote the letter above.

71. From Tom MacDonald / Fionn MacColla (EUL Gen.2094/3/1261 a&b)

The Schoolhouse
Torlum
By Lochboisdale
South Uist
2 December 1945

My dear Chris,

Many thanks for your letter, & many apologies for delay in answering it. To begin with I received it when I was laid up in bed with a severe cold or mild 'flu or something; then six weeks ago I received notification of my appointment to a school in Barra & the intervening period has been filled with intermittent alarms of impending departure, packings, etc., followed by partial unpackings when the alarms proved false, & all this superimposed on the normal hectic order of things has left us even less time than usual for correspondence. Your own course of life appears to have been no less crowded & involved of late, so you will understand. It was good to hear, however, that you hope to be able to give yourself up to writing again very soon, & I hope that can be arranged. I wish it could be arranged in my own case, but by all indications I should say my writing days are pretty well over – before they'd quite begun, as you might well say. I have been able to do practically nothing for a year & a half to the book I told you of, which remains less than half done, & short of some drastic lessening of the pressure upon my time & nervous energy, it looks like being another *And The Cock Crew* which was exactly eleven years & two months from commencement to publication – although not worked upon more than a tenth of that time, of course. You will see therefore how it is impossible for me to do anything for *The Voice of Scotland* [1]on this occasion. I should like to say I'd do something for the succeeding issue, but as the next few months are rather uncertain I'd be better to say merely that I hope to do so. Incidentally I shall be glad to subscribe to the periodical if you will kindly put me on the list. Good luck to it & to all the pro-Scottish activities of all good men!

Many thanks for your kind & encouraging remarks about *And The Cock Crew* – you will have seen the book by now, I take it. I'm really the last person to pass judgement on it at the moment – am in fact inclined to be somewhat scunnered at it: you will know the feeling, I suppose. I should have liked to go through it again, had I ever had the time, if only to purge out some affectations of style etc., which irritate me, & there are some parts which not only recall rather painfully, but show,

I fear, rather too clear signs of the intense mental & emotional strain due to causes having nothing to do with the writing of the book under which I was nevertheless compelled to write it. However, I suppose I'd not have been satisfied with it in any event: I daresay one ought not to be. I certainly hope it sells well for thereon probably depend the chances of the next ever getting written. And I hope it may serve to do some good to the general cause by clarifying some folks' notions of the particular causes of our national dereliction.

It is possible that I may be on the mainland during the coming holidays & if so I should hope to get through to Glasgow to see you, when all sorts of matters can be discussed much better than by letter. I really have to come, for medical & other reasons, though of course the question of cost is a formidable one. (Which is one reason why I should advise you against coming to the Isles, if that is still your intention. With one thing & another you can add some forty to fifty per cent to the cost of living.) I am pretty spry again, all the same, & with a little less pressure of other things would be very active creatively.

I had the pleasure on Friday last – appropriately enough, St Andrew's Day – of a visit from Robert MacIntyre[2] on his way to the Airport. He had apparently been doing 'locum' for the North Uist medico, & was then on his way home.

I must close now. I do so with renewed thanks for your encouraging words, with the hope that Valda, yourself & James Michael continue to enjoy health & good fortune, & in the hope that I may perchance be seeing you soon in person.

Yours aye,
Tom.

PS I hardly expect now that we shall flit before the holidays, but in any event a letter addressed to me here would be forwarded.

[1] *The Voice of Scotland* had resumed publication in December 1945.
[2] Robert D. MacIntyre (1913-1998) was the first Scottish Nationalist to be elected to Westminster (at a by-election in Motherwell earlier in 1945). He lost the seat at the General Election.

72. From David Martin (EUL Gen.2094/6)

4 Heath Hunt Rd
London NW3

10 December 1945
Dear Comrade Grieve,
A brief answer, this, to your letter of the 5th. I am happy that you will carry through the book-plan – very happy.

Re the financial side: I am pleased you are quite frank about it. I feel that I shall perhaps be able to manage you the £50/-/- you need to keep *The Voice of Scotland* in the press. It may take me just a few days to see what can be done – please, dear friend, allow me these. As to the other side the P. Press[1] payments if they do the book – I feel sure they will – this is still open and I do really feel that if they like your opening of the novel they will be generous. However, I shall be there ...

I don't think just now I can lay my hand on much more than the £50 I hope to obtain. Hope it helps a little.

Hasta luego.[2]

David Martin.

How does MacColla's novel strike you? The subject seems to me well chosen but a little less hatingly approached. It should have moved from the first page on a more vigorous plane. But it's good, nevertheless, I think. DM.

[1]   'the P. Press' was the Pilot Press.
[2]   'see you later'.

73. From David Martin (NLS Acc.7361/16)

4 Heath Hunt Road
NW3
19 December 1945

My dear Grieve,

I am sorry for the delay – I am afraid it could not be speeded. I enclose herewith £50/-/- in the hope that this will be of some little help. I have heard from Pilot Press that they are looking forward to hearing from you when your first Chapters are ready.

I myself am working at the rate of 3500 words a day to complete my first book of prose before the end of the year. May 1946 be strong for you and the things you value and wish well!

Fraternally yours,

David Martin.

74. From Albert D. M. Spencer (EUL Gen. 2094/5/2153)

Flat 11
No. 6 Colville Sq.
N. Kensington
London W11
n.d. [1945]

Dear Mr Grieve,

The quotation from your speech in today's *Daily Mail* is just another example of Scottish incompetence. The trouble with you[,] sir, and many other Scots, is that you talk far too much. To blame the English for Scottish slums is just another 'get out' and typical of your type.

Take a tip from us proud English[,] Mr Grieve. 'Button up, and get on with the job.'

And shoulder your own troubles, we have bottle fed you people and other people far too much.

Yours etc.,

Albert D. M. Spencer.

75. From Edward Gaitens (EUL MS2948.6 ff.9-10)

Room 214
Great Eastern Hotel
Duke Street
Glasgow
n.d. [c.1945]

Dear Chris,

I was sorry to have appeared so dead to your eager reading of your 'Lament' on Sunday.[1] I felt I was utterly ungracious and I was deeply embarrassed inside myself while I was with you, and for some time after. Forgive me and blame it on the dumb state of my head which afflicts me so frequently and for too long. When I'm like that I cannot even read an ordinary book. The impact of print, the thinking about thoughts and images intensely irritates me and I throw down the book in anger and despair. I have been told that this condition is anemia of the brain. So I was quite unable to survey the vast architecture of ideas in your 'Lament' which seemed to glitter and dart every way at once. But I have read it since and have been moved by its warmth, ardour and subtle aspirations. You chose a noble theme and sometimes you nobly rise to it. I think you can still achieve 'the bird-like leap' to that ancient nobility of Scotland's childhood and youth, but I feel you would have accomplished a truly great poem on that exalted and exquisite theme if you had given it a longer gestation in yourself. Sometimes I think you should have just gone away like Rilke, and lived only for Poetry. But you are a tolerant, hospitable and social being and that would have been harder for you than it was for him.

Where is the Soul of Scotland noo? I sometimes feel for it in vain. Has it been industrialised and commercialised out of existence? Or has Religion, which should have watered it and made it flower, rendered it dry and barren?

I still like your Scottish lyrics best. I am now reading *Annals of the Five Senses*. 'Café Scene' made me feel queer. I have felt somewhat as you did then – for different reasons – perhaps because I thought too little, instead of too much. I am ever straining after poise and because I strain it never comes. Poise should come like the dawn in one of your moorland scenes. Then is seen joy without fever, flawless balance, accomplishment without haste. That which Nature possesses surely we all will someday find!

Turner is coming up to-morrow for three weeks and I should like to bring him out to-day week if you're being at home. I don't think 'Tributary' will prove tough going for your vigorous brain. In your work and his I see many resemblances of attitude and feeling.

I started work on Tuesday as a railway-booking clerk in College Goods Station.

Now I must try and get a small flat like I had in London where I can invite men like yourself to sit and talk till three in the morning if we want to!

Edward

---

1   'Lament for the Great Music' (*C. P.* I, pp.462-482).

76. From William MacLellan (EUL MS2954.16 f.11)

William MacLellan
Publisher
240 Hope Street
Glasgow C2
14 January 1946

My Dear Chris,

Had Robt Kemp of BBC in here on Friday & he is anxious to meet you.[1] He will be thro' a bit this week as his play is being done at Citizens' so wonder if you could spare an evening to have a meal. P'haps Valda could let me know a date & will see if it suits Kemp. I'm not free Wed. and have suggested Fri. or Sat. to Kemp.

Kemp represents my 'line of least resistance' which I keep trailing after & seems keen to do more contemporary stuff.

Congrats on *Voice of Scotland*.[2] The printing is a great improvement on Black's standards. I hope the editorial gets to the right people – it stirred me up & I wish the step which follows righteous indignation could be taken, whatever it may be.

You weaken yr argument in music hopelessly by omitting Chisholm, of course. He is the only person here who has mastered the Symphonic form – wish you had heard the July performance. Nan will play some piano music soon, I hope.[3]

Also it has to be admitted now freely that Whyte's[4] performances have recently become the very best being done on the air, far ahead of Boult etc.[5] Listen some time & give credit for actual achievements in our midst, that's the only way self-respect & confidence in our national idiom will be strengthened. Whyte to me is giving recently the intellectual detail of musical thought that one would expect in our idiom and which is best expressed to date in Lomond's Beethoven.[6] His interpretations are almost too heavy with detail & his recitals are very exhausting for that reason.

You will be wanting to cast a brick or two at MacLeod's new Scottish National Film Studios so will keep you informed.[7] In the meantime if you have any idea on how the illusion of poetry & beauty might be better cast on a screen & thus take the film nearer to being an art form, do formulate it, for we want you on the literary advisory panel. The great thing is that most of the founders are fully national conscious & the absence of Bridie & Co. is a useful guide to our aspirations there.

Hope to see you this week.

Yrs,

Bill.

1   *Victory Square* by Robert Kemp (1908-1967) opened at the Citizens' Theatre on 15 January 1946. Kemp, a BBC producer, was best known for his adaptation of Sir David Lindsay's *Ane Satyre of the Thrie Estaits* which was performed at the Edinburgh Festival in 1948, and for his adaptations into Scots of Molière's *L'Ecole des Femmes* and *L'Avare* as *Let Wives Tak Tent* and *The Laird o' Grippy* respectively.

2   The issue was vol.2, no.2 (December 1945), the first of the second series. It was published by The Caledonian Press, Glasgow.

3   Nan (Agnes) Walker was his wife. They had married in Glasgow Cathedral in 1943.

4   Ian Whyte was in charge both of BBC Music in Scotland and conductor of the BBC Scottish Orchestra.

5   Sir Adrian Boult (1889-1983) was the first conductor of the BBC Symphony Orchestra 1930-1950 and principal conductor of the London Philharmonic 1950-1957.

6   Frederic Lomond (1868-1948), Scottish pianist and composer. He published *Beethoven: Notes on the Sonatas* (Glasgow, 1944) and left fragments of an autobiography, *The Memoirs of Frederic Lomond* (Glasgow, 1949).

7   Joseph MacLeod was Managing Director of Scottish National Film Studios, an early attempt to establish a Scottish film industry. William MacLellan was a member of the inaugural group which met on 3 November 1945. Offices were taken at 121 St Vincent St, Glasgow. MacLeod resigned early in 1947 as the initiative did not attract enough capital.

77. From T. S. Eliot (EUL MS2967/3)

[Faber headed notepaper]
Faber & Faber Ltd Publishers
24 Russell Square
London WCl
4 February 1946

Dear Mr. Grieve,

I have had your Joyce poem a long time. I found my Board indisposed to take it on but I am afraid I have been hanging on to it and brooding over it by myself from time to time to try to think whether anything could be done. It is a magnificent tribute to language and even the least sympathetic critic could not deny that it is an astonishing piece of work. I don't believe that more than a very few people would read it because I don't think that more than a very few people have the right infatuation with language. But I still don't see what can be done and I at last reluctantly return it. Have you thought of Nicholson and Watson as a possible publisher?

With deep regrets and best wishes,

Yours sincerely,

T. S. Eliot.

78. From Neil M. Gunn (EUL MS2948.15 f.41)

Braefarm House
Dingwall
Ross-shire
6 February 1946

Dear Christopher,

I have been travelling in the North & come back to find *The Voice* that breathes o'er Scotland – shouts might be better! – and my own name under 'Good-bye Twilight'.[1] This is handsome of you & I hasten to send due & proper acknowledgements. I have used Sibelius in many sic an argument myself so the matter of the poem is familiar, though it would be exhilarating to have a good-going discussion about it all, not forgetting the musical highbrows who deplore that so great a musician should have composed so much commonplace stuff! And your reference to Kafka has its point too, even if he thought all his writings should be burned. There's no bottoming the old human mind!

I was in Glasgow since I saw you last, but unfortunately got waylaid by some medical friends & failed even to do the business I should have done. I saw Taylor Elder, the painter, when he was here some time ago & he was full of interesting news & ideas. If you see him give him our regards & say we are still waiting for his promised epistle. We enjoyed him very much.

I gather you are in grand trim yourself & carrying on the old fight in the best style. Fine!

I have no idea when I'll be down again but if I do heave in sight you'll have to take me places and be spoken to wide, large and handsome.

All the best!

Yours,

Neil.

---

[1] 'Goodbye Twilight' was first published in *The Voice of Scotland* vol. 2, no. 3 (March 1946). *C.P.* II, pp.1124-1126.

79. From Denis Saurat (EUL MS2960.3 f.10)

22 Queen's Gate Gardens
London SW7
26 February 1946

Dear Grieve,

Thank you for Silver[1] – *part* of his essay is useful.[2] But I want a thorough going attack on religion as such from an intellectual rationalist materialist Marxist angle – rationalist chiefly; and *I am not getting that*. 3 or 4 essays have been sent in, but they all avoid the main issue to stress sociology, or economics, or psychology or politics. I want *you* to say: religion is wrong; religion is altogether a mistake, and this is why. *How* the mistake arose is irrelevant. I have had too many explanations of the origin of it; your point should be to prove it is wrong.

Now, buckle to and hurry up; you will be a hero. There does not seem to be *one* bona fide unbeliever left.

Affectionately,

D. Saurat.

[1]   Robert S. Silver (1913-1997) was born in Montrose . He became Professor of Mechanical Engineering at Heriot-Watt University in 1962 and was appointed James Watt Professor of Mechanical Engineering at Glasgow University in 1967. His best-known non-scientific publication is *The Hert o Scotland*, sub-titled *Robert I, King o Scots*, which was first published by the Saltire Society in 1986. An amended and expanded edition was published by the Scottish Cultural Press in 1995.

[2]   Saurat's plan for a book on religion in the post-second World War era reached galley proof stage but was unpublished.(Cf. Robert S. Silver, 'Student culture in the 1930s and aquaintance with CMG' in *Edinburgh Review*, Edinburgh, 1986, pp. 63-75).

80. From Paul Potts (EUL MS2958.9 f.6)

6 Belsize Square
Swiss Cottage
London NW3
7 April 1946

Dear Chris,

Orwell and I will be in Glasgow for a day or part of one in roughly, the second week in May, on our way to spend the summer on Jura.[1] George would like to meet you very much and I would love to see you again so could you send me your home address or phone no.

My regards to your family.

Yours etc.,

Paul Potts.

The following is the condition of broadsheet sales.[2]

Sold on the sidewalks to date	657
To you	50
To New York City	25
To Winnipeg, Manitoba	25
To the literary gang, newspapers etc via post	48
To myself	12
Lost dirtied torn etc while selling	7
	854
On hand	146

[1] It is not known whether Potts and Orwell met MacDiarmid on this occasion. MacDiarmid was included in Orwell's list of 38 journalists, writers and actors who in his opinion were '[...] crypto-communists, fellow-travellers, or inclined that way and should not be trusted as [anti-communist] propagandists.' On 2 May 1949 he enclosed this list to Celia Kirwan who worked for the Information Research Department of the Foreign Office. MacDiarmid was described as 'Dissident Communist but reliably pro-Russian.' *The Guardian*, 21 June 2003.

[2] This refers to sales of MacDiarmid's ' Speaking for Scotland' broadsheet (1939) but the figures don't add up correctly.

81. From George Campbell Hay (NLS Acc.7361/1)

10557059 Sgt. Hay
Carstairs Military Hospital
30 June 1946

Dear Christopher,

I'm sending you on this French pome for *The Voice of Scotland*.[1] I wrote it in Algeria in 1943, but you'll find it still has plenty of meaning. Glad to see the translation from the Greek got through safely.

Probably I'd have been able to send you along more, but I unfortunately had a nervous breakdown which put me in hospital for a matter of two months, and sent me home from Salonica via Athens and Naples. At present I'm up (or down) here at Carstairs convalescing a trifle dreichly and awaiting discharge with some eagerness, but unfortunately unable to write a scrape. Surroundings and company are not at all conducive to composing, or even thought, for they are utterly cretinous and wearing.

When do the Faber anthology and your long poem come out? I have a copy of the second on order and looking forward very much to reading both.

Looking forward to seeing you some time, either here or in Glasgow or Edinburgh.

Le mias is deagh dhùraidh,

Suas Alba,

Deòrsa.[2]

PS I've printed it, so the typesetter won't be likely to make any mistakes. I enclose a Gaelic poem, as well, along with translation.

[1] *The Voice of Scotland*, vol. iii, no. 1 (September 1946) included six poems by George Campbell Hay: ' Three Poems from Modern Greek', 'The Prince's Army' and 'Europe's Piteous Plight' in Gaelic and English, and 'Epreuve de Doute', pp.12-19.

[2] 'With respect and kindest regards / Up Scotland / George'.

82. From O. H. Mavor (James Bridie) (EUL MS2955.5 ff.2-3)

[On 'The Citizens' Theatre Ltd.' headed notepaper]

16 Roman Road
Dumbartonshire
13 July 1946

My dear MacDiarmid,

Your many friends, present and emeritus, are well aware that a person has only to make a successful attempt to do something for the Arts, Industry or Commerce of Scotland to become an immediate target for your bile. At the same time I am flattered that you should have devoted ten pages of your recent pamphlet to an attack on me.[1] I should have been more flattered if the other twenty-four pages had shown a vestige of merit or if the attack itself had evidenced a little more regard for the facts of the case, the laws of controversy, and the canons of English composition. Good sense and good manners were hardly to be expected.

Three years ago a group of Glasgow men determined to provide for Glasgow a resident company of professional players with a theatre of their own. They have provided this theatre. Both personally and by implication they have invited and continued to invite Scottish authors to try their hand at the difficult art of play-writing. Bearing in mind that the toad, ugly and venomous, has yet a precious jewel in its skull I sent you a civil request to participate to which you did not do me the courtesy to reply. I am still waiting for a sign that your nest of national socialist geniuses is prepared to do a hand's turn to help the Scottish Drama. I have only your word that they are capable of doing so – a word on which I have learned not to place very great reliance.

The offer is still open. I knew it would be said that London-trained actors cannot perform Scottish plays. Even if this were true we must make a beginning somewhere. Under the present deplorable conditions London is the only place where the average actor can undergo the discipline that perfects him in his life's work. It is only by founding and supporting theatres outside London that we can provide that discipline without the taint of London faults and follies. But such a theatre must have a nucleus of trained actors until we can establish a training school of our own. Acting is not, with all respect to Mr. Wilkie,[2] a part-time hobby.

In any case, if you know anything at all about it, which I gravely doubt, you should know that in any proper kind of theatre the play makes the actors. If you give us plays you will be at liberty to attend rehearsals and mould the play to your heart's desire.

If your answer to this is that I, James Bridie, sit like Cerberus in the manger stopping all these brilliant works as they arise I must simply give you the lie. You have a poor opinion of my work and to that opinion you are fully entitled but I don't think you can deny me a certain mean level of technical competence. It is on the grounds of technical competence alone that I have taken it upon myself to oppose the production of any play offered to the theatre. You lie explicitly when you say that I either publicly or privately have ever said that I had no use for the propaganda of ideas. So long as I am connected with this theatre I will object as strongly as I can to the production of any string of political clichés masquerading as a play; but that is entirely another matter. I am old-fashioned enough to believe that aesthetic values can be separated from political theory. That is the only really honest point of difference between us. It should surely make me less impervious to works of art with whose theme I do not happen to agree.

It is advanced as proof of my alleged dictatorship that a number of the plays presented have been original works by myself. I rather think the number is four and I make you a present of the fact that an Ibsen and a Molnar[3] were also adaptations by me. All my original works were invited by the Board; one of them was withdrawn from the Old Vic who wished to include it in their repertory of Shakespeare, Chekhov, Ibsen and Rostand.[4] Each of these plays was a free gift to the company. It is a matter of opinion whether four out of forty is too large a proportion; but while we are on the topic I think that the proportion of MacDiarmid in the current *Voice of Scotland* is even more considerable. I also reflect that, even in my college magazine days, I never wrote anything quite so bad as the McGonagallese insult to Queen Mary:[5] that I would have been beaten in school for turning out an exercise in such atrocious French as 'Tristan and Iseult'.[6] I have never pretended to write great plays, but you, sir, have written great poetry. I beg of you to be a little more respectful to yourself.

It is only the consideration mentioned in my last sentence but one that has led me to waste so much time in replying to you and your foolish little friend, the Honours graduate and ex-member of the Rutherglen Repertory Theatre. Let me assure you in conclusion that the Citizens' Theatre is by no means on its last legs. With this thought I leave you to crow in your own little midden my dear *orphelin d'Orage*.[7]

Yours faithfully,

O. H. Mavor.

---

1 Mavor refers here to an unsigned editorial in *The Voice of Scotland*, vol.II, no.4 (June 1946).
2 Robert Blair Wilkie contributed 'The Citizens' Theatre: A Nuisance and A Menace' to the same issue, pp. 2-8. He published *Remembered Radiance* (Macdonald: Edinburgh, 1956).
3 Ferenc Molnar (1878-1952), Hungarian dramatist and novelist.
4 Edmond Rostand (1868-1918), French playwright whose greatest success was *Cyrano de Bergerac* (1897).
5 'Die Grenzsituation', *C.P.* II, p.1331.
6 *C.P.* II, pp.683-684.
7 'Orphan of Orage'. Perhaps it was at this time that Bridie wrote 'The Blighted Flyting of James Bridie and Hugh MacDiarmid' which included the lines ' The puddock in the wall-e'e, ugly and venemous, / Carries a gaud in its skull.' (NLS Acc.11309)

83. From Joan Littlewood (EUL MS2965.11 f.16)

Theatre Workshop Ltd[1]
3 Robert Street
London WC2

Dear Christopher,

There has been a terrible setback. An hour ago Ewan was taken away under military escort. It is just six years since he deserted. I was warned a week or so ago that some ill-disposed person was likely to go to the police in London. It is symptomatic of the hatred some of the Party people have for him.[3] I am still stunned by tonight's happenings but as far as I can see the only hope is to plead extenuating circumstances at the court martial. He was a sick man in the Army – that can be one plea. I can get doctor's notes to prove that he has been ill a good deal since. Secondly, he could build up an 'artistic neurosis' story, I should think. I don't know how much he can be depended upon, he has never been able to compromise in any way, I mean, make himself pleasant or very tactful.

I have a letter from his captain saying that he would be far more useful outside the army.

I am sorry to bother you with our personal troubles. I know your advice will help me.

The colonel and his wife[4] have been quite reasonable, naturally they want it kept as quiet as possible. I must do everything in my power to get his sentence lightened because he is constitutionally incapable of living an army life for long. I asked him to leave here when we heard that someone in London was threatening to go to the police but he seemed incapable of going off on his own. He had lived as a hermit for five years and he would not face going off to be on his own again.

What a mess we are in.

I don't think the company will be hurt by all this, after all he will be charged as Jimmie Miller. Mike has power of attorney for all his writing.[5] It is possible, I suppose, that there will be publicity. I think we can avoid it.

Please let me know how you see it. I think I should use all the letters and publicity he has had. Do you agree?

Yours,

Joan.

---

1   MacDiarmid became one of the three directors of the Theatre Workshop in 1946. The others were William MacLellan and J.F. Ford.
2   This letter was misdated '1947'. This is clearly wrong since Jimmie Miller was released on 8 March 1947. (*Joan's Book*, London, 2003, p.274).
3   With regard to the person who may have informed on Jimmie Miller, Joan Littlewood writes, 'Ben [Ellis] was reluctant to rehearse the deserter until he received a letter from Jimmie wishing him luck and saying that his arrest had been a question of mistaken identity. The James Miller on their list was a much older man. Someone had told the police that there was a deserter named Miller in our company, calling himself MacColl. Who could have done such a thing? Someone who knew us. I didn't want to think about it.' (*Joan's Book*, p.232).
4   'The Colonel and his wife' were Colonel and Ruth Pennyman of Ormesby Hall. They were hosts to Theatre Workshop at this time.
5   'Mike' was Michael Thompson, then Business Manager of Theatre Workshop.

84. From Joan Littlewood (EUL MS2965.11 f.9)

> Theatre Workshop Ltd
> 3 Robert Street
> LONDON WC2
> Ormesby 23 December 1946

Dear Christopher,

Thank you for your letter. I wrote a reply yesterday but didn't send it because I hadn't heard anything coherent from him. I now have his address.[1] For three days there was no word. I couldn't trace him though I tried half a dozen barracks and police stations. The Army's Gestapo methods are most effective.

He is now caged up in a room with seven other men awaiting court martial. I've advised him to get hold of King's Regulations and the Army Act, but from the sound of things they are not treated as if they have any human rights whatsoever.

The Colonel here saw the Police papers and practically told me outright that Ewan had been informed on. I haven't told Ewan this.

I wonder if the records M.I.5 have of him will be at the disposal of the court martial?

I think the first thing is for me to get hold of as many letters as I can which state that Ewan's work is worth something. His defending officer can produce these at the court martial.[2] Then, if the sentence is heavy – whatever it is for that matter – we can start a public campaign.

I think the main thing is to prove the value of his work at the court martial. Up till now I suppose the whole thing has followed a routine – as a deserter he must face the court martial, there's no getting round that but I must shift heaven & earth to get a light sentence. I know he couldn't stand a couple of years of the glasshouse which must be about the most awful hell on earth.

If, Chris, you could let me have such a letter from yourself and from any other writers and artists who would be prepared to do this. Separate ones rather than a signed collective letter. I hope this won't be a worry to you, you have helped us a lot already. I don't know whether it would be safe to send such letters to him. I hear that letters are opened. It might be better if I collected them all and dish them to him, personally.

I will write Bill MacLellan and tell him what's happened.

My love to you and Valda.

Thank you both for your understanding.

Joan.

---

[1]   Ewan MacColl's address was: Private Miller J. H. / 3772842 N.W. No 2 I.T.C. / c/o Guard Room / Wingate Lines / Parkhall Camp / Oswestry / Salop.

[2]   Cf.EUL MS2965.11 f.10 29 December 1946, letter from Littlewood to MacDiarmid: 'Ewan has got over the first reaction to this business and is getting his perspective back. They've put him in uniform. For a day or two I thought he was going to lose his reason. We both felt as if we'd lost ourselves. Anyway, I've started things moving now and Bill [MacLellan]

is putting a spur into the publication of the plays. I intend to fight this business until he's free. For over a week he received none of my letters but now we've made contact we feel a lot better. He's got *Lucky Poet* with him, he says it's the best book for that place. .. .'
Also EUL MS2965.11 f.10 16 January 1947, letter to MacDiarmid: '...Ewan is at home on compassionate leave. He will be there until Jan 24 when he goes back to Oswestry Camp. I have tried every angle I could think of – I've got medical evidence from the doctor and specialist who attended him when he deserted, & from Kendal Hospital where he was a year ago – and a psychiatrist's report. I have some testimonials, not enough though ...'
Ewan MacColl's court martial, due on 17 February 1947, was cancelled on medical grounds, and he was released.

85. From David Orr (EUL MS2958.5 ff.36-37)

4 Hope Street
Leith
Edinburgh 6
[1946]

Dear Christopher,

I was hoping I might see you kinda casual like in either Edinburgh or Glasgow one of these days but it is a sort of needle in the haystack chance. It's unfortunate that one has to write to keep in touch with one's friends, see how much better it would have been if you had been like Duncan Bàn,[1] calling round the country and reciting your poems in the good old bardic way, it would have saved me lots of bother, & see the fun we would have had.

Since seeing you I have been to the Shetlands, and the bonnie isle, where Glibie,[2] Johnnie Geordie,[3] & a few others were enquiring kindly for you, and hoping to see you soon. There's not much difference, the sea the dotted isles, and Auld Williamson[4] just as of yore, but the auld laird & his lady are gone,[5] but it seems sma' change a' the same. The lassies just as bonnie, indeed bonnier, gave me a richt warm welcome, tea hame-baked scones, and whisky, everything was grand, my supply of John o' Groats lasted not so badly. The herrin fishing had just finished & was very successful, so too was the hairst, it also was good, the one trouble was the shortness of my stay, but next time I'll stay longer if no' for guid.

The Coop are going ahead as you know, they were bargaining with Johnnie Shearer for his butcher's business, some say he had a blank cheque, some that he had been offered £500, but a near relation informed me he had been offered £4000 for business and croft, enough to mak' the auld laird gie a bit grump or turn. There is also some talk of Hay's selling out lock, stock & barrel of their whole Shetland business, to the Coop, but that was just a side whisper, & was not generally known in Whalsay.

I saw Jamie Arthur,[6] I called at his house twice, he seems to be holding on, & probably will manage to hold his own for a time yet, I didn't discuss the Coop business with him, but he was in good form, & was organising for the first post-war regatta.

Altogether I had a fine stay, weather was perfect, food – butter, meat, fish, vegetables, eggs etc. & no' a coupon to show. I went up to 17 stone, & it wasna the whisky to blame.

In a Scottish sense things have been a bit quiet, Sydney Smith is writing some articles for John Bull, one appeared on Rosyth, & he has another on Leith, written under James Gow.

I saw Scott-Moncrieff's play,[7] not much drama about it, so topical it could hardly go outside of Scotland, but in the philosophy of the 'Storm-Cock',[8] a poor churning note in winter is better than nothing, and it is but a first trial, and if not so entertaining as Bridie's 'it all depends what you mean',[9] it has at least more grit.

As to the SNP there is not much to say, it continues to follow events from a safe distance, & I feel it has lost a lot of ground during the last few months. I find it difficult to attend Council meetings & am considering resigning, there was always a better personal association when you were there, and I just don't feel like running through to Glasgow to sit listening to (or for) cerebral manifestations.

How is the writing going? I suppose it is just as difficult if not more so than ever, at least I have not seen any more Scottish things except *Scoop*'s publication.[10]

I saw Sorley MacLean, he is speaking at Glasgow to the Gaelic Society soon, he was in good fettle, but he had just seen Davie who has been appointed to a post in Belfast where he is first man in Moral Philosophy, there being no Professor, he has £650 a year, & he seemed to be in very good heart according to Sorley.

Trust you are keeping well and hope to see and hear from you soon. With every regard.

Yours,

David.

---

[1] Duncan Bàn MacIntyre.
[2] 'Glibie' or 'Gliebie' was John Irvine, captain of *Valkyrie*. He was born in a small cottage called 'The Glebe' below the manse – whence his nickname.
[3] 'Johnnie Geordie' was John G. Anderson who sold MacDiarmid his cottage at Sudheim or Sodom.
[4] Possibly Jimmy Williamson of Brough, father of Lizzie, Dr Orr's housekeeper.
[5] 'The auld laird & his lady' were Mr and Mrs W. A. Bruce.
[6] Arthur was a General Merchant.
[7] *The Fiddler Calls the Tune* was produced at The Alhambra, Glasgow, 22-27 June 1946.
[8] The 'Storm-Cock' reference is to MacDiarmid's poem 'The Storm-Cock's Song' (*C.P.*, I, p.565).
[9] James Bridie's play *It Depends What you Mean* was performed at Westminster Theatre, London from 2 October 1944-10 March 1945.
[10] *Scoop* was published by Scoop Books Ltd. Four issues of *Scots Writing* were published by Scoop Books Ltd, Glasgow between 1943 and 1947.

86. From Edwin Muir (EUL MS2955.19 f.21)

THE BRITISH INSTITUTE

Director
EDWIN MUIR   Č.j.ref.   PRAHA II
                                                                Panská 7
                                                                Kaunický palác
                                                                10 February 1947

Dear Christopher,

If I may still call you so after our long feud, in which you will give me the credit of
never having taken part (but it does not take two to make a feud), I am now writing
to ask if you would care to contribute some poems either new or old, to a Czech
literary quarterly which wishes to bring out a Scottish number.[1] It is edited by the
veteran Czech poet, Seifert,[2] one of the best now living, and I have been asked to
help in getting together poems, short stories, etc. for this number. I sincerely hope
you will send something, even if it is to me, whom you may regard merely as a
middle man in this emergency. We seem to have been at odds for a long time; I think
that is quite unnecessary, seeing that we once used to be friends. At any rate, any
grudge you may have against me should not affect your decision in this case. With
kind regards and best wishes.

Yours ever,
Edwin Muir.

C.M. Grieve Esq.,
c/o Messrs William MacLellan Ltd.,
Glasgow,
Scotland.

---

[1]   A later letter from Muir (16 June, 1948) indicates that 'the Scottish number of the Czech
      Literary Review will not appear' (EUL MS2955.19 f.22). Therefore it would appear that
      MacDiarmid did send something.
[2]   Jaroslav Seifert (1901-1986), poet and journalist.

87. From William Tait (NLS Acc. 7361/18)

                                                                'Ravenscourt'
                                                                Lerwick
                                                                Shetland
                                                                9 July 1947

Dear Mr. Grieve,

I am enclosing a rendering into Shetlandic of Villon's 'La Belle Heaulmière' which
I hope you will consider for publication in *The Voice of Scotland*. I have appended
a glossary which should enable anyone able to read Lallans to understand the
poem. The spelling adopted is roughly but not extravagantly phonetic: the main
difficulty has been what to do with the sound usually represented by 'ø'. Apart from
typographical difficulties, I am all against using extra-alphabetical symbols; and

throughout the poem I have used 'oe' rather than the usual Lallans 'ui', which has a quite different pronunciation. If possible, this should be printed as a digraph.

I got your present address from Peter Jamieson, Editor of *The New Shetlander*. I can't help wishing that, now that one or two of us are trying to stimulate some sort of a literary flowering in Shetland, we still had you in the Islands, as your help and advice would have been invaluable. At the very least, I hope we can show that the Norn leid is capable of a much wider range of expression than has ever been attempted in the past, and rescue from the comparative oblivion of Jacobsen's Dictionary some of the lovely words fast disappearing from our speech.

I suppose a poem of 300 lines would be too long even for *The Voice of Scotland*? I have one, in English not in Shetlandic, of which I should very much like your opinion. I call it 'Scorched Earth'[2] and it is, briefly, the story of an imaginary German invasion of Scotland in 1940, if Hitler had struck West instead of East. The poem opens and closes in a still neutral Moscow where a group of short wave listeners hear the story told by a member of the beleaguered Scottish Army still holding the Highland line against superhuman odds. Incidentally, I have taken the liberty of introducing, though not of course by name, George Davie as one of the characters. Even if the poem were not so long, the current anti-Russian campaign would render its acceptance by most periodicals very unlikely. If I can have your permission, I should be very glad to send it to you to get your comments, even if these should be quite unfavourable.

Yours sincerely,
William J. Tait.

P.S. Sorry no foolscap envelopes to be had in Country shop where I am presently holidaying. W.J.T.

---

[1] 'Les Regrets de la Belle Heaulmière' was published in *The Voice of Scotland*, vol. iv, no. 1 (September 1947), pp. 21-25.
[2] 'Scorched Earth (1941)' –'1942' in the 'Contents' – was included in Tait's *A Day Between Weathers*, sub-titled 'Collected Poems 1938-1978' (Edinburgh:Paul Harris, 1980), pp. 114-122. 'Les Regrets de la Belle Heaulmière' was also included, pp.61-63.

88. From Jessie H. Grieg (NLS Acc. 7361/18)

Old Ballikinrain
Balfron
21 July 1947

Dear Mr MacDiarmid,
I have just listened to your broadcast. I am a Scotswoman, Glasgow born & bred, & it has always made me feel rather ashamed that when my countrymen, & especially my townsmen, get on the air they sometimes adopt an aggressive and rather rude attitude to their listeners and are dogmatic & crude in expression.

You certainly excelled in these things tonight.

If you really feel so annoyed about Edinburgh and its Festival, would it not have been better to state your views a little less rudely? In my opinion Glasgow people are kindly, hospitable & courteous. Their reputation for kindliness & hospitality to our fighting men of all nations was unequalled. Do you have to try to spoil that & put yet another weapon into the hands of our Edinburgh friends by being so unjust & so unreasonable in your statements?

This Edinburgh Festival may have many faults, but in my opinion it is a brave effort to put Scotland on the artistic map. In these days when our young people are flocking to hear good music, & thirsting for something to satisfy their need for beauty & self-expression through the arts, it seems to me that the narrow & prejudiced view you have taken of the Festival & the manner in which you have expressed it should be severely criticised.

Yours faithfully,

Jessie H. Greig.

89. From Peter Thomson (EUL MS2976)

The British Broadcasting Corporation
Head Office: Broadcasting House, London, Wl
Broadcasting House
Queen Margaret Drive
Glasgow W2
29 July 1947

Dear Sir,

Sorry for the delay in replying to your letter of 8th July, but I have been tied up with numerous outside broadcasts recently.

I should like to thank you for your kind offer to supply reports and results of Cricket, Football and Rugby, etc., and the members of our Sports Department will be glad to call on your assistance when any sports item of interest takes place in your area.

Our standard rate of payment for telephoned reports is 5/-for 50 words.

Yours faithfully,

Peter Thomson.

90. From Mary C. Dott (NLS Acc.7361/18)

The Scottish National Party
59 Elmbank Street
Glasgow C2
30 December 1947

Dear Mr Grieve,

I have your letter of 19th instant and I am sorry at the delay in answering. I was not in Glasgow last week and so the correspondence has been held up.

"CONSCRIPTION IS THE BADGE OF THE SLAVE" published by the Scottish Resistance Committee [1948]. '2000 needed for Sunday' in MacDiarmid's handwriting. By permission of the National Library of Scotland.

BURNS SAID

Ye hypocrites are these your pranks
to murder men and give God thanks?

~~~~~~~~

OUR ANCESTORS SAID in the Arbroath Declaration, in the year 1320—

'For so long as one hundred of us shall remain alive, we will never submit to English domination.'

~~~~~~~~

WHAT DO YOU SAY?

~~~~~~~~

Rally to All Meetings of

SCOTTISH RESISTANCE

Published by Scottish Resistance Committee (Secy., G. Hamilton, 271 Bilsland Drive, Glasgow. Printed by the Caledonian Press, 793 Argyle Street, Glasgow, C.3.

With regard to your membership of the Party, I would suggest that you discuss it with Miss Jean Drummond, the Secretary of the Glasgow Central Branch, or Mrs C. L. Gibson, the Treasurer of the Branch, so that the matter may be cleared up satisfactorily.

The organiser tells me that you are not on the current list of members of Glasgow Central Branch but, as you explained to me when we last met, as you did not have a receipt for the subscription you paid it is possible there has been a misunderstanding somewhere.

You can quite appreciate that, as Secretary of the Party, I cannot tell at any given moment who are members and who are not. Until the last day I saw you my own impression was that you had not been a member of the Party for some years.

With kind regards to the Grieve family and the compliments of the Season to your good self.

I am,

Yours for Scotland,

Mary C. Dott.

National Secretary

91. From Burns Singer (EUL MS2976)

C.M. Grieve Esq.
c/o *Carlisle Journal*
Carlisle
England
[1947]

Dear Chris,

Sorry my poor wearridden brain forgot to let me come. But here's my better half with all the thought in the world sent over to you. I wish I had seen you, as chances are I won't again since I don't intend to return to this snaky lochy country. The rest is prose (*Hamlet* or something like that). Since I'm broke in Paris I half hope you might send me the addresses of anyone who is likely to be able to give me a meal in return for a partisan dissertations on the S. Ren. If you find immediate time & desire to send me an introductory letter could you send it 'c/o Clubbe littéraire de la France, 94[?5] Boulevard Raspail, Paris'.

Yours in a teary time,

(Your likely G.I. friend & admirer)

Jimmy Singer.

P.S. Only existing copy of enclosed chunk of prose (or poetry?).[1]

---

[1]   P.6 of a TS survives (EUL MS2976 unsorted).

92. From Robert Blair Wilkie (NLS Acc.7361/19)

99 St Andrew's Road
Glasgow S1
30 January 1948

Dear Chris,
There will be a full-scale meeting of the Resistance Committee on *Tuesday* night at the above address at 7pm.
  Business will be
  (a) Statement and review of the Camlachie Bye-Election.[1]
  (b) Consideration of the future activities & programme of the Resistance Committee.
  Warmest regards.
  Robert.

[1] Robert Blair Wilkie was the Independent Scottish Nationalist candidate at the Camlachie By-Election in January 1948. He came fourth out of six candidates and received 1320 votes. The Resistance Committee also supported Hugh MacDiarmid when he stood as an Independent Scottish Nationalist in Kelvingrove in the General Election in 1950. He received 639 votes and came last of four candidates in the Election on 23 February.

93. From Ronald K. R. Taylor (NLS Acc.7361/19)

Kindrogan
Enochdhu
Blairgowrie
Perthshire
Albainn
2 May 1948

Dear Hugh MacDiarmid,
The first general meeting of the Clann Albainn Society will be held in Central Halls on Thursday, 3 June at 6.30 p.m., the main business of the evening being the election of the office-bearers for the coming year.[1]
  The following have been proposed or have signified their intention of accepting office: Hon. President, Douglas Young; Hon. Vice-Presidents, William Power, Peter F. Anson,[2] Nigel G. Tranter,[3] William MacLellan; Chairman, J. Foster Forbes F.R.A.I., F.S.A. Scot.
  Would you be prepared to give your name as an Hon. Vice-President or (?) assist us in our task of proving that the Gaidhealtachd is more than a glorified deer-forest or recreation ground for tired business-men?
  Yours for Scotland,
  Ronald K. R. Taylor.
  Secretary, Clann Albainn Society.

The first Clann Albainn Society had been a small nationalist secret society formed in 1930. Lewis Spence recorded in the *Daily Record*, 21 May 1930: 'On the 10th May, 1930, as some Scottish political historian of the future may in a weak moment record, six men foregathered in a Glasow hotel and resolved on the formation of a Scottish secret society – Clann Albainn'. The names of these men have never been discovered nor any primary document relating to the aims of the society. MacDiarmid gave the name Clann Albann to the five parts of a projected poem of which sections appeared in *First Hymn to Lenin and Other Poems*, *Second Hymn to Lenin* and *Scots Unbound and Other Poems*. The aim of the second Clann Albainn Society was to restore arable land which had fallen out of cultivation. To this end a search was made for suitable crofts to take over and the site of the first settlement was at Durnamuck, Dundonnell, Wester Ross. Douglas Young withdrew as Hon. President as he was going to be out of Scotland for nearly six months and his place was taken by the Countess of Errol. MacDiarmid agreed to be an Hon. Vice-President. Rona Lorne Black, daughter of Robin Black and later wife of Ronald K. R. Taylor, was Hon. Treasurer. Other members included Eric Linklater, Dr Agnes Mure MacKenzie and Hon. David Watson.[4] Bulletin no.6 of the Society recorded in 1949: 'The first pioneer team is in the field and doing a grand job of work. One 10-acre croft is already drained, cleared and ploughed, and a small vegetable garden reclaimed. That sounds little enough for four men to have accomplished in three months; but think it over. Winter on the exposed coast of Wester Ross – lashing rain, fearsome gales, transport difficulties, and no modern machinery. Apart from a tractor hired for some ploughing, the rest of the work has been done with spades, picks and scythes. [...] We have bought a boat which cost us £12, we have a hen or two and soon hope to have our first in-calf heifer. But more cattle, more poultry, seeds and manures, timber and cement are only some of the things required. [...] We have now launched an all-out drive to raise our first target of £10,000. [...] As the first holding is now ready, the first permanent settler will move in in May [1949].' (NLS Acc 3721/37/1309). Rona Lorne Black, now Mrs R. L. Taylor, has told this editor in a telephone interview in January 2009 that the second Clann Albainn was ultimately unsuccessful through lack of funds though one man had obtained a croft through the Society and that it had remained in his family. Previously Scoraig had been identified as a possible site of a settlement. Scoraig was on the north side of Little Loch Broom, Durnamuck was on the south side.

[2] Peter F. Anson (1889-1975) was an artist and author who devoted his life to his interest in the sea.

[3] Nigel G. Tranter (1909-2000), historian and prolific author of historical fiction.

[4] Hon. David Watson, advocate.

94. From Robert MacLellan (EUL MS2954.14 ff.5-7)

Robert MacLellan
High Corrie
Isle of Arran
Scotland
20 June 1948

Dear Chris,

Thank you for your letter regarding 'The Flouers o Edinburgh'.[1]

Always after finishing a play I leave it for a long time then go back to it, bearing the opinions of my friends in mind, and revise it. My copy is out at the moment with a critic whose judgment I value very highly, but should be back in a few days. When it arrives I'll carry out my revision.

It seems to be clear from what you say that in the second act I fail to make the curtain convey beyond question that Charles' election prospects are completely damned.[2] I can remedy that in a few lines. No one will then expect the third act to deal with the election, as you and a few others seem to have expected, and the third act will then be received, like the first two, without the handicap of being approached with mistaken pre-conceived ideas. It seems obvious that if one approaches an act expecting it to deal with a subject which it hardly touches, and with anxiety in one's mind as to its quality, having heard an opinion that it goes off the rails, one is likely to wander into speculation every few lines, instead of absorbing it as it comes, with the consequence that one may miss much that is in it. The third act does, in fact, contain not only the implication of 'the two people of the old order, seeing nothing for it but to console each other in the general abandonment of all the values for which they have stood', but also a 'hint that the battle may not be lost altogether, that there may be a refluence of the old spirit'.

I do think that if I am a little less 'subtle' in the second act, and make it clear from the curtain lines that Charles' election prospects are utterly damned, there need be no fear of the third act failing to convey the play's intention. However, I will re-read the play with the necessity of clearing its intention at the forefront of my mind, and point any lines or passages which from that viewpoint seem slack or weak. I see that I shall have to make more of the fact that the younger generation is left at loggerheads with itself, and I must in some way during the final Dowie scene make the audience think of Robert Burns and yourself, without mentioning either of you by name.[3] But I do not think it would be wise, in fact it would be fatal, to put an explicit declaration of *our* faith into the mouths of any of my 18th century characters. The play is an interpretation of a period, and during that period our countrymen sold the pass. The older generation, in as far as it felt the need to resist the new order, was defeated at Culloden. The younger generation toed the line.

Don't worry about Mitchell's[4] ability as a producer. I prophesy that before long he will be acknowledged the best in Britain. The reason why the scripts are in London is that since the company is playing there, they must rehearse there. The play is to open in Edinburgh. It is booked for the Kings on the 8th September, but I hear rumours that it is to open the week before that in Princes Street Gardens, during the Festival. I feel uneasy about that but will thrash it all out when I next see Mitchell.

We'll have a good talk with you next time I'm up. I don't think you need worry much about the 'Flouers' not getting over. I'll do all I can to point its intention, and so will Mitchell.

Thank you very much indeed for your help, and for being so anxious.

With best wishes from us all, to all.

Sincerely,

Robert.

PS Met a cousin of yours not long ago, who seemed rather awkward about being related to you until he found that I was a fervent admirer. Then he basked in the reflected glory! He called you 'Christie Grieve'. We all do too now. R.

1   'The Flouers o Edinburgh', sub-titled 'A Comedy of the Eighteenth Century in Three Acts', is set in the years 1761-2. There are topical references to the Treaty of Union and Culloden, whether to speak and write English or Scots, 'Moderates' in the Kirk, David Hume, John Home the dramatist, Dr Johnson and Allan Ramsay.
2   Charles Gilchrist had expected to win a seat at Westminster for Lanerick Burghs by granting favours; however, his methods were employed more quickly by another candidate.
3   'the final Dowie scene' in the third act refers to the Rev. Daniel Dowie who says, 'Oor ain dialect, Captain, is aa richt for a bit sentimental sang, but for the higher purposes of literature is inadequate.' Robert MacLellan, *Collected Plays Volume One* (London and New York, 1981), p.230.
4   Robert Mitchell.

95. From Edward Gaitens (EUL MS2948.6 ff.11-12)

134 Bothwell Street
Glasgow C5
21 September 1948

My Dear Christopher,

Once again I must say how deep a pleasure it was to be crouse and canty with you and Valda again after so long a time. And how cheerful it was to find you both so handsome with attractive health. Valda is a revelation in youthful beauty and a constant refreshment for the eye that looks for character and not callowness, or comeliness painted on.

I had a very nice letter from Haliburton yesterday, saying I would be in time if I sent a 1000 [word] article by Tuesday, so I sent him one to-day.[1] I do hope his Magazine soon becomes a monthly and a thoroughly good one for Scotland's sake. Then, of course, you should be the well-paid Editor of that distinguished journal.

I 'phoned the B.B.C. this morning to ask about short stories. It appears that a Mr Lee is in charge and that Richardson is in Edinbro.[2] I am determined to have at least three of my stories broadcast and I shall be frankly grateful for your help in the matter. Quite apart from the question of payment I think that some of the stories in my book should have been broadcast from Scotland a long time ago. [Frank] O' Connor is constantly reading his stories both on the Third Programme and from Radio Eiréann and sometimes they are no better than ornamental anecdotes. If Scotland is broadcasting really poor stuff then it's time someone took a good look at my genuine article. London & Glasgow have refused these stories before but I may get by this time. But I have decided for the time being to sidetrack Mr Lee as I don't want to waste time and possibly get rejection by giving them to the wrong man. So if you can find time for a word to Richardson about me while in Edinbro, I shall appreciate it.

I have been reading again your Anthology for the past week and gained much excitement and vision from your translation of 'The Praise of Ben Dorain'. I went to sleep the other night with my entire consciousness filled with a fair-sized mountain, teeming with the life of all the seasons, and in my mouth was the brave iron savour of mountain springs and in my nostrils the ironic scent of heather and peat and moss, like the ironic smile of an old man of the mountains who has become acquainted in solitude with the heights and depths of life and the subtleness of the human heart. And the 'winsome hinds' frisked about in my head while their parents browsed and lowered and raised their antlered heads.

I suppose it is thirty years since I was thrilled by the sight of moving antlers on a mountain-slope at the far side of a glowing loch, but I saw them clearly and was thrilled again the other night. And it is over twenty years ago since I saw, when walking with Charles, at four o'clock of a summer's dawn, round a bend of a road swinging in from the Rhine, a young fawn leap across our path. His small hoofs made no sound and in that unparalleled silence his flashing appearance and vanishing was sacred and awe-inspiring. We saw his radiant colour and form and stood in amazed delight hoping he would appear again.

While reading of Ben Dorain that fawn leapt across my vision again and I was overcome as supremely with inspired wonder as I was when I actually saw him. In the reflective hours of middle-age happenings as wonderful as that revisit us more vividly than when we saw them through the puzzled eyes of youth. And I believe we enjoy more profoundly such happenings as the years come on us, just as I find that I now read with more exquisite pleasure great books that I devoured voraciously in my youth. Really it is very good being fifty and I hope I'll live till I'm eighty with a mind and heart so stored with experience that I shall be the wealthiest man of my time.

Willie Power said the other day that your notes to the poems were excellent.

I hope I shall see you on Wed. and my love to Valda.

Edward.

---

[1] Not identified.
[2.] The producers were A.P. Lee and Robin Richardson.

96. From Douglas Young (EUL MS2961.18 f.42)

36 McLaren Road
Edinburgh 9
6 November 1948

Dear Chris,

Herewith the report of Dylan Thomas' speech to the Scottish PEN, the week after your disjune,[1] in which he referred to yourself and the Lallans matter in quite a reasonable way. I had not time to type it before going to Italy, nor since my return till now. If you are getting out an issue of *The Voice of Scotland* dealing with the disjune, then certainly this should go with it.[2]

I have nothing of interest for the next *Voice*, but in any case you will be short of space.

I am trying to get the Makars started again this winter, with the short-term objects of raising funds for a bicentenary statue to Fergusson, and of offering a disjune next year to Sir Wm Craigie, now over eighty,[3] whose services to the language ought to be honoured by other than the academic. As Sydney [Goodsir Smith] and I see it, Albert Mackie is the most suitable Preses, being of good public standing in Edinburgh and Glasgow, as well as well up in the tongues, and a competent man of affairs. For secretary we favour Alex Scott, whose position as first lecturer in Scots Literature makes him in a way the natural focus for the type of work the Makars must do. Maurice Lindsay has too many other irons in the fire, and is sometimes not too tactful. I hope if you see him you will support the line favoured by Sydney and me, i..e, the Mackie-Scott axis. I also wish to bring in the newer writers, who have taken over the neo-Lallans canon ready-made, and can concentrate on content without too much trouble for language, i.e., Kincaid,[4] Thurso Berwick,[5] etc. Lindsay seems not to favour their poetry or their politics. Again on this point I hope you will show him the need for considerable numbers to sustain even a small literary club, and also of the publicity value in the working class of their factory jingles, as I believe you term them.

On the political question, the SNP has now decided to exclude from ordinary membership any member of an organisation whose object is the furtherance of its own political, social or economic programme. Specifically they have included in this excommunication the Scottish Socialist Party of O[liver] Brown, and the Scottish Convention. Simultaneously, they have resiled from the old policy of fighting by-elections etc., and are concentrating on municipal work and trade union activity. The constitutional change seems singularly inept in relation to the new emphasis on local and infiltratory tactics. I have told Kirkcaldy nationalists that I won't stand there again under SNP auspices unless the SNP can endorse forty candidates throughout Scotland at a General Election.[6] I haven't time to nurse it as an Independent. What I am trying just now to get going is a series of local Scottish Assemblies, one for each constituency, to bring on one platform the sitting MP and the prospective candidates of other Parties, also spokesmen of Parties without candidates, to call them to account on the Scottish issue. Each constituency must form a committee of local public men, all Parties or none, to run the thing, and reconvene after a due interval to keep the pressure up. I also favour a liaison group to be called Friends of the National Assembly, which will finance and pressurise the (originally Convention) Assembly.

Hope to see you 28th at the MacLean affair.[7]

Yours for Scotland,

Douglas Young.

---

[1]   The occasion of the 'disjune' was the presentation to MacDiarmid of the portrait by David Foggie completed in Edinburgh in 1933. The event, hosted by the Makars' Club, took place in the Scotia Hotel, Edinburgh on 28 August 1948. On this occasion T.S. Eliot

wrote to the chairman, Albert Mackie, 15 August 1948, regretting that he was unable to be present, and concluding, 'It will eventually be admitted that [MacDiarmid] has done more also for English poetry, by committing some of his finest verse to Scots, than if he had elected to write exclusively in the Southern dialect.' (*MacDiarmid*, p. 396).

2 There were reports of the 'disjune' and also of Dylan Thomas's address to the Scottish PEN Centre on Saturday, 4 September 1948, also in the Scotia Hotel, in *The Voice of Scotland,* vol. v, no. 2 (December 1948), pp.19-25 and continued on p.32.

3 Sir William Craigie, philologist and lexicographer, 1867-1957.

4 John Kincaid (1909-1981) was one of the four contributors to *Fowrsom Reel,* sub-titled 'A Collection of New Poetry', and published for the Clyde Group by the Caledonian Press, Glasgow, in 1949.MacDiarmid wrote the Introduction.

5 'Thurso Berwick' (Maurice Blythman) (1919-1981) was also a contributor. The others were Freddy Anderson and George Todd.

6 Young had been an SNP candidate at a by-election for Kirkcaldy Burghs in 1944 and also at the General Election in 1945.

7 'The MacLean affair' was the commemoration of the twenty-fifth anniversary of the death of John MacLean on 30 November 1923. The John MacLean Society was formed on this occasion.

97. *From John Kincaid (EUL Gen.2094/3/1032)*

106 Haywood Street
Lambhill
Glasgow NW
15 December 1948

Dear Chris,

The meeting of the Renaissance Society will be in Glasgow Unity Theatre Centre at 7pm, Friday first.[1]

As you recommended, I went up to see Mrs Norrie Fraser at the Golden Eagle Press on Tuesday, but the 'springing' of the idea on her seemed to take her aback, rather, and she asked for a day's grace to arrange things.[2] I came away thinking of the problem of communication, when it suddenly struck me that Unity had plenty of room, and was, moreover, within a stone's throw of the State bar! So I went along and fixed it up that way, and posted the notices to all concerned.

I had an anxious letter this morning from Alexander Scott in which he wondered if I'd fixed up a meeting place and if members in Edinburgh and elsewhere had been circulated. I am writing to further assure him.

It strikes me that the first real business this Society must tackle is to hammer out a broad path as to how the Renaissance Society is to be promoted, and that that also should decide which matters we discuss and which we don't discuss. I for one should very much like to hear the points of view of all the members about the Renaissance conception.

Best wishes to yourself, Valda, and Michael.

Yours aye,

John Kincaid.

1   The Renaissance Society was formed in November 1948.
2   Mrs Norrie Fraser was Secretary to the Scottish Reconstruction Committee. She and A.I. Milton jointly edited *The New Scot* which was published monthly by The Golden Eagle Press, Glasgow, from 1945-49.

98. From Sydney Goodsir Smith (EUL Gen.2104/4/55-56)

18 Royal Terrace
Edinburgh
Sunday [1948]

Dear Chris,

Just a short note suggesting that if you are not spending next weekend in Oxford you might like to return via Edinburgh. On Friday 19th at 6:30pm at the Abbotsford (back room) we are having a gathering of the Makars to expand the Club into an association including what can conveniently be called the Renaissance writers – in other words, not just the Edinburgh Lallans Loons but also the Gaels and those who use English like MacCaig etc. This society to meet monthly in Glasgow and Edinburgh alternately, to discuss matters of interest in Scottish Literature as a whole, and producing an annual publication of our proceedings & contributions from all members. Such an annual demonstration might have a greater impact on the general life & thought of Scotland than anything hitherto produced. Also, the association is intended to heal the existing or potential breaches between East & West, Highland & Lowland, Politicals & Aesthetes, Lallansers & Anglicisers etc. etc. To provide a forum where one will be able to meet fellow-writers & discuss matters of general import.[1]

Thereafter, after a year or so, it might be even further extended to include artists in other fields, painters, composers etc. – all of whom could have (and especially among the different genres of writers) great and mutual fecundating influences.

No more for now.

All the best,

Sydney

1   The Makars' Club proposed a 'style sheet' for the Spelling of Scots at its meeting on 11 April 1947 in a hostelry in Edinburgh. This 'style sheet' was published in The *New Alliance and Scottish Review*, vol. 8, no. 2 (May 1947). The magazine was published monthly from April 1946 to August 1951 and bi-monthly September-October 1951 (last issue).

99. From Norman MacCaig (EUL MS2953.7 f.3)

7 Leamington Terrace
Edinburgh 10
8 February 1949

Dear Chris,

Here are the lyrics I've threatened you with for so long. Will you like them? I don't know; but I do know you're interested in whatever's going on, and anyway I'd rather be abused for my present faults than my past ones. And surely, surely, this'll put an end to loose talk about Apocalypticism!

If you're going to the next meeting of the Reniassance Soc. it'll save you the bother of posting these back if you let me have them then. At any rate, I hope you *will* be there, for many other reasons.

Best wishes,

Norman MacCaig.

100. From Mrs Bryce (NLS Acc. 7361/20)

'The Next of Kin of War Deceased Organisation'
(Scotland)
GLASGOW BRANCH
Affiliated to 'The National League of British Parents [for Allowances and Pensions]'
(England)

COMMITTEE:

President	Secretary	Treasurer
Mrs Lawson	Mrs. A. Bryce	Mr. J. Espie
353 Paisley Road	776 Argyle Street	689 Dalmarnock Road
Glasgow C5	Glasgow C3	Glasgow SE

776 Argyle St
Glasgow C3
6 June 1949

Dear Mr Grieve,

I enclose one of our leaflets, you will see we are holding a Public Meeting on June 19. We extend to you and the Members of your Party a cordial invitation to come along and help by your support to make the Meeting a success. I am sending out invitations to all other interested Organisations, Party's, etc etc.[1] I hope to hear from you that we can count on you and your Members to accept our invitation. I understand that *again* on the occasion you were to address our Members you would be absent unavoidably. Best wishes for your Party.

I remain,

Yours sincerely,

Mrs Bryce.

---

[1]   A letter from Mrs Bryce to Mrs Grieve, 2 August 1945 (NLS Acc. 7361/16) indicates that MacDiarmid had expressed support for the Organisation to Mr Bryce at the time of the 1945 Election. 'The Party' would therefore be the Scottish National Party.

101. From O. H. Mavor (James Bridie) (EUL MS2955.5 f.4)

Rock Bank
Helensburgh
Dunbartonshire
19 July 1949

My dear Chris Grieve,

I am busy with the reply to your diatribe.[1] I am making it as fierce as I can, but I am a much milder man than you and it may not come off.

You are, of course, outrageously wrong in almost every respect but I don't think you will mind that, or mind having it pointed out to you. I will send you the manuscript in a day or two.

All the best,
Ever yours,
O. H.

[1] MacDiarmid's 'diatribe' in *The Galliard* in 1949 has been reprinted in *The Raucle Tongue* III, pp.151-153.

102. From Robert Garioch Sutherland (EUL MS2960.21 f.4)

90 Constance Crescent
Hayes
Bromley
Kent
6 September 1949

Dear Mr Grieve,

Here is a copy of the 'Chuckies',[1] which I beg you to accept with my homage to you whose poems set me going about 15 years ago: an obvious enough remark, but there seems no harm in saying what is true. I wish, however, that I had done more in those 15 years or so, however.

Yours sincerely,
Robert G. Sutherland.

[1] The reference is to Garioch's *Chuckies on the Cairn*, poems in Scots and English, Chalmers Press, 1949.

103. From Sean O'Casey (EUL MS2958.1 ff.1-2)

Tingrith
Station Road
Totnes
Devon

9 October 1949

C.M. Grieve, Esq.
My dear Christopher,
First, greetings to you as ucht mo chroidhe.[1] It was very good to hear from you, though I've often heard of you. If you can, let me have *The Voice of Scotland*, or, better still, let me know the amount of annual subscription, & I shall be glad to listen to Scotland's Voice for a year once a day; & longer, till she holds her own place among the Nations. What a comment it is on our 'Western Civilization' that neither Scotland nor Wales has a voice or a vote among the 'United Nations'! Anyway, you've done a man's work in making Scotland's voice heard among her own people, and those out in the world; & many other nations whose knowledge of Scotland was something like 'Roamin' in the gloamin', or 'Keep right on to the end of the road'. And what a passionate & lyrical voice it is – the Scotland of the past, the present, the future.

As for that 'grievance', it was mentioned to me long ago by someone connected with MacLellan's, and I associated it with my acquaintanceship with McElroy, & what happened to you through him. When I came first to England, I was just a gaum, having practically no experience; possessed only of an honesty I thought all had as well as myself. McElroy was, I knew, something of a business rascal, but he was a character, and, in my mind then, a friend to artists. I thought he was standing by you through Peggy, & he gave me his word of honour that this was all he had in mind. It was long after, through conversations with his son that I discovered what an untrustworthy man he was. I for a long time was sure he'd never do anything mean or underhand to an artist. I was just a gaum.

I honestly don't remember receiving a letter from you asking me to try to get you in touch with your children. What I do recollect is that you asked my advice about a young lass of Shetland;[2] whether you would or would not hold her fast, seeing you were anxious about your children, & still had a gradh[3] for Peggy.

Well, Chris, a chroidhe, I decided not to reply. That was a such a delicate and personal problem (in my mind) that I thought any interference on my part would make matters worse. I was not in touch with McElroy; not for a long time before that. It is certainly a monstrous thing that you haven't had the opportunity of seeing & getting to know your children. They have been deprived of a great experience, &, I am sure, of much joy and spiritual encouragement. To me there is no meaner thing in existence than the power of money giving an opportunity to the meanest to hurt the noblest amongst us. There is nothing for this sort of thing but the fire and the sword. I know myself what poverty and insecurity are only too well. I knew these things always; I know them now. I could have freed myself from them had I been content to do what others wanted. (The artist is free in democratic countries!) I've refused many film offers, one of 100,000 dollars for a scenario, feeling that my soul & integrity are worth more to me (and maybe to the world) than that sum, or that sum ten times multiplied.

I can't come, unfortunately, to the London Peace Conference. Years of intermittent silicosis have pulled my heart about, and I have to go cannily now. I am doing a little for the Peace Conference to be held in Plymouth; but can't risk a speech. It is a nuisance, but it cannot be helped. Anyway, I'm getting on now – I shall be seventy next March – and it is as well that younger hearts should plunge into the struggle.

As far as I know, McElroy is still alive & kicking. I understand he is living somewhere in Chelsea with a Maggie Madison, who used to be his 'secretary', but I learned years afterwards that she was something else to him as well. I learned too, from his son, that he was anxious for me to take her up, & relieve him of her. Many things that come to my mind confirm that view, though I would as quickly go to bed with a telegraph pole as I would with poor Maggie. McElroy was the most egoistic & selfish mortal that ever crossed my path.

Where Peggy is, I haven't the slightest idea, nor have I heard of her for the last 16 or 17 years. If you like, I'll write to McElroy's son, Conn – though he may be dead, for for years he has been drinking himself to death –. If anyone knows, he'd know. But, maybe, you'd just as well be ignorant of these things – for, of course, the children. You certainly should know where they are and what they do. Why don't you write to Pritt about the legal aspect? I'm sure he'd advise you.

I am very sorry indeed that I can't see you in London. Ever since I met you, I have had you in my affections. Eileen sends her warm regards.

Believe me, Chris, a chroidhe,[4]

Yours affectionately & with deep admiration.

Sean.

---

[1] Literally ' from the bosom of my heart' ; ' from the bottom of my heart'.
[2] Valda wasn't 'a young lass of Shetland'; she was Cornish.
[3] 'gradh' – 'love'.
[4] 'a chroidhe', literally 'my heart'; ' my friend'.

104. From Ewan MacColl (EUL MS2965.11 f.108)

Theatre Workshop
England
All Communications Should Be Addressed To The General Manager: Gerald C. Raffles

151 Bury Old Rd
Manchester 8
[1949]

Dear Chris,

I was able to contact Douglas Young prior to his departure and have given him a note of hand to my German publishers so everything should be alright. The news about your new domicile's great – we'll chalk one up for the Laird![1] I expect that when you are settled in your output will exceed Lope de Vega's. Our Highland trip was completely satisfying – spent five weeks (and only £6) in a dying civilization – toured and camped in Morar, Glenfinnan, Mallaig, Skye and Wester Ross. Heard an old fisherman recite Duncan Ban and Alastair MacDonald and William Ross. Heard a tinker singing in Shelta, songs which, she said, were older than the mountains of Ross. I still haven't recovered my equilibrium.

Glad you've started work on *Macbeth*.[2] I'll be glad when it's written. I'm beginning to feel like a woman must feel in the final stages of pregnancy. Please let me have the result of your researches as soon as possible.

T.W. is playing at the Edinburgh Festival after all. We have got a small hall (quite unsuited for theatrical performances) which we will have to adapt to our needs. Unfortunately it is too small and too primitive to 'take' 'The Other Animals' so we are playing a mixed programme. During the first two weeks we'll be presenting a programme consisting of three short plays – 'The Proposal' by Chekhov,[3] 'The Love of Don Perlimplín for Belisa in the Garden' by Lorca and 'The Flying Doctor' by Molière. For the final week we'll be playing my new play 'Landscape with Chimneys' – this is a very simple work on the housing problem and I don't know how it will go. I hope we shall have you and Valda in the audience. I'll be interested to hear your views on the Lorca play.

Incidentally, do you know anyone in Edinburgh who could help us with digs for the period or part of the period. The entire city seems to be booked up and the few places that are left are quite beyond our means. Is Dr David Orr still living in Edinburgh? He was helpful the last time we played there. If he is, could you let me have his address along with that of any other character you can think of. This is a rather urgent matter, Chris.

The Kulturbund have invited us to play Eastern Germany. We are hoping to go there in January 1950. Do you think you might come with us?

Love to Valda – hope she got her share of the July sun.

Yours aye,

Ewan.

---

[1] 'We'll chalk one up for the Laird!' is a reference to MacDiarmid's move to the laundry cottage attached to the Duke of Hamilton's mansion of Dungavel in the autumn of 1949. In the following year Dungavel House was bought by the Coal Board as a residential training school for young miners.

[2] Ewan MacColl makes two other references in letters to *Macbeth*. In an undated letter, EUL MS 2965.11, f.105, he writes, 'The more I think about *Macbeth* the more I am convinced that we have the subject of a great Scots play. I am looking forward to working with you.' In another undated letter, ibid. f.109v., from 13 Wilmslow Rd., Withington, Manchester 20, he writes, 'There doesn't seem to be much chance of my getting up to Glasgow in the near future but I am still very keen on doing the Scots *Macbeth* so perhaps we can fix a date after the Scandinavian tour – that is if you are still interested.' In *Joan's Book*, Joan Littlewood records that she had written to MacDiarmid to ask him to write '[...] the true story of the Great King Macbeth and Gruach his queen, their resistance to the Saxons and the long march they led to save the Scottish army from annihilation[...]' (p.300).

[3] A one-act farce written in 1888-9 and first performed in 1890.

The 1950s

1. From Lida Moser (EUL Gen.2094/4/1600)

Friday, 24 February 1950

Dear Hugh,

I love you – I think of you and I try to think with you – When I left Glasgow – I rode on London Underground standing and I read *Voices of Scotland*– The trip home was dreadful – I love the sea – only when I stand on the shore or bathe in it – but in a ship – it reduces me to utter helplessness, and makes me too aware of how far from the real live human being I want to be – I am. In fact now that I think of it – I do not care for many of the carriers that take you off your feet for purposes of transportation. They're things I bear with only in view of the final destinations – and are tolerable because of the other poor souls sharing the experiences.

Last night I looked for a coffee grinder for Valda – and then went to hear Dylan Thomas read poetry.

I have many lovely pictures of you – I'm sending you some – but I can't send you all – because *Vogue* asked me to keep them undercover – until after their article appears which should be in May or June – I think it will be very nice and that you'll be very pleased with it.[1] Here is a stamp for Michael –

Love – Lida

[1] The Vogue article 'Scottish Talents' appeared in July 1950. The text was by Eric Linklater and was illustrated by Lisa Moser's photos of seventeen Scottish authors, artists, musicians, and public figures. MacDiarmid is shown standing among fallen trees and bracken at Dungavel.

2. From George Blake (NLS Acc. 7361/1)

East Devon Lodge
Dollar
Clackmannanshire
10 April 1950

Dear Christopher,

May I – even over several gulfs of misunderstanding – say how glad I was that you had been offered, and had received, the Civil List Pension?

This is a right thing. As I get older I get more and more sick of myself as a commercial novelist, earning easy money easily. The hell of it is that I write to the limit of a small capacity. I envy, more bitterly than you might imagine, your genius and integrity.

Yesterday, by a coincidence, I was re-reading *Circumjack* and laughing again over your fancy about the plaque on the wall of your Langholm School – Believe me, most sincerely do I trust that the little bit from the State will set you free again – A lyric or two again? You should hear my young daughter aged 15, mummlin out *Ae weet forenicht i' the yowe-trummle* –.[1]

Fraternally,
George Blake.

[1] The first line of 'The Watergaw' (*C.P.* I, p.17).

3. From George Blake (EUL Gen. 2094/1/49)

East Devon Lodge
Dollar
Clackmannanshire
21 April 1950

Dear C.M.G.,

Blessings on your frosty pow for your letter. I was happy to receive a message so candid.

Don't worry about chaps like me or about your instinct to assail us. I have always been truly fatalistic about that sort of thing: simply knowing, as I said before, that my range is necessarily small – essentially journalistic or expository. Indeed, in the 58th year of my age, I have come to see that my job should have been social and economic history, and now rather bitterly regret that circumstances denied me the academic training. My novels are only a way of blowing off this condensed steam. Like you, I don't read fiction; my bug is the social thinking of 19th century Scotland, when all the wild asses of the devil trampled over our land, left us a shambles and, I fear, fatally wounded the old Scotland.

As for Royal and Ducal condescendences, what the hell?[1] The poet is unique, a rare accident. There is much to be said for the survival of Patronage into these times, when no other accommodation is as yet in sight. If the house in the pine wood was the Duke's doing, then I take off my hat to him.

My young daughter has just kissed me goodnight. She has blushed and wants you to know that she is happy and excited about your suggestion. We call her Sally, but her true Christian names are rather pleasant – Ursula Mary – after her two grandmothers.

All good fortune. Spare the nerves in useless controversy – 'for none was worth my strife'.[2] And give us more and more poetry and of pure aesthetic excitement and fun.

G.B.

[1]   The Grieves stayed in the laundry cottage of Dungavel House, the property of the Duke of Hamilton, from the autumn of 1949 into January 1951.
[2]   'I strove with none; for none was worth my strife:
     Nature I loved, and, next to nature, Art.'
     - Walter Savage Landor, 'Dying speech of an old Philosopher' (1853).

4. From Mary Ramsay (EUL MS2958.12 ff.19-20)

11 Saxe-Coburg Place
Edinburgh 3
17 October 1950

Dear Chris,

I saw Tom Murray this forenoon & he tellt me you're awa to the USSR neist ook.[1] I

Scottish Art and Letters 5 - 1950.
© The Fergusson Gallery, Perth and Kinross Council.

tellt him ye'd nae doot gie's aa a shog whan ye got back – aiblins ane to the USSR i the bygaun.

I went in to ask T.M. gin they had ony further news o oor speir after the Wallace Letter[2] (see enclosed) – you'll maybe ken that I fand oot that aa the Municipal Archives o Lübeck war seized by the USSR army (they had been taen to the country somewhere 'for security') & the Scottish-USSR society undertook to make enquiries. T.M. has been in touch wi the Soviet Ambassador, but so far naething has come o't. He's tae ask the delegation to gang to Russia neist ook to tak the matter up whan they're yonder, but I thocht I micht as weel gie a scrieve to yoursel. The Soviet Ambassador recognised the importance o the document. Had it fa'en intil the hannds o the Yankee soldiery it wad been destroyed nae doot like aathing else, but wi the USSR army ane can hope siclyk documents wad be keepit & transportit to Russia. Gif occasion offers you'll aiblins speak o the matter amang friens o Scotland ower yonder.

I hear your laddie is a C.O. for Scotland's sake. It's to lads like him we maun luik the day for help to our belovid cintra. For us auld yins, our day's by, but we hae aye our blessings to gie to the youngsters that pit Scotland abune aathing else.

I hear ye're aye at Dungavel.

Love to Valda & yersel.

Aye wi ye for Scotland.

Mary Ramsay.

[1]   MacDiarmid was one of the three delegates who were elected to represent the Scottish-USSR Society at the November celebrations in Moscow in 1950. The others were David Campbell and George Hamilton. They left London on 26 October and arrived back on 11 November.
[2]   The Lübeck Letter is held at Archiv der Hansestadt Lübeck. It was displayed at Holyrood in the 'For Freedom Alone' exhibition in August 2005. The Letter is the only surviving document issued by William Wallace (1297) and was sent to advise European trade partners that Scottish ports were open for trade as Scotland had been freed from English control.

5. From Jack Lindsay (NLS Acc. 7361/52)

Arena
28 Southampton Street
[London] WC2
Friday [October 1950]

Dear Hugh MacDiarmid,

I have only got your letter on my return from Czechoslovakia and of course I would have replied earlier.

At Prague I noted that you were flying to Moscow, and was very pleased. I hope you had a chance to meet Tikhonov[1] whom (you will have gathered from my book) I like very much indeed as poet and man.

I see you say you'll be at Sheffield.[2] Hope to see you then. So for the moment.
Yours fraternally,
Jack Lindsay.

[1]   Nikolai Tikhonov (1896-1979): Soviet poet. Lindsay's book was *Three Letters to Nikolai Tikhonov* (London, 1950).
[2]   MacDiarmid went to the World Peace Conference in Sheffield the day after his return from Moscow. However, it only lasted one day (November 13) as several hundred foreign delegates had been refused entry into Britain. It was transferred to Warsaw (November 16-22).

6. From F. G. Scott (EUL MS2959 f.144)

44 Munro Road
Jordanhill
Glasgow W3
21 November 1950

Dear Christopher,

I'm returning the books as soon as I've found time to do so – I have Burges in bed with the doctor attending her – he says she's been over-working herself – has symptoms of cardiac trouble and high-blood pressure – and *must* keep in bed until he allows her to resume housework. She's been in bed now for about 10 days and I've had a real pigsty time of it.

Lovey has of course arrived in New York and her messages so far are all superlatives of delight and amazement.

I'm sorry I haven't time to discuss the enclosed books – he seems (Lukács)[1] to think that everybody who lived before 1848 was a kind of blind-bat that couldn't see the light – the really great geniuses of the past had just wee glimpses of what was coming, but we all have to wait till Lenin & Stalin pin a medal on Gorki, and such like, and we'll all fall on our knees – 'All Hail! Joe!' – Or something like that. I was chiefly pleased to learn from Lukács that Sir Walter Scott, and Tolstoi and a few other semi-imbeciles were quite passable in their own way and day, but was sad to learn that he couldn't put me on anyone else I didn't know about already.

Ever,
F.G.

[1]   Georg Lukács (1885-1971): Hungarian philospher and literary critic who had brief involvement in the governments of Béla Kun in 1919 and Imre Nagy in 1956.

7. From Norman MacCaig (EUL MS2953.7 ff.11-12)

7 Leamington Terrace
Edinburgh 10
11 July 1951

Dear Chris,

Your friend Howard Gurney[1] called on me for a half-hour visit and told me about the scheme to hold ceilidhs. I've passed on the information to Hector MacIver[2] thinking he might be useful – but he was so drunk I doubt if he remembers anything about it. I didn't see Sam and have failed to get him on the phone, so I'll write him tonight. I've been in hospital since Monday the 2nd, having lumps cut out of my tongue, so my activity has been a bit restricted. I intend to go off on holiday this Friday, if I can chew; so I'm polishing off, rather brusquely, the most necessary bits of correspondence that are cluttering up the mantelpiece.

I return the book with thanks – we discussed it when you were through here, you remember – and also the great, the prodigious, the extravagant (in a way) 'Once in a Cornish Garden'.[3] It gallops along. It goes off like a fuff of fireworks with its crimsons and peach colour and prune colour and all the rest of the fiery nonsense. The nonsense turns out to be something other, however, if I see rightly – you are after a kind of unity of experience that's possible only to a man who understands the observable world of objects and the mental world of ideas as they are in themselves, without throwing over them his own shadow. You are as much interested in the method (seeing straight and thinking straight) – being a didactic sort of character – as in the experience itself, which keeps your attempt to express it on a strictly intellectual level; the fact that it is an experience of this sort, however, gives your writing an intellectual value of a philosophic sort and not a scientific one – and that's its overlap into 'poetry'. In fact, you're trying to show in a clear and intellectual light something that people generally try to reveal through the technicolour mists of a sprawling emotionalism. No wonder you don't like what's called 'mysticism'.

Is this all nonsense? I could work it out better and certainly express it better if I had more time. But this handling of what looks like a transcendental theme in terms of strict observation and precise rationalism is something that fascinates me, and which I find a good deal of in your later work, as well as in this poem. When it comes off, it really is 'philosophical poetry' and the bird is no longer divided.[4]

I'm to be away for a month; but I look forward to seeing you again in August. Give our regards to Valda. And thank you for letting me see the poem.

Yours,

Norman.

---

[1] Howard Goorney (1921-2007), actor . One of the original members of Joan Littlewood's Theatre Workshop Company. He wrote *The Theatre Workshop Story* (London, 1950).
[2] Hector MacIver was Head of English at the Royal High School, Edinburgh.
[3] 'Once in a Cornish Garden', *C.P.* II, pp.1102-1109.
[4] 'The Divided Bird', *C. P.* II, pp.712-720.

8. From J. Douglas Geddes (NLS Acc.7361/22)

167 Hunts Cross Avenue
Woolton

Liverpool
18 October 1951

Dear Chris,

I do not know whether this missive will reach you, as I do not know your address, for certain, or whether you will remember me. But, I think you will.

Do you remember certain nights, shot with often lurid, saffron-hued interludes, in the Liverpool Press Club, nigh on 20 years ago, when you were on the Liverpool Organisation?[1] And, do you remember one called J. Douglas Geddes, who, when crimson-robed lightning struck through clouds of thought at one's senses, tried to stand by in heavy seas? Well, it is he.

I have often thought of you, but seeing that my acquaintance with you must have only occupied a tiny spot of your life, I have refrained from writing, till now. But, in consequence of certain happenings, akin to those which I have mentioned, having occurred, I am impelled to 'drop you a line'.

I saw your photograph in *Vogue* some little time back, and have picked up your address out of a newspaper. I am glad to see you faring so well, as, at one time, I thought the heavy seas of Fate may have engulfed you.

I will not write of myself, except to say that I am battling with a momentary crisis, but I would like to hear from you to compare notes.

If you would be so kind as to write, I shall be obliged.

Yours most sincerely,

J. Douglas Geddes.

[1] MacDiarmid was Publicity Officer to the Merseyside Corporation 1930-1.

9. From David Daiches (EUL MS2946.11 f.1)

53E Bateman Street
Cambridge
19 January 1952

Dear Mr Grieve,

Many thanks indeed for your letter. I am sorry to hear of your wife's illness, and hope that she is now fully recovered. It must have been a difficult time for you.

I am glad that you liked the collection of essays.[1] I was, of course, limited in space and further hemmed in by the fact that the book is to be used as a textbook in American colleges. The choice of your own essay was not difficult for me: I don't quite know why, but that particular piece of yours had stuck in my mind very vividly ever since I first read it in *At the Sign of the Thistle* when that book came out in 1934 (I think). As a matter of fact, that collection of your essays in a sense launched me on my literary career, for it was the first book I was ever given to review for a serious professional literary journal. It was late in 1934 that I met Hamish Miles in London (he was then editor of *Life and Letters*): I had just taken my degree at Edinburgh and was looking for some literary work. He asked me to do some reviewing for him, and gave me your book to begin with. But I need hardly tell you that I have not depended on review copies for reading your work, either in verse or in prose!

I am finding Cambridge reasonably congenial, and am enjoying my work here. I hope eventually to get back to Scotland – both my wife and I want to settle down there within a few years; we have had enough of wandering around – and nourish the hope that I might get one of the Scottish Chairs in English within the next five or ten years. What a chance there would be to do some real house cleaning and get some new vigour and life into literary studies in Scotland! I know one would have a hard fight against every kind of lethargy and vested interest, but it would be exciting, and well worth doing. Think of what the Chair of English at Edinburgh or Aberdeen might be made into, as a living influence on Scottish letters, with some imagination and courage! But this for your private ear.

I see *Botteghe Oscure* occasionally, but have not yet seen the issue with your long poem in.[2] I shall get a hold of it. And I am interested, too, in your collecting some of your prose again, even though the prospect of getting a publisher these days for prose essays is not bright. But I hope something comes of it.

I'm glad you have managed to get together with Kenneth and Sheila Buthlay. I'm very fond of both of them – she was my secretary when I was at Cornell and he was doing graduate work under me – and I think something will be heard of him some day. He wrote me of meeting you, and I wish I could have been there. I was in Scotland in the summer, in Cullen, on the Moray Firth, where we often spend the summer (my wife's people are farmers in that neighbourhood), and had a few days in Edinburgh on my way down to Cambridge in early September; but I met almost nobody. I shall be in Scotland again this summer, and perhaps briefly in the spring, but my plans are still vague. I hope to see and talk with you anyway, when next I go north.

With all good wishes,
Yours sincerely,
David Daiches.

1   The book was *A Century of the Essay* and MacDiarmid's contribution was 'Life in the Shetland Islands'.
2   *Botteghe Oscure* 1-25, 1948-1960, was edited by M. Caetani and G. Bassani in Rome and included work in Italian, English, French, and Spanish. 'Once in a Cornish Garden' appeared in *Quaderno* VIII, pp. 192-199.

10. From Samuel Marshak (EUL MS2966)

Moscow
28 March 1952

To Mr C. M. Grieve ('Hugh MacDiarmid')
Scottish-U.S.S.R. Society National Council
42, Frederick Street
Edinburgh 2

My dear Mr. Grieve,

This is to express my deep gratitude for your charming present – the books on the life and works of one of the greatest poets of the world, Robert Burns. You could not find a better gift to one who loves and admires the Bard of truth and liberty.

May the friendship between our peoples grow to win the fight for peace all over the world.

Please accept, dear friend, my best wishes and most sincere thanks.

Ever yours,

S. Marshak.

11. From Irwin MacDonald Urling (NLS Acc. 7361/23)

730 State St
Baden
Penna
28 March 1952

Dear Sir,

Your 'Dour Drinkers of Glasgow' in the March *Mercury* did more to put in words the Scottish feeling than anything outside of Burns.

Since I was a child I've tried to put a name to the spirit which led my great-aunt, Frances MacDonald Wallace, when asked what she had against a family she had no time for, to answer: 'They're the finest kind of people ... but to Hell with them'.

I'm always eager to hear discussed one question: 'Did we make the Presbyterian Church what it is, or did it make us what we are?'

Looking forward for more straight off the sawdust.

Yours very sincerely,

Irwin MacDonald Urling.

12. From Muriel K. Doughty (NLS Acc.7361/52)

18 Nugent Road
Sowhitowine
Bournemouth
4 June [1952]

Dear Sir – May I say how we sympathize with & admire your dear son for his refusal to pay the £5 fine & for choosing prison rather than agreeing to be called up.

Free England! & failing absolutely to maintain the 1st principles of Freedom! May God give to your son & to many more of our youth the Grace to suffer in His name for the truth's sake & let us pray that:-

1. The Church may outlaw War.

2. That the parents may refuse any longer to allow their sons to pass through the fire to Moloch – may no longer *push* them in.

3. That the young men & women may refuse any longer to kill, mutilate & mar their fellow men at the bidding of any Government.

May God help us.

(Mrs) Muriel K. Doughty

13. From Ian Hamilton Finlay (EUL MS2949.21 f.21)

Drum Na Keil
Dunira
Comrie
Perthshire
3 July 1952

Dear Christopher, and Valda,

Marion and I were delighted to get your letter. We knew you had moved to a new – and Biggar – house, but otherwise had not heard how you were. We hope Valda is keeping better, and that there is good news about Mike. We saw a photograph in the paper, of yourself, Valda, and Muirhead, an old man who seemed almost tragical, as tranced thus in the newspaper's black and white.

Marion and I are fine, except, of course, financially. Marion paints as much as possible. I also, and I do some writing (mostly stories, in a kind of blurred or wet-day neo-cubist style). Previously I was a pine-exponent, with a broad brush. Now we both want to work more naturalistically.

We sometimes see Crombie;[1] and we have a weekend in Glasgow once or twice a year. That is generally enough. The pub I go to is the *Cockburn* (around Bath Street area), but I imagine you must, if you go anywhere, go somewhere else.

We hope you are getting on, very well, and that your new house is suitable. We were *truly delighted* to get your letter, and hope you will drop us a line again fairly soon. Have you been writing, Christopher?

I think Marion will be writing to you fairly soon. If you would be interested I would send on one of my stories. I cannot send any drawing or picture as we both have a very small output, due in Marion's case to our lack of finances, and in my own case to that and, in addition, a fretful temperament.

I have read a good many books in the last years. I was quite amazed by Zola's *Germinal*. Among painters, we both prefer the Northerners, Durer, Rembrandt, the Germans, new and old. I am for the Scots-German alliance. The Franco-Scottish alliance strikes me as tosh. That is what comes of living at a mountain-altitude.

With love to all,

Yours,

Ian (Finlay).

---

[1] R. Crombie Saunders, poet, editor and teacher.

14. From Sean O'Casey (EUL MS2958.1 f.4)

Tingrith
Station Road
Totnes
Devon
18 August 1952

My dear Chris,

Your letter telling of a changed address was put away in a safe place to be answered when some work I was doing was done. Then the safe place couldn't be remembered, &, after many a hunt, is hiding from me still. I'm sending this via your publisher, MacLellan's. I've read your *A Kist of Whistles* a number of times, & have enjoyed it immensely, though some of it is away above & beyond the stretching out of my mind. As well as being a wonderful poet, you are a wonderful scholar too. You have a mind as keen and receptive as the mind of Joyce; much more poetical, & roses glow redder when you pass them, too, as they did for Rubén Darío.[1] Your hymning of nationality finds a ready & eager response in my soul; the remembrance of things past (not Proust's little group) in the deeds of men & women of Eirean, Cymru, and Albain. Groping, groping only for me: for you the clear and coloured vision, seen more clear & coloured more brightly in the vigorous & lovely things you write. If you get comfort in Aneurin[2] & Lochiel,[3] so do I in the remembrance of Owen Roe,[4] Fiach Macaich O' Broin,[5] Wolfe Tone,[6] Parnell,[7] & the big, lumbering loveliness of Jim Larkin.[8] Your 'Hostings of Heroes'[9] is a grand song, man: a trumpet-song with the roll of many drums beside it. Your 'The Kulturkampf'[10] a gusty chant choir-sung by a new-born Scotland. A lot of your 'The Divided Bird'[11] is beyond me. You have, for instance, a knowledge of mathematics & music that I haven't got. Your saying, 'All men are ripe for the highest any man knows',[12] is agreeable to me. I like it with all my heart. But not me: too old, now (72); but though I can never be a scholar, I can still learn, man; & am learning from *A Kist of Whistles*, and greedily enjoying the tuition, too. But I get your 'Off the Coast of Fiedeland'[13] all right, though your poem of the seas ('The Wreck of the *Swan*')[14] has more than one shiver in it, even though the green of the sea & night's darkness be brightened by the gold glints in a lassie's bonnie brown hair.

Well, Chris, a gradh, your book's beside me as I work, I will go on reading it till I reel the whole of it into my mind. It is a grand book in my opinion & in my imagination, too.

I read a note about you & your boy in *The Daily Worker*. I hope things are going all right with you & him. If you are getting up a fund for his defence, I shall be delighted to send on a guinea. It would be a lot more, an I could spare it. And [Hugh] Walpole isn't the head of Letters. There I disagree with you. There's a helluva & a heavenly lot more in *A Kist of Whistles* than in all that Walpole wrote. And, me lad, there are still sons of Lochiel in Albain; & the brightest & bravest is a lad that the Lord named Chris Grieve, & the lad himself named Hugh MacDiarmid.

My love to you.

As ever,
Sean.

1   Rubén Darío (1867-1916): born in Nicaragua, Darío was the founder of Hispanic modernism, the first to introduce the rhythms of the French Parnassians and symbolists.
2   Aneirin (late 6th century). *Y Gododdin,* the epic poem about the defeat of the Britons against the Saxons was composed by (or ascribed to) him.
3   Donald Cameron of Lochiel (b. about 1550) was the warrior of the Cameron clan against the MacIntoshes.
4   Owen Roe [O'Neill] (d. 1649) was the most outstanding Irish general. Victor of the Battle of Benburb in 1646 over an army made up of Scots and Ulster Scots under General Munro.
5   Faich Macaich O'Broin was chief of the junior branch of the O'Byrnes and won the Battle of Glenmalure in 1580 against an English force; later betrayed and killed in 1597.
6   Wolfe Tone (1763-1798): Irish nationalist and political writer who took his own life while under sentence of death on 1 November 1798.
7   Charles Stewart Parnell (1846-1891): leader of the Irish Home Rule Party and supporter of the Irish Land League.
8   Jim Larkin (1874-1947): leader of the Irish Transport and General Workers' Union.
9   *C.P.* I, pp. 692-693.
10 *C.P.* I, pp. 694-704.
11 *C.P.* I, pp.712-720.
12 A line from 'The Divided Bird', *C.P.* I, p.716.
13 *C.P.* I, pp.723-728.
14 *C.P.* I, pp.728-734.

15. From Mary Ramsay (EUL MS2942.1 f.42)

11 Saxe-Coburg Place
Edinburgh 3
13 October 1952

Dear Chris,

I saw in the press that Mike's case was deferred to suit David Watson. I had not heard anything, till then. If you can let me have a p.c. to say when it is to come up again I should like very much to go as a supporter. It does help the lads I think when there are plenty of friends in Court. How do you feel? Or rather, how does Mike feel about that?

Have you seen the enclosed papers? In the questionnaire Booklet I think at least three out of the five questions could be answered emphasising the need for small free nations (pledged to Neutrality I feel) especially Scotland & Wales to start with! I think we could have a good opportunity for propaganda if as many Nationalists as possible would fill in a page with such messages, & a small donation would be well spent on such propaganda.

I may see you & Valda if Mike's case is coming up here.

Yours in haste,
Mary.

Christine MacIntosh, née Grieve, his daughter, c. 1952.
By permission of Christine MacIntosh.

PS I gather I shd. keep track of the booklet as they're issued according to numbers.
small – free – nations

16. From Archie Lamont (EUL MS2952.8 f.8)

Jess Cottage
Carlops
by Penicuik
19 November 1952

Dear Grieve,

I don't want to see MacLellan as I think his running of *Scottish Journal*[1] is just reducing sales of more valuable types of Nationalist propaganda. His apologetics for the N. of S. Hydro-Board[2] are about as bad as Compton MacKenzie's *Eastern Epic*[3] & Linklater on Korea.[4]

I'm sorry you have to truckle to them.

Tell Michael I'm remembering him, but think I'd better not face the 7 a.m. fogs!

I'd like to see an article on Douglas Social Credit vis-à-vis Communism, and a statement of what a Communist programme for Scotland might be. It wouldn't need to be so austere as for China. The best of the Douglas articles was the one with the poem[5] but it seemed to be more applicable to G. Plekhanov[6] or Ludwig Feuerbach[7] than to C. H. Douglas.

However, it does let me say you are Communist of the 'Theses on Feuerbach'[8] phase of Marx, much more so than 'First or Second Hymns to Lenin'.

I was in Ireland and later I was ill so no wonder you didn't see much of me. I badly want to have a talk with you personally.

Yours sincerely,

Archie Lamont.

---

[1]   Twelve issues of *Scottish Journal* appeared between No. 1, September 1952 and No. 12, January-April 1954.

[2]   *Scottish Journal* No. 3, November 1952, carried an account of the opening of the Glen Affric Hydro-electric scheme, 'To Tea with the Turbines', p.4.

[3]   London, 1951.

[4]   *Our Men in Korea*, London, 1952.

[5]   MacDiarmid contributed three articles to *National Weekly* (Glasgow, 1948-1953) after the death of Major C.H. Douglas on 29 September 1952. These appeared on 11 October, 25 October and 8 November that year. The poem in the third article was 'Beyond Argument' (*C.P.* II, 1364).

[6]   G.V. Plekhanov (1856-1918) was a leading advocate and interpreter of Marxist ideas in Russia during the late nineteenth and early twentieth centuries.

[7]   L.A. Feuerbach (1804-1872) was a German philosopher who studied under Hegel but later turned from Hegel's philosophical idealism.

[8]   The eleven 'Theses on Feuerbach' were probably written in April 1845. Karl Marx: *Selected Writings,* ed. by David McLellan (Oxford: Oxford University Press, 1977), pp. 156-158.

17. From Christine MacIntosh (EUL MS2954.6 f.1)

Maryfield Hosp.
Dundee
12 December 1952

Dear Christopher,

It was a shock to receive your letter today after such a lapse of time, but how *very* glad I am that you wrote.

To bridge the gap of years is never easy and I shall not attempt to try in this letter. Suffice it to say that I have not forgotten you – indeed you are always much in my thoughts – and I look forward to a meeting with you early in the New Year.

I will be seeing Walter and my mother in the near future as we are joining forces at Christmas. This I tell you to explain why I do not suggest an earlier meeting.

Our son, Donald Alistair Ross, is a fine husky youngster with the promise of a fair share of the devil lurking in his eyes. But we have also another child, a daughter of three – Elspeth Margaret Catriona by name – who is now very like the young daughter you will remember best.

I hope my use of your Christian name has neither hurt nor offended you but it comes more readily to my tongue.

You will understand why I have written so brief a letter but I did just want to let you know at once how much I appreciated having your letter.

As ever,

Christine.

18. From Tom Scott (EUL Gen.2094/6)

43 Knightsbridge
London SW1
28 February 1953

Dear Chris,

Be weill thankit for yir couthy letter... the waarst o the problems are like tae rise later whan the buik has taen on beuk an shape. Then I'll be gled tae hae yir advice on several maitters. I'm enclosin a hantle o ma Baudelaire versions tae gie ye a taste o ma ain owresettins.[1] Ma wee buik *Seeven Poems o Maister Francis Villon* is oot,[2] an Peter Russell[3] will be forwardin ye a complimentary copy, if he hesnae duin so forenent this.

Yin o the perennial problems o coorse is the question o a mair or less standart spellin... it's mebbe ower suin in the developement o the language tae try an tichten up on sic maitters though, an although I see a lot o forms I dinnae much like personally in the gear that's comin in, I hev nae clear enough notions tae recommend tae ither fowk ... indeed I'm gey fashed whiles masel tae ken whit form is best, haein an ee tae etymology an soond baith. Yae thing I'm suir o' ... the fewer the apostrophes the better, but I cannae think o a satisfactory equivalent tae 'ne'er'. Tae ma mind, Will Soutar had mebbe the shairpest sense o Scots word-forms o us aa. He obviously wes able tae gie it lang thoucht an consideration lyin yonder in his bit box, mair likely than mair active fowk hae time for; but he only sairs as an example o scrupulous attention til't. It'll be a lang while afore the last word is said on the maitter.

I hae notit aa yir names an addresses o owresetters, for which, much thanks. I hadnae hard o Hay's illness... I hope he's no beyond revivin ...it kin o pints the hellish urgency an inherent tragedy o this maitter o language, which must be a hundred times waur for the Gaelic chiels than for us laalanders. Incidentally Lallans is lousy as a name... it reminds ye o a coo chewin the cud. Whye no juist Scots... or Laalan Scots or the like? I dinnae think Burns or Stevenson deserve tae be gien sic authority on maitters o spellin.

I hae seen mony o yir ain translations o coorse ... ye maun hae hundreds I daur say ... I wad like best if ye were tae mak yersel an anthology o whit ye think are yir best, whit ye like best, an send them on ... unless it were book-length in itsel I wad prent the lot as ye send them. Goodsir Smith I hae written tae an wait word. I tried tae get Young tae dae this anthologie himsel, him the obvious chiel for't, but I got nae reply ... fowr months or so syne, so I expect naethin frae him, whitever the reason. If a man's ower thrang tae answer a letter o that nature within fowr months, he's lost tae poetry as near's damn it. Aa the same I wrote him again the ither day. Tait wrote tae me an he sent me some guid Baudelaire an Villon. I've had poems frae the Magyar frae William Auld[4] o Glasgow, a Baudelaire paraphrase frae a Brian Foster o Southampton University, a sliver o Pindar frae Garioch tae whom I'll haand on yer message whan I see him, a bit o von Platen an Horace frae Edwin Morgan, a Labe frae W. M. Lindsay o Cupar, an some Horace frae G. F. Cunningham o Alva. I wish I could get some Dante, Goethe, Sappho, Homer, an the like, for whit I waant tae shaw an encourage is the extraordinary poetic range o the auld leid... it can cover near every range o genuine feelin... it only baulks at sophistication an falsity. Even Baudelaire in his dandiest moods is automatically chastened an realized bi the Scots. I've duin the Paolo an Francesca episode masel,[5] an the Sappho fragment *Deduke men a selanna*.[6] So faur there's no enough variety in the stuff reachin me, no enough o the very greatest, which is the maist important test o the language an wad shaw the lines alang which waark should move, if Scotland is to achieve a new gret poetry o her ain. Incidentally, I hev also translatit frae Scott ... a suggestive activity ... we could thus save some o oor best writers frae mediocrity. Somebody should certainly pit L.G. Gibbon intil its correct spellin insteid o the bastard form he gied it; but that mebbe belangs tae the future. We need prose as weill.

I wrote tae Mackie at the address gien in *Who's Who* but hevnae heard yet. Scott an the ithers I will write. I hae access tae Soutar's anthologie, but for the Simpson[7] I'll hae tae gang tae the British Museum... mebbe if you wadnae mind lendin me yours it wad be that much the better... I wadnae keep it lang. Are folks aye at 37 Wilson Street,[8] Perth; or hev I got it wrang?

Incidentally, hev ye an idea o a better-knawn publisher than Peter Russell, wha micht at the same time hae mebbe hauf the verve an guts at gettin something duin? It should really gang oot frae a big an famous press, if possible. But they're aa hauf deid, it seems tae me.

Whan ye mak yir ain selection, an if ye hae a crack aboot this anthologie wi ony o yir freens, I hope ye will bear in mind I'm ettlin chiefly tae shaw whit the auld leid can dae wi the grettest an best-knawn poetry in the waarld; that's ma chief concairn, poems that will bring oot the leemitations an possibeelities o the leid rather than new ideas or the like.

It has surprised me hoo guid a reception I hev had here in London wi ma reading o Scots poems, an frae established poets in response tae ma ain owresettins... people as various as T.S. Eliot, Kathleen Raine, William Empson,[9] John Hayward,[10] an Edwin Muir hae been encoragin; ditto George Barker an some o the younger men. Robert Lowell,[11] the American poet, told Princess Caetani o *Botteghe Oscure* that ma Baudelaire an Villon were the best English [sic] translations he had seen.

On the ither haand, the *Weekly Scotsman, Scotsman, Observer, Sunday Times* an *Times Lit Sup* hev either refused, ignored or not received a copy o the wee letter o announcement o the anthologie which eventually got intae the *Statesman*. Even the *Statesman* hadnae published it until Janet Smith[12] heard me read at the ICA[13] an wrote me for the ballat o the fires,[14] which had been written only that eftirnuin. Then she got them tae prent ma letter ... itherwise it wad never hev been prentit onywhaur.

I enclose twa three original poems tae.

Yours aye.

Tom Scott.

PS Criticism welcomed, if ye can be bothered.

[1]   A group of ten of Tom Scott's translations into Scots from Charles Baudelaire (1821-1867) is included in *Pervigilium Scotiae* (Scotland's Vigil), (Buckfastleigh:Etruscan Books, 1997), pp. 10-19, with a note by Heather Scott, p.45.

[2]   Tunbridge Wells, 1953, in an edition of 195 numbered copies; François Villon (c.1431-after 1463).

[3]   Peter Russell (1921-2003), poet, translator, publisher, and editor of *NINE* (1949-1956).

[4]   William Auld (1924-2006), poet, mainly in Esperanto.

[5]   *European Poetry in Scotland,* ed. by Peter France and Duncan Glen, (Edinburgh: Edinburgh University Press, 1989), p. 74 (from the *Inferno*, Canto 5, of Dante Alighieri, 1265-1321).

[6]   Ibid.; 'Doun gaes the muin'; Sappho (7th century BC).

[7]   Margaret Winifride Simpson published *Keys of Morning*, poems in English and Scots.

[8]   27 Wilson Street.

[9]   William Empson (1906-1984), poet and literary scholar.

[10]   John Hayward (1907-1967), editor and scholar.

[11]   Robert Lowell (1917-1977), poet, translator and playwright.

[12]   Janet Adam Smith (1905-1999), anthologist, John Buchan scholar and co-translator of books on climbing.

[13]   Institute of Contemporary Arts, London.

[14]   Not identified.

19. From Tom Scott (EUL Gen.2094/6)

43 Knightsbridge
London SW1
25 March 1953

Dear Chris,

I got a copy of *The National Weekly* the other day, so presume you got the Baudelaire all right. Thanks for the most encouraging remarks about my Scots work ... I begin to feel gey isolated up here; the wee Villon is four weeks old and yours is the only word so far, except for a mention in *Times Lit Sup* French section this week – article 'Translator's Task' saying I had demonstrated Villon can be carried over into Lallans with greater ease than suddron. Not much but something. Russell seems to be disappointed in response so far. I would dearly like, if you can be bothered, any critical remarks you care to make. I think the price o the book[1] will be a stumbling-block to enthusiasm. Had it been a bob[2] or so I'd have peddled it round the doors myself.

Re Lallans and Anglo-Scots ... too bloody right an good for you. I would like from now on to do what little I can to see to it that Scots can never again be suppressed, become an all-purpose language again ... especially be developed as a prose medium, for that will take it the next stage to the people. I'm glad my letter provided some grape-shot for the cause.

I think I mentioned to you this notion of mine to try putting some Anglo-Scottish prose into Scots ... re-spelling Gibbon, 'Wandering Willie's Tale',[3] *House with the Green Shutters*,[4] *Weir of Hermiston*,[5] and the like; what do you think? If half a dozen writers undertake to do a spot of this kind of work in their spare time, the outlook would soon be considerably brighter, don't you think... such translation would stimulate original prose writing ... but it calls for team work really, else three or four would be doing the same book. I have done some experiments in this direction ... It's astonishing how the rhythm of Scott's poetry suddenly takes on meaning when you give it even a rough makin over into Scots... it seems to flower, to become organic, and you see what power underlay these thin surfaces.

The anthology is steadily growing... I wish you would chivvy up Smith if you see him, an Alexander Scott ... both have not yet replied; ditto T. S. Law.[6] I'm finding difficulty getting information about M. W. Simpson ... have you any? So far I have a lot of things from W. J. Tait, Douglas Young, Sir Alex. Gray,[7] your own to come (or would you rather let me choose from your publications?), Smith not yet, M. W. Simpson bags of stuff to be gone through at the Museum, but OK wanted. The rest are just bits and pieces by amateurs which would make a background or chorus ... one each say, with twenty or thirty pages to the professionals. Would you advise trying to make it all-in rather than contemporary? Or leave that to a better scholar than myself at a later date? Any other suggestions? Fraser[8] gave me some garbled news over the phone about your thinking I was wrong trying to get *ad hoc* stuff, which really I am not. Be glad if you will write soon anent these matters.

Yours as aye,
Tom Scott.

What about Maurice Lindsay?

Real problem is a publisher and/or backer. Another problem is men who should be enacting a renaissance literature in the fullest sense are far too busy dain other things.

1 8/6 (42.5 new pence).
2 A shilling (5 new pence).
3 From *Redgauntlet* (1824); Sir Walter Scott (1771-1832).
4 1901; George Douglas Brown (1869-1902).
5 1896; Robert Louis Stevenson (1850-1894).
6 Thomas Sturdy Law (1916-1997), poet in Scots.
7 Sir Alexander Gray (1916-1968), poet, translator and writer on economics and politics.
8 G. S. Fraser (1915-1980), poet and critic.

20. From Norman MacCaig (EUL 2953.7 ff.21-22)

Ward 13
Royal Infirmary
8 July 1953

Dear Chris,

I need hardly say I found this interesting, partly for a reason which you might claim to be secondary, that it's bloody well written. However, as I write that, I know it isn't true, as long as 'well written' means that the writing approximates to the complete expression of the matter – *with nothing added*. So long as rhythm, metaphor, associations and allusions encrust what is to be said with the thinnest of irrelevant gold-leaf, they are not only mere ornament and unnecessary but a blemish on the writing and a failure in expression of what lies under them. A concept is a concept is a concept, as Stein would say: we get far enough away from it when we put it into the barest minimum of words at all. The intrusion of the dangerously emotive, no matter how seriously intended as illumination and clarification of the concept, introduces what is foreign to it, and whatever is added to the bare statement widens the space between what is written and the thing written about – so that, indeed, the thing written about becomes another thing altogether. It might be a good thing, but it is not the concept that was a concept that was a concept.

I believe all this, and I believe you do too. *But*, it seems to me, that a deliberate because intellectually formalised decision to reject, for example, the patterns of strict rhythm and stanza form means a suicidal, or at any rate self-maiming, attempt to limit the means at one's disposal. I know there are other rhythms than iambic pentameters acatalectic and that the prose paragraph has its own complex of balanced relationships as much as a verse stanza has; but whether these slacker rhythms and patterns can produce the tension we associate with poetry is pretty doubtful. On the other hand, I agree with you also in saying, 'All right, it isn't poetry, in the accepted sense. Either extend the meaning of the word "poetry" to cover such writing or give it a new name'. I would extend the meaning of the word, for such writing as your James Joyce poem is certainly more nearly related even to the conventional idea of poetry than to prose.

I think one of the deceiving things is a matter of scale. The limits that produce the tension are not the so many lines of a stanza form but the totality of the poem, and the separate elements involved are not poetic 'feet' or phrases or lines but the paragraphs. In the same way, as I see it, this tension is also partially created, not by the juxtaposition of noun and epithet, or phrase and phrase, but by the repulsion and attraction of great blocks of ideas. It is almost as though such poetry were attempting, not to build a house with bricks, but to construct a city with houses.

However, it's ridiculous always to talk about the *differences* between this sort of poetry and the usual, as though there were nothing in common. The passage you quote in this typescript[1] seems to me to share the virtues of both, though of course not extended enough to give the result of accumulation which is an essential quality of the complete poem.

Anyway, it's *interesting*. And how many flossy little lyrics are that?
Norman.

The doctor's just been round and has agreed to my going home today.

[1]   Though the subject of 'this typescript' is unknown, the letter has been included because it gives MacCaig's views on 'this sort of poetry and the usual'.

21. From Albert D. Mackie (EUL MS2962.11 f.27)

27 Blackford Ave
Edinburgh 9
5 February 1954

Dear Chris,
Many thanks for your letter. Here are the facts. Although, in common with most people connected with The Scotsman Publications, I have been apprehensive of the influence of this financier, Roy Thomson from Canada, I have made an honest endeavour to fit in and keep the paper going. I have carried out his typographical (economy) instructions and played delaying tactics on other economies which threatened to affect my staff (two pens have run out on me & I have fallen back on my Biro). Despite my discretion and his great show of affability, it is obvious now that from the beginning he has been stalking me for the kill. On Saturday morning after the edition, he called me up to tell me he had appointed an editor from London who would start on the 15th. He made an insulting offer of a *Scotsman* job (unspecified) at a Salary (unspecified) 'much less' than I was getting. I said I would not work for him for *any* less. I had £1750 a year, yet he sacked me with £500, although an editor is entitled to 9 months' salary. I'm sorry I wasn't able to do more for Michael & hope he does well. I'll get by. Love to Valda.

Bert.[1]

[1] 'Bert' was Albert D. Mackie, editor at that time of the *Evening Despatch* (Edinburgh).

22. From Norman MacCaig (EUL MS2953.7 f.29)

7 Leamington Terrace
Edinburgh 10
10 May 1954

Dear Chris,

I have your other books safe and will hand them over to you when we meet.

Please give our thanks to Valda (keeping a proper share for yourself) for our excellent wee night on Saturday. It's always a pleasure and a relief, somehow, to meet the pair of you. – it shakes my growing conviction that *everybody* is a tedious fool lifted off the ground only by his pretensions.

We hope to see you soon.

Norman.

23. From Denis Saurat (NLS Acc.7361/26)

permanent address
504 Regina
Cimierz
Nice (A.M.)
France
5 July 1954

My dear Grieve,

I was delighted to receive your letter. Of course I referred to you as a great poet in Amsterdam, since my theme was how languages of few readers, being more genuine, less "lied in" as someone said[,] can be a source of regeneration.

I am deep in work of a rather occult nature which I suspect would not meet with your agreement. I published last year a book on *l'experiénce de l'au-delà*,[1] which presents experimented & experienced facts *re* the existence of spirits. But never mind.

Besides this, just now, I am undergoing the resurrection of the language of my tribe: a few people on a mountain side near Spain (now all dead or gone away scattered); their peculiar linguo was never written by any one – I left them at the age of three – and now, in dreams, I receive complete poems in that language – a romance dialect carrying words & ideas of the Middle Ages. The last poem is over 300 lines long – on Cathar themes.[2] I shall send it to you when published – but it carries a *tabou* against being translated into any other language. It's about chastity: the chief Cathar preoccupation in 1000-1300 (and *not* mine at all).

I can assure you your political or other views do not worry me at all; any more than mine worry you. You are a great poet, and that is enough for me. I have studied Milton's ideas enough to know they have little enough to do with his poetry.

I am thrilled at the prospect of your *Joyce*. Please send it to me, as soon as you can – even in proof; I am so keen to see it: it looks like being your masterpiece. Each man ought to have totally different ideas from every other man.

I am glad you & your wife are well. All our family are getting along reasonably.

Every affectionate wish to you both from both of us.

Denis Saurat.

One thing horrifies me: the thought that it is nearly always raining where you are – RAINING. Please write to tell me it is not so. I can no longer live out of the sunshine.

1   *l'experiénce de l'au-delà* – the experience of the other world. The book, with this title, was published by La Colombe in Paris in 1951.
2   Cathars formed a heretical Christian sect in some parts of Western Europe in the 12th and 13th centuries. Saurat published two works in Occitan in 1954: *Ac digas pas. Poëma ante-catar*, Tolosa, Institut d'estudis occitans, and *La Bierjo Ihi diguec*, Avignon, Aubanel.

24. From Neil M. Gunn (EUL MS2948.15 ff.45-46)

Kerrow House
Cannich
Beauly
Inverness-shire
15 December 1954

Dear Chris,

I am just back from Edinburgh and find it good to get your letter.[1] On Saturday I tried to contact Norman MacCaig but learned he had gone to see you. I had to stop in Edinburgh because I was attending rehearsals of my broadcast on the Clearances. Than writing, how much better to have tossed around a few theories and ideological differences (though you are beginning to sound suspiciously like a fellow who has found a Heaven, complete with puritanical theology) as we used to do in talk long ago. I have such a pleasant memory of those early adventuring times that I did not want it to be confused with or damaged by ambiguous snatches of criticism heard on the air or elsewhere. Somehow when I wrote to you[2] I had not thought of an unscripted talk afterwards cut to a time measure, but now you explain much.

My ear caught your expression 'the Nineties' and I wondered what on earth you were getting at, or what you were now trying to make yourself believe. Even your change of emphasis to Celtic Renaissance – or Twilight – does not help much, though it's got so hackneyed that the old laughter did have an innings! I thought we had been at the burial of that long ago. I can even vaguely remember a night when, after dealing fairly faithfully with the beauteous Twilight, you came to its support with a poem by Fiona MacLeod on, I think, Women. Our agreement was complete.

Round about that time I even wrote a short story about it, from the subjective angle, which appeared in *The Cornhill [Magazine]*. That must be going back some thirty years. Yet here you are, rousing what has been long buried by all, trying to make a living Aunt Sally of it and flogging it to death once more. Can you wonder that I was astonished enough to search for some sort of motive? Certainly you seem to have been hard-driven to find or manufacture an 'opposite' for your materialism!

However, please don't think I am taking your position too lightly. And an argument never came amiss yet. But I sort of look at you twice – it's long since we really talked – at the rigid way you stick to your own thesis, at your positively solemn intolerance! Surely even in your Marxist dialectic you should make some sort of effort at getting your thesis and its anti into a synthesis. When you talk about irreconcilable opposites I begin to wonder about your dialectic. But then I admit I have the kind of mathematical mind that gets bothered over a lack of rigour in reasoning. Even in that broadcast you said that art came from the unconscious, but, a little later, that materialism was all. Which is like having irrationalism and rationalism at the same time. Not a bad idea when it is taken far enough! I could trot out analogies from the sub-atomic world of physics. Your rigid standpoint and the opposing one you condemn may be but two aspects of a whole. The word 'synthesis' has for me sometimes a 'synthetic' flavour, but the physicist's complementarism is as acceptable as his experimental results. He does the doings and shows you the results. When thought or criticism takes that kind of slant then I am all there. In fact I find scientific penetration here – as at the other end with its four-dimensional space-time continuum – more fascinating than most modern poetry I have read, to put it mildly.

You talk of 'the scientific attitude to nature'. Of course. But what I'd like you [to] tell me then is where poetry comes in. What can the poet *add* to the physicist's equation? To what is already perfect in form and communication? The content can't be tampered with. What is it then that the poet adds and how do you include that within your concept of materialism? So with nature in the obvious way. A colour photograph beats any artist or any poet bent on describing what he sees. If the poet *should* add nothing, then what is his function? For do you think that I or any tolerably educated person am going to have the poet's words on quanta or waves rather than the physicist's?

And when I come to Renaissance of any kind or time I am bothered in the same way. You are against Edwin Muir, you say. And presumably also against T. S. Eliot and Joyce and Proust and Dostoevsky and all those who have been concerned with the spiritual and the humanistic. Do you include them in 'the Nineties' also? In whole or in part – and where do you draw the line? And can you be so certain of any given situation seeing that science moves? The rationalism of last century is not now to me what it was as a lad. Things have happened to the constitution of the atom since then! But I have said more than enough, probably – or not nearly enough. But it springs from a very genuine interest in what you may have been thinking.

I know quite well what you mean about my name not appearing in Renaissance articles abroad. In the current *Listener* I see a new Oscar Wilde Society has been formed in New Delhi. Oscar will beat you to it yet! Even if I am never asked to speak at an Oscar Society. Which sounds like the time for another round.

But – more important – it was nice to hear from you and know that you are alive and kicking. Daisy and I are pretty fit at the moment. We had a baddish spell some months ago but are now getting around in good style. I think I got my trouble from chasing deer over frozen mountains. The years of the Lord have a way of getting on your back.

With all good wishes,

Yours,

Neil.

You talk in the usual fashionable way about Yeats's 'early work': what about his late work, about 'A Vision' with its spooks & astrology[?]

[1] Neil Gunn refers here to MacDiarmid's letter of 10 December 1954, (*Letters*, pp.270-272).

[2] This reference is to his own earlier letter of 27 November. *Neil M. Gunn: Selected Letters*, ed. by J. B. Pick, (Edinburgh: Polygon, 1987), pp. 119-120.

25. From William MacLellan (EUL MS2954.16 f.49)

William MacLellan
Publishers Limited
240 Hope Street
Glasgow
23 December 1954

Dear Chris,

Perhaps you could give Eliot the information he requires about the quote.[1] He must be having second thoughts! If you'd rather do it thro' me let me know the details.

Did not get over Sunday as was at Council Meeting of the Scot – USSR Soc. Marshak hopes to be over for the Burns celebrations & other writers & a Scot. Local Gov. delegation is planned for the autumn – viva Kinloch.

I see they minuted disapproval of your attack on him!

A friend has picked up a wonderful bargain for us – a sleek black & silver S.S. Jaguar such as Nan is always talking about.[2] We put the hat around the families & borrowed enough but I'm sure it's too low set to get up the hill.

Will take you a run on Sunday maybe W.P.[3]

Yrs,

Bill.

[1] T.S. Eliot had objected that words which he had written in a letter to MacDiarmid on 24 April 1941 had been quoted in the invitation to subscribe to *In Memoriam James Joyce* which MacLellan had sent out.

[2] In a later letter to MacDiarmid MacLellan wrote: 'I know my own position must look rather affluent in the Jaguar & German maids, but it is all done on a sort of Hire Purchase

system of credit with traders which allows one to live beyond one's means. This, I know, is quite irrelevant but I'd hate it to be considered that such things are possible by publishing poetry without standard agreements as advised by Sir Stanley Unwin & his *Authors & Artists Year Book* breed.' (EUL MS2954.16 f.55 in biro).

3 Weather permitting.

26. From Joseph MacLeod (EUL MS2966)

<small>CARD IN INK FROM JOSEPH MACLEOD, 46 QUEEN ST, EDINBURGH 2</small>

n.d. [1954]

For 14 years I had only one devotion: poetry. For 26 years after that I had only two: poetry and my wife. My wife died a fortnight ago. If you have any imagination left in you, you will understand how cruel is your cheap and hasty bits of newspaper-filling about my life-work.[1] Why have you become so mean that you must try to damage anything Scottish that is not your own?

Joseph Macleod

1 MacDiarmid's article was 'The Poetry of Joseph Gordon MacLeod', published in *Scottish Journal*, no.11 (Nov.-Dec. 1953).

27. From Edward Boyd (NLS Acc.7361/26)

21 Tay Crescent
Riddrie
Glasgow E1
30 March 1955

Dear Hugh MacDiarmid,

I saw the other day in Fisher's bookshop in Hope Street that you had resumed publication of *The Voice of Scotland*, and, remembering that in June 1947 you were good enough to print one of my poems in the same magazine, I decided to test empirically that old saw about lightning striking in the same place twice. So I am enclosing several poems for your consideration, plus a short story called 'Prelude' in the Grassic Gibbon manner – but Gibbon with an Ayrshire accent. I don't know whether you use short stories or not but if you don't, then you can send it back.[1]

It's nice to see *The Voice of Scotland* again. One gets so tired of magazines – nae names nae polis office – which are non-political, non-sectarian, non-controversial and, inevitably, non-entities.

With best wishes,
Yours sincerely,
Edward Boyd.

1 *The Voice of Scotland*, vol. iv, no. 2 (July 1955), included two poems by Edward Boyd. *The Voice of Scotland*, vol. iii, no. 4 (June 1947), had published his 'The Niddity-Noddin' Chesbow'.

28. From Muriel Rukeyser (NLS Acc.7361/26)

436 East 88th St
New York City 28
[April 1955]

Dear Hugh MacDiarmid,

The wonderful poem has come – it moves me deeply to see it appear; and the lapse of time since you wrote the *Hymn* is moving in all that has not happened. I wish we could at least have had one first meeting during this time.

This poem is full of your deep sources; for me it has stood, these years, with the centre of your poetry. A 'deepest source'.

It is a great gift that you should put my name on it. I am on fire with pride in it, in the richest humility.

This is my New York address – I shall be back there again from San Francisco, with my young son, by September 10th. And I should like very much to stay in touch with you now, and I hope to do that.

With every wish –
Muriel Rukeyser.

29. From Michael Grieve (NLS MS27151 f.27)

Jamieson & Munro Ltd
Printers, Publishers and Wholesale Stationers
40 Craigs
Stirling
[August1955]

Dearest Dad,

Just read the review of the Joyce poem in this week's *Listener*.[1] Very glad that it is so favourable despite the damned nonsense in the last ten or twelve lines. With one of the papers at last under way let's hope the others follow suit in the near future.

A propos Thornton Wilder.[2] Was talking to John Tonge who says that Wilder is very enthusiastic about the poem, been reading Ian Rodger's[3] copy, and that there is to be a luncheon party in your honour given by Wilder at his hotel on Wednesday coming. Daresay, however, that John will have written to you by now.

Met a young Dutch female journalist in Vienna, she speaks about four languages, etc., saw her in London and think she will be coming out to Brownsbank this Sunday. Hope that won't break up any plans. If you wish to go to the commemoration in Edinburgh just phone me up and we can as easily see each other there although the speakers seem a pretty platitudinous lot. Was at a similar event at the Abbey Craig this week. You probably saw it reported in *The Bulletin*. At the end, after trailing miserably through two verses of 'Scots Wha Hae ...' the song had to be abruptly stopped as the sixty people there did not know the words ...

All love to you both,
Mike.

1   This was an unsigned review of *In Memoriam James Joyce* in *The Listener*'s 'Book Chronicle', 25 August 1955, p.303.
2   MacDiarmid is shown with Wilder and Caroline Rait at a lunch party in Edinburgh during the International Festival in *Hugh MacDiarmid: a festschrift* (Edinburgh, 1962) and *MacDiarmid: an illustrated biography* (Edinburgh, 1977). In both places, the date is given as 1959.
3   Ian Rodger made several contributions to *The Voice of Scotland* : a poem,'The Wall', to vol. vi, no.2 (July 1955); another poem, 'Thinking all round the clock of the earth', to vol. vi, no.4 (January 1956); and an essay, 'The Poetry of Artur Lundqvist', with 'Gie us a dream', a translation of a Lundqvist poem to vol. vii, no.2 (July 1956).

30. From Robert Garioch Sutherland (EUL MS2960.20 f.6)

90 Constance Crescent
Hayes
Bromley
Kent
19 September 1955

Dear Mr Grieve,

Thank you for your very encouraging letter, which makes me think you might like a copy of the whole of *Jephthah*,[1] so I'm sending it to you. It is certainly a fine gloomy tragedy, very Calvinist and Scottish, and I think it would be impressive on the stage. I sent it to the Glasgow Citizens' Theatre, but having seen their programme for this winter I see it is not at all surprising that they voted against performing it. The Cambridge Society means to give a reading of it. I can't be there, as it is in the middle of the week, but I shall be interested to hear how they get on. The *Baptist* must certainly be done, but it will take time. *Jephthah* took four or five months of evenings.

Enclosed is a second copy of 'Disparplit',[2] with slight improvements; I should be glad if you print the second version.

I have thought of getting out a collection for some time, but we shall see. I really do think there is hope that I will do better work soon, but as I read somewhere lately, you were saying that the job of writing poetry has to be learned. Though I have always known that, I still don't know how to set about learning it, and never know clearly what is best to do next. But I'm trying now to be scientific or rather to use ideas from science & to get scientific and commonsense meanings going at once. I wish I could get shades of meaning in Scots: sometimes with luck I find words with an English meaning that strikes anyone at once, and a more exact meaning in Jamieson, e.g., the hierodules are nou *arrayit*.

Anyhow, I'll keep bashing away, and your encouragement helps a lot.

Yours sincerely,

Robert G. Sutherland.

Saw a wonderful play: *Waiting for Godot*, by James Joyce's secretary, I forget his name.[3] Some play. Breaks all the rules: fearfully sad, when not comic; hard to say which bit is one or the other.

[1]   *Jephthah*; and, *The Baptist* translated frae Latin in Scots by Robert Garioch Sutherland frae George Buchanan (1506-1582), Edinburgh, 1959.,
[2]   'Disparplit' was published in *The Voice of Scotland*, vol. iv, no.3 (October 1955).
[3]   Samuel Beckett, winner of Nobel Prize for Literature in 1969.

31. From R. Crombie Saunders (EUL MS2960.2 f.17)

Tom na Voil
Balquhidder
Perthshire
23 September 1955

My dear Chris,
I'm a lazy bugger at writing letters but I must tell you how much I liked *In Memoriam James Joyce*. 'Liked' seems a silly word. But it's a most exciting and impressive work. I did not recognise one in fifty of the references but I found the book continually illuminating. The references, of course, don't need to be recognised to have their effect. (Most of your reviewers seem to have overlooked the subtitle of the book – 'A *Vision* of World Language').

I now go back and start rereading it. At least to ponder over those many passages where you are so surely grappling with what you have called 'the root of the matter'. And to enjoy those 'flights into the image' like the triple-feathered arrow and the peacock with the five-foot tail. You are undoubtedly the only man living who could have written an adequate 'In Memoriam' to Joyce. You're the only one in his class.

I'm doing a piece about it for *Forward*,[1] but *Forward* readers being in the main simple and non-literary souls it will of necessity be slight and superficial, though you can be sure I will make clear how good I think it is.

I blush when I think how I used to criticise your 'new' poetry. How patient you were with the impertinence of your juniors! But I think it was probably a mistake to publish excerpts from this sort of work. It requires the full canvas for the parts to be seen in their proper relations and importance.

I remember you once said, discussing your new writing, that the poetry was 'in the intensity of the thought'. Then I knew what you meant; now I see what you meant. Our indebtedness to you is greater than ever.

As ever,
Crombie.

[1]   *Forward* was a Scottish weekly Socialist newspaper which had been started by Thomas Johnston in 1907. The first edition of his *Our Scots Noble Families* was published by *Forward* Publishing Co., Ltd in 1909. Johnston later became Secretary of State for Scotland.

32. From Walter Dunlop (EUL Gen.2094/1/469)

Walter Dunlop
27 rue Vignon
Cormeilles-en-Parisis
Seine-et-Oise
Saturday, 24 September 1955

Dear Mr Grieve,

I have had a letter from Norman Buchan,[1] suggesting I might contribute to *The Voice of Scotland* with some notes from France.

As regards possible subjects for such notes, we have *l'embarras du choix*, but if you are interested in the idea, here are some suggestions.

There is Aragon's campaign 'pour une poésie nationale' – narrowed down in fact to a return to the alexandrine and sonnet, with other classical forms admitted.[2] This could be discussed either by itself, or better in a panorama of French poetry since the last period well-known to the English-speaking world – the poetry of the Resistance – with tangent references to such other forms of expression as painting, song, etc.

That is a vast subject, and various elements in it could be taken out for closer study. But I think the general picture should be given first, and could be 'done' in one article.

Some notes on Paul Eluard, 'with particular reference' to his last years.[3]

The whole intellectual scene in France today, with the re-emergence at the surface of Left-wing lights other than Marxist. This subject, however, would be less easy to treat in clear and simple fashion, being itself neither clear nor simple.

From one complication to another: North Africa. Among other things, it helps French intellectuals to look at themselves and one another and see where each stands.

François Mauriac,[4] by the way, after his appeal for the Rosenbergs[5] has also put his oar in over North Africa.

This brings me to the enclosures. The Hikmet poem, although nearly thirty years old, is still good on the movement of the Asian and African peoples for national independence. You might like to use it, either by itself or with the Iffet Halim poem.[6] The latter is not so good, but the two together have that 'Voice of Asia' touch which is lacking in all that Europeans can write on the subject.

Still not knowing how far you may be interested in translated material, I send also part of some unfinished notes, which I could knock into shape, on Nicolás Guillén.[7] I saw Guillén several times about the translations, and he is, of course, keen to find a way through the English-language wall.

I will stop my suggestions there meantime.

You may remember that we met once or twice during the winter 1949-1950, chiefly over the matter of a petition for Nâzim Hikmet.[8] It will interest you to know that, a month before Nâzim's liberation, the text of the petition, 'We the undersigned Scottish intellectuals...', was published in Turkish in Istanbul, in the *ad hoc* journal *Nâzim Hikmet*, the same issue containing an article signed 'A Scottish Student'.

I had hoped to pay you a visit during my short stay at home over Easter (was told off for not doing so by Tzara,[9] who wanted news of you), but was frustrated, as of most of what I had thought to pack into ten days. I hope I can repair the fault on my next homecoming, and in the meantime look forward to reading you.

Yours very sincerely,
W. Dunlop.

1   Norman Buchan (1922-1990), Glasgow teacher, one of the organizers of the Edinburgh People's Festivals 1951-1954, Labour M.P. 1964-1990.
2   Louis Aragon (1897-1982), poet, novelist and writer on art.
3   Paul Eluard (1895-1952), poet.
4   François Mauriac (1885-1970), major French Catholic novelist.
5   Julius and Ethel Rosenberg were executed in the US for spying for the USSR, 19 June, 1953.
6   In October 1955 MacDiarmid published Walter Dunlop's translations of 'A lion pacing an iron cage' by Nâzim Hikmet and 'The riddle of India' by Iffet Halim Oruz, in *The Voice of Scotland,* vol vi, no. 3 (October 1955).
7   Nicolás Guillén (1902-1989), Cuban poet.
8   Nâzim Hikmet (1902-1963), Turkish poet.
9   Tristan Tzara is regarded as 'the father of Dada'. In two further letters Dunlop says he hopes to see Tzara soon and will pass on MacDiarmid's greetings (29 December 1955) and encloses a book from Tzara to MacDiarmid (16 April 1956).

33. From Thornton Wilder (EUL MS2962.10 f.56)

[in red pencil]

Rome
10 December [1955]

Cher Maître
A happy Christmas to you – but above all, a fruitful rich Rabelaisian, Dantesque Joycian New Year – in which you give us abounding pages – lyrics with your right hand and satire with your left.

Ever cordially
Thornton Wilder

34. From Alexander Scott (EUL MS2960.5 ff.22-23)

The Saltire Review
of Arts, Letters and Life
Gladstone's Land
483 Lawnmarket
Edinburgh 1
16 March 1956

Dear Sir,

As you have already attacked Maurice Lindsay at considerable length in the Editorial of the current *The Voice of Scotland*,[1] it would be super-rogatory for a shorter version of the same to appear in the correspondence section of *The Review*. Abuse of the critic does not constitute an adequate rebuttal of his criticisms.

When Maurice Lindsay was asked to review *In Memoriam James Joyce*, I was unaware that a MacDiarmid-Lindsay feud was still 'on'. I assumed that it had dwindled away like a similar difference between Lindsay and myself.

As to publication of the review,[2] all writers who are asked to contribute to *The Saltire Review* are given *carte blanche*. Far from seeking to impose any kind of 'line', I hope that their views may stimulate discussion, and that from the consequent clash of opinion something like the truth may emerge.

Had I shared your extremely low estimate of Lindsay's abilities as a critic, I should not have asked him to review your book. But my own view of his capabilities lies somewhere between your present attitude towards him and the entirely different outlook on his talents expressed in your introduction to his *Hurlygush*,[3] which places him extremely high. Didn't you once say in *A Drunk Man* that the right place to be was 'whaur extremes meet'?

It seems to me a sign of vitality that *IMJJ* should provoke reviews ranging from the obloquy of *Saltire* to the eulogy of *The Voice*. Mere mediocrity would have been received with tepid praise all round, as usual in Scotland.

I am sorry you should regard my publishing Lindsay's review as 'a deliberate insult'. Should I want to attack a writer's work, I am perfectly capable (as shown by past performances) of striking out for myself, without the assistance of any hired assassin.

Should you wish to comment upon Lindsay's review without dragging in personalities, I shall be glad to publish your letter, although I'm afraid that to the general public the spectacle of a writer defending himself against a reviewer always appears somewhat ludicrous. The best defence is surely silence.

Yours faithfully,
Alexander Scott.
Editor.

---

[1]   Vol. vi, no. 4, pp. 1-8.
[2]   *The Saltire Review*, vol. 2, no. 6 (Winter 1955), on pages 77 and 79. Lindsay referred to '[...] this long, tedious, vulgar piece of bombastic pretentiousness [...]'.
[3]   *Hurlygush* (Edinburgh:Serif, 1948); MacDiarmid's introduction pp. 11-13.

35. From Alexander Scott (EUL MS2960.5 f.24)

The Saltire Review
of Arts, Letters and Life
Gladstone's Land
483 Lawnmarket
Edinburgh 1

C. M. Grieve, Esq.

10 April 1956

Dear Sir,[1]

Thank you for your letter of 19 March. Since your first letter had no indication to the contrary, I assumed that it was intended for publication, and my remark about 'abuse of the critic' was offered in explanation of not doing so. I am sorry you should choose to regard it as insulting.

Maurice Lindsay was not my first choice to review your book. Originally the commission went to Burns Singer, but for reasons unknown to me he failed to send in his copy. I couldn't ask Daiches, as he had already reviewed it in *Lines*;[2] nor MacCaig since he was a 'character' in the poem; nor Young, because he isn't a critic anyway; and finally by a process of elimination the choice fell on Lindsay, who had at least written appreciative1y on your work in English in the past.

I don't know who wrote *The Glasgow Herald* articles – nor, indeed, did I see them, as I was up north most of last summer. I hear the BBC are trying to get Auden to review your book on *Arts Review*.

Should your plans for future publications mature, *The Saltire Review* will review them as a matter of course, whether or not review copies should be sent. Other reviewers may look on them more favourably than Lindsay regarded the Joyce book.

Yours, etc.,

Alexander Scott.

Editor.

[1] 'Dear Sir' in the letters of 16 March and 10 April had changed to 'Dear Chris' by the time of the letter of 6 June 1956.

[2] *Lines Review* 9, Edinburgh (August 1955), pp. 22-26.

36. From Christopher Hill (NLS Acc. 7361/27)

2B Rawlinson Rd
Oxford
22 November 1956

Dear Mr. Grieve,

Thank you very much for your letter, and for signing.[1] The letter had already gone into the *Daily Worker*, but I have sent your signature in to be added. If it is not printed in the *Daily Worker* within a reasonable space of time, we had proposed to send the letter to the *New Statesman* and *Tribune*, as I presume Victor Kiernan[2] explained to you. All but one of the 17 signatories of the letter have agreed to this. May I assume that you too agree unless I hear from you to the contrary?

With best wishes and many thanks.

Yours sincerely,

Christopher Hill. (ink)

[1] Christopher Hill refers here to the letter which criticised the Executive Committee of the Communist Party of Great Britain for their support of the Soviet action in Hungary

which commenced on 30 October. The letter was published in the *New Statesman* on 1 December. MacDiarmid's signing of this letter and his private letter to John Gollan, General Secretary of the CPGB, on 15 November, in which he expressed complete support for the position taken by the Executive, have often been cited as an example of his contradictions.

2   Marxist historian.

37. From Sean O'Casey (EUL MS2958.1 f.5)

Flat 3
40 Trumlands Road
St. Marychurch
Torquay
Devon
12 January 1957

My very dear Chris,

Thanks for your sympathy, and for Valda's & Michael's good sympathy, too. We've suffered a bitter blow, and my heart is bruised. Niall was 21, a gallant lad, grand sense of humour, gay, and reliable. He bid fair to become a first-class biologist. He was deeply troubled over the tragedy of Hungary, & couldn't find a reason for the Soviet action. He came from London to talk with me about it, but couldn't agree with my view that it was a sad necessity. I insisted he should have his own opinion, while I held on to mine. We shook hands & embraced, thank God, deciding that each opinion was sacred. He came down with his sister, Shivaun, for the holidays, driving a small van, and a few days later he was dead.

I listened to *Drunk Man* on the Third [Programme], and enjoyed it immensely. I have your tribute to Joyce, but haven't read it yet. I was in hospital for 5 months; two big operations, &, in between, an attack of bronchial pneumonia; so I was left pretty low after it all; but after 6 months, I began to pull out, & am now fairly fit, and trying to get away from the recent shock of losing a lad I dearly loved. Eileen was with him all the time, & gave him great comfort, so that he died a brave boy.

My deep love to you, Chris, to Valda, & to your Michael.

As ever,

Sean.

38. From Gordon McLennan (NLS Acc.7361/28)

The Communist Party
Scottish Committee
57 Miller St
Glasgow C1
20 February 1957

Dear Comrade MacDiarmid,

This is a note to inform you that the Scottish Committee of the Party, at its meeting on Sunday, decided unanimously to support your readmission for membership of the Party.[1]

We will be getting in touch with you to issue you with a Party Card.

Best wishes.

Yours fraternally,

Gordon McLennan.

Secretary

[1] In a letter to the present editor, 8 November 2002, Gordon McLennan writes of his interview with MacDiarmid at Brownsbank after he had applied for readmission, 'It was the first time I met Chris & [I] was impressed by his warmth, humour, friendship, modesty & clear political stance. It was an impression confirmed in all my experience with Chris in subsequent years when he took on various commitments for the Party, including being a Parliamentary candidate in Kinross and West Perthshire, where Sir Alec Douglas-Home was the Conservative candidate.'

39. From Barbara Niven (EUL MS2957)

Wednesday [February/March 1957]

My dear Chris,

I was delighted with your letter and concentrated contents. It's wonderful news about China, the most right of arrangements![1] I half-knew, no more.

I knew first about your regularised position with the C. P. (regularised? you?) from Gordon McLennan who was deeply impressed by your conversation with him. I'm very happy about it. Shall see J. R. Campbell to propose a letter from you saying why, if you agree.[2]

Understand from Ewan that he has your poem packed up ready to send & will be doing it to-day.

Wonderful, also, to see you before you go. Please allow a day or two at the least, the very least, before you leave. And Valda. Tell her she must come to us for longer this time – on the way there or back or both.

I was about to write, anyway, to know if you could come (with at least half the fare paid – it was to be then) to one of these monthly meetings organised by John Berger[3] & Peter da Francia,[4] and read some of your poems, talk, whatever you decide. Perhaps this could now be arranged on one of your transits to China.

Love to you both from us and the others.

Barbara.

[1] MacDiarmid went to China for five weeks in April and May 1957 in a group from the British-Chinese Friendship Society, without Valda.

[2] *Daily Worker* published 'Why I Rejoined' by Hugh MacDiarmid, 28 March 1957. J.R. Campbell was the then editor.

[3] John Berger (b. 1926), art critic, novelist, painter and author.

[4] Peter de Francia (b. 1921), artist, writer and teacher. Retired as Professor of Painting at the Royal College of Art in 1987.

40. From Helen Cruickshank (EUL MS2962 f.43)

EPISTLE TO HUGH MACDIARMID

Dear Chris, Dear Hugh, dear Everyman,
Chief Pillidacus o' your Clan,
Richt prood am I this day tae scan
The mornin papers,
An see ye'll yet wear hood an goon
For a' your capers.

An wha's mair richt than *you* to be
In sic a learned companie
As Science, Law, Philosophie,
(An eke Releegion)
For ye're a compound o' the three
In my opeenion.

For 'deed, ye're *Christ*opher, nae ither
An cairry Gude upo yer shouther,
Ye fecht the battles for yer brither
To ease his weird.
Ye sing, preach, sweir, cajole (whiles blether)
Fegs, ye're no feared.

Ay, ye're a singin fechtin bard
That dings doon idols, shard on shard,
Wi verbal clypes, an nae clinch barred
Ye coonter Evil,
Yer dunts sae savage, fell an hard
Wad fleg the Deevil.

But noo, a warld's wonder see!
Ye hinna flegged the Varsitee,
They're giein you an LL D
As honoured poet,
An Science, Law, Philosophie,
An *Plebs* shall know it.

Inscribed in affection and pride
H. B. C. 16 March 1957

41. From Norman Kemp Smith (EUL Gen. 2094/5/2137)

14 Kilgraston Road
Edinburgh
18 March 1957

Dear Mr Grieve,

I greatly rejoice to hear that the University is proposing to honour itself & you, by the conferring on you of its Ll.D; & look forward to be present on the happy occasion of your capping. I am glad too that my good friend, Max Born,[1] is being similarly honoured.

George Davie I hope to be seeing next week.

Yours sincerely,

N. Kemp Smith.

[1] Max Born (1882-1970) was a German-born physicist and mathematician who was instrumental in the development of quantum physics.

42. From Enid 'Mamie' Fullerton (EUL MS2950 f.40)

Astley House
[128 Heaton Moor Road]
Heaton Moor
Stockport
17 April 1957

Dear Christopher,

I hope this will catch you up somewhere in Wales, before you go on your marvellous tour – Brussels, Warsaw, Moscow and Peking – 'with magic in each name'. Thank you for your interesting letter, which I was delighted to get. I'll come up to Edinburgh for your Honorary Degree bestowal. Do I need a ticket? You won't be too surrounded, all of the time, for me to be able to have a word with you? It well could be that no one present met you longer ago than I did. I think 1913! I am very happy that you are having this recognition, and I hope I shall be able to congratulate you in person.

I am looking forward to hearing from you. My very best wishes for your journey, and my warmest regards to Valda, whom I look forward to meeting on the 5th July.

Mamie.

43. From Fang Cheng Ping (NLS Acc.7361/27)

7 May 1957

Mr Grieve:

I have phoned up Mr Vepallen (the author of *In The Ceylon Tea Garden*) and have told him all that you asked me to say in this morning. He said that he would be free tomorrow morning and would come here to meet you at 9:00am. Therefore please wait for him tomorrow morning around nine o'clock.

Your programme for tomorrow morning is as follows:

1) 10:00 or 10:30 going to see the old observatory.

2) 12:00 or 12:30 having lunch with Mr Fong (editor-in-chief of the *Chinese Literature.*)

Good night.

Fang Cheng Ping.
(your interpreter)

44. From William MacLellan (EUL MS2954.16 ff.71-73)

William MacLellan
Publishers Limited
240 Hope Street
Glasgow C2
26 August 1957

My Dear Chris,

Apologies for that unskilful phrase about the fivers.[1] I meant that *you* must find it distasteful but I suppose it could be interpreted adverbially in your present mood towards the irresponsible type of publisher you clearly consider me to be.

Your letter raises very fundamental issues on the relationship between publisher & author which can have significance far beyond our own little situation & we must try to clear up the illusions that exist either in my mind or yours if we are to work happily together, as you gave me reason to hope might be possible before I left for Moscow, upon other work in the future.

You may find it tiresome to hear me attempt to explain some of the difficulties associated with the work of literary publishing but clearly some sort of basis of understanding must be created.

Is your view now that the Joyce poem was a piece of dishonest practice because I took on liabilities which I have so far failed to discharge & that further the issue of a second edition with all the attendant expenditure of paper, time & binding was also irresponsible? Further do you honestly think that my best action now should be to let 'The Knowe'[2] & take a flat in town & sell the car & if need be the whole business & take a job as manager of a print factory somewhere?

If all the books on my shelves were sold I could pay my creditors many times over but that takes time & I suggest it is wiser to hold on to the goodwill (& the inevitable illwill) that has been created at this address & hope that the break will come. Publishers have to be gamblers. So too are authors whether they like it or not & all I ask is that writers I deal with appreciate the gamble that is taken on their behalf.

You say our fundamental difference lies in the fact that the publisher calls for the return of his outlay first before the author. That is *not* the point. Can you tell me where the cash has to come from to pay the author except from the working capital of the publisher, if the receipts from sales do not cover the outlay. For instance, say a book costs £450 for the 1st edition & the royalties amount to £50 & sales £375. At this stage the publisher has had to pay out £75 on printing which he has not been able to recover & if royalties are paid a further £50. All this is provided by working capital.

To retrieve this loss he puts out a reprint costing say £250 which means his total capital outlay is now £375 plus the royalties that become due as sales proceed. Another £50 royalties & £375 sales, leaving another £50 debit to carry over to the third edition.

That is roughly the position I find myself in – only I have no working capital except the day to day turnover of the jobbing printing business. Your fivers therefore, as I tried to explain, have in fact nothing to do with the economy of the book at this stage & depend on the prosperity of the printing.

Quite absurd, I agree, but finance is all mad & we are mad if we allow ourselves to be distracted by this madness from getting on with things that seem important to us & publishing your poetry does frankly seem an important thing for someone in Scotland to be doing in a manner that sends it the whole world over.

That is the kind of organisation I tried to create here, however imperfect it may be financially & I offer it in all humility for your service at all times.

Perhaps all this may merely confuse the issue still further but I hope you see the real point at issue & not the surrounding matters associated with commercial publishing practice which have little to do with our problem in Scotland. The legality of your claim is not in doubt. The practical issue still haunts us as to how to get the money with which to pay these royalties.

Yours,
Bill.

¹   This appears to refer to an earlier undated letter, 'These £5s that you have to wring out of me so distastefully are taken from the printing business as 'the Joyce' is still not earning royalties' (EUL MS 2954.16 f.104v.).
²   MacLellan's house at Thankerton, near Biggar.

45. From William MacLellan (EUL MS2954.16 ff.74-77)

William MacLellan
Publishing Limited
240 Hope Street
Glasgow C2
31 August 1957

Dear Chris,
Each successive letter just adds to the fog & seems to produce less & less sympathy for our respective positions. Obviously you don't believe my statement on the *Joyce* sales submitted to you & conveniently forget you added 25% to the poem on the backs of the galleys of the first proofs & so rocketed the costs my retail price was originally based on. Actually I'm not ruthless & businesslike enough in permitting such things to pass.

Anyway you are not inclined to admit that I could be in financial difficulties or out of pocket as far as publication of your work is concerned so it is a waste of time pressing the point further.

I don't know what you mean by 'alienate' because I'm still on speaking terms with all my early collaborators but I cannot feel that in your present mood you even grant the possibility that any group gathered round me. A printing press is an entity in itself & that is all you or any other writer is interested in. I *never* mattered & lack the drive as yet to make any contribution of my own. However, your letters have that poetic fire & strong feeling about real values which acts as a stimulant and incentive to do better. Your instinctive desire to stir the stagnant is something I enjoy and accept.

We can't all be MacDiarmid's & even you cannot live at the same high level as 'Doctor' C. M. Grieve in your personal life & relationships as you achieve in the cold high solitudes of creation. If there is ever any point that we have reached together at this higher level, apart from those sections of your poetry that have moved me utterly (but which you consider me incapable of feeling as you intended) I should say it lies at the heart of this duality. You say MacDiarmid is greater than Grieve – Art is more than Life. My disagreement with you lies there. The living Grieve, the total man, is what the content of Art is ultimately concerned with. That is why my concern is for the control of the passions & mental processes & the refinement of action as a result.

Regarding Literary Values & my shortcomings in this field I would not quarrel with you – for me, you alone are the contemporary Literary Movement in Scotland & all the stars in the tail of the comet, which you are right to draw after you, because you cannot easily avoid it, mean very little to me & seem to contribute nothing to the forward drive of thought.

As for intellectual & aesthetic standards I would not give house room to your views on painting & music & dance. Through Valda, I know your views on Chisholm as a composer, Nan as a pianist, Donald as a painter[1] & the Celtic Ballet Movement.[2] These are the things you see me solidly behind & abominate my attempts to encourage & advance by what you call pulling strings.

Time will tell whether my aesthetic judgment is so faulty. There is a quality of 'faith' necessary in such matters – a word I can perhaps use in writing to one of the great metaphysical poets of the day.

As far as persistent publicity stunts are concerned, there is an art or craft in presentation which I'm still learning the hard way. It is, I agree, a mistake to push anything mediocre & I'm surprised to know that many people associate me with so many mediocrities of no account. There's just a touch of the pot & the kettle here.

Meg Morris gets the same criticism – we overdo the publicity angle & receive mention in excess of what is deserved but that is partly the fault of the press that will never have anything to do with worthwhile art.

As far as Nan's PRO work goes, there is sometimes a tinge of jealousy – 'how does she get this & that!' They do not see the nights & nights of correspondence & thought which can go into the simplest tour & presentation of one artist.

There was a time when the hard things you say about my character would have hurt but I think I know myself well enough to recognise what is true & false about your estimate. I ran into Eva Gibbon's husband at the Garden Party yesterday – he is interested in phrenology & 'did' my head on the spot. It would seem there is little we can do about our bumps but use them to the best advantage and all the characteristics are evidently there on the old cranium – the tendency to manipulate half-a-dozen things at a time; work through other people; lack of capacity to concentrate on one job etc., etc., *ad purgatorum*.

However all that is beside the point. There can be no dramatic parting of the ways for us as mutual interests bind us together at least till the *Joyce* poem edition is sold out. Facts are more real than words & all the letters we write cannot alter the position here at Hope St where books can be printed & distributed conveniently, if at little profit in the early stages of distribution.

We never had much aesthetic intercourse – in all the years we only twice reached any real heights in discussion together. Like all artists, your first concern is what you have created & the desire to have it in recognisable form. If I can assist in that process you will use me again despite the rubbish that I do to keep the pot boiling. I'm surprised you take all that stuff seriously, Chris. You know perfectly well I don't drop standards at the vital points where bigger literary values are at stake such as was the case with Bob MacLellan's verse play.[3]

We are down in Glasgow for some days to let Nan through to Edinburgh for her 'contacts'.

Will do what I can also about the royalties with as little recourse to the prods as I can possibly contrive.

Yours,

Bill.

[1]   'Donald' was Donald Bain.
[2]   Margaret Morris was the director of the Celtic Ballet Movement.
[3]   Robert MacLellan's verse play was *The Carlin Moth* which was first published by William MacLellan in 1947 in a collection of one-act plays entitled *North Light*. Republished in Robert MacLellan, *Collected Plays Volume One* (London and New York, 1981).

46. From Samuel Marshak (EUL MS2966)

Moscow
Vorovsky Street 52
10 November 1957

My dear MacDiarmid,

This is to congratulate you most heartily on the honour awarded to you by Edinburgh University.

I always remember our friendly meetings both here and in Scotland and look forward to seeing you again.

With best wishes,

James Barke and William Gallacher. 'J.B. with Willie Gallacher M.P. - after the culmination of the greatest 1930s Hunger March.' (In Barke's writing)
By permission of The Mitchell Library, Glasgow City Council, (Box 12A) and of Alastair Barke.

Sincerely yours,
S. Marshak.

1   MacDiarmid first met Marshak during his visit to the USSR in 1950. They met again
     when Marshak came to Scotland with Madame Anna Elistratova and Mr Boris Polevoi
     in January 1955, not 1950 as given in *MacDiarmid : a festschrift* and in *MacDiarmid: an
     illustrated biography*.

47. From David Boadella (NLS Acc.7361/29)

476 Woodborough Road
Nottingham
18 March 1958

Dear Mr Grieve,

Let me hasten to congratulate you upon a first-class issue of *The Voice of Scotland*. The article by Cyril Barrow is quite surprisingly good, and the remarks in your editorial were very flattering and considerate.[1] I have taken the opportunity to order several copies from your publishers, and I sincerely hope that when the next issue of 'Orgonomic Functionalism' appears later this month, your circulation for the current issue will be increased. I should be interested to know how big your circulation is, and would like to know some details of articles published in previous issues.

You may be interested to know that in Reich's middle period in Germany he worked in very close connection with the German Communist organisations, & was a most energetic public speaker. My own feeling is that Reich, even more than Lenin, is a successor in twentieth century terms to the work of Christ, both in the sense of a man with revolutionary *healing* techniques, and as one who re-interpreted the meaning of the phrase, 'Save ye become as bairns again'.[2]

You may like to know that yours is the first journal of any standing in Britain to publish in full the facts about Reich's 'judicial murder', and to give his work a decent coverage.

Yours sincerely,
David Boadella.

1   *The Voice of Scotland*, vol. viii, nos.3-4 [1958], carried the articles 'A Rebel's Death' by
     Cyril Barrow, pp. 8-14, and 'The Work and Persecution of Dr Wilhelm Reich' by David
     Boadella, pp. 15-19.
2   Wilhelm Reich was an Austrian and (after 1939) US pyschiatrist and psychoanalyst,
     known as one of the most radical figures in the history of psychiatry. He built 'orgone
     energy accumulators' which his patients sat inside to harness reputed health benefits.
     When Reich violated an injunction obtained by the US Food and Drug Administration
     against the interstate sale of the 'accumulators', he received a two-year jail sentence and
     died of heart failure just over a year later and before he could apply for parole. Several
     tons of his publications were burnt by the F.D.A..

48. From Nan Barke (EUL Gen.2094/1/73a&b)

5 Redhouse Close
Bentley Heath
Knowle
Warks
8 April 1958

Dear Christopher Grieve,

Being on the doctor's sick list is my only excuse for not writing earlier to thank you most sincerely for the tribute you paid at my husband's grave-side.

From all quarters I have been made aware of how worthily you acquitted yourself on that never-to-be-forgotten day, and this has indeed been a consolation to me in my sorrow. I shall be eternally grateful to you for the services you have rendered to my sons and myself.

Yours sincerely,
Nan Barke.

Someone gave me the impression that you would let me have a copy of your notes sometime and I should be most interested if you could – for reading at some future date.[1]

Thank you.

[1] 24 March 1958

TEXT of C. M. GRIEVE'S SPEECH at NEW KILPATRICK CEMETERY, BEARSDEN, at the COMMITTAL SERVICE of JAMES BARKE, Author.

I have little to add to the splendid tribute Willie Gallacher paid to James Barke at the Crematorium; but I certainly endorse every word of it.

We all come to mourn a good friend and comrade and a very able Humanist and great Scotsman, and to express our sympathy in their bereavement with his widow and his two sons, Alasdair and Allan, and other relatives and friends. I do not come to pay tribute to James Barke. His life and work have done that, and will continue to be a sufficient testimony to his great qualities. All we can do is to recognise that and profit by it. His name is secure in the annals of Scottish Literature and will be forever linked with that of our national Poet, Robert Burns, to whose life and work he devoted so much untiring research and of which he wrote so fully in his great quintet of novels, an achievement which will be further enhanced by the posthumous publication of a sixth volume in the series.

The great Russian writer, Maxim Gorki, asked: 'Masters of Culture, what side are you on?' James Barke never had any difficulty in making his choice. He was one of the all too few Scottish writers of his generation who made the same choice that all the great line of Scottish radical writers have made, from Barbour to Sir David Lyndsay right down to Burns and since; that great line of Scottish writers who sided with the working class and lived and wrote for the Social Commonwealth. That line includes Thomas Muir and the martyred Friends of the People, and all those Scotsmen and Scotswomen since who have been animated by the cause of Social Justice; and James Barke takes his unchallenged place in it. For all time his name will be on the roster of those Scottish writers who constitute our true national tradition and our only hope now and for the future.

James Barke has gone from us at a sadly early age, yet in his too brief lifetime he accomplished a great deal of work in various departments of literature – drama, fiction, autobiography and politics. His mortal remains have been consumed by fire, but the flames have been unable to touch much fine gold twice refined contained in his writings and in our recollections of his warm, generous personality, and these form a precious legacy that will pass indestructibly down the generations.

The great German poet, Goethe, said that Death exists for the enrichment of life; and I think all of us will agree that it is well that what can be destroyed should be destroyed, and only the indestructible remain. Much that is quintessential of James Barke has not been, and never will be, destroyed, but remains as a model and an incentive to Scots now and henceforward. Let gratitude mingle with our grief then, and may pride infused with our sorrow strengthen us to recognise his achievement and follow his example in the things that matter.

We have lost a fine comrade. Let us then all the more close our ranks and redouble our efforts in the great cause in which he and we have been united and in which his spirit will continue to play its part though the body through which it operated is no longer numbered among the living. He was a man who in his own way, with great courage and resource, fought against the Powers and Principalities of Darkness, and now that we have lost him, we should realise all the more the need to follow his example and to gird our loins and acquit ourselves as men. Karl Marx said that the meaning of life is struggle – let us then struggle all the more to make up for the fighter we have lost. That would have been James Barke's own wish, and to the extent to which we can carry it out we can transform this sad scene here today into a powerful reinforcement of our common cause which will be James Barke's greatest reward and the only one he would have desired in his heart of hearts.

He loved Scotland. Earth of Scotland, rest lightly on a very true and distinguished son.

Good-bye, James. Here by your grave we pledge ourselves to redoubled effort for the great Scottish and great human values we had in common.

(Mitchell Library, Glasgow City Council, Barke Papers, Box 12A).

49. From A. S. Neill (NLS Acc.7361/29)

Summerhill School
Leiston
Suffolk
11 April 1958

Dear Mac . . . but I ay think of you as Grieve o' Montrose ... Gord, what an age since Minnie Anderson took me to meet you on the – what was it? *Montrose Standard*?

It was good to see you take up Reich in *The Voice [of Scotland]*. Ta also for reprinting my letter in *The Times Ed. Supp.*[1] Not surprised to read that you are barred from *The G[lasgow Herald]* and *The Scotsman*. I guess I am too, or nearly so. How much is just

Scottish? I don't think the Farfar[2] paper has mentioned my name in over 40 years, but that didn't surprise me. If the *Dundee [Courier and Adver]tiser* did years ago I fancy it was because J. B. Salmond was on the staff ... his death the other day was a real blow to me.

I'm visiting the Muirs near Cambridge later on this month. Edwin has at last come into his own but I hear that Minnie (now Willa) has had a few operations.

I'll hae a shottie at your magazine warning you that if any bloody politics enter its pages I'll – I'll tak in *The Glasgow Herald*. Since USSR education left *The Road to Life*[3] way and became mass character-moulding I lost all belief in Communism. Trouble is that if a man hates both sides what in hell can he do? My own sad feeling is that there needn't be any trouble in deciding, for the hate merchants will destroy the world and that is a hell of a fear when one deals with bairns, one's own included.

I'll be meeting John Aitkenhead[4] at a co-ed conference next week. He is always the only guy with a kilt ... my legs are no that shape and I fancy it wud be kinda cauld aboot the knees.

I canna find your letter and hope you didna speer onything.

All the best.

A. S. Neill.

found yr letter

[1] MacDiarmid reprinted Neill's letter of 6 September 1958 in his editorial, vol. viii, nos. 3-4, [1958], pp. 4-6.
[2] 'Farfar' is Forfar, Neill's birthplace.
[3] A. S. Makarenko (1888-1939) wrote *The Road to Life*, translated by Stephen Garry, London, 1936.
[4] John Aitkenhead was Head of Kilquhanity House School.

50. From David M. Craig (EUL MS2978)

198 Grange Loan
Edinburgh 9
4 June 1958

Dear Mr Grieve,

I went into the Castle Wynd Printers for *Voices* yesterday & he told me the deadline for the next issue. I thought that a version of my part in a broadcast discussion (with Maurice Lindsay) on 'Is a separate Scottish Literature desirable?' ('Scottish Life & Letters', June 11 coming) might be acceptable to you for the next *Voice*.[1] The printer seemed to think I could give copy straight to him, but I thought that my argument is so counter to your own positions that you might, if you publish my article at all, consider replying to it yourself. What might be called 'Scottish literary nationalism' seems to me a real clog on thought in Scotland; I feel I've only recently groped my way out of it myself, & in this article I try to evoke the fallacies in such 'nationalism' & what I take to be the desirable alternative.

Yours sincerely,
David M. Craig.

1   'Is a separate Scottish literature desirable?' was included in *The Voice of Scotland*, vol.
ix, no. 2, which was the last published issue of the magazine. MacDiarmid made some
comments in reply in his Editorial. Craig also contributed several other essays to this
third series of *The Voice*: 'Hugh MacDiarmid's Poetry' in vol.vii, no. 1 (April 1956)
(followed by MacDiarmid's 'Reply to Criticism' in the same issue); 'Burns and Scottish
Culture' in two parts, vol.vii, nos. 3-4 (October 1956- January 1957) and viii, nos. 1-2
(April-July 1957); 'Stevenson and the vanished Scotland', vol.viii, nos.3-4 [1958]; and
'Literature and native language', vol.ix, no.1 [1958].

51. From Boris Polevoj (EUL MS2966)

[Translated from Russian]

Moscow
18 December 1958

Mr Hugh MacDiarmid
Dear friend,
As you know, I am not a poet and never in my life have ventured to compose a
single line of poetry, but nevertheless I dare to send to the glorious poet of Scotland
heartiest greeting of Soviet poets and somewhere at the end join my own greeting
of a prose writer. Please accept my very best wishes for the New Year, let it bring you
happiness and first of all – new poems, which really constitute the true happiness
of an artist.
   Yours,
   Boris Polevoj.

52. From Michael Grieve (NLS MS27151 f.44)

Partickhill Road
Glasgow
Friday [1958]

Dearest Dad and Mum,
Very glad to find you back on the ball when I arrived home, Dad – but try and take
care for a little.
   I sat up last night to do the enclosed. I hope it is all right despite having to do half
of it in candlelight as the bloody shillings ran out again!
   I have typed THREE copies – 1 for America; 1 for you, and the last one for
reference for myself. On it, I have copied out instructions regarding starting and
ending poems, etc., from your pink-sheeted original.
   On p.5 of the typescript I couldn't decipher the last word 'In Memoriam Liam ...';
on p. 6 'The ... Olympian'.[1]

The only other query is that on p.8 you have 'Glasgow' (to be taken from *Impavidi*)[2] and on p.10 you have 'Glasgow 1960' also from *Impavidi* – I take it they are separate poems?

Whenever you say the word, I'll get going and might get quite a lot of the 'straight' typing like the 'Drunk Man' done before you arrive from Bulgaria. Anyway, let me know what is doing as soon as you can.

All going well I think I'll be deputy features editor of the *Record* before I'm next home – but will let you know. There is nothing much been happening here – was sent an advance copy of Kurt Wittig's book for review.[3]

I think I will be making a flying visit from Carnoustie to Stirling tomorrow (Saturday) as I have just seen that John Wilson, the *Stirling Observer* photographer who almost came to our wedding before the numbers were cut, has died. Spoke on the phone to Alf and Bet (both asking very warmly after you both) and they said he had just died in his sleep. He was only fifty-five, Think, therefore, I'll be attending the funeral. Hope everything is going all right – will be writing at beginning of week and will let you know when we're likely to be through again – I'm working on the Sunday.

All my love to you both.

Mike xxx (in ink).

1   'In Memoriam Liam Mac'Ille Iosa' and 'The Oon Olympian' were the full titles.
2   'Impavidi Progrediamur' or ' Haud Forrit' remains unpublished in the way MacDiarmid intended (NLS MS 27025 and NLS MS 27026). Titles of parts are given in Index of Titles, *C.P.* II, p. 1462.
3   *The Scottish Tradition in Literature* (Edinburgh, 1958).

53. From Lydia Pasternak Slater (EUL MS2958.22 f.53v.)

A card without date or postmark [1958][1]

Dear Mr MacDiarmid

First of all I would like to thank you for your very nice introduction and your flattering appreciation of my translations.[2] Secondly I do so hope you will understand how anxious I am not to add any new burden onto Boris' shoulders by this booklet – I feel that it is *essential* to drop every political allusion – left or right – and keep strictly only to the subject: the poems. I have upset Mr Russell, I am afraid and will probably upset you too; needless to say I am even more upset myself. Please do not be cross with me! And many thanks once again! (Also for *The Voice of Scotland*!)[3]

Lydia P. Slater.

1   The card showed three drawings by Leonid Pasternak, her father. It was found among Peter Russell's letters to MacDiarmid, so presumably he forwarded the card.
2   *Poems by Boris Pasternak*, Peter Russell, Fairwarp, 1958. MacDiarmid's introduction has been reprinted in *The Raucle Tongue* III, pp. 408-410.
3   MacDiarmid published seven of her translations in *The Voice of Scotland*, vol ix, no. 2 [1958].

54. From Neil M. Gunn (EUL MS2948.15 f.48)

Kerrow House
Cannich
Beauly
12 January 1959

Dear Christopher,

Thank you very much for sending *Jabberwock*.[1] Yes, I remember now writing my piece, & am glad to see it fit into the page – & the tribute – so neatly. I think the lads have done you proud. Together with MacCaig's broadcast, it salutes an occasion of honour fairly handsomely.

The one thing I might cavil at a little bit, perhaps, is the section on 'MacDiarmid on Scotland'. Whoever was responsible for choosing the quotations would have done your work more credit if he had included at least one or two paragraphs exemplifying creative elements. That old bit about schoolmasters, for example, – you start off by saying that you had two superb teachers. Recently I listened in to a broadcast – good, I thought – on Lewis Grassic Gibbon, in which I heard your own voice to excellent effect. Here again was the wonderful schoolmaster. I could multiply this by other recorded instances of a similar kind in recent times. But even sticking to yourself & Gibbon: that *two* leading Scottish writers in different parts of Scotland should by chance have had *three* teachers of high distinction out of an army of so-called belly-crawling nitwits & worse is so against the laws of mathematical probability that it surely becomes absurd? Indeed I was beginning to think that my early boyhood was exceptional in a headmaster who was regarded as the natural enemy!

I liked the contribution by David Orr, even if I could not help smiling when he got to mentioning 'essence' and 'personality' in a way reminiscent of Ouspensky-Gurdjieff,[2] for if he thinks that readers will understand him, he's an optimist! In recent years I have been exploring such regions of the psyche with much interest, but when I tried in every way I could, in book & essay, & by every parallel or analogy I could think of from science & the arts, to get across one single manifestation of a certain real, if rare, psychic event, I was met by the blank wall. Though I can imagine the private comments!

However, all this merely sets me talking in a way reminiscent of an older day.

I did hear you had been out East & I am sure you would have enjoyed it all. Daisy & I were in Denmark last summer. *Inter alia*, I wanted to see from the inside how the Danes ran their agricultural cooperatives, for I had in recent years given a lot of time, on the Crofters Commission & elsewhere, to Highland crofting conditions.

So there's a lot of leeway to make up, one way or another, should we find ourselves making a night of it once again. I have no fixed date for Edinburgh, but something is bound to happen to draw me there soon.

Again with thanks for *Jabberwock* & with every good wish for health & more power to you both.

Neil.

---

[1] *Jabberwock,* vol.5, no.1, featured 'A Tribute to MacDiarmid'. It was dated 1958.

Peter D. Ouspensky (1878-1947), a Russian philosopher who left Russia after the Bolshevik Revolution, was an exponent of the teachings of George I. Gurdjieff (1877-1949), a Greco-Armenian philospher whom he met in Moscow in 1915. Gurdjieff re-established his Institute for the Harmonious Development of Man at Fontainebleau from 1922 to 1933 (originally at Tiflis).

55. From Kenneth Rexroth (EUL MS2962.7 f.57)

L'Atelier
Vallon des Gardes
route Tholonet
Aix en Provence
Bd R France
[January 1959]

Dear Hugh MacDiarmid,

Hope you made the Burns celebrations lively & significant. I'm sure you did. Wasn't that hilarious about the postage stamp? This chauvinism – I guess 'little nation chauvinism' should be the term – is incomprehensible to Americans – who learn Burns in school, whether their ancestry is Polish, Negro or Red Indian. England's leading literary critic once stared at me in mute incomprehension when I said you were generally considered around the world the most important non-Fascist poet in the British Isles (a crack at T. S. E.). He said, 'Why no one whatever reads that incomprehensible gibberish except a few of Grieve's disciples who have memorized a Scots dialectic dictionary!'

And these are the people who when you say everything in England from the morning porridge to the evening's savory tastes like the same thing – say, Shepherds' Pie – say, 'What about the Negroes in the South?'

Even the most bigoted Southerners are proud of Negro Spirituals & jazz. – But the English won't even honor the greatest poetry of the 18th century. If he were alive today he'd be lucky to get a gold-plated medal like Tensing.

Sad, Muir's death. He was the last thoroly *bona fide* expression of Scots Presbyterian sensibility (*not* a contradiction in terms) the world will ever see. He was young to die – nowadays people tend to live out their 'allotment'.[1] He certainly unleashed something by his 'discovery' of Kierkegaard. Although I guess most of our intellectuals didn't know that but got Kierkegaard through Sartre. I am sure the Existentialists of Iowa and Adelaide never read either Muir – or Emerson [2]– or J. G. Huneker[3] on Kierkegaard.

That's all – just chat. We'll be in Europe for 3 months more – may see you yet.
Best.
Kenneth Rexroth.

[1] Muir *was* over seventy.
[2] Ralph Waldo Emerson (1803-1882), US essayist, philospher and poet best remembered for leading the Transcendentalist movement of the mid-19th century.
[3] J.G. Huneker (1857-1921), US critic of music, art and literature.

56. From Joyce Williams (NLS Acc.7361/30)

Flat 7\
38 Arterberry Road\
Wimbledon\
London SW20\
October 1959

Dear Hugh

I daresay you'll be surprised to hear from me once more. I've been re-reading your 'drunk man', & suddenly & strongly wished to communicate! Where is your new Lallans poem??? Do let me know when it comes out, so I can buy it & recommend it!

I've just been in Spain at least in Basque country (Euzkadi). I was so struck by the poverty amid all the sunshine & lush grass. Franco was in S. Sebastian & every mountain road was double-checked by police. I think it is a pity the U.S. gives relief to Spain because it simply means Franco stays put, I suppose. A wonderful place though. Extremes like Ireland. And nothing to do with the Church either, just the temperament of the people. They have the same detached attitude that could make Pearse[1] say 'Ireland is the sow that eats her own farrow'. I met Pearse's sister once she lives outside Dublin in St Enda where he had his Gaelic school. His profile very melancholy & Spanish-looking dominated every wall – she had the house *unchanged* since 1916 even his dog was stuffed on a chair in the gloom of an antimacassared horsehair sofa'd drawing room. I patted it & had a great shock. She is a recluse & looks very like the photos of Pearse, a gloomy withdrawn noble face. On a high horse.

Anyway – let me have a line sometime – By the way what do you think of the Lunik?[2] Has it, also, got '... *a wunnerfu' finger / For the back-lill o' Daith!*'?[3]

Very best wishes to you.

Joyce Williams.

[1]   Padraic Pearse (1879-1916), teacher, poet, critic, propagandist, orator, dramatist. Nationalist leader of the uprising of 1916. Executed.
[2]   On 12 January 1959 a Soviet Lunik flew past the moon into orbit round the sun. It was the first spacecraft to escape from Earth's gravity.
[3]   'Prelude to Moon Music', *C.P.* I, p. 24.

57. From Helen Cruickshank (EUL MS2946.9 ff.67-68)

4 Hillview Drive\
Corstorphine\
Edinburgh 12\
17 December 1959

Dear Chris,

Some time ago someone said to me that I was about the only person he knew whom Grieve had never attacked. I replied, 'Don't worry: my turn will come!'

And it has, and I don't grumble, for of course I provoked it myself but only because you provoked the sleeping AMV. in me to protest at certain features of your 2-column-long letter in *The Scotsman* last week. (I've mislaid the cuttings & can't quote precise date.)[1]

Your later letter of Wed. this week is much more reasonable, & you have to thank me for giving you the opportunity of making a clearer & more acceptable statement of your position. Your final jape about 'sour grapes' is, I fear, merely petty; & certainly irrelevant. I have 'never-ever' tried to exalt my own exceedingly small talent into anything bigger than it is, but *that* isn't worth arguing about, & I don't propose to do anything about that. In fact, I have restrained a doughty champion from entering the lists.

The funny thing is that the only other letter I ever wrote to *The Scotsman* was occasioned by you too: at the time when your name was under editorial ban, I managed to introduce it in their columns in connection with a correspondence which had cropped up over the word 'ashypet'. Thus I contrived to quote from your 'Cophetua' poem[2] with author's name attached.

Now. I hope the whole subject will be dropped, altho' I think anything that brings literary argument into public notice as a vital issue is all to the good.

Better to 'keep the pottie boiling' than be an ashypet lass shivering over a dead fire.

I still hope I may welcome Valda & you to my house, as of yore. I'm in a muddle just now, clearing up after a big party of art students, & not yet having had time to tackle my own Xmas correspondence (now, alas, augmented by letters from folks who reacted to my recent *jeu d'écrire*).

Tell Valda, if she's shopping, there's always a tin-opener here for the unexpected guest. And a warm fire.

My sister-in-law is coming for New Year weekend, with her lovely dog; otherwise, I expect to be alone.

With love to both, & please, don't spit it back in my face. It might ricochet!
Yours,
Helen.

---

[1] Helen Cruickshank refers here to MacDiarmid's letter to *The Scotsman*, 12 December 1959, which was published on 16 December 1959, *Letters*, 806-7.
[2] *C.P.* I, p. 30.

The 1960s

1. From Elspeth Schubert (NLS MS27011)

Svartviksringen 17
Saltsjöbaden
Sweden
28 February [1960]

Dear Mr MacDiarmid,

I was wondering whether the letter I wrote you some weeks ago has ever turned up? I wanted to know what you thought of the financial aspect of our work on *Aniara*.[1] Pending your decision, I have now written to Hutchinsons to say that I am willing to 'go ahead', as they put it, on the basis of the fee offered by the Council of Europe (approx. £150 per head) but that I would like them to consider making a further payment *if* & *when* the book sells in over 3000 copies. This was on the advice of Bonniers, the publishers here. What do you think?

Now about the poem itself. I am working on it, but am very much bothered as to the best way of tackling our collaboration. If I translate each line of verse as it stands, i.e., retaining the rhythm, stress, metre & so on, the result will be an appalling jumble of bad writing & extra words pushed in to make it *scan* – also very confusing for you. Isn't the best plan for me to do a *prose* translation of each song, sending you at the same time a copy of the song in question *in Swedish*, with ten beats in each line underlined? Harry Martinson has emphasised over & over again that the 'narrative lilt' of the poem must be strictly adhered to (most of it is in iambic verse, ten beats to a line). He breaks away, of course, at intervals, and this is why it seems important to me to give you a clear picture of the *Swedish* verse as it stands. Here is an example, in the first line of the first canto:

> Mitt första möti med min Doris lyser
> u __ u __ u __   u __ u __ u
> My first encounter with my Doris shimmers
> u __ u __ u __   u __ u __   u

Obviously neither 'encounter' nor 'shimmers' are the best words here, but I give them in order to emphasise the rhythm.

May I ask whether you know any Swedish at all? And have you been sent a copy of Harry Martinson's own analysis of the poem? A great help in the translation is, or will be, my contact with Martinson's biographer, Dr Tord Hall, who can interpret most of the 'inner meanings' & mathematical terms, both real and imaginary!

With best wishes, & looking forward to hearing from you.
Sincerely,
Elspeth Schubert.

---

[1] Harry Martinson, *Aniara: A Review of Man in Space and Time,* adapted from the Swedish by Hugh MacDiarmid and Elspeth Harley Schubert was published in London in 1963. *Aniara* had been published in Swedish in 1956.

2. From Michael Grieve (NLS MS27151 f.53)

34 Redcliffe Gardens
London SW10
1 March [1960]

Dearest Mum and Dad,

It wasn't till I arrived home last night that I learned about the accident[1] – and what a shock it was. We only knew because Deirdre's[2] mother had phoned to ask how you were getting on, thinking we knew all the time.

However, thank God it wasn't much, much worse. I spoke to the nurses in both the wards and they said you were 'comfortable' – such a silly bloody word, really. Then phoned Norman and learned more of the whole business.

Remember the last time I met Ted Brookes I said to Deirdre that he was a bad driver, especially with a drink in him (he then gets the speed mania which is the main cause of accidents when drinking.)

I hope when you both get out – this weekend? – you will both try and take it as easy as possible for at least a week. The shock lasts quite a long time.

Thought of coming up, but there is nothing much I could do in a day or two and the situation is a bit complicated with my notice being in. But if, when you leave, you find that you are still shaky, let me know and I'll manage to get a week one way or another.

I had just arrived back to listen to the second half of your broadcast, Dad, when Deirdre told me ... so I wasn't able to hear it for trying to find out what happened. Let me know in detail when you're fit what happened.

There is no more news about when we will be freed from our contracts – but hope it will not be too long.

We went up to Norwich on Saturday and had a look round – an interesting town but terribly dull countryside. Flat and open most of the way.

I'm keeping in touch with Norman so will know what is happening. Hope things turn out all right and neither of you is too shaken up – Norman said something about cuts and your nose, Mum. Were you sitting in the back seat?

All our love, writing soon,
Mike xxx

[1] Dr Edwin Brookes of Workington crashed his car into a telegraph pole near Brownsbank.
[2] Michael's wife.

3. From Brigita Tempest (EUL MS2966)

17 Robins Court
Chinbrook Road
London SE12
17 April 1960

Dear Chris,

I wanted to write you straight after I heard your talk on the Third Programme and your slander about Hristo Botev,[1] but decided to cool off first. But I can see that even time couldn't calm me. Now let's speak very frankly, Chris.

I am the person who knows perfectly well why you went for your three months' holiday in Bulgaria. It wasn't to eat strawberries and rest at the Black Sea. The Union of Writers invited you because you asked to be invited. (I was present at the meeting when you posed the question to the group of secretaries.) You proposed to translate Botev, our great (and truly great) poet. The Union of Writers agreed to your proposal and I remember very well our private discussion: how nice it's going to be for you to live for six months or so in the seclusion of the forest at Borovets, where the writers' rest-home is, where far from the temptations of the city, but still with plenty of strawberries, you could work hard and repay the kind hospitality of the Bulgarian people. But, oh no, when I came back from Sofia in January this year I collected very detailed descriptions [of] how you did everything except sit and work on the translations of Botev. The little scandals about money matters, the caprices etc, etc. I won't go into details about them. What could I answer to all this, when you didn't even consider on your return to England to ring or drop a line or come to see me. You never wrote to me during your three months stay in Bulgaria, you didn't go and visit my friends who were so kind to you during your first visit to Bulgaria when they treated your sunburn, when they went round the chemists' shops to buy medicaments, when I neglected my child so that I could be with you and Ewan to help you and introduce you to writers, visit their homes etc., etc.

And here it comes, your sneering opinion, expressed where else but on the Third Programme of the B.B.C. (those great friends of the People's Democracies). Of course, the little 'ha, ha' of the interviewer about Botev was in full harmony with your 'brave' abuse of Botev. You know perfectly well that the B.B.C. is not the place to argue about Botev. It's so rarely that the name of Bulgaria can appear in England and it's always in connection with slanders and misrepresentations. I expected from you, the Communist, who spent three months rejoicing on holiday under the Bulgarian sun at hospitable Bulgarian tables, at least a sense of responsibility. Why didn't you tell the B.B.C. that it took you three whole months of holidaying in Bulgaria to realise at the end that Botev is not 'great'? For heaven's sake, you went there to translate him and you should have been able to decide in your cottage in Scotland whether it was worthwhile going to Bulgaria in connection with Botev.[2]

I'm not arguing with you about the greatness of Botev because it will take me too long and it must include your incredible praise of Ezra Pound in the same talk. But I am arguing about the hidden truth about your going to Bulgaria, which you never mentioned.

The Bulgarians are not grateful to such friends. We have a proverb: 'He ate the porridge and kicked the table'. Until now we have survived all kinds and varieties and ingenuities of abuses and slanders, so this one is just one more.

I hope you are feeling well and engaged in worthwhile translations. Pity that Ezra Pound writes in English.

Yours,
Brigita.

1   Christo Botev (1848-1876) is still regarded as the national poet of Bulgaria. He was a *haidouk*, a Bulgarian partisan against the five-hundred-year-old Turkish occupation. He was killed leading an uprising, after a landing on the Bulgarian banks of the Danube.

2   In *One of Ben's* (1993), Maurice Shadbolt gives an account of a literary dinner in Sofia in 1959 in which MacDiarmid explained to him why he was so slow in translating Botev: 'Well, for one thing, he's no bloody good ... He's a national icon, not a poet.'

4. From Elspeth Schubert (NLS Acc.7361/1)

> Svartviksringen 17
> Saltsjöbaden
> 18 August [1960]

Dear Mr MacDiarmid,

Thank you very much for your letter, which explained things to me. I have not been able to type out the 10 Cantos (40-50) of *Aniara* & send them to you yet, as I have had an invasion of my family from abroad, and no domestic help. But they all are ready, I hope to get them off early next week.

This is to tell you that I expect to be in Scotland from Sept. 7th – 15th, staying at the George Hotel, Perth – and I think we should really try to meet sometime during that week, to discuss matters – I could come into Edinburgh one day to meet you, if that would ease things? But I think it quite essential that we should have a talk & decide definitely on the course of the 2nd half of the poem.

All being well, I should be back in Stockholm on Oct. 10th after my Canadian journey. It would be a splendid thing if, other things being equal, you could come to Sweden then, meet Martinson, & get the poem finally gone over, & ready for publication around Christmas or in the early spring. These are only suggestions, but I would be glad to hear your views, also, if possible, by return, whether we can meet in Scotland.

Sincerely,
Elspeth Schubert.

5. From 'Maurice Girodias' (Maurice Kahane) (EUL MS2976)

> The Olympia Press
> 7 Rue St-Séverin
> Paris 5
> 23 August 1960

Dear Mr MacDiarmid:

I should have written to you earlier about the copy of NIGHT by Francis Pollini which was confiscated by the Scottish Postal authorities of which we were informed by their French counterparts.[1]

I received a cutting of the article in the *Manchester Evening Chronicle* yesterday and learnt that you had even been questioned by the Police. I wish to say how sorry I am for any inconvenience unwittingly caused you. The book contains nothing of a morally offensive nature; even the language in some of the soldiers' dialogues is a good deal milder than in most war novels.

We are now waiting for further information from the French postal authorities before deciding upon a course of action but it is our intention to initiate legal proceedings, if at all possible, against the seizure and, more particularly, against the destruction of the copy sent you which, we understand, has been effected by the British postal authorities. Our London Solicitors inform us that the book cannot possibly be declared obscene under the present rulings of the Obscene Publications Act, 1959 [,] but they add that the Act does not obtain in Scotland where, apparently, some archaic law still gives the local Post office or Customs censors unlimited and uncontrolled power.[2]

We shall keep you informed of developments and, in the meantime, wish to thank you for your statements following this incident. I hesitate, in the circumstnces, to suggest we send another copy but we might arrange to have one sent to you from London if you wish.

With all good wishes.

Yours sincerely,

Maurice Girodias.

---

[1] A press release from The Olympia Press in August 1960 stated that Francis Pollini's first novel *Night* had been seized by the British postal authorities in Scotland and by the Irish Customs in Dublin. The copy which the Press had sent to Alex Neish, editor of *Jabberwock*, had been seized in Edinburgh. Another copy sent to Hugh MacDiarmid had not only been confiscated but destroyed. MacDiarmid had been questioned by detectives at his home and even a letter to him from the Press had been seized. Brendan Behan had been informed by the Irish authorities that a copy sent to him had also been confiscated.

[2] The Press claimed that *Night*, a war novel depicting the life of American POWs in a Chinese camp in North Korea, had been widely regarded as a book of great literary merit and considerable informative value. The Obscene Publications Act, 1959, did not apply in Scotland where two copies had been seized. The Olympia Press had been the first to publish Nabokov's *Lolita* in 1955. The book had been banned in 1956 by the French authorities and it had taken Olympia more than three years of litigation before the ban had been revoked.

6. From Bertrand Russell (EUL MS2958.20 f.1)

from: The Earl Russell, O.M., F.R.S.
Plas Penrhyn
Penrhyndeudraeth
Merioneth

Dear Mr MacDiarmid,

The rapidity with which we are moving towards a nuclear calamity convinces me that events are moving too quickly for the present policy of our Campaign. It is my conviction that the effectiveness of our Campaign is becoming dependent upon its endorsing a programme of civil disobedience.

I am going to make a statement at the first suitable opportunity expressing the hope that the Campaign will become convinced of the necessity of such a programme.

I should like to ask your support in carrying this into action. A group of one hundred persons called 'The Committee of 100' – for civil disobedience against nuclear warfare – is being formed and I should be grateful if you would join me on it. Could you favour me with an early reply?[1]

Sincerely yours,

Bertrand Russell.

[1] MacDiarmid did join the committee of 100 and spoke in Trafalgar Square, London on 18 February 1961 on its behalf.

7. From Muriel MacSwiney (EUL MS2962.6 f.26)

18 Passage des Princes
Paris 2
21 November 1960

A Chara dhil[1]

I should have written to you years ago but am anything but a quick person with the pen. I often saw your letters in *The Scotsman*, an excellent paper, you will I think know my name? I am the widow of Terence MacSwiney, mayor of Cork, who died of hunger strike in Brixton prison in 1920. I knew my husband through being in the Irish Freedom movement which I joined in 1915. He had started work long before the War of 1914 in the Celtic Literary Society with a handful like himself. I was also very active in Connrad na Gaelige;[2] having been born in a town like my husband I had to learn our own language. In 1922-23 on my second visit to the U.S.A. (a very different place to what it is now), I joined the Women's [International] League for Peace and Freedom, Jane Adams, Mrs. Frances Villard, widow of [the] founder of *N. Y. Nation*, etc.[3]

In the early autumn of 1923 on my return to Ireland Jim Larkin,[4] who had recently been released from Sing Sing, founded a new Trade Union in Dublin and for all Ireland. The workers asked me to join it, which I regarded as an honour, this T.U. was affiliated with the Soviet Union, I have therefore always regarded myself since then as a member of the Communist Party. Now as you will know there is none in Eire, only in the North.

I went to Germany with my little daughter at the end of 1923; after some years I joined the Party there, a foreigner could at the time, the Weimar Republic was a democratic state, socially and culturally, although extremely capitalist and therefore bankrupt economically.

Now I am a member of the English Party (have been since 1933 when I naturally left my home in Germany, we were nearly all the time in Heidelberg). I live in Paris where I was after leaving the Nazis, until the war. I was naturally not neutral in the war because I was strongly anti-Fascist and pro-Soviet. I don't think I have ever been on the same side as England for anything else.

Now, what is I believe the most important question at the present time, Peace & Laïcité. I have really been a freethinker or I believe I should say athiest, since the age of fifteen when I was in an English convent, my family were fanatical pro-English imperialist, and everything Irish was inferior and vulgar, so we were all sent to English convents.

I was very ignorant but well up in the Catechism. I found that it was impossible to command my thoughts as one is ordered to do, also it hit, I think, my economic sense that God, omnipotent and omniscient, should create people whom he knew he was going to damn. I spoke to several priests both in England and Ireland who treated me kindly because my father was an industrialist, but who could not convince me of what no doubt they did not believe. I did not leave the Vatican church until 1922 formally. At that time I proclaimed this as publicly as possible.

My daughter was kidnapped ten years later.[5] In July 1932, when the world Eucharistic Congress was held in Dublin, all help was refused to me by the Eire government which had entirely gone over to Rome. I'll send you an account of this, there were several other cases. I never saw my child again.

I came back to live in France in 1951. I now belong to La Ligue des Droits de L'Homme and La Ligue Française de L'Enseignment, nothing else here.[6] I should very much like to meet you, are you ever in Paris or in London? There is a faint possibility that I shall be on a very brief visit to Scotland this winter, I don't yet know. I was only once in Scotland (in 1930 I think) with a German friend. I thought it somewhat like Ireland only that you have real mountains and we only have samples.

I am a strong disciple of the great Carlyle, and had the luck to read him when I was young.

I belong to no religion and have suffered much persecution for this, I allow however the fundamental right to everybody to belong to whatever creed or not they think best. I was particularly interested in your attitude and principle on this subject. There was a letter in *The Scotsman* from some idiot, who thought he was making fun of you by relating that your son had been married in the R. C. Church.[7] You replied admirably saying that as your children had been brought up entirely freely this marriage was in accordance with your principles.

It is however most deplorable that there is such a landslide now towards Rome. It is caused by the help given the R. C.s by non-Catholics. If you talk to them about this they say that they have 'Catholic friends' which we all have. Montgomery Hyde[8] who was still in the House of Commons when the school subvention to private Roman schools was being debated a year ago said absolutely nothing against. He was reproached last summer in Dublin about this by Senator Skeffington[9] and he gave the usual rejoinder, 'I have Catholic friends'.

It is charming however that Kennedy's majority is now almost invisible.[10] I know that some writers don't write letters; whereas others like Carlyle write wonders; I hope you belong to the latter category, or that at any rate you will send me two words on a post card saying if there is a possibility of meeting you before we are all blown up.

I work here also with the Breton autonomists and I know the very numerous Breton Communists both here and in Brittany. Would you have any literature? It can be in English or even Scotch Gaelic (a few Bretons know this), describing your amicable relations with the Communist Party.

I am personally good friends with the present I.R.A. in Ireland, practically all the youth either belongs to them or sympathises; most are gone to other lands, it being impossible for almost anyone to earn their living at home. The I.R.A. are sincere and honest which no Irish government has been, but they will not have national health, or religious toleration. I have pointed out to them several times that Wolfe Tone who is rightly their great hero was a Freethinker. No good, if it is a case of shooting somebody they gladly disobey the Vatican, if it is a case of anything else including birth control, they obey slavishly, no difference with De Valera.

It is a hopeless policy with regards to getting the North in, but useful against English Imperialism, it is yet another place where troops are kept.

Is mise

Le meas mòr

Muirgheal Bean Mhic Suibhne – Muriel wife of MacSwiney.

[1] A Chara dhil (in Roman letters) –Dear Friend.
[2] The Gaelic League.
[3] The International Congress of Women met at The Hague on 28 April 1915 and formed the Women's International League for Peace and Freedom to express their opposition to the First World War and consider ways of ending the conflict. There were delegations from Europe and America, and from 'enemy' and neutral countries.
[4] Jim Larkin (1874-1947), Irish labour leader. He had sailed to US in late October 1914 to raise funds necessary to rebuild the Irish Transport and General Workers' Union. In late 1919 he was arrested on a charge of criminal anarchy and sentenced to between five to ten years in prison but released in early 1923 and deported back to Britain.
[5] Muriel MacSwiney does not reveal that her relationship with her daughter Máire in Germany had been distant for eight years, e.g., Máire had been five years at a boarding school and only spent the summer holidays with her mother. When an aunt, a co-guardian, came to see her in Germany in 1932, she hurriedly chose to return to Ireland with her aunt. She never met her mother again. Máire MacSwiney Brugha's *History's Daughter* (Dublin: The O'Brien Press, 2006).
[6] The League for the Rights of Man and the French Educational League.
[7] Michael and Deirdre Grieve were married in the Church of Scotland in Carnoustie, not in a Roman Catholic Church.
[8] H. Montgomery Hyde (1907-1987), author and barrister, was Unionist MP for North Belfast from 1950 to 1959.
[9] Owen Lancelot Sheehy-Skeffington (1909-1970), politician and university teacher. He was a senator in Eire from 1954 to 1961 and again from 1965 until his death.

The reference to 'Kennedy's majority' is to John F. Kennedy's narrow margin over Richard M. Nixon in the 1960 US Presidential election.

8. From George Campbell Hay (EUL MS2951.2 ff.37-38)

6 Maxwell St
Edinburgh 10
4 December 1960

Dear C. M. Grieve,

Dr Alasdair MacLean told me recently that he had seen you last autumn, and that you would like me to come through and pay you a visit. I was delighted to hear it.

Most likely he told you that I am working at the National Library now. I look after Scandinavian Literature, and Scandinavia is about as congenial a foreign clime as any Scot can find, especially linguistically from the point of view of Scots (one can hardly class Eire as foreign, although I don't mean that in the way a true-bred Englishman would mean it.) It's a business of going through the year's catalogues and selecting for buying the best books they have to offer. There are endless catches about issues and editions, trilogies with one general title and three separate ones, and books in Swedish which turn out to be translated from Icelandic – for instance, if you do not know the author already you can't tell whether a man called Andrésson is a Swede or an Icelander, and people often don't bother to state simply that a book is a translation though all they need to do is to add 'tr.' in English or 'övers.' in Swedish. Factors of that kind make the day's work quite a lively affair, but I'm not going to bore you with any more details. The rest of my work is cataloguing old British and Foreign books before 1700 – one comes across such things as the Latin translation of 'The Cherry and The Slae'[1] and Argyll's Declaration issued from Campbelltown when he landed there in 1685,[2] or for that matter James VI's Latin treatise on the mutual duties of the monarch and the people.[3]

The person responsible for Celtic manuscripts is Donald MacDonald from North Uist (he has several namesakes), and I know him pretty well by now. The Keeper of Printed Books is a Mr David Lloyd, a very patriotic Welshman, a native Welsh speaker, a man with Gaelic and Irish, and a member of the Irish Gaelic League (Connrad na Gaeilge). That is good company to begin with, and everyone in the place, workmen and all, is extremely pleasant. There is absolutely no Edinburgh snobbery in the National Library.

Any queries about Gaelic and Irish books usually come my way, and that is a refreshing kind of a thing to be dealing with in the course of a day's work. Manuscripts and Printed Books are two quite separate spheres.

Over the past three or four months I have been continually taking half-mornings off, because a succession of appointments and interviews obliged me to do so. Until my holidays come round in March I'll need to keep to a steady routine for I am only a beginner and I don't want to try the patience of the Library authorities. Would it be convenient for you if I visited you in March some time, although I do admit that that is a longish time away? I'll be going to Dunure (from where my father's forebears moved to Tarbert), and from there to Tarbert. Disgracefully enough, I've never been in Dunure yet, although I was alongside a Dunure skiff in Loch Ranza once, and her crew told me that there were still Hays in Carrick.

Any writing I do has to be at the weekends, or on an occasional evening, but that is not so bad as it sounds. Jotted down in outline I have the makings of another book of Gaelic poetry, which should be complete in two or three years. Recently I had twelve Gaelic poems on my hands simultaneously, and most of them will appear in *Gairm*.[4] It's a great problem when you're halfway down Lothian Road, and a third of a verse and two syllables of the last line tumble down from the slates on top of you.   If bits of a tune put in their appearance as well it's worse. What are you to do? Tear a poster off the front of the Usher Hall and write on the back of it? Go into a restaurant and write on a menu? A member of the Irish Bardic School would have lain down in a bus shelter with a stone on his chest. But you would get tired carrying a stone about with you all the time. Such is poetry at times. (I'm writing a Gaelic poem about it which I thought of halfway down Lothian Road. I jettisoned the tune opposite and got a fast grip of the words.)

I'll write something in Gaelic suitable for *The Voice of Scotland*, and let you have it as soon as is possible. A lot, though not all, of what I have been writing recently is humorous and local – in Tarbert Gaelic some of it. But it would be wise to keep Tarbert flourishing in a literary way (to put it so), and make it one more secure mooring-point for those who care for Scotland and the Highlands, just as Lewis is. And in any case Gaelic literature emanating from so far south is a muckle great spoke in the wheel of the Ascendancy.

Yours aye,

George Campbell Hay.

PS I am enclosing one of the humorous Tarbert poems, which I mentioned, along with a translation into Tarbert 'English'. It is rather slight, but is a genuine enough picture of the Loch Fyne men, and you may find it of some use. However, if you do think it on the slight side just disregard it.

[1]   'The Cherry and the Slae' was first published in 1597, Alexander Montgomerie (?1545-?1611).

[2]   In 1685 Archibald Campbell, 9th Earl of Argyll (1629-1685), conspired with James, Duke of Monmouth to overthrow King James VII and II who had just acceded to the throne. He returned to the west of Scotland from Holland but was unable to gather the forces he had intended and was captured and executed.

[3]   Did Campbell Hay mean George Buchanan's *De Juri Regni Apud Scotos* (1579) ?

[4]   Gaelic Quarterly, edited by Derick Thomson, Glasgow, 1952-2002.

9. From Alan D. Bush (EUL MS2942.19 f.1)

Alan Bush
25 Christchurch Crescent

Radlett
Hertfordshire
30 December 1960

Dear Hugh McDiarmid,

Our paths have never crossed up to the present time. But I am writing to you now with a proposition for our collaboration, which I sincerely hope that you will consider favourably.

At the next Congress of the Communist Party during the Easter weekend an evening concert will be held in the St Pancras Town Hall. It has been suggested that the concert should end with a specially-written choral work, the text of which should deal at least in part with the situation of the socialist, colonial and imperialist countries at the present time, somewhat along the lines of the resolution recently passed at the conference of Communist Parties held in Moscow. The Party did me the great honour of asking me to compose the music, which I have enthusiastically agreed to do.

I am writing to you to ask whether you would write the text. It would be a work in which a choir, a youth choir, a solo singer and a speaker could be involved. The musical portion of the work cannot be lengthy, because there will not be the time to prepare a long choral section, or an elaborate part for the youth choir. The solo part could be longer, but if it is very long, it is likely that it will become boring. On the other hand, the speaker could, in the middle of the work have five to ten minutes, if necessary (nearer five than ten, if possible!) The whole work should not in any circumstances last more than 15 minutes.

If you would give your consent in principle, we could then go into the form of the work in greater detail. For the moment, therefore, I will say no more except that I do most sincerely hope that you will accept this proposal. I know of no one whose collaboration would give me greater joy, and I think that the idea of a Scottish and an English artist, working together in such a project for the Party should be greeted with great enthusiasm in general.[1]

Awaiting your reply, which I hope to receive soon,

Yours fraternally.

Alan D. Bush.

[1]   The work, 'The Tide That Will Never Turn', was published in *Artery* 13, edited by Jeff Sawtell, Winter 1977/8, pp. 17-19.

10. From Edward Gaitens (EUL MS2948.6 ff.14-16)

19 Camphill Avenue
Glasgow S1
2 April 1961

Dear Chris,

It was by the merest freakish chance that I learned of your second unfortunate accident in which again fate chose to injure your valuable head.[1] Yesterday my landlady gave me some old newspapers to light my fire. One was last Thursday's *[Daily] Mail* and as I looked idly through it kneeling by the grate I was startled to see your photograph and report of your accident. I'm so glad it was no worse – not quite so serious as last year's crash – but bad enough I'm sure and I hope it has not left you with irremediable headaches which can be such a bore and creative setback.

I was deeply and sadly stirred by your powerful and sensitive poem, 'The Glen of Silence',[2] in the American *Nation* of January 7th. That was a brilliant and most dramatic likening of that glen's silence to the silence of foetal death. It made me think of the deserted villages of Ireland also. Much blood has flowed under Communist, Fascist and Imperialist bridges since we were young in the First World War and there must be now many a glen the world over whereon that sad silence lies – where tyranny and oppression has swept ruthlessly through.

Is it not largely faults in the Highlanders themselves that have left them an 'unevolved people'? Ireland has attained at least partial nationhood in spite of her loss of stamina through decades of emigration and flights of thousandfold hordes of the Wild Geese and deaths of countless thousands of her people through famine and rackrenting under English rule.

I do not see the Highlander through the romantic lenses I once viewed him by. The citified Highlander so often becomes a different being and my experience of Highlanders as landlords and landladies in Glasgow have been among my most disagreeable and unfortunate experiences from every human aspect and my years as a door-to-door canvasser in talks with hundreds of Highland folk I learned that the majority of them couldn't care less for the beauty of their glens and hills and were only too glad to get far away from them to a good job or prosperous business in any city anywhere. Has there ever been any deep spiritual cohesion among the Highlanders? Even to-day I meet individual Highlanders who express hatred for members of other clans, the MacDonalds for the Campbells etc. They are old unwearying hatreds and sometimes I feel they were the corrosive poison that helped to disintegrate Scottish unity – hatreds that ended in treachery of Highlandmen fighting for England against their own land. The clans often appear to me like petty nations within a nation whose resolute spiritual amalgam could have created a wonderful unified country.

I hope Valda is very well and I send her my kindest regards.

Edward.

---

[1]   MacDiarmid had been struck by a car in Edinburgh on 29 March.
[2]   *C.P.* II, pp. 1310-1312.

11. *From R. S. Thomas (EUL MS2962.10 f.10)*

Eglwys Fach
Machynlleth

9 August 1961

Dear Mr MacDiarmid,

Thank you so much for your kind letter and permission to use your two poems.[1]

I am glad to hear your *Collected Poems* are in the offing and shall look forward to reading them. I wish I had known your address sooner, as we must have passed quite close to your place in April on our way north. It would have been nice just to call for a while.

Yours sincerely,

R. S. Thomas.

---

[1]   R. S. Thomas included ' At my Father's Grave', *C. P.* I, p.299, and 'Harry Semen', *C. P.* I, pp. 483-5, in *The Penguin Book of Religious Verse* which he edited in 1963.

12. From M. L. Rosenthal (EUL MS2967/9)

87 South End Road
London NW3
14 August 1961

Dear Dr Grieve,

Just a note to tell you the sad news (for me) that I won't be able to make it to Scotland after all. This is a great disappointment to me, for I've been looking forward to seeing you in your native habitat all year. Two developments, or rather three, prevented; an unexpectedly protracted lecture tour in Germany, participation in the Poetry Festival here, and the terrors o' Bank Holiday traffic. And now, it seems, the end of our year has arrived – we sail for home on the nineteenth (this coming Saturday), and I can but be grateful for the day we spent in one another's company when you were last in London.

Please let me have a note this week if there is anything you'd like me to do on your behalf when I get back to the United States. (We arrive on the 25th). I have heard nothing about your book, and so don't know whether or not you've been receiving proofs. The whole state of your book is something I want to look into at once when I get back.[1]

My little book on Pound (*A Primer of Ezra Pound*) will be out shortly in this country and a copy will be sent to you.

With best wishes and highest personal regards –

Yours ever,

M. L. Rosenthal.

---

[1]   Hugh MacDiarmid's *Collected Poems* were published in 1962. At the time The MacMillan Company, New York, agreed to publish *Collected Poems* M. L. Rosenthal was their poetry adviser.

13. From Elspeth Schubert (EUL MS2967/7)

Svartviksringen 17
Saltsjöbaden
Sweden
16 October 1961

Dear Mr Grieve,

I have just sent off the manuscript of your version of *Aniara* to Hutchinsons, with the notes, suggestions etc. which have been worked out in consultation with Harry Martinson.[1] He has a strong wish that the introduction to the poem, i.e., the first Canto (by the way, are these to be called Songs or Cantos?) should be as 'majestic' as possible – hence the suggested new version of Verse 1. You will use your own judgment whether the remainder of this first Song needs alteration, to correspond?

I have sent Hutchinsons a list, together with the manuscript, of the various suggestions, and you will yourself find in the text a number of small points which I have tried to make clear there. If there are any points with regard to which you are in doubt, do please let me know.

May I say here that I find your treatment of my original translation very liberal and sensitive – and the more I read *Aniara*, the more fascinated I become! I should be very glad to hear from you sometime, your own opinion of the poem, as such?

I am sure you will agree that a foreword by a Swede who knows the whole background, and is also an expert on the terminology and on natural science, must be included in the publication? Martinson himself has suggested his biographer, Dr Tord Hall of Uppsala University, who has written a book on *Aniara* – and this seems to be an excellent suggestion, and one which we ought to accept.

Hoping that you and your family are well, and that I shall hear from you in due course.

With kind regards.
Sincerely yours,
Elspeth Schubert.

[1] MacDiarmid here appears to have made a satisfactory translation from Elspeth Schubert's literal translation, which he failed to do from the literal translations of Hristo Botev's poems made for him by Hungarian scholars.

14. From Neil M. Gunn (EUL MS2948.15 f.49)

Dalcraig
Kessock
Inverness
20 November 1961

Dear Christopher,

I very much appreciated your tribute to myself & to the old days on Saturday night's 'Scottish Life & Letters'.[1] When you referred to some of our sessions that lasted into the morning, I had an involuntary picture (& not the only time) of a split-second decision I once took on a steep incline in – was it St. Cyrus? We had gone north from Montrose in my car to visit F.G. Scott, & you, not too sure of the way, suddenly indicated a steep road on my right. I swung the car at it, all out, & a few yards from the top saw two posts in front indicating no thoroughfare for traffic. With the lucidity engendered on these occasions I decided she could scrape through – & she did. Otherwise the Renaissance might have had a shattering blow! You'll have forgotten the critical moment because you weren't driving.

You sounded in good voice, & I hope you are both keeping well & enjoying life. We are now in a cottage on the Beauly Firth & enjoying our days in a freedom that positively seems to expand.

Again with my best acknowledgements of your warm & friendly 'remembrance of things past' & all good wishes for the future.

Yours,
Neil.

[1]   Radio programme.

15. From Donald Bain (EUL MS2948.2 f.12)

49 Hillhouse Street
Glasgow N1
6 December 1961

Dear Chris,
I am truly happy about the event this Saturday Dec. 9. Personally I feel that you are the right choice to [do] justice to my old friend J. D. Fergusson.[1]

The ignorance of art authorities in the U.K. regarding the contribution Fergus made to the modern movement in Europe is appalling. London takes the view that there are no artists in Scotland. People like [Alan] Davie[2] who have become Londonised and sooked in with certain authorities just don't count, all such painters are able to do is to exploit fashionable trends, they are quite incapable of making a statement of their own. No one was more aware of this than Fergus, he lived long enough in London to know what goes on there. And I can say that he wasn't very happy about living there.

When I was searching among his papers for material for the catalogue I discovered one of your books dated '1928' with an inscription on the flyleaf written by you for him. When in France he knew Guillaume Apollinaire[3] and many other writers, Francis Carco[4] in particular, who experienced great emotion from the work of Fergusson.

I remember Fergus telling me of being in a Paris café at a time when the leading Russians of the Revolution were making their plans, and that it was interesting to Fergus because the painters had already started their revolution, and the Irish too were in the same café. Outwardly everything calm, no one would have guessed the implications. Fergus used to say, 'Only in Paris could this happen'.

He also told me that he saw some of Picasso's early, and at that time revolutionary, works, the beginnings of the latter's Cubist period. Fergus was very much for Picasso, and never got tired of saying so.

Of course you are well aware of Fergusson's association with John Middleton Murry and Katherine Mansfield.[5] When some paintings were sent to the National Gallery of Scotland after Fergusson's death with a view to purchasing for the national collection, they declined. I was shocked to learn that Baxandall[6] the director didn't consider Fergusson's work important, just because Baxandall hadn't read anything about Fergusson or his work in any recent anthologies on modern art. This of course is a typically English outlook. *Bon courage* for Saturday –

Best wishes.

Yours,

Donald Bain.

[1] MacDiarmid opened the J. D. Fergusson Memorial Exhibition.
[2] Alan Davie b.1920, painter.
[3] Guillaume Apollinaire (1880-1918). His reputation rests principally on the two main collections of lyric poetry published in his lifetime – *Alcools* (1913) and *Calligrammes* (1918).
[4] Francis Carco (1886-1958) was a Fantaisiste poet, dramatist, art critic, and biographer, but is remembered particularly as a novelist.
[5] Katherine Mansfield (1884-1923) was married to Middleton Murry from 1918 until her death.
[6] David Baxandall (1905-1992) was Director of the National Gallery of Scotland from 1952 to 1970.

16. From Elspeth Grant Cameron (EUL Gen.2094/1/253)

The Scottish Association for the Speaking of Verse
Glasgow Branch

64 Woodcroft Avenue
Glasgow W1
8 December 1961

Dear Hugh MacDiarmid,

I have always been hoping to have the opportunity to meet you to thank you in person for the wonderful tribute you sent me for my Edwin Muir Memorial Meeting.[1] It was so wonderful and touching a tribute that I had it typed and copies of it given to his relatives at the meeting. I never knew Edwin; only his nieces but I loved all my tributes from far and near.

I know you would have loved to have been with us and made your apologies. Everything passed off exceedingly well and we had 250 there despite the fact that it was New Year Sunday.

My friend Robert Blair Wilkie was there and helped me in the stewarding.

Wishing you a happy Festive Season and good Health – and writing! – in the New Year.

Yours very sincerely,

Elspeth Grant Cameron.

Hon. Sec.

PS Now I have the notion to organize a Weekend Conference at Whit Weekend 1962 or 1963 in Edinburgh or Newbattle Abbey College. Will let you know if it materialises as I should want you to be there if in Scotland at the time. You *are a must*! E.G.C.

[1] The Edwin Muir event was on 3 January 1960 at 3 pm in St Andrew's Lesser Hall, Glasgow, the first anniversary of Muir's death. A 50-word message had been requested.

17. From Donald Bain (EUL MS2948.2 f.13)

49 Hillhouse Street
Glasgow N1
11 December 1961

Dear Chris,

I thank you for your contribution in defence of Scottish culture, but I'm wondering if it penetrated the materialistic cloud in most minds. Probably more dangerous and sterilising than a radioactive one.

In today's *Glasgow Herald* there was an abbreviated report, it would be hard for any sub[-editor] to take the guts out of what you had to say. We know only too well that it was the voice of the writers in France which spread the information about their fellow-artists, the painters, throughout the world.

Those in authority at Kelvingrove made a complete mess of the hanging of the Exhibition, typical of the YES men, afraid of losing their jobs, completely dominated by local government officials. If you had seen the simpering and social climbing effort by Jean Roberts[1] and her retinue when Lord Snowdon[2] opened the Scottish Painting Exhibition, it was enough to make any honest man BOKE.

It was amusing to hear on Saturday that bloody little chancer Dr Miller,[3] a speug has much more intellect.

The whole position of the arts in Scotland looks quite hopeless at the moment. The people who could be trusted to send a telling Exhibition of Scottish Painting abroad would never get the opportunity. Only the loud mouths who have the ear of officialdom would get the opportunity and make a mess of it, the ingratiating bastards. I would rather regard that sort as enemies than friends.

The bit of blurb that [Emilio] Coia[4] had printed in *The Scotsman* just won't bear serious examination. He's hoping it may be useful to him, the wee man who tries to be everybody's friend. I remember well when Bill [MacLellan] took me into the Glasgow Art Club for lunch and Coia was belching forth on art and declaring that there wasn't a painter worth his salt in Scotland (except his wife,[5] slyly hinted). I mentioned Fergus.

His reply was, 'A painter in the manner of Cézanne'.[6]

He got his answer.

Another time although he wrote up the Civic Arts Exbibition he said he was against it in principle. I told him, 'A cunt like you can't afford to have principles'.

I tell you, Chris, we don't need such people, the main thing is to get the paintings to France and let them speak for themselves.

I just can't bear to think about the way that works by members of the group 'The Glasgow School' have been allowed to sink into obscurity. I have hopes that this Fergusson Exhibition will act as a spearhead.

With best wishes.

Yours aye,

Donald Bain.

[1] Jean Roberts (1895-1988) was Lord Provost of Glasgow from 1960 to 1963.
[2] Antony Armstrong-Jones b.1930, photographer, created Earl of Snowdon in 1961. He was married to Princess Margaret from 1960 to 1978.
[3] Dr Maurice J. Miller J.P. (1920-2001) was Labour M.P. for Kelvingrove from 1964 to 1974, and for East Kilbride from 1974 to 1987.
[4] Emilio Coia (1911-1997), portrait painter, caricaturist and art critic.
[5] Mrs Marie Coia, flower painter. Exhibited at the Royal Scottish Academy between 1960 and 1968.
[6] Paul Cézanne (1839-1906), Impressionist artist.

18. From Compton MacKenzie (EUL MS2954.8 f.25)

31 Drummond Place
Edinburgh 3
11 January 1962

My Dear Christopher,

How good of you to write. I had subscribed to THE KIND OF POETRY I WANT[1] and had already read it with pleasure and admiration when I got your letter. My copy is number Thirty-Two, which pleases me as a good omen for the octaves of my autobiography. I'm working on Number One now. Chrissie will be writing soon to thank you for your letter, but she and I have both been overwhelmed with kind wishes. I hope we'll be seeing you soon.

Love to Valda,

Yours ever affectionately,

Monty C. M.

Ours has been a long unbroken friendship.

[1] Edinburgh, 1961. Printed by Dr Giovanni Mardersteig on the hand-press of the Officina Bodini, Verona.

19. From David Orr (EUL Gen.2094/4/1746)

air mail from ORR
S.S. PRO?E
Near Aden
3 May 1962

Dear Christopher,

I was glad to have your letter at Rangoon, and regretted that I was unable to see your phiz on television with Muggeridge[1] if that's how you spell his name. I hope that the Printers are getting on with *A Drunk Man* but I shall soon be home, when we should get things going.[2]

Hope like myself you lapse but seldom as far as drink is concerned & when you do – it's not a lapse. We have had a wonderful trip so far. The Sea of Arabia has been like a mill pond and we should be good till we get [to] the Bay o' Biscay & even that shouldn't be too bad at this time.

I haven't made up my mind what to do when I get home, but I should like a run to Torridon to see Joey [Shepherd][3] and our few old friends in that district.

Hope your chores are a bit easier now & that Valda is recovered from the flu, she has been a good wife –, sometimes, keep 'sometimes' out if you read this to her.

I understand this ship is to do but one more voyage, so I was thinking of going with her but I haven't fully made up my mind, if I do I shall miss the Festival, but that won't matter much, though I should not like to miss any official affairs in which you are involved.

Well, well parting time is near.

Wishing you both the best.

Yours aye,

David.

---

[1]   Malcolm Muggeridge (1905-1990), journalist, author, satirist, media personality, soldier-spy and in his later years a Catholic convert and writer. As Lord Rector of Edinburgh University he refused to support the call for contraceptive pills to be available at the University Health Centre, and resigned.

[2]   The 200 Burns Club reprinted *A Drunk Man Looks at the Thistle* for MacDiarmid's 70th birthday.

[3]   Josephine ('Joey') Shepherd's late husband was John MacNair Reid, the dedicatee of 'Depth and the Chthonian Image'. Dr Orr's second wife had died prior to this cruise.

20. From Walter Grieve (EUL MS2948.14 f.1)

30 St George's Road
Deal
KENT
9 June 1962

Dear Christopher,

I regret to inform you that my mother, Margaret Piller (née Skinner) died peacefully yesterday evening after a brief illness. The funeral will take place at Barham Crematorium on June 13th at 10.30 am.

It is a great pity that my first letter to you should contain this news, but I sincerely believe that you would wish to know. I hope that we may meet during this summer if I can get up to Scotland.

Yours sincerely,

Walter Ross Grieve.

21. From T. J. Douglas MacDonald / Fionn MacColla (EUL MS2965.5 ff.105-106)

40a Morningside Park
Edinburgh 10
26 June 1962

Dear Chris,

I'd have replied to your letter immediately only that I have had the deuce of a job tracking down a copy of *The Albannach*.[1] Everyone I approached had had a copy but had had it either pilfered or borrowed and not returned, and it was only at long last that I obtained the copy I am enclosing, which as you will see was a gift from the late W. D. MacColl to Iain Gillies. I hope that the delay has not interfered in any way with your plans for the disposal of your scanty free time at the present juncture.

Incidentally, you will be interested to hear that last year William Gillies,[2] son of Iain and grandson of our old friend Liam, took first place in the University Bursary competition – a half-holiday for Oban High School, where John MacLean, brother of Sorley, is Rector – and that this year his sister Anne *repeated the process*![3] Another half-holiday, of course, and constituting, I should imagine, an 'all-time' record – brother and sister first in the 'Bursary Comp.' in succeeding years. Incidentally Willie Matheson, whom doubtless you know or remember from the old days, brother of Professor Angus Matheson and lecturer in Gaelic at Edinburgh, who set and corrected the Gaelic papers in the aforesaid 'Bursary Comp.', told Mamie – who works nowadays in the School of Scottish Studies – that William's Gaelic in his papers was absolutely flawless. I don't know what he said in that context about Anne's, but he did say that in her Essay paper in Gaelic she wrote about *The Albannach*! Anne didn't mention this on any of her frequent visits to us during her time here, but she did mention it to me over the phone from Oban when I was ringing up to enquire whether they had a copy, and on hearing what I wanted it for, i.e., to send to you, bade me tell you as the opinion of one of the younger generation that she thought it was 'fabulous' – apparently a term much in use by that younger generation. She's pretty fabulous herself, this eighteen-year-old: James B. Caird, whom I saw last night, told me that the chap who marked her English papers had been showing them round as the sort of paper one only encounters once in many years. All this merely by the way.

I thought I had a copy in my collection of old issues of *The Free Man* of the issue in which you originally wrote about *The Albannach*, but have not been able to find it. I turned up however a large extract from it which I had copied out with, I fear, reprehensible haste and carelessness – and over which I then spilt tea – as well as a mention of the book which I came upon by chance years later in a copy of *The Voice of Scotland*. I am sending them to you in case they should be of interest to you in the context of the present matter. I can't help reflecting on how your prophecy that I should 'dine late and in exceedingly small company' seems to have been fulfilled. It would be true to say, as I daresay you know already, that for thirty years I have never at any time had the conditions in which writing of any quality whatever could reasonably be expected – and haven't got them yet, nor any prospect of getting them. So that the (at least) twenty books which I should certainly have written in the intervening period had I had any sort of a chance, have simply not been written, and the (at least) ten which I still have it in me to write will almost certainly never be written either. A pretty shocking example, come to think of it, of the state of this cultural dunghill of a Scotland you and I have both had to live in all our lives, and quite unthinkable in any other country whatsoever. However that's an old tale upon which, if I mistake not, I have frequently heard you expatiate yourself!

I need not say how happy I am that *The Albannach* will re-appear with an Introduction by yourself, the pre-eminently suitable person to write it for a number of reasons, important among them the fact that you were instrumental in its appearing in the first instance. I have made only the slightest verbal changes in it in view of its re-publication, being well aware that only a touch or two of a so much more mature – if not indeed senile – hand would simply destroy its quality.

I feel it is mere presumption for me to ask if you could write the Introduction next week – when I see you say you will be freer in the matter of time – but this has come upon me all of a sudden and the publishers, Michael Slains, give me to understand they want to have it out by October,[4] so that they may be able to issue a new, big novel of mine by December. Do therefore please forgive the seeming importunity. (I may mention that *And The Cock Crew* will be out again by the end of next month – I returned the final proofs some time ago – and that I am verbally contracted to deliver another book to the same publishers, in this case Burns of Glasgow, for issue by this time next year.[5] I have not written a word of it and have simply no idea how I am going to write it, labouring as I am under the necessity of teaching classes of forty in order, just barely, to make ends meet, and finding that in itself so enormously exhausting that recently I was slung into the Royal Infirmary on suspicion of an incipient coronary thrombosis – the severity of my blood pressure is apparently 'fabulous'.

I need not say how very shocked I was to hear about Peggy. I had not seen or heard of her for thirty years and was totally unprepared for the news. I extend you my most heartfelt condolences.

Please excuse the obvious shortcomings of this letter. I fear it must seem 'muggy' and confused, owing to the fact that, as usual, my brain is reeling with fatigue. Perhaps you will acknowledge receipt of this by a p.c., so as to set my fussy mind at rest in the matter of its safe delivery.

All affectionate remembrances from us both.

Yours ever,

T. J. Douglas MacDonald.

1   *The Albannach* was first published in London in 1932.
2   William Gillies is Professor of Gaelic in The University of Edinburgh.
3   Anne Lorne Gillies is a singer and Gaelic scholar who has been a Parliamentary candidate.
4   *The Albannach* was not, in fact, reprinted until 1971, by Reprographia, with a Foreword by 'Fionn MacColla' himself. Michael Slains published *Ane Tryall of Heretiks* in 1962, again with a Foreword by 'Fionn MacColla'. No 'new big novel' appeared at this time.
5   *And the Cock Crew* was republished by John S. Burns in 1962, but 'another book' did not appear the following year.

22. From Jonathan Knight (EUL MS2962.6 f.22)

The University
Reading
Department of Microbiology
Professor: B.C.J.G. Knight, D.Sc.
7 August 1962

Dear Hugh MacDiarmid,

I look forward very much to your *Festschrift*,[1] which is due to appear – according to K. Duval – on 11 August – which I assume is on or near your birthday: many happy returns of it!!

I've been reading and re-reading your *Collected Poems* (Macmillan, New York) ever since you kindly sent it to me. I look forward to the day when there will be a neat pocket edition of it – a slightly fuller glossary would help the semi-literate – on India paper, easy to slip into a pocket and carry everywhere (what a bombshell!). This we must look forward, too – it's a *must*.

I find quotes and curses for so many things in your poems that I'd like always to carry it around. There is so much to dig out of what you have written – useful stuff for living. I'm not one of those who believes that 'poets' (with or without a capital 'P') have very much more *original* to say than other human beings. But that poets may say what they want to say rather better – more evocatively – than most other kinds of writing, their phrases more loaded, more conducive *to thought in their readers* – this I will maintain. Besides Stendhal, whom I read again and again because I repeatedly find that some experience – some perception new to me has already been noted and used by Stendhal in his 'fictions' – besides his writing, yours is to me certainly the best, the densest in concentration of thought + feeling that I can find today. You combine too, so much scientific knowledge and outlook with your poetry of human perception and feeling, which I think is at present unique. And which I think points a way forward. I want to say: 'There is something added to my life; some things I thought I was alone in seeing and feeling, but could not, did not, express, nor thought noteworthy; yet here are you expressing it inimitably, vividly, livingly; other things which I've *not* met before; things which make life worth living to the end, *transforming things*, things to make others live, too ... A concentrated store of life and living.

All best wishes.

Yours ever,

Jonathan Knight.

P.S. Please accept offprint herewith.

[1]   *MacDiarmid : a festschrift*, edited by K. D. Duval and Sydney Goodsir Smith, was published by Duval (Edinburgh, 1962).

23. From Comtesse Eileen de Vismes (NLS MS27156)

Greetings telegram 11 August 1962

GWO C 21 GTG London X E 24 EZH

Greetings, Grieve,
Brownsbank,
BIGGAR Lanarkshire.

Love and many thanks for still being with us

Eillen Contesse de Vismes[1]

[1]   Spacing on the telegram copied exactly – also spelling of her name. MacDiarmid refers to her in *The Company I've Kept*, pp. 17-18. as Comtesse Eileen de Vismes.

24. From William McCance (EUL MS2953.8 f.26)

'Sunnyside'
Barr
by Girvan
Ayrshire
14 August 1962

Dear Chris,

I enjoyed the party the other night and it was good meeting you and at last meeting Valda. I think she liked me. Anyhow I liked her. I am glad to see that you are getting this spate of recognition. I have been following it in the Press. Recognition is perhaps not exactly the right word. The curse of criticism is that most critics choose their own little narrow plank to walk and are so damned frightened to fall off it, in case they get a ducking before they reach its end and their final plunge into oblivion, that they fail to realize that artists are not concerned with walking a plank but with living a life, sometimes painfully, and dying with good grace. As a painter they accuse me of being more of a sculptor because I draw on all the senses, visual, tactile & kinaesthetic, in the structure of my design, throwing my rhythms backwards and forwards in space, in order to get a complex unity linked biologically with man's evolutionary supremacy over all other animals as a non-specialist, who has not succumbed to his immediate environment for immediate advantage. It's a biological necessity with me. But most critics get no further than the decorative pattern of the peacock's tail. Man is not limited in space. Yet the critics would like us to walk the plank with them to our doom and the betrayal of our species. So don't fash yourself with some of their haverings. Just get a bit angry. And now I'll finish. You haven't too much time on your hands these days.

Yours aye,

Mac.

P.S. Margaret[1] & I are coming over on Tuesday for the Writers' Conference that day so I hope we shall see you and Valda.

---

[1] Margaret Chislett was to become McCance's second wife. He had been married to Agnes Miller Parker, the engraver, from 1917 to 1955. He re-married in 1963.

25. From Douglas Dunn (NLS MS27155 ff.124-126)

Douglas Dunn
15 Greenhead Road
INCHINNAN
Renfrewshire
n.d. [c.1962]

Dear Christopher Grieve,

On Wednesday evening I was angry (and perhaps rash) as to rise and speak regarding the 'contemporary condition of Scottish Literature', which was the title of your address, although, chronologically, it bore little relevance to what you said.[1] I asked your views on Nepotism in Scottish poetry, as emphasised through *New Saltire*. I enclose an actual letter from M. Magnusson[2] regarding my own manuscripts which he kept for about seven months without so much as a word regarding their safe receipt, although the customary stationery was included.

This letter is a result of my belief that you misinterpreted the purpose of my remarks. It is very fashionable for young writers to rise and sensationally deride their elders e.g. Trocchi / Scottish literature in general, Yevtushenko[3] / Kruschev,[4] Ehrenburg / Sholokhov,[5] etc., etc. It is so fashionable that I *demand* you know I take no part in it. I am a gentle, unassuming person and there is no place in my personality for sensationalism. I am not bitter that Scottish journals should reject me; perhaps I am a very poor poet: the people are the deciders of that; (there is little a poet's confidence can do for his own reputation.) But, in my unaccustomed anger over your pomposity (which was so out of keeping with the pathos of some of your poetry) I must, I feel, voice myself, for my own peace of mind and satisfaction that I have done so.

I do not expect an answer to this, but perhaps you will be good enough to return Magnusson's letter, for which I enclose the necessary stationery. I also enclose some 'poems', furtively, perhaps as if you might not notice them as you read this.

You pointed out on Wednesday that you would not use them for certain eliminatory functions which you would not mention. *I* shall not compliment you by saying I hope you shall wipe your arse with them.

Yours *sincerely*,
Douglas Dunn.

PS It would be almost too melodramatic is I receive certain brown-smeared MSS in about a week's time!

[1] Professor Dunn recalls that the event was chaired by the late Dr W. R. Aitken and may have been promoted by either the County Libraries Circle or the Scottish Library Association.
[2] Magnus Magnusson was editor of *New Saltire* 5-11, Edinburgh, August 1962-April 1964.
[3] Yevgeny Yevtushenko b. 1936, outstanding Soviet poet.
[4] Nikita Khruschev (1894-1971) was First Secretary of the Communist Party of the Soviet Union (1953-1964) and Chair of Council of Ministers (1958-1964).
[5] Mikhail Sholokhov (1905-1984), Soviet novelist, Nobel Prize Winner for Literature in 1965. *And Quiet Flows the Don*, first published in USSR in 1929, and in English in UK in 1934, remains his best-known work.

26. From John Gawsworth (NLS Acc.7361/34)

35 Sutherland Place
[Paddington] W2
11 January 1963

Dear Chris,

I have not yet got the 'Festschrift' fixed up with a publisher as I am still at work on the Checklist to complete it. In the meantime, I wondered would you sign 40 copies (& keep 10 as fee) if, with your permission, I issued your essay, as from my Twyn Barlwm Press, separately?[1]

As with *Five Bits of Miller* it would be very strictly limited[2] – and only for collection & libraries: I could rid me of my 30 & it would help me out a bit. This ruddy old diabetic crawls now to the Labour Exchange, damn it.

Let me know – I have had a printers' quote for an 8-page pamphlet and enough 'possible' orders to cover that printing & let you hold on to 10 copies (*quarter* of the edition). Trust you'll agree.

As ever
John [Gawsworth]

1   'When the Rat-race Is Over' was placed and dated 'London June 29, 1962' on the front cover, presumably Gawsworth's fiftieth birthday. 'Forty numbered copies of this opuscule have been privately printed by the Twyn Barlwm Press, 35 Sutherland Place, London, W.2., each signed by Hugh MacDiarmid & John Gawsworth'.

2   *Five Bits of Miller* was privately published by MacDiarmid in an edition limited to forty numbered copies, in 1934.

27. From Muriel Rukeyser (EUL MS2962.7 f.67)

The Blue Bell
Belford
Northumberland
26 August 1963

Dear Valda and Hugh MacDiarmid – or would you rather be called Christopher? –
That was beautiful, meeting you at last the other day. Now I am on the train, on the way to Alnwick again – and, if it is good for you, I'd like to take you at your word and try to find you this weekend, in Candymill or Edinburgh.

My son and I are at the Blue Bell, Belford. Would you call me there, collect, morning or evening? If you reach me, splendid; if not, would you leave a number and I'll try to call you back – or come to that place on Saturday.

Love,
Muriel.
Belford 203
(the train's in my writing)

28. From Freddy Anderson (EUL Gen.2094/6)

47 Coxton Place
Garthamloch
Glasgow E3
c.23 October 1963

Dear Chris,
Once again I take up this rather noisy nuisance of a quill to 'pen' you a few lines regarding the old subject again, yet not merely regarding 'Oiney'[1] but things in general. About this book first, or better still, my respects to Valda and yourself – I understand that Michael is married long since, not of course that such a step puts him in a world outside my best regards. I trust you are all keeping in the best of form. You will remember Harry Keir,[2] it was he who first introduced me to you off Byres Road! As you perhaps know Harry has not been keeping well these past few years, but he is contemplating a part-time job and is arranging an Art Exhibition of recent work plus the collection in Annan's for sometime in the near future. I was speaking to him by phone recently and am due to see him this week. I had told him I was in

correspondence with you and he asked me to pass his regards to you all. To continue in this rather gossipy vein, which I trust you won't find unbearable, another artist – writer this time – I have been in touch with recently is Helen Fullerton.[3] Lawrence and Wishart published a collection of her poems some time ago, a book entitled *My Country*. She sent you two of the poems, but on reading through her book again last night, I was greatly moved by the remarkable beauty of some of her work. 'The rose and the pimpernel' after Aragon's 'la rose et le réséda' seemed to me a lovely thing. I do not know the original but, if it carries the spirit as surely it should of her English interpretation, it must be a splendid poem. Others of her poems are exceptional, but I do not think the two which she sent to you are by any means the best of her work. She is now a student of geology etc. at Gilmorehill by the grace of the Government, but is working on a ballad-opera, or something of the like, based on her experience of a few years in the Hydro Scheme at Glen Shira. Her make-up will never allow her to lay aside the pen.

Regarding my book, Matt McGinn[4] had been in touch with Bruce Dunnet, the folk-song agent in London of The Singers' Club, who asked to see it, and I did a rather foolish thing and sent it to him a number of months ago. I wrote him two letters recently, the second one asking for it its return, but both my letters have been completely ignored. I'm just left to gnash my teeth, or whatever remains of them at this day and age. In fact, although I have not told him so, I want to withdraw the book completely. On reflection I felt I had not done justice to the subject on hand, and for the fourth time, I re-started it and am presently engaged on it. I want Oiney to be a unique sort of character between boy and adult moving about twentieth century Ireland and elsewhere among all the contradictions of an even 'madder' environment than his own immediate thinking. My greatest difficulty is not so much the capture but the retention of this elusive thing. And even now as I write a comparison comes to me to illustrate the point. There are many stories as you will know in Irish literature and folk-lore regarding the poor Irish peasant catching the leprechaun and the eyes of the former are gleaming at the prospects of the crook of gold when suddenly the cunning wee rogue by some simple device distracts his attention and, this achieved, makes his escape. It is this precisely which happens to me. At those times when I am *most confident* of having captured Oiney, the rascal proves to be more rubber-boned than the famous Hynds. However, here I go again though there are sometimes I feel I am more of a prison warder than a writer. That's a Behan one for you.[5]

After this long spiel, I am gradually reaching the main point of the literary side of my letter. Almost eighteen months ago, on my return from a most miserable but revealing experience in London, William MacLellan engaged on the production of some series of poetry, suggested that I might like to contribute a slender volume, based to some extent on the Peace and anti-Polaris poems and ballads which I had been getting out as single broadsheets in the Holy Loch campaign.[6]

[1] *Oiney Hoy* was finally published In Edinburgh in 1989.
[2] Harry Keir (1902-1977), painter mainly in wash drawings but also occasional oils, figure

subjects and genre. *Woman at a Jawbox* (1933), People's Palace, Glasgow.

3   MacDiarmid published Helen Fullerton's poem 'Backies' in *The Voice of Scotland*, vol.vii, no.2 (July 1956), pp. 25-26. It was included in *My Country*, London, 1957, pp.17-19, as also her translation of 'La Rose et Le Réséda', pp.26-28.

4   Matt McGinn (1928-1977), Scots folk-song writer and singer. *Fry the little fishes*, fiction in English, (London, 1975).

5   A reference to Brendan Behan (1923-1964). His plays *The Quare Fellow* and *The Hostage* were first produced in 1954 and 1958 respectively. Autobiographical writings: *Borstal Boy* (London, 1958) and *Confessions of an Irish rebel* (London, 1965).

6   Freddy Anderson's letter breaks off here.

29. From Maurice Lindsay (EUL MS2953.3 f.108)

Greenbank
Annan
Dumfriesshire
[30th April 1964]

My dear Chris,

You and I have known each other for twenty-one years, during which time we have had our differences. But we have always agreed on at least two things: on our love for Scotland, even where that love may have been forced by circumstances to take on temporarily an inverse form: and in the pursuit of poetry.

You have ranged freely and splendidly over vast mountain ranges, while I have scaled only a few modest hills. But in gratitude for these years of friendship, I should like to dedicate this book to you.[1] May I?

Yours aye,
Maurice.

P. S. Could you please return the galleys in the enclosed envelope? – M.

1   The book was *One Later Day*, London, 1964. It was dedicated 'To Dr C. M. Grieve (Hugh MacDiarmid)/ with respect and affection'.

30. From Alexander Trocchi (Trocchi Estate) [1]

17 May 1964

Dear Mr MacDiarmid,

While there have been and will be aspects of life and art upon which we cannot be in accord, it seems to me there must be a few vital issues upon which we can hardly fail to be in agreement, and I, for my part, am most sorry that the particular circumstances in which we first met one another were such as to bring the former into prominence and distract our attention from the latter. Amongst this latter is our common revolt against the smug philistinism of many of our countrymen. That the good folk of the Edinburgh establishment should take pride in smothering the literary side of the festival this year is for both of us, I am sure, bloody shocking evidence of their barbarism. I believe too that we are agreed that they shouldn't be allowed to get away with it, that it is a scandal and could be a dangerous precedent. I am writing to inform you that I shall be doing all in my own power to help Haynes[2] make a success of an 'unofficial conference' and to express my personal hope that you will be with us, in your rightful place at the head of our shock troops, in Edinburgh this summer. I am certain we can do much more than was ever done 'officially', and at much less expense, if we can be together in this, for poetry and sanity, now. Next time I am in Scotland I hope I shall have the opportunity of meeting you privately. Really, I am not in the least anxious to continue a public sniping match with a man for whom I have always had the profoundest respect.[3]

[1]   This letter was published in Alexander Trocchi, *Invisible Insurrection of a Million Minds*, ed. by Andrew Scott Murray (Edinburgh: Polygon, 1991, pp. 205-6.) MacDiarmid received it; he wrote to Trocchi, 8th June 1964, 'I was in Canada for a month and only got back here on Saturday - to find your letter of 17th inst among my accumulated mail.' (*New Selected Letters*, p.395). Clearly he meant 'ult.' for 'inst.

[2]   Jim Haynes established the Paperback Bookshop in Charles St, Edinburgh in 1959 and the Traverse Theatre in 1963. He was also co-organiser of the first Edinburgh International Writers' Conference in 1962.

[3]   Trocchi also wrote letters on 7 August 1964 and 26 August [1964] in efforts to meet MacDiarmid privately. It is clear from MacDiarmid's letters of 26 August 1964 and 31 August 1965 (*New Selected Letters*, pp. 398-9 & p.411 respectively) that these efforts, and at least one later effort, were unsuccessful.

31. From Alexander Trocchi (EUL MS2962.10 f.12)

6 St Stephen's Gardens
London W2
7 August 1964

Dear Hugh MacDiarmid

I shall be in Edinburgh at the beginning of the second week of the confabulations. I'd like very much to see you soon after my arrival. Would you please leave instructions with Jim Haynes about the best way of contacting you? Or, if you have time, let me have word here?

I'm attaching something that keeps me very busy presently.[1] I hope you will approve.

Yours,
Alex T.

[1]   Trocchi attaches his scheme for a round robin of writers. (EUL MS2962.10 f.13). He also attaches his contribution to the round robin along with a list of 52 names of poets, novelists and critics (mainly). (Ibid. ff.14-16).

32. From Sybil Thorndike (EUL MS2976)

98 Swan Court
Chelsea SW3
19 August 1964

Dear Mr Grieve,
Thank you so much for your charming letter (which has reached me at Cambridge, as I am on tour with a new play). And thank you for your good wishes. We have splendid news of John and Patricia from Melbourne, and we are hoping that they will be home for Christmas – it is ten years since John has been home, though we have been to Australia. I *love* your poetry & have enjoyed so many of them – I have your full book.[1] I'll give John & Patricia your message. Bless you & thank you.
   Yours very sincerely,
   Sybil Thorndike.

   I've learnt some of yours & hope you will let me do some at a theatre with fee, of course!

[1]   Sybil Thorndike read from MacDiarmid's *Collected Poems* at Foyle's Literary Luncheon on Thursday 14 March 1965 when W. A. Foyle presented him with the William Foyle Poetry Prize for 1962.

33. From Victor J. G. Határ (EUL MS2966)

6 Glenhurst Avenue
Highgate Road
London NW5
26 August 1964

Dear Mr Grieve,
The afternoon I spent with you and Mrs Grieve were one of the best memories I took home from Edinburgh this year. You were most kind indeed to someone who has been introduced to you as a 'Fascist beast' (Fascist sounds all right but why 'beast'?) yet who will prove a loyal friend as he was a biased, partial and committed admirer of your poetry in the past. After all, on the sweeping Mercator map of the Republic of Writing, a few degrees of longitude and latitude to the Left or to the Right what do they matter as long as we do not try – as we do not – to cheat by words? And that is, I think, the crux of the matter.
   Mes sentiments les plus respectueuses à Madame, très cordialement à vous, vôtre Victor J. G. Határ.

34. From Alexander Trocchi (EUL MS2962.10 f.17)

c/o Haynes

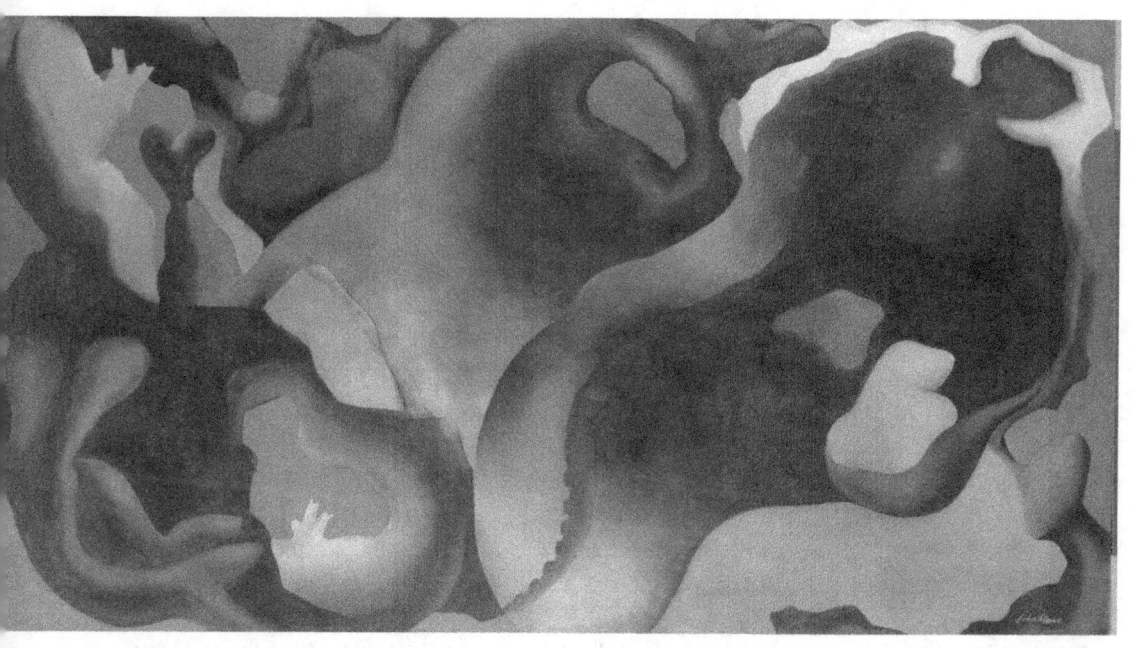

'A Point In Time'
By permission of The Scottish National Gallery of Modern Art and of A. D. Currie, W.S., for Sarah Johnstone.

12.30 pm 26 August [1964]

Dear Hugh,

Will you please try to look in this afternoon at the Traverse if you don't already intend to do so? I should be most grateful. Moreover, to meet you properly is one of the reasons I am here. Whether you come this afternoon or not, I still would like to see you. Will you let me have some sort of reply through Abercrombie.[1] Thanks.

Alex Trocchi.

PS Sorry I couldn't get here in time for Monday.[2]

[1]   Not identified.
[2]   The unofficial Poets' Conference opened in the Traverse Theatre on Monday 24 August 1964, and continued for four days. MacDiarmid attended the conference on the Monday only.

35. From William Johnstone (EUL MS2951.9 f.40)

William Johnstone OBE
Satchells Farm
Lilliesleaf
Nr. Melrose
Roxburghshire
19 September [1964]

Dear Christopher,

M. Reid [of the Reid Gallery] rang me from London.[1] He wants to use one of the six poems as an introduction to my exhibition as it seems to relate so intrinsically to the paintings. Acknowledgement will be made to you and to [Kulgin] Duval and suitable reference.[2] He asks about permission and I told him because of the urgency to go ahead as I was certain you would be agreeable. Would you square Duval on this too? It seems to me that it would be to his advantage. The exhibition opens on the 15 Oct. so there is little time to spare.

Would you clear this as soon as possible? Have not got the proofs for the limited Edition but I have been heavily engaged with my exhibition in London. They tell me the edition is going along and before long will be able to let you see proofs. Think it might be very interesting.

Have been reading about you but think you should be sitting by the fire smoking your pipe. It must be terribly exhausting all this political stuff and you are a great poet.[3] We take the pictures to London next Friday in a Thames van. Mary does the driving and it is a long drive.

Don't exhaust yourself. Your description of the Prime Minister was very funny.

As ever,

William Johnstone.

PS The poem is 'A Point in Time'.[4] There is a party in the Gallery on the 13 October – Do come.

Alex Clark, left, and Hugh MacDiarmid leaving Parliament Square on 21 December 1964 after a hearing in the Election Court of MacDiarmid's appeal to have the result in Kinross and West Perthshire declared void as he had not equal broadcasting time with Sir Alec Douglas-Home.
By permission of the MacDiarmid Estate.

1   The Exhibition in the Reid Gallery lasted from 14 October to 7 November 1964.

2   *Poems to Paintings by William Johnstone* was published by Kulgin Duval, 112 Rose Street, Edinburgh in 1963 in an edition of 100. MacDiarmid had written the poems in 1933. There are eight poems in the series, not six as Johnstone recalls here. The cover design 'Self Portrait' was by Johnstone.

3   MacDiarmid contested Kinross and West Perthshire on behalf of the Communist Party in the General Election on 15 October 1964.

4   *C.P.* II, p.1069.

36. From Sydney Goodsir Smith (EUL MS2960.16 ff.105-106)

18 Royal Terrace
Edinburgh
Friday
[1964]

Dear Chris,

Gent's Natty Suiting (1912 vintage - once belonging to my papa and now the only decent one I have - you will note the Natty Narrow Trousering of the Unmentionables or Inexpressibles) follows by parcel post. It is a bit wide round the corporation for me - which I find v. useful for dinner parties with much wine-bibbing. No doubt you will have ample opportunity to test its merits in this respect.[1]

I should like to have accompanied you to my All-ma Mate-her but I fear funds will not permit same. However, you can do me a favour by entering Oriel College by dirkness and pissing against the Provost's dwelling (Sir David Fucking Ross, by God, foul nitted Airstwatailion) which is on your left as you enter the port Quadrangle - a function that was aince my chiefest and nightly pleisure. The foul and ever-to-be-execrated Ross (black be his faa!) occurs in Carotid, [2] if you recollect, as Sair Drysquid Runts, Provokit, Puirlost and Peeriboss o Glauriaul or Hairyhole Cullage, Eggsfried and Vice-Chainseller o the Inverityshitty o Cocksfraud, Page 66, Quart Fitt.

You'd better take a copy of *CC* down with you and present it with due solemnity to the Oriel Coll. Library or perhaps to the Bodleian.

Hoping you have a reasonable time to finish your drinks. Will be through to Glasgow next week-end almost certainly.

Thine

Auk.

1   Perhaps the occasion was MacDiarmid's proposal of the motion, 'Extremism in the defence of Liberty is no vice; moderation in the pursuit of Justice is no virtue' in the televised debate from the Oxford Union on 3 December 1964. He was supported by Malcolm X, and opposed by Lord Stoneham and Humphrey Berkeley MP.

2   Sydney Goodsir Smith here refers to *Carotid Cornucopious,* Printed by the Caledonian Press, 793 Argyle Street, Glasgow, and issued by them only to members of the Auk Society in 1947.

37. From Glyn Jones (EUL Gen.2094/2/985)

158 Manor Way
Whitchurch
Cardiff
7 January 1965

Dear Hugh MacDiarmid,

In September, 1964, I bought and read Professor Buthlay's book on your life and work in Oliver and Boyd's 'Writers and Critics' series. There the Professor quotes a poem entitled 'Perfect'. Now the words of that poem, all except the first line, were written by me, as prose, and published by Cape in 1937, in a collection of my short stories entitled *The Blue Bed*. The earliest appearance of your poem that I can trace in print is 1939.[1]

I have written to my agent and to Oliver and Boyd about this matter. In the current issue of the *Times Literary Supplement* I see 'Perfect' again in full. I have written, therefore, to the editors pointing out what I have just pointed out to you.

Perhaps you would like to comment on all this.

Yours sincerely,

Glyn Jones.

I might add that the *Times Literary Supplement* has received another letter, from a person unknown to me, pointing out that the words really belong to me.

[1] This appearance was in Hugh MacDiarmid, *The Islands of Scotland* (London:Batsford, 1939), p. x .

38a. From Nguyen Xuan Sanh (EUL MS2966)

Hanoï le 19 February 1965

Cher monsieur Christopher Grieve,

Les actes de nouvelle guerre excessivement graves des U.S.A. contre notre République démocratique de Vietnam continuent encore.

Le fait qu'ils viennent d'envoyer de grandes vagues d'avions à réaction pour bombarder et mitrailler Viviblines, Donghoï, et Vines les 7,8 et 11/2 a grossièrement dérangé les principes les plus élémentaires du droit international.

Mais cher monsieur bien aimé, l'ármée populaire et la population vigilante des endroits sous-mentionnés ont lutté avec fierté et ont remporté glorieusement de nouvelles grandes victoires.

Nous sommes sincèrement émus du soutien profondément fraternel des peuples et des écrivains des cinq parties du monde.

Comme un ami vietnamien qui vous a rencontré en septembre 1959 en Bulgarie – lorsque vous et moi nous étions tous invités de l'Union des écrivains bulgares à Sofia –, je vous demande de vouloir bien élever votre voix pour exprimer votre adhésion à notre juste cause, de vouloir bien écrire de nouveaux poémes pleins de feu sur la lutte sans merci de notre peuple contre les envahisseurs américains, sur notre foi inébranlable en la victoire finale.

Cher monsieur, notre amitié est bien grande. À vous, mes meilleurs voeux de bonne création littéraire. Vos souvenirs restent toujours vivants au plus profond de mon coeur.

Au revoir et à bientôt.

Sincèrement votre

Nguyen Xuan Sanh

poet

Vietnam Writers' Union HANOI D. R. Vietnam

38b. From Nguyen Xuan Sanh (EUL) [translation]

Hanoï

19 February 1965

Dear Mr Christopher Grieve,

The extremely serious acts of renewed war by the USA against our Democratic Republic of Vietnam still continue.

The fact that they have just sent great waves of jets to bomb and strafe Viviblines, Donghoï and Vines on the 7th, 8th and 11th of this month has crudely shattered the most elementary principles of international law.

But dear sir, the People's Army and the vigilant population of the above-mentioned places have fought with pride and gloriously won great new victories.

We are sincerely moved by the profoundly fraternal support of the peoples and writers of the five continents of the world.

As a Vietnamese friend who met you in September in 1959 in Bulgaria – when you and I were both guests of the Bulgarian Writers' Union in Sofia – I ask you to raise your voice to express your support for our just cause, to write fiery new poems on the merciless struggle of our people against the American invaders, on our unshakeable faith in final victory.

Dear sir, our friendship is very strong. My best wishes to you for good literary creativity. My memories of you always remain vivid deep in my heart.

Good-bye until we meet again.

Sincerely yours

Nguyen Xuan Sanh

poet

Vietnam Writers' Union HANOI D. R. Vietnam

39. From Tom Scott (EUL MS2960.6 f.58)

12 St Vincent Street

Edinburgh

6 April 1965

Dear Chris,

Still no word from our pals owre the waater. I've written them again to-day. What a way to run a business.

The Finlay[1] lobby swells daily – now nearly twenty letters from Europe and America. A young Scot told Oxford in an eight-page letter that either I should be made to print Finlay or they should get another editor – the name of Morgan being mentioned as a concrete 'safe' man. It's comic, and it's libellous. Another says your friend Prof. Rosenthal is printing F. in a forthcoming anthology – are you in it?[2] And I suppose Lindsay will HAVE to print him in the forthcoming Faber book.[3] But this attempted force has hardened me, and it has hardened Oxford – he's had it as far as this book is concerned.[4] His friends have queered the pitch.

I had a specimen page of the Dunbar from Oliver & Boyd the other day – looks quite good.[5]

Aye,

Tom.

---

1   Ian Hamilton Finlay (1925-2006).
2   M. L. Rosenthal (1917-1996) wrote *New Poets: American and British Poetry since World War Two*. There were references to, and quotations from, Finlay in Chapter 5, 'Contemporary British Poetry'.
3   *Modern Scottish Poetry: An anthology of the Scottish Renaissance*, enlarged second edition (London: Faber & Faber, 1966).
4   *The Oxford Book of Scottish Verse*, edited by Tom Scott and John MacQueen was published by the Clarendon Press, Oxford in 1966. Ian Hamilton Finlay was not represented.
5   Tom Scott, *Dunbar: A Critical Exposition of the Poems*, (London, 1966).

40. From Tom Scott (EUL MS2960.6 f.59)

Did you know also that *Poetry Scotland* is being revived
on a British or Arts Council grant? Edited by – guess –
Lindsay, Bruce, and Morgan, published Edinburgh
University Press. It's to be an annual.[1]

12 St Vincent Street
Edinburgh
9 April 1965

Dear Chris,

I don't know any more about the Rosenthal anthology than I've told you, except that Auden and Wilbur[2] are also to be in it – for F. respectability at last – but Lindsay is revising the Faber *Modern Scottish Poetry* volume. I thought you'd know. I don't see how L. can avoid putting something of Finlay's early work in, or Morgan's: but if he intends putting in also this concrete rubbish, then I too would be prepared to refuse permission. If we all did that, it would force an issue – but how many will be willing to do so. It only needs Smith, MacCaig, Crichton Smith, say, Alex Scott – six

THE THREEPENNY OPERA

Prince of Wales Theatre
programme 10p

The opening night of the production of Hugh MacDiarmid's translation of Bertolt Brecht's
The Threepenny Opera in the Prince of Wales Theatre, 10 February 1972.

of us – and the Faber book would be in trouble. I hope it needn't come to that, and I hate having to think like this – but the very identity of poetry is at issue, and if we don't take a stand, these bastards will use us to get their rubbish through, to OK it with the gullible purblind public.

This shibboleth 'internationalism' is another form of bourgeois escapism – not a true international, but cloud-cuckoo-land. I have attacked it in today's *Scotsman* – my letter gelded as usual. All this is symptomatic of the collapse of values in the west. But as the enemy organize, so must we.

Aye,

Tom.

---

1 *Scottish Poetry 1-9*, 1966-1976. Vols 1-6 were edited by George Bruce, Maurice Lindsay and Edwin Morgan and published by Edinburgh University Press. Vols 7-9 were edited by Maurice Lindsay, Alexander Scott and Roderick Watson and published by Glasgow University Press (7) and Carcanet, Manchester (8 and 9).

2 Richard Wilbur (b. 1921), professor, poet and translator.

41. From Stefan S. Brecht (NLS MS27153 f.82)

737 Washington St
New York City 14
NY
12 April 1965

Dear Sir,

I heard from Dr Czech, the UK representative of the Bertolt Brecht estate, to my great pleasure, that you were working on a translation of my father's *Threepenny Opera*.[1] As there is interest in this country, also, for a publication of this work, and as the local translations are not so good, I would appreciate a word from you, at your convenience, as to the veridity of this information. –

I have long urged Mr Cullen of Methuen's and Dr Czech, to approach you about translating such other works of my father's as the *Caucasian Chalk Circle*, but of course if you are working on the *Threepenny Opera*, there would be no sense in that … at the moment …

Assuring you of my respects.

Stefan S. Brecht.

---

1 The *Threepenny Opera* opened at Prince of Wales Theatre in London on 10 February 1972 and was attended by Hugh MacDiarmid and Valda.

42. From C. R. Honig (EUL MS2970)

as from 32 Claigmar Gardens
London N3

30 August 1965

Dear Hugh MacDiarmid,

I should like personally and most cordially to invite you as honoured guest to an In Memoriam Martin Buber symposium which is taking place on Thursday, 23 September 1965 in the Royal Albert Hall with the participation of a large number of philosophers, writers, psychoanalysts, anthropologists, and poets as well as, 'leider auch'[1] as Goethe would have said, theologians. One of my vice-Presidents is Sir Herbert Read, another Sir Isaiah Berlin,[2] a third Prof. Cleanth Brooks,[3] cultural attaché of the American Embassy, etc. etc. Whether you have or have not read Buber,[4] I don't know. Neither do I care what you think of him (if negatively, then you don't know him...!) But I do know *you* as a great poet and Scotsman – and I shall be most happy to meet you and welcome you here. If you wish to say a few words at the Symposium (5 minutes alas!) please let me know. Could you perhaps if you wish send me some of your work and some prose – for a review I am preparing for our forthcoming magazine.

Whom would you suggest to be invited from the Communist countries? – and who you think might come. I should like to see some of them and have a real Existential Buberian-Dialogue. Any likelihood of having here G. Lukács? Will he come? Perhaps you might write to Lukács and others and invite them. I have written to Arnold Zweig.[5] Do write right away.

C. R. Honig

Camille R. Honig was General Secretary and Founder of the International Martin Buber Society and Institute, London.

[1] leider auch – unfortunately also.
[2] Sir Isaiah Berlin (1909-1997), Russian-British philospher and historian of ideas.
[3] Cleanth Brooks (1906-1994) was an influential US literary critic.
[4] Martin Buber (1878-1965) was one of the greatest Jewish philosophers of modern times. MacDiarmid showed his interest in Buber's work in *Lucky Poet*, pp. 158-162. In a later letter, n.d., following MacDiarmid's answer (*New Selected Letters*, pp.411-412) Honig wrote, 'Yes. Buber had great admiration for you *and* your work which he sometimes had difficulties in understanding if it was in Scottish.' (NLS Acc. 7361/52).
[5] Arnold Zweig (1887-1968), novelist.

43. From Kenneth Buthlay (EUL MS2842.20 f.71)

Dunira
Whim Road
Gullane
East Lothian
5 January 1966

Dear Chris:

Do you remember, I mentioned to you that I was thinking of writing something about phonaesthetic aspects of language for the dissertation I have to do in applied linguistics? I've now begun to work on this, and I'd like to include something about differences in sound between Scots and 'standard' English as they appear to a poet who has written extensively in both.

Would you please let me know how you feel about this from your experience? Are there any particular sounds in Scots to which you find yourself specially responsive? If so, could you say what sort of qualities characterise these sounds as compared with their English equivalents (if any)? And is there any factor in your creative processes you feel to have been connected with the sounds of Scots as such?

Apart from your own experience as a writer – I don't suppose you know of anything that has already been written about the specifically phonetic side of verse in Scots, do you? I haven't come across anything except for one item about Burns, but I find it hard to believe that there's really *nothing* worth reading on the subject.

With best wishes for the new year to Valda and yourself from all of us.

Yours aye,

Kenneth.

44. From William MacCance (EUL MS2953.8 f.38)

28 The Avenue
Girvan
Ayrshire
30 August 1966

Dear Chris,

I am so sorry I haven't written to you for such a long time, especially when you had just got over your severe bout of 'flu, and were still under the weather. I do hope that you have now recovered now that we have had a moderately good summer. I felt rather depressed, partly because of a persistent form of sinus trouble, but mostly through my disappointment with my visits to Edinburgh in search of a gallery suitable for the kind of exhibition I have in mind – a retrospective show somewhat similar to the ones I had in Reading and London.[1] None of the private galleries I saw were in any way suitable. I had hoped that perhaps it might be possible to have an officially sponsored exhibition through the Scottish Committee of the Arts Council, but I have no contacts of any kind in Scotland apart from you and Kulgin. After all I could be thought of as the 'father of modern art' in Scotland, since I was the first Scottish-trained artist to paint an 'abstract' picture and other experimental works throughout my painting life. I am almost an individualised history of modern art from the early Twenties until the latest American rash that seems to prevail now amongst the younger painters, with which I am out of sympathy. My work is so experimental and personal, besides being technically & aesthetically varied, that I cannot introduce myself to the Scottish public by sending a few works to mixed exhibitions or the R.S.A. for they would not be at all representative of my development.

Recently however there seems to be a new venture by Richard Demarco who has started a gallery in Edinburgh which will be run on non-profit-making lines, and which seems to me a possibility if I can get him interested in my work.[2] The chief reason I went South after the First World War was because of the rather contemptuous & sneering attitude adopted by my contemporaries at the Glasgow School of Art to my early recruitment to the very lively modern attitude which was surging throughout the Continent and in London but did not seem to find any reaction in Scotland apart from this scathing attitude of the Establishment and my fellow-students. I well remember the contemptuous attitude of Sivell and MacGlashan, both of whom became leading members of the establishment later on.[3]

Margaret recently visited the Demarco Gallery and was very impressed by it. The chief drawback I may have will be my age, since I think the scheme is primarily for the benefit of the younger painters. Still, I think my work would be stimulating to the younger painters since they would see the continuous linking of the earlier movements with some of the saner experimental work now being produced; for I think the American rash is on the way out. It hasn't enough life or body in it for survival value.

Forgive this preoccupation with my personal worries, Chris. But you can perhaps understand the mental conflicts I feel regarding this problem of exhibiting. There is nothing I would like better than having my work seen in Scotland; more to have it seen than having an exhibition as a commercial gesture. You are the only Scot who has seen a comprehensive exhibition of my work when you delighted me by coming all the way to Reading for that purpose. You made it a red-letter day (or week-end) for me. And you know the variety of work I can show.

I was glad to see that your books are still finding a wider & wider appreciation throughout Europe & America. Margaret's father died recently so she is spending most of her holiday at present at Chippenham in Wiltshire with her mother & one of her sisters to help them out with things. I am alone here at present but she will be returning on Sunday. When she comes back I shall hope to visit Edinburgh again, but before that I shall try writing to Demarco, who is director of this gallery I have mentioned. Unfortunately Kulgin will not return from the Continent before early November. Hope again, Chris, that you have fully recovered. Our affection & regards to you & Valda.

Yours,

Mac.

[1]   The Reading Exhibition was in 1960, and the London Exhibition at Foyle's was in 1961. A retrospective Exhibition was held at the Scottish National Gallery of Modern Art in September 1990.

[2]   Richard Demarco (b.1930) used the gallery space of the Traverse Theatre for three years. He then ran the Richard Demarco Gallery from 1966 to 1992 and has since continued under the auspices of the Demarco European Art Foundation.

[3]   Robert Sivell (1889-1958) and Archibald MacGlashan (1888-1983) were (with Benno Schotz) founders of the Glasgow School of Painters and Sculptors in 1919.

45. From Georg Seehase (NLS Acc.7361/37)

Karl-Marx-Universität
Institut für Anglistik und Amerikanistik
Leipzig C1
Universitätsstr 3-5
15 December 1966

Dear Dr Grieve,

I have to apologise for being so late thanking you for your kind letter and the deeply moving poem. 'Is It Nothing to You'[1] is welcome, not only for the purpose of the book *Vietnam in dieser Stunde*[2] but also, if I may say so, for the purpose of my lectures on progressive English poetry after the 1930s. As it is so difficult to obtain specimens of that poetry any poem of this kind is most gratefully accepted.

Let me close with two questions – first: can I be of some use to you (sending you books from the GDR etc.)? – and second: is there any possibility of you coming to Leipzig next year to be our guest at the Institute?

Looking forward to your answer,

With best wishes,

Yours sincerely,

Georg Seehase.

[1]   The poem to which Dr Seehase refers was first published in English in *The Revolutionary Art of the Future*, Manchester, 2003. The MS copy in the National Library of Scotland was untitled. The editors provided the title, 'Aberfan and Viet-Nam'.

[2]   *Vietnam in dieser stunde* – Vietnam in this hour.

46. From Nathaniel Tarn (EUL MS2961.3 ff.1-2)

21 Kidderpore Gardens
London NW3
27 December 1966

Dear Mr. MacDiarmid,

I have been wondering, since your reading in London at the Jeanetta Cochrane Theatre, how best to write this letter – for that which declares, around one's eighteenth year, may do little more than confess two decades later. Well then: simplicity.

I discovered your work about a month before the reading and, since then, have spent my time both marvelling at my blindness and blessing it for the late, inestimable harvest of joy it has brought me. I think we are all asleep in this part of these islands and still asleep despite your bugles & pipes loud all these years. We are poisoned. I had believed, had allowed myself to believe, or been trapped into believing, that the kind of poetry you want – which is the kind of poetry you have indeed given us and are – was impossible. And this, like leukemia, was killing *me*: for it was also the poetry I wanted. Well, I shall not say what I shall or shall not do from this time forward with your help (for no one should prophesy outside the crucible) but I must thank you nakedly for changing the chemistry of my life and I declare myself from now your missionary – since, through madness, you still require such creatures in this South. Now I have spoken and shall go on speaking of this here, and let it be to good effect.

I am sending you – as an offering to be kept or discarded – a piece of Neruda I have recently done, knowing the Spanish, and a short piece on poetry and science, written in a night and never revised, which would have been very different had I then known your work.[1]

And a question: will you not admit a little, despite your 'jury of incontrovertible detail' that poets *make* the myths they need? The Spanish priests made much of the Amerindians as Jews, the better to pour the lead of their own sins into their wounds. Well, since I have realized the meaning of the Celtic belt this country wears, I *will* my fathers, the jury, to be Celts. Like that. Let it come, from the past, out of Fabre d'Olivet if need be, and for the future, from Karl Marx and Sigmund Freud and Albert Einstein and Emile Durkheim[2] and Claude Lévi-Strauss,[3] great poets all, and many more, if need be, this myth is constituted. History being the Natural History of man. And poetry being, at any moment, more than the whole future can dream in one dream.

I have been three times round the earth, lived with the Maya of Guatemala, the Burmese and the Shans of the China Border, the Japanese and most nations of Europe, yet never been to Scotland. Another madness, quite clearly. I wait on a young friend[4] in Edinburgh whose vice is to disappear into France the moment I declare my intention of coming North. (We have vacations at the same time of year and he is bilingual and half-French as I am). If I can do this, sometime in January, I wonder whether you would allow me to visit you? I have never made such a request before but then where are the eagles in their own skies? Something too much of this.

You are honoured, Mr. MacDiarmid, at this desk, in England.

Yours sincerely,

Nathaniel Tarn.

---

[1] Tarn published his translation of *The Heights of Macchu Picchu* by Pablo Neruda in 1966 (Cape, London). The short piece on poetry and science may be the first piece (1964) in his *Views from the Weaving Mountain: Essays in Politics and Anthropology* (University of New Mexico Press, 1991).

[2] Emile Durkheim (1858-1917), a founding father of modern sociology.

[3] Claude Lévi-Strauss (1908-2009), structural anthropologist.

[4] Kenneth White was the 'young friend'.

47. From J. R. Campbell (EUL Gen.2094/1/266)

20 Saffron Close
Hendon Park Way
London NW4

Dear Chris,

I think you are over-modest about the book.[1] Apart from the section I had reservations about, I think it is very good indeed. Some people who have read it here regard it as something new and fresh and have talked about it.

The *[Morning] Star*, incidentally, sat on my review for about three weeks. It should have been published three weeks before. Instead it came out at the very end of the queue.

I think it could go on selling for quite a time.

Give me a ring whenever you are in this 'benighted Imperial capital' (as MacLean once called it) and I will try and have a 'crack' with you.

A Happy New Year!

Yours fraternally,

J.R. Campbell.

---

[1] The book' was *The Company I've Kept* (London, 1966).

48. From Professor P. H. Butter (EUL Gen.2094/1/229a&b)

Ashfield
Bridge of Weir
Renfrewshire
4 January 1967

Dear Dr Grieve,

I am most grateful to you for reading my book with such care and for writing to me frankly and fully about it.[1] I will not now continue the argument on the thing about which we disagree (Muir's integrity, the value of his poetry). But I would just like to say that in what I wrote on page 133 I did not intend to do anything so impertinent as to blame you for turning in the 1930s to English, nor did I mean to deny the value of what you have done in your (mainly) English poems. My point – rather an obvious one, I am afraid – is that what a poet does in his work is more important than what any critic (even the poet himself as critic) says. Argument is of little weight in comparison with demonstration. After your work in Scots in the 1920s there was no point in arguing whether Scots could be used for writing important poetry in the twentieth century; the thing had been done. But it was still possible to ask how many things could be done in Scots, whether a poet could express in it the whole range of what he wanted to say. The answer had to be given by the poets, not by the critics. Your answer, the answer which most of your published poems since the mid 1930s seems to give, is that a wide-ranging poet cannot do in Scots all that he wants to do.

This old controversy is rather tedious and I am glad that in the article on Muir you are planning you intend to deal with his poetry rather than with the language question. There has not been much good critical writing on Muir, and some good close criticism of his poems would be welcome. The best article I have come across is John Holloway's in *The Hudson Review* (reprinted in his *The Colours of Clarity*).[2]

With best wishes for 1967.
Yours sincerely,
Peter Butter.

---

[1]   The reference here is to *Edwin Muir: Man and Poet* (Edinburgh, 1966).
[2]   London, 1964.

49. From Nathaniel Tarn (EUL MS2961.3 ff.3-4)

21 Kidderpore Gardens
London NW3
31 January 1967

Dear Mr and Mrs MacDiarmid,

I am back at this desk in London, wondering, as usual, what I am doing here. Just now, returning from a lecture to schoolchildren, on the North Circular Road, there was a hawk hovering so close to the road, I stopped the car & caused confusion. I am not entirely exiled!

How long did I spend with you? Much more than four wonderful hours. To begin with, all the preparation *towards*. Then the visit itself. Then the whole night, lying on my steel trapeze high up in a railway carriage, unable to sleep for the excitement, and turning over in my mind the diamond of your welcome. I think I must have gone off to sleep about a moment before the rough shake and the 'Kings Cross, sir' & the tea & biscuits shoved under one's nose. I am most grateful to you for having spent your precious time on us, and that so warmly & so generously.

Now the portrait (which my wife likes very much, & the children begin to ask) & the books are here in the treasure boxes.[1] You must forgive my 'collecting' disease. I disciplined myself to the extent of forbearing to ask Mr MacDiarmid to sign 'Fire of the Spirit' pamphlet[2] he so generously gave me, because I felt I had asked enough. (No doubt, the disease will return & I'll ask him another time!)

I am turning over the possibility of writing a piece for *Critique*, a magazine in Paris, devoted entirely to book-reviewing of the most serious order & unique of its kind – to coincide with the 2nd edition of the *Collected* perhaps. It depends on many things which I cannot foresee yet: too often I undertake too much & work beyond my strength. But if 'yes', then I may write with a question or two. I may write also about publishing: for the moment, am studying the checklist at the back of the *festschrift* volume, to look into reprint possibilities. I need hardly say that, for the series, an original essay would be my highest hope (a poem too high?). All that must be left to you ...

After Mr MacDiarmid's uncomplimentary remarks on Tarn-the-puddle, we decided to rebaptize ourselves MacLoch. The nineteen-twentyish hero of French detective fiction was called 'Fantomas': a cross between 'Mandrake the Magician' & 'Superman'. How do you like 'Fantomas MacLoch', temporarily at any rate? My friends, the Whites, were mainly reponsible for this! Are they not delightful people?

Forgive, too, my messy eagle. I could have done better but for Mr MacDiarmid's unfriendly comments (!) as well as the strength of your daemon HUISKAY, the national drink. 'Tis a fierce & magnificent beverage but one needs practice. Especially if one is going to sketch.

Well: I need hardly say that you are welcome here, *whenever*. 'Your house' as the Spaniards say.

For me Hugh MacDiarmid is just born and I delight in him as the worlds are said to delight when a Buddha is born. I hope you know that. A Frenchman wrote, in an article a few weeks ago, 'Poetry enables me to live myself in justice'. Pas mal?

In justice then, and in gratitude, yours,
Nathaniel Tarn.

---

[1]   In a letter to the present editor Tarn writes: 'I had been buying everything I could of M's in Edinburgh bookshops and acquired a very large pencil portrait on cardboard which I still have.' (19 July 2007).
[2]   Sub-titled 'Two poems by Hugh MacDiarmid', Glasgow, 1965. The two poems were 'By Wauchopeside ' and 'The Diamond Body'.

50. From David Murison (EUL MS2955.22 f.6)

The Scottish National Dictionary
27 George Square
Edinburgh 8
12 April 1967

Dear Christopher Grieve,

Many thanks for your kind and interesting letter of the 10th. Curiously enough, Hilda[1] and I had been seeing Helen Cruickshank on Sunday with Bruce Watson[2] and his wife (Hilda's sister) and were speaking of you. Helen told us of your American and European tour and we were speculating on the adamantine nature of the constitution needed to stand up to the ordeal. I hope you survive unscathed from the unlimited American capacity for listening to speeches – a kind of verbal porousness or spongiosity.

Yes, I'm glad to have had the chance of saying something about your *pars maxima* in the Lallans movement in *New North*[3] though I was given only 1500 words and you can't say much in that compass – just about the length of one of your sentences in *Lucky Poet*! However I *did* mention that you were returning to Scots, having castigated you somewhat for abandoning it, after you had seen the light. As you say, you did tell me that a year or two ago. I am making the point, rightly I hope, that you were inspired into Scots by Jamieson's Dictionary and realised that there were untapped poetic resources in Scots that a trite and exhausted English could not provide, and that with you, in a sense, the words had preceded the ideas, and not the other way round as one supposes poetry to work. This, of course, is not in the least to decry your poetry, as you will well understand, but merely to express the process. I say 'undoubtedly it was the renewed acquaintance with the old words that released in him not only the inarticulate poetry but the frustrated Scot'. I hope that's a fair and true statement of the position in regard to *Sangschaw* and its successors. I then speak of your theory of Lallans, 'Back to Dunbar', etc., the opposition it aroused and how the impulse you gave has been carried on by Smith, Young, Garioch and others. Then I go on to speak of similar movements abroad, Afrikaans, Nynorsk, Hindi, Urdu, Faeroese, Hebrew, etc. and the possibility of doing the same for Scots, lamenting the fact that there can be no real permanent hope for the language until Scots writers start reconstructing *prose*, as Sir William Craigie pointed out in 1926. And I leave the question of the desirability of the thing to the reader's own conscience, crediting you with forcing the issue to the forefront of Scottish letters.

That's all I had space for. The whole question of rebuilding Scots is of course a frightfully complex and difficult one and it will need a generation of research and a lot more academic recognition before it can be done. But it is good to know that you are turning back into the old ways and your influence is so immense and seminal that it could give a tremendous fillip to the whole movement once again. Good luck to you and I hope the *Dictionary* will be of some service again in the process!

By the bye, our nephew, young Rory Watson, is writing a Cambridge thesis on you and your language and I think has been in touch with you. He will be very glad of any guidance you can give him.[4]

With best wishes for your tour and all kind regards to both of you from us twa.
Yours sincerely,
David Murison.

[1] His wife.
[2] Professor of Chemistry in the University of Aberdeen.
[3] *New North* was an Aberdeen University student publication.
[4] Roderick Watson, Professor of English at the University of Stirling, is a nephew of the late Hilda Murison, sister of Bruce Watson's wife.

51. From Alexander Scott (EUL MS2960.5 f.40)

5 Doune Gardens
Glasgow NW
4 July 1967

Dear Chris,
Many thanks for your letter about *Void*.[1] I'm sorry for the delay in replying, but it never rains without pouring, and I had to go up to Aberdeen last week to see my mother, who had been taken back into hospital with a suspected thrombosis. However, I'm glad to say that the diagnosis has been more favourable – poor circulation due to anaemia.

I agree with you entirely about 'Whuchulls'[2] and 'By Wauchopeside', and go most of the way towards agreeing on 'Depth and the Chthonian Image', which I read again recently while working on the *A Lap of Honour* proofs.[3] The trouble about writing brief survey articles like the one in *Void* is that in order to cover the ground at all one has to wear seven-league boots and make large general statements to which there are bound to be individual exceptions. Perhaps I assumed too easily that your reason for turning from Scots to English in the mid-Thirties was dissatisfaction with the former as a language for intellectual discourse. I was led on to making this assumption by my view that some of the more abstruse poems in *Scots Unbound* weren't entirely satisfactory; but if general critical opinion shows that I'm in error, I shan't really be displeased.

Naturally I'm delighted that you approve of the article as a whole. My own view is that the passages in praise of your work tend towards understatement rather than towards flattery. How can one possibly flatter the closest approximation to perfection that imperfect humanity can make? It's a distinction to share the same century with you.

The production of *Right Royal* at Perth now seems quite definite – it's to be the first play of a new season of Scottish drama, which is to include a version of Grassic Gibbon's *Sunset Song* made by Ian Munro. Distinguished company.

I was able to send Duncan Glen the typescript of my new verse collection last week. Provisionally it's called 'Hairst', but perhaps that's a title that claims too much.[4] Anyhow, he has written back in the most complimentary terms, and intends to publish it once his other projects, already advertised, are off his hands.

Recently I've been involved in negotiations to launch a new Scottish arts review with Arts Council backing, and as a result of sticking my neck out for 'Renaissance' writing I've managed to get Robert Garioch appointed to the editorial group. If all goes well, the first issue ought to be out in the spring.[5] I hope I'm not being too subjective in feeling that just at present there's a moving-forward spirit about, after a long period of stagnation.

Love to the Valda, and all good wishes to you.

As ever,

Alex.

---

[1] *Void*, edited by Ewan Scott, Alexander Scott's younger son, and fellow-students at Sussex University, appeared on only one occasion, April 1967.

[2] *C.P.* II, pp. 1087-1093.

[3] London:MacGibbon & Kee, 1967.

[4] The collection, provisionally called 'Hairst', was published as *Cantrips* (1968).

[5] Alex Scott refers here to the formation of *Scottish International*; Robert Garioch became an editorial adviser. The first issue was published in January 1968 and it ran until March 1974 in varying formats and frequency.

52. *From Ted Hughes (EUL MS2963 f.33)*

Court Green
North Taunton
Devon
21 July 1967

Dear Mr MacDiarmid,

Thank you for coming to the Festival. I hope you enjoyed it and thought it was worth it.[1]

I'd have liked to talk to you in a leisurely way, but I met nobody at that Festival for more than 5 minutes – distracted minutes too.

If I'm in Edinburgh, as I hope to be, this next year, I'll ask your permission to call on you.

All the best meanwhile, and to your wife,

sincerely,

Ted Hughes.

[1] Hughes refers here to MacDiarmid's readings at Poetry International 1967 in the Purcell Room and Queen Elizabeth Hall, Southbank, on 14 and 16 July respectively.

53. *From Barbara Niven (EUL MS2957)*

Wednesday 9 August [1967]

My dear Chris,

It's strange to be greeting your triumphant 75th birthday from this distance but even as I say it I realise that it's no distance at all.

What I am acutely aware of as it comes is a microscope's view, sharp as that, of what you have given to me, among the thousands of lives you have changed and opened doors and grasps for. It's like a time I've suddenly remembered in the War when the Germans were bombing Manchester throughout a night and I was in the small house where [I] was living and when sizes were reversed and instead of feeling small with the immensity of the sky and the noise I became large, an undefeatable centre of life, not just rejecting fear but revelling in my possession. That is how I feel when I think now of you and your birthday, I can only think of it through the centre of myself, it insists upon concentrating into that small space.

That is because you have given me so immeasurably much and because my love for you, which Valda and Ern have understood with such generosity as a necessity of my life, is really a recognition – within my own capacity – of what you are and what you mean for life and for penetration of the future.

How wonderful to be able to say happy birthday, Chris, with the whole of one's being.

Barbara.

54. From Donald Bain (EUL MS2948.2 f.14)

49 Hillhouse Street
Glasgow N1
10 August 1967

Dear Chris,
My sincere congratulations to you achieving seventy-five.
The pressures, misunderstanding apathy bigotry.
Not least the means to maintain life.
Hoping you will have tranquillity
to enjoy life your own way,
satisfaction of creative works
truly appreciated,
more years of contemplation for a dedicated artist.

With best wishes.
Yours Aye,
Donald Bain.

55. From R. S. Thomas (EUL MS2966)

Aberdavon Vicarage
Pwllheli
Caerns
13 August 1967

Dear Hugh MacDiarmid,
It was good of you to write. I expect Dr Beattie[1] explained that owing to my recent move here, I was unable to visit your exhibition as originally arranged. Months of removing, and general settling in have successfully banished the Muse. I don't know whether it will condescend to return. This is a good place with relics of long habitation, but with an infestation of English visitors at present. There was no need to thank for the preface.[2] You are one of the poets I re-read, which is the only criterion of poetry.
   Yn gywir iawn,[3]
   R. S. Thomas.

---

[1]   Librarian of the National Library of Scotland.
[2]   R. S. Thomas wrote the preface to the catalogue of the Exhibition at the National Library of Scotland from 3 July – end September 1967.
[3]   yours very sincerely.

56. From Willa Muir (NLS MS27148 ff.88-90)

47A Paultons Square
Chelsea
London, SW3
September 13 (I *think*) [1967]

My dear Christopher,

Very many thanks for your letter, and for telling me you won't object to my stories about you. But I *have* made three small corrections because of what you told me: I have scored out the hypothetical £400 in your pocket when you came to lift the Coronation Stone: I have changed your vendetta with Edwin, which I had called 'personal', into a 'literary' vendetta, and I can't remember at the moment what the third point was that you made and that I have corrected. I do remember you vividly, which in itself is an affectionate compliment. But I never said you and Peggy *quarrelled* over the farmers' whisky, and I carefully said you didn't drink much, but that a little whisky overset you – which I think was true at that time. O my dear Chris, what I have missed out!! For instance, your taking out your new false teeth and shoving them up on the mantelpiece, saying: 'I canna be doing wi' thae things!' I have a lot of memories of you.

I want to tell you something about Peggy which I have kept to myself till now. After Edwin died she suddenly rang me up from Walmer. She sounded tearful, but as I was tearful too that didn't surprise me. What did distress me was that she went on to ask if I would *let* her come to see me, and not turn her from my door. That was terrible. I urged very strongly that she should come and that I should be glad to see her and that she could stay for some nights if she liked. Here she became incoherent, even maudlin, so that I suspected she was drunk, but she promised to come. She did not come. As she had given me her address I wrote to her, asking her again to come, but she did not answer. That was the last I heard of her. Now that you tell me that she had become an alcoholic I can understand the incident: what an unhappy finish for a pretty and intelligent girl. Yes, I did hear of her death – I forget who told me. (I have always regretted that she did not turn up.)

You see, Christopher, when I have once liked people I go on having a 'tendre' for them, and whatever -isms they use to live by don't matter to me. Some wit, I forget who, said that all -*is*ms sooner or later become *was*-ims, and I think so too. The atmospheric envelope around this planet is filled with impalpable, invisible, inaudible radiations that make our climates of belief; we contribute to them daily and are daily affected by them usually without knowing it, and the fighting -isms seem to be relatively superficial. This may be a peculiarly feminine attitude, which you won't appreciate, since you enjoy the fighting, but it's the way I am made and I can't help it. In the same way I shared only some of Edwin's beliefs: what he called the Fable I called the Unconscious: he knew very well that I did not believe in personal immortality, for instance, but that made no difference to our relationship, because we loved each other *as we were*. He was religious in a much wider sense than orthodox Christianity – to call him a Christian poet, in the Church sense of the word, is to confine his flow of wine to an inadequate pint pot. You and he probably had more in common at a deeper – or higher – level than you think.

About Gavin[1] – he's on the up and up. He and his wife are living in Ely: she's been made the Matron of an Ely maternity home, and he's lecturing on maths and physics in Huntingdon Technical College, where he seems to be much beloved. His address is 'Verona', St John's Road, Ely, Cambs. They are living in luxury – I mean, oil central heating and all that; but they have no children, only two cats called Caesar and Hamlet. Apparently I shall never be a grandparent, unlike you. Gavin has got a newfangled hearing-aid, almost invisible, without any dangling cord, and has gained in confidence. He is now learning to drive their car. And he has got himself an A.R.C.M. – quite a feat for a deaf man. I am not worried about him now. Well, that's plenty for today.

Yours, as aye,
Willa.

---

[1]   Son of Willa and Edwin Muir.

57. From Anthony Ross (EUL)

SCOTTISH INTERNATIONAL
Review Incorporating FEEDBACK

20 September 1967

Dear Dr Grieve,

I would very much like to see you and discuss this new magazine which is to appear in January with support from the Scottish Arts Council, Scottish Television, and The Saltire Society. Its title expresses an idea which you have long represented, and when you have more information about what is aimed at we hope you will honour us by becoming one of the five Trustees who will act as intermediary for the Arts Council and the Review. We are asking Alex Gibson of the SNO to become a fifth and think of resting there.[1]

Your visit to Hungary went well, I hope. It was good to see you in such form on television. I saw only a few minutes of one of the programmes – but good.

As regards meeting, I could come down to Biggar if you prefer. And also could bring Robert Tait with me.

One thing more – which to me is very important about this venture. It is giving an opportunity to the under-Thirties especially. The role in which I see us older people is one of support with criticism of course, and essentially encouraging.

With all good wishes.

Yours ever,

Anthony Ross O.P.

1   Neither MacDiarmid nor Alexander Gibson became a Director. MacDiarmid explained the reasons in 'Greeks Bearing Gifts', in the first issue of *Catalyst* (December 1967), p.6.

58. *From Iain Crichton Smith (EUL MS2960.14 f.12)*

42 Crombie St
Oban
Wednesday [1967]

Dear Christopher Grieve,

I take it as a very great compliment that you should have written me such a long letter knowing how busy you are. And, in fact, I have often thought of writing to you before but was too diffident and too shy. What I would have said if I had written to you was simply that I, like so many others, consider you a very great poet indeed, that you have opened avenues of experience and light that we ourselves hadn't seen, that I admire you for your unremitting devotion to your art in spite of the difficulties it must have caused you and that in comparison with you I feel remarkably trivial.

My essay on you is a personal reaction to your poetry and I hope that you don't think that anything I have said detracts or seems to detract in any way from my opinion of you as by far the best Scottish poet of this century and one of the major poets of this century. I have, I hope, made my view of you clear in the essay, such as it is.[1]

With regard to what I said in it, I believe that your lyrics are your finest achievement. I agree that you would have to go on. One cannot write lyrics forever and I said that with a mind like yours you were bound to go on. Nevertheless I still believe that your lyrics are your finest achievement. Let me be quite clear about this: I'll put it this way. I can imagine how many of your other poems came to be written. I cannot imagine how some of your lyrics were written. They seem to me to be, if you will forgive the word, pure inspiration, imaginative through and through. Again, let me put it this way: if I were to pick from your poems the ones that I myself (had I the talent) would prefer to have written I would choose ones like 'The Watergaw' and 'The Bonnie Broukit Bairn'. As I said in my essay I do not know anywhere of poems like these. They have what I was forced to call a hallucinatory quality, visionary and human at the same time.

I don't usually write defences of what I write (the little that I do write) but I write this to make you believe, if you did not do so before, that my admiration for your work is no lower than that of any other man, that I say this not out of any flattery but after due consideration and reading over many, many years, and that I would want you to appreciate this. For you and Sorley MacLean of this century my admiration and allegiance are total.

Yours sincerely, and with many thanks for your letter.
Iain C. Smith.

PS May I also send you at this time my best wishes for your birthday and may you have many more!

---

1 Iain Crichton Smith's *The Golden Lyric: An Essay on the Poetry of Hugh MacDiarmid* was published by Akros Publications in Preston in 1967.

59. From Arno Reinfrank (EUL Gen.2094/5/1899)

45 Goldhurst Terrace
London NW6
1 January 1968

Dear Hugh MacDiarmid,
I wish you 'well over the flu'!

This is splendid news that you plan to come to London on 12th January. I'll be pleased to see you wherever you wish but invite you, also on my wife's behalf, with your good wife and any friends to come for Lunch or Supper to our place.

With regards to the quotation from your contract with MacLellan's I feel that I have to inform all the Accounts Departments concerned to send their fee to the publishers directly who'll have to settle accounts with you. But this, I want to talk over with you when you're here.

I'll be away in Paris from 4th until 10th/11th January. If it's not too much trouble please phone us any evening after your arrival in Golders Green which is only an 8d bus ride away from my place.

I'm really sorry that Volk and Welt's selection turned out unsatisfactory.[1] However, it may be better than nothing at all and I won't mention it when writing to them *re* the list. Your poetry stands for coming centuries and it won't be the last selection published in the GDR! Since I know that you had to put up with much more serious silliness during your lifetime, I am sure that you'll just grin and bear it. What else could one do?

The thought that we soon can meet makes me really happy!
Yours sincerely,
Arno Reinfrank.

---

1 The selection published by Volk and Welt Verlag was *Ein Wind Sprang Auf*, translated by Heinz Kahlau and Günter Kunert, with an afterword by Hans Petersen (Berlin, January, 1968).

60. *From Vladimir Serafimovich Vakhrushev (EUL Gen.2094/5 2350a&b)*

URSS
Saratov region
Balashov
Marxa 67
28 Vakhrushev VS
22 March 1968

Dear Mr MacDiarmid,

I am a teacher of foreign literatures (mainly French, English, American, German and Italian plus Cervantes and Lope de Vega, etc) at a small pedagogical institute, the town of Balashov. It is situated 200km from Saratov, a big Volga city. Our river is ХОПЁР,[1] a tribute of the Don. Sholokov often goes fishing up this river. Reading modern English literature I came across your verses some years ago. The Scottish language is very difficult for me! I've never seen a text-book of Scottish. Still I read something: R. Burns, W. Scott's novels (only a few), Naomi Mitchison's historical novels, etc. I wrote an essay, 'The Image of Lenin in English poetry of the 30s', where your two Hymns to Lenin and 'Seamless Garment' are the main object of my study. Now I send you this essay in a separate envelope.[2] If you read Russian (as I think you do), will you be so kind as to give me your opinion on my views?

Recently I read *The Company I've Kept*. A very curious book! By the way, I was born in the Kirov (former Vjatka) region and in Kirov (it is a big city now) we have MacLean Street. Only in Russian one says УЛИЦА МАКЛИНА,[3] it sounds just like a Russian family-name, so MacLean is a Russian in Kirov. Only a few know he was a Scottish Communist.

As for your poetry, I say, first of all, that it is but very poorly known in the Soviet Union (see page 72 of the reprint of my essay) whereas it is of great interest to us because MacDiarmid is keenly interested in Russian culture. Hence his many translations of Pushkin,[4] Tjutchev,[5] Blok,[6] references to Dostoevsky, etc. At first this interest was connected with the romantic quest for a salvation-hero, a new Christ who would save the Scottish people from degradation (parallel with Dostoevskian notion of НАРОД БОГОНОСЕЦ,[7] 'the God-bearing people'). Then in the 20s[8] comes a Soviet theme. 'Etika preobrazhennavo Erosa'[9] is, evidently, a phrase from A.M. КОЛЛОНТАИ [Kollontai] [10] writings (I've not read her books, but I know that she advocated a new free sex social relations moral, something like ДОРОГУ КРЫЛАТОМУ ЭРОСУ (room for a winged Eros!) etc.

Then I point out that to me Lenin's image in MacDiarmid's poetry seems to be a core of the poet's inner contradictions caused by the alienation effects. The essence of this contradiction is: accepting wholly Lenin's political creed, the poet cannot (though he strives, at least, on the conscious level) reconcile with this creed his own inner understanding of what art means to him. And this cleavage is caused by the immense gulf between working people and intelligentsia in the bourgeois society. The poet is already on the highest peaks of culture, but the common reader does not understand him. He longs for a swifter victory of the workers' cause, but the Scottish and Eng. proletariat is very far from beginning a Socialist revolution. Etc. etc.

Then I begin to analyze 'The Skeleton of the Future',[11] 'Etika ... Erosa', two Hymns. I say, e.g., that admiring Lenin does not make the poet to accept dogmatically his ideas (and that was alas! the way many English Marxists took especially in the 30s – as I point out at the beginning of my essay). Then I speak on the comparison of Lenin's image with the figure of Christ, etc. (it is very bad that the editor of the magazine wiped out what I say on how Lenin is compared with Rilke). At the end I disagree with the final thoughts of your 2nd Hymn ('Ah, Lenin, politics is bairns' play / To what this [the poetry] maun be!') I say that this doesn't correspond with the above statements of the poem and is not true generally.

Yours sincerely
Vladmir Vakhrushev.

[1] Hoper (979km long).
[2] Vakhrushev's article 'Stikhi o Lenine Mak-Daiarmide' was published in *Nauchnye Dokledy Vysshei Shkoly*, 5, pp.68-79, 1967.
[3] Ulitsa Makleena.
[4] Alexander Pushkin (1799-1839).
[5] Fyodor Tjutchev (1803-1873) was the last of the great Romantic poets of Russia, following Alexander Pushkin, and Mikhail Lermontov.
[6] Alexander Blok (1880-1921).
[7] Narodbogonosets.
[8] 1930s.
[9] *C.P.* I, pp. 407-411. In a note to the title MacDiarmid gives the meaning as 'Ethics of the Transfigured Eros'. (In 'Author's Note' to 'Mature Art', March 1938, NLS Acc. 12074/1, ff. 9-13[13].) But in a letter to Hamish Henderson, 12 July 1951, Hugh MacDiarmid defined 'etika preobrazhennavo erosa' as 'the ethics of brotherly love', adding 'but the phrase has a religious overlay, the basis of the brotherliness being a presumed Heavenly Father'. (EUL E84/67). Neither of these definitions matches the meaning of the poem. Vakhrushev considers that the phrase comes from A. M. Kollontai.

However, in his article 'Forms of Culture in Hugh MacDiarmid's "Etika Preobrazhennavo Erosa" in *International Journal of Scottish Literature,* Michael Whitworth writes, ' "Etika Preobrazhennago Erosa" was a work by the exiled Russian philospher Boris Petrovich Vysheslavtzev (1877-1954), published in Paris in 1931. It is almost certain that MacDiarmid knew of the work only through an article by Nathalie Duddington that appeared in *The New Atlantis* in January 1934 [...]. In Duddington's review the second word of Vysheslavtzev's title is mistakenly given as 'preobrazhennavo' and MacDiarmid followed her error . Duddington's translation of the title was "Ethics of the Transfigured Eros"; Vysheslavtzev's philosophy, or Duddington's account of it, is relevant primarily to the poem's references to spiritual aspiration and the sublimation of the self in a larger force.' (Pp. 1-18 [3], issue 5, Autumn/ Winter, 2009, www.ijsl.stir.ac.uk).
[10] Alexsandra Mikhailovna Kollontai (1872-1952) was one of the most popular Bolshevik leaders and made Commissar of Social Welfare in the first Soviet Government. She later became an Oppositionist and was given Ambassadorial posts, first in Norway (1922) and, later, in Sweden and Mexico.
[11] *C.P.* I, p. 386.

61. From W. A. S. Keir (EUL MS2951.11 f.14)

4 Marine Terrace
Aberdeen
15 April 1968

Dear Chris,

I have been asked by Secker & Warburg to do a kind of memorial volume of Burns Singer's poems and prose.[1] It is rather an embarrassing assignment as G.S. Fraser was asked first and did a very good editing job but they feel he was out of sympathy with him both as a poet and critic and as a human being, so I am expected to take over. So somehow I will have to attempt a personal memoir to please all parties, especially his widow, and my own conscience – by no means easy. I can, however, cope with the poetry section, and also with the criticism as a whole (there is a surprising amount from the *T.L.S.*) But in this section his essay from *Encounter* on you, 'Scarlet Eminence', will take pride of place, and here I would be very glad of your own comments on it if you could be bothered.[2] I myself thought it first class, but I seem to remember that apart from the title and some factual errors at the beginning you had reservations, though my memory may be letting me down here. Anyway I would be very glad of any comments you care to make about this article or about Jimmie Singer in general – and you will, of course, be paid for anything you wish to write. (They seem at the moment to be over-generous if anything).

I am glad to read in the papers that you are about it and about – I had heard earlier that you had been ill, but that is a couple of months ago. Also I passed Tom Crawford[3] in the corridor in King's this morning as I was dashing to a lecture and he had just time to say he had seen you with Middleton,[4] whom I liked very much. He didn't take long to sum up the academics at a conference here. He saw them like insects sending out feelers or antennae measuring their colleagues, where to attack, where to submit, where to wound, where to placate. So I have watched them for years.

Warm regards to Valda and to you from us both.

Yours sincerely,

Walter (A.S. Keir).

P.S. If you don't want to write anything about the *Encounter* article – a very short comment would do – even an indication if you thought he was on the right (or wrong) lines would help. Also if you haven't a copy I could lend you mine.

---

[1] Keir edited *The Collected Poems of Burns Singer* (London: Secker & Warburg, 1970) for which MacDiarmid wrote the preface. Keir wrote an introduction, pp. xix-xlvii.

[2] Burns Singer, 'Scarlet Eminence', *Encounter,* vol. viii, no. 3, (March 1951), pp. 49-62.

[3] Tom Crawford (b. 1920) Aberdeen University scholar of Scottish literature.

[4] O. E. D. Middleton, New Zealand writer, short stories mainly.

62. From Tom Scott (EUL MS2960.6 f.103)

59 The Promenade
Edinburgh 15
18 April 1968

Dear Chris,

Many thanks for your note. It is indeed a relief to have a three-year breather, for the history gets more and more demanding,[1] and nothing distracts like money-grubbing – and there are my other projects.

We're still up to the eyes here, with painters in, Heather[2] working like a Trojan herself, yet we still pick our way among the boxes. When we're settled you must come here[+] for a pow-wow as you say: actually we're nearer as the crow flies, though of course we ain't no crows.

Now that you are the chief of 1320 Club (of which I am a member), it occurs to me that efforts ought to be made to reprint C. H. Douglas's *Plan for Scotland*,[3] and to re-examine his whole theory of social credit. Clearly this is the real crux of our time – the hand that controls the issue of credit rules the world. Marx was culpably silent on the biggest issue of all. Not only social democracy but even communism can be hamstrung by the bloody usurers, and all attention shd be directed at them and their villainous activities.

I enclose my latest effusion.

Aye
Tom

[+]We overlook the Firth – yesterday a pair of fulmars inspected us for a nesting site!

[1] Scott refers here to his history of Scottish Literature which remains unpublished.
[2] His wife.
[3] This may refer to *Reconstruction*, the Glasgow *Evening Times* articles of 6, 13 and 27 May 1932 on Social Credit by Major C. H. Douglas, reprinted by K.R.P. Publications Liverpool, 1943, or to a previous article in the same paper by Major Douglas, 11 March 1932, which was headlined, 'Social-Credit Scheme for Scotland/ National Dividend of £300 per Family/Major Douglas presents his plan.'

63. From Ella Saurat (EUL Gen.2094/5/2019)

13 Bolton Gdns
London SW5
30 April 1968

My dear Hugh

What joy I had in reading your book – 'The Company I have Kept'. I found this highly analytical book quite by chance. What generous and prophetic words you find about Denis and all the great members of the inspired group of yesterday and today – I felt so close to your way of thinking when you said about 'no use for the latter occult religious vein of my husband'. If only we had remained here instead of mixing with pseudo-rich Catholic folk in Nice. What a charming photo of you in your front garden in the 'Times Literary Supplement' of 8. March with long article. Shall we ever meet again? I go to London P.E.N. often also to Avignon to help found the Provençal P.E.N. two years ago

With my greetings

Ella Saurat

64. From T. W. Atkinson (NLS Acc.7361/39)

Cornell Modern Indonesia Project
Department of Asian Studies
Cornell University
Ithaca
New York 14850
29 June 1968

Dear Dr Grieve,

I have again been reading, with great emotion, you're *The Company I've Kept*. As a (temporarily) expatriate Scot, I have again been deeply moved by the passion of your writing and your love of our country and nation.

However, my intention in writing to you is not merely to express my thanks for your books and your poetry. Indeed, the only way in which anyone can thank you for your work is by getting up and marching!

There is one particular question to which, if you will, I would like a reply. On page 127 of my edition of *The Company I've Kept*, you refer to 'John Murdoch (the crofters' leader – MacLean's agrarian counterpart)'. I personally have no knowledge of John Murdoch, and I can find no reference to him in our very extensive library here. Could you please give me a clue about him? Where did he live, and when? Did he write, and is there any writing about him?[1]

I am interested because, purely on the basis of your passing reference to him, it would seem that he should be better known, and that he will have relevant lessons for Scotland today. I have it in mind that a biography might be a worthwhile effort.

My own home is in Ardnamurchan, and I shall return there. From 1945 to 1961 I was an adviser to the Republic of Indonesia, and saw that crippled nation lifting itself from the degradation of colonial exploitation to an honoured and influential place among the free nations of the world. In 1965, a fearful reaction struck, and, mounting over the bodies of not less than one million men, women and children, there is now a militarist fascism in power there, lining up meekly for the handouts of surplus western production and capital.[2] As an academic I cannot say these things bluntly to my students, but I am saying them soon in a book. That will possibly be the end of my academic career.

The link between the silent slaughter in Indonesia and John Murdoch is in fact quite close. Basic to the Indonesian massacre was the demand of the peasants for land reform. They demanded land and they received death, and their children died, too.

I would, then, be very grateful for any scrap of information you can give me on John Murdoch. This will place me even more in your debt, but we all owe you much even now, for the pleasure – and great pain – evoked by your poetry.

I have tried to think of a way of remitting at least return postage to you. Perhaps this attached Kennedy 50c piece will do. They are quite rare, and it is said that they will become valuable.

With great respect,

Sincerely,

Tom Atkinson.

[1]   John Murdoch (1818-1903) was born in Ardclach, near Nairn and brought up in Islay. He was an Inland Revenue officer in Dublin where he was involved in Irish nationalist politics. He retired to Inverness and founded *The Highlander* newspaper (1873-1881) to promote the crofters' cause during the Land Agitation. The Mitchell Library, Glasgow, holds his unfinished autobiography in five notebooks.

[2]   The reference is to the coup led by General Suharto and to the massacres of Communists, Communist suspects and peasants which followed.

65. From Duncan Glen (EUL MS2948.9 f.89)

14 Parklands Avenue
Penwortham
Preston
Lancashire
6 July 1968

Dear Chris Grieve,

I have been trying to find a moment to write to you for about a month or more. Originally it was to let you know that James Annand[1] had offered to bring you sheets of *Early Lyrics* [2] for signing but of course all that is long past and more recently I have wanted to thank you for your very kind inscription in the copy you signed for me. *Early Lyrics* has been (and is) a big success, I've had a lot of enquiries and some of the shops have been buying two dozen. I sent out about a thousand of a 'catalogue' I've had printed as well as a card for *Early Lyrics* and this has been a big success in getting orders. Alex Scott's excellent piece in *The Scots Independent* no doubt also helped.[3] James Annand has told you about Maurice Lindsay. I am the man in the middle but quite enjoy the situation. I have also been the man in the middle between Alex Scott and Tom Scott. As you will know they are at each other's throats and I get both sides of the 'case'. I've been quoting 'The Jolly Beggars' to them but they can fight it out if they want to. I don't like lawyers being brought in.

I thought Alex Scott's piece in *The Scots Independent* well done. I remember thinking too when James first sent me his essay that you were the conscience of all of us who were attempting to do anything for Scottish literature. I know that applies to me although living up to your standards means also showing the good 'MacDiarmid' characteristic of being 'mysel' and oorsels.

No doubt Alex will send you a copy of his *Cantrips* but as its publisher I'd like also to send you a copy and enclose it with my kindest regards although I'll not write that on it as you may want to use it yourself if Alex sends you a copy.

I'm introducing Scots prose into *Akros* [4] when I can give people enough courage to try their hand at it. The December issue is a translation number with a new translation of 'The Praise of Ben Dorain' by Iain Crichton Smith as the main poetry item.[5] If you could spare time to give me a piece on either a Gaelic poet or poetry or on some aspect of poetry translation I would be very pleased to have it although I should not create work for you as I expect you have more than enough already.[6] I'm planning the March 1969 issue[7] as an all-Scots number including the prose but I'm trying to introduce Scots prose into all issues.

With kindest regards as always,
Duncan.

[1] James K. Annand (1908-1993), teacher and poet.
[2] *Hugh MacDiarmid : Early lyrics* with a memoir of George Ogilvie by Hugh MacDiarmid, edited with an introduction by J. K. Annand, was published in Preston on 1 June, 1968.
[3] 1 June 1968.
[4] Duncan Glen edited 51 issues of *Akros* from 1965 to 1983. 'Adsum' contributed Scots prose to Number 9 (January 1969) and Number 10 (May 1969). The editor and 'Carrubers Close' also wrote in Scots in Number 10.
[5] The issue was Number 9 (January 1969).
[6] MacDiarmid did not contribute to this issue.
[7] Number 10.

66. From Gaye Poulton (EUL MS2967)

23 August 1968

Dear Mr MacDiarmid,
I am writing just to let you know that, on behalf of Glyn Jones, we are giving permission to The Bodley Head to reprint 'Perfect' in an anthology of poetry they are preparing for publication next spring and we are asking for the following note to be included:

'These lines (with the exception of the first) appear in the short story by Glyn Jones, "Porth-y-Rhyd", from his collection of short stories, *The Blue Bed*, published by Jonathan Cape. They have been rearranged by Hugh MacDiarmid to make the above poem which he has called "Perfect" and are reprinted here by permission of Glyn Jones and Jonathan Cape Limited.'

Yours sincerely,
Gaye Poulton.
Permissions.

67. From Iain Crichton Smith (EUL MS2960.14 ff.1-5)

42 Crombie St
Oban
Argyll
5 November 1968

Dear Christopher Grieve,

Thank you for your detailed and interesting letter, & also for the enclosed essay by Mr Weston which I now return.[1] On the whole, it seems to me to be an explication of the poem, rather than a creatively critical article though within its limits it's very sound and it sticks very closely to the text.

I have written about four or five pages on 'The Drunk Man'. I see it quite clearly as facing the following problem: To select is to be untrue to life. Not to select is to face the possibility of extinction. The attack on the bourgeoisie, as I see it, is related to the fact that the bourgeoisie have made a selection out of the possibilities of life which is too attenuated. The poet must remain open to all possible experiences but in doing this his psyche is bombarded by forces of such intensity as might / would destroy him. I find it extremely interesting that you should compare this to a 'psychedelic trip' because on a certain level I believe this to be true, but the problem raised is a crucial one. Logically, it is a paradox. In living, it can only be lived through. That is why I consider this poem to be 'existential' and comparisons between it and other poems aesthetically seem to me to be irrelevant. I am *not* sure about the ending, but the rest of it I think I follow (to say one 'understands' it is a compliment to the power of the mind which the poem seems to me to undermine.) I would also imagine (as you say) that it would be practically impossible to write another poem of this intensity for the reasons you have given since I feel that it is not an argumentative poem: it is a poem on which the poet's life is staked. It is not (in my opinion) like 'The Waste Land' which is more distanced and 'aesthetic' and less raw. By saying that I am of course saying that it is closer to life than Eliot's poem is.

I hadn't realised how involved you were in various tasks when you wrote this poem, but it is highly probable that if you hadn't been involved in such tasks the poem would have lacked the necessary tension.

I am interested above all in how much you manage to do with simple properties – the thistle, moonlight and the drunk man. And another thing which interests me is the question posed by the drunk man as to whether the thistle is in 'reality' outside, or whether he himself is the thistle. I was wondering whether this kind of formulation had something to do with Einstein's relativity and how far, if at all, you would have been conscious of such a thing at that time. I notice too that you refer to Rilke in one or two sections (not in this poem, I think in the next one) and as far as I understand Rilke he was interested in the internalisation of what lay outside.

However, I do *not* wish to be 'aesthetic' about this poem, since I feel that whole approach is wrong.

In any case, I was going to do a number of essays which would include one on *Confessions of a Justified Sinner* (a work of the highest genius in my opinion),[2] R. L.

Stevenson (all his work), something on yourself, something on Edwin Muir, M{c}Caig, Bruce, some modern Scottish novels, Modern Gaelic poetry, & *The House with the Green Shutters*[3] (i.e. to say, important Scottish work.)

Thank you very much for your most helpful letter and the essay which I herewith return.

Yours sincerely,

Iain C. Smith.

[1] Crichton Smith appears to refer here to a typescript of the essay published as *Hugh MacDiarmid's A Drunk Man Looks at the Thistle* by John C. Weston (Preston, 1970).

[2] James Hogg, *The Private Memoirs and Confessions of a Justified Sinner* was first published anonymously in Edinburgh in 1824.

[3] George Douglas Brown, *The House with the Green Shutters*, (London, 1901).

68. From Roderick Watson (EUL Gen.2094/6/2394a-c)

63 Glisson Road
Cambridge
24 June 1969

Dear C. M. Grieve,

I was glad to see you in Cambridge, for that talk to the English Club, – and I think that the evening went down well with the undergraduates. I had wondered earlier just how many of them would be in any kind of sympathy with your work. The growing influence of modern American poetry from Pound to Carlos Williams and along that line seems to have given another perspective to students here, and thus encouraged a more critical attitude to 'English' poetry than one might expect. Which *must* be good.

I'm writing in the hope that you can help me in connection with a study I've done of your first published book – *Annals of the Five Senses*. I hope that this doesn't cause you too much trouble. There are three main points that concern me.

1. Mr W. R. Aitken has noted that *Annals* was listed in the *English Catalogue* for 1921, as an edition published by Foulis of Edinburgh. Clearly, this must have fallen through, and the book finally published at Montrose in 1923. But am I right in assuming that this means that the MS for *Annals* must have been ready by 1921? – or at least part of it?

2. I have taken it that the prose passages in *Annals* are essentially a series of studies and experiments in the nature of your own sensibility, projected upon the various characters. The book remains, of course, the experimental work of a young writer, but I believe that despite this, and the 'mosaic' of quotations you use, the sensibility that invests the studies is very close to you, and to much of your later poetry (although it would appear in different guises).

Perhaps you could throw some light on how you regarded *Annals*. Am I right in giving some importance to the book for its first part in the development of your sensibility as a poet, and to your level of involvement with it at the time? And how do you see it now?

3. Had you read Gregory Smith's book *Scottish Literature: Character and Influence* (pub. 1919) when you were writing *Annals*, and, if so, were you aware of being much influenced by his analysis of the Scottish psychology in your treatment of the characters in the *Annals*, or did these come from your own interests at the time?

I would be very greatful if you could answer some of these questions. But I understand, of course, that your time (if not patience) for such matters must be limited. Also, the circumstances of the composition of *Annals* are a while off now.

I had dinner with Marie Singer[1] the other month, by the way, after meeting her for the first time at the evening she arranged at her house when you were in Cambridge. I hadn't known that she was here until then. She does a great chicken with red peppers!

Thank you.

Yours sincerely,

Rory Watson.

PS I've enclosed a s.a.e. since all this is by way of a professional enquiry from me – but please answer at your convenience only, or use the stamp for something else!

[1]   Widow of Burns Singer.

69. From Hamish Henderson (EUL MS2951.3 ff.69-71)

As from University of Edinburgh
27 George Square
Edinburgh 8
[Bavaria, Germany]

Dear Chris,

As you may recall, I told you in the Traverse last year that I've been working on an essay – or rather a series of essays[1] – which attempts to survey your later poetry through the eyes (so to speak) of the people who have contributed to it, e.g., Gramsci,[2] Karl Kraus,[3] etc.

I have often wondered if you know (or have guessed?) who wrote the unsigned article in the TLS ('Satirist in the Modern World', 8 May 1953) which you turned into a poem in *In Memoriam James Joyce*?[4]

There are two reasons why, continuing to work on one of these essays in the quiet of the Bavarian countryside, I've suddenly decided to ask you this direct question. The first is just natural curiosity, which you may feel like satisfying, or not, just as you wish. The second, however, springs from an extensive reading – and re-reading – of Karl Kraus himself, which I've undertaken in connection with this work. I don't know how familiar you are with Kraus's own work; not very familiar, I imagine, because of the paucity of translations. Much of his best work has to be sought out, in the pages of *Die Fackel* [5] and other magazines. But it is really astounding at how many points the life and work of Karl Kraus touch the life and work of Hugh MacDiarmid.

It would take a longish letter to do anything like justice to this theme; however, here are a few general headings: attitudes to religion, politics and the state; overmastering interest in linguistics and the power of the word; assaults on a philistine late-capitalist society; neglect (sometimes total) by the press, even when his name was put forward by Sorbonne professors for the Nobel Prize; sharp-edged polemics; his poetry.

Here is one incident, which ties up with the general line of my essay 'Alias MacAlias' in the last *Scottish International*.[6] When Brecht's *Die Dreigroschenoper*[7] was staged in Berlin, the dramatic critic Alfred Kerr[8] accused Brecht of plagiarism, because he had used twenty-five lines of a Villon ballade,[9] and had credited the poet but not the German translator. Karl Kraus leapt to the defence of Brecht, saying (in *Die Fackel*) that Brecht had more originality in the little finger of the hand which had lifted twenty-five lines of Ammer's translation of Villon than Kerr (the critic) had in his whole body ... He then carried the war into the enemy's camp by recalling that during World War One this same Alfred Kerr had published a lot of drum-thumping chauvinistic rhymes under the pseudonym 'Gottlieb', and added 'Kerr has had worse luck than Brecht, in that it has never occurred to anyone to reveal that he *didn't* write the rhymes signed 'Gottlieb'.

There is even a parallel to your own early flirting with Catholicism, for Karl Kraus was actually received into the Catholic Church in 1911, although he left it again a few years later.

For me, the most interesting thing about Kraus is his championship of spoken poetry; he was an early wave in the carrying stream which has given poetry back to the spoken (and sung) word in the last three decades. As Paul Schick[10] has pointed out, 'His readings influenced his own creative work [...]. The unity of word, sound and content explains the enormous effectiveness of his language – an effectiveness which even his enemies could not call in question'.

The main difference between Karl Kraus and Chris Grieve resides in the languages with which they have had to cope. Chris Grieve has operated, in the main, through the English language, that great estuary on which so many craft can ride, although, of course, he also did his famous salmon-leap upstream in the Lallans peat-burn. Karl Kraus, on the other hand, had to deal with the German language, that extraordinary mixture of the angelic and the diabolic; the language, which, more than any other I know, seems to have taken off, and to have enjoyed a separate existence over and above the life and tradition which brought it into being. His lifelong struggle with this sinuous word-monster invites comparison with your own half-century long 'Ringkampf'[11] with intractable Scottish philistinism.

Best wishes to Valda.

Yours aye,

Hamish.

---

1   These essays never appeared. The material was used in a paper given by Henderson at the MacDiarmid Symposium in 1972, and also in his article, 'The Langholm Byspale', which appeared in *Edinburgh City Lynx* magazine in 1978.

2   Antonio Gramsci (1891-1937) was a founder-member of the Communist Party of Italy in 1921 and a member of the Italian parliament from 1924 until his arrest in 1926. At his trial the prosecutor stated: 'We must prevent this brain from functioning for twenty years.' In jail he wrote the thirty-two 'Prison Notebooks'. MacDiarmid refers to him as 'That heroic genius, Antonio Gramsci' in *In Memoriam James Joyce, C.P.* II, p. 745.

3   Karl Kraus (1874-1936), Viennese satirist.

4   The article had been written by Erich Heller. MacDiarmid's 'poem' in *In Memoriam James Joyce* begins, 'And, above all, Karl Kraus', *C.P.* II, p. 737 . In the fourth edition of his *The Disinherited Mind* (London, 1975, p.x.) Heller pointed out that the passage '[...] consists of 157 lines of which 149 are taken from my essay [...].'

5   *Die Fackel* (The Torch) appeared from 1899 until Karl Kraus's death, though latterly at irregular intervals.

6   *Scottish International* 6, April 1969, pp. 59-61.

7   *The Threepenny Opera.*

8   Alfred Kerr (1867-1948) was one of the most influential German dramatic critics of the years 1895-1920.

9   François Villon b.1431.

10   Paul Schick was the author of *Karl Kraus : Mit Selbstzeugnissen und Bilddocumenten* (With Autobiographical Writings and Images).

11   'struggle'; 'wrestling-match'.

70. From Kenneth White (EUL MS2961.13 ff.18-19)

Studio 40
Résidence d'Aspin IV
64-PAU
7 October 1969

Dear Hugh MacDiarmid,

Many thanks for your last letter. I'd normally have replied much sooner, but, first, I knew you were to be away in Canada for a while, and then I myself have been away from Pau for about three months.

Although I'd come to expect nothing from the Arts Council, the definitive news from them was irritating, if not disappointing – especially along with what you told me about their dishing-out large sums of money elsewhere. As to their policy, I don't understand it any more than you do (my 'case' seemed pretty good), but I could make a guess. Maybe I don't seem 'Scottish' enough to them (wasn't it Yeats who said that there was nothing more monstrous than nationality defined in narrow terms?) I don't live in Scotland, I don't contribute to the Scottish magazines, my books aren't published in Scotland, and I don't write 'about' Scotland... That's possibly enough to warrant, if not a refusal, at least a prejudice. That they should make a serious study of my books is probably too much to ask – though there they would see characteristics that, if we're to use national terms at all, would have to be called 'Scottish'. It's as a Scottish poet that I'm known in France, where, I've been told, I'm the only younger English-speaking poet with any reputation at all. You remember how Thoreau says he would have defined himself vis-à-vis the nationalists – as a Transcendentalist?[1]

Well, I'm a transcendentalist Scot ... (how's that for a grotesque appelation?)

Well, to hell with the Arts Council. I'm still here, living and working away. And I'll still be here when the Arts Council crew will be well and truly forgotten. So far as economic circumstances are concerned, I've got myself a job up in Paris, at the Sorbonne, for next year, and shall be moving up there soon, while maintaining my attachments to Pau. Marie-Claude[2] will keep the studio going here in Pau, for neither of us wants to live again for any length of time in Paris. I'll be there during the University terms, then, trying to earn enough cash to come back down here.

Once again, thanks for proposing me for the bursary. All the very best to Mrs Grieve and yourself.

Kenneth White.

[1]   Henry David Thoreau (1817-1862) was in his own words, ' a mystic, a transcendentalist and a natural philosopher to boot'.
[2]   His wife.

The 1970s

1. *From Compton MacKenzie (EUL MS2954.8 f.31)*

31 Drummond Place
Edinburgh 3
29 January 1970[1]

My dear Chris,

How kind of you to remember my birthday. Your letter was a great pleasure. I am sorry to hear you have been having a bad time with your health and I can easily understand your *temporary* allergy to pen and paper. I think both of us might be forgiven for that. I have no doubt it is only temporary. My own health has been splendid except for my wretched eyes and reading through a magnifying glass a print two inches from one's vision is exhausting. However I am halfway through my last Octave[2] and when that is finished I shall not attempt to write anything which needs previous reading.

Fortunately for me my beloved Lily[3] has mastered my horrible handwriting and reads it when I can't read it myself.

Do come and see us sometime with dear Valda to whom I send my love. Our friendship has never been interrupted. We shall not get away to France before June when I hope to have finished Octave 10.

All good things to you for 1970 and the rest of the 'seventies.

Yours ever

Monty C. M.

I do think 'Sir Compton' might be given up!

[1]   Compton MacKenzie's last letter to MacDiarmid was written on 5 January 1971.
[2]   Mackenzie wrote *My Life and Times* in ten volumes (1963-1971).
[3]   Lilian (Lily) Mackenzie MacSween was Mackenzie's second wife whom he married in 1965 after the death of his first wife Christine (Chrissie) MacKenzie MacSween in 1963.

2. *From Serge Fauchereau (EUL Gen.2094/2/531)*

Serge Fauchereau
129 rue des Ecoles
60 MONTATAIRE. Oise
France
21 March 1970

Monsieur,

My friend Garech Browne[1] entreated me to write to you as he knows I am very interested in your work; in fact he had me write my address on a letter he wrote to you last week when he was in Paris. I am sorry to say it is impossible to find any of your work (as well as any other foreign poetry) in Paris. Two years ago I managed to lay a hand on your *Selected Poems*[2] and *A Lap of Honour*[3] and was so enthusiastic I published two or three pages on your work in the magazine *Les Lettres Nouvelles* (May 1968), along with translations of two poems. I don't think you have ever seen that, possibly you would like to see the translations at least, I don't know. Anyway my problem now is that I would like to make a larger presentation of your poetry, and since two books are issued now it is a good opportunity. Here Maurice Nadeau[4] or Aragon (you probably know him) would be glad to see that. If you could suggest MacMillan or MacGibbon and Kee to send me one or two books I would be very glad and grateful to you. Thus I could translate some poems. Above all I would hate to bother you with my little problems.

Yours very truly,
Serge Fauchereau.

[1] 'Garech Browne' was Hon. Garech de Brun, member of the Guinness family and the founder of Claddagh Records.
[2] MacMillan published *Selected Poems* in 1934; Fauchereau probably meant *Collected Poems* (1962).
[3] MacGibbon and Kee published *A Lap of Honour* in 1967.
[4] Maurice Nadeau (b. 1911) was a literary critic, editor and author who wrote *Histoire du surréalisme* (Paris, 1945).

3. From David Black (EUL Gen.2094/1/108)

16 St Nicholas Road
Brighton
3 April 1970

Dear Hugh MacDiarmid,
It was a great pleasure to meet you on Thursday. Now back in Brighton, I felt I'd like to send you a copy of my more recent book – not at all in the expectation that you will like it! but more to gratify my own vanity to think that you will have had a chance to see it.

I hope sometime we'll have a chance to talk about things in more depth than breadth. It seems to me we have quite a few areas of disagreement, notably on the twin questions of Stalinism & Robert Garioch! (Absurd as that juxtaposition seems, I suspect it points to something rather central.) I'd be glad to work these out a bit at our next meeting.

Kindest regards, meanwhile, to your difficult wife!
And to yourself also,
David Black.

PS Just got this copy from the publisher – it seems, I'm sorry, to have been rather messily stored.

4. From Barbara Niven (EUL MS2957)

54 Trinity Church Square

London SE1

9 April [1970]

My dear Chris,

Your *More Collected Poems* have just come and I – we – are delighting in them.[1] They are in fact almost snatched from hand to hand. Thank you with all my heart.

There are so many there that are tied into my life with threads that are always there and alive, but now at this moment painfully and splendidly so. The wonderful 'In Memoriam' to Rilke,[2] the 'Divertissement Philologique',[3] 'Plaited Like the Generations of Men'[4] – what's the use? I'd be repeating the 'Contents' list. But deeply known and loved ones are there in such numbers – ones that have changed my life.

Also, some I didn't know – 'Up to my Eyes in Debt',[5] for instance with that extraordinary twist that is the tone of your voice, from the macrocosm to the microcosm with wit as the binder. And something I'd forgotten, the way you 'use' America, bang into the 20th century from John Donne.

I saw the review by James Brogan,[6] didn't think it lived up to its (true) title of dazzling but who am I to complain of that?

I wonder if Valda has decided to go to Canada with you? I realise it's only 2 or 3 weeks off now. Tell me when you're going?

Our love to Valda and to you – with all the edge of countless memories of the Shetlands in it. Sometimes I think I possess a positively Proustian 'memory', if that's the word.

Barbara.

[1]   *More Collected Poems* (London: MacGibbon & Kee, 1970).
[2]   *C.P.* I, pp. 416-419.
[3]   *C.P.* I, pp. 340-346.
[4]   *C.P.* II, pp. 871-889.
[5]   *C.P.* I, p.252.
[6]   Not identified.

5. From Basil Bunting (EUL MS2945 f.5)[1]

Shadingfield
Wylam
Northumberland
30 April 1970

Dear Christopher

It's as well to know the worst in advance, so I'm sending you a carbon of the 'review' Cookson demanded for *Agenda*.[2] I don't think much of it. I always hated writing reviews. Since there's not much limit to my admiration of your poetry, I don't think you'll find anything offensive in it, though I know well that even the most favourable reviews can be stupid enough to annoy anyone. If you do find anything objectionable, please board Cookson and tell him to suppress it: I've already told him I don't give two hoots about having such things rejected. On the other hand, by dwelling on the long didactic poems and saying nothing worth mentioning about Scottish nationalism or communism I hope I may recruit a few more readers for Hugh MacDiarmid.

I hope your health has held up to this long unending perpetual infinite winter – and Valda's. I'm lethargic and dismayed by it, but bodily pretty well. I've been promising myself a car trip up the North Tyne and by Hawick and Peebles to enjoy looking at you and hearing your growly voice, but the chance never seems to come. The bottle of Glenfiddich is nearly empty drinking healths to you.

I expect I'll have to go to Canada to keep meat on the table by September, but nothing is fixed or clear yet. They gave me a Civil List pension, very civilly: £250 less income tax at unearned rate, which should leave enough to pay for cigarettes AND matches. Sima's legs are tired of carrying her weight,[3] and I imagine there'll be some kind of medical bill to meet soon. That exhausts my stock of gossip.

Anyway, good luck stay with you for many years.

Yours ever,

B. Bunting.

---

[1]   Basil Bunting first met MacDiarmid at 17 Keats Grove, Catherine Carswell's house in London, in 1934.

[2]   'Thanks to the Guinea-Worm', Bunting's review of *More Collected Poems* (1970) and *A Clyack-Sheaf* (1969) appeared in *Agenda,* vol. 8, nos. 3-4 (Autumn-Winter, 1970), pp. 117-121.

[3]   Sima Alladadian (b.1931) was Bunting's second wife.

6. From W. S. Graham (EUL MS2948.12 f.4)

Madron
Penzance
Cornwall
England
[before 19 May 1970]

Dear Christopher Grieve,

I write to you with true affection & good respect to thank you for your letter to me after all those long changing times.[1]

I only wish that I had had the pleasure and vitality of your company during those last, what, twenty years. I have grown up into some degree of knowing the worth of your words.

What you say about *Malcolm Mooney's Land*[2] is very generous and, coming from you up there and *up there*, is doubly valuable to me here in my place of the moment.

What a pity you did not get me down here when you came. Nessie[3] and I think of you often at various unexpected times. Good luck to your Canadian visit. I well remember Valda. I send my (can we say?) love to her. In a kind of way I am trying to send my love to you but what could I make the words do to show that?

I am reading with Ted Hughes & Heaney at the Book League on 19th May.[4] To see you there would be a great pleasure. Nessie will be with me.

With good Scots heart towards you,

W. S. Graham

[1] W. S. Graham met MacDiarmid at The New Art Club in Glasgow in 1942.
[2] *Malcolm Mooney's Land* was published on 23 March 1970.
[3] Agnes Kilpatrick Dunsmuir ('Nessie') (1909-1999) was married to W. S. Graham. She was also a poet.
[4] Ted Hughes was unable to come and was replaced by George Barker.

7. From Hamish Henderson (EUL MS2951.3 ff.80-81)

University of Edinburgh
School of Scottish Studies
27 George Square
Edinburgh
EH8 9LD
9 June 1970

Dear Chris,

Thank you for your letter about the Karl Kraus passage. I imagine you will have heard from David Wright[1] by now, and I hope that everything has been 'redded up' to Erich Heller's satisfaction, and your own.

As I think I mentioned in an earlier letter, I now have enough material to do a sort of mini – 'Road to Xanadu'[2] on the origins of the whole business – including passages from articles by Kraus which appeared originally in his magazine *Die Fackel* and were reprinted in collections like *Die Chinesische Mauer* (The Chinese Wall). As you are aware, Kark Kraus's method was often merely to *quote*, without any verbal additions of his own, except sometimes an ironic title and sub-title. For example, in his article *Die Weisse Kultur* (White Culture) which he sub-titles *Warum in die Ferne schweifen?* (Why roam around in foreign parts?) he juxtaposes an article from a Berlin newspaper about 'undesirable' pen-pal contacts between German 'Mädchen' and Negroes in the German colonies with a series of 'with a view to marriage' adverts in the German press which reveal a whole ugly world of sex and the cash nexus reminiscent of those surgical cartoons of Grosz[3] which appeared just after World War One ('Engineer with Diploma desires to meet Protestant lady of means – not under 25 000 marks!')

Last night I was re-reading the very interesting double number of *Akros* about you and your work, and I noticed a reference (in your conversation with Glen) to the 'draining of the Po marshes' as one of the achievements of Mussolini which impressed people outside Italy.[4] (You also mentioned this in a letter to *The Scotsman* a couple of years ago, and I alluded to your statement in my reply, but unfortunately the para. was cut in the published letter.)[5]

No doubt, when you refer to the 'Po marshes', you mean the Pontine marshes, which are – or rather were – between Rome and Naples. This is a minor point. However, it should be remembered that the plan which the Fascists utilized was drawn up in 1919 by the 'Genio Civile' – the Engineering Dept of the Civil Service in Rome – four years before Mussolini seized power. Furthermore, the Fascist 'drive', accompanied by countless publicity fanfares, did not take place till 1932 – nine years *after* you wrote the two articles 'A Plea for a Scottish Fascism' and 'A Programme for a Scottish Fascism'.[6] It seems to me a matter of some importance that this obfuscation should be cleared up, for Italian Fascism obviously impressed you as an *idea* when it emerged in the early 1920s; it is therefore regrettable that political and social events should be hauled in to confuse the issue, which is surely the demonstrable and revealing influence which a political ideology had on you.[7]

This influence is, of course, very understandable, given the conditions in Scotland after World War One. Wouldn't you agree that the key to your 'Fascist' articles is to be found rather 'in the slums of Glasgow' than in the Pontine marshes?

Best wishes.

Yours aye,

Hamish.

P.S. I have often wondered if you came across the books of the philosopher Giovanni Gentile in the 1930s and if so, what you thought of them.[8]

1   David Wright (1920-1994), poet and anthologist, editor and translator.
2   John L. Lowes (1867-1945) wrote *The Road to Xanadu* (1927), sub-titled 'a study of the ways of the imagination'.
3   George Grosz (1893-1959) painter, draughtsman and illustrator. Valued for his caustic caricatures.
4   Vol. 5, no. 13, April 1970, p.33.
5   MacDiarmid's letter, 4 March 1968, to which Henderson refers, is given in *The Armstrong Nose,* subtitled 'Selected Letters of Hamish Henderson', Edinburgh, 1996, pp.167-8. The paragraph cut from Henderson's reply (really two paragraphs), 9 March 1968, is given in the same place, p.170.
6   The two articles appeared in *The Scottish Nation* nos. 5 and 7, 5 June and 19 June, 1923.
7   In 'Programme for a Scottish Fascism' MacDiarmid wrote: 'Just as Fascism in Italy must incline to the Left, as has been pointed out, just because nationalism is opposed to capitalist materialism, so already in Scottish literature and religion tendencies are manifesting themselves to meet Labour half-way and make common cause in the interest of 'Scotland First'". Hugh MacDiarmid, *Selected Prose,* ed. by Alan Riach (Manchester: Carcanet, 1992), p. 36.
8   The fascist philosopher, Giovanni Gentile (1875-1944), was executed by Italian partisans.

8. From Ronald Stevenson (EUL MS2960.20 f.64)

Townfoot House
West Linton
Peeblesshire

Dear Chris,

Kulgin [Duval] has just brought me the fine new edition of *A Drunk Man*.[1] Hearty congratulations!

Aeons have elapsed since I visited Brownsbank. With F. G., I qualify to be the only other 'whole and seldom man' in these airts: certainly 'seldom' in the *other* sense (alas!) and I hope reasonably whole. But I have visited you often in my work; have lived whole days with you. I tell you straight – with not an ounce of flattery – that your poetry is the major fructifying influence on my work for Scottish music.

You'll welcome the news, I know, that my new song-cycle, *Border Boyhood* (settings of your prose) is to be performed at the 1971 Aldeburgh Festival.

Marjorie said only the other day 'Let's go and see Chris and Valda sometime soon!' We'll do that; and I know there'll be no hard feelings.

Love to you both,

Ronald.

PS Tomorrow (Sunday) at 11.20pm on Radio 4, I broadcast the 'Kreutzer' Sonata with Leonard Friedman. – R.S.

---

[1] The de luxe edition published by Bodoni Press, Verona.

9. From George Bruce (EUL MS2944.1 f.15)

> 25 Warriston Cres.
> Edinburgh
> EH3 5CB
> 8 December 1970

Dear Chris,

I have been away over the weekend and out thereafter otherwise you would have had my thanks, my very sincere thanks, for your too generous remarks about my poems. I take credit for one perception in that book, my recognition in the poem dedicated to you, written in 1942, that you had created 'the canon of a giant art' as a response to the needs of the time and as a disclaimer of the devitalised pseudo-poetry that was still hanging around, fairly polluting the mental atmosphere. I had no doubts where you were then. Not that I did not admire the early lyrics and *A Drunk Man*. Your comment on the 'repetition complex' of the Scots has stuck with me over the years. Alas it is too true.

Whether or not the confidence which you generated will have, nearly thirty years later, a useful outcome in me, now, I cannot tell. At present I am writing social and political poems. If I think any are worthy I'll let you see them.

I was very glad to be of some help to you as a taxi-man. As ever I greatly enjoyed your company – the both of you – as we say North of Aberdeen.

Yours aye,

George.

10. From John Dickie (EUL Gen.2094/1/404)

99 Cranwich Road
London N16
30 March 1971

Dear Dr Grieve,

Some months ago you were kind enough to help me with a study I was doing of your work. That study has been completed and was accepted by the university for my teacher's certificate. I am now working on my education degree, and as a natural continuation of that work, I am engaged on a thesis attempting to plan strategies for teaching Scots in our schools. Doing some work in a non-certifcate school at home in Wigtownshire produced some very useful results. Children who could not write creative 'standard English' found themselves able to express themselves in their own language. A free and powerful language was created that owed little to 'formal English'; as so many Black people are now doing, our children were able 'to tell it as it is'. The children used the language to get back at all those who were seen to oppress them, the teachers, the polis; the whole set-up that serves to suppress their abilities and send them into what is nothing more than agricultural wage slavery was exposed in a forceful way.

However within their anger there was also an element of cultural oppression, their language was not as free as it should have been, they're still victims of perhaps the most pernicious manipulators of public opinion in Scotland, the fearsome D. C. Thomson organisation. What I wanted to ask you was how important do you think *The Sunday Post* is. I know that sounds a faintly silly question but it seems to me that it wields an awful lot of influence, particularly amongst workers, who rely heavily on the 'fitba' pages. Have you ever had any experiences with that organisation? They seem remarkably unwilling to help students, even with the simplest of questions.

I'm sorry to waste your time with a seemingly trivial question, but to me it seems important because if we're ever to get anywhere then that particular kailyard has to be razed to the ground, and I would welcome your comments on them.

I'd have sent you a copy of my study but I hardly think it was worth the posting. I'm afraid (again) that I've said little original about your work. The only thing perhaps worth pursuing is your relationship to Trotskyism. It seems to me that there is a great deal in common between your views on literature and art and some of those accredited to Trotsky, yet I can find no comment in your work on Trotsky. Have you published your views on him anywhere? I would of course carefully separate the thoughts and actions of Trotsky from those of his so-called followers.

Anyway, I'd like to thank you for enabling me to get my certificate and my degree, not that I am terribly impressed by the sorts of bits of paper that liberal institutions such as Sussex dole out, but thanks anyway for helping me to get a few years valuable study done.

Very Best Wishes.
Fraternally,
John Dickie.

11. From Marguérite and Félix Paknadel (EUL MS2960.3 f.12)[1]

34 rue du 4 Septembre
Aix en Provence 13
29 April 1971

Dear Christopher and Valda,

Thank you with all my heart for the very sweet letter you wrote me about my mother. What fortunate circumstances that you were all able to meet in Aix: it was indeed a very happy time for my mother and you know well how attached she and my Father were to Scotland to their Scottish friends and how far back this affection goes.

May I add that my husband and myself were very happy to make your acquaintance or rather in my case to renew it and to see you both, looking so well, in our house. I hope that some day you may come again. May we send you our warmest regards and thank you again for your sympathy.

Affectionately,

Marguérite and Félix (Paknadel).

[1] Marguérite and Félix (Paknadel) were the daughter and son-in-law of Denis and Ella Saurat.

12. From George Bruce (EUL MS2944 ff.16-18)

25 Warriston Crescent
Edinburgh
EH3 5LB
15 May 1971

Dear Chris,

How good of you to send me your congratulations about the Fellowship. It's for one year only – I'm under no illusions about the possibility of a harvest of real writers. That can't be, but to get some young people made more alive to the quality of writing that has been achieved here, that is another matter. I know I am not appointed to lecture about you but to win confidence in your achievement, to get some few to grasp the largeness of your enterprise, this is a point of beginning to which I shall direct all who come my way. And in view of the fashionable nonsense that is blowing across the face of Scotland just now, and is accepted by some as having been gusted from Parnassus – I believe I shall have a useful enough job to do.

I saw you on television the other night. You did very well despite an interviewer who was playing for sensation, who had no proper respect for you, and who seemed incapable of developing any line at all. Some of his remarks were crass. I take the strongest exception to his irrelevant and silly remark about your age. I wish these current affairs people would stick to their current affairs, in which they can chirp away at politicians who are fair game. But the attempt to devalue a man who has won through to eminence by the deployment of his imagination on the worthiest objective of all – to create a new poetry for his country and mankind – and who for this end gave up all prospect of worldly advancement, is utterly abhorrent.

I note your remark about 'not' giving the public what it 'wants' and applaud it to the echo. In the discussion in *Bookmarks* I found myself in the company of two men, one a bookseller, one a popular writer, who actually thought it strange that I should challenge their assumption that the bigger the sales the surer guarantee of the quality of the book. If this were so quite clearly there is no point in having the Arts Council involved in any way in the encouragement of writers. But as you and I know only too well, the odds are that the reverse proposition is nearer the truth in the devalued society in which we live. Unfortunately the presence of two such ignorant people – clearly they had not read the most elementary treatises on this subject (Q.D. Leavis on *Fiction and the Reading Public* for instance) [1] made discussion of the subject at a serious level impossible.

It's a fine day here. I hope it is the same with you. I hope you keep well. My love to Valda.

George.

[1]   London, 1932.

13. From Duncan Glen (EUL MS2948.9 f.155)

AKROS
from Duncan Glen
Akros Publications
14 Parklands Avenue
Penwortham
Preston
Lancashire
England
PR1 OQL
13 November 1971

Dear Chris,

I hope you are now fit and well after your convalescence. It seems a long time to me since I visited you in hospital and if you have been having to be lazy I expect it seems as long to you. My own laziness is growing on me and I am *almost* beginning to like it. At any rate I have been easing up although I had a busy day yesterday with Raymond Gardner of *The Guardian* here to interview me for one of his 'talking to' pieces. 'Hugh MacDiarmid' naturally came into our talk. I seem to remember saying both how your fight and work had given us all a chance to be ourselves and yet at the same time you were such a powerful influence that we younger Scottish poets had to fight against being swamped by your influence. Of course a lot of poets have turned nasty to defend themselves from your influence – not that they would admit (some of them!) that they were responding to your influence!

I am wishing to enclose copies of my latest two productions which may interest you – my *The Individual and the Twentieth Century Scottish Literary Tradition* and *Feres*.[1]

I have received one set of proofs of *Hugh MacDiarmid: A Critical Survey*[2] and I am trying to get other sets so that I can send you one.

I hear from Alex Scott that Mike and he are making good progress with your new book of poems.[3] I am looking forward to it.

All good wishes to you and Valda from all here.

Yours,

Duncan.

---

[1] Duncan Glen's pamphlets were published in 1971.

[2] He edited Hugh MacDiarmid: *A Critical Survey* (Edinburgh and London:Scottish Academic Press, 1972).

[3] The 'new book' mentioned was *The Hugh MacDiarmid Anthology,* ed. by Michael Grieve and Alexander Scott (London:Routledge & Kegan Paul, 1972).

14. From Morven Cameron (EUL MS2954.4 f.4)

> 11 Belmont Crescent
> Glasgow W2
> 13 December [1971]

Dear Dr MacDiarmid,

How enormously kind of you to write and say what you did. I was tongue-tied and quailing when I wrote you first, and felt I sounded like an elderly and foolish virgin. Anyway, I hope you won't mind if I send my/your poem to *The Scotsman*? (I've never dared say 'poem' before, only 'verses', but you've put courage in me.)[1]

You met my father once, years ago, when he went out to see you with my sister and my *ex*-brother-in-law, Finlay MacDonald[2] – he cherishes the memory, and joins me in hoping that you live to be a hundred at least. I'm sure your wife's jaw will acquire a mobility to cope with the situation.

If you don't mind, I'll drive out to Biggar to hand something in to you before Christmas – not to deave you with long visits from unknown folk.

Is it safe for me to say, since I'm 40 and you're 80, I love you? As anyone worth his/her salt in this country must. Whether it's safe or not: I'll take the risk, since I come from that country whose hills are older than the Himalayas.

My very best wishes and many many thanks for your courtesy and generosity.

Yours sincerely,

Morven Cameron.

P.S. I work in the Girls' High School here and I'm enclosing a wee thing I wrote as a 'divert'. And another.[3] But I don't *expect* an answer, for I know you've far too much to do – it's only for fun.

1   Morven Cameron's poem 'For Hugh MacDiarmid' appears in Gordon Wright's *MacDiarmid: An Illustrated Biography* (Edinburgh,1977), p.145.
2   Finlay J. MacDonald, radio producer and, in later life, writer of Hebridean reminiscences.
3   The poems she refers to here are 'Christmas, Glasgow 1971' and 'Address to the Senior Staffroom' (EUL MS2954.4 ff. 5-6.).

15. From Eric Mottram (EUL Gen.2094/4/1603)

UNIVERSITY OF LONDON KING'S COLLEGE
from 15 Vicarage Gate
London W8
Strand WC2
26 January 1972

Dear Mr MacDiarmid,

Thank you very much for 'At James Joyce's Deathbed'; I will happily put it into *Poetry Review*'s summer issue, which I am building now. The copy and the (tiny) cheque will be coming from the Poetry Society once the issue is out. I enclose your manuscript, as you requested – I've made a copy for actual publication.

I do hope you have made a good recovery from your recent setbacks: I was highly perturbed to hear of it, and feel doubly grateful that you wrote and sent the poem. The sense of hope through process of change and growth in your poem is exhilarating – but that old sense of the people other than that 'infinitesimal percentage' worries me, as ever. It's constant in your work, and I've always appreciated the way you handle it. Muriel Rukeyser sends her best wishes to you and your wife – she read excellently here recently – and I mention her because, as you know, her work has always been in this sense socialist – from those Thirties beginnings, which your '[Third] Hymn to Lenin' dedication recognises. How to get the Clydeside workers into a poem possibly, without either condescension or *Socialist Worker* fulsomeness: this is I take it near the issue. Poetry is such a class matter in this country. No one could, for instance, make that George Jackson song like Bob Dylan recently did – so simple and straightforward, taking it for granted that that is what a poet does – just writes the song of the moment, as well as the complex statement of the context of the political moment, in another kind of work.

One thing more: forgive me if I'm dense but is the reference on p.2 of the MSS to 'Gandaparla'?[1] I want to get it right in the printing.

It's a marvellous hopeful poem – the very sense of ease in the movement is itself moving to me, carrying the intelligence information with it, without affectation. Thank you.

Yours sincerely,
Eric Mottram.

1   The reference was to 'Gaudaparla', the teacher of Govinda, Sankara's own teacher, according to Vedantic tradition.

16. From Brian Campbell (NLS Acc.7361/43)

Knocktower
Knockvennie
by Castle Douglas
Stewartry of Kirkcudbright
7 August 1972

Dear Chris,

We have just been listening to 'The Drunk Man' on the Scots Programme of the BBC. Though I have read the poem many times I have never before heard Tom Fleming's rendering of it. We felt we must write immediately to tell you how great was our pleasure in it & how deeply we were moved. Monica suddenly said of you: 'he plays on the nerves of the unconscious & gives words to the sores of one's heart'. A spontaneous reaction with which I heartily agree. Heard in the whole the poem is a wonderful experience, comparable with Beethoven's Fifth. I cannot say more except 'Thank you'.

By another post you should receive a more potable appreciation. Meanwhile every good wish for your 80th birthday and for many more.

Yours aye,

Brian.

P.S. My brother asks me to include his good wishes also.

17. From Donald Bain (EUL MS2948.2 f.15)

49 Hillhouse Street
Glasgow
G21 4HS
9 August 1972

Dear Chris,

It is good to know that you have survived the pressures of life, including Art and Literary politics, to be truly independent one has to suffer.

I haven't been immune myself and I still go my own way, in spite of all kinds of attempts to belittle my statements in paint.

But within the past two years a young Glasgow man, W. R. Hardie, who is Keeper of Art at the Dundee Art Galleries is organising an exhibition of my works, which will open at Dundee in December and then go on tour.[1] Twenty years ago in August M. Paul Lorion opened my first retrospective exhibition and you proposed a very sincere vote of thanks. One of Jacques Villon's remarks was: 'For a painter the toughest are the first seventy years'. Well I'll be 69 next March. Fergusson used to say to me: 'If you live long enough you'll be a great success', but one begins to wonder just what success means, some satisfaction in confounding some of the so-called critics, and then kicking them in the teeth perhaps, not putting the boot in physically.

With best wishes for the 11th.
Yours aye,
Donald Bain.

1   *Donald Bain: A Scottish Colourist* (Glasgow:William Hardie Ltd, 2000) gives the dates of 'An Exhibition of Paintings and Drawings, Donald Bain, Dundee City Art Gallery and Tour' as 1973-1974.

18. From John Donovan (EUL Gen.2094/1/420)

Post Card

24 Kilmaurs Rd
Kilmarnock
10 August 1972

Dear Mr Grieve,
Congratulations on your 80th birthday but not on your declaration that you 'would sacrifice a million people any day for one immortal lyric'. (Quoting you on Lewis Grassic Gibbon).[1]
Sincerely yours,
John Donovan.

1   MacDiarmid made the comment in his article 'Lewis Grassic Gibbon' written in 1944, published in *Scottish Art and Letters* 2, 1946, pp. 39-44.

19. From Eric Mottram (EUL MS2970)

UNIVERSITY OF LONDON KING'S COLLEGE
Strand London WC2R 2LS
Department of English
12 August 1972

Dear Mr MacDiarmid,
I hope you liked how your fine poem appeared in the Summer *Poetry Review*: it was grand to have you in it and I am deeply grateful.[1] But this is really a personal letter, greeting you, I like so many others, on your eightieth birthday. Tom Pickard once gave me *The Fire of the Spirit* as a gift: it is one of the most prized books I have – 'Diamond Body' is a poem I return to again and again. What your work has meant to me, as a poet and writer, is that ability to make over scientific and philosophical information into fine poetry, to speak of this directly and without making too much of a surface puzzle of it. It struck me again this week when I discovered 'On a Raised Beach' in *The Penguin Book of Longer Contemporary Poems*:[2] it moved me deeply again – 'The rocks rattling in the bead-proof seas' – 'The deadly clarity of this "seeing of a hungry man"' – there it is. And I have always appreciated that interior action between rejection of mob standards and need for a defined socialist position, which

I find as the central dialectic in your work again and again. So without going on about it, and risking the obvious, let me wish you creative happiness for the future, and offer my thanks for your poetry. Any time you have anything for *Poetry Review*, you have only to post it off.

Yours sincerely,
Eric Mottram,
editor, *Poetry Review*.

1   *Poetry Review* had just published 'At James Joyce's Death-bed', vol. 63, no. 2, pp. 102-105.
2   David Wright edited *Longer Contemporary Poems* (Harmondsworth, 1966).

20. From Timothy Cribb (NLS Acc.7361/43)

Churchill College
Cambridge
CB3 ODS
17 October 1972

Dear Mr Grieve,

First, please convey my regards to your wife. Did she by any chance encounter Marin Sorescu in Romania?[1]

Next, please accept best wishes from John Holloway, who is hopeful of meeting you when you're in Cambridge next month.

Second, is it all right to picture your face on the cover of the *Cambridge Review* if I can get a suitable photograph? If so, I shall approach Duncan Glen who may be able to put me in the way of the photographs used in the *Akros* booklet of 1970 based on his conversations with you in 1968.

That issue of the *Review* is the second of this term, & comes out in the sixth week, not long before your visit. Copy deadline for the printers is the end of this month, i.e., Monday 30th October, though if it comes any earlier that makes it easier for them. If you discover that you can't in fact make the deadline, could you please let me know before the end of the month, so that the editors can reorganise their copy for the issue?

The first issue of term comes out this Friday, so you should receive it next week. I don't know what's in it (except for the film review, which I commissioned) save that its theme is radical philosophy.

Are plans for your visit organised in any detail? As you can imagine, I'd be honoured and delighted to organise a party for you in Churchill, or elsewhere, to which you could invite whomever you wished, submitting to be lionised or rejoicing in escape to a small group as your inclination prompted. I imagine the English Faculty will organise a reception after your reading. Probably there will be little time for other celebrations.

I'm reading *Lucky Poet* with great delight & excitement. I came to the part which works from 'Diamond Body In a Cave of the Sea' through quotations from

Wordsworth & other references to Thaisa's revival in *Pericles*: that had a most startling effect of a sudden fusion, discovery, familiarity, strangeness & unification. I immediately Xeroxed the pages for discussion with my first year students at their first meeting & was lucky enough to find that among them was one who had read St John of the Cross & some Eastern mysticism in connection with *Four Quartets*, so we had an illuminating conversation.

Sorry, I don't mean to embarrass you.

I've heard from Donald Saunders,[2] my old student we met in the Pewter Pot. He has some poems in the December *Akros* which I look forward to seeing.

With warmest regards,

I am,

Yours sincerely,

Timothy Cribb.

PS Ian Grant has got engaged.

[1]   Marin Sorescu (1936-1996) published over twenty collections of poetry in Rumania.
[2]   Donald Goodbrand Saunders (b.1949) is the son of R. Crombie Saunders.

21. From George N. Reid (EUL MS2963.59)

George Reid
21 Hamilton Drive
Glasgow
G12 8DN
7 January 1973

Dear Chris

LION AND DRAGON

Herewith the notes on this programme, as promised by Marjorie Orr.

I shall phone you on Tuesday to confirm the arrangements, and also – if I may – to get some idea of what you are likely to say.

A car will collect you from Browns Bank at 1 pm on Friday, and will take you home again in the evening.

Looking forward to meeting you again.

Sincerely,

George [in biro].

GEORGE N. REID

PS The fee is £40. G.

The Scottish Agency for Film . Television . Radio . Press & Magazines .

22. From Margaret Morris (EUL MS2948.2 f.9 r.&v.)

now at 4 Clouston St
Glasgow
G20 8QS
7 July 1973

Dear Chris,

I get news of you from the Scotts, I have never forgotten the wonderful speech you made at the Memorial dinner to Fergus![1]

I have *just* finished a *biography* of Fergus![2] – & I wondered if you would consent to write an introduction?[3] – I can think of no one else Fergus would like to do it! – ?

It *need*n't be long – but as long as you like! – !

I can let you see a duplicate copy of the book if you wish –

It *is* a good book!!! – *because* there is so much of *Fergus own* writing in it!

Perhaps Valda can let me know how you feel about this?

Sincerest good wishes

always to you both,

Meg.

[1] The Memorial Dinner was held on 9 March 1962.
[2] Her biography was *The Art of J. D. Fergusson* (Blackie, 1974). The full title of the biography was '*The Art of J. D. Fergusson 1874-1961*. A Biased Biography by Margaret Morris with his own letters essays and notes. Fully illustrated in Colour, half tones and line drawings.' MacDiarmid opened two Fergusson Exhibitions. He opened the Memorial Exhibition on 9 December 1961 and the Centenary Exhibition on 11 October 1974.
[3] MacDiarmid did write a Foreword.

23. From Logie Barrow (NLS Acc.7361/44)

58 Hill Court
Putney Hill
London SW15
19 August 1973

Dear Mr MacDiarmid,

To avoid wasting your time: I am writing this letter under the impression that you are also sometimes known as C. M. Grieve. If this not so, then the rest is a long-winded joke.

I noted your address from *The Guardian*, after coming across a remark of C. M. Grieve's in a 1951 *Reynolds News*.[1] You had recalled a 1912 conversation with Tom Mann,[2] where Mann mentioned that Blatchford had consciously plagiarised much of *Merrie England*[3] from 'Elihu' Washington.[4] I had read similar rumours from Keir Hardie[5] (via D. Lowe's book).[6] But I had previously discounted them: after all, when did Hardie and Blatchford ever miss a chance to stick knives into each other?

I would be surprised if you were to like what Blatchford later came to represent, any more than I do. But mudslinging never shed much light. And I'd be controversial if claimed that even his 'reputable' work was unoriginal in any sense.

Have you any firm, even checkable, convictions that Blatchford's *Merrie England* involved plagiarisation? Until reading you, I had believed he didn't need to plagiarise – that he merely distilled what he had been saying in the *Clarion* and *Sunday Chronicle* with what numbers of early-1890s socialists were saying, but in a far less clumsy style than 'Elihu's'.

If you have time to give me an opinion, I would be very interested and very grateful.

Yours sincerely,

Logie Barrow.

[1] E.M.W. Reynolds founded his newspaper in Chartist times in the 1840s. It survived as a Socialist Sunday paper into the 1960s.

[2] Tom Mann (1856-1941) was a trade union leader. He joined the Social Democratic Federation in 1885, the British Socialist Party in 1917 and the Communist Party in 1920. At the time MacDiarmid met him he had recently founded the Industrial Syndicalist Education League in May 1910. It is intriguing to note that MacDiarmid pasted into a scrapbook an article entitled 'What is Syndicalism?' which had appeared in the *Edinburgh Evening News,* 23 March 1912 (he notes in ink). The author is given as a member of Edinburgh University Fabian Society. (EUL MS2236).

[3] Robert Blatchford (1851-1943) founded *Clarion,* a weekly socialist newspaper, in 1891. It serialised Blatchford's *Merrie England* (1893) and ran until 1931.

[4] 'Elihu' was the pseudonym of Samuel Washington, a pamphleteer of the Independent Labour Party.

[5] James Keir Hardie (1856-1915) founded the Independent Labour Party in 1893. He was a pacifist, opposed the Boer War, and also opposed Britain's involvement in the First World War.

[6] David Lowe published *Souvenirs of Scottish Labour* in 1919.

24. From Allen Ginsberg (EUL MS2966)

London 20 August 1973

Dear Chris & Valda – Here are 3 photos from Rotterdam – I'll bring the Biggar rolls to USA and develop them there – leaving in a few hours – love from Allen Ginsberg.

25. From Basil Bunting (EUL MS2945 f.8)

Shadingfield
Wylam
Northumberland
13 November 1973

Dear Chris,

I'm glad you survived a week with us and the jolting of my car. You certainly made an impression on our dinner guests. Both the university ladies have commented very cheerfully. And I hardly need say that Sima and I enjoyed having you about.

I liked Oliver Edwards[1] when I met him at Sligo. I don't remember the lady you mention by her name, though, since she repeated my story about the suicidal cat and the Bard, no doubt I'd remember her by sight.

I'm sorry the Newcastle Festival people are what they are. So far as I'm concerned, don't worry about them. I knew them of old, and if I'd known you were on their programme I'd have warned you of them in advance. When first I came across them they were all Belfast people, with no connection at all with Newcastle beyond the determination to exploit its people as much as they could. I don't think they can have changed much.

When I got home from Biggar (a good, fast drive) I found I'd forgotten to decant from the car the book I took to look at in the cottage overnight. So I annexed it temporarily, read it with some amusement, and here it is back again. Thank you for the loan of it, though perhaps you never knew you'd unconsciously lent it.

I'm playing hell with the London Poetry Secretariat for cheapening poetry. I've a good mind to resign from the Poetry Society presidency, since that institution is ultimately responsible for the Secretariat and its fees, but I'll hang on till things get worse. I never had the oriental humility of the begging bowl.

It seems to me that every kind of reactionary is flourishing just now. The infection spreads quickly from politics to morals to literature. I've been patient all my life, but it's got progressively harder to resist the conviction that nothing short of the guillotine will ever make this island tolerable. Certainly government from London by the southern well-off blind men is not endurable, so that I was pleased by the self-possessed woman from Govan[2] though I daresay her ideas are not likely to be fearfully intelligent.

Please give my affectionate greetings to Valda. And I look forward to our next glass of Glenfiddich together, whenever it may appear.

Yours ever,

B.

---

[1]   Oliver Edwards had participated in the Ezra Pound commemoration at Queens University, Belfast on 21 February 1973.
[2]   Glasgow district.

26. From G. Singh (EUL Gen.2094/5/2107)

Queen's University of Belfast
Italian Department
[1973]

With the Compliments of Professor G. Singh
It was very kind of you to go through the typescript version of your tribute to Pound.[1] I am taking the liberty of sending you my book on Montale[2] – I remember Montale telling me that he met you once – which I hope you would accept.

    G. Singh.

1   MacDiarmid's tribute to Pound at the commemorative symposium was published in *Paideuma*, vol.3, no.2 (Autumn 1974), 151-153.
2   G. S. Singh, *Eugenio Montale: A Critical Study of his Poetry, Prose and Criticism* (New Haven and London:Yale University Press, 1973).

27. From Norman MacLeod (EUL MS2955.1 f.58)[1]

West End Hotel
Palmerston Place
Edinburgh
7 October 1974

Dear Chris & Valda – My meeting you was one of the great memorable moments of my life. I wish I lived near you so that I could see you again from time to time. I send my love to both of you – affectionately – Norman.

I will send you the book I said I would & also next issue of *P.M.*[2]

1   MacDiarmid's correspondence with Norman Macleod started in 1935.
2   *Pembroke Magazine.*

28. From Edwin Morgan (EUL MS2955.18 ff.25-26)

19 Whittingehame Court
Glasgow
G12 0RG
16 February 1975

Dear Christopher Grieve

It was a great pleasure to receive your letter, which I would have answered long before, but for the pressure of the University work this term. A mid-term holiday gives me a breathing-space to catch up with some of my correspondence. I was sorry that your health did not permit reading at Ayr. The thing went quite well, and a surprisingly large audience for a Saturday afternoon (my train from Glasgow was full of people going to the races) patiently sat through a mort of poetry plus recitations from Burns.

I was interested by what you wrote about being a loner and 'eschewing intimacy'. Quite apart from the point of being true to yourself and, as you say, practising what you preach, it is obviously no bad thing as an antidote to all the couthy-ites and pawky-ites who have been so rife in Scotland – 'like a dog when it loves you', as you once said. I also think it's important to preserve a kind of creative solitariness and not to be always discussing literature with kindred spirits (though my Philip Hobsbaum would not agree). Nowadays the pressures on even a moderately successful writer are legion, and demands to do this and that and go here and there would cripple originality and drain energy if they couldn't be at times resisted. Conscience does make it hard to resist, though, in the sense that when a community shows a genuine interest the writer naturally wants to reciprocate if he can, and not just with a bit of charisma but with the possibility of being useful. At any rate I feel this – I'm not sure whether in a missionary or a theatrical spirit, or both! I remember you once wrote to the effect that poetry, though created as poetry, becomes eventually either entertainment or education, which struck me as a forceful but perhaps resistible view. I'm not sure that poetry can't remain poetry even while it is being delivered – like a load of luscious pink Texan grapefruit – to an audience, or being conveyed – piece by piece on a bright travelling roller – into the understandings of a class. I think what you call 'mass indifference' is what one must keep chipping away at. Chinks of light here, crumblings of apathy there, sudden links seen, moments of possibility, seeds and growth points ... these I believe in.

I stand corrected about 'The Watergaw'[1] and I am sorry to have helped to perpetuate the misreading, which of course as you know is quite common. I have always much admired the other poem, 'At My Father's Grave',[2] which has the true yet moving impersonality of art, and where what you call your 'inhuman' attitude reaps far-reachingly. A correspondent in Dublin wrote to me recently about 'the arctic MacDiarmid' (meant as a term of awed praise), which I think both is and is not true. You have an extraordinary strength which comes from isolated exploration, but if it's arctic or antarctic, it's more Scott than Amundsen, and the vulnerabilities and checks remain as productive, as seed-casting, as the eye for horizons. Or so I think – but I am using too many metaphors!

Well, if my essays have in any way interested or helped you I am honoured as well as pleased. I hope you have recovered from the 'flu and are yourself again.

My very best for 1975 to Valda and yourself –
Sincerely yours
Edwin Morgan

[1]   *C.P.* I, p.17. The misreading of the Watergaw' has been the presumption that 'the last wild look' was given by his first wife.
[2]   *C.P.* I, p.299.

29. From Charles Nicoll (EUL MS2957 f.30)

226 Tresta Road
Glasgow
G23 5DD
28 February 1975

Dear Chris,
To meet such keen wit and humour is, at 83,[1] a pleasing experience and one which I appreciate. I am a little sorry my portrait appears a bit refined but I take comfort from the fact that there are many facets to a strong character. Actually I shall always remember you best with a great shaggy mane blowing in the wind on the Clydeside.

A magnificent picture and one which I loved. I envy your luxuriant growth. My friend, Willie Montgomery, who was with me the day we visited you at Brownsbank said of you, 'He has the head of a lion'. I thought that very appropriate. Regarding the pictures around the walls of your cottage, I remember them very well. All of them were most striking and most interesting because they showed each artist's interpretation of different aspects of your character but the most effective one, I thought, was that which you loaned to Michael Donnelly for your 80th birthday celebration exhibition in the People's Palace in Glasgow. I am working on another landscape just now but when it is finished I have an urge to paint another portrait of 'Poet Hugh MacDiarmid' but more on the lines as I remember you on Clydeside.

I am glad to know that you and Mrs Grieve are now recovering from the 'tartan flu' although still feeling the after-effects. I hope these will pass quickly. It is, as you say, ironic that anything of a Scottish nature should strike adversely at Hugh MacDiarmid.

I note with particular interest that you are being honoured with the freedom of the town of Cumbernauld in April. Since the conferment of your doctorate the long-overdue honours are now falling on you and I am glad that, at last, suitable recognition is now being given to the leading Scottish poet of our time. I would like very much to be in Cumbernauld at that time with my camera. I am sure that photographs taken of that occasion will be unique. If any events of this occasion are public there is the possibility I could get one or two shots. Even though I may not get very close I could use a telephoto lens. I shall keep a lookout to see if the date is announced publicly.

How thoughtful it was of you to ask of my daughter.[2] She is married and has a boy and girl. Her husband is a lecturer at Glasgow University but he has had tempting offers from America after he had been over there in connection with his job. Now Nettie and I are wondering just what is going to transpire.

This letter is a bit longer than I intended when I began it so I shall close it now and wish you and Mrs Grieve good health and happiness.

Yours truly,

Charles Nicoll.

[1] MacDiarmid was still 82 at the time.
[2] Janette Nicoll.

30. From Archie Lamont (EUL MS2952 f.22)

Jess Cottage
Carlops
Penicuik
EH26 9NF
20 April 1975

Brock's article leads to Maurice Barrès[1] and Ezra Pound. I wish you'd do an essay on that pair vis-à-vis Lenin and Maritain[2] & the Puritans (Carlyle etc.)

Dear Chris,

I've been meaning to pay a visit to give you a talk on the successive 'contradictions' that mark the evolution of each genus of plants, vis-à-vis your Caledonian synantisyzygy thing. One of the problems is your evolution as a Communist. Actually about 1929 I thought you might mutate into some intelligent form of Christianity, and I was greatly disappointed when it was Fionn MacColla who – on grossly inadequate grounds, lack of experience, and a third-rate authority called Wüst[3] – took that plunge. At least, I thought, Chris's style of writing seems adapted to him climbing the *Sartor Resartus* tree![4] I still had hopes for Russian communism myself in 1931, but it wore off by 1936 and the murder of Gorki.[5]

Anyhow your second conversion to Communism in 1956 was intelligible if not in terms of armed strategy in Hungary, at least because Krushchev was rising to power as First Secretary of which, as careful students, you (and I) were aware. Unfriendly critics might say that conversions are due more to frustrations, drunken, sexual, or just sheer contrariness; and you certainly don't like being hedged into a fixed position as I once learnt to my cost in 1945 after the June election when you resigned from the S.N.P. Council, it seemed to me because I was trying to force you into a campaign against peacetime conscription.

You're an old warhorse, you know, like Compton MacKenzie & Derrick Boothby[6] & Hugh Ryan;[7] and I'll be duly cautious not to offend you too much.

Communism is more than Stalinism or even Leninism or Brezhnev's imperialism in Uzbekistan, Tajikistan etc. where the Russian imperialists have closed down the mosque schools and set the inhabitants who remain to grow cotton & tobacco for their overlords further north – just like the cotton-field coolies of the U.S.A.

Communism means Communes; and you'll like the relics of Dr A.J. Brock's decentralism in the enclosed pamphlet *Constitution for Free Scots*.[8] Is Communism really individualism as applied to the small group? After your Lenin poems did you drift into the World Language idea, and lose contact with something? I'll phone some decent day.

Archie.

I was getting letters from Sydney [Goodsir] Smith just before he died about a pamphlet on Scots & Irish poets. I see you've published a bibliography. I'd like to see this when I call on you.

---

[1] Maurice Barrès (1862-1923), novelist, journalist and right-wing politician.
[2] Jacques Maritain (1882-1973) was France's leading 20th century Catholic philosopher.
[3] Georg Adolf Otto Wüst (1890-1977), German oceanographer who, by collecting and analyzing many systematic observations, developed the first essentially complete understanding of the physical structure and deep circulation of the Atlantic Ocean. *Ency.*

Brit. Vol. 12, pp.784-5. But was this the authority who influenced Fionn MacColla?

4   Thomas Carlyle, *Sartor Resartus* (1843).

5   Suspicions have been expressed about the manner of the death of Maxim Gorky.

6   Major F.A.C. Boothby ('Derek'), founder member of the 1320 Club, served thirteen months in 1975-6 of a three-year sentence for conspiracy to import explosives for the purpose of damaging property in connection with the Army of the Provisional Government of Scotland.

7   Dr Hugh Ryan founded Scottish Action in 1935.

8   *Constitution for Free Scots* was published by The Scottish Secretariat from Lamont's address c.1975. Dr A.J. Brock M.D., Inverkeithing, contributed a short paper, 'A Federal Scotland', pp.27-29.

31. From Mary 'Mamie' MacDonald (EUL MS2954.3 f.15)

51 Warrender Park Road
Edinburgh
EH9 1EU
1 July 1975

Dear Chris,

I hope you will forgive the familiarity, but I can think of you by no other name, chiefly because we talk so much about you, and the very happy memories, I especially, have of these early days in West Claremont Street when you used to stay with us on your occasional visits from Whalsay. So many years have passed since then and the memory to you must be a very dim one, but it all made such a tremendous impression on me that I shall always treasure these memories and although we had one brief meeting at poor Helen's funeral I retain the warmest affection for you and the joy your visits brought with them. So all this made your letters to Tom and to me all the more touching. It was so kind of you to write and although I don't think Tom has realised it – although your letter was opened and presumably read to him by a nurse – he is too ill to take anything in. He is suffering from hypertension and is still very much on a knife edge, and the prognosis is poor. He is very heavily sedated, but still his brain refuses to stop, and although I desperately refuse to believe that the worst can happen, I try to steel myself for it.

Anyway, I would like you to know how very often we talked about you. Although your views were so directly opposed in many things he always spoke of you with such affection and was constantly quoting things you had said. And I know that in the early days – dating back to Montrose, no doubt, you were his hero and his inspiration. He is still a fairly young man – 69, but he lived, and is now perhaps dying, a poor tortured soul, frustrated all his life because he felt he never achieved what he had set out to do. In one review of yours you said something like 'he would dine late and in an exceedingly small company', and how right you were.

There is little point in keeping you informed of his progress as he has a couple of good days when things seem hopeful, and then a relapse, but apparently this is how the illness goes, and there is absolutely nothing the doctors can do but try to keep his blood pressure stable which isn't easy when dealing with a temperament like his.

Again my sincere thanks for your concern and if he does make a recovery I shall certainly let you know. Three of the family flew over from Canada but they are not allowed to see him and even I have to restrict my visit to a couple of minutes.[1]

I hope you are both well.

Love,

Mamie.

---

[1] Tom MacDonald ('Fionn MacColla') died on 20 July 1975.

32. From Mary 'Mamie' MacDonald (EUL MS2954.3 f.16)

51 Warrender Park Road
Edinburgh 9
2 August 1975

Dear Chris,

Thank you so much for your kind letter. I would just like you to know that Tom's last action before he got a stroke that ended his life, was to post a letter to you. I had offered to do it for him, but he said he'd like to see it go into the pillarbox himself. This confirms what I said in my last letter to you, that he had the greatest affection for you, and was exceedingly touched at your concern for his health.

It's a great comfort to know that others are sharing the burden of our sorrow with us. Life is going to seem very dull and monotonous after living for nearly forty years with that vital spirit.

My kindest regards to you both.

Yours very sincerely,

Mamie.

33. From Robert Murdoch Struthers (NLS Acc.7361/46)

The original typing of this letter has been retained.

Flat 7, 17 Castle St
Barnstaple
N Devon
8 August 1975

Dear Hughie, (Ignoring your real name.),

I'M half puggled, having whisky & a rotten bannnana for breakfast, plus a few scrumpies.

(What a start to a kind of letter!)

Worse to come. I have had an ulcer cut out, followed by pneumia, then I have cancer of the lung. (THE bloddy doctor like a withch said ha-ha-your liver will get you. I accused him of witchcraft!)

Now what can you make of all this true nonsense?

Ive been very ill so my typing is .... NOW I'm going back to 1936 when I landed on Whalsay off the valkirie. I called on you & you kindly gave me your other cottage in Sand Voe.[1] We visitted it & had a builder on the job but with marriage & getting awater supply a difficulty it fell through. (Too long a story in my puggled mood.)

However IHAVE A BONE TO PICK WITH YOU. You never came to see me in Hawkhead!![2]

I suppose you know that wee rab, R. B. Wilkie was my best man & I was slightly upset when he inferred that you more or less ignored him, LAST TIME.

Politics I would imagine.

I must explain why I'm writing this. Yesterday you were on telli & b.w. missed it. I thought it was today (puggled again).

I suppose you know I'M a member of the Society of Authors & Brit. League Of Dramatists. I'LL keep my trap shut aout that.

Now, when it comes to poetry I had better clamp doon: aiblins (that' the stuff!) I WOULD BE HANGED!

What I've admired most about you.... Can you guess?

WHAT YOU WROTE ABOUT THE BANK OF ENGLAND. I wish I had copied it. It ought to be emblazoned ALL OVER THE COUNTRY.

I congratulate on your apparent good health

I'm only 75 & I have said enough.

You look the same as you did in 1936.

If I do wrte again I hope to be more coherent & less scrumatised (new word.) I would liked to have used more lowland scots to please you. Dinna fret.

Well, BARD,

Peace be with you,

Old age is no joke!

Yours most cordially,

Robert Murdoch Struthers (full of scrumpy).

[1]   It appears that MacDiarmid did have an option on the other cottage in Sand Voe.
[2]   Hawkshead was a psychiatric hospital.

34. From Margery Palmer McCulloch (EUL Gen.2094/3/1239)

12 Meadow View
Cumbernauld
Glasgow
G67 2BY
1 February 1976

Dear Dr Grieve,

I wonder if you would give me permission to photocopy some poems from *Collected Poems* which are not reproduced in other more readily obtainable anthologies of your work. I am preparing a postgraduate thesis on your poetry at the University of Strathclyde and I have been unable to purchase a copy of *Collected Poems*. I have been working with a University Library copy since the autumn, but as this in danger of being recalled for another reader, it would be most helpful to me if I could photocopy the poems not obtainable elsewhere. The photocopies would be solely for my own use while preparing my thesis. I should be very grateful if you would let me do this.

I wonder if I could come to Biggar and have a talk with you sometime? I have come to the Scottish poetry tradition in a roundabout way – after training as a singer, a degree in English Literature and Language from London University, and two small boys – but I still feel the shock and excitement which the discovery of your Penguin *Selected Poems* gave me.[1] You sent me off on a musical discovery road too. After reading your essay on Francis George Scott,[2] I set out to find some of his songs and eventually tracked down the Saltire edition to a dusty top shelf in Bayley & Ferguson's at the ridiculously low price of £1.05.

I think these songs are very fine indeed – I have especially enjoyed learning 'To a Ladye'[3] and your own 'The Innumerable Christ',[4] 'First Love'[5] and 'Lourd on My Hert'.[6] He seemed to be able to leave the poem with its own identity intact and yet to bring out its essence even more powerfully by his setting of it. I don't think I had appreciated to the full the marrying of satire and lyricism in 'Lourd on My Hert' until I began to sing Scott's setting of it. I would very much like to talk to you about him and your relationship with him in the early Scots lyrics.

I live in Cumbernauld, which is not too far away by car, and I could come to Biggar at any time convenient to you.

With best wishes.
Yours sincerely,
Margery McCulloch.
(Mrs Margery McCulloch)

[1]   Ed. by David Craig and John Manson (Harmondsworth, 1970).
[2]   Edinburgh:MacDonald, 1955.
[3]   *The Poems of William Dunbar*, ed. by W Mackay Mackenzie (London:Faber & Faber, 1937), p. 99.
[4]   *C.P.* I, p. 32.
[5]   *C.P.* I, p. 434.
[6]   *C.P.* I, pp. 204-5.

35. From Per Skjaeveland (EUL Gen.2094/5/2112a&b)

From: Per Skjaeveland (Mr)
              Fylkessjukehuset
              5401 Stord
              Norway

To : The Scottish Poet
Hugh MacDiarmid

Dear Sir,

Recently I bought *The Hugh MacDiarmid Anthology* edited by Michael Grieve and Alexander Scott, 1972. To my surprise I find in the poem, 'Gairmscoile',[1] the name 'Wergeland',[2] twice.

It is general consent in Norway that Wergeland is a major poet, who would probably have been world-famous if he had written in English or another major language. But I thought he was very little known outside Scandinavia, and did not know that he had made such an impact upon a poet like yourself.

Now I am so daring to ask you how you came to know Wergeland, and if you have written about him in other connections?

Perhaps you know that Wergeland in 1838 wrote a small play with a story from Scotland, *Campbellerne (The Campbells)*, and in this play he also translated a few poems by Robert Burns. I am thus pleased to know that some inspiration has come the other way across the North Sea.

Robert Burns, of course, is fairly well-known in Norway. After Wergeland, he has been translated by the poets Olav Nygard,[3] André Bjerke[4] and Hartvig Kiran[5]. The great Swedish poet, Gustaf Fröding[6] also translated several poems by Burns.

I came to love Burns through the translation by Kiran, published to the Burns Jubilee in 1959. But I found it difficult to read his poems in the original form. In 1961, however, I visited Edinburgh. Then I bought a long-playing record, 'An Evening with Robert Burns'. When I listened to that while reading the poems in a book, it was far easier to appreciate the original text.

It was through Burns I became interested in your poems as well.

For when I, in June 1975, visited Edinburgh once more, I bought the record, 'The Legend & The Man', where you read poems by Burns and yourself.[7] I liked very much the way you read Burns, but I found it difficult to understand your poems by ear alone. Therefore I have bought this anthology where I have found most of the poems on the record.

I must admit that I do not take your poems easily. I am in no way a literary person myself. I belong to the medical profession, being a radiologist in a small hospital on an island on the Western coast of Norway, south of Bergen. But I do not take umbrage to your Scottish language, on the contrary. As you may know, we in Norway have two closely related standard languages, Bokmål and Nynorsk. Nynorsk is my language, and this is the minority language, based on dialects and more close to old Norse. The Bokmål, on the other hand, is more related to Danish, is used by the majority, and has, on the whole, more social prestige. And when I read the word notes on the bottom of the pages, I recognise with joy a lot of words which we in Western Norway will pronounce almost in the same way. For instance 'bairn' for 'child'; 'grat' for 'wept'; 'ken' for 'know'; 'brenn' for 'burn'; 'haill' for 'whole'; 'ain' for 'own'; 'keek' for 'peep' and so on. But I miss an explanation of the word 'Gairmscoile', which I do not understand, nor can I find it in my dictionary.

Back to Wergeland. I would guess that the poem which you may refer to in

'Gairmscoile' is 'Følg kallet', which means, 'follow the call, live after thy vocation', or something like that. It is right that Wergeland was of Scots strain, as you say in your poem, his mother's mother's father was the Scot, Andrew Christie. His father's family was from Western Norway.

Norwegian scholars have pointed to the fact that some Norwegian authors and poets, like Olav Duun,[8] Knut Hamsun[9] and Jakob Sande,[10] may have more in common with their brethren on the North Atlantic Coasts – like Halldor Laxness[11] in Iceland, William Heinesen[12] in the Faroe Islands and Robert Burns in Scotland – than with authors in Sweden or on the Continent.

Anyhow, I am impressed by the cultural connection Burns – Wergeland – MacDiarmid.

I recognise that, even though you sound very vigorous on the record, you are now an old man, and may not find time or occasion to answer letters like this. But perhaps your son, the co-editor of the anthology, Mr Michael Grieve, might send me a few words about your connection with Henrik Wergeland?

I wish you good health and all the best for many years still.

Yours sincerely,

Per Skjaeveland.

[1]   'Gairmscoile' (school-call in Gaelic), *C.P.* I, pp. 72-75, was first entitled ' Braid Scots An Inventory and Appraisement', dedicated to Edwin Muir, and published in *The Scottish Chapbook,* vol. 2, no. 3 (Nov.-Dec. 1923), pp. 63-67.
[2]   Henrik Arnold Wergeland (1808-1845).
[3]   Olav Nygard (1884-1924), poet.
[4]   André Bjerke (1918-1985), poet and author of mystery novels.
[5]   not identified.
[6]   Gustav Fröding (1866-1911).
[7]   Major Minor Records, London, 1968.
[8]   Olav Duun (1876-1939).
[9]   Knut Hamsun, Norwegian novelist, 1859-1952, Nobel Prize for Literature, 1920.
[10]   Jakob Sande (1906-1967).
[11]   Halldor Laxness, Icelandic novelist, 1902-1998, Nobel Prize for Literature, 1955.
[12]   William Heinesen, Faeroese novelist, 1900-1991.

36. From Jessie Kocmanová (NLS Acc.7361/47)

Jessie Kocmanová
603 00 Brno 1
Kalvadova 4
Czechoslovakia
23 June 1976

Dear Chris,

I feel terribly guilty for not having written you for so long and every time I am in Prague Ian Milner[1] curses me for not being able to tell him anything about you. The number of times I've sat down to write you and then been interrupted. However, I feel I must tell you about some work I've just finished.

I was asked by some people at a Spanish University to write an article on some aspect of literature and the working class for a symposium publication. (Arnold Kettle[2] and David Craig both spoke at the conference). So I did what I've been meaning to do for a long time and took another look at *A Scots Quair*.[3] (I'll send you a copy of the article by separate post.) I must say it made a far greater impression on me than it did away back in the Thirties and certainly I would rate it higher than most of the highly-praised unnecessary stuff that gets itself written and published today. What one wouldn't give for that unfinished novel he was said to be working on when he died. I suppose it really was destroyed according to his wishes, as Ivor Brown says in his introduction? I came to the conclusion, too, that the weak spots are not at all where the critics have alleged them to be – in the last book – but somewhere in the middle, and lie in the development of Chris Tavendale into a middle-class woman, and not in the character of young Ewan at all. Also I have been interested in some parallels to *The Antiquary*,[4] and above all, in its debt to *A Drunk Man*. Perhaps you think this is nonsense and typical literary criticitis, seeing influences all over the place, but I'm convinced it's not, and the next thing I hope to get down to is a consideration of *A Drunk Man* itself.[5]

I was in London for quite a time in summer 1974 and was very sorry I didn't get up to see you – but I was spending the time copying an unpublished Morris MS in the BM. That bore some fruit – I was asked to contribute to the special Morris double number of *Victorian Poetry* and wrote about this MS – his attempt in the 1870s at a contemporary novel which nobody had ever bothered to read properly and which to my mind demonstrates why he later went on to write his prose romances because he couldn't be bothered with the sort of thing the Victorian novel was trying to do.

I do hope, Chris, that you're keeping well and don't find all this rigmarole of mine too boring. As regards family, Vincie is still running his picture gallery business in London and working madly hard – he's become a real expert in Victoriana. Krista has married a nice Frenchman in Paris and would be happy but for some bad health, the result of her unsettled life for so long. Her husband's family is too *haute bourgeoise* for words but he is not and they go trotting around on business trips to places like Senegal. Anna is getting married in August and Jindra is already happily married and we have added bits to the house and turned it into three separate domiciles, or rather, we are in process of doing this and the building materials are all over the place, with me thumping at my typewriter in the middle of chaos. Otherwise, I've no doubt you are well informed as to how things are with us here. Some things could be worse, others could be much, much better.

I'm longing to hear from both you and Valda and curse the fact that I can't just pop over and see you without filling in all those idiotic forms. Also I'm kept very busy as I now run the literary side of the Department.

I shall be glad of even the tiniest note. Love to you both, and all yours.

You are both very often in my thoughts.

Ever,

Jessie.

[1] Ian Milner (1911-1991) was a New Zealand Marxist who taught at the Charles University in Prague from 1951. With his second wife Jarmila he translated several volumes of the poetry of Miroslav Holub and Vladimir Holan; and also many poems by other Czech poets. He contributed an essay on Grassic Gibbon to *The Marxist Quarterly*, 'An Estimation of Lewis Grassic Gibbon's "A Scots Quair"', vol. 1, no.4, pp. 207-218, (London, October 1954).

[2] Arnold Kettle (1916-1986) was the first Professor of English Literature with the Open University 1970-1981. He had previously been Professor of Literature in the University of Dar es Salaam 1967-1970. He was a pioneer of the Marxist criticism of the novel and published *An Introduction to the English Novel* in two volumes, London, 1951, 1953. He also edited *Shakespeare in a Changing World* : *Essays* [by various contributors], London, 1964. He was a C.P. member for fifty years.

[3] Kocmanová wrote 'a brief note' on Grassic Gibbon in the Journal of the Faculty of Philosophy of the University of Brno in 1955 and '"A Scots Quair" and its Relevance to the Scottish Proletarian Struggle of the Thirties' in *English Literature and the Working Class*, ed. by Francisco García Tortosa and Ramon Lopez Ortega (Seville: University of Seville, 1980), pp.77-93.

[4] By Sir Walter Scott (1771-1832).

[5] Cf. Kocmanová, '"Drunk Man Looks at the Thistle": Literary Landmark?' in *The Scottish Marxist* vol.15 (Winter 1977), pp. 6-18, and 'Hugh MacDiarmid, Grassic Gibbon, and the Class Commitment of Scottish Literature in the Twenties and Thirties' in *Hungarian Studies in English*, vol.13 (1980), pp. 59-69.

37. From Robert S. Warren (EUL Gen.2094/5/2374a&b)

31 Ponsonby Road
Milehouse
Plymouth
PL3 4HP
1 September 1976

Dear Mr MacDiarmid,

May I congratulate you on your appt. as the President of the Poetry Society.

I expect you will not remember me, after all these years, but I well remember you.

We used to meet during the 2nd World War when I was Admiralty Overseer at Scott's Shipbuilding Co. Ltd., Greenock, and you were in the Admiralty Stores at the Albert Harbour in Greenock.

I lived then at Bishopton, and you I believe lived in or near Glasgow, and we would often travel home together on the bus which ran from Largs to Glasgow.

We would board the bus outside Scott's Yard – remember?

I have always remembered that you paid me a compliment one evening on the bus – you said 'Warren you're the only decent Englishman I have ever met', or words to that effect.

One rather 'rash' statement you made was – 'After the war I will send you a "book" of my poems'; I would have liked that!

I have often read about you in the newspapers since, and have always been interested in things you have said and done.

After the War I had to return to Devonport with my wife and daughter, but we all have some very pleasant memories of Scotland.

Of course I am now retired (since 1962), so I suppose I am now an 'Ancient Briton'.

When I knew you it was as Mr Greaves, and not your professional name, Hugh MacDiarmid.

I think one of the 'bosses' at the Albert Harbour then was Lt the Hon John (?) Hankey R. N. (or was it R. N. *V. R*.?) with whom you were associated, I think, and he was the son of the late Lord Hankey, one of the Lords of Appeal in Ordinary.

His father, as you might well imagine, must have been a right 'Pillar of the Establishment'.

With every good wish.

Yours sincerely,

Robert S. Warren.

38. From Kenneth White (EUL MS2961.13 ff.30-31)

Résidence d'Aspin III
64000 PAU
France
11 October 1976

Dear Hugh MacDiarmid,

Well, we did not talk a great deal when we met, but that is no matter. I for my part had just left my folks, with a lump in my throat not conducive to dialectics. Then, I felt you'd probably done enough talking with the TV team. And anyway I like that old Chinese (or is it Japanese?) poem:

They spoke no word
the host, the guest
and the white chrysanthemums

In fact, though, I've been doing quite a lot of talking with you since I got back. About your 'East-West Synthesis' poems, we didn't stop at Castlelaw[1] on our way that night from Biggar, being anxious to get to Edinburgh, where I intended to go the next day to Updike's.[2] But the next day I didn't get round to Updike's after all – I met an old friend in the vicinity of Rose Street ... But I did get hold of your *Metaphysics and Poetry*[3] and the *Contemporary Scottish Studies*. (I'll write to Updike *re* the 'Poems of the East-West Synthesis'.)

Since my return I've written a review of the *Metaphysics and Poetry*, a review which extended into an essay: 'The Metaphysical Landscape'. The review will go to *Poetry Information*, the essay belongs in a book of essays I'm working on, but I may send it to Walter Perrie at Lothlorien for possible publication as a pamphlet. It's a dialogue with yourself, and a statement of my own position – I think it could interest you. It's time anyway I was publishing in my home country. In France here I'm known as a Scots poet, but in Scotland I'm probably something nearer the Abominable Snowman. Still, far-outness has its joyance, as you very well know.

I'll be sending you the odd sign in any case, from whatever provenance (two or three books, prose and poetry, come out in Paris this autumn; and a long poem-sequence is about to go into printing in London). This little note is just to say how glad I was to see you again, and in such fine fettle. Best regards to Mrs Grieve. Oh, by the way, Marie-Claude's pupils don't think the President is dishy at all – they prefer Alain Delon.

Salud!

Kenneth White.

PS The photos Marie-Claude took are not yet developed – if they're any good at all I'll be sending copies.

K.

[1]   The bookshop and press of Alex. Frizzell.
[2]   John Updike, Booksellers.
[3]   *Metaphysics and Poetry*, from a conversation with Walter Perrie, Hamilton, 1975.

39. From Eliot Weinberger (EUL Gen. 2094/6/2403)

The Montemora Foundation Inc.
Box 336, Cooper Station
New York
N. Y. 10003
USA
25 October 1976

Dear Mr MacDiarmid,

Roger Guedalla has forwarded your manuscript of 'Diamond Body' and 'Here is the Gate' for *Montemora*.

'Diamond Body' has long been one of my favourite poems – one of the essential poems, I think, of the century – and I am astonished that it has never been published in the US. It will be a great honour to include it in our third issue, scheduled for January.

I naturally recognised 'Here is the Gate' as an excerpt from 'Plaited Like the Generations of Men' – another favourite poem! I am, however, trying to avoid truncated texts in *Montemora*, and wonder if there are other works, poetry or prose, unpublished or unknown in the US, that we might use in its place.

In my reading of literary history, the UK and Ireland have produced three master poets in this century: Yeats, Bunting, and yourself. It is incredible that the latter two are so little known to American readers. I hope that *Montemora*, in its small way, will help change this terrible situation. (We are also publishing a long interview with Bunting in Number 3.)

Please consider *Montemora* as a reliable outlet for your work, and a good friend.

My best to you ---

Eliot Weinberger

40. From S. H. Quothquar (NLS Acc.7361/4)

22 February 1977

Dear Who? the mcdiarmid?

I listened last night to your vapourings on the telly, all about Scottish culture etc. How the hell do you think such metaphysical rubbish is going to help to fill the bellies of the Scottish workers which is all that they really want apart from a wee dram occasionally?

Mon, yer a puir stupid old bugger. You should quit all your havering and disappear quietly into the mists of Celtic limbo where you belong. As for the Anglophobia which it was mentioned you had spent most of your life doing – what a waste of a lifetime indulging in sae negative an emotion to no good purpose. You are a disgrace to a great people and a great country as well as being a miserable old curmudgeon. Get thee gone, thou cream-faced Communist loon! Scotland will be better without thee!

Silly Old Bugger

S. H. Quothquar

41. From Mary ('Mamie') MacDonald (EUL MS2968)

Islay
20 May 1977

My dear Chris,

I know the above will make you happy.[1] Naturally I am delighted about it, for it may help the publication of his other three novels along with masses of manuscripts which he'd given up as he never believed they'd get into print. It will be interesting to see if they'll attempt the pronunciation of the Gaelic names! They'll have a job. It's sad it's come so late. In a notebook he'd written, 'I've failed in everything I've tried to do'. He was 67 then. How true is the old Gaelic saying in his case, 'If you want praise, die'.

I heard you were going into hospital again on the 11th of May so I hope you are feeling fit and that the treatment isn't too unpleasant.

I looked around in vain for Gordon [Wright's] book[2] before I came 'home' for 10 days to Islay, a really beautiful place. The book must have been delayed, but it should go like hot cakes once the summer visitors and the Festival crowds descend on the Capital. I've ordered a copy and I'll be honoured if you'll autograph it, as it is something I want to leave for my youngest son, John-Ogilvie, his father's double, all 6' 4" of him, and who is a great admirer of your work. I just discovered this when he was up at Easter. He works in London.

Tom and I had a week in Montrose the October before his death – he said he wanted to see it *once* more. We walked around the old haunts and, standing near Foreman's house, he quoted your poem about him.[3] In fact I heard an awful lot of your poetry from him all our married life so there's little wonder I've his favourite pieces off by heart!

I also found a poem in *The Montrose Standard* (1927) on Edwin & Willa Muir, you & Tom by 'Mossgiel Minor'. The paper I put in the Nat. Library but I made a copy of the poem which I have in Edinburgh & will send it to you. From what I remember I think it was C. P. Robertson who wrote it. Wasn't he the Episcopalian minister? I know Tom had a very high regard for him.

I've taken these 10 days to catch up on much neglected correspondence. The sun shines every day but there is a biting wind so I can't sit around. Ruth [McQuilllan] is keeping house till I return so I hope she and the cat are getting on well together. It gives her some freedom to have a place of her own for a couple of weeks and gives me peace of mind.

My brother and his wife who live in Bermuda have retired here for 8 months in the year and have a spare flat so it allows me to come back to my native soil for a few days each year – but mighty little Gaelic is spoken today. Keep well and take care.

My love to you and Valda.

Mamie.

1   Mrs MacDonald's letter was written below and on the back of a letter from the Souvenir Press Ltd which told her that Lady Antonia Fraser had chosen their reprint of *And The Cock Crew* as her 'Pick of the Paperbacks' for a review programme, 'Read All About It', the last in that current series, which would be broadcast on 5 June that year.
2   *MacDiarmid : An illustrated Biography,* Edinburgh, 1977.
3   The poem to which Mrs MacDonald refers was sub-titled 'MacDiarmid's Curses' in *Collected Poems* (1962). It begins, 'Here in the hauf licht hoo I've grown!', *C.P.* I, p. 234. It was part of *To Circumjack Cencrastus* (1930).

42. From Tommy Mearns (NLS Acc.7361/48)

18 McKie Avenue
Dumfries
29 June 1977

'Sincere congratulations and best wishes to you on reaching your 85th birthday from your old-time Printer's Devil.... Tommy'.

Dear Christopher,

Tommy Mearns, now a retired Clergyman staying in a Corporation house in Dumfries sends you his warm and sincere congratulations on your approaching 85th birthday. It is many years since we worked together on the *Montrose Review*. I think we both started and left about the same time, so we must have had seven years working on the *Review*. I well remember the birth of *The Scottish Chapbook* and *Northern Numbers*, then came our biggest job together, *The Scottish Nation*. What a fight you had during those years. And you even offered to contest Dundee if George Bernard Shaw would contest a General Election. But he withdrew, and you did likewise. Amid all your troubles you kept the heid! I only once saw you get angry, and that was the day I pulled a proof copy of your leader in the *Review* and it was laid up on a galley and James Foreman began editing your article by cutting bits out. After he had finished scoring bits out he handed the galley proof over to you asking you to make amendments, but you simply rolled the proof into a ball of wastepaper and threw it to the end of the room saying quite audibly, 'Write the damned thing yourself'. You went off to your room, and James Foreman asked me to pull another proof, and after a very small correction he let the editorial pass.

I remember how kind and understanding you were with me when I told you I was thinking of going into the Congregational Ministry after I had taken an Arts degree. At that time I was in Dorward's Orphanage, but you put in a good word for me with the Governor of 'the Hoosie' and he allowed me the full use of the boardroom at weekends to allow me every opportunity to swot up the Greek language and other studies. *Many thanks for opening doors for me when I required them open*. Some of your own push and struggle was passed on to me and kept me going.

I took Economics in my M.A. degree and I also have you to blame for this. Some years ago after the First World War I remember a gentleman coming into the *Review* office to invite all of us to buy saving stamps. I think he was one of the landed gentry. All the staff including yourself were brought into the front office to hear this luminary present his case for national savings. We all listened carefully, and Jim Foreman asked for questions. You immediately obliged by stressing the need to let capital go round more quickly and not tie it up and prevent honest and good circulation of the currency, if we were ever to overcome unemployment. After you had delivered your manifest contribution Jim Foreman was quite red in the face, and he turned to me and said, 'Well, Tommy, what do you think then?' I replied, 'I think exactly the same as Mr Grieve. It is the only way to solve unemployment'. Jim Foreman looked at me in disgust, and turned to the speaker and said that would be enough for the day. That was the first time I realised that you and I together could move mountains.

I remember one day I went into the back room to tell you we were one page short for *The Scottish Chapbook* that month. You immediately lit up your thick black and took out your short pencil and wrote out a lovely poem about a wee bairn. It was all over in five minutes, about three or four verses only. It was the finest wee poem I ever clapped eyes on. I could see you were a born poem: you had the feel of reality in your bones and you could translate it into meaningful words. The title of that poem was 'The Bonnie Broukit Bairn' if my memory serves me right.[1]

I saw all along in those early years how necessary the revival of Scots Arts and Letters was because we had nothing in Scotland to base a true political revival upon, unless it were the old I.L.P., but even that lacked the depth of vision required. It was essential for Scotland's future that you, Christopher, should keep up your cultural end of the bargain, and this you did magnificently, but not without much heart-searching at times, but this heart-searching is good for all of us at times, dear brother.

I am quite looking forward to seeing your book when it comes out on July 5th. I hope it gets good press and television coverage. Last time I met you face to face was on a railway platform, Dumbarton station, during the war years. You were going round the platform trying to spot a man with a match. You wanted a light, and when I held my lighted match into your face, I almost dropped with excitement because I had never met you face to face since we left the *Review* about the same time. I was going up to the University on some matter, and I told you about a book review I had missed, and later on you spotted it somewhere and sent it to me. Many thanks for that favour. I think you told me you were a cook on a tramp steamer during the war which was on at that time. That must have been around 1944!

I trust you and your goodwife will keep well during your festive celebrations. I hope you will appear on television to tell us at least a part of your story, although you don't like talking about yourself. *We really have to get you 'wound-up' to do it!* Let us see you in your shining armour, and damn your critics! You have a right to every bit of yours, because you had to make it for yourself as you went along. It was either that or Scotland would have lost a National Bard. My life has been greatly enriched by knowing you in those earlier years when you were under all manner of pressures, but you were determined to survive and win through gallantly and honestly for Scotland's sake only. All I can say now is, 'Dull would he be of soul who could pass by a sight so touching in its majesty'.

My wife joins with me in sending you and your wife our very best wishes for a happy and enjoyable honouring of your life-work on the publication of *MacDiarmid An Illustrated Biography.*

Wishing you both good health and much happiness.

Yours sincerely,

Tommy Mearns.

God's blessing on you both.

[1]   After 55 years Tommy Mearns's memory seems to have let him down with regard to 'The Bonnie Broukit Bairn', which was first published in *The Scottish Chapbook*, vol.1, no.5 (December 1922) as IV in the series 'From "A Kist o' Whistles"'. 'Cophetua' as V of 'From "A Kist o' Whistles"' and 'To One Who Urges More Ambitious Flights' are also on the same page.

43. From Charles Nicoll (EUL MS2956 f.37)

226 Tresta Road
Glasgow
G23 5DD
11 July 1977

Dear Dr Grieve,

I have received your biography from Gordon Wright Publishing and have had a first reading of it. I found it extremely interesting reading but also very harrowing in a number of instances. I felt disturbed at the hardship you suffered during all the period from 1945 while in Glasgow and I had known nothing of it. The account of your accident in London when you were toppled from the upper deck of a bus was horrifying. Indeed, to picture this happening made me actually shudder. After reading right through the book the evidence is clear that, in a material sense, Fate did not deal with you kindly. Indeed this seems to have been the fate of many of the most gifted writers, musicians and painters. What really makes me angry about this is the fortunes which these works are sold for by mercenaries long after the authors have died. I saw an example of this during a visit to my daughter in America this year. In a bookstore there was quite a display of the works of the Dundee poet.[1] Yet they laughed him to scorn during his lifetime and they still laugh at his memory but all the time they are coining in the money from this man's writing. This sickens me.

But to get back to your biography – it also leaves me with the feeling that there is still a great deal more to be told and probably told better in an autobiography because, there, it is the person who is speaking from the pages and, therefore, a better understanding of the person is obtained. The book is well illustrated and the pictures give life to the wording in connection with them. The picture of you at work in Mechans came out quite well but I prefer the one on page 68 of yourself along with Francis George Scott which I took on the occasion of a visit to my home, at that time at Shakespeare Street, Maryhill. To me this looks the most natural with no hint of a pose whatsoever. Indeed it was this picture that took my mind back to the happy occasions we had together and the discussions I so much enjoyed.

Do you remember the efforts made to get a popular cultural movement going among a broader mass of people when cultural leaders like Dr Honeyman of Glasgow Art Gallery, William MacLellan, publisher, Ian Whyte of the BBC orchestra, and Douglas Young rallied to your call? It fell through because you were transferred to the Navy and you were the driving force behind the movement. These are the days I now look back on as among the most enjoyable in my life so I'll close by saying, 'Thanks for the memory'.

I am,

yours sincerely,

Charles Nicoll.

PS For years I signed my name with one 'l' at 'Nicol', but on retiring it was pointed out to me my birth certificate showed it with two 'l's. C. N.

---

[1]   William McGonagall.

44. From Benno Schotz (NLS MS27155 f.49)

> 2 Kirklees Rd
> Glasgow
> G12 0TN
> n.d. [probably August 1977]

My dear Christopher,

It was nice to have your note, though quite unexpected. It was good to know that you are as active as ever and have not lost your sense of humour.

I enjoyed seeing you and Valda at Michael Wright's and to have the chance of a few words with you.

The Press has been voluble about your approaching 85th birthday and I am writing to send you my warm greetings and good wishes for the 11th. Mine is later in August also, but I will be a year older than you. The inner spirit of revolt and anger at the stupidity of those who rule us helps us both to carry on with an optimism few can understand. To be an individualist today is not given to many people, and to demand attention to very few indeed. You are of this small breed, and I salute you and wish you many more years of health and strength to carry the torch of freedom into the darkest corners of our habitat.

One day Michael will take me on a pilgrimage to visit you and Valda, and this will be a happy occasion for me.

With respect, love and affection.

Benno.

45. From Alexander Moffat (NLS Acc.7361/48)

41a Broughton Street
Edinburgh
EH1 3JU
30 September 1977

Dear Dr Grieve,

I have been asked to write about your *Twenty Poems by Hugh MacDiarmid with Twenty Lithographs by William Johnstone* for *Art Monthly*.[1] (A London art magazine – the only one interested in what is happening in Scotland.) I know that you have been a friend of William Johnstone's for fifty years or more and have championed his work for all of that time, but I wonder if you feel that there is something special about the new collaboration. I should be very interested in hearing from you about this.

I should also like to take this opportunity to approach you about the possibility of coming out to paint your portrait. As you may know, I have painted some of the Scottish poets in the past, most notably Norman MacCaig, and I should very much like to do something of you – more than anything else in fact. Recently I painted the actor Bernie Scott as William Soutar for the film *The Garden Beyond* and as a result of this I am now planning a painting of yourself and the real Soutar. I think that this would be an important picture to do. Of course, you'll look a lot younger in this particular painting.

I hope this letter doesn't take up too much of your time.

With very best wishes.

Yours sincerely,

Alexander Moffat.

---

[1]   Edinburgh, 1977. Moffat's review, 'A collaboration', was published in *Art Monthly* 14 (December 1977-January 1978).

Platform Party at the Celebrity Concert to honour Hugh MacDiarmid on his 85th birthday
in the Music Hall, George Street, Edinburgh on 13th August 1977, sponsored by the
Scottish Trades Union Congress and supported by the Scottish Arts Council.
By permission of the National Library of Scotland and of Stewart Ferguson.

From left to right in the background are Terry Neason (?), Iain Cuthbertson, John McGrath,
—, Hugh MacDiarmid, Ronald Stevenson, Henry Stamper, Patricia McCue, Bill McCue,
Jimmy Milne, —, Elizabeth MacLennan, —, Dave Anderson, Valda Grieve (off stage).

46. From Patrick Crotty (EUL Gen.2094/1/351a&b)

1 Ashe Quay
Fermoy
Co. Cork
Ireland
11 November 1977

Dear Dr Grieve,

I hope you are well and have recovered from the birthday celebrations! I'd like to enlist your aid, if you have time and are not bogged down with commitments. I'm working on the 'Clann Albann' poems at the moment: you say, in the author's note to *Scots Unbound*, that the contents of that volume belong, with those of *First Hymn to Lenin*, to the opening, or autobiographical, book of 'Clann Albann'. My questions relate to 'Depth and the Chthonian Image' from *Scots Unbound*.

1. (Perhaps a silly question). 'Depth etc.' is linked to the 'Muckle Toon' poems in its development of their water symbolism etc. Is it linked in its setting also, i.e., was the ruined mill of the poem's subtitle in the vicinity of Langholm, or indeed anywhere?

2. Does the word 'epopteia', used in this and other poems of the early Thirties, refer to illumination in general or to illumination in the secrets of the dead as revealed to initiates at Eleusis, in particular? If the latter is the case, then 'chthonian' in the poem's title refers to the Chthonian gods who yielded up their secrets to the Eleusinian initiates. (?)

I'd like to take this opportunity to say how much I enjoyed your speech at the end of the birthday concert in August. All the genteel half-baked nonsense of the Labourites was 'like rook blown awa'' by your speech which made what would otherwise have been a night of mindless sentimentalism more than memorable to me. Thank you!

Please give my very best wishes to Valda. Again, hoping you are well.

Yours sincerely,
Patrick Crotty.

47. From John Montague (EUL MS2955.15 f.13)

25 Grattan Hill
Cork
27 November 1977

Dear Christopher,

Last night we had a crowd of young people in, dancing and talking, and Pat (Crotty) showed me your letter, so generous and so brave. It brought back many memories, all of them heartening. As it happens I have been thinking of you a lot these last months, and not only because I have been trying to drag Pat's thesis out of him; he is the best student I have had in convivial chat over the bottle but the formalities of critical writing bore him, as they do us all! But I had begun to work on a broadcast on Sorley [MacLean] and trying to find someone in Scotland to do the cover for Sydney [Goodsir Smith's] record (there has been so much talk about the misprints or Anglicizations in the *Collected Poems* [1] that I wanted to clarify the issue).

Working on these two tasks, you were often in my mind, because after all, they are the only two who occasionally reach your level of intensity; and both are finally lyric poets, Sydney obviously, but even Sorley is more *emotional* than metaphysical (don't tell him I said that, but I feel it is true). And as I passed through London to work on *The Rough Field* [2] record I saw Tim O'Keeffe and discussed the *Complete Poems*. [3] I wish there were some way it could be hurried along but he and Martin [Green] are living & drinking on a shoestring. But while it is great to see one's own monument unveiled, you know that nearly everyone who cares has tracked down the work over the years. Right across the world (I should say 'left'!) you are recognised as a great poet. When Garech and I first spoke of poetry, your name came up first, and when I got drunk with John Berryman [4] he insisted *A Drunk Man* was the only masterpiece suitable to our footless condition and recited tracts of it, oceans of it!

And as well as being a great poet, you have been a great example. I don't think I would have tried something like *The Rough Field* without your continual proof that poetry can deal with *anything*, provided there is passion and intelligence. I remember a very intense conversation we once had, in Biggar, in which we seemed to agree about such things, and I don't think it was the good whisky alone. Your example was especially warming for someone suspicious of English literary imperialism, like myself: you showed me I was not alone in my refusal to bow to the metropolis, nor do I yet.

And so, as I work on, you will always be with me. When I found refuge in Cork, my first thought was to bring you, and your visit here has become a legend, something to fire the young forever. You will have found that in Pat but it applies to the young poets as well. It would have been nice if you had both come back especially as we now have a house in Cork where, as last night, we could have a splendid time.

Garech is somewhere in the East, still unmarried. Paddy Maloney [5] is a kind of superstar of Celtic Pop, still playing well but overextending himself in the competitive concert world. I write away steadily and have two largish prizes in the last two years. I have not been back to Edinburgh since; I miss Sydney's presence, and also I try to curtail my wanderings. Nora Clarke is still alive, lonely but brave; [6] Evelyn is very fond of her. To end this rambling letter, Christopher, I would like to wish you some success with your new treatments and let Valda be assured that there is always a welcome for her here. A student brought a Highland Malt last night; I raise a parting glass in your honour.

Gratefully,

John (Montague).

[1]   London, 1975.
[2]   *The Rough Field : 1961-71* is now in its sixth edition.

3   *Complete Poems* was published by Martin Brian and O'Keeffe, London, on 28 September 1978, in two volumes.
4   John Berryman (1914-1972), US poet.
5   Paddy Maloney was the leader of The Chieftains, the Irish traditional instrumental group.
6   Nora Clarke was the widow of Austin Clarke.

48a. From Eugène Guillevic (EUL MS2961.13 f.57v.)

On the back of a letter from John Montague to MacDiarmid, 'end of 1977'.

Guillevic, a Celt & Communist

Cher Poète,
Permettez à un poète Breton, bien que d'expression Française, de vous addresser à travers landes, menhirs et dolmens, ses felicitations et ses voeux de vous voir continuer longtemps votre belle oeuvre.
   Guillevic.

48b. From Eugène Guillevic (Translation)

Dear Poet,
Allow a Breton poet, though writing in French, to address to you across wastes, menhirs and dolmens his congratulations and his good wishes to see you continuing your fine work for a long time to come.

49. From Sacheverell Sitwell (EUL MS2966)

Weston Hall
Towcester
Northamptonshire
n.d.[1977]

Dear Hugh MacDiarmid
Please allow me to write and thank you for allowing 'Ulysses' Bow' to appear in the little *Hand and Eye*.[1] How much I admire and envy the language you write in, with all the additional sounds and possibilities that have run out of English!
   It is very satisfying that our mutual old friend Kaikhosru Sorabji seems at last to be receiving some of the admiration he has so long deserved, and refused! The pianist Yonky Solomon is a most devoted and doughty performer – and I have not heard anything like it in the Wigmore Hall since the great days of Busoni's recitals there in 1924-5.
   With greetings and renewed thanks.
   Yours,
   Sacheverell Sitwell.

[1] 'Ulysses' Bow' appeared in *Hand and Eye: an Anthology for Sacheverell Sitwell*, ed. by Geoffrey Elborn in 1977. 'Ulysses' Bow' first appeared in *The Lucky Bag* in 1927, *C. P.* I, pp.171-172. Geoffrey Elborn was born in 1950.

50. From Basil Bunting (EUL MS2945 f.9)

107 Striding Edge
Blackfell
Washington
Tyne and Wear
15 January 1978

Dear Chris,

Somebody said you were ill. I hope that's not true. But it reminded me that I'd neither written to you nor seen you for quite a long time, which is out of tune with what I feel.

Of course there are reasons (as well as excuses). When they were celebrating your birthday I remembered how embarrassed I was by the letters when they were celebrating mine, and thought it better not to add to the pile, which must have been enormous. And since then I've had nothing of my own to chronicle but misfortunes, which aren't cheering matter for the post.

You and I must be the last survivors of Orage's literary young men. There can't be very many survivors of Pound's. And the world hasn't taken very much notice of us. You'll be remembered, right enough, for quite a few centuries, but it would be nice if they'd thought on to remember you while you can still enjoy it. I listen in vain to the honours list for the O.M. or the knighthood they ought to have given you long since, and I get very angry every summer when the Swedish academy passes over both you and Zukovsky, thus making asses of themselves. (Solzhenitsyn – I ask you!)[1]

Now I'm living in a house Northern Arts has from the new town here – not a badly planned house, inside, but the nastiest place I've ever had to inhabit. I couldn't live otherwise, couldn't pay a rent, let alone buy a cottage to die in. The ghost of a stroke has left my right side numb – can't hold a needle, can't help dropping my cigarette, which complicates life for an old man all alone. I keep the car going, but it is so many miles to anything that can be called the country that I'm discouraged from using it as much as I did and would like to. All the same, when the nights are lighter I'll come over Carter or through Liddesdale to see you, if I may. Can you still polish off enough Glenfiddich to keep cheerful?

Please give Valda my affectionate greetings; and for you affection and admiration keep step.

Yours ever,

B.

[1] Alexander Solzhenitsyn (1918-2008), novelist and historian. Nobel Prize for Literature in 1970.

51. From Alan Riach (EUL Gen.2094/5/1931)

85 Whitehill Lane
Gravesend
Kent
[early 1978]

Dear Christopher Grieve,

My deepest thanks for your two poems, and your letter.[1] That the poems are in Scots, generous, but taut, will, I think, get the magazine off on the right footing. When it is finally printed, I shall send you on a copy.

We had a marvellous evening with Sorley and Robert Garioch, which grew more and more enjoyable as the night grew deeper.[2] Bert Davis drove them down on the 30th, arriving at 4 o'clock, and we were talking and drinking until 3.00 am; and they set off at 9.00 am the next morning!

I am travelling to Scotland myself in a week's time for the duration of the holiday, and I would dearly have liked to have seen you again, but from what you say in your letter I imagine you may be under some pressure just now, and receiving as few visitors as possible. At least, I shall phone to ask after you when I do get back. The radio/neutron therapy has had a beneficial effect on a headmaster I know here, and it is far more effective than chemico-therapy. It seems that that is your best chance, and I hope it is as effective as it can be.

Give my best wishes to your wife Valda, and my deep regards I send to yourself.
Yours ever,
Alan Riach.

[1] ' My Sailor Son Comes Home' (after the German of Stefan George), *C.P.* II, p.1307, and 'Under The Hallior Moon', *C.P.* II, p.1313, were printed in *Gallimafray,* edited by Alan Riach and David Richards (Cambridge, 1978).
[2] Riach and a fellow-student, Christopher Larsen, organised a poetry reading at Churchill College, Cambridge, in 1978.

52. From Christine MacIntosh (EUL MS2954.6 f.118)

Lakefield College School
13 April 1978

Dear Dad,

It was so very good to see you again despite the sadness of knowing you to be ill and in pain. Just to have you there in your own chair by the fire with your spirit undimmed by your recent very debilitating troubles was a joy.

On the way back on the plane it came to me that all too often words that should be spoken are left unsaid until too late. So before this is so, I want you to know that I do, did, and always have, admired you as a man and loved you as a father.

Walter's birthday went off very well and he is now all set for the second fifty years. A great pity Deirdre couldn't be there too but it was lovely to have Michael.

He must be very sad about the loss of Garscadden to Labour after all his efforts. I saw the paragraph in our morning paper today. I'll be writing to him very soon – also a letter to Valda is next on the agenda. My address to the Mothers' Guild of the School was – if I may say so – an outstanding success and was extremely well received by the largest turnout they have ever had. So I think I should be pleased with my work. I had a good time doing it and received a lovely bunch of deep red carnations as well as my free luncheon.

25 April

Time seems to have escaped me since I got back to work. Rory[1] competed this week in a Music Festival where he won two firsts. He sang in the Changed Voices Class as a tenor and was given an excellent adjudication and also in the Baritone under 21 years where again the adjudication was very complimentary. He was invited to sing then in the 'Concert of Festival Stars' but could not accept as he was participating in a Model United Nations Assembly for four days as part of the Ugandan Delegation where I believe he distinguished himself by organizing 4 'kidnappings' and 2 'assassinations'. All in all he enjoyed the experience thoroughly.

Had a long letter today from the Farrars who send love to you both. Elspeth[2] phoned last night to let me know that Dan's father is in hospital, having suffered a stroke. He is making progress but also faces surgery on his prostate gland which has been causing him difficulty.

My love to you all and keep working on that date in July – I'm keeping it free. Will write to Valda soon.

Much love from all here. Christine.

---

[1]   Her son.
[2]   Her daughter.

53. From Douglas Sealy (EUL MS2960.7 ff.6-7)

[late April-early May 1978]

A UISDIN MHIC DHIARMAID
(recté Giolla Chríosd Mac a' Ghreidhir)
Salud!

A MESSAGE FROM ONE OF THE DAMNED (A Schoolteacher: Parasite on the Body of Education but aware of Higher Things such as Poetry and Politics but much preferring Poetry) to be filed under fan-mail.

This is just a little note to say that having been hospitalized for the past fortnight – nothing serious – I find myself whiling away the long watches of the night by repeating to myself those lines of yours that seem to have stuck in my memory like burrs. I can remember nearly all of *Sangschaw*, some of *Penny Wheep* and there are lines from *A Drunk Man* that stand as heich forenenst the sun stupendous as a windlestrae! And of course there is 'North of the Tweed'[1] from *Cencrastus* and the famous lyric by Alias MacAlias 'Perfect' by Hugh MacDiarmid, Fernan de Rojas and Glyn Jones. I used to know the whole of Crombie Saunders' selection by heart (for its size an excellent selection, crammed with meaning like a Jack-in-the-box – open any page and something jumps up and hits you). I have had it brought in to me and am re-impressing on the electric circuitry of my brain such noble poems as 'Harry Semen', 'Depth and the Chthonian Image' and 'Stony Limits'.

As one of the world's great quoters you will forgive me if I offer a short quotation from John Cage: 'As I see it, poetry is not prose simply because poetry is in one way or another formalised. It is not poetry by reason of its content or ambiguity but by reason of allowing musical elements (time, sound) to be introduced into the world of words. Thus, traditionally, information no matter how stuffy (e.g., the sutras and shastras of India) was transmitted in poetry. It was easier to grasp that way'.[2] It is the time and sound that make the works I have mentioned so memorable (and of course the content) – they are so much more highly organised in those regards than in *In Memoriam JJ*, à mon avis. And if all the books in the world were to be destroyed these poems could be reconstructed from the memories of men. This note is turning into a lecture! – What I really want to express is simply the gratitude I feel towards you as I fall asleep murmuring such lines as

> Not since Ezekiel has that faw sun ringed
> A worthier head; red as Adam you stood
> In the desert, the horizon with vultures black-winged,
> And sang and died in this still greater solitude[3]

I retain vivid memories of your visit to my house. I trust that you and Valda are in good health.
Douglas Sealy.
Turloch, Thormanby Rd, Howth, Co Dublin

---

[1]   *C.P.* II, pp.269-271.
[2]   John Cage, *Silence: Lectures and Writings* (London, 1968). Sealy quotes from 'Foreword', p. x.
[3]   From 'Stony Limits', *C.P.* I, p. 422.

54. From Kaikhosru Shapurji Sorabji (EUL MS2960.17 f.41)

The EYE; Townsend
Corfe Castle
Wareham
Dorset
16 June 1978

My dear Dr Grieve,
I am very distressed to hear from our dear Norman [Peterkin] that you have been so ill and had so many operations. He tells me that when he saw you, you were

better; that I rejoice to hear! Norman tells me you asked after me with your usual kindness VASTLY APPRECIATED! Although I do not write often that doesn't mean I'm forgetful of my old friends. NOT A SCRAP. BUT these days my eyes aren't up to much after the vast amount of huge scores I've written and am apt to wriggle out of letter-writing when I didn't oughter! I don't know if Norman told you that somebody came from Canada on purpose to microfilm all my unpublished works thousands of pages of huge scores … which they took away from my home here and brought back when the job was done assisted by an adorable and devoted young friend without whose invaluable assistance the thing could never have been accomplished. I finished a spell of writing of some six years duration and hope I shan't have to write any more … some six major works but NOT any enormous full scores any more … but all the same several VERY large piano works. *Cui bono?* All one can say is with the loathsome Luther *Gott helfe mich ich kann nicht anders* …

By the way do you know the THREE GREAT LIES … or at least three of them … many others of course?? …

British fair play …

French politeness

Christian charity …

with which bright thought I'll leave you for this nonce with all affectionate greetings and well-wishings from yours as always

AND WITH APOLOGIES FOR MY VILE TYPING!!! … MUCH WORSE NOWADAYS.

Kaikhosru Shapurji Sorabji

55. From Basil Bunting (EUL MS2945 f.14)

107 Striding Edge
Blackfell
Washington
Tyne and Wear
24 June 1978

Dear Chris,

I'm wondering what the prospects are for your Dublin voyage. I hope you can make it – pain gone or diminished – and can show those untamed Irishmen the civilised, efficient way to rid the world of whisky by drinking it all up. That's true teetotalism.

By the way, some to me unknown person whose copy of my book I signed some time ago at some public function has thought it right to send me the price of a couple of bottles of the stuff. The first time *that* has ever happened to me.

I've agreed to review your complete works for *Agenda*, so I am waiting almost as anxiously as you for their appearance. I'll have nothing new to say, I fear, having said it all before in the same magazine, but it would be a shame to let the occasion pass without a shout, particularly seeing what fools the mass of the critics are.[1]

I'm also looking forward to your oriental adventures. What a country, Egypt! I remember a boy on Tanta railway station with a beautiful clean nightie on and a rose in his hair. I'd have jumped from the train if I hadn't been so broke, he was so pretty – and I'm normally only moveable by canny young lasses. Should I warn Valda to keep a sharp eye on them? Also there was a session in a café in Alexandria, with one boy cleaning my shoes, another opening oysters at my right hand and a third at my left shelling prawns. The wine was good, the sun not too hot, and my Arabic just equal to a few broad jokes. But I daresay you'll be shepherded by the rich and famous, who will think you far too respectable for any fun.

My only news is that a publisher seems to be thinking, very cautiously, of doing my *Pious Cat*, but is at odds with me about illustrations. A Canadian ex-pupil turned up here, pleasant enough for two days. And I read, very badly, in Leeds to quite a crowd. Jonathan Williams[2] is back in Dentdale, but I haven't seen him yet.

Please give Valda my love. With luck I might manage another afternoon at Brownsbank sometime in July or August. And to you, better health and cheerful days.

Yours ever,

B.

[1]   Bunting contributed 'Hugh MacDiarmid Lost' to *Agenda* 16 (3-4), 1978.

[2]   Jonathan Williams (1929-2008), poet and author of a variety of literary works.

56. *From Seamus Heaney (EUL MS2962.4 f.58)*

191 Strand Road
Dublin 4
6 July 1978

Dear Chris and Valda,

Congratulations.

I am sorry not to have seen you but I am sure you feel by now you have seen enough. I have to go off on the 8:15a.m. train to Belfast in the morning so I just want to add my grain of pleasure to the strand and to say, like Molly, yes, yes, yes to the new doctor.

With love and gratitude to you and yours,

Seamus Heaney.

57. *From Alex McCrindle (EUL MS2953.11 f.96)*

38 Trinity Church Square
London
England
SE1 4HY
n.d. [August 1978]

Dear Chris,

I'm sorry I forgot about your birthday! Belatedly, Many Happy Returns!

I agree with you about the lack of reviews of *The Socialist Poems*.[1] I wrote a letter to the *Morning Star* quoting 'Reflections in an Ironworks'[2] in connection with some news item. I hoped to remind those responsible that they had not yet reviewed your book but nothing has happened.

I have now written to the features editor, Bob Leeson, asking him what has happened.

Good to see that *The Scotsman* has at least reported your Dublin trip and reviewed *The Socialist Poems*.

I'm hoping to get to Edinburgh before I go to Spain but if I don't I shall come up afterwards.

Jessica[3] is pregnant and they are moving to Fife quite soon.

Jean[4] is going to live in Derbyshire.

But only here can I get so much work! Perhaps I ought to stop work?

Love to you both.

Alex.

PS Disappointing about the *Complete Poems*.[5] I know the feeling. I recorded a play specially written for me by C. P. Taylor[6] just before the last General Election.[7] It's now being shown on 27 August!

[1]   *The Socialist Poems of Hugh MacDiarmid* was edited by T. S. Law and Thurso Berwick (London, Henley and Boston, 1978).
[2]   *C. P.*, I, p. 555.
[3]   Catherine and Jessica were twin daughters of Alex McCrindle and Honor Arundel, his second wife .
[4]   Jean was Alex McCrindle's daughter by his first marriage.
[5]   *Complete Poems* was published on 28 September 1978, nineteen days after MacDiarmid's death.
[6]   C. P. Taylor (1929-1981) was a prolific writer for both theatre and television.
[7]   'The last General Election' was on 10 October 1974.

58. From Joseph Chiari (EUL MS2947 ff.34-35)

15A Westleigh Avenue
Putney
London SW15
2 September 1978

My dear Chris,

I was very moved by your letter; it brought me great joy. I know what it cost you to write it, and I appreciate your affection, as you can always count on mine. Then, it shows also that nailed on your Tree, as you are, your mind and heart are still strong and I think that God, who loves you more than he loves all the Holy Wyllies of our hypocritical world, will keep you this side of the earth, for a good while yet. He knows that you are still needed among your people for whom you have been Father, brother and lover, all in one. In our egalitarian age, devoted to worshipping the herd, the masses, I still believe that peoples and nations, every now and then, throw up from their entrails, from their history, men and women who sum up their past, see their future, and fully understand their destiny. These people are for me, typical heroes of tragedies, for their own people are slow to understand them, and take up their tents and follow them, so they let them die on solitary rocks, nailed to trees or on lonely hillsides. Knowledge, the knowledge imparted by these extraordinary men, seemed only to strike their own people as a slanting, dying light, once they themselves have practically disappeared beyond the horizon. This is what Hegel meant when he said that the owl of Minerva only appeared at dusk. You are at the dusk of your life, a marvellous and courageous life, and your light has anything but set. I can guess your suffering, I know what it takes you to write a letter; I have like you spent a good deal of my time in Hospitals; in fact I am going in again at the end of the month for another operation. So, my good friend, if I say that I admire your courage, I vaguely know what this kind of courage is, for I have spent many nights, with only a night light, and every now and then the muffled footsteps of a nurse along the corridor. I am convinced, Christopher, that God willing, you and I, Valda and Joy, will again be together next year chatting, and drinking whisky together.

I am sad to hear about your collected poems. It is a downright shame that they keep you waiting so long before you can see your own work, and worse still, before the rest of the world can see it, and derive joy and profit from it. Publishers are, on the whole, scoundrels, yet, there are some who are human. Ann Stevenson, a Scot who loves your poetry and Gaelic poetry, will review my poems for the T.L.S. I was very pleased to hear this piece of news. I forgot to tell you that I wrote a short memoir on T. S. Eliot in which I said that, in spite of your different social and political attitudes, you were the poet he admired most. That will come out next year, and I shall bring you a copy. Before that I shall send you, when it comes out, a book on *Picasso*. The Spaniards, like the Scots, have a sense of tragedy, and as a Corsican, I feel great affinities with them. I have just been reading Pablo Neruda, and he loved Chile, with the passion with which you love Scotland, and myself Corsica and Scotland, so much so that I have always felt that I should like my bones to find their final rest in Scotland on the banks of Loch Achray in the Trossachs.

I hope that Valda has a very good holiday in Spain. She needs it, for, alas, she has a great deal to do to look after you, but thank God you have her. I can say the same for Joy. I hope that you have a pleasant, or rather, as easy a time as it is possible with your son. I am, as you know, most happy to hear from you, and whenever you can, even a few short words, which I know, cost you a lot, are welcome.

Meanwhile, courage, my good friend, and to this wish, we join our affection for you both.

Love.

Yours ever.

Jo.

From left to right, Walter Grieve, Michael Grieve, Valda Grieve and Walter Bell at the unveiling of the commemorative plaque to Hugh MacDiarmid on the wall of Langholm Library, 14 September, 1980. Walter Bell was chair of the Hugh MacDiarmid Memorial Committee. (*The Scotsman*)

Letters to Hugh MacDiarmid which have previously appeared in print:

Appendix B of Maurice Lindsay, *Francis George Scott & The Scottish Renaissance* (Edinburgh: Paul Harris Publishing, 1980) has a 'Survey of the Letters from F.G. Scott to Hugh MacDiarmid' in small print but does not include or annotate any complete letter, pp.184-212.

Four letters from George Ogilvie, dated 10 February 1925, 17 January 1928, 1 May 1928 and 31 October 1932, in *Hugh MacDiarmid-George Ogilvie Letters,* ed. by Catherine Kerrigan (Aberdeen: Aberdeen University Press, 1988), pp.115-116,129-130,135-136,146-147.

One letter from D.S. Mirsky, dated 25 June 1934, in 'D.S. Mirskii and Hugh MacDiarmid: A Relationship and an Exchange of Letters' by G.S. Smith, published in *Slavonica,* vol.3, no. 2, ed. by Yekaterina Young (Sheffield: Academic Press, 1987), pp. 49-60 [54].

Two letters from Hamish Henderson, dated 5 July 1969 and 9 June 1970, in *The Armstrong Nose,* ed. by Alec Finlay (Edinburgh: Polygon, 1996), pp.174-6 and 196-7.

One letter from Sir Patrick Geddes, dated 19 October 1925, in *Cencrastus* 75, ed. by Raymond Ross (Edinburgh, [2003]), p.48.

Parts of two letters from Catherine Carswell, dated 17 May 1936 and 7 October 1938, in *Nationalism and Modernism,* ed. by Margery Palmer McCulloch (Glasgow: Association for Scottish Literary Studies, 2004), pp.366-7 and pp.376-7.

Six letters from Valda Grieve, dated [10 September 1935], 17 September 1937, 9 February 1942, 1 June 1942, [January 1945], 15 March 1945, in *Scarcely Ever Out of My Thoughts*: *The Letters of Valda Trevlyn Grieve to Christopher Murray Grieve* (Hugh MacDiarmid), ed. with an Introduction by Beth Junor (Edinburgh: Word Power Books, 2007), pp.49-50, 87-88, 99-100, 131, 158 and 157.

Eight letters from Sorley MacLean, dated 16 February 1935, 17 July 1935, 10 January 1940, 12 May 1940, 25 May 1940, 8 March 1941, 15 June 1941 and 23 February 1942 in *The Correspondence Between Hugh MacDiarmid and Sorley MacLean,* ed. by Susan R. Wilson (Edinburgh: Edinburgh University Press, 2010), pp.127-128, 142, 178-180, 182-3, 185-7, 191-194, 197-199 and 199-201.

Biographical List of Correspondents

Mary Baird Aitken lectured for the Workers' Educational Association on Clydeside in Motherwell, Coatbridge and Greenock in the 1920s. She published a novel, *Soon Bright Day* (Glasgow, 1944), and an article, 'The Poetry of Hugh MacDiarmid', in *Scottish Art and Letters*, no.4, ed. R. Crombie Saunders (Glasgow, 1949). Other MSS had been prepared for the press: 'The Windswept Tree', a novel of Edinburgh University life before the First World War, and a collection of essays on Scottish and European literature which she had contributed to the *Scottish Educational Journal*.
Letter: 24 October 1943.

W. R. Aitken (1913-1998) followed a career in librarianship and became Reader at the University of Strathclyde. He was joint editor (with Michael Grieve) of MacDiarmid's *Complete Poems* (London, 1978). He had been dismissed as editor of *The Student* after two issues in 1933 for publishing MacDiarmid's article, 'A Stone Among the Pigeons'.
Letters: 25 September 1933; 6 November 1939.

Guy A. Aldred (1886-1963) was born in London and settled in Glasgow in 1919. He was the best-known anarchist in the Scotland of his time. In the First World War he was imprisoned as a conscientious objector for three years. He was a founder of the Anti-Parliamentary Communist Federation in 1921 and of the United Socialist Movement in 1933. He also founded and edited *The Spur* (1914-1921), *The Commune* (1923-1929), and *The Word* (1938-1963). He stood unsuccessfully in local and parliamentary elections. World Microfilm Publications have issued his books and articles.
Letter: 23 September 1936.

Esther Amall worked for Gilbert Wright (London) Ltd, literary agents.
Letter: 3 July 1940.

Freddy Anderson (1922-2001) was born in County Monaghan and settled in Glasgow after the end of the Second World War. He was a poet, playwright, novelist and political activist. He was a member of the Clyde Group, with 'Thurso Berwick' (Maurice Blythman), John Kincaid and George Todd, and the Group published *Fowrsom Reel: A Collection of New Poetry* in Glasgow in 1949. Anderson also published *At Glasgow Cross and Other Poems* (Glasgow, c.1987); *Krassivy, A Play About the Great Socialist, John MacLean,* (Glasgow, 2005); and *Oiney Hoy*, a satirical, Irish novel (Edinburgh, 1989).
Letter: c.23 October 1963.

John G. Anderson was skipper of the herring sail boat *Research* at Symbister Harbour, Whalsay.
Letters: 4 November 1935; 16 October 1937.

Roy Armstrong (1902-1993) was senior lecturer in the Extra-Mural Department at Southampton University. He was a conservationist and in 1970 he opened the Weald and Downland Open Air Museum at Singleton, near Chichester. His books included *Sussex* (1961, revised 1974) and *Traditional Buildings Accessible to the Public* (1979).
Letter: 5 June 1940.

Terence Ian Fytton Armstrong ('John Gawsworth') (1912-1970), poet and editor. He was MacDiarmid's host at 33 Great James Street for some weeks in the spring of 1935. Dedicatee of 'The Little White Rose'(*C.P.* I, p.461).
Letters: 14 March 1935; 28 July 1941; 2 April 1943; 11 January 1963.

L. W. Arthur was officer in charge at the Ministry of Labour and National Service Employment office in Lerwick at the time of MacDiarmid's industrial conscription.
Letter: 7 January 1942.

Tom W. Atkinson (1922-2007) was born in a small mining village in County Durham. From 1941-1946 he served in the RAF's Servicing Commandos whose task was to set up new airfields immediately behind front lines. Atkinson's final posting was to Indonesia, and while there he and others began to publish *Indonesian Information* in support of President Sukarno's newly-independent government. After demobilisation in 1946 he continued to publish this bulletin in London on behalf of the Indonesian government until 1950. Then for a decade he was speech-writer to Sukarno in Jakarta. In the 1960s and 1970s he and his wife ran a family hotel in Ardnamurchan and, later, a small organic farm in West Wales. For a semester in 1968 Atkinson was a visiting professor at Cornell. He founded the Luath Press in Barr, Ayrshire in 1981 and published seventeen works including his own *South West Scotland*; *The Northern Highlands: the empty lands*; *The West Highlands: the lonely lands*; and *The North West Highlands: roads to the Isles*, which are all still in print.
Letter: 29 June 1968.

Donald Bain (1904-1979) was a self-taught artist in the Colourist tradition. He was a devotee of French painting and stayed in Paris and the South of France for short periods in 1946-1947, 1950 and 1963. He was an opponent of academic art and the art establishment. His first exhibitions were at the New Art Club and New Scottish Group in Glasgow in the 1940s. These were followed by exhibitions in France, Italy, Germany, North and South America as well as in Scotland. *Donald Bain: A Scottish Colourist* (Glasgow:William Hardie Ltd:, 2000) accompanied the exhibition at the Collins Gallery, University of Strathclyde in the same year. Bain also illustrated many of the literary publications of the 1940s and 1950s.
Letters: 6 December 1961; 11 December 1961; 10 August 1967; 9 August 1972.

W. Ballingall was a patient in Gilgal Nursing Home in Perth at the same time as MacDiarmid in 1935.
Card: 23 October 1935.

Marie de Banzie (b.1918) trained as a ballet dancer (with Margaret Morris's Celtic Ballet) as well as an artist at Glasgow School of Art. A painter in oils, she was a founder-member of the New Art Club (1940) and secretary of the New Scottish Group from 1943 to 1945. She contributed illustrations to *Scottish Arts and Letters* 1944-1950. Her painting, *Shadow,* was reproduced in *New Scottish Group* (Glasgow, 1947).
Letter: 12 March 1945.

Nan Barke (née Agnes Coats) married James Barke in 1926. They had two sons. She also acted as his secretary and was the licensee of Daljarrock House which was turned into a Hotel 1947-52 when they lived there. They moved back to Glasgow in 1955.
Letter: 8 April 1958.

Professor Sir Ernest Barker (1874-1960). Classicist and political theorist.
Letter: Easter Sunday 1931.

Logie Barrow (b.1945), historian. He published *A Short History of the British Labour Movement* (London, 1969), *Independent Spirits: Spiritualism and English Plebeians, 1850-1910* (London, 1986) and (with Ian Bullock) *Democratic Ideas in the British Labour Movement 1880-1914* (Cambridge, 1996).
Letter: 19 August 1973.

David M. Black studied philosophy at Edinburgh University and now lives and works in London. He is a psychoanalyst and Fellow of the British Psychoanalytical Society. He has published several collections of poetry including *Collected Poems 1964-87*, and *Love as Landscape Painter* in 2006 (translations from Goethe). He edited *Psychoanalysis and Religion in the 21ˢᵗ Century: Competitors or Collaborators?* (2006).
Letter: 3 April 1970.

Robert ('Robin') MacKelvie Black (1895-1963) was the publisher of *The Free Man* (main series) from 1932-1934. He founded the groups of Free Scots (Social Crediters) in 1933 and *Scottish Cycling News* in 1934. From 1935-6 Black published thirty issues of *New Scotland* (*Alba Nuadh*, which incorporated *The Free Man*) and continued *The Free Man* in much reduced form in the 1940s.
Letters: 1 March 1934; 'Monday' [March 1934]; 17 September 1935.

George Blake (1893-1961) was a novelist, journalist and publisher. *The Shipbuilders* (1935) is his best-known novel. He was seriously wounded in the First World War.
Letters: 6 March 1931; 3 July 1937; 10 April 1950; 21 April 1950.

David Boadella (b.1931), psychotherapist. His principal works are *Spiral Flame: a Study in the Meaning of D. H. Lawrence* (Nottingham, 1956); *In the Wake of the*

Reich (London, 1976); *Wilhelm Reich: the Evolution of his Work* (London, 1985); and *Lifestreams: an introduction to the biosynthesis* (London, 1987).
Letter: 18 March 1958.

Gordon Bottomley (1874-1948). Poet and playwright.
Letter: 29 November 1932.

Edward Boyd (1916-1989). Writer for stage, screen, radio and TV. He published a collection of poems, *Night Flight* (Glasgow, 1945).
Letter: 30 March 1955.

Stefan S. Brecht (1924-2009) wrote *The Bread and Puppet Theatre*, sub-titled 'Peter Schumann and the modern morality play' (London, 1986) and *The Theatre of Visions* (on Robert Wilson) (London, 1994).
Letter: 12 April 1965.

Ern Brooks (1911-1993) was a painter and illustrator and Barbara Niven's husband. Together they visited Whalsay in 1938 and 1939.
Letter: 'Tuesday'[12 September 1939.] with Barbara Niven.

George Bruce (1909-2002) was a poet, teacher of English in Dundee and, from 1946-1970, a BBC producer in Aberdeen and Edinburgh. He was appointed as the first creative writing fellow at Glasgow University in 1971 and for the next twenty years was a visiting professor at several universities in the US and Australia. He was born in Fraserburgh and his first volume, *Sea Talk* (Glasgow, 1944), made his reputation as the poet of Buchan. *Today Tomorrow: Collected Poems 1933-2000*, edited by Lucina Prestige and prefaced by Edwin Morgan, was published in Edinburgh, 2001. 'MacDiarmid at Eighty-Five', Bruce's BBC Radio Scotland interview, was published in *The Thistle Rises: an anthology of poetry and prose by Hugh MacDiarmid*, ed. by Alan Bold (London:Hamish Hamilton, 1984).
Letters: 8 December 1970; 15 May 1971.

J. U. Bruce may have been the Matron at Gilgal. MacDiarmid belonged to a bridge party which met in the Matron's room in Gilgal.
Letter: 15 December 1935.

Mrs Bryce was secretary of the Glasgow branch of 'The Next of Kin of War Deceased' organisation (Scotland).
Letter: 6 June 1949.

Basil Bunting (1900-1985) is best known for *Briggflatts* (1966), a long, semi-autobiographical, deeply Northumbrian poem. *Complete Poems* (Newcastle, 2000).
Letters: 30 April 1970; 13 November 1973; 15 January 1978; 24 June 1978.

Alan D. Bush (1900-1995) was a Communist composer. A poetry text entitled 'Cantata 1917-1977', by Hugh MacDiarmid and Alan Bush, was published in *Artery*, 13 (Autumn-Winter 1977), pp. 17-19. He was Professor at the Royal Academy of Music 1925-1978.

Letter: 30 December 1960.

Kenneth Buthlay (1925-2009) has been Professor of Scottish Literature in the University of Glasgow and a lifelong MacDiarmid scholar. He wrote the first critical monograph *Hugh MacDiarmid* in the Writers and Critics series (Edinburgh and London, 1964, extended 1982) and edited, with an introduction, *The Uncanny Scot*, subtitled 'A selection of prose' (London, 1968). Buthlay wrote a number of important essays in *Scottish Literary Journal*, e.g., 'The Appreciation of the Golden Lyric' in vol.2, no.1 (July 1975), 'Some Hints for Source-Hunters', vol.5, no.2 (December 1978) and 'The Ablach in the Gold Pavilion' in vol.15, no.2 (November 1988). He was editor of the *Journal* from 1985 to 1990. He also contributed the introductory essay to Gordon Wright's *MacDiarmid: An Illustrated Biography* (Edinburgh, 1977). Perhaps his most notable achievement is the annotated edition of *A Drunk Man Looks at the Thistle* (Edinburgh: Scottish Academic Press, 1987).

Letter: 5 January 1966.

Professor P. H. Butter (1921-1999) published three works relating to Edwin Muir: a short critical study in the Oliver and Boyd 'Writers and Critics' series in 1962; *Edwin Muir: Man and Poet* (Oliver and Boyd, 1966); and *Selected Letters*, which he edited for Hogarth in 1974.

Letter: 4 January 1967.

James B. Caird (1913-1989). Teacher of English and H. M. Inspector of Schools. Lifelong enthusiast for and critic of Scottish literature. Council member of the Association for Scottish Literary Studies 1970-86.

Letter (with Robin Orr): [1932].

Elspeth Grant Cameron worked in an honorary capacity for the Scottish Association for the Speaking of Verse and also for the Saltire Society.

Letter: 8 December 1961.

Morven Cameron (1930-2002) was a teacher and successively Head of English at Wellington School, Ayr, the Glasgow High School for Girls,and finally Laurel Bank School for Girls . She wrote the Preface to the 1975 edition of *Voices of Our Kind: An Anthology of Contemporary Scottish Verse* (Edinburgh and Glasgow).

Letter: 13 December 1971.

Brian Campbell, teacher and joint editor (with four others) of *Eleventh Hour Questions* (Edinburgh, 1937). In 1936 he played a role in trying to reconcile MacDiarmid and the Scottish District Committee of the Communist Party.

Letters: 'Sunday' [April 1934]; 7 August 1972.

John Ross Campbell (1894-1969) was a Paisley Communist who was wounded in the First World War. As editor of *Workers' Weekly* in 1924 he published his 'Open Letter to the Fighting Forces' which asked them not 'to shoot strikers in industrial disputes'. Campbell was charged under the Incitement to Mutiny Act but the Attorney-General later withdrew the case. The first Labour Government lost a vote of confidence on 8 October that year. In 1925 he was sentenced to six months' imprisonment under the same Act. Campbell, along with William Gallacher and Harry Pollitt, opposed the 'change of line', i.e., that the Second World War was a war between 'two Imperialist groups of powers' and not an anti-Fascist war, in the debates in the Central Committee of the CPGB on 2 and 3 October 1939. He was editor of *The Daily Worker* in 1939, assistant editor from 1942 to 1948 and again editor from 1949 to 1958.
Letter: [1966].

Monica Campbell, wife of Brian Campbell, was organising secretary of the Scottish Joint Committee for Spanish Relief, established in February 1938.
Letter: 6 December 1938.

Stewart Carmichael (1867-1950) travelled widely before returning to Dundee where he established himself as part of a vibrant, artistic circle which included John Duncan and David Foggie. He occupied his city centre studio in the Overgate for nearly forty years. He was the subject of an article in *The Scottish Educational Journal* on 25 December 1925.
Letters: 29 November 1926; 21 January 1927.

Catherine Carswell (1879-1946), novelist and biographer. She published *Open the Door* (1920); *The Camomile* (1922); *The Life of Robert Burns* (1930); *The Savage Pilgrimage: A Narrative of D. H. Lawrence* (1932); *The Tranquil Heart: Portrait of Giovanni Boccaccio* (1937).
Letters: 28 February [1934];17 May 1936; 8 August 1936; 2 November 1936; 1 November 1937; 28 August 1938.

John Casey ('Sean O'Casey') (1880-1964). His best-known plays remain the 'Dublin' or 'Abbey' trilogy: *The Shadow of a Gunman*, first performed in 1923, *Juno and the Paycock* (1924), and *The Plough and the Stars* (1926). The concluding volume of his six-volume autobiography was dedicated to MacDiarmid.
Letters: 9 October 1949; 18 August 1952; 12 January 1957.

Joseph Chiari (1911-1989). During the years of the Second World War, Chiari was Free French representative in Scotland. Later he worked in England as a University lecturer and then as French Consul in Southampton. He published almost forty books in Britain and the USA, and two in Paris. His *Collected Poems* (1978) were prefaced by his 'old friend', Hugh MacDiarmid.
Letter: 2 September 1978.

Richard Church (1893-1972), poet, novelist, essayist. He published many volumes of verse from 1917 onwards, mainly of a Georgian nature, and both adult and children's fiction. He also published three volumes of autobiography, 1956-1964.
Letter: 10 August 1941.

Aonghas Cleireach / Angus Clark (1881-1945) was descended from a line of quarryworkers. In 1907 he left Ballachulish to take up a post as cashier to the British Steam Navigation Company Ltd, later taken over by P & O. He resigned from a senior position with P & O to return to Scotland in 1936. In London he had been Chair of the East Ham branch of the Labour Party but left to join the National Party of Scotland. He was active in the Scottish National Party after his return to Scotland.
Letters: 17 January 1934; 'Tuesday night' [23 January 1934]; 19 March 1934.

David Craig (b.1932). Poet, novelist, critic, editor and author of books about climbing, crofting and the exploration of the 'great rocks'. He has published five collections of poems and three novels, *King Cameron*, *The Unbroken Harp*, and *The Rebels and the Hostage* (with Nigel Gray). His main critical works are *Scottish Literature and the Scottish People* (1961), *The Real Foundations* (1973) and *Extreme Situations*, sub-titled 'Literature and Crisis from the Great War to the Atom Bomb' (with Michael Egan) in 1979. Craig edited the first Penguin selection of MacDiarmid's poems (with John Manson) in 1970 and also edited *Marxists on Literature* (1975). *Native Stones* appeared in 1987, *On the Crofters' Trail* in 1990 and *Landmarks* in 1995.
Letter: 4 June 1958.

Timothy Cribb, b.1939, fellow of Churchill College, Cambridge. He contributed 'The Cheka's Horrors and "On a Raised Beach"' to *Studies in Scottish Literature*, vol.28 (1985), pp.88-100.
Letter: 17 October 1972.

Patrick Crotty, editor, scholar and translator from Irish. He selected *Modern Irish Poetry: an anthology* (Belfast, 1995). His essays on MacDiarmid include 'From Genesis to Revelation: Patterns and Continuities in Hugh MacDiarmid's Poetry in the Early Thirties' in *Scottish Literary Journal*, vol.15, no.2 (November 1988), pp.5-23, and 'Still mair dazzlin' Hugh: A Reading of "Harry Semen"' in *Études écossaises* 4 (1997), pp.71-92.
Letter: 14 November 1977.

Helen Cruickshank (1886-1975) was a poet and civil servant. She gave practical help and encouragement to other writers, notably Hugh MacDiarmid. Her collections were *Up the Noran Water* (1934), *Sea Buckthorn* (1954) and *The Ponnage Pool* (1968). *Collected Poems* (1971) was followed posthumously by *More Collected Poems* (1978). Her *Octobiography* was also published posthumously (Montrose, 1976). Her poem 'Epistle to Hugh MacDiarmid' was dated 16 March 1957, the day she read in the papers about Edinburgh University's award of an Honorary Degree to MacDiarmid.

Letters: 18 June 1936; 23 November 1938; 16 March 1957 (poem); 17 December 1959.

Nancy Cunard (1896-1965). Poet, editor, publisher, memoirist and correspondent to newspapers and magazines. She edited *Negro* (London, 1934), *Authors Take Sides on the Spanish Civil War* (London, 1937) and *Poems for France* (London, 1944). In 1928 she founded Hours Press in the barn of her house at La Chapelle-Reanville and published Ezra Pound's *A Draft of XXX Cantos* (1930) among other works. She wrote memoirs of Norman Douglas (London, 1954) and George Moore (London, 1956). In 2008 François Buot published his biography *Nancy Cunard* (Editions Pauvert).
Letter: 26 March 1944.

Dr M. C. Not identified.
Letter: 23 August [1936].

David Daiches (1912-2005) was the son of a rabbi and brought up in Edinburgh. After teaching at the University of Chicago and Cornell University he came back to Britain in 1951 to work at Cambridge. He was Professor of English and Dean of the School of English and American Studies at Sussex University from its foundation in 1961 until his retirement in 1979. From 1980 until 1986 he was director of the Institute in Advanced Studies in the Humanities at Edinburgh University. He was the author of many critical, historical, biographical (and autobiographical) works, including studies of Burns, Fergusson, Scott and Stevenson. His essay, 'Hugh MacDiarmid in Scottish Poetry', in *Poetry* (Chicago), vol.72, no.4 (1948), and his introduction to the second edition of *A Drunk Man* (Glasgow, 1953) were influential.
Letter: 19 January 1952.

George Elder Davie (1912-2007) lectured in Philosophy at Queen's University, Belfast, and at Edinburgh University. His principal works are *The Democratic Intellect: Scotland and Her Universities in the Nineteenth Century* (1961); *The Crisis of the Democratic Intellect: The Problem of Generalism and Specialisation in Twentieth-Century Scotland* (1986); and *The Scotch Metaphysics* (2001).
Letters: 1 October 1935; 21 August 1936; [December 1936]; 15 June 1937.

Elizabeth Dawson, (formerly Grieve, née Graham) (1856-1934), Hugh MacDiarmid's mother, had been a domestic worker before her marriage to James Grieve, a postman. They lived first in Arkinholm Terrace, Langholm, moved to Henry Street in 1896, and then to Library Buildings in 1899. Elizabeth was employed as caretaker to the Langholm Library, in the same building and above the post office. Her husband died in 1911, and when MacDiarmid rented a house four miles out of Forfar, where he was a journalist, she moved in to keep house for him. In 1918 she married James Dawson, a forester, of Lammermuir Lodge, Whittingehame, East Lothian. After his death in 1932, she lived at Laurie's Close, Waterbeck.
Letter: 20 April 1933.

John Dickie is currently researching the life of his uncle George Dickie ('Jack Brent'), a native of Whithorn, who was seriously wounded at the Battle of Jarama in 1937.

Letter: 30 March 1971.

Arthur Donaldson (1901-1993) was born in Dundee. He emigrated to the United States in 1923 and returned to Scotland in 1937. He founded the Scottish Neutrality League in 1938 and worked as a poultry farmer at North Halket, Lugton, Kilmarnock where he was arrested under Regulation 18B of the Defence Regulations, on 3 May 1941, and detained in Barlinnie until the middle of June. MacDiarmid, Sydney Goodsir Smith and George Scott-Moncrieff all joined the SNL, although Goodsir Smith changed his mind before 1939. Later Donaldson became a newsagent in Forfar and Provost of the town. In 1964 he was SNP candidate for Kinross and West Perthshire when MacDiarmid was the Communist candidate.

Letter: 6 April 1939.

John Donovan. Not identified.

Letter: 10 August 1972.

Mary C. Dott, lifelong Scottish nationalist.

Letter: 30 December 1947.

Caroline Doughty, wife of Charles Doughty.

Letters: 8 March 1936; 26 June 1936.

Muriel K. Doughty. Precise relationship to Charles Doughty not identified.

Letter: 4 June [1952].

John Drummond translated three of Ezra Pound's pamphlets from Italian into English – *Oro e Lavoro* (i.m. Aurelio Baisi, Rapallo, 1944) was published in London as *Gold and Work* in 1951, *Carta da Visita* (first published in Rome in 1942) was published in London as *A Visiting Card* in 1952, and *L'America, Roosevelt e le cause della guerra presente* (1944) was published in *London as America, Roosevelt and the cause of the present war* in 1951.

Letters: 14 December 1934; 16 January 1935.

Walter Dunlop had a literary correspondence with MacDiarmid as a young man, writing from Paris.

Letter: 24 September 1955.

Douglas Dunn (b.1942), poet and professor, editor and translator. His first book *Terry Street* (London, 1969) has been followed by several collections, including *Elegies* (London, 1985) which won the Whitbread Book of the Year Award. His *New Selected Poems: 1964-2000* was published in London in 2003. He has edited *The*

Faber Book of Twentieth-Century Scottish Poetry (London, 1992) and *The Oxford Book of Scottish Short Stories* (Oxford, 1995), and also published selections of Byron (London, 1974) and of Robert Browning (London, 2004). His translation of Racine's *Andromache* was published in London in 1990.

Letter: [1962].

T. S. Eliot (1888-1965), poet, critic and publisher. Nobel Prize for literature in 1948.

Letters: 8 February 1938; 8 June 1938; before 17 September 1938; 24 April 1941; 28 August 1945; 4 February 1946.

The Hon. Ruaraidh Erskine of Mar (1869-1960) edited *The Pictish Review*, a twelve-page monthly review, from November 1927-June 1928. Mar had previously edited the bilingual *Guth na Bliadlina* ('The Voice of the Year') from 1904-1925 and *Scottish Review* from 1914 to 1920. He was a founder-member of the National Party of Scotland as a representative of the Scots National League.

Letters: 21 October 1937; 13 November 1937; 7 August 1938; 24 September 1945.

Barker Fairley (1887-1986) was Professor of German, University of Manchester, 1932-1936, and subsequently Professor of German, University of Toronto, 1936-1957. He published *Charles M. Doughty* (1927), and *The Dawn in Britain* (1935); also *Goethe* (1932), *Heine* (1954) and his translation of *Faust* (1970).

Letter: 29 May 1935.

Serge Fauchereau b. 1939, art critic who has published in London and Paris. In London he has published *Malevich* (1992), *Mondrian and the neo-plasticist utopia* (1994) and *Fernand Léger: a painter in the city* (c.1994). In Paris his publications included *Expressionisme, dada, surréalisme et autres ismes* (1976), *Théophile Gautier* (1972), *Les peintres révolutionnaires Mexicains* (c.1985), *Moscou 1900-1930: Moscow in Art* (1988), and *Sur les Pas de Brancusi* (1995).

Letter: 21 March 1970.

J. D. Fergusson (1874-1961) was a Scottish Colourist. In the final third of his long career his style has been described as Celtic Expressionism. He designed the geometric cover of *Scottish Art and Letters*, of which he was Art Editor for all five issues, 1944-1950. He also created the decorations for MacDiarmid's *In Memoriam James Joyce* (Glasgow, 1955). In 'A Note on the Decorations' Fergusson wrote: 'The Ogam Alphabet was an indigenous script of old Ireland named after Ogma the Celtic God of Literature and Eloquence [.] The Decorations are composed of Joyce's initials in Ogam and other characters together with other symbols that convey Joyce's concern with music, creation, feeling and his native Ireland [.] J. D. F. 7th November 1954.'

Letter: 8 February 1944.

Ian Hamilton Finlay (1925-2006), poet, short story writer and visual artist. After his early poems (*The Dancers Inherit the Party,* 1960) and short stories (*The Sea-Bed and Other Stories,* 1962) Finlay became involved with the international movement known as 'concrete poetry' and transformed a neglected croft at Stonypath, Dunsyre into a literary-philosophical garden complex.
Letter: 3 July 1952.

Vincent Flynn (1909-1991). Vincent Flynn and his wife, Ann F. Smith, were members of the Glasgow Workers Theatre Group who visited Whalsay in 1938. Vincent Flynn became General Secretary of SOGAT.
Letter: 19 May 1938.

Enid 'Mamie' Fullerton. It is not known where Enid Fullerton first met MacDiarmid in 1913. She refers in one letter to reading *The Southern Reporter,* a Borders newspaper. She met him again when he addressed Manchester University Literary Club on 10 May 1935.
Letter: 17 April 1957.

Edward Gaitens (1897-1966) published *Growing Up and Other Stories* (1942) and *The Dance of the Apprentices* (1948). He spent two years in Wormwood Scrubs as a conscientious objector during the First World War and worked at unskilled jobs.
Letters: 17 September 1945; [1945]; 21 September 1948; 2 April 1961.

J. Douglas Geddes, probably a journalist in Liverpool while MacDiarmid was there in 1930-1931.
Letter: 18 October 1951.

Sir Patrick Geddes (1854-1932) was professor of Botany at Dundee, 1888-1919. In 1885 he established the Edinburgh Social Union which was dedicated to the improvement of the quality of city life. In 1895-6 he published the four issues of *The Evergreen: Northern Seasonal* which helped to generate a cultural revival in the form of a Celtic revival among Scottish artists. Geddes's *camera obscura* was installed in the Outlook Tower on Castlehill in Edinburgh and the Tower was a meeting place for groups and clubs. In the 1920s he established the Scots College at Montpellier.
Letter: 19 October 1925.

Allen Ginsberg (1926-1997), author of *Howl*. His *Complete Poems 1947-1997* was published in London in 2009, and *Deliberate Prose: Selected Essays, 1952-1995,* edited by Bill Morgan, appeared in London in 2000.
Letter: 20 August 1973.

'Maurice Girodias' (1919-1990) was the son of Jack Kahane. He assumed his mother's surname. He launched the Olympia Press in 1953 though he sometimes

reverted to the Obelisk imprint. He brought together 'The best of *Olympia*: an anthology of tales, poems, scientific documents and tricks which appeared in the short-lived and much-lamented *Olympia*' (London, 1966). With Peter Singleton-Gates he wrote *Black Diaries*, an account of Roger Casement's life and times with a collection of his diaries and public writings (with illustrations, including portraits, maps, an endpaper plan and facsimiles), Paris, 1959. He also published *Une Journée sur la Terre* (Paris, 1977).
Letter: 23 August 1960.

Duncan Glen (1933-2008) was Professor of Visual Communication in Trent Polytechnic from 1978-1987. He was a lifelong supporter of the work of Hugh MacDiarmid, the author of the first biography, *Hugh MacDiarmid and the Scottish Renaissance* (Edinburgh, 1964) and of the centenary *Hugh MacDiarmid: out of Langholm and into the world* (Edinburgh, 1992). He also edited *Selected Essays of Hugh Macdiarmid* (London, 1969) and *Hugh MacDiarmid: A Critical Survey* (Edinburgh and London, 1972). His magazine *Akros* ran for fifty-one issues from 1965 onwards and included the 'Special Hugh MacDiarmid Issue', numbers 13-14 (April 1970), and another double MacDiarmid issue, numbers 34-35 (August 1977). Later another magazine, *Zed$_2$O*, ran for over twenty issues. His *Collected Poems 1965-2005* was published in 2006.
Letters: 6 July 1968; 13 November 1971.

Oliver St John Gogarty (1878-1957) was a surgeon and a senator in the Irish Free State from 1922 to 1936. His *Poems and Plays* was collected, edited and introduced by A. Norman Jeffares (Gerrards Cross, 2001). *Sackville Street and Other Stories* (London, 1988) comprised *As I Was Going Down Sackville Street* (first published in 1937), *it isn't this time of year at all!* (1954) and *rolling down the lea* (1982).
Letter: 4 March 1928.

W. S. Graham (1918-1986): *New Collected Poems*, ed. Matthew Francis (London, 2005); *The Nightfisherman – Selected Letters of W. S. Graham*, ed.by Michael and Margaret Snow (Manchester, 1999)
Letter: [before 19 May 1970].

Fredric Grant was director of the Project Theatre in Glasgow.
Letter: 3 January 1933.

J. L. Grant published *Male and Female* (London, 1933), a novel founded on part of the life of D. H. Lawrence. In 1934 he became Organising Secretary of The International Hostel and Language Centre in Hildenborough, Kent.
Letter: 5 March 1934.

Jessie H. Greig. Not identified.
Letter: 21 July 1947.

H. J. C. Grierson (1866-1960) was Professor of English at Aberdeen from 1894 to 1915 and at Edinburgh from 1915-1935. Among his best-known works were *English Parnassus: an anthology of longer poems*, edited with W. MacNeile Dixon (Oxford, 1909); *Background of English Literature and other collected essays and addresses* (London, 1925); and (with J. C. Smith) *A Critical History of English Poetry* (London, 1944).

Letter: 28 October 1925.

John Grierson (1898-1972) was a documentary film maker. His best-known films were *Drifters* (1929) and *Night Mail* (1936). In 1939 Grierson was invited to form the National Film Board of Canada and in 1946 he was appointed as Director of Mass Communication at UNESCO in Paris. In 1950 he became head of Group 3, the film-producing arm of the National Film Finance Corporation. From October 1957 to late 1967 he presented *This Modern World* for Scottish Television, making 350 programmes over the period.

Letter: 5 October 1934.

Andrew Graham Grieve (1894-1972), MacDiarmid's younger brother, followed a career in the Inland Revenue.

Letter: 3 September 1934.

Margaret (Peggy) Grieve, née Skinner (1897-1962) was MacDiarmid's first wife whom he described in conversation in his later years as 'the love of his life'. They married in 1918 and divorced in 1932. She became for a time the partner of William McElroy, coal factor, and worked in London as secretary and then director of his business. She lived in Scotland 1938-1939. During the Second World War she worked at the Ministry of Fuel and Power. She made a brief second marriage to Harry Piller.

Letters: 12 March 1934; 4 May 1934; 12 May 1934; 20 September 1935; 1 October 1935.

Michael Grieve (1932-1995) was Hugh MacDiarmid's son by his second marriage. He was a journalist by profession and became an Arts producer for Scottish Television. He registered as a conscientious objector on Scottish nationalist grounds in 1950 and served a six months' prison sentence in 1952. A lifelong nationalist, he edited the *Scots Independent* in the late 1960s, stood for the SNP in Glasgow Govan in 1970 and was SNP Vice-Chairman for Publicity for several years. With W. R. Aitken, he co-edited MacDiarmid's *Complete Poems* in 1978, and with Alan Riach, the second Penguin selection in 1993.

Letters: 27 March 1942; [August 1955]; 1958; 1 March 1960.

Valda Grieve (1906-1989) was born in Bude, Cornwall. Her maiden name was Valda Trevlyn Rowlands. She left Cornwall in 1928, worked as a shop assistant in Bristol, and moved to London in 1930. She met MacDiarmid in 1931 and they married on 12 September 1934. She was the mainstay of their subsequent life in London, West Sussex, Longniddry, Edinburgh, Whalsay, Glasgow, Dungavel and Brownsbank. In the 1940s she worked for short periods in Lyons' book department and in John Smith's bookshop. Her poem, 'To Hugh MacDiarmid, on his 80th birthday' was published in *The Scotsman*, 12 August 1972, and later included in Gordon Wright's *MacDiarmid: An Illustrated Biography* (Edinburgh, 1977). Single poems were published in wrappers: *High Death* (Falkland, 1970); *A Sea-Girl's Cry* (Preston, 1971), previously in *The Scotsman*, 11 July 1970; *Grey Ghost* (West Linton, 1976); and *Why?* (West Linton, 1978).

Letters: 10 September 1935; 17 September 1937; 9 February [1942]; 1 June [1942]; [January 1945]; 15 March 1945.

Walter Ross Grieve (1928-2011) was MacDiarmid's son by his first marriage. He became a mining engineer and worked for the National Coal Board for twenty-five years. Later he became managing director of a research company and, in 1981, a consultant engineer in Cincinnati, Ohio.

Letter: 9 June 1962.

Carmel Haden Guest was the dedicatee of 'The Burning Passion (*C. P.* I, pp.303-5). MacDiarmid gave her name as a referee in his application to join the Communist Party in 1934. Her son was shot through the heart in the Spanish Civil War and in 1939 she edited *David Guest: A Scientist Fights for Freedom* (1911-1938) for Lawrence & Wishart, London. She was active in PEN and ILD (International Labour Defence). Ivor Montagu (1904-1984), writer and film producer, was her nephew.

Letters: [late July/early August 1932]; [late July/early August 1932].

Eugène Guillevic (1907-1997) published over twenty collections of poetry, almost all with Gallimard. *Terraqué* (1945) and *Carnac* (1961) are the most highly regarded. He was a member of the French Communist Party from 1942 to 1980. John Montague translated *Carnac* into English (Newcastle Upon Tyne, 1999).

Letter: [late 1977].

Neil M. Gunn (1891-1973). Novelist and author of short stories and articles. He published over thirty books of which the novels *Butcher's Broom* (1934), *Highland River* (1937) and *The Silver Darlings* (1941) are among the best-known. His last book was an autobiographical work, *The Atom of Delight* (1956).

Letters: 21 December 1933; 26 December 1934; 19 May 1938; 9 July 1938; 6 February 1946; 15 December 1954; 12 January 1959; 20 November 1961.

Victor J. G. Határ (1914-2006), Hungarian poet, novelist, philosopher, essayist and playwright who lived in England from 1956 to 1989 and worked for the Hungarian Department of the BBC from 1957 to 1976.

Letter: 26 August 1964.

George Campbell Hay (1915-1984) was an outstanding poet in Gaelic, English and Scots (although he was not a native Gaelic speaker), and also a translator from several languages. He received a classical education at Fettes College, Edinburgh and at Oxford University. After initially hiding in the hills of Argyllshire for over six months from October 1940 into May 1941, he finally enlisted in the Royal Army Ordnance Corps and was based in North Africa, Italy and Greece as an education officer. At Kavalla in 1946 Hay was mistaken for a Communist during the Greek Civil War and was involved in '[...] a terrific to-do, knives and carabines and all the rest.' [...] He was invalided out to Carstairs Military Hospital and his mental health was never secure afterwards. Dr Michel Byrne has edited *Collected Poems and Songs of George Campbell Hay* in two volumes (Edinburgh, 2000), which include a short biography, 'A Stey Brae an' Bonnie', quoted above in George Campbell Hay's own words, in vol.2, pp.3-59 [41].

Letters: 14 November 1938; 7 September 1939; 4 August 1940; 30 June 1946; 4 December 1960.

Seamus Heaney (b.1939), winner of the Nobel Prize for Literature in 1995.
Letter: 6 July 1978.

Hamish Henderson (1919-2002), poet, folk-song collector, composer, socialist and Scottish Nationalist, and teacher at the School of Scottish Studies in Edinburgh from 1952 to 1987. His *Elegies for the Dead in Cyrenaica* was first published in London in 1948 and, after other editions, is included in *Collected Poems and Songs*, edited by Raymond Ross (Edinburgh, 2000). His translation of *Prison Letters* by Antonio Gramsci was published in book form, after many delays, by Zwan Publications, 1988. *Alias MacAlias*, Henderson's writings on song, folk and literature, was published in Edinburgh in 1992, and his controversies with MacDiarmid over the merits of folk-song are recorded in *The Armstrong Nose*, a selection of his letters edited by Alec Finlay (Edinburgh, 1996). *Etruscan Reader 2* (Buckfastleigh, 1997) gave then unpublished selections from the work of Tom Scott, Sorley MacLean and Hamish Henderson. Henderson's 'Freedom Come All Ye' is one of the best-known contemporary songs in Scotland. Timothy Neat has written *Hamish Henderson: A Biography* in two volumes (Edinburgh, 2007 and 2009).

Letters: 5 July 1969; 9 June 1970.

T. Henderson, editor of *The Scottish Educational Journal*.
Letter: 7 November 1932.

J. F. Hendry (1912-1986), poet, prose writer, translator and editor. Two wartime collections of poetry, *The Bombed Happiness* and *The Orchestral Mountain* (1943) were followed by two later collections, *Marimarusa* (1978) and *A World Alien* (1980). Prose works: *The Blackbird of Ospo: Stories of Jugoslavia* (1945) and *Fernie Brae* (1947). He co-edited the three anthologies of the 'New Apocalypse', *The New Apocalypse* (1939), *The White Horseman* (1940) and *The Crown and the Sickle* (1943); and edited *The Penguin Book of Scottish Short Stories* (1969). Hendry also

wrote *Your Career in Translating and Interpreting* and *The Sacred Threshold* (1982), a critical biography of Rilke.
  Letter: 22 October 1938.

Nigel Heseltine (1916-95) was the son of Philip Arnold Heseltine ('Peter Warlock'). He included MacDiarmid's 'On Reading Professor Ifor Williams's "Canu Aneurin" in Difficult Days' in *Wales*, vol.8, no.9 (August 1939), and 'Poetry Like the Hawthorn' in *Wales*, no.11 (Winter 1939-1940). He published poems and short stories as a young man but later abandoned creative writing and worked as an international civil servant with the Food and Agriculture Organisation of the United Nations for twenty years. His later works were non-fiction, including autobiography, travel and agronomy.
  Letter: 10 October 1939.

Christopher Hill (1912-2003), outstanding historian of the English seventeenth century. After a career mainly at Balliol College, Oxford he became Master in 1965. After his retirement he was a Professor with the Open University from 1978 to 1980. He was a member of the Communist Party from 1934 to 1957.
  Letter: 22 November 1956.

Lancelot Hogben (1895-1975), biologist. He was Regius Professor of Natural History in the University of Aberdeen 1937-1942. Thereafter he was a professor at Birmingham from 1942 to 1961. He was vice-chancellor of the newly-founded University of Guyana from 1963 to 1965.
  Letter: 22 June 1938.

C. R. Honig was General Secretary and Founder of the International Martin Buber Society and Institute, London.
  Letter: 30 August 1965.

Stuart Hood (b.1915), novelist, translator and author of books on radio and television. After the War years, which included a year - 1943-1944 - in an Italian partisan group, Hood joined the BBC in 1946. In the 1950s he was head of the General Overseas Service, and from 1961 to 1964 Controller of Programmes (Television). Later he became Professor of Film and Television at the Royal College of Art from 1974 to 1978.
  Letter: 28 July 1939.

Ted Hughes (1930-1998), poet and prose-writer. He was appointed Poet Laureate in 1984.
  Letter: 21 July 1967.

N. C. Jack was Hon. Sec. of South Edinburgh Branch of the National Party of Scotland at the time MacDiarmid failed to be reinstated in the NPS.
  Letter: 31 May 1933.

L. L. Johnson was secretary of Shetland Labour Party in the 1930s.
Letter: 26 September 1938.

William Johnstone (1897-1981), painter and teacher. Two of Johnstone's best-known paintings, *A Point in Time* (1927-1937) and *Ode to the North Wind* (1929), were celebrated in MacDiarmid's *Poems to Paintings by William Johnstone* (1933 – published 1963). He was Principal of Camberwell School of Arts and Crafts (1938-1946) and Principal of Central School of Arts and Crafts (1947-1960). Johnstone had been born into a farming family in Denholm, Roxburghshire and returned to the Scottish Borders as a full-time sheep farmer in 1960. His autobiography *Points in Time* was published in 1980.
Letters: 7 July 1942; [1943], 19 September [1964].

Glyn Jones (1905-1995), short story writer, novelist and poet. He began his literary career as a prose-writer with two collections of short stories, *The Blue Bed* (1937) and *The Water Music* (1944), and his *Collected Stories* was edited by Tony Brown in 1999. The most important of his three novels are *The Valley, The City, The Village* (1956) and *The Island of Apples* (1965). His *Collected Poems* was edited by Meic Stephens in 1996.
Letters: [June 1939]; 9 October 1939; 7 January 1965.

Gwyn Jones (1907-1999), novelist, scholar and editor. He published extensively on Welsh and Viking subjects (including translations of sagas). *Collected Stories of Gwyn Jones* was published in Cardiff in 1997. He selected *The Oxford Book of Welsh Verse* (Oxford, 1977) and (with Islwyn Ffowc Elis) *Classic Welsh Short Stories* (Oxford, 1992). With Thomas Jones he translated *The Mabinogion* (London, 1993). *Background to Dylan Thomas: and Other Explorations* was published by Oxford University Press in 1992.
Letters: 31 August 1939; 12 September 1939.

Jack Kahane (1889-1939), proprietor of The Obelisk Press in Paris, from 1929-1939.
Letter: 2 November 1938.

W. A. S. Keir lectured in English at Aberdeen University. He contributed two essays to *MacDiarmid: A Festschrift* (Edinburgh, 1962) and edited *The Collected Poems of Burns Singer* (London, 1970), with an introduction (pp.xix-xlvii) and a Preface by MacDiarmid. He also gave broadcast talks and wrote reviews.
Letter: 15 April 1968.

W. Kennedy T. D. was a member of the Dáil Eireann, or Irish Parliament.
Letter: 4 November 1931.

Roderick Watson Kerr, journalist, published *The Polite Educator: Political satires*, Porpoise Press broadsheets, second series 4 (Edinburgh, 1925), and *Style of*

Me: Letters of Eula from the USA, Compiled and illustrated by RWK (London, 1945). He is represented in *In Flanders Fields,* ed. by Trevor Royle (Edinburgh, 1990).
Letter: 6 January 1936.

Peter Kerrigan (1899-1977) was a Glasgow engineer and chairman of the Glasgow Central Strike Co-ordination Committee in 1926. He was a member of the Executive Committee of the Communist Party of Great Britain from 1927 to 1929 and from 1931 to 1965, and successively Scottish Secretary, National Organiser and Industrial Organiser. He led Hunger Marches from Scotland to London in 1934 and 1936 and was a Political Commissar with the International Brigade. The character of Jock MacKelvie in James Barke's *Major Operation* (1936) was drawn from Barke's assocation with Kerrigan. In the pages of *Alba Nuadh* (*New Scotland*) Kerrigan was involved in exchanges of 'letters to the editor' with MacDiarmid in 1935 and 1936.
Letter: 25 January 1939.

John Kincaid (1909-1981) published *Measures for Masses* (Glasgow, 1944) and was one of the four authors (with George Todd, 'Thurso Berwick' and Freddy Anderson) of *Fowrsom Reel* (Glasgow, 1949).
Letter: 15 December 1948.

John L. Kinloch, founder of the non-party Clan Scotland Youth Movement in 1934 and Secretary of the SNP at the time MacDiarmid left the Party in 1945. He was a pioneering advocate of youth cruises.
Letter: 14 October 1945.

Jonathan Knight (1904-1981) was Professor of Microbiology at the University of Reading.
Letters: 7 August 1962.

Jessie Kocmanová, née Scott (1914-1985) was born in Edinburgh and was one of the distinguished group of students at the University there at the time of Hugh MacDiarmid's candidature for Lord Rector in 1936. (Cf. John Manson, 'You are the only man', in *Cencrastus* 67, Edinburgh, n.d., pp.43-46). In 1936, also, she painted a watercolour inspired by *A Drunk Man Looks at the Thistle,* shown in black and white in *MacDiarmid: An Illustrated Biography* (Edinburgh, 1977), p.72. Kocmanová published articles on Grassic Gibbon and MacDiarmid in several journals and also translated *Red Glow Over Kladno* by A. Zápatocky who had been a leader of the Communist rising in Kladno in 1920 and became president of Czechoslovakia in March 1953.
Letter: 23 June 1976.

Charles Lahr (1885-1971) was a German anarchist who came to London in 1910 to avoid conscription. He was interned (in Alexandra Palace) during the First World War and also briefly in the Second, and remained stateless. In 1925 he founded the Red Lion bookshop in Red Lion Street, London. His Blue Moon Press published

booklets including 'O wha's been here afore me, lass', the lyric from *A Drunk Man Looks at the Thistle*. His shop was frequented by Grassic Gibbon, MacDiarmid and many other writers, and he and his friend Margaret Bressler were the witnesses at MacDiarmid's second marriage ceremony.
Letter: 17 June 1941.

Archie Lamont (d.1985), geologist, pacifist and nationalist, author of many pamphlets published by The Scots Secretariat and fourteen of the twenty-one parts of *Scottish Journal of Science*, 1965-1984. He taught geology at the University of Birmingham for many years.
Letters: 14 October 1938; 19 November 1952; 20 April 1975.

F. R. Leavis (1895-1978) was one of the major critics of English literature in the twentieth century, giving his name to the Leavis school of criticism. He was a fellow of Downing College, Cambridge, and taught there from 1927 to 1962, becoming Reader in 1959. He principal works were *New Bearings in English Poetry* (1932), *Revaluation* (1936), *Education and The University* (1943), *The Great Tradition* (1948), *The Common Pursuit* (1952) and *D. H. Lawrence: Novelist* (1955), all published in London by Chatto and Windus. The dates of the first editions are given here. He was one of the founding editors of *Scrutiny* (1932-1953) and reviewed MacDiarmid's *Second Hymn to Lenin and Other Poems* (1935) in vol.4, no.3 (December 1935), p.305. In 1965 Leavis became Honorary professor at the new University of York, and in 1969 he was visiting professor, and in 1970 Churchill professor, both at Bristol.
Letter: 9 January 1939.

Jack Lindsay (1900-1990), prolific Communist novelist, historian and biographer of Australian origin.
Letter: 'Friday' [October 1950].

Maurice Lindsay (1918-2009) was a poet, editor, critic, broadcaster and conservationist. He edited *Poetry Scotland* (Glasgow, 1943-1946), and also *Modern Scottish Poetry: An Anthology of the Scottish Renaissance 1920-1945* (London, 1945) and later extensions of the work. MacDiarmid introduced his *Hurlygush: Poems in Scots* (Edinburgh:Serif, 1948) but a rupture soon developed over Lindsay's careerism, as MacDiarmid saw it. MacDiarmid's 'A Soldier's Farewell to Maurice Lindsay', first published in *The National Weekly*, 28 June 1952, was a masterpiece of invective. Periods of mutual respect between the two men were punctuated by disagreements on other occasions. Lindsay's *Complete Poems 1940-1990* was published by Aberdeen University Press in 1990, and later single collections followed. Lindsay edited John Davidson's *Selected Poems* with a preface by T. S. Eliot and an essay by Hugh MacDiarmid (Glasgow, 1961). His prose works included *Francis George Scott and the Scottish Renaissance* (Edinburgh, 1980), and works descriptive of different areas of Scotland. In 2005 he co-edited (with Lesley Duncan) the *Edinburgh Book of Twentieth Century Scottish Poetry*. He was Programme Controller and chief interviewer of Border Television, 1961-1967, and Director of the Scottish Civic Trust, 1967-1983.

Letters: [1943]; 30 April 1964.

Eric Linklater (1899-1974) was the author of over twenty novels, thirty short stories, and three volumes of autobiography. In *Magnus Merriman* (London, 1934) the character of Hugh Skene is modelled on Hugh MacDiarmid.

Letter: 20 January 1933.

Joan Littlewood (1914-2002), theatre director – Theatre Union and Theatre Workshop. *Joan's Book* (London, 2002).

Letters: [March 1940] with Jimmy Miller ('Ewan MacColl'); 23 January 1941; 17 May 1945; 16 December 1946.

Norman MacCaig (1910-1996), poet, editor, primary school teacher and, later, university teacher. His early work, *Far Cry* (London, 1943) and *The Inward Eye* (1946), which he disavowed, was followed by many mature collections. *The Poems of Norman MacCaig*, edited by Ewen MacCaig and introduced by Alan Taylor, was published in Edinburgh in 2005. MacCaig selected and edited *Honour'd Shade: an anthology of new Scottish poetry to mark the bi-centenary of the birth of Robert Burns* (Edinburgh, 1959) and, with Alexander Scott, *Contemporary Scottish Verse 1959-1969* (London, 1970).

Letters: 14 August 1938; 8 February 1949; 11 July 1951; 8 July 1953; 10 May 1954.

William McCance (1894-1970) was the youngest of eight children. His father, a miner, was killed in the pit when McCance was fifteen. He was imprisoned as a conscientious objector in the First World War. He was the second controller of the Gregynog Press in the 1930s (the first was Robert Maynard). The first book printed under McCance's direction was *Comus* in 1931. In 1944 McCance became a lecturer in typography and book design in Reading University. McCance was a supporter of the Social Credit Movement. Some of his images from the 1920s have been described as having a 'machine aesthetic', e.g., *Heavy Structures in a Landscape Setting* (1922), *Study for a Colossal Steel Head* (1926) and *Machine Moloch* (1928).

Letters: 22 October 1932; 9 January 1933; 25 January 1933; 14 August 1962; 30 August 1966.

W. D. MacColl (1880-1959) died one day short of his 79th birthday. His brother in Paris, Harry MacColl, had made him an allowance. MacDiarmid had given him a copy of *Annals of the Five Senses* in London in 1931. MacColl also met Valda and Michael on their visit to Glasgow late September – early October 1938.

Letter: 18 August 1937.

John M. MacCormick (1904-1961) was a founder-member of the National Party of Scotland in 1928 and Hon. National Secretary when MacDiarmid failed to gain reinstatement in 1933. MacCormick supported the merger of the National Party of Scotland with the Scottish Party in 1934 to form the Scottish National Party. He left in 1942 when Douglas Young was elected chairman. He then founded the all-Party Scottish Union (later Scottish Convention) which organised a National Covenant advocating a Scottish Parliament within the UK. His memoir, *The Flag in the Wind*, was published in 1955.

Letter: 10 May 1933.

Alex McCrindle (1911-1990) was an actor and lifelong member of the Communist Party. Among his roles were 'Jock' in the later 1940s BBC Light Programme thriller *Dick Barton Special Agent* and 'General Dodonna' in the 1977 *Star Wars* film. McCrindle read MacDiarmid's poems with Norman MacCaig and John Laurie in 'The Lallans Makars', a programme produced by Ewan MacColl and broadcast on the BBC Third Programme on 23 June 1952. In 1961 he was the driving force behind the renovation of the cottage at Brownsbank. His second marriage was to Honor Arundel who wrote children's fiction and Marxist criticism. They had three daughters. McCrindle had another daughter by his first marriage.

Letter: [August 1978].

Margery Palmer McCulloch is a scholar who has published widely on Scottish literature. She met and corresponded with MacDiarmid in 1976-1977 when first beginning postgraduate research into his poetry. She is currently co-editing a *MacDiarmid Companion* for Edinburgh University Press.

Letter: 1 February 1976.

Mary MacDonald was married to T. D. MacDonald.

Letters: 1 July 1975; 2 August 1975; 20 May 1977.

Thomas Douglas MacDonald ('Fionn MacColla') (1906-1975), teacher and novelist. *The Albannach* (1932), *And the Cock Crew* (1945), *At the Sign of the Clenched Fist* (1967), *Too Long in This Condition* (1975), *The Ministers* (1979) and *Move Up, John* (1994) have been the major publications of his work.

Letters: 20 July 1936; 2 December 1945; 26 June 1962.

William McElroy, coal factor who made money from the sale of waste abandoned around the pits closed in the General Strike of 1926. He funded the transfer of two plays by Sean O'Casey from Dublin to London. In O'Casey's *Purple Dust* (1940) McElroy is characterised as Cyril Poges whose young mistress, Souhaun, may have been modelled on Peggy Grieve. He was the dedicatee of MacDiarmid's poem 'Charisma and My Relatives'(*C.P.* I, pp.301-302).

Letter: 4 October 1933.

Sir Alexander MacEwen (1875-1941), lawyer and leading Scottish Nationalist. He was a candidate in a by-election in 1933 in the Kilmarnock division of Ayrshire. He published *The Thistle and the Rose: Scotland's Problems Today* (Edinburgh, 1932), and *Act Now for the Highlands and Islands* (with John Lorne Campbell of Canna) (Edinburgh, 1939).
Letter: 12 September 1939.

Graham MacGibbon, Scottish nationalist.
Letters: 5 December 1933; 15 January 1934; 12 February 1934.

Alexander McGill was a journalist and playwright. He contributed an article on MacDiarmid to the *Glasgow Herald* on 4 April 1925. There are references to McGill in *The Scottish Educational Journal*, 1925-1926. R. F. Pollock's Lennox Players produced McGill's *Pardon in the Morning* in 1924; the play had been published in *The Northern Review*, June-July in that year.
Letter: 17 September 1925.

James Pittendrigh MacGillivray (1856-1938) had been King's Sculptor in Ordinary for Scotland since 1921. He was also a poet in English and Scots who privately printed his collections *Pro Patria* (1915) and *Bog Myrtle and Peat Reek* (1922).
Letters: 12 March 1936; 29 March 1936; 14 April 1936.

William Duff McHardy (1911-1999) was a supporter of MacDiarmid's candidature for Lord Rector of Aberdeen University in 1933. He was Professor of Old Testament Studies at London University from 1949 to 1960 and Professor of Hebrew at Oxford from 1960 to 1978. He was also one of the editors of the New English Bible.
Letter: 13 November 1933.

Christine Macintosh (b.1924) is MacDiarmid's daughter. She trained as a nurse and married Alastair Macintosh who belonged to Brora. They left Dundee in 1955 and emigrated to Georgetown, Ontario where she still lives. She became Matron of Lakeland College School there.
Letters: 12 December 1952; 13 April 1978.

Compton MacKenzie (1883-1972) was knighted in 1952. His early novels, which included *Sinister Street* (1913), formed the basis of a literary career in fiction, travel, biography, essays, poetry and journalism. Between 1937 and 1945 he published the six-volume *The Four Winds of Love* which followed the life and loves of the hero, John Ogilvie. He also wrote a series of comedies about the Highlands and Islands, e.g., *Whisky Galore* (1947) and *Rockets Galore* (1957). From 1963 to 1971 he published the ten volumes of autobiography *My Life and Times*. In 1928 he joined the National Party of Scotland and was elected Lord Rector of Glasgow University in October 1931, standing as a Scottish Nationalist.

Letters: 24 March 1928; 20 April 1928; 29 April [1928]; 10 October 1932; 11 January 1962; 29 January 1970.

Albert D. Mackie (1904-85) was editor of the *Edinburgh Evening Despatch* from 1946 to 1954. His best-known poem, 'Molecatcher', was included in MacDiarmid's *Golden Treasury of Scottish Poetry*. He published *Poems in Two Tongues* (Edinburgh, 1928) and *Sing a Sang o Scotland* (Glasgow, 1944).
Letter: 5 February 1954.

Douglas MacKillop. Correspondent from Moscow.
Letter: 20 March 1937.

Sorley MacLean (1911-1996), teacher of English and outstanding Gaelic poet of the twentieth century. *O Choille gu Bearradh (From Wood to Ridge): Collected Poems in Gaelic and English* was published in 1989. *Ris a' Bhruthaich: The Criticism and Prose Writings of Sorley MacLean* had been edited by William Gillies and published by Acair, Stornoway in 1985. An annotated edition of his *Dàin do Eimhir (Poems to Eimhir)* by Christopher Whyte was published by the Association for Scottish Literary Studies in Glasgow in 2002.
Letters: 16 February 1935; 17 July 1935;10 January 1940; 12 May 1940; 25 May 1940; 8 March 1941; 15 June 1941; 23 February 1942.

Robert MacLellan (1907-1985) wrote plays, short stories and poems in Scots. His plays included *Toom Byres* (1936), *Jamie the Saxt* (1937), *Torwatletie* (1946), *The Flouers o Edinburgh* (1948), *Young Auchinleck* (1962) and *The Hypocrite* (1967). *Linmill Stories* collected his short stories (Canongate Classics, 1990). The poem 'Sweet Largie Bay' won an Arts Council prize in 1956 and a long poem 'The Arran Burn' was televised in 1965. His book on the Isle of Arran was published in 1969.
Letter: 20 June 1948.

William MacLellan (1915-1996), publisher and cultural activist in Glasgow, particularly in the 1940s and 1950s. National Organiser of the Dunedin Association for the encouragement of the Scottish Creative Arts. The Advisory Council was Dr Erik Chisholm, Dr Henry G. Farmer, J.D. Fergusson, C.M. Grieve, John MacKechnie and Compton MacKenzie.
Letters: [1944]; 22 August 1945; 4 January 1946; 23 December 1954; 26 August 1957; 31 August 1957.

Gordon McLennan (1924-2011) was General Secretary of the Communist Party of Great Britain from 1956 to 1975.
Letter: 20 February 1957.

Joseph MacLeod (1903-1984) was a news reader in the Second World War and author under his own name and 'Adam Drinan'. *Selected Poems : Cyclic Serial Zeniths*

from the Flux was edited by Andrew Duncan (Hove, 2009).
  Card: [1954].

Norman MacLeod (1906-1985) was an American poet whose grandfather went out from Raasay. MacDiarmid reviewed his *Thanksgiving Before November* (The Parnassus Press, New York) in *Outlook*, July 1936, pp.82-84, reprinted in *The Raucle Tongue* III, pp.550-552, under the title 'A Scottish-American Communist Poet'. MacLeod included MacDiarmid's poems 'A Golden Wine in the Gaidhealtachd' and 'One of the Principal Causes of War' in his *Calendar: an anthology of 1941 poetry* (1941). MacLeod's poem 'C. M. Grieve Speaks of Ancestors' was published in *Wales*, vol.8, no.9 (August 1939).
  Letter: 7 October 1974.

Harold MacMillan (1894-1986), later Earl of Stockton, was Prime Minister from 1957 to 1963. He is perhaps most popularly remembered for his speech about 'the wind of change' in Africa and his encomium, 'You've never had it so good!' with reference to living conditions in Britain. He wrote to MacDiarmid in his role as publisher.
  Letter: 28 March 1940.

Florence Marian MacNeill (1895-1973) was the author of *Scots Kitchen: Its Traditions and Lore*, with old-time recipes, first published in 1929, and *The Silver Bough: A Four-Volume Study of the National and Local Festivals of Scotland* (Glasgow, 1957-68). Her other works included *Iona: A History of the Island* (London, 1920); *The Road Home: A Novel* (London, 1932); and *Book of Breakfasts, with Menus, Recipes and Breakfast Lore* (London, 1932).
  Letter: 23 November 1932.

Mrs MacSwiney (1893-1982) had been married to Terence MacSwiney (1879-1920), Mayor of Cork, who died on hunger strike in Brixton Jail . He had written *The Principles of Freedom* (New York, 1921; Cork, 2005).
  Letter: 21 November 1960.

James Malcolm knew MacDiarmid when the latter was working on *The Free Man* in Edinburgh from September 1932 to April 1933.
  Letter: 14 February 1934.

George Reston Malloch (1875-1953) was the subject of an article in the *Scottish Educational Journal*, 18 September 1925. MacDiarmid published two of his plays from Montrose in 1925, *The House of the Queen* and *Thomas the Rhymer*.
  Letter: 8 June 1924.

Samuel Marshak (1887-1964), poet and translator, prose-writer and critic. He was the best-known Russian translator of Robert Burns into Russian and also translated Shakespeare's sonnets and poems by Blake, Wordsworth and Keats. He first met MacDiarmid in Moscow in 1950. He visited Scotland in 1955 and is shown in a grouping in *MacDiarmid: An Illustrated Biography* (Edinburgh, 1977), p.83, though the date given there is 1950.

Letters: 28 March 1952; 10 November 1957.

David Martin (1915-1997) was born Ludwig Detsinyi in Budapest. He served as a medical volunteer in the International Brigade. In 1949 he moved to Australia where he continued his career as novelist, poet, playwright, journalist, literary reviewer and editor. MacLellan published Martin's *Battlefields and Girls* in 1942 and Martin edited *Rhyme and Reason* for The Working Writers' Association in 1944. MacDiarmid's poem, 'The Bourgeoisie, 1939-1943', was included in the latter. (*C.P.* II, pp.1321-2).

Letters: 9 October 1945; 10 December 1945; 19 December 1945.

Osborne Henry Mavor ('James Bridie') (1888-1951) was a medical doctor and dramatist. In addition to writing over forty plays he was actively involved in founding Glasgow Citizens' Theatre in 1943 and the first College of Drama in Scotland in 1950. *The Devil to Stage: Five plays by James Bridie* was edited by Gerard Carruthers for the Association of Scottish Literary Studies in 2005.

Letters: 4 March 1943; 29 May 1945; 13 July 1946; 19 July 1949.

Tommy Mearns was MacDiarmid's 'printer's devil' in Montrose and later qualified as a Congregationalist Minister.

Letter: 29 June 1977.

Nan Mercer (later Milton, née MacLean) (1913-1996), daughter of John MacLean (1879-1923), published *John MacLean*, London, 1973 and edited *John MacLean: In the Rapids of Revolution*, London, 1978.

Letters: 6 August 1936; 22 August 1936.

Jimmy Miller ('Ewan MacColl') (1915-1989), playwright and writer and performer of folk-songs and ballads. *Journeyman: An Autobiography* was published in 1990, nine months after MacColl's death. His unpublished novel was 'The Damnable Town'. *Class Act*, sub-titled 'The Cultural and Political Life of Ewan MacColl', by Ben Harker was published by Pluto Press, London in 2007.

Letters: [March 1940] with Joan Littlewood; [1949].

J. H. Miller-Wheeler (Harry Miller) (1910-1963), secretary of the Scottish Socialist Party, which was founded on 16 May 1940, and editor of *The Scots Socialist*. He was an apprentice draughtsman in 1926 and served his time in Drysdale's (Glasgow). During the Depression he worked in the drapery trade in England and returned to Drysdale's in 1937. At the time of his death Miller was chair of the Drafting Commission for a Constitution of Self-Governing Scotland (for the Scottish National

Congress). In his obituary in *Forward Scotland* (November 1963) MacDiarmid wrote that the magazine ' [...] involved enough work for any ordinary man, but Harry was at the same time building up a high reputation in his own professional field of design and publicity. This culminated in the unique appointment found for him in the last months of his life on the staff of Glasgow University'.
Letters: 20 September 1940; 4 January 1941; 18 May 1941.

Ex-Prince **D. S. Mirsky** (1890-1939) taught Russian Literature at King's College, London, from 1922 to 1932. He had previously served in Denikin's White Army. He joined the Communist Party in 1931 and returned to USSR in 1932. In 1937 he was arrested and sentenced to eight years in a labour camp on suspicion of espionage. He died there in hospital. MacDiarmid dedicated his 'First Hymn to Lenin'(*C.P.* I, pp.297-299) to Mirsky in 1931 and he was also one of three dedicatees of *In Memoriam James Joyce* in 1955. Mirsky's major works in English translation are *Contemporary Russian Literature 1881-1925* (1926), *Pushkin* (1926), *A History of Russian Literature* (1927), *Lenin* (1931) and *The Intelligentsia of Great Britain*, trans. Alec Brown (1935). *D. S. Mirsky: A Russian-English Life, 1890-1939*, by G. S. Smith was published by Oxford University Press in 2000.
Letters: 26 October 1931; 25 November 1931; 25 June 1934.

James Leslie Mitchell ('Lewis Grassic Gibbon') (1901-1935) published seventeen books in seven years from 1928 to 1934, including *Scottish Scene* (1934) with Hugh MacDiarmid. He wrote ten novels, two collections of short stories, and four works of non-fiction. The three Scottish novels, *Sunset Song* (1932), *Cloud Howe* (1933) and *Grey Granite* (1934), are collectively known as *A Scots Quair*. His contributions to *Scottish Scene*, collections of short stories, previously unpublished poems, a selection of essays and notes, and an unfinished Scottish novel, *The Speak of the Mearns*, posthumously published in 1992, have been brought together in *Smeddum*, ed. Valentina Bold (Edinburgh, 2001).
Letters: 21 January 1933; 11 August 1933; 31 August 1933; 10 September 1934; 12 January 1935; 30 January 1935.

Rhea (Rebecca) Mitchell (1900-1977) married James Leslie Mitchell in London in 1925. They had been neighbours as children and attended Arbuthnott School and Mackie Academy, Stonehaven. Rhea Mitchell entered the civil service.
Letter: 3 April 1935.

Naomi Mitchison (1897-1999), prolific novelist and observer of African affairs. Her best-known novels are *The Corn King and the Spring Queen* (London, 1931) and *Bull Calves* (London, 1947). Later publications included *What Do You Think Yourself? Short stories* (Edinburgh, 1982), *The Cleansing of the Knife: poems* (Edinburgh, 1985), and *Among You Taking Notes: The Wartime Diary of Naomi Mitchison 1939-1945*, ed. Dorothy Sheridan (London, 1985).
Letter: 2 November 1932.

Alexander Moffat (b.1943) studied at Edinburgh College of Art 1960-1964. A love of Léger's paintings and a commitment to socialism led him to work in an engineering factory and as a photographer until 1968. He was subsequently director of the New 57 Gallery in Edinburgh from 1968 to 1978. A year later he joined the staff of Glasgow School of Art where he was head of painting from 1992-2005. His work has been the subject of many exhibitions and has been selected for major British collections. His portraits of many of Scotland's best-known writers culminated in *Poet's Pub* (1980). In 2008 Luath Press, Edinburgh published a series of conversations with Alan Riach (and Linda MacDonald-Lewis) entitled *Arts of Resistance: Poets, Portraits and Landscapes of Modern Scotland*.
Letter: 30 September 1977.

John Montague (b.1929), poet and editor. His volume *The Rough Field*, first published in Dublin and London, is now in its sixth edition. He edited *The Faber Book of Irish Verse* (London, 1974). His *Collected Poems* have been published (Oldcastle, 1995) and *Selected Poems* (London, 2001). His translation of *Carnac* by Eugène Guillevic appeared in 1999 from Bloodaxe.
Letter: 27 November 1977.

Edwin Morgan (1920-2010) has been the most prolific and varied Scottish poet since MacDiarmid. *Collected Poems* was published in Manchester in 1990 and has been followed by more individual volumes; *New Selected Poems* was published in 2000. His *Crossing the Border: Essays in Scottish Literature* was also published in 1990 and *Collected Translations* in 1996. Among many other works he has edited *Scottish Satirical Verse: An Anthology* (1980) and made verse translations of Edmond Rostand's *Cyrano de Bergerac* (1992) and of *Beowulf* (2002). His essay on MacDiarmid in the 'Writers and their Work' series was published for the British Council (Harlow, 1976), and he included three essays on MacDiarmid in *Crossing the Border*, viz, 'James Joyce and Hugh MacDiarmid', 'MacDiarmid's Later Poetry Against an International Background' and 'MacDiarmid at Seventy-Five'. The latter had also been included in his *Essays* (Cheadle, 1974).
Letter: 16 February 1975.

Margaret Morris (1891-1980) was the founder of the Margaret Morris Movement and of the Celtic Ballet. She was married to J.D. Fergusson (1874-1961).
Letter: 7 July 1973.

Lida Moser (b.1920) was born in Manhattan of Russian parents and worked as a photo-journalist.
Letter: 24 February 1950.

Eric Mottram (1924-1995), poet, critic and editor. He published *Selected Poems* (1989). His critical works include *Penguin Companion to Literature*, no.3 (Harmondsworth, 1972) (the USA section edited by E. M. and Malcolm Bradbury and Latin America by Jean Franco); *William Faulkner* (London, 1971) and *The Rexroth Reader*, selected with an introduction (London, 1972).

Letters: 26 January 1972; 12 August 1972.

Edwin Muir (1887-1959), poet and novelist. His seven collections of poems (1925-1956) have been collected in *The Complete Poems of Edwin Muir* (1991). His three novels are *The Marionette* (1927), *The Three Brothers* (1931) and *Poor Tom* (1932). Edwin and Willa Muir translated Franz Kafka's *The Castle* (1930) *The Trial* (1935) and *America* (1938), and also works by other authors. The publication of Muir's *Scott and Scotland* in 1936 ended the friendship between MacDiarmid and Muir. *An Autobiography* was published in 1954 by the Hogarth Press in London.

Letters: 6 November 1932; 8 January 1933; 9 September 1933; 17 January 1934; 10 February 1947.

Willa Muir (née Anderson) (1890-1970). *Imagined Selves*, edited and introduced by Kirsty Allen (Edinburgh, 1996), comprises *Women: an inquiry* (1925), *Imagined Corners* (1931), *Mrs Ritchie* (1933), and *Mrs Grundy in Scotland* (1936). *Living with Ballads* was published in London in 1965 and *Belonging: A Memoir* also in London in 1967.

Letter: 13 September 1967.

J. S. Muirhead was a partner in the legal firm Baird Smiths, Muirhead and Guthrie Smith.

Letter: 20 March 1923.

R. E. Muirhead (1868-1964), lifelong Nationalist and supporter of Nationalist papers and organisations.

Letters: 25 February 1939; 23 October 1939.

David Murison (1913-1997) was editor of the Scottish National Dictionary from 1946-1976 and was one of MacDiarmid's supporters for Lord Rector of Aberdeen University in 1933.

Letter: 12 April 1967.

A. S. Neill (1883-1973), free school educationist and author.

Letters: 8 March 1943; 11 April 1958.

Victor Neuburg (1883-1940) was the proprieter of the Vine Press in Steyning, Sussex. By 1933 he was back in London where he edited the Poetry Corner of the *Sunday Referee* and was the first editor to publish Dylan Thomas.

Letter: 7 December 1932.

Thomas Evan Nicholas (1878-1971) was known in Welsh as 'Niclas y Glais', 'Nicholas from the Glais', the small village of Glais, near Clydach in the Swansea valley where he was minister of the Welsh Independent Chapel from 1904-1914. He was a poet and socialist orator in the Welsh language. During the First World War he served two Welsh Independent chapels in Cardiganshire. In 1918 he resigned from the active ministry and trained as a dentist. He was a founder-member of the Communist Party and remained a member till his death.

Letter: 18 October 1938.

Charles Nicoll was MacDiarmid's foreman at Mechans in the Copper Shell-Band Section from 1942 to 1944. He was a member of Partick Camera Club and took several published photographs of MacDiarmid at work at Mechans.

Letters: 9 November 1944; 6 February 1945; 28 February 1975; 11 July 1977.

Barbara Niven (1895-1972) was an artist and friend of MacDiarmid from their first meeting in 1935 in Manchester until her death. She managed the *Daily Worker* Fighting Fund from 1942-1967.

Letters: 2 August [1938]; 12 September [1939], with Ern Brooks; 27 September [1939]; 26 January [1940]; 25 November [1940]; 'Wednesday' [February/March 1957]; 9 August [1967]; 9 April [1970].

Stanley C. Nott (1887-1978), director of the Unicorn Press (in 1932) but defaulted in paying his share capital. He published MacDiarmid's collection of essays *At the Sign of the Thistle* (1934) and *Second Hymn to Lenin and Other Poems* (1935).

Letter: 19 May 1935.

George Ogilvie (1871-1934) was Head Teacher of English at Broughton Junior Student Centre from 1904-1928.

Letters: 10 February 1925; 17 January 1928; 1 May 1928; 31 October 1932.

A. R. Orage (1873-1934) was editor of *New Age* from 1907-1922 and of *New English Weekly* from 1932 to 1934. MacDiarmid was a reader of and contributor to both.

Letter: 27 July 1933.

David Orr was the doctor on Whalsay during the first five years of the Grieves' stay and returned as a locum for some months in late 1939 and early 1940. Later he had a practice in Leith.

Letters: [1946]; 3 May 1962.

Robin Orr, teacher, brother of David Orr.

Letter: (with J. B. Caird): [1932].

Marguérite and **Félix Paknadel**, daughter and son-in-law of Denis and Ella Saurat.

Letter: 29 April 1971.

D.J.F. Parsons, one of six directors of Lawrence and Wishart Ltd.
Letter: 14 July 1936.

Kenneth Patchen (1911-1972), American poet who wrote, 'My blood inheritance is of English, Scotch, Irish, and French strains (probably others of which I am unaware).' (*Twentieth Century Authors*, New York, 1942). He was for several years a migratory worker and had a major operation on his spine in 1951 after an incapacitating illness for many years. Cape published his *Selected Poems* in London in 1968. In 'Homage to Kenneth Patchen' in *The Outsider*, Winter 1968-1969, MacDiarmid wrote, 'I had encountered his poetry in the early 1930s when I was living on a small island in the Shetland archipelago off the North East of Scotland. We had exchanged a letter or two then. [...] His social protest, his pacifism, his whole political stance, is much to my liking.' (Reprinted in *The Raucle Tongue* III (Manchester, 1998), p.493).
Letters: August 1936; April 1937; 23 July [1937]; 20 May 1939.

A. J. B. Paterson was sales manager at Routledge.
Letter: 15 January 1936.

D. Pearson. Not identified.
Letter: 4 June 1932.

Fang Cheng Ping was MacDiarmid's interpreter in China in 1957.
Letter: 7 May 1957.

Ruth Pitter (1897-1992), poet and craftswoman. *A Mad Lady's Garland* (1934) was her first volume to attract public attention.
Letter: 20 August 1937.

Boris Polevoj (b.1908), novelist and short story writer. His best-known work, *The Tale of a Real Man* (1946), was based on the exploits of the pilot A. P. Mares'ev, and widely translated. From 1941-1945 he was a war correspondent for *Pravda*. He visited Scotland in 1955 and is shown in a group in *MacDiarmid: An Illustrated Biography* (Edinburgh, 1977), p.83.
Letter: 18 December 1958.

Paul Potts (1911-1990), Canadian poet. He published MacDiarmid's 'Speaking for Scotland' as Broadsheet No. 3, August 1939, in a series of broadsheets he edited (London: Lumphen Press). MacDiarmid wrote the foreword to Potts's *A Poet's Testament* (London, 1940), and included an extract from the first chapter in *The Voice of Scotland* vol.2, no.1 (June-August 1939), with two of Potts's poems. Potts's collection *Instead of a Sonnet* was published in London in 1944. *Dante Called You Beatrice: An Autobiography* was published in London in 1960.
Letter: 7 April 1946.

Gaye Poulton was in charge of 'permissions' at Jonathan Cape Limited.
Letter: 23 August 1968.

Ezra Pound (1885-1972), poet who coined the term 'imagism' in 1912 and published a variety of innovative works in London in the 1930s. Although damaged by his commitment to Mussolini's fascist politics, and his anti-semitism, Pound's reputation rests on the *Cantos*. *The Letters of Ezra Pound 1907-1941*, edited by D. D. Paige, was first published in New York in 1950, and then in London in 1951. *Literary Essays of Ezra Pound* was edited with an introduction by T. S. Eliot (London, 1954).
Letters: 7 December [1934]; 28 December [1934].

William Power (1873-1951), journalist and literary critic. Author of *Literature and Oatmeal* (London, 1935) and autobiography *Should Auld Acquaintance* (1937). He was President of Scottish PEN from 1934 to 1938 and chair of the SNP from 1940 to 1942. He came second in the Argyll by-election in 1940 with 7308 votes.
Letter: 3 April 1936.

Sadie Pritchard (née McLellan) (1914-2007) was the sister of Robert MacLellan. She was an artist in stained, engraved and sand blasted glass and taught at Edinburgh College of Art.
Letter: 'Saturday' [5 May1945].

John Purves (1877-1961), Reader in the Italian Department of the University of Edinburgh and one of the founders of the Department.
Letter: 17 February 1936.

S. H. Quothquar. Not identified.
Letter: 22 February 1977.

Mary Ramsay, University teacher and Scottish Nationalist. She published *Doctrines Médiévales Chez Donne, le poète métaphysicien de l'Angleterre, 1573-1631* and *Calvin and Art*, considered in relation to Scotland (Edinburgh, 1938).
Letters: 7 August 1936; 20 May 1941; 17 October 1950; 13 October 1952.

I. J. C. Rankin was a patient in Gilgal Nursing Home at the same time as MacDiarmid in 1935.
Card: 23 October 1935.

Herbert Read (1893-1968): poet, literary critic and writer on art. He was Professor of Fine Art in the University of Edinburgh 1931-1933. An anarchist, he was knighted for his services to literature in 1953.
Letter: 5 February 1933.

George N. Reid (b. 1939) was a broadcast journalist and TV producer for the BBC. He became SNP MP for Clackmannan and East Stirlingshire (1974-9) and an MSP from 1999 to 2007. He was Presiding Officer in the Scottish Parliament (2003-2007).
Letter: 7 January 1973.

John MacNair Reid (1895-1954) was a journalist, novelist, editor and poet. His best-known novel *Homeward Journey* (Edinburgh, 1934) was reprinted as a Canongate Classic with an introduction by J. B. Pick (Edinburgh, 1988). Two more novels were published posthumously in Ilfracombe, *Tobias the Rod* (1968) and *Judy from Crown Street* (1970). He also edited *Scottish One-Act Plays* [by various authors] (Edinburgh, 1935). His earlier collections of poetry were *The Gleam on the Road*, a Porpoise Press broadsheet (Edinburgh, 1928), and *Symbols, and Other Poems* (London, 1933). MacNair Reid was the dedicatee of MacDiarmid's 'Depth and the Chthonian Image', *C.P.* I, pp.346-353
Letter: 9 March 1936.

Arno Reinfrank (1934-2001), poet and translator of 'On a Raised Beach' into German as 'Die Höhe Felsen Küste' (total-hirsch verlag: Berlin, c.1970).
Letter: 1 January 1968.

Kenneth Rexroth (1905-1982) became involved in the Communist Party's John Reed Clubs in the 1930s. In 1938 he shifted his Communist-based political ideologies to ecologically-informed pacifism. Later he became known as the 'father' of the Beat generation. In the 1960s Rexroth supported both civil rights struggles and the anti-war movement. Rexroth published volumes of his own poetry and of his translations from Chinese, Japanese and French poems. His *New British Poets: An Anthology* (New York, 1949) included nine of MacDiarmid's poems.
Letter: [1959].

Keidrych Rhys (1915-87) was born William Ronald Rees Jones; the Ceidrych was a small river near his birthplace. He started the Magazine *Wales* in 1937 and was better known for his work on behalf of other poets than for his own work. He edited two selections of verse by poets in the armed forces, and also *Modern Welsh Poetry* (1944) which represented the work of thirty-seven poets. His own collection, *The Van Pool*, was published in 1942.
Letter: 1 April 1939.

Alan Riach (b.1957) is a poet, critic and scholar. His collections include *This Folding Map* (Auckland University Press/Oxford University Press, 1990), *An Open Return* (Untold Books, New Zealand), *First and Last Songs* (Auckland University Press / Chapman Books, Edinburgh, 1995), *From the Vision of Hell: An Extract of Dante* (Kirkcaldy, 1998), *Clearances* (Christchurch and Dalkeith, 2001) and *Homecoming* (Edinburgh, 2009). Edinburgh University Press published his *Hugh*

MacDiarmid's Epic Poetry in 1991 and his *Scotnotes: the Poetry of Hugh MacDiarmid* was published by the Association of Scottish Literary Studies (Glasgow, 1999). He is currently general editor of Carcanet's MacDiarmid 2000 project which has published thirteen volumes of MacDiarmid's poetry and prose with more volumes planned. Riach has also published important essays, including 'Les coléoptères de l'intelligence: Hugh MacDiarmid and Paul Valéry' in *La Nouvelle Alliance*, edited by David Kinloch and Richard Price (Grenoble, 2000) and 'The Idea of Order in "On a Raised Beach": The Language of Location and the Politics of Music' in *Terranglian Territories*, edited by Susanne Hagemann (Frankfurt am Mein, 2000).
Letter: [1978].

Edgell Rickword (1898-1982), poet and editor. His *Collected Poems* was edited by Charles Hobday (Manchester, 1991). A. Young edited *Essays & Opinions*, 1921-1931 (Cheadle, 1974) and also *Literature in Society*, essays and opinions II. Rickword was co-editor of *Calendar of Modern Letters*, 1924-1927, editor of the third volume of *Left Review*, February 1937 to May 1938, and editor of *Our Time*, vol.4, no.4 (November 1944) – Vol.7, no.1 (August 1947). He was a Communist Party member from 1934 to 1956. Charles Hobday wrote Rickword's biography *A Poet at War* (Manchester, 1989).
Letters: 'Sunday' [May 1934]; 19 September 1936.

Macha Louis Rosenthal (1917-1996), poet, editor and critic, was Professor of English at New York University 1961-1987. He arranged MacDiarmid's reading at the New York Poetry Centre in 1967.
Letter: 14 August 1961.

Anthony Ross (1917-1993), Dominican priest and Scottish nationalist. He was Superior in the Dominican Chaplaincy in Edinburgh from 1959 to 1977 and was elected Lord Rector of Edinburgh University 1979-1982.
Letter: 20 September 1967.

Florence Ann Rowlands was Valda Grieve's mother.
Card: 24 May 1933.

Muriel Rukeyser (1913-1980), American poet whose work in *The Nation* attracted MacDiarmid's attention. *Muriel Rukeyser Reader*, ed. Jan Heller Levi; with an introduction by Adrienne Rich was published in New York and London in 1994. Her *Life of Poetry*, with a new foreword by Jane Cooper, appeared in Ashfield, Massachussets in 1996. *Collected Poems of Muriel Rukeyser*, ed. Janet E. Kaufman and Anne F. Herzog; with Jan Heller Levi was published in Pittsburg in 2005.
Letters: 5 August 1938; [1955]; 26 August 1963.

Bertrand Russell (1872-1970), philosopher, journalist and political campaigner.
Letter: 22 September 1960.

George W. Russell ('AE') (1867-1935), poet, mystic, dramatist, editor and essayist on Irish national questions. He wrote the Introductory Essay to *First Hymn to Lenin and Other Poems* (1931) and made the crayon drawing used as a frontispiece. His *Collected Poems* was published in London in 1926.
Letters: 3 November 1925; 22 January 1934; 19 June 1934.

Lady Margaret Sackville (1881-1963), poet and playwright. She was the first President of Scottish PEN in 1927 and had been the first President of the Poetry Society in 1909.
Letter: 12 January 1929.

J. B. Salmond (1891-1958) was editor of *The Scots Magazine* from 1927 to 1948.
Letter: 9 February 1932.

Nguyen Xuan Sanh (1920-2009), Vietnamese poet and member of Vietnam Writers' Union.
Letter: 19 February 1965.

R. Crombie Saunders (1914-1991) was a poet, editor and teacher. He published *The Year's Green Edge* (Baltimore, 1955) and *XXI Poems* (Edinburgh, 1955) and edited *Selected Poems of Hugh MacDiarmid* (Glasgow, 1944) and the first four issues of *Scottish Art and Letters* with J.D. Fergusson as Art Editor (1944-8). He also edited the Scottish Socialist weekly *Forward* 1951-6.
Letter: 23 September 1955.

Denis Saurat (1890-1958) was director of the French Institute in London from 1924 to 1950 and from 1926 onwards he lectured in literature at King's College, London. He acclaimed MacDiarmid's lyrics in his article in April 1924, 'Le groupe de la "Renaissance écossaise"' in *Revue anglo-américaine*, pp.295-307. His translation of 'The Watergaw' had been previously published in *Scottish Nation*, 19 June 1923; and his translations of 'The Eemis Stane', 'The Bonnie Lowe', 'Feery-o'-the-Feet' and 'Cophetua' appeared in *Scottish Chapbook*, vol.2, no.1 (August 1923). His translations of 'The Watergaw', 'The Eemis Stane' and 'Crowdieknowe' appeared in *Adam*, September 1948. MacDiarmid was particularly influenced by Saurat's *The Three Conventions* (New York: Lincoln MacVeagh / The Dial Press, 1926) and *The End of Fear* (London: Faber and Faber, 1938).
Letters: 15 March 1927; 21 November 1932; 5 February 1945; 26 February 1946, 5 July 1954.

Ella Saurat, wife of Denis Saurat.
Letter: 30 April 1968.

Benno Schotz (1891-1984) was born in Estonia. Head of Sculpture and Ceramics Department in Glasgow School of Art, 1938-1961, he was essentially a modeller of portraits, and considered his Head of MacDiarmid (1958) as 'the high-water mark' of his portraiture. He was appointed HM Sculptor in Ordinary for Scotland in 1938. His autobiography *Bronze in My Blood* was published in 1981.

Letter: [August 1977].

Elspeth Schubert made literal draft translations of Martinson's *Aniara*.
Letters: 28 February [1960]; 18 August [1960]; 16 October 1961.

Alexander Scott (1920-89), poet, editor, critic, biographer and playwright. He was the first Head of a separate Department of Scottish Literature in a Scottish University (Glasgow). *Collected Poems of Alexander Scott* was edited by David S. Robb (Edinburgh, 1994), and Robb also wrote *Auld Campaigner: A Life of Alexander Scott* (Edinburgh, 2007). Scott edited William Soutar's *Diaries of a Dying Man* (Edinburgh, 1954) and also wrote his biography *Still Life* (London, 1958). He co-edited several works: *Contemporary Scottish Verse 1959-69* with Norman MacCaig (London, 1970); *The Hugh MacDiarmid Anthology: poems in Scots and English* with Michael Grieve (London, 1972); and *Neil M. Gunn: the Man and the Writer* with Douglas Gifford (Edinburgh, 1973). His plays included *Untrue Thomas: a play in one act, being a sequel to the Ballad of Thomas the Rhymer* (Glasgow, 1952) and *Shetland Yarn: a Comedy in One Act* (London, 1954).

Letters: 16 March 1956; 10 April 1956; 4 July 1967.

Francis George Scott (1880-1958), school teacher from 1898-1925. Lecturer in Music at Jordanhill from 1925 to 1946. He composed the settings of many lyrics by MacDiarmid, Burns and other Scottish poets. The correspondence between Scott and MacDiarmid shows that Scott was the first to read and comment on MacDiarmid's poems. He was the dedicatee of *A Drunk Man Looks at the Thistle* (1926).

Letters: 11 December 1927; 7 May 1932; 15 May 1932; 28 July 1932; 5 February 1933; 5 February 1934; [with regard to Scott's Irish visit in 1933]; [early 1935]; 1 September 1936; 2 October 1936; 6 September 1937; 12 June 1938; 5 July 1938; 20 April 1940; 21 April 1940; 21 August 1940; 14 September 1940; 7 October 1941; 8 August 1943; 21 November 1950.

John R. Scott, lighthouse keeper.
Letter: 13 January 1940.

Tom Scott (1918-1995), poet in Scots and English, translator and scholar. Though some of his 'longer' poems, e.g., 'The Ship' and 'At the Shrine o the Unkent Sodger', were collected in *The Selected Shorter Poems of Tom Scott* (Agenda / Chapman Publications: London / Edinburgh, 1993), *The Tree: an animal fable* (Dunfermline, 1977) and *The Dirty Business: a poem about war* (Barr, 1986) remain uncollected. *Seeven poems o Maister Francis Villon* (Tunbridge Wells, 1953) remains a landmark in translation into Scots. Some previously unpublished translations were included in Scott's section of *Etruscan Reader* 2 (Buckfastleigh, 1997) with Sorley MacLean and Hamish Henderson. Scott co-edited with Professor John MacQueen the *Oxford Book of Scottish Verse* (Oxford, 1966) and also edited *Late Medieval Scots Poetry* (London, 1967) and *Penguin Book of Scottish Verse* (London, 1970). His prose works were *Dunbar: A Critical Exposition of the Poems* (London, 1966), and (for younger people) *Tales of King Robert the Bruce* (London, 1969) and also (with Heather Scott) *True Thomas the Rhymer and other tales of the Lowland Scots* (London, 1971). A comprehensive history of Scottish literature, written forty years go, remains in MS in the National Library.

Letters: 28 February 1953; 25 March 1953; 6 April 1965; 9 April 1965; 18 April 1968.

Edward Scouller (b.1892) was a critic and short story writer. As a teacher he was active in adult education and later gave occasional lectures at Newbattle Abbey College.

Letter: 10 February 1937.

Douglas Sealy (b. 1929), teacher and critic. He contributed the essay 'Hugh MacDiarmid and Gaelic Literature' to the *Festschrift* in 1962.

Letter: Late April / early May 1978.

Georg Seehase, professor at Karl-Marx Universität in Leipzig.

Letter: 15 December 1966.

Burns Singer (1928-1964) was born in New York and brought up in Glasgow. From 1951 to 1955 he worked as a laboratory assistant in the Marine Research Laboratory in Torry, Aberdeen. He then went to London where he contributed to *Times Literary Supplement, The Listener, Encounter* and other literary periodicals. He published *Still and All* (1957), his only collection of poetry, *Living Silver: An Impression of the British Fishing Industry* (1957), and *Five Centuries of Polish Poetry*, co-translated with Jerzy Peterkiewicz (1960) – all in London. James Keery edited his (latest) *Collected Poems* with a brief introduction (Manchester, 2001).

Letter: [1947].

John Singer was an English poet who lived in Glasgow in the 1940s. Two collections of poetry were published in Glasgow, *The Fury of the Living*, with an introduction by MacDiarmid, in 1942, and *Storm and Monument: Second Poems* in 1947. He edited three issues of *Million*, 1943-6; *New Short Stories* 1944 and 1945-6; and *Holiday Book* (1946), all published by MacLellan.

Letters: 6 October 1942; 30 June 1943.

G. Singh (1929-2009), scholar of Italian literature, e.g., Leopardi and Montale, and also of Eliot, Pound and the criticism of F. R. and Q. D. Leavis

Letter: [1973].

Sir Sacheverell Sitwell (1879-1988), poet and writer on art, architecture, music and literature. He also published volumes of autobiography among his more than sixty books.

Letter: [1977].

Elizabeth Skinner was Peggy Grieve's mother.

Letter: 22 December 1938.

Per Skjaeveland was a radiologist who was interested in Scottish and Norwegian literature.

Letter: 22 February 1976.

Lydia Pasternak Slater (1902-1989) was the sister of Boris Pasternak (1890-1960). MacDiarmid wrote the Foreword to *Poems by Boris Pasternak* which Peter Russell published in 1958. It was reprinted in *The Raucle Tongue* III, edited by Angus Calder, Glen Murray and Alan Riach, Manchester, 1998, pp.408-410. MacDiarmid published 'Seven Poems, by Boris Pasternak Translated by L. Slater' in *The Voice of Scotland*, vol. ix, no. 2 [1958].

Letter: [1959].

Iain Crichton Smith (Iain Mac a' Ghobhainn) (1928-1998) was a poet, novelist and short story writer in English and Gaelic. His *Collected Poems* was published in Manchester in 1992 and followed by another collection, *The Leaf and the Marble* in 1998. His first and still the best-known of his many novels was *Consider the Lilies* (London, 1968) which focussed on the eviction of an old woman from her croft. *Black Halo: the Complete English Short Stories, 1977-1998* was edited with an introduction by Kevin MacNeil (Edinburgh, 2001). *Towards the Human: selected essays*, with an introduction by Derick Thomson, was published in Edinburgh in 1986. His first book in Gaelic, *Bùrn is Aran* (*Bread and Water*), a collection of poems and short stories, was published under his Gaelic name (Glasgow, 1960), and he translated Sorley MacLean's *Poems to Eimhir* into English (Newcastle upon Tyne, 1971) and also Duncan Ban Macintyre's 'In Praise of Ben Dorain' in *Akros*, vol.3, no.9 (January 1969). In the 1980s Crichton Smith was a much-respected writer in residence at the University of Aberdeen.

Letters: 'Wednesday' [1967]; 5 November 1968.

Norman Kemp Smith (1872-1958), professor of Logic and Metaphysics at Edinburgh University.

Letters: 22 December 1937; 18 March 1957.

Sydney Goodsir Smith (1915-1975), Scots poet and prose author, playwright, critic and artist. His *Collected Poems 1941-1975* was published by John Calder in London in 1975 with an introduction by Hugh MacDiarmid. *Carotid Cornucopius (The first 4 fitts) by Gude Schir Skidderie Smithereens* was published by The

Caledonian Press in Glasgow in 1947 for the Auk Society, and extended editions by Macdonald in Edinburgh in 1964 and 1982. Goodsir Smith's *The Wallace (A Triumph in Five Acts)* was published and performed in Edinburgh in 1960. He edited *Robert Fergusson 1750-1774 (Essays by Various Hands to Commemorate the Bicentenary of his Birth)* (Edinburgh, 1952); *Hugh MacDiarmid: A Festschrift* (with Kulgin Duval) (Edinburgh, 1962); and Robert Burns's *The Merry Muses of Caledonia* (with James Barke and J. DeLancey Ferguson) (Edinburgh, 1959), also for the Auk Society. *The Drawings of Sydney Goodsir Smith, Poet* was collected by Ian Begg and edited by Joy Hendry, and published for the New Auk Society by Chapman Publishing, Edinburgh, in collaboration with Tuckwell Press, East Linton, in 1998.

Letters: 1 November 1941; 'Sunday' [1948]; 'Friday' [1964].

M. F. Somerville was Organiser for the Scottish Union of Ex-Servicemen and Women which was a short-lived attempt to form an alternative to the British Legion in the mid-1940s. He is shown in photos of several Nationalist demonstrations in Gordon Wright's *MacDiarmid: An Illustrated Biography*. He published *Scotland and the Common Market* (Scots Secretariat Publications, no.80).

Letter: 14 March 1944.

Kaikhosru Shapurji Sorabji (Leon Dudley Sorabji) (1892-1988), composer and pianist. He was the son of a Spanish-Sicilian mother and a Parsi father. His best-known work is *Opus Clavicembalisticum* which MacDiarmid, the dedicatee, described in *The Company I've Kept* as being '[...]in three parts, twelve sub-divisions, 252 pages [...]', p. 39, and taking two hours to perform. Sorabji banned all performance of his works in 1940 but lifted the ban in 1976. He published music criticism in *The New Age* and *New English Weekly*. His books were *Around Music: Essays* (London, 1932) and *Mi Contra Fa: The Immoralisings of a Machiavellian Musician* (London, 1947).

Letters: 7 March 1931; 29 May 1938; 16 June 1978.

William Soutar (1898-1943), poet and diarist. He wrote in Scots and in English and published ten slim volumes of poetry. An eleventh, *The Expectant Silence*, which he had prepared for the press, appeared in 1944. *The Collected Poems of William Soutar*, edited with an introduction by Hugh MacDiarmid (London, 1948), was a misnomer as several of the original volumes had been omitted. W. R. Aitken selected *Poems in Scots and English* (Edinburgh, 1961), and also made a new selection, *Poems of William Soutar* (Edinburgh, 1988). Tom Hubbard edited *A Bairn's Sang and other Scots Verse for Children*, illustrated by Sheila Cant (Edinburgh, 1999). *Into a Room: Selected Poems by William Soutar* was edited and with an introduction by Carl MacDougall and Douglas Gifford (Glendaruel, 2000). Alexander Scott edited *Diaries of a Dying Man* (Edinburgh, 1954) and also wrote a critical biography of Soutar, *Still Life*. Another volume, *The Diary of a Dying Man*, edited by Joy Hendry, was published in Edinburgh in 1991.

Letters: 25 February 1934; 23 July 1937; 19 December 1940; 18 February 1941; 16 December 1941.

Albert D. M. Spencer. Not identified.
Letters: [1946].

Ronald Stevenson (b.1928), composer and pianist, was a friend of MacDiarmid's for the last twenty years of his life. His MacDiarmid settings include *Border Boyhoood* which was commissioned and performed by Sir Peter Pears and the composer at the 1972 Aldeburgh Festival. *Passacaglia on DSCH* (published by Oxford University Press and recorded by EMI), his Second Piano Concerto (*The Continents*, performed at the London Promenade Concerts in 1972), and his Violin Concerto (commissioned by Yehudi Menuhin) are among his renowned works. As a pianist Stevenson has performed all over the world.
Letter: 19 July 1970.

Robert Murdoch Struthers had visited the Grieves in Whalsay and also knew them in Glasgow.
Letter: 8 August 1975.

Norman Suddaby knew the Grieves in West Sussex.
Letter: 29 November 1939.

Robert Garioch Sutherland ('Robert Garioch') (1909-1981), poet, translator and teacher. His *Collected Poems* was edited by Robert Fulton (Edinburgh 2004). Fulton also edited *A Garioch Miscellany* (Edinburgh, 1986). Garioch's translation from Latin of the plays by George Buchanan, *Jephthah; and, The Baptist* was published in 1959. His one prose work, *Two Men and a Blanket: Memoirs of Captivity* (about his experiences as a prisoner of war) was published in Edinburgh in 1975.
Letters: August 1934; 6 September 1949; 19 September 1955.

William J. Tait (1919-1992) was an outstanding poet and translator in Shetlandic. *A Day Between the Weathers: Collected Poems, 1938-1978*, was published in Edinburgh in 1980.
Letter: 9 July 1947.

Nathaniel Tarn (b.1928) is a poet, translator, critic, editor and anthropologist. He has some thirty-five publications in these disciplines, including lately: *Selected Poems* (Wesleyan University Press, US); *Recollections of Being* (Salt, UK); *Avia* (Shearsman, UK); *Ins & Outs of the Forest Rivers* (New Directions, US) and *The Embattled Lyric: Conversations & Essays in Poetics & Anthropology* (Stanford University Press, US). His translations include work by Pablo Neruda, Victor Segalen, Cuban poets and many younger writers in French and Spanish. In London in the 1960s he was a founding editor of Cape Editions & Cape Goliard. He moved to the US in 1970, worked widely in academia and retired to New Mexico in 1985.
Letters: 27 December 1966; 31 January 1967.

Henry Grant Taylor (1914-1999), MacDiarmid's honorary private secretary from 15 January 1938 into 1940.
Letters: 20 November 1937; 22 January 1940.

Ronald K. R. Taylor (1925-1995) joined the SNP in 1940 and was a lifelong nationalist. During the Second World War he was an apprentice officer in the Merchant Navy. In 1948 he was the prime mover in setting up the second Clann Albainn Society, which aimed to restore crofts in Wester Ross. From 1951 to 1989 he and his wife lived in Drumnadrochit. He worked on Hydro-Electric schemes at Loch Awe and Glenmorriston and later became Clerk of Works with Highland Region Roads Department.
Letter: 2 May 1948.

Brigita Tempest was married to Peter Tempest who translated Nikola Vaptsarov, *Selected Poems* (London, 1954). Vaptsarov (1910-1942) was shot by Fascists in Sofia.
Letter: 17 April 1960.

Dylan Thomas (1914-1953) was the most celebrated Welsh poet of the century. Latest editions of his work include *Collected Poems 1934-1953*, ed. by Walford Davies and Ralph Maud (London, 2000); *Collected Stories*, ed. by Walford Davies, introduced by Leslie Norris (London, 2000); *The Dylan Thomas Omnibus: Under Milk Wood, Poems, Stories, Broadcasts* (London, 2000); *Portrait of the Artist as a Young Dog* (London, 2001); *The Film Scripts*, ed. by John Ackerman (London, 1995); *The Collected Letters of Dylan Thomas*, ed. by Paul Ferris (London, 1985); and *The Love Letters of Dylan Thomas* (London, 2003).
Letter: October 1938.

R. S. Thomas (1913-2000), poet and vicar. He shares with Dylan Thomas the position of being one of the two greatest Welsh poets writing in English in the twentieth century. His *Collected Poems 1945-1990* was published by Dent in 1993 and *Collected Later Poems 1988-2000* was published by Bloodaxe in 2004. He also wrote four autobiographical works, three in Welsh, and edited five books of verse. *The Man Who Went into the West*, sub-titled *The Life of R. S. Thomas*, by Byron Rogers, was published by Aurum Press Ltd, London in 2007.
Letters: 9 August 1961; 13 August 1967.

Peter Thomson, Head of Outside Broadcasts at BBC Scotland in the 1940s and later.
Letter: 29 July 1947.

Watson Thomson was assistant editor of *The New Atlantis*.
Letter: 27 January 1934.

Dame Sybil Thorndike (1882-1976), actress, published *Religion and Stage* (London, 1928), *Lilian Baylis* (personal recollections with Russell Thorndike) (London, 1938) and *Favourites*, a personal selection of English poetry (London, 1973).
Letter: 19 August 1964.

John Tonge ('A. T. Cunninghame') was an art critic and journalist. He published *The Arts of Scotland* in London in 1938. In Alexander Moffat's *Poets' Pub* (1980) he is represented coming down the stair in recognition of the stimulus which his conversation about the 1930s had given to younger writers and artists.
Letter: 29 January 1935.

Henry Treece (1911-1966) published six collections of poetry, short stories, historical fiction and novels for children. However, he was best known for founding with J. F. Hendry the short-lived movement which came to be known as The New Apocalypse and later the New Romantics. Dylan Thomas was a strong influence and Treece wrote the first study of Thomas, *Dylan Thomas: Dog Among the Fairies* (1949).
Letter: 7 November 1939.

Alexander Trocchi (1925-1984) was born in Glasgow and graduated in Philosophy at Glasgow University in 1947. He edited the journal *Merlin* in Paris from 1952-1955. His first novel, *Young Adam*, was published there by the Olympia Press in 1954 under a pseudonym. In 1956 he went to the US where he published *Cain's Book* in 1960 (in England in 1963). In 1961 Trocchi returned to Britain. At the Edinburgh Festival Writers Conference in August, 1962, MacDiarmid denounced writers such as Burroughs and Trocchi as 'cosmopolitan scum'. Trocchi's translations include several works from French.
Letters: 17 May 1964; 7 August 1964; 26 August [1964].

Irwin MacDonald Urling. Not identified.
Letter: 28 March 1952.

Vladimir Serafimovich Vakhrushev published a book on Thackeray and a general work on English literature.
Letter: 22 March 1968.

H. A. Valette translated some of MacDiarmid's poems into French.
Letter: 6 April 1936.

A.R. Duy Vinycomt ('Michael') was left in charge of the Grieves' effects when they hurriedly left Thakeham, Sussex in August 1932.
Letter: [1936].

Comtesse Eileen de Vismes. In *The Company I've Kept*, MacDiarmid records that he once 'loaned' her 5d at Speaker's Corner in Hyde Park. 'Then, in 1962, on the occasion of my seventieth birthday, I received a greetings telegram from her – but it gave no clue to her address' (p.18). The 'maison de Vismes' can be traced back to the 12th century A.D.
Telegram: 11 August 1962.

Fredric J. Warburg (1898-1981) was Junior Managing Director at Routledge.
Letters: 29 May 1935; 25 July 1935.

Robert S. Warren was Admiralty Overseer at Scott's Shipbuilding Co. in Greenock during the Second World War.
Letter: 1 September 1976.

Sir George A. Waters, editor of *The Scotsman* (1924-1944).
Letter: 8 November 1938.

Roderick Watson (b.1943), poet and scholar. Professor of English at the University of Stirling. He was one of three poets represented in *Trio* (New York, 1971), and also published *True History on the Walls* (Edinburgh, 1977). His latest collection is *Into the Blue Wavelengths: love poems and elegies* (Edinburgh: Luath Press, 2004). He wrote the MacDiarmid unit for an Open University Course (Milton Keynes, 1976) and he co-edited (with Alan Riach) MacDiarmid's *Annals of the Five Senses and other stories, sketches and plays* (Manchester, 1999). *The Literature of Scotland* was published in Basingstoke in 1984 and he edited and introduced *Poetry of Scotland: Gaelic, Scots and English, 1380-1980* (Edinburgh, 1995). With Martin Gray he wrote *The Penguin Book of the Bicycle* (London, 1978).
Letter: 24 June 1969.

Eliot Weinberger (b. 1949), editor, translator and commentator on current events. His introduction to the publication by New Directions in 1993 of Hugh MacDiarmid's *Selected Poems*, edited by Michael Grieve and Alan Riach (Manchester, 1992), was included in his *Karmic Traces 1993-1999* (New York, 2000). He wrote *9/12 New York After* (Chicago, 2003) and *What I Heard about Iraq* (London, 2005).
Letter: 25 October 1976.

Mrs Dyke White was married to the cartoonist, Dyke White.
Letter: 14 April 1934.

J. A. White was an editor at Methuen and Co. Ltd.
Letters: 26 January 1944; 3 April 1944.

Kenneth White (b.1936) was born in Fairlie, Ayrshire and studied French, German and philosophy at the Universities of Glasgow, Munich and Paris. His first books were published in London by Cape. In the 1960s White settled in France, first in the Pyrenees and then on the coast of Brittany. He began publishing again, in Paris. From 1983-1996 White held the Chair of Twentieth-Century Poetics at Paris-Sorbonne. He founded the Institut International de Géopoétique in 1989. OPEN WORLD, subtitled 'The Collected Poems 1960-2000', was published in Edinburgh in 2003. In the introduction White wrote, 'In the poem, without going back to myth, metaphysics or religion, I tried to get out beyond personal poetry and social poetry and linguistic poetry, into what I called 'world poetry', poetry concerned with *world*, that is, what emerges from the contact between the human mind and the matter-energy of the universe' (p.xxvi).

Letters: 7 October 1969; 11 October 1976.

James H. Whyte (1909-62) edited and published *The Modern Scot* vols 1-6 in St Andrews, 1930-6, and was subsequently literary editor of *Outlook, 1936-1937*. He returned to US in 1938, opened the Whyte Bookshop and Gallery in Washington D.C., and acted as president between 1938 and 1955. Later he moved to Maryland and was active in local history and journalism. He published *The Uncivil War* on the American Civil War. He was the dedicatee of 'On a Raised Beach' and one of the dedicatees of *In Memoriam James Joyce*.

Letters: 12 November 1932; 25 June 1936; 10 September 1936; 27 September 1936.

Thornton Wilder (1897-1975), dramatist, novelist, Charles Eliot Norton Professor of Poetry at Harvard 1951-1952. *The Alcestiad* was produced at the Edinburgh Festival in 1955.

Letter: 10 December 1955.

Robert Blair Wilkie, a lifelong Scottish nationalist who was expelled three times from the Scottish National Party. He was a founder-member of the Scottish Resistance Committee and contributor to *The Voice of Scotland*, vol.2, no.4 (June 1946). Wilkie graduated in English Language and Literature in the late 1930s and taught English in Clermont Ferrand in the early 1950s. For a period he was Curator of the People's Palace, Glasgow. *Remembered Radiance*, his book of English poems (with one in Scots), was published in Edinburgh in 1956 with a foreword by Hugh MacDiarmid.

Letter: 30 January 1948.

Joyce Williams. Not identified.
Letter: October 1959.

T. H. Wintringham (1898-1949) served in the First World War. He was a member of the Communist Party from 1923 to 1938. Wintringham was charged under the Incitement to Mutiny Act of 1797 and imprisoned for six months between November 1925 and April 1926. He was twice wounded in the International Brigade in Spain.

In July 1940 he became Director of the Guerrilla Warfare Training School in Osterley Park which inspired the training of the Home Guard. Later he joined the Common Wealth party and came close to winning North Midlothian in a by-election in 1943. Biography: *The Last English Revolutionary*, by Hugh Purcell (Stroud, 2004).

Letter: 5 July 1934.

Wendy Wood (1893-1981), writer, artist and Scottish Nationalist. She is best remembered as the leader of the Scottish Patriots. A good deal of her writing celebrated the places of Scotland. She published two autobiographical works: *I Like Life* (Edinburgh, 1938) and *Yours Sincerely for Scotland: the Autobiography of a Patriot* (London, 1970). Two other works celebrated crofting: *Mac's Croft* (London, 1947) and *from a Highland Croft* (Edinburgh, 1952).

Letters: 25 May 1938; October ? [1939].

George Woodcock (1912-1995) wrote and edited several works on anarchism and also many works on Canada and Canadian literature. His early works included two books of verse, *The White Island* (London, 1940) and *The Centre Cannot Hold* (London 1943); *William Godwin: A Biographical Study* (London, 1946); *Incomparable Aphra: A Biography of Aphra Behn, with portraits* (London 1948); and *Anarchy and Chaos* (London, 1944). He also wrote several pamphlets on housing, agriculture, railways, ethics and other questions. His autobiography was titled *Beyond the Blue Mountains* (Markham: Ontario, 1987).

Letter: 8 February 1940.

Gilbert Wright (London) Ltd was a firm of literary agents.

Letter: 29 March 1939.

W. B. Yeats (1865-1939), poet, playwright, essayist. Winner of the Nobel Prize for literature in 1923. He was an Irish nationalist and senator in the Irish Free State from 1922 to 1928. MacDiarmid met him in Dublin and Yeats included four of his poems in *The Oxford Book of Modern Verse 1892-1935* in 1936.

Letter: 4 March 1934.

Douglas Young (1913-1973) was a Classical scholar and a Scottish nationalist. He taught at the University of Aberdeen before the Second World War and at the University of Dundee from 1947 to 1968. Subsequently he became Professor of Greek at the University of North Carolina from 1969 until his death. Young published two collections of poems in Scots, *Auntran Blads* (Glasgow, 1943) and *A Braird o Thristles* (Glasgow, 1947), and *Selected Scottish Verse 1851-1951* (Edinburgh, 1952). He also translated three plays into Scots, *The Puddocks* (Tayport, 1957) and *The Burdies* (Tayport, 1959), both from Aristophanes, and *The Oresteia of Aeschylus* (Norman, [1974]). *Chasing an Ancient Greek* (London, 1950) was subtitled 'discursive reminiscences of an European journey'. *A Clear Voice: Douglas Young, poet and polymath* (Edinburgh, 1977) formed a selection from his writing with a memoir and was edited by his daughter Clara Young and his former colleague David Murison. During the Second World War, Young was imprisoned on two occasions for refusing conscription on Scottish nationalist grounds. He was chair of the SNP from 1942 to 1944 and came second in the Kirkcaldy Burghs by-election in 1944 with 42% of the vote.

Letters: 23 November 1939; 11 February 1941; 14 January 1943; 6 November 1948.

Index

'Elihu' (Samuel Washington), 527, 528
Eliot, George, 21, 282
Eliot, T.S., ix, 35, 45, 46, 94, 123, 201, 204,
206, 209, 219, 223, 234, 279, 285,
305, 306, 312, 346, 377, 403, 409,
410, 503, 562, 574, 583, 595, 600
Elis, Islwyn Ffowc, 581
Elistratova, Madame Anna, 428
Elliott, Walter, 80
Eluard, Paul, 415, 416
Emerson, Ralph Waldo, 435
Empson, William, 403
Engels, Friedrich, 298
England, Robert, 119, 123
Ernst, Max, 122, 124
Errol, Countess of, 373
Erskine of Mar, Hon. Ruaraidh, 27, 28, 29,
197, 198, 199, 200, 222, 348, 574
Este, Ginerva d' 117, 118
Etruscan Books, 403, 579, 600
Eunson, Johnny, 317
Evans, Admiral Sir E.R.G.R., 256
Evans, George Ewart, 242, 244

F

Faber & Faber Ltd, 305, 356, 477, 537
Fabre d'Olivet, Antoine, 122, 123, 484
Fagan, Abraham, 242
Fairley, Barker, 134, 135, 148, 208, 209,
229, 317, 574
Farmer, Henry G., 338, 345, 587
Fauchereau, Serge, 511, 512, 574
Fellowes, Horace, 286
Fenollosa, Ernest Francisco, 122
Ferguson, Aitken, 238
Ferguson, J. DeLancey, 258
Ferguson, John, 21
Fergusson, J.D., xi, 287, 333, 338, 345, 455,
456, 458, 574, 587, 591, 598, 602
Fergusson, Robert, 377, 572
Ferris, Paul, 604
Feuerbach, Ludwig A., 400
Finlay, Alec, 564, 579
Finlay, Ian Hamilton, ix, 396, 477, 575
Fisher, Bill, 307
Flaubert, Gustave, 208
Fleming, Ian, 65

Fleming, Tom, 523
Flynn, Vincent, 202, 575
Foggie, David, 377, 570
Folengo, Teofilo, 147
Forbes, J. Foster, 372
Forbes, Lillias Scott, x, xii (formerly
Chisholm)
Ford, J.F., 362
Foreman, James, 157, 158, 546
Forrest, J. Reid, 65
Forward Publishing Co. Ltd, 414
Foster, Brian, 402
Fox, Ralph, 109
Foyle, W.A., 470, 482
France, Peter, 403
Francia, Peter de, 420
Francis, Matthew, 576
Franco, General Francisco, 163, 240, 272,
273, 304, 305
Franco, Jean, 592
Fraser, George S., 258, 405, 498
Fraser, Lady Antonia, 545
Fraser, Mary (Mrs George Dott), 225, 226
Fraser, Mrs Norrie, 378
Frazer, Sir J.G., 122, 123
Freud, Sigmund, 52, 213, 484
Friedman, Leonard, 517
Frizzell, Alex., 543
Frobenius, Leo, 122, 123
Fröding, Gustav, 538, 539
Fullerton, Enid, 422, 575
Fullerton, Helen, 467, 468
Fulton, Robin, 603
Furness, Alan, 170

G

Gaitens, Edward, ix, 346, 347, 354, 355,
375, 376, 451, 452, 575
Gallacher, William, 165, 166, 167, 168, 180,
181, 429, 570
Galsworthy, John, 18, 54, 132
Gardner, Raymond, 520
Garman, Douglas, 174, 178
Gaulle, General de, 286, 288, 313
'Gawsworth, John' (Armstrong, Terence Ian
Fytton), xi, xxix, 130, 310, 326, 465,
466, 566

615